Introduction to
Law Enforcement
and Criminal Justice

Introduction to Law Enforcement and Criminal Justice

Henry M. Wrobleski
Normandale Community College
Bloomington, Minnesota

Karen M. Hess
Normandale Community College
Bloomington, Minnesota

Criminal Justice Series

West Publishing Company
St. Paul • New York • Los Angeles • San Francisco

PHOTO CREDITS

Chapter 1—Minnesota Historical Society
Chapters 2, 4, 5, 6, 7, 8, 10, 11, 12, 13, 14, 15, 16—Ekm-Nepenthe; Bob
   Eckert, John Maher, photographers
Chapter 3—Jeroboam; Jeffrey Blankfort, photographer
Chapter 9—San Diego Police Department
Section One—Minnesota Historical Society
Sections Two, Three, Four—Ekm-Nepenthe

COPYRIGHT ® 1979 By WEST PUBLISHING CO.
                50 West Kellogg Boulevard
                P.O. Box 3526
                St. Paul, Minnesota 55165

Printed in the United States of America

Library of Congress Cataloging in Publication Data
Wrobleski, Henry M   1922-
   Introduction to law enforcement and criminal justice.

   (Criminal justice series)
   Bibliography: p.
   Includes index.

   1. Law enforcement—United States.   2. Criminal justice, Administration
of—United States.   I. Hess, Karen M., 1939- joint author.   II. Title.   III. Series.

HV8138.W76   364'.973   78-31922

ISBN 0-8299-0250-3

*To those who have
dedicated their lives
to
the advancement
of human rights.*

Preface

The future of our lawful, democratic society depends in large part upon those of you currently in the field of law enforcement and those of you preparing to enter this field. The law enforcement officer is responsible for assisting those in distress, providing services to persons who request them, preserving peace and order in the community, preventing unlawful acts, and apprehending those who violate the law. These complex responsibilities must be met under constantly changing conditions and in a manner which assures the rights of the individual. Increased technology, industrialization, urbanization, and mobility have brought new problems to law enforcement requiring the law enforcement officer to be knowledgeable in a wide variety of areas.

Introduction to Law Enforcement and Criminal Justice provides basic information which should serve as an overview of the entire field as well as a solid foundation for future course work. The content in each chapter could easily be expanded into an entire book or course, but the basic concepts in each area have been included. You will be introduced to the history of law enforcement, the nature and importance of civil rights and civil liberties, and crime as it exists in the United States, including juvenile delinquency and organized crime. After familiarizing yourself with this general background of law enforcement, you will learn about the agencies engaged in law enforcement activities, the general organization of most police departments, and the goals most seek to accomplish, as well as the image of the law enforcement officer. Next you will study the complex role of the police officer in depth— the functions performed in fulfilling extremely difficult responsibilities, including traffic, patrol, community service, and investigation. Then you will be introduced to the police officer's role in the criminal justice system, from the investigation and search through the arrest and the court trial. Finally, you will learn about the requirements for becoming a police officer, what occurs during the recruitment, probation, and training period; what opportunities in law enforcement are available to members of minority groups and women; and, briefly, what the future of law enforcement may hold.

Important court cases and decisions are presented throughout the book rather than being isolated in a single chapter. Likewise, modern advancements in law enforcement are integrated into chapters rather than presented as a separate subject. The content of the book is based on the results of five years of classroom research among police officers and pre-service students as to what subject matter is most important and useful to the future police officer. The book itself has been classroom tested and reviewed by several experts in the field.

The book recognizes the importance of women in law enforcement. The fact that the authors have chosen to use the masculine pronoun when a pronoun is called for should in no way be construed as implying bias. The pronouns *he* and *him* are used simply for clarity and directness; using *he or she* and *him or her* is cumbersome and, for mature readers, unnecessary.

HOW TO USE THIS BOOK

Introduction to Law Enforcement and Criminal Justice is more than a textbook; it is a learning experience requiring your active participation to obtain best results. You will get the most out of this book if you first familiarize yourself with the total scope of law enforcement: read and think about the Table of Contents and what is included. Then follow these steps as you read each chapter:

1. Read the objectives at the beginning of each chapter:

DO YOU KNOW□ □ □
□ What the basic instrument of government is?

Think about your current knowledge on each question.
What preconceptions do you hold?

2. Read the chapter (underlining or taking notes if that is your preferred study style).
   a. Pay special attention to all information that is shaded:

> The United States Constitution is the Basic Instrument of Government and the Supreme Law of the United States.

   The key concepts of each chapter are highlighted in this manner.
   b. Look up unfamiliar words in the glossary at the back of the book.

3. Answer the questions presented in the Check Points throughout the chapter:

☑ CHECK POINT
1. **What is the basic instrument of government?**

Read the answers immediately following the questions and evaluate your responses. If your answers do not agree with those given, reread the preceding information. Sometimes you may still disagree with a given answer—and you may be right. More than one answer is possible for many of the questions presented. The main thing is that you have a plausible, supportable response to the important questions raised.

4. When you have finished reading the chapter, re-read the list of objectives given at the beginning of the chapter to make certain you are able to give an educated response to each question. If you find yourself stumped, find the appropriate material in the chapter and review it.

5. Finally, complete the Application at the end of each chapter. These application exercises provide an opportunity to use the concepts in actual or hypothetical cases. After you have made your responses, compare them with the sample answers provided.

Good reading and learning!

Acknowledgements

We would like to thank the following individuals and organizations for their contribution to *Introduction to Law Enforcement and Criminal Justice.*

Thank you to Larry Gaines, Eastern Kentucky University; Professor George Green, Mankato State University; Robert Ingram, Florida International University; Glen Morgan, Lincolnland Community College; Professor Frank Post, Fullerton College; Jack Spurlin, Missouri Southern State College; and Larry Tuttle, Palm Beach Junior College for their helpful reviews of the manuscript and their suggestions for changes. A special thank you to Professor Post for his valuable additions, particularly in the areas of law enforcement agencies and the police career.

Thank you to the administration and staff of Normandale Community College for their assistance and support during the classroom testing of the manuscript, to the students in Law Enforcement 050 for using the manuscript as a text and providing ideas and suggestions, and to Pamela Reierson, media specialist, for her invaluable assistance in locating sources and information.

Thank you to the Department of Justice; the Federal Bureau of Investigation; the Federal Drug Enforcement Administration; the International Association of Chiefs of Police; the Law Enforcement Assistance Administration; the Minnesota Attorney General's Office, Civil Service Department, County Attorney's Association, Governor's Commission on Crime Prevention and Control, and State Highway Department; the National Council of Christians and Jews; the National Safety Council; and police departments of Philadelphia, San Diego, and St. Louis Park; and the publishers for permission to include their materials in our text.

Finally, thank you to our families and colleagues for their support and assistance during the development of *Introduction to Law Enforcement and Criminal Justice.* A special thank you to Adina Wrobleski for her careful, thorough review of the entire manuscript.

Contents in Brief

Contents

Introduction to
Law Enforcement
and Criminal Justice

Section One
Background

The chapters in Section One present the rich heritage of law enforcement, and how our laws and our system of enforcing them evolved from ancient to modern times (Chapter 1). An integral part of the evolution was the insistence upon individual civil rights and civil liberties, concepts embodied in the U.S. Constitution and Bill or Rights (Chapter 2).

Rules for conduct within society and laws regarding violations of these rules have been clearly specified in our criminal statutes, which not only define crimes but prescribe punishments. The crimes range from violent Index Crimes such as murder and rape to costly white-collar crime, to the illegal use, possession, and sale of narcotics and dangerous drugs. The multiple causes of crime and factors influencing juvenile delinquency and drug abuse underscore the complexity of the crime problem (Chapter 3). In addition, although not a crime in itself, organized crime, with its corrupting and strong-arm tactics, poses a direct threat to our national security and a difficult challenge to individuals in law enforcement (Chapter 4).

It is within this context that the modern law enforcement officer functions. An awareness of the heritage of law enforcement, the basic rights of citizens, the types of crimes occurring in the United States and their multiple causes contributes to effective performance of law enforcement responsibilities.

1

The Rondo Street Police Station, located at Rondo and Western Avenue in St. Paul, Minnesota, in 1900. Note the four staff officers on the right and how their uniforms differed from the patrolmen. Photo courtesy of the Minnesota Historical Society.

A Brief History

The Evolution of Modern Law and Law Enforcement

1

DO YOU KNOW □ □ □

- □ What a law is?
- □ When and why law enforcement began?
- □ The origins of features of our law enforcement system such as:
  - The police baton and the officer's shield?
  - The offices of sheriff, constable, and justice of the peace?
  - General alarms and citizen's arrests?
  - Jury by peers, grand jury, and due process?
  - Separation between enforcing laws and judging offenders?
  - Division of offenses into felonies and misdemeanors?
  - Local responsibility for law enforcement?
  - Paid law enforcement officers?
  - Women in law enforcement?
- □ The significance of the Frankpledge system, the tithing system, Leges Henrici, the Magna Carta, and the Watch and Ward System?
- □ How law enforcement has traditionally responded to increased crime?
- □ What significant contributions to law enforcement were made by Sir Robert Peel?
- □ Where and when the first police department was established in England and what it was called?
- □ What systems of law enforcement were brought from England and adopted in the United States in colonial New England and the South?
- □ When and where the first modern American police force began and what it was modeled after?
- □ When and how state and federal law enforcement agencies originated in the United States?
- □ What effect the Jacksonian philosophy had on law enforcement in the 1900s?

3

☐ What organizational systems of law enforcement have been tried in the United States and which have been most successful?

☐ What five levels of law enforcement are currently operating in the United States?

☐ How to define and differentiate: law, custom, moral law, common law, criminal law, civil law, tort, equity, statute, crime, misdemeanor, and felony?

☐ What law takes precedence if two laws conflict?

☐ Where police get their power and authority and what restrictions are placed on this power and authority?

> *The historian is a prophet looking backward.*
> —Schlegel

INTRODUCTION

A brief look into the history of laws and law enforcement will give you answers to many of the preceding questions. The heritage of law enforcement is a source of pride as well as a guide to avoiding mistakes in the future.

Specific dates and events are not as important as acquiring a sense of the sequence or chronology of how our present-day laws and system of law enforcement came into existence. As you read, watch for information related to the preceding questions. You may want to take notes or to underline in your book. Periodically you will be asked to answer questions to assess your understanding of the material.

LAW

We all have an idea of what a law is; we all have to live by laws or face the consequences. We may *not* all know how laws originated, what they cover, or how they are enforced.

Technically, laws are made and passed by the legislative branches of our federal, state, county, and city governments. They are based on customs, traditions, mores, and current need.

> LAW refers to all the rules of conduct established *and* enforced by the custom, authority, or legislation of a group, community, or country.

Notice that law implies both prescription (rule) and enforcement by authority. It might seem that the term *law enforcement* is redundant since law refers to both the rules and their enforcement. But, in the United States, those who enforce the laws are NOT the same as those who make them. This has not always been true.

PRIMITIVE AND ANCIENT LAW

Even the cavemen had certain rules they were expected to follow or face death or banishment from the tribe. The customs depicted in early cave-dwelling drawings may well represent the beginning of law and law enforcement.

> A system of law and law enforcement began earlier than 2000 B.C. as a means of controlling human conduct and enforcing society's rules.

The earliest record of ancient man's need to organize and standardize rules and methods of enforcement to control human behavior date back to approximately 2300 B.C. when the Sumerian rulers Lipitshtar and Eshumma set forth standards on what did and did not constitute an offense against society. A hundred years later, the Babylonian *King Hammurabi established rules for his kingdom that designated not only offenses but punishments as well.* In fact, Hammurabi established the oldest known building code. Although the penalties prescribed were often barbaric by today's standards, the relationship between the crime and the punishment are of interest.

Figure 1-1. The Oldest Known Building Code.

FROM THE CODE OF HAMMURABI (2200 BC)

IF A BUILDER BUILDS A HOUSE FOR A MAN AND DOES NOT MAKE ITS CONSTRUCTION FIRM AND THE HOUSE COLLAPSES AND CAUSES THE DEATH OF THE OWNER OF THE HOUSE–THAT BUILDER SHALL BE PUT TO DEATH. IF IT CAUSES THE DEATH OF A SON OF THE OWNER–THEY SHALL PUT TO DEATH A SON OF THAT BUILDER. IF IT CAUSES THE DEATH OF A SLAVE OF THE OWNER–HE SHALL GIVE TO THE OWNER A SLAVE OF EQUAL VALUE. IF IT DESTROYS PROPERTY HE SHALL RESTORE WHATEVER IT DESTROYED AND BECAUSE HE DID NOT MAKE THE HOUSE FIRM HE SHALL REBUILD THE HOUSE WHICH COLLAPSED AT HIS OWN EXPENSE. IF A BUILDER BUILDS A HOUSE AND DOES NOT MAKE ITS CONSTRUCTION MEET THE REQUIREMENTS AND A WALL FALLS IN–THAT BUILDER SHALL STRENGTHEN THE WALL AT HIS OWN EXPENSE.

Source: Masonry Institute, 55 New Montgomery Street, San Francisco, California 94105.

About 1000 B.C. in *Egypt,* public officers performed police functions. Their weapon and symbol of authority was a staff topped by a metal knob engraved with the king's name. *The baton carried by the modern police officer may have its origin in that staff.*

The *Greeks* had an impressive form of law enforcement called the *epohri.* Each year at Sparta a body of five epohrs was elected and given almost unlimited powers. They were the highest executive power in the land, being investigator, judge, jury, and executioner. These five men also presided over the Senate and Assembly, assuring that their rules and decrees were followed. One problem with this system, however, was that it promoted corrupt enforcement.

Like the Greeks, the Romans had a highly developed system for the administration of justice. In the Roman Empire during the first century A.D., public officials (called *lictors*) acted as bodyguards for magistrates. When the magistrate ordered, the lictor would bring criminals before him and carry out the magistrate's prescribed punishments, even the death penalty. Their symbol of public authority was a *fasces*, a bundle of rods tied by a red thong around an axe, which represented their absolute authority over life and limb. Within the city of Rome itself, however, the fasces had no axe because there was a right to appeal a capital sentence (Hall, 1974, p.119).

Figure 1-2.
Fasces.

From the Greek Plato came the idea that punishment should serve a purpose rather than just being retaliation. This was further developed in the mid-1700s in England to the idea that, to be just, fair, and reasonable, punishment must fit the crime. (Note the similarity between this concept and the relationship between the crimes and punishments set forth by Hammurabi in 2200 B.C.) This relationship is the basis of *equity* and the basis of law in America, as we will discuss later in this chapter.

Traces of Roman law are still evident in parts of Europe and the United States, for instance, the "Law of the Roman Catholic Church" and Canon Law which sets forth practices regarding marriage, contracts, and court procedures.

☑ CHECK POINT

1. What is a law?
2. When and why did law enforcement begin?
3. What features of our law enforcement system originated in ancient civilizations?

*Answers

1. Law refers to all the rules of conduct established and enforced by the custom, authority, or legislation of a group, community, or country.
2. A system of law and law enforcement began earlier than 2000 years B.C. as a means of controlling human conduct and enforcing society's rules.
3. Features of our law enforcement system which may have originated in ancient civilizations include: establishing specific penalties for specific offenses (Hammurabi), the modern police baton (Egyptian staff), and having punishment serve a purpose (Plato).

ENGLISH LAW AND LAW ENFORCEMENT

In the fifth century A.D. the famous knights of King Arthur's court roamed through Britain suppressing wrongs, enforcing rights, and safeguarding travelers. *Their shields, which they would die to protect, may be the origin of the shield worn on the modern police officer's uniform.*

Throughout the *Anglo-Saxon Period* it was assumed that the King's Peace

---

*Drawing of fasces by Ione Bell.

pervaded the entire country. England was divided into fifty-two separate shires (counties), which were the primary political subdivisions of England. The king appointed a person in each shire to act on his behalf as a reeve (the Anglo-Saxon word for *judge*). The *shire-reeve* had two primary duties: (1) responsibility to the king for insuring law and order within the shire, and (2) serving as the judge of cases brought before him. *The name shire-reeve has been contracted over the years to become sheriff.*

The occupation of the German tribes (Anglia and Saxony) were not for war as with most other nations, but for settlement and development of the people in a new country. Every male, unless excused by the king, was enrolled for police purposes into a group of ten families known as a *tithing*. To maintain order in the tithing, they had a leader or chief tithingman who was the mayor, council, and judge all in one. Society was so basic at this time that they needed to enforce only two laws: laws against murder and theft.

Any victim or person who discovered a crime would put out the "Hue and Cry" (Lunt, 1938), for example, "Stop, thief." Anyone who heard the cry would stop whatever he was doing and help capture the suspect. *This may be the forerunner of both the general alarm and the citizen's arrest.*

> The tithing system established the principle of collective responsibility for maintaining local law and order.

When capture was made, the suspect was brought before the chief tithingman, who determined innocence or guilt plus punishment. Theft was often punished by civil restitution or working off the loss by bondage or servitude— *the basis for civil law, restitution for financial loss* (Lunt, 1938).

As the size of the tithings increased and reached the size of ten times ten or one hundred families, they were called *hundreds*. If the village was near the coast, log walls or fortresses were built, and the settlement became known as a borough or walled tithing or hundred. The chief tithingman of each hundred was called the *head constable*; the chief of each tithing was called a *petty constable*. The modern English policeman is a descendant of these constables. *In the United States, constable is the title of an officer whose duty is to maintain the peace, arrest offenders, serve writs, and execute warrants.*

In 1066 the *Norman Conquest* of England occurred. In September of 1066 an invading army from Normandy, France (the same beaches from which the Allies began the invasion of Europe during World War II), began the invasion and conquest of England. The French culture, language, and government were superimposed over the English, basically Germanic, people.

In December of 1066 the Duke of Normandy was crowned King of all England—King William I. He changed the form of local government (that centered around each castle) into a strong central government, a dictatorship. He substituted mutilation for the death penalty and instituted the wager of battle to decide who was right and wrong. That is, a person accused of a crime could challenge the accuser to a battle; the winner won his case, presumably the result of God's judgment.

In addition, the Normans modified the tithing system into the *Frankpledge* system, which refers to the guarantee for peace maintenance that the king demanded from all free Englishmen.

> The *Frankpledge system* required loyalty to the king's law and mutual local responsibility in maintaining the peace.

Descendants of William I created *circuit judges*, a system brought to America in the form of Circuit Judge Roy Bean in the area west of the Pecos. With establishment of circuit judges and courts, the shire-reeves and constables were relieved of their judicial powers and left with the task of enforcing the law. Less than one hundred years later, in 1166, *trial by jury of one's peers was established along with a grand jury responsible for investigation and for indictments as we know them today.* According to Lunt (1938), the juries, called Assizes, were designed to settle disputes over ownership or possession of land. Their decisions were final; there was no appeal.

Also in 1166 Henry the Law-Giver put forth his famous *Leges Henrici* (Laws of Henry).

> The *Leges Henrici* made law enforcement a public matter and separated offenses into felonies and misdemeanors.

Offenses against the King's peace, arson, robbery, murder, false coinage, and crimes of violence were classified as felonies.

Fifty years later, in 1215, King John signed the *Magna Carta*, a bill which provided that all cities and villages would have their liberties and customs, that every man was entitled to trial by jury, and that state and local governments should be separated.

> The *Magna Carta*, similar to our Bill of Rights, gave Englishmen due process of law.

In 1285 King Edward I set up a curfew and night watch program which allowed for the gates of Westminster, then capital of England, to be locked. This would keep the city's occupants in and unwanted persons out. Bailiffs were hired as night watchmen to enforce the curfew and guard the gates. Edward I also mandated that groups of one hundred merchants be responsible for keeping peace in their districts, *thus making law enforcement a local responsibility.*

With an ever-increasing population and a trend toward urbanization, society in England became increasingly complex. Law enforcement became truly a collective responsibility. If a man's next-door-neighbor broke the law, the man was responsible for bringing the law-breaker before the shire-reeve. This prompted the development of a system under which the hundred would decide yearly who would be responsible for maintaining law and order. Responsibility rotated among community members. It was inevitable that some people, not wanting to serve their turn, would seek other members of the hundred to serve in their place for pay. *This was the beginning of the system of paid deputies appointed to be responsible for law and order.* The paid deputy system was then formalized so that those whose turn it was to pay for protecting the hundred met and appointed the law enforcers.

During the fourteenth century the *office of Justice of the Peace was established to replace the shire-reeve.* The Justice of the Peace was assisted by the constables and by three or four men knowledgeable of the country's laws. At first the Justice of the Peace was involved in both judicial matters and law enforcement, but later his powers became strictly judicial. He was responsible for settling matters of wages, prices, conditions of labor, and *pre-trial preliminary hearings* to determine if there was enough evidence to keep a man in jail to await trial. The Justice of the Peace eventually became the real power of local government (Lunt, 1938).

With the passing of feudal times and rise in the power of the church, the unit of local government in rural areas progressed from the hundred to the parish, that is, the area in which people lived who worshipped in a particular parish church. Once each year the parish appointed a person to be parish constable and to act as their law officer. This system of maintaining law and order in rural Britain lasted from the Middle Ages until the eighteenth century.

> During the Middle Ages, the Parish Constable System was used for rural law enforcement; the Watch and Ward System was used for urban law enforcement.

Developments in urban England required a different system of law enforcement. With urbanization came commerce, industry, and a variety of buildings, usually made of wood since England was primarily forest land. For purposes of fire prevention, the town guild appointed men known as the *Watch and Ward who patrolled at night on fire watch. They assumed the coincidental responsibility of preventing people from breaking into houses and shops.*

Although the Watch and Ward System was primitive and not too effective, it was adequate until the Industrial Revolution (1750) began. About the same time famine struck the rural areas, and large numbers of people moved from the country into the towns seeking work in weaving and knitting mills and in factories. Many, however, failed to find work, and England experienced much unemployment, poverty, and crime.

In addition, political extremists often aroused mobs and incited them to march upon Parliament. These mobs were usually unruly, destructive, and indifferent to the safety of local residents and their property. The government had no civil police force to deal with mob violence, so they ordered a magistrate to read the "riot act," which permitted the magistrate to call on the military to quell the riot.

The use of a military force to repress civil disobedience did not work very well. Soldiers hesitated to fire on their own townspeople, and the townspeople, who actually paid the soldiers' wages, resented being fired on. Consequently, when the riot act was read and the military were called into action, citizen unrest usually mounted.

In addition to unemployment, poverty, and resentment against use of military force, the invention of gin and whiskey in the seventeenth century also caused a great rise in violent crimes and theft.

> The government responded to the increase in crime by improving street lighting, hiring more watchmen, and greatly increasing the severity of punishment for all kinds of crime.

In 1736 a law was passed requiring every gin and whiskey seller and manufacturer to purchase exhorbitantly priced licenses. This law did not stop the flow of gin and whiskey, but instead greatly increased the corruption of the constables. Since the constables were often employed in the liquor trade, it was impossible for them to honestly enforce the regulations governing taverns and inns. Additionally, the London watchmen who were responsible for regulating the morals of the townspeople were highly susceptible to bribes and payoffs.

Around 1750 Henry Fielding, an English magistrate and novelist (author of *Tom Jones*) was instrumental in establishing the *Bow Street Runners, the first detective unit* in London, and an indicator of the increasing problems faced by law enforcement officials.

Parliament was justifiably concerned about poverty, unemployment, lawlessness, and general conditions. Five Parliamentary commissions of inquiry met in London between 1780 and 1820 to determine what should be done about the public order. It was not until Sir Robert (Bobbie) Peel was appointed Home Secretary that the first really constructive proposal was brought before Parliament.

Peelian Reform

Sir Robert Peel, often referred to as the "father of police administration," proposed a return to the Anglo-Saxon principle of individual community responsibility for preserving law and order. He proposed that London have a body of civilians appointed and paid by the community to serve as *police officers.** Parliament agreed, and, in 1829, the Metropolitan Police of London was organized.

---

*The name *police*, introduced into England from France, is derived from the Greek word *polis* meaning "city." Originally, in continental Europe, the term included all activities of a state which had not been segregated into special administrative branches. By the middle of the eighteenth century, the scope of police activity had narrowed to two main classifications: security police, charged with preserving the individual from dangers threatening his person or property, and welfare police, charged with fostering the public welfare by promoting interest beneficial to society.

Peel's principles for reform called for: local responsibility for law and order; appointed, paid civilians to assume this responsibility; and standards for these individuals' conduct and organization. His proposals resulted in the organization of the Metropolitan Police of London.

Many of the fundamental principles of Peelian Reform are as applicable today as they were in 1829:

Police must be stable, efficient, and organized militarily.

Police must be under governmental control.

The absence of crime will best prove the efficiency of the police.

The distribution of crime news is essential.

The deployment of police strength by both time and area is essential.

No quality is more indispensable to a policeman than a perfect command of temper; a quiet, determined manner has more effect than violent action.

Good appearance commands respect.

The securing and training of proper persons is at the root of efficiency.

Public security demands that every police officer be given a number.

Police headquarters should be centrally located and easily accessible.

Policemen should be hired on a probationary basis.

Police records are necessary to the correct distribution of police strength.

Although most of these principles make sense to us in the twentieth century, they were not readily accepted in nineteenth century England. During the first few years of Peelian Reform, strong opposition was encountered. In addition to this opposition, Peel was faced with the problem of finding a building for the newly created London Police. He chose an abandoned building that had been built many years before for the Scottish nobility to use when they visited London. This building housed the London Metropolitan Police, and it became known the world over as Scotland Yard as canonized by A. Conan Doyle in his Sherlock Holmes mysteries.

Peel eventually became a national hero, and his reforms led to increased status and prestige for all who entered a career in law enforcement. His principles also became the basis of police reform in many large cities in America.

London Metropolitan Police (1829)

The London Metropolitan Police were uniformed for easy identification —top hats, three-quarter length royal blue coats and white trousers—and were armed only with a truncheon. They were obviously *not* soldiers as they had no guns. They were (and still are) called "Bobbies" after Sir "Bobbie" Peel.

Unfortunately, the London Metropolitan Police were not popular. Soon after the force went on street duty in 1829, a London mob assembled, prepared to march on Parliament. A police sergeant and two constables asked the mob leaders to send their people home. The police, trained to be courteous but firm, did their job properly; however, the mob did not disperse. Instead they attacked the sergeant and constables, killing the sergeant and critically injuring the constables. A jury of London citizens, after hearing evidence clearly indicative of a cold, brutal murder, returned a verdict of justifiable homicide. In time, however, the effect of the policemen discharging their duties with professional integrity created a respect for the law which still exists today in England.

City and Borough Police Forces (1835)

With the coming of broad public use of the steam engine and railways and the building of better roads, many criminals moved from London to provincial cities such as Birmingham, Liverpool, and Manchester. Soon the citizens of these cities demanded some police organization similar to that of London. In 1835 Parliament enacted permissive legislation allowing (but not requiring) every city or borough* over 20,000 people to form a police force. The act called for the town council, a body of elected representatives who administered the city's affairs, to appoint from its members a watch committee to (1) appoint a chief of police, (2) appoint the officers of the force, and (3) administer the force.

County Police Act (1839)

The counties had no collective system of local government larger than the individual parish, yet they, too, felt the need for an organized police force. This prompted Parliament to pass the County Police Act (1839) giving magistates the responsibility to fix the strength of the force and to appoint and dismiss the chief constable. Unlike his borough counterpart, the parish magistrate, once appointed, had absolute rights of appointment over his subordinates. The new force was paid for by citizens' taxes.

The County Police Act produced an uneven response. Only fifteen of the fifty-two counties had adopted it by the end of 1840. Reluctance to implement the legislation came from several sources, the most important being financial interests. The decision rested with the magistrates, the principle landowners in each county, and they had a vested interest in keeping taxes down.

Women Enter Law Enforcement (1883)

In 1883 the London Metropolitan Police appointed two women to supervise women convicts. Their numbers and functions later expanded.

---

*Unincorporated township.

In 1905 a woman was attached to the London Metropolitan Police force to conduct inquiries in cases involving women and children. Each year an increasing number of police matrons were hired.

Around 1914 considerable public concern arose in favor of the employment of women police as part of the organization for the prevention and detection of crime. The Penal Reform League passed a resolution urging the appointment of women police constables with powers equal to those of men constables in all county boroughs and the metropolitan boroughs of the County of London (Chapman and Johnston, 1962).

Soon after, the Criminal Law Amendment Committee and the National Vigilance Association sent delegates to interview the Secretary of State on the subject. Delegates were then appointed by the Women's Industrial Council to serve on the Parks Committee of the London Council.

Early in World War I, two separate movements for women police began. The Women Police Volunteers was formed and later came to be called the Women Police Service. In 1920 the group split into the Women's Auxiliary Service and the Women Patrols of the National Union of Women Workers of Great Britain and Ireland. The present official women police are largely a direct continuation of the Women Patrols (Chapman and Johnston, 1962).

☑ CHECK POINT

1. What features of our law enforcement system originated in England?
2. What is the significance of the tithing system?
3. What is the significance of the Frankpledge system?
4. What is the significance of Leges Henrici?
5. What is the significance of the Magna Carta?
6. What is the significance of the Watch and Ward System?
7. How did English law enforcement officials respond to increased crime?
8. What significant contributions to law enforcement were made by Sir Robert Peel?
9. Where and when was the first police department established in England and what was it called?

*Answers

1. Features of our law enforcement system which originated in England include:
   a. Officer's shield may have originated in the shields of King Arthur's knights during the fifth century A.D.
   b. Office of sheriff originated in the position of the shire (county) reeve (judge) appointed by the king during the Anglo-Saxon period.
   c. General alarm and citizen's arrest may have originated in the cry raised by any member of a tithing who witnessed a crime.
   d. Office of constable originated in the title given to the head of the English hundred.
   e. Circuit judges and courts established separation between enforcing laws and judging offenders.
   f. Trial by jury and grand jury were established in 1166.
   g. Due process was provided to the English people in 1215 through the Magna Carta.
   h. Local responsibility for law enforcement is noted throughout English history; Leges Henrici made law enforcement a public matter in 1166.

i. Paid law enforcement officers began in England when the hundred decided to use a system of selecting yearly who would be responsible for maintaining law and order. Some chose to pay others to serve in their place.

j. Office of Justice of the Peace was established in the fourteenth century.

k. Women in law enforcement began in 1883 when two women were appointed to the London Metropolitan Police to supervise women convicts.

2. The tithing system established the principle of collective responsibility for maintaining local law and order.

3. The Frankpledge system required loyalty to the king's law and mutual local responsibility in maintaining the peace.

4. Leges Henrici made law enforcement a public matter and separated offenses into felonies and misdemeanors.

5. The Magna Carta gave Englishmen "due process" of law. (It is similar to our Bill of Rights.)

6. The Watch and Ward System was the first system used for urban law enforcement. It was originally intended primarily for fire prevention!

7. English law enforcement officials responded to increases in crime by improving street lighting, hiring more watchmen, and greatly increasing the severity of punishment for all kinds of crime.

8. Peel's principles for reform called for local responsibility for law and order; appointed, paid civilians to assume this responsibility; and standards for these individuals' conduct and organization. His proposals resulted not only in general reform but in the organization of the London Metropolitan Police.

9. The first police department established in England was the London Metropolitan Police, established in 1829.

EARLY LAW ENFORCEMENT IN THE UNITED STATES

Many features of British law enforcement were present in early American colonial settlements. In New England, where people depended on commerce and industry, the night watchman or constable served as protector of public order. In the South, where agriculture played a dominant role, the office of sheriff was established as the means of area law enforcement.

> New England adopted the night watchman or constable as the chief means of law enforcement; the South adopted the office of sheriff.

Most of the watchmen and sheriffs were volunteers, but many were paid to serve in the place of others who were supposed to patrol as a civic duty.

Many different types of law enforcement were tried in many different parts of the country. Almost all used some kind of night watch system, with little or no protection during the day. Boston established the first night watch in 1636, followed in 1658 by New York's "rattle watch," so called because the watchmen used rattles to announce their presence and to communicate with each other (Folley, 1973). As in England, the early night watches were seldom effective. Usually members of the watch were citizens who rotated the responsibility among themselves and who often hired any substitute they could find, no matter what his character. Further, it was also common for a person to be sentenced to be a watchman as a form of punishment for a misdemeanor.

Daytime policing came into existence in 1833 in Philadelphia, followed by Boston in 1838, Cincinnati in 1842, and New York in 1844 (Folley, 1973). Due to a continuing increase in crime during the daytime, New York City hired an assortment of watchmen, fire marshals, and bell ringers to patrol during the day and night. In 1833 legislators from New York City visited the London Metropolitan Police Department and were so highly impressed that in 1844, New York City followed the pattern set in England fifteen years earlier by Sir Robert Peel.

> In 1844 New York City established the first modern American city police force.

The night watch and the daytime forces were combined into one force working around the clock.

Soon other police forces similar to that in New York developed including forces in Chicago, Cincinnati, New Orleans, Philadelphia, Boston, Baltimore, and San Francisco.

In spite of patterning themselves after the London Metropolitan Police, New York police officers vigorously protested against wearing uniforms. It wasn't until twelve years later that New York adopted a full police uniform and became the first uniformed law enforcement officers in the country. Likewise, although Henry Fielding established the Bow Street Runners (the first detective unit) in 1750, it was over a hundred years later before American police agencies recognized a need for detective units. In 1866 Detroit established the first detective bureau, followed by New York in 1882, and Cincinnati in 1886.

When city police were first established, their only contact with their departments was face-to-face meetings or messengers. However, during the 1850s telegraph networks linked police headquarters directly with their districts, making unnecessary the daily meetings between the captains and the commissioners. Several decades later a modified telegraph system linked the patrolman directly to his station. A fire-alarm system, first introduced in Boston, was adopted for police use. Call boxes placed on city street corners became a common sight. These boxes were equipped with a simple lever which signalled the station that the officer was at his post. A bell system was then added that allowed the patrolman to use a few simple signals to call an ambulance, a "slow wagon" for routine duties, or a "fast wagon" for emergencies. The introduction of a special "Gamewell" telephone into the call box in 1880 made this a truly two-way communication system, greatly improving the contact between the patrolmen and their station house.

The Civil War brought new problems of social control. Municipal forces tried to meet these problems by organizing new divisions and specializing the force. As centers of population became increasingly urbanized and fringe areas became incorporated suburbs of the hub city, a trend developed to add forces to the police organization rather than to centralize or consolidate them.

Consequently, newly-developed fringe cities had their own forces which, rather than improving efficiency, fostered complex, uncoordinated relationships, compartmentalization, and inefficiency.

Establishment of State Law Enforcement Agencies

In 1835, when Texas was still a republic, the Texas provisional government established the Texas Rangers.

> The Texas Rangers (established 1835) were the first agency similar to our present day state police.

The Texas Rangers were actually a military unit established into three companies which were responsible for border patrol. The apprehension of Mexican cattle rustlers was a primary task. (Folley, 1973, p.64).

Massachusetts became the next state to establish a state law enforcement agency by appointing a small force of state officers in 1865 to control vice within the state. The state also granted them general police powers; therefore, Massachusetts is usually credited with establishing the first law enforcement agency with general police authority throughout the state.

Establishment of Federal Law Enforcement Agencies

Several federal law enforcement agencies were created by Congress to meet demands created by the changing conditions of the nation.

> Among the earliest federal law enforcement agencies were: United States Marshals, Immigration and Naturalization Service, the Secret Service, and the Internal Revenue Service.

The oldest federal agency is the U.S. Marshals Office, created in 1789. Thirteen U.S. Marshals were assigned to President George Washington's Attorney General. As the nation began to grow westward, the U.S. Marshals were the main law enforcement in the territories and made some men famous, such as "Wild" Bill Hickok, Matt Dillon, and Wyatt Earp. When the Civil War ended (1865) and most of the territories had become states, the U.S. Marshals became the bailiffs of the U.S. District Courts, where violations of federal crimes are tried.

The U.S. Justice Department also established other federal law enforcement agencies such as the Immigration and Naturalization Service (1891), of which the Border Patrol is a well-known division.

The Treasury Department also established federal law enforcement agencies which are still well known today. The Secret Service was created in 1865 to control the flood of counterfeit currency bankrupting the war effort. After President McKinley was assassinated in 1901, the Secret Service was authorized to protect the President and his family.

Another well-known federal agency established within the Treasury

Department was the Internal Revenue Service (1862) and its famous Intelligence Division agents whose income tax evasion cases brought long prison sentences to such infamous criminals as Scarface Al Capone, Vito Genovese, and many others.

LAW ENFORCEMENT IN THE 1900s

Although there have been dramatic changes in law enforcement, many features from the past still exist, including the positions of sheriff and constable. The sheriff and constable, elected officers, were usually the chief law enforcement officers in their areas. The sheriff was generally responsible for the entire county, the constable for a smaller area such as unincorporated townships and villages. They were usually elected for two to four years and were not eligible for reelection, thus eliminating their potential to gain too much control over those who elected them. Through the years the office of constable has been slowly disappearing. However, the office of sheriff remains today with very similar functions; that is, he is responsible for police protection primarily in the unincorporated areas of a county.

Just as in earlier times in other countries, corruption became a problem in law enforcement in the 1900s. The Jacksonian* philosophy, which placed rewards in the hands of victors, led politicians to staff many of the nation's police forces with incompetent people as rewards for support, "fixing" arrests, or assuring that arrests were not made, and securing immunity from supervision for certain establishments or people.

> The Jacksonian philosophy encouraged politicians to reward their "friends" by giving them key positions in police departments.

With so many second-rate, low potential, spoils-motivated personnel within the police department, corruption, theft, shake-downs, and related problems hindered effective administration of law enforcement in many American cities.

Reform movements began early but moved slowly against the solidly entrenched political "untouchables."

> Cities sought to break political control by a variety of organizational techniques, including the election of policemen and chiefs, administering forces through bipartisan lay boards, asking states to assume local policing, and instituting Mayor-Council or Council-City Manager Municipal Government—which have proved to be the most effective thus far.

The *election of the municipal chief of police* was common with the establishment of local departments. Remembering the corrupt officials who served

---

*Andrew Jackson was President from 1829-1837.

as long as they pleased the king, the people elected police officials to serve short terms so they would not have time to become too powerful or corrupt. But this system had its drawbacks. Not only were the officials not in office long enough to become corrupt, they were not in office long enough to gain proficiency in their job. In fact, officials would just get to know their own officers and have enough experience to run the police department when their terms would expire. Additionally, since terms were so short, officials kept their civilian jobs and generally devoted most of their time to them, giving only spare time to running the police force. This system lacked professionalism; the position of police chief became a popularity contest. Therefore, it was decided that a permanent police chief, qualified with experience and ability, was the best way to have effective law enforcement. Today the elected police chief system remains in only a few cities.

In the mid 1800s *administrative police boards or commissions* were established. They were made up of judges, mayors, and private citizens who served as the head of the police department with the police chief following their orders. The rationale was that the chief of police should be a professional and keep his job continuously, but that civilian control was necessary to maintain responsibility to community needs. This system lasted many years, but it had serious weaknesses. The board members often proved more of a hindrance than a help, and the system fostered political corruption.

As a reaction against local boards, and in an attempt to control corrupt police agencies, *state control* of local agencies was developed in some areas of the country. It was believed that if the state controlled local agencies, citizens would be assured of adequate and uniform law enforcement. While some cities still operate within this framework, most cities and states found this was not the answer to the problem because the laws were not equally enforced. In some areas the laws were underenforced and in other areas, overenforced. The system also lacked responsiveness to local demands and needs. Therefore, control was again given to the local government in most instances.

The next system to be tried was the *commission government charter*. Commissioners were elected and charged with various branches of city government. This system, also on the decline, was as inadequate as the administrative police board.

The most efficient and prevalent current local system is the *mayor-council or council-city manager municipal government*. The former is very efficient when the mayor is a full-time, capable administrator. The latter assures more continuity in the business administration and executive control of the overall operations because a professional, nonpolitical administrator is managing the affairs of the community. Either way the chief of police is selected on the basis of merit.

Largely because of civil service and a grassroots inspired groundswell of general reform, most police forces have shaken the influence of corrupt politics. In contrast to conditions at the turn of the century, appointment to the forces and police administration generally is vastly improved. Police recruitment, discipline, and promotion have been removed from politics in most cities.

Communications involving police service have also greatly improved. The radio and patrol car transformed the relationship between the police and the public and offered increased protection for everyone. The continuous expansion of the telephone in the 1960s and 1970s made it easier for people to call the police. Police dispatchers were added to tie radio systems directly into telephone networks. The use of fingerprint systems and the increased employment of policewomen as well as many other advances occurred at an accelerated pace.

However, despite the advanced technology which greatly improved the police officer's ability to respond to requests for aid and increased his mobility, the basic strategy of police has not altered.

> Crime waves in metropolitan areas cause cities to improve their street lighting, increase the number of police officers on the streets, and demand more severe punishment for the convicted criminals.

This should sound very familiar! One important change has occurred, however. In the last three decades, the human factor has assumed greater importance as police agencies cope with the tensions and dislocations of population growth, increasing urbanization, developing technology, the civil rights revolution, changing social norms, and a breakdown of traditional values. These factors have enormously complicated law enforcement, making more critical the need for truly professional police officers.

Today's local police officers must be aware of human factors and understand the psychological and sociological implications for their community. They must deal with all citizens, rich and poor, young and old, in ways which will maintain their support and confidence. They must provide a variety of services while protecting life, property, and personal liberty. They must be law enforcement generalists with a working knowledge of federal, state, county, and municipal law, traffic law, criminal law, juvenile law, narcotics, liquor control, and countless other areas.

Development of State Law Enforcement Agencies in the 1900s

Most state police agencies established prior to the twentieth century were created as a response to a limited need such as the control of vice. Such was not the case in Pennsylvania.

> The first modern state police agency was the Pennsylvania Constabulary, which originated in 1905 to meet several needs.

As noted by Folley (1973 p. 66), the Pennsylvania Constabulary (1) provided the governor an executive arm to assist him in accomplishing his responsibilities, (2) provided a means to quell riots occurring during labor disputes in the coal regions, and (3) improved law enforcement services in the rural portions of the state where county officials were generally ineffective. Governor Pennypacker's rationale for the first need to be met by such a state agency is vividly described by Katherine Mayo (1917, pp. 5-6):

In the year 1903, when I assumed the office of chief executive of the state, I found myself thereby invested with supreme executive authority. I found that no power existed to interfere with me in my duty to enforce the laws of the state, and that by the same token, no conditions could release me from my duty so to do. I then looked about me to see what instruments I possessed wherewith to accomplish this bounden obligation—what instruments on whose loyalty and obedience I could truly rely. I perceived three such instruments—my private secretary, a very small man; my woman stenographer; and the janitor ... So I made the state police.

Humorous as it may sound, there was a large element of truth in the governor's thinking. Further, the labor riots were real and had to be faced. Perhaps most important, however, was the emphasis on rural law enforcement and the establishment of a uniformed mounted force offering protection in even the most remote areas of Pennsylvania. The Pennsylvania state police served as a model for other states and heralded the advent of modern state policing.

Development of Federal Law Enforcement Agencies in the 1900s

The most important federal law enforcement agency created in the twentieth century is the Federal Bureau of Investigation, better known as the FBI.

The world-famous Federal Bureau of Investigation was not created by the U.S. Congress until 1908. Six attorney agents were hired, but they were not allowed to use guns. In 1924 J. Edgar Hoover was appointed Director, and he completely reorganized the Bureau. Shortly thereafter it reached national stature. The FBI has jurisdiction in three general areas encompassing some 180 different criminal matters: (1) crimes involving national security, (2) interstate crimes, and (3) crimes on the high seas. The importance of the FBI as well as other federal and state agencies will be discussed in detail in Chapter 5.

☑ CHECK POINT

1. What systems of law enforcement were brought from England and adopted in the United States in colonial New England and the South?
2. When and where was the first modern American police force begun and what was it modeled after?
3. What state and federal law enforcement agencies originated prior to 1900? After 1900?
4. What was the Jacksonian philosophy and how did it influence law enforcement in the 1900s?
5. What organizational systems of law enforcement were tried in the United States to reduce corruption? Which has been most successful?

*Answers

1. New England adopted the night watchman or constable as the chief means of law enforcement; the South adopted the office of sheriff.
2. New York City established the first modern American city police force in 1844.

3. The first agency similar to our present state police was the Texas Rangers (1835). The first modern state police agency was the Pennsylvania Constabulary (1905). Among the earliest federal law enforcement agencies were: United States Marshals, Immigration and Naturalization Service, Federal Drug Enforcement Agency, the Secret Service, and the Internal Revenue Service. The most important twentieth century federal law enforcement agency is the FBI.

4. The Jacksonian philosophy held that "to the victor belong the spoils." This philosophy led many politicians to reward friends by giving them high-ranking jobs in law enforcement, resulting in much corruption.

5. Cities have sought to break political control by a variety of organizational techniques including the election of police chiefs, administering forces through bipartisan lay boards (administrative police boards), asking states to assume local policing, using commission government charters, and establishing Mayor-Council or Council City Manager Municipal Governments which select the police chief on merit—the most effective system to date.

CURRENT ORGANIZATION OF LAW ENFORCEMENT

Having traced the history of law enforcement from its ancient roots, through its British influences and colonial America, to the present time, let's look at what has resulted from the developments of the past. From the preceding historical overview, you probably have a fairly good idea of the complexity and diversity which exists within law enforcement.

American police forces may be classified according to the level of government that each serves, but no uniform pattern of police administration exists at any of the five levels of government, and no mechanism exists to coordinate the activities and goals of the agencies which differ greatly in size, jurisdiction, and operational methods.

> The five levels of government authorized to have law enforcement agencies result in the presence of (1) township and special district police, (2) municipal police, (3) county police, (4) state police, and (5) federal police.

Township and Special District Police

The United States has approximately 19,000 townships which vary widely in scope of governmental powers and operations. Most townships provide a very limited range of services for predominately rural areas. Some townships, often those in well-developed fringe areas surrounding a metropolitan complex, perform functions similar to municipal police.

Not all townships have their own police force. Many rural townships have few law enforcement problems and purposely avoid appropriating funds for local police protection, relying instead upon the sheriff or state police (or both) for preventive patrol and criminal investigation.

When small, essentially rural townships enter the policing field, a variety of difficulties arise. In addition to jurisdiction conflicts and the resulting diffusion of responsibility, a general lack of coordination results from having two or more government agencies, at different levels, actively policing the same area. The small township department, with its limited financial support, cannot offer complete police services, provide specialized services, nor police the area continually, but if there *is* a township police force, regardless of its adequacy, township residents and officials cannot exert as much pressure on the county governing body to expand the sheriff's force to bring about better general county police protection.

Many townships have only a one-man police force similar to the resident deputy system frequently found in sheriff's departments in which one man must police vast, sparsely populated regions. This man serves as a "jack-of-all trades" and is on emergency call day and night. His home may serve as headquarters. Because of the informality of township policing, rural township police personnel are often neither carefully selected nor fully trained for police duties in today's complex society.

Municipal Police

The United States has over 40,000 police jurisdictions and approximately 450,000 police officers, all with similar responsibilities, but with limited geographical jurisdictions. The least uniformity and greatest organizational complexity is found at the municipal level due to local autonomy, that is, the independence of local governmental units to control their own police departments.

The majority of these police forces consist of fewer than ten men who provide resident deputy-type police service rather than emergency-oriented service. Some personnel of very small forces are appointed with little attention to their mental or physical fitness for the work, and many such personnel have never received any formal police training and lack proper supervision and discipline.

In contrast are police agencies in large metropolitan areas such as New York City, which have over 30,000 officers who are highly qualified and trained to perform demanding duties which police officers in smaller agencies rarely encounter. Likewise, many suburban areas are now hiring career-minded, progressive police officers who bring with them dedication, education, and a high degree of competency in human relations and technical skills.

Suburban police departments have different policing problems than small towns and large cities, just as a small town police department is far different from that of a city of several million people in terms of organization, structure, and discipline.

County Police

There are about 3,065 county governments in the United States. In most counties the sheriff is the principal county law enforcement officer. He is usually elected locally for a two- or four-year term. Qualifications are set by state law, and the salary is usually set by the legislature or the county board. The sheriff's powers and duties are also established by state law. Each sheriff is authorized to appoint deputies and, working with them, to assume responsibility for providing police protection as well as a variety of other functions including (1) keeping the public peace, (2) executing civil and criminal process throughout the county,* (3) keeping the county jail, (4) preserving the dignity of the court, and (5) enforcing court orders.

The sheriff operates freely in the unincorporated portions of the county and works with the municipal police departments in incorporated areas. The sheriff also works closely with the state police or highway patrol and township personnel in unincorporated portions of the county.

In some states the coroner or medical examiner is, by statutory provision, the chief law enforcement officer of the county. When this occurs, a sheriff's department usually has the traditional combination of criminal and civil duties to perform.

State Police

Two types of state police agencies exist. Some, like the Michigan State Police, have general police powers and may enforce all state laws. Others, like the California Highway Patrol, direct their attention to enforcement of traffic laws upon public highways (Germann, Day, and Gallati, 1973). As noted by Adams (1968), each state differs from all others in its state police agencies, depending on its history and evolving law enforcement needs. From the Texas Rangers in 1835 to the present, new agencies have been formed and old agencies reorganized to meet the changing requirements of the states.

Usually *state police agencies*, although often having general police authority, do not work within municipalities which have their own forces, except upon request. These state forces generally do not enter local labor, political, or other mass disturbances or potentially disastrous situations unless asked by the local sheriff or police chief.

Most *highway patrol agencies* enforce state traffic laws and all laws governing operation of vehicles on public highways in the state. They usually operate in uniform, drive distinctively marked patrol cars and motorcycles, and engage in such activities as (1) enforcing laws regulating the use of vehicles, (2) maintaining preventive patrol on the highways, (3) regulating traffic movements and relieving congestion, (4) investigating traffic accidents, and (5) making surveys and studies of accidents and enforcement practices to improve traffic safety (Adams, 1968). Since state highway patrols are a recent development, not subject to the mistakes of the past, they have a professional quality found in few law enforcement agencies at other levels of government.

A governor may send state highway patrol or state police personnel to a locality to preserve the peace. This occurred in Mississippi and other southern states during mob actions prompted by efforts to racially integrate public schools. On two such occasions (Little Rock, Arkansas, in 1957 and Oxford, Mississippi, in 1962), National Guard units and regular U.S. Army military personnel were ordered by federal authorities to assist state and local police in maintaining civil order.

The increasing responsibilities of state police are considerable. They often work in cooperation with the National Guard to restore order in mass disturbances. They have assumed responsibility from county sheriffs for policing traffic on major highways, and they assist the sheriff or small-town

---

*Such as serving civil legal papers and criminal warrants.

police officer in solving crimes requiring the use of specialized equipment. Further, many state police or highway patrol organizations administer the duties of the state fire marshal's office.

In addition to state police or highway patrol forces, some states have organized special departments for the regulation of movies and for other forms of censorship, alcoholic beverage control units, laboratories for criminal investigation evidence analysis, and central clearing-houses for criminal identification and criminal modus operandi. Also some states have special divisions to enforce fish, game, and conservation laws and a bureau which compiles and publishes criminal statistics.

Federal Police

Federal police came into being with the creation of the various federal departments following the American Revolution. Most federal agencies are attached to specific departments of the Executive Branch of government and have duties confined to the interests of the parent department. For example, the Justice Department has the United States Marshals and the Federal Bureau of Investigation; the Post Office Department has Postal Inspectors who investigate offenses connected with the mails; the Treasury Department has the Internal Revenue Service, the Secret Service, and the Bureau of Customs. The Military Services have Intelligence and Security Divisions. The Central Intelligence Agency is a separate agency which is concerned with our national security. Most of these agencies will be discussed in greater detail in Chapter 5.

In addition to agencies connected with specific departments, the federal government has several other special units, including those which police federal buildings and national parks.

Of all the federal law enforcement units, the Federal Bureau of Investigation comes closest to functioning as a national police force. Its broad charge is to exercise full police jurisdiction over all federal crimes which are not the immediate and special concern of other federal police agencies. The diverse character of the Bureau's work makes it necessary to have regular contact with police at every level of government.

The numerical strength, powers, and scope of operation of the FBI has increased greatly in recent years. Its jurisdiction has often been enlarged by Congress, and the federal government regularly makes use of its broadened enforcement powers and personnel. These developments are the inevitable response to the ever-broadening scope of operations, the increased mobility, and the increasingly effective techniques of modern criminals to elude apprehension.

Some of the legal instruments fashioned by Congress to increase the efficiency and broaden the scope of the FBI's operation include: (1) the National Stolen Property Act, (2) the Fugitive Felon Law, (3) the National Bank Robbery Act, (4) the Federal Kidnapping Statute—prompted by the Lindbergh case of 1930, and (5) the White Slave Act—covering interstate prostitution.

Overlap

Police agencies of the five governmental levels can be found operating in any given spot in America. For example, you can find: (1) several federal police establishments operating as much as 4,000 miles from Washington, D.C. (2) one or more state-wide police service, (3) the county sheriff and his county police force, (4) the township constables and town police constables or marshals, (5) village police or marshals, (6) city police forces that range in size from 10 to 39,000 officers, (7) special park and turnpike police, (8) special district police, (9) independent state and county detectives, identification, communication, and records agencies, and (10) numerous others of less direct relationship to the official police function.

The evils of overlapping jurisdictions and the pitfalls of competition when two (and often many more) forces find themselves investigating the same offense pose serious problems to law enforcement and highlight the need for education and professionalism.

☑ CHECK POINT

1. **What five governmental levels of law enforcement are currently operating in the United States?**

*Answer

1. Five governmental levels of law enforcement are township and special district police, municipal police, county police, state police, and federal police.

LAWS AND CRIMES

Thus far we've been talking quite generally about law enforcement, and we've used the words *law* and *crime* frequently. Before leaving our historical overview, let's clarify our understanding of these terms and other closely related terms which have evolved right along with law enforcement.

Law

Recall that we began this chapter with a discussion of what law is:

> Law is a body of rules for human conduct which are enforced by imposing penalties for their violation.

Laws define man's social obligations and determine the relations of its members to society and to each other. The purpose of law is to regulate the actions of individuals to conform to the way of life that the people's elected representatives or the community consider essential.

Social or Moral Law

Often obedience to law is obtained through social pressure—ridicule, contempt, scorn, or ostricism. Such methods are called moral or social sanctions, and the laws they enforce are called moral or social laws.

Moral or social laws are laws made by society and enforced solely by social pressure.

Moral or social laws include laws of etiquette, "honor," and morality. When moral laws break down and social sanctions fail to obtain conformity, other laws may be enacted and enforced.

Customary Law

The beginnings of law are found in social habit or custom. Custom is simply precedent—doing what has been done before. In early times custom, religion, morals, and the law were intermingled. Some early customs have, over the centuries, become law.

Customary law is law based on habit or precedent; it is equivalent to common law.

Some customary laws were enforced physically rather than morally, the violator being expelled from the community, sacrificed to the gods, or hanged. Other violations of custom which were not felt to be harmful to the whole community were punished by the injured group or the injured individual with the aid of his family (self-help, vengeance, feud). As long as such acts of vengeance, although regarded as right by the victim, might lead to retaliation, the sanction behind the rules of custom were still purely moral. But when the community began to protect those who had taken *rightful* vengeance, these persons became agents of the community. This kind of self-help met early society's needs in all cases in which a violation was apparent and the right to take vengeance or redress was clear. It did not provide a way to settle controversies. Therefore courts were established to interpret customs and settle controversies.

The growth of customary law was accomplished by court decisions; its rules were found in the tradition, the recollection, or the written record of judicial precedents. Popular custom was replaced by judicial custom. Legally, however, precedents or decisions are not law, but only evidence of the law. Even if the precedent or decision is written, the law in them is "unwritten."

Equity

With the establishment of judicial and legislative authorities, the factors that produce law in modern time became operative. There was, however, an intermediate stage of development in both Roman and English legal history which is known as *equity*.

> Equity means to resort to general principles of fairness and justice whenever existing law is inadequate.*

Neither the Roman praetors nor the English chancellors made rigid rules like legislators; instead they found law in the decisions of single cases as judges do. They did not, however, regard themselves bound by precedents. The new rules were not regarded as law at first, but rather as arbitrary assertions of governmental power. However, both in Rome and in England, equity, following its own precedents, soon developed a new body of judicial custom recognized as law. In England and in the United States, today equity is recognized as judge-made law, that is, a legal ruling by a judge based on fairness.

> Equity requires that the "spirit of the law" take precedence over the "letter of the law."

As noted by Ferguson and Stokke (1976, p. 64): "The rule of thumb in construing penal statutes is that criminal statutes are not to be strictly construed, but rather should be interpreted so as to promote fairness and justice. When construing penal statutes, one must take into consideration the 'spirit of the law, not the letter of the law.' " This imperative to justice is echoed by Germann, Day, and Gallati (1972, p. 16): "In order that justice might prevail, the strict letter of the law is not always satisfactory; often equity must be considered, and legal justice corrected or supplemented by reference to the spirit of the law rather than to the letter of the law."

Common Law

In a nontechnical sense, common law describes the law generally used in the absence of a specific law.

> Common law is what is considered right by local custom.

Common law is a term also frequently used in both medieval and modern times to describe the great body of English unwritten law.

In England common law was the term applied to the laws and customs of the realm applied by the royal courts. It was defined as the customary law of England *set by the judges* as disputes arose. This was in contrast to local custom, equity, or ecclesiastical (church) law. When Parliament supplemented and modified the existing legal principles, the term *common law* was used to describe the law in force before, and independent of, any acts of the legislature. When it is said that a certain doctrine exists by common law, common law is contrasted with statute and equity.

---

*In the U.S., equity describes a system of rules and doctrines supplementing common and statutory law and superseding laws which are inadequate for fair setttlement of a case.

Common law had three classifications of crimes: treason (the worst crime), felony (second in severity), and misdemeanors (including all minor offenses). We will discuss these terms more fully late in this chapter.

The common law brought to the United States by the early settlers and established in the various colonies forms the basis of modern American law. The common law of the states has one exception, Louisiana, which established and kept the system of French civil law.

The federal courts worked out certain principles of the common law along lines of their own. In the United States, as in England, the body of the common law has developed with growing industrial conditions, yet it has been restricted from time to time by the statutes of the states or the federal government. The common law on a given point is always replaced by a statute covering the point. The statute takes precedence.

Statutory Law

In an advanced society, legislation becomes an increasingly important agency of legal development. The United States, as well as many other countries, has largely succeeded in replacing common law (unwritten law) with statutory law (legislated and written law). However, much of our law still rests upon judicial precedent; that is, common law and case law. Case law is a collection of summaries of how statutes have been applied by judges in various situations. Such judicial rulings persist in cases of equity and when points of law come before the courts which were not anticipated by the legislators. In these cases the judges' rulings will, for all practical purposes, be treated as law.

> Statutory law is law passed by the legislature. It may be passed at the federal or state level, and at either level it includes constitutional and ordinary law.

Federal constitutional law is based on the United States Constitution, its amendments, and interpretations of the Constitution by the federal courts. Ordinary federal law consists of acts of Congress, treaties with foreign states, executive orders and regulations, and interpretation of the preceding by federal courts.

State constitutional law is based on the individual state's constitution, its amendments, and interpretations of them by the state's courts. State ordinary law consists of acts of the state legislatures, decisions of the federal courts in matters not governed by federal law, decisions of the state courts in interpreting or developing the common law, executive orders and regulations, and municipal ordinances.

In addition, in most states, each county and city is given the right to make and pass laws for its local jurisdiction, providing the law does not conflict or pre-empt the state's laws. The basis of the local ordinances (laws) are primarily enacted to protect the individual community.

Order of Authority of Law

If two laws conflict, a set order of authority has been established.

> The order of authority of law is: the federal Constitution, treaties with foreign powers, acts of Congress, the state constitutions, state statutes, and finally, common law.

When a statute is rescinded, the common law on that point again becomes of force, unless there is an older, unrescinded statute, in which case that revives.

Criminal Law and Crime

> Criminal law defines crimes and fixes punishments for them.

Criminal law includes rules and procedures for preventing and investigating crimes and prosecuting criminals; regulations governing the constitution of courts, the conduct of trials; and the administration of penal institutions.

American criminal law has a number of unique features. In establishing criminal law, the federal government and each state government are sovereign within the limits of their authority as defined by the Constitution. Therefore, criminal law varies from state to state. Although there are many differences, most of them have a tradition derived from English common law. There is no federal common law jurisdiction in criminal cases, however (*U.S. v. Hudson*, 11 U.S. [14 Cranch] 32 [1812]).

> A crime is an action which is harmful to another person and/or to society and is made punishable by law.

The statutes that define what acts constitute social harm are called *substantive criminal law*, for example, a statute defining homicide. A substantive criminal law not only defines the offense, but also states the punishment. The omission of the punishment invalidates the criminal law.

In most countries crimes and punishments are expressed in statutes. Punishments include removal from public office, fines, exile, imprisonment, and death. Unless the act of which a defendant is accused is expressly defined by statute as a crime, no indictment or conviction for the commission of the act is legal. This provision is important in establishing the difference between government by law and arbitrary dictatorial government.

Crime, then, is an action which violates a law which expressly indicates that it is a criminal offense. It may be either an action forbidden by criminal law, or an act of omission, a failure to do what the law requires. As defined by law, a crime includes both an act and *intent* to commit the act. Criminal intent involves an understanding of the act and *voluntary* commission of it.

People who are insane, people who are forced to commit criminal acts, and legal minors are *not* criminally liable for their actions because they are not capable of committing the act freely and voluntarily, nor are they conscious of their conduct.

Criminal law in the United States generally defines seven classes of crimes. It includes offenses against (1) international law, (2) the dispensation of justice and the legitimate exercise of governmental authority, (3) the public peace, (4) property, (5) trade, (6) public decency, and (7) persons.

And, like English law, American criminal law also classifies crimes with respect to their gravity as treason, felonies, and misdemeanors.

> <u>Felony</u> refers to serious crimes, generally those punishable by death or by imprisonment in the state prison or penitentiary.*

No crime is a felony unless made so by statute, or unless it was a felony under common law. Formerly a felony was a crime punishable by forfeiture of the criminal's lands, or goods, or both. In addition, other punishment might be added, according to the degree of guilt. In England for a long time most felonies were punishable by death.

> <u>Misdemeanor</u> is a term applied to any crime other than treason or a felony.

The criminal codes of the states vary in their classification of offenses that are considered misdemeanors. Examples of crimes usually defined as misdemeanors include libel, assault and battery, malicious mischief, and petty theft. Prosecution for a misdemeanor is generally by information and not by indictment.** Persons found guilty of committing a misdemeanor are usually punished by a fine or by imprisonment in a county or city jail, not in a state prison or penitentiary.

In some states the distinction between felonies and misdemeanors is practically discarded, the punishment for each particular crime being prescribed by statute.

The same situation existed under common law. Although under common law a crime was generally classified as treason, felony, or misdemeanor, many offenses could not be defined exactly, so the rule was adopted that any immoral act harmful to the community was, in itself, a crime, punishable by the courts. Crimes were classified as *mala in se* (bad in itself), based to a large degree on religious doctrine, or as *mala prohibita* (bad because it is forbidden). A *mala in se* crime is one which is so offensive that it is obviously criminal, for example, murder or rape. A *mala prohibita* crime is one which violates a specific regulatory statute, certain traffic violations, for example. These would not usually be considered crimes if no law prohibited them.

---

*The court or jury may inflict a lesser punishment.
**Through a preliminary hearing rather than a grand jury hearing, as we will discuss in Chapter 15.

In most cases, crimes (including treason) which are *mala in se* are called felonies and are punished more severely than those which are *mala prohibita*, most of the latter falling in the category of misdemeanors.

Civil Law and Torts

Civil law refers to all other noncriminal restrictions placed upon individuals. It seeks not punishment, but restitution.

Although laws vary from state to state, generally such actions as trespassing, desertion of family, slander, failure to make good on a contract, or similar actions against an individual would be covered under civil law.

A tort is a civil wrong for which the court will seek a remedy in the form of damages to be paid.

As Prosser notes (1955, p. 7):

A tort is not the same thing as a crime, although the two sometimes have many features in common. The distinction between them lies in the interests affected and the remedy afforded by the law. A crime is an offense against the public at large, for which the state, as the representative of the public, will bring proceedings in the form of criminal prosecution.... A criminal prosecution is not concerned in any way with compensation of the injured individual against whom the crime is committed.... The civil action for a tort, on the other hand, is commenced and maintained by the injured person himself, and its purpose is to compensate him for the damage he has suffered, at the expense of the wrongdoer.

Sutherland and Cressey (1978, p. 8) clarify the distinction between a tort and a crime:

The conventional view is that a crime is an offense against the state, while, in contrast, a tort in violation of civil law is an offense against an individual. A particular act may be considered as an offense against an individual and also against the state, and is either a tort or a crime or both, according to the way it is handled. A person who has committed an act of assault, for example, may be ordered by the civil court to pay the victim a sum of $500 for the damages to his interests, and may also be ordered by the criminal court to pay a fine of $500 to the state. The payment of the first $500 is not punishment, but payment of the second $500 is punishment.

POLICE POWER

Without means of enforcement, the great body of federal, state, municipal, and common law would be empty, meaningless. Recall that the term *law* implies not only the rule, but also enforcement of that rule. It has been said that: "Common to all forms of society are the requisites of authority and power. *Authority* is the right to direct and command. *Power* is the force by means of which others can be obliged to obey" (Germann, Day, and Gallati, 1969, p. 9).

Police power is a term used to describe the power of the federal, state, or municipal governments to pass laws regulating private interests to protect the health and safety of the people, to prevent fraud and oppression, and to promote public convenience, prosperity, and welfare.

> Police power is derived from the U.S. Constitution, U.S. Supreme Court decisions, federal statutes, state constitutions, state statutes, state court decisions, and various municipal charters and ordinances.

Police power was defined by the United States Supreme Court in 1887 as "embracing no more than the power to promote public health, morals, and safety" (Mugler v. Kansas 123 U.S. 623, 661). Others have defined police power as the force used by the state to preserve the general health, safety, welfare, and morals.

For example, narcotic laws are passed to preserve the people's health. Any person who abuses narcotics or drugs by taking them without medical prescription and in proper dosage jeopardizes his mental and physical health. Traffic laws are passed to preserve the general safety and to make the highways safe for the motoring public. Gambling laws are passed by the legislature to protect the welfare of the individual and the family from financial loss. Likewise, juvenile laws are passed to protect the welfare of the juvenile from his parents, guardians, relatives, or other people who would place his physical and mental welfare in danger. Finally, legislation prohibiting prostitution and obscenity is passed to "protect" the public's morals.

All levels of government grant their *legislative* branches the right and power to make laws. The *executive* branches of government are created to enforce these laws while the *judicial* branches interpret what the laws mean and how they are to be enforced.

The police power of the federal government is based on authority granted by the United States Constitution. The general grants of power, such as the power of Congress, the legislative branch of government, to provide for the general welfare of the United States by law, are restricted by other provisions of the Constitution taken from the English Bill of Rights or from the political experience of England and America.

The police power of the states is delegated to them by the federal government in Article X of the Bill of Rights. There is no single source of police power. The Tenth Amendment of our Bill of Rights gives the states those powers not delegated to the federal government. Since the power to organize police forces is not delegated to the federal government, this authority is given to the individual states and their subdivisions, that is, their cities, counties, and townships. Therefore, police power ultimately rests with the people since their elected representatives create the laws which the police enforce.

Because each state is responsible for its citizens' health, safety, and general well-being, the usual procedure has been to assign these functions to municipal police departments in the cities and to sheriffs and constables in the rural areas of the state. Within the limits established by state constitutions, state legislatures may define the powers and duties of police officers in the state. However, police officers' authority and powers cannot conflict with the provisions in the Fourteenth Amendment of the Constitution which guarantee citizens equal protection by due process of law. Therefore, police officers can exercise only the powers and authority specifically granted by legislative enactment.

> Police power is restricted by the Constitution, by the Fourteenth Amendment, and by the courts.

The authority, powers, duties, and limits of the police officer are usually determined by each state for all police officers, state, municipal, and rural. Most states fulfill their responsibility for preserving the public peace, detecting and arresting offenders, and enforcing the law by giving cities the authority to appoint municipal police officers. Although these municipal officers are concerned with enforcing city ordinances, enforcing state statutes is their most important job.

Police authority and power are broad in scope and include maintaining the peace, licensing trades and professions, regulating public service corporations' rates, and enforcing health regulations such as quarantines, compulsory vaccinations, and segregation of people with contagious diseases. State laws and judicial decisions also determine the civil and criminal liability of police officers who step beyond their legal powers in discharging the duties of their office.

Although the state legislature passes laws, the courts, the judicial branch of government, decide the purpose and character of the statutes as well as whether or not these statutes conflict with the Constitution or are contrary to proper public policy. Since the courts continuously review laws, police authority and power cannot easily be corrupted nor controlled by private interests.

The courts determine what police authority and power is appropriate. Acceptable police power requires that the regulations are (1) reasonable, (2) within the power given to the states by the Constitution, and (3) in accord with "due process of law." The requirements of the Constitution and "due process" are discussed in the next chapter.

☑ CHECK POINT

1. Define and differentiate the following terms:

   a. Law
   b. Moral or social law
   c. Customary law
   d. Equity
   e. Common law
   f. Statutory law
   g. Criminal law
   h. Crime
   i. Felony
   j. Misdemeanor
   k. Civil law
   l. Tort

2. What takes precedence? Put the following in their order of authority:

   a. Common law
   b. Federal constitutional law
   c. State constitutional law
   d. State statute
   e. Federal statute

   a. Spirit of the law
   b. Letter of the law

3. Where do police get their power and authority?
4. What restrictions are placed on this power and authority?

*Answers

1. a. Law is a body of rules for human conduct which are enforced by imposing penalties for their violation.
   b. Moral or social laws are laws made by society and enforced solely by social pressure.
   c. Customary law is law based on habit or precedent; it is often equivalent to common law.
   d. Equity means to resort to general principles of fairness and justice whenever existing law is inadequate. It requires that the "spirit of the law" take precedence over the "letter of the law."
   e. Common law is what is considered right by local custom.
   f. Statutory law is law passed by the legislature, either at the state or federal level, including both constitutional and ordinary law.
   g. Criminal law defines crimes and fixes punishments for them.
   h. A crime is an action which is harmful to another person and/or to society and which is made punishable by law.
   i. Felony refers to serious crimes, generally those punishable by death or by imprisonment in the state prison or penitentiary.
   j. Misdemeanor is a term applied to any crime other than treason or a felony.
   k. Civil law refers to all other noncriminal legal restrictions placed upon individuals. It seeks not punishment, but restitution.
   l. A tort is a civil wrong for which the court will seek a remedy in the form of damages to be paid.

2. The order of precedence is:
   b. Federal constitutional law
   e. Federal statute
   c. State constitutional law
   d. State statute
   a. Common law

   a. Spirit of the law
   b. Letter of the law

3. Police power comes from multiple sources: the U.S. Constitution, U.S. Supreme Court decisions, federal statutes, state constitutions, state statutes, state court decisions, and various municipal charters and ordinances.

4. Police power is restricted by the Constitution, by the Fourteenth Amendment, and by the courts.

SUMMARY

Our current laws and the means by which they are enforced have their origins in the distant past, perhaps as far back as the cave dwellers. Laws and law enforcement began several thousand years B.C. as a means of controlling human conduct and enforcing society's rules. Many features of our present system of law enforcement have been borrowed from the Greeks, Romans, and particularly the English.

The early American settlers brought with them several features of English law and law enforcement including those found in Leges Henrici, which made law enforcement a public matter, and in the Magna Carta, which provided for due process of law. Law enforcement in Colonial America was frequently patterned after England's Watch and Ward System and later after the London Metropolitan Police and the principles for reform set forth by Sir Robert Peel.

Although law enforcement was generally considered a local responsibility, the early beginning of state law enforcement agencies occurred with the establishment of the Texas Rangers, and the early beginning of federal law-enforcement agencies with the establishment of U.S. Marshals. After the turn of the century other state agencies, notably the Pennsylvania Constabulary, and other federal agencies, notably the Federal Bureau of Investigation, were established.

Currently five governmental levels of police agencies operate in the United States: township and special district, municipal, county, state, and federal, each with its own activities and goals, and each differing greatly in size, operational methods, and jurisdiction.

Just as our current methods of enforcing the laws have slowly evolved, so have the laws themselves. In the beginning most laws were set by a ruler or were moral or social laws, enforced by social pressure. This was followed by customary law—law based on habit or precedent. Next equity entered the legal system with its emphasis on fairness and justice, on the "spirit of the law" rather than the "letter of the law." Common law, what is considered right by local custom and established by judicial decision, was the main type of law for several centuries. Finally, however, statutory law replaced most common law. Statutory law consisted of laws passed by federal and state legislatures regarding both constitutional and non-constitutional (ordinary) matters.

As the legal system developed, a distinction arose between an action which was considered a crime and one which was not considered a crime even though it did violate a law (tort). This division was reflected in the establishment of two separate bodies of law: criminal law and civil law. Criminal law defines what action constitutes a specific crime and establishes punishments for each. Civil law, on the other hand, sets forth laws which citizens are expected to obey, but if they do not they are not considered "criminals." Civil law seeks to establish restitution for a wrong against an individual.

Laws, by their very definition, imply both the rule and its enforcement. To ensure enforcement, police have been given power and authority from local, state, and federal sources; but they are also restricted in their use of this power by the Constitution, the Fourteenth Amendment, and the courts. They have the power to enforce the laws so long as they do not violate the civil rights and liberties of any individual—the subject of the next chapter.

APPLICATION

You have been asked to speak to a sixth grade class on the "History of Our Laws and Law Enforcement." What facts will you include in your talk?

DISCUSSION QUESTIONS

1. What common problems have existed throughout the centuries for people in law enforcement?
2. How have these common problems been approached at different points in history?
3. What demands are made on the modern police officer which were not present twenty or thirty years ago?
4. What is the difference between someone seeking vengeance on his own for a wrong against him and a court imposing a fine or prison sentence on a wrongdoer?
5. Why was there no law enforcement during the daytime for many centuries?
6. Why did it take so long to develop a police force in England? In the United States?
7. Is there any level of law enforcement that is not really needed?
8. Should police officers be appointed or elected?
9. If a person's reckless driving of a car injures another person who dies two weeks later as a result of the injuries, could the reckless driver be charged for a crime, sued for a tort, or both? How would the type of charge affect the possible consequences faced by the reckless driver?

REFERENCES

Adams, T. F. *Law enforcement.* Englewood Cliffs, New Jersey: Prentice Hall, Inc., 1968.

Chapman, S. G. and Johnston, Colonel T. E. St. *The police heritage in England and America.* East Lansing: Michigan State University, for Community Development and Services, Continuing Education Service, 1962.

Eldefonso, E.; Coffey, A.; and Grace, R. C. *Principles of law enforcement.* (2nd ed.) New York: John Wiley & Sons, 1974.

Ferguson, R. W. and Stokke, A. H. *Concepts of criminal law.* Boston: Holbrook Press, 1976.

Folley, V. L. *American law enforcement.* Boston: Holbrook Press, 1973.

Germann, A. C.; Day, F. D.; and Gallati, R. B. *Introduction to law enforcement and criminal justice.* Springfield, Illinois: Charles C. Thomas, 1969, 1972, 1973.

Golden high school encyclopedia, Vol. 10. Golden Press, 1961.

Hall, J. *Dictionary of subjects and symbols in art.* New York: Harper and Row, 1974.

Knudten, R. D. *Crime in a complex society.* The Dorsey Press, 1970.

Lunt, W. E. *History of England.* New York: Harper and Brothers, 1938.

Mayo, K. M. *Justice to all: The story of the Pennsylvania state police.* New York: G. P. Putnam's Sons, 1917.

Owings, C. *Women police.* Montclair, New Jersey: Patterson Smith Publishing Corp., 1969.

Prosser, W. L. *Handbook of the law of torts.* (2nd ed.) St. Paul: West Publishing Company, 1955.

Quinney, R. *Criminology.* Boston: Little, Brown & Company, 1975.

Rubinstein, J. *City police.* New York: Farrar, Straus & Giroux, 1973.

Saunders, C. *Upgrading the American police.* Washington, D.C.: The Brookings Institution, 1970.

Sutherland, E. H. and Cressey, D. R. *Criminology.* (10th ed.) New York: J. B. Lippincott Co., 1978.

Universal standard encyclopedia, Vol. 18. New York: Unicorn Publishers, 1954.

Freedom of speech, the right to peaceful assembly, and the right to petition the government for redress of grievances are some of the liberties guaranteed to the people of the United States in the first ten amendments to the Constitution.

Civil Rights and Civil Liberties

The American Creed

2

DO YOU KNOW □ □ □

☐ What civil rights and civil liberties are?

☐ What contributions the Magna Carta made to our Constitution and our system of justice?

☐ What the Declaration of Independence says about civil rights and civil liberties?

☐ What the basic instrument of government and the supreme law of the land is?

☐ What the Bill of Rights is?

☐ What specific rights are guaranteed by the First, Second, Fourth, Fifth, Sixth, Eighth, and Fourteenth Amendments?

☐ What four guarantees are included in due process?

☐ What the difference is between the Fifth and the Fourteenth Amendments?

☐ When changes in our institutions and statutes are necessary and how they can be made?

As you read this chapter, watch for answers to these questions.

The welfare of the people is the chief law.
—Cicero

INTRODUCTION

My country 'tis of thee, sweet land of liberty . . .
From every mountain side, let freedom ring.
U.S. Supreme Court Censures Government on Illegal Wiretap

One nation, under God, with liberty and justice for all.
Discrimination Claimed in Job Firing

We hold these truths to be self-evident: that all men are endowed by their creator with certain unalienable rights; that among these are life, liberty, and the pursuit of happiness.
Police Embarrassed as a Result of False Arrest

Between the idea and the reality . . . falls the shadow . . .
T. S. Eliot

We are surrounded by symbols of freedom, liberty, and justice. The Statue of Liberty, a gift from France to celebrate the central theme in American development, our money, our coins, our stamps, our patriotic songs, our oaths of office, all echo our belief in freedom, liberty, and justice. Yet sometimes what we believe does not match reality. We are still striving to achieve *civil rights* and *civil liberties* for all Americans.

Civil rights are those claims which the citizen has to the affirmative assistance of government. *Civil liberties* are an individual's immunity from governmental oppression.

Although we have not completely achieved our ideals of freedom, liberty, and justice for all, we are far ahead of other countries and have come a long way since the founding of the United States. Much of our progress can be traced to developments in England, as seen in the preceding chapter. Of special significance is the historic Magna Carta.

THE MAGNA CARTA*

Our modern system of justice owes much to the Magna Carta, a decisive document in the development of constitutional government in England. In later centuries, it became a model for those who demanded democratic governments and individual rights for all, including the United States. In its own time, however, the greatest value of the Magna Carta was that it checked royal power and placed the king under the law.

*Based upon material from *The World Book Encyclopedia.* © 1978 World Book-Childcraft International, Inc.

40

The *Magna Carta*, a model for democratic government and individual rights, laid the foundation for:
—Requiring rulers to uphold the law.
—Forbidding taxation without representation.
—Requiring due process of law, including trial by jury.
—Providing safeguards against unfair imprisonment.

When the Normans conquered England in 1066, able kings ruled the country for more than a hundred years with no real controls over their power. However, when John became king in 1199, he abused his power by demanding more military service from the feudal class, selling royal positions to the highest bidder, and increasing taxes without obtaining consent from the barons—actions all contrary to feudal custom. In addition, John's courts decided cases according to his wishes, not according to law.

In 1213, a group of barons and church leaders met near London to call for a halt to the king's injustices. They drew up a list of rights they wanted King John to grant them. After the king refused to grant these rights on two separate occasions, the barons raised an army and forced him to meet their demands. On June 15, 1215, King John signed the Magna Carta.

The Magna Carta contained sixty-three articles, most requiring the king to uphold feudal law. The articles initially benefited only the barons and other members of the feudal class, but they later became important to all people. Some articles granted the church freedom from royal interference, and a few guaranteed the rights of the rising middle class. Ordinary freemen and peasants, although making up the great majority of England's population, were hardly mentioned in the charter.

The charter required the king to seek the advice and consent of the barons on all matters important to the kingdom, including taxation. Later such articles supported the argument that no law should be made nor tax raised without the consent of England's Parliament.

Other articles of the Magna Carta became foundations for modern justice. One article, for example, required that no freeman should be imprisoned, deprived of property, sent out of the country, or destroyed, except by the lawful judgment of his peers or by the law of the land. The concept of due process of law, including trial by jury, developed from this article.

Although the Magna Carta included several articles designed to keep the king under the law, additional measures were also taken to assure this control. A council of barons was formed to make certain the king abided by the articles. If John violated the charter, the council had the right to raise an army to force him to follow the charter's provisions. Almost immediately this right was exercised, as the king refused to abide by the charter. John died in the ensuing war, and in the years that followed, other English kings wisely agreed to the terms of the charter which became recognized as a fundamental part of English law.

During the 1500s, members of Parliament viewed the charter as a constitutional check on royal power and cited it as legal support for the argument that there could be no laws or taxation without the consent of Parliament. They also used the charter to demand guarantees of trial by jury, safeguards against unfair imprisonment, and other rights.

In the 1700s, colonists carried these English ideals regarding legal and political rights to America where they eventually became part of the framework of the United States Constitution.

☑ CHECK POINT

1. Define civil rights.
2. Define civil liberties.
3. List at least three contributions made to our Constitution and system of justice by the Magna Carta.

* Answers

1. Civil rights are those claims which the citizen has to the affirmative assistance of government, for example, the right to due process, protection from cruel and unusual punishment, and so on.
2. Civil liberties are an individual's immunity from governmental oppression, for example, freedom of speech, freedom from unreasonable search and seizure, and the like.
3. The Magna Carta laid the foundation for (1) requiring rulers to uphold the law, (2) forbidding taxation without representation, (3) requiring due process of law, and (4) providing safeguards against unfair imprisonment.

THE QUEST FOR CIVIL RIGHTS AND CIVIL LIBERTIES IN THE UNITED STATES

The Europeans' original immigration to the new world was heavily motivated by a desire to escape the religious, economic, political, and social repressions of traditional European society. North America was seen early as a land where individuals could get a new start, free to make of themselves what they chose.

Sometimes, however, reality did not fully coincide with the American creed of individual freedom, as seen in the treatment of the American Indian, the importation of slaves, the establishment of state churches, and the repressiveness involved in episodes such as the Salem witchcraft trials. Nevertheless, the spirit of liberty and justice remained strong. As noted by Gunnar Myrdal (1944): the American creed is the national conscience; a body of beliefs about equality, liberty, and justice which most Americans believe in, in spite of the fact that America has, and always has had, multiple wrongs.

In the 1760s when the British began taking away rights which Americans had come to feel were naturally theirs, the American Revolution resulted. In effect, the United States was born out of a desire for—indeed, a demand for—civil rights and civil liberties.

Civil rights and civil liberties are recurring themes in America's development. Our initial institutions reflected a high concern for the individual human spirit. Our founding fathers showed strong commitments to positively guarantee those rights which Americans had fought and died to protect in the American Revolution. These values were strongly stated in our most basic document: The Declaration of Independence.

THE DECLARATION OF INDEPENDENCE

The Declaration of Independence is not only a statement of grievances against England, it is a statement of alternative basic premises underlying man's freedom. As Thomas Jefferson phrased it in the Declaration, the United States was demanding "the separate and equal station to which the laws of nature and of nature's God entitle them." In powerful rhetoric, Jefferson asserted:

We hold these truths to be self-evident: —That all men are created equal; that they are endowed by their Creator with certain unalienable rights; that among these are life, liberty, and the pursuit of happiness. That, to secure these rights, governments are instituted among men, deriving their just powers from the consent of the governed; that, whenever any form of government becomes destructive of these ends, it is the right of the people to alter or to abolish it, and to institute new government.

In other words, the purpose of government is to secure the peoples' unalienable rights, including life, liberty, and happiness—on an equal basis, since "all men are created equal."

> The Declaration of Independence asserts that all men are created equal and are entitled to the unalienable rights of life, liberty, and the pursuit of happiness. It further asserts that governments are instituted by and derive their power from the governed.

The Declaration, however, was principally a statement of ideals and intentions; its importance, therefore, is more as a philosophy than as a concrete governing mechanism. The *Constitution* afforded the mechanism for achieving the goals of the Declaration. The Declaration and the Constitution are two parts of one whole, one breaking away from old government and calling for a new one, and the other creating that government, a carefully developed mechanism for the achievement of the principles contained in the Declaration.

THE UNITED STATES CONSTITUTION

The Constitution was drafted by the Constitutional Convention of 1787 and, following its ratification by the convention in two-thirds of the states, became effective in 1789.

> The United States Constitution is the basic instrument of government and the supreme law of the United States.

The Constitution states that the legislative, executive, and judicial departments of government should be separated as far as is practicable, and that their respective powers should be exercised by different men or groups of men. The legislature makes the laws, the executive branch, of which law enforcement is a part, enforces the laws, and the judicial branch determines when laws have been violated. The United States Constitution does not require that the three branches of government be separated on the state level, but all state constitutions require it in varying degrees.

The Constitution is divided into seven major articles:

Article 1—Sets forth the structure and functions of Congress.

Article 2—Establishes the executive branch of government.

Article 3—Delineates the judicial power of the United States Supreme Court and other courts that Congress may establish.

Article 4—Describes the duties of the states to the federal government and to each other.

Article 5—Provides for amendments to the Constitution and describes the procedures which must be followed.

Article 6—Provides for the taking of the oath of office for all federal and state legislative, executive, and judicial officers. It also contains the Supremacy Clause which provides that the Constitution, laws, and treaties of the United States are the supreme law of the land and that all states are bound by it.

Article 7—Deals primarily with the method of ratification of the Constitution which was completed in 1789.

When the first Congress of the United States convened on March 4, 1789, it had before it 103 amendments to the Constitution submitted by the states, forty-two amendments proposed by minority groups within the states, and bills of rights submitted by two states. After deliberating on these proposed amendments, Congress reduced them to twelve to submit to the states. Two failed to be ratified; the others became the first Ten Amendments. They went into effect on December 15, 1791, and are known as the *Bill of Rights*.

THE BILL OF RIGHTS

The Constitution, adopted in 1789, organized the government of the new nation, but it contained very few personal guarantees, and, consequently, some states refused to ratify it without a specific Bill of Rights. In 1791 the ten amendments, with personal guarantees included, came into effect. They became known as the Bill of Rights, a fundamental document describing the liberties of the people and forbidding the government to violate these rights.

> The Bill of Rights protects a person's right to "life, liberty, and the pursuit of happiness." It forbids the government to violate these rights.

Man is considered to have inborn rights which a government may not deprive him of. Government has only limited powers which are delegated by the people.

Initially the Bill of Rights applied only to the federal government. It was not until the Fourteenth Amendment was adopted that it became possible for the United States and Congress to end state actions which violated the human rights of its citizens, as will be discussed shortly.

Individual constitutional rights are clearly specified in each amendment. Some are of more relevance to individuals in law enforcement than others. Of special importance are the First, Second, Fourth, Fifth, Sixth, Eighth, and Fourteenth Amendments.

☑ CHECK POINT

1. What does the Declaration of Independence say regarding civil rights and civil liberties?
2. What is the basic instrument of government and the supreme law of the land in the United States?
3. What is the Bill of Rights? What does it consist of and what does it do?

*Answers

1. The Declaration of Independence asserts that all men are created equal and are entitled to the unalienable rights of life, liberty, and the pursuit of happiness. It further asserts that governments are instituted by and derive their power from the governed.
2. The United States Constitution is the basic instrument of government and the supreme law of the land.
3. The Bill of Rights consists of the first ten amendments to the Constitution. It protects a person's right to "life, liberty, and the pursuit of happiness," and forbids the government to violate these rights.

THE FIRST TEN AMENDMENTS (THE BILL OF RIGHTS)*

The First Amendment

Congress shall make no law respecting an establishment of religion, or prohibiting the free exercise thereof; or abridging the freedom of speech, or of the press; or the right of the people peaceably to assemble, and to petition the Government for a redress of grievances.

> The First Amendment guarantees:
> —Freedom of religion.
> —Freedom of speech.
> —Freedom of the press.
> —Freedom of assembly and petition.

*Adapted from *The Layman's Guide to Individual Rights Under the United States Constitution.*

Religion. Two guarantees of religious freedom are provided: (1) No law may be enacted which establishes an official church that all Americans must accept and support or to whose tenets all must subscribe or that favors one church over another and (2) no law is constitutional which prohibits the free exercise of religion. In short, citizens are guaranteed freedom to worship as they see fit.

Freedom of Speech. The Supreme Court has ruled that the protections afforded by the First Amendment do not extend to all forms of expression. Highly inflammatory remarks spoken to a crowd which advocate violence and clearly threaten the peace and safety of the community, or present a "clear and present danger" to the continued existence of the government are not protected. Obscenity, too, is unprotected by the First Amendment, although the Court has held that the mere possession of obscene materials in the home is not punishable.

Courts have also recognized that "symbolic speech" involving tangible forms of expression such as wearing buttons or clothing with political slogans or displaying a sign or a flag is protected by the First Amendment.

Finally, the courts have frequently condemned censorship by requirement of official approval or a license in advance of speaking. While citizens are free to make speeches on the public streets, they may be prevented from doing so when they use a loud, raucous amplifier in a hospital zone or when the location chosen for the address is likely to interfere with traffic. Thus, freedom of speech is not an "absolute."

Freedom of the Press. The First Amendment also guarantees the right to express oneself by writing or publishing one's views. The founding fathers recognized the importance of a free interplay of ideas in a democratic society and sought to guarantee the right of all citizens to speak or publish their views, even if they were contrary to those of the government or the society as a whole. Accordingly, the First Amendment generally forbids censorship or other restraint upon speech or the printed word.

As with speech, freedom to write or publish is not an absolute right of expression. The sale of obscene materials and libelous printed materials are not protected. The Supreme Court has ruled, however, that public figures cannot sue for defamation unless the alleged libelous remarks were printed with knowledge of their falsity or a reckless disregard for the truth.

Broadcasting, including radio, television, and motion pictures, receives the protections of the free press guarantee and is subject to its limitations.

Assembly and Petition. Americans have the right to assemble peaceably for any political, religious, or social activity. Public authorities cannot impose unreasonable restrictions on such assemblies, but they can impose limitations reasonably designed to prevent fire, health hazards, or traffic obstructions. The Supreme Court has emphasized that freedom of assembly is just as fundamental as freedom of speech and press. Thus, while no law may legitimately prohibit demonstrations, laws or governmental actions may legitimately restrict demonstrations to certain areas or prohibit the obstruction and occupation of public buildings.

Picketing has also been protected under the free speech guarantee; however, it may be reasonably regulated to prevent pickets from obstructing movement onto and from the involved property. Picketing on private property has been upheld, but only where the property is open to the public and the picketing relates to the business being conducted on the property.

The right of petition is designed to allow citizens to communicate with their government without obstruction. When citizens exercise their First Amendment freedom to write or speak to their Senator or Congressman, they partake of "the healthy essence of the democratic process."

The Second Amendment

A well regulated Militia, being necessary to the security of a free State, the right of the people to keep and bear Arms shall not be infringed.

> The Second Amendment guarantees the right to bear arms.

Citizens are guaranteed the right to protect themselves from disorder in the community and attack from foreign enemies. This right to bear arms has become much less important in recent decades as well-trained military and police forces have been developed to protect citizens. No longer do they need to rely on having their own weapons available, yet attempts to limit this right are strenuously opposed by many citizens, as evidenced in the current gun control controversy. No matter what police officers' views are on gun control, they are obliged to enforce the laws passed by Congress.

The Supreme Court has ruled that state and federal governments may pass laws prohibiting the carrying of concealed weapons, requiring the registration of firearms, and limiting the sale of firearms for other than military use. Thus, it is illegal to possess certain types of "people-killing" weapons such as operable machine guns and sawed-off shotguns of a certain length.

The Third Amendment

No Solider shall, in time of peace be quartered in any house, without the consent of the Owner; nor in time of war, but in a manner to be prescribed by law.

Before the Revolution, American colonists were frequently forced to provide food and lodging for British soldiers. The Third Amendment prohibited continuing this practice.

The Fourth Amendment

The right of the people to be secure in their persons, houses, papers, and effects, against unreasonable searches and seizures, shall not be violated, and no warrant shall issue, but upon probable cause, supported by Oath or affirmation, and particularly describing the place to be searched, and the persons or things to be seized.

> The Fourth Amendment forbids unreasonable searches and seizures and requires probable cause.

In some countries, even today, police officers may invade citizens' homes, seize their property, or arrest them whenever they see fit. In the United States such actions are prohibited by the Fourth Amendment which protects individuals and their property from unreasonable search and seizure by law officers.

In most instances a police officer is not allowed to search the homes of private citizens, seize any of their property, or arrest them without first obtaining a court order, a *warrant*. Before a warrant will be issued, the police officer must convince a magistrate that he has *probable cause*—good reason—to believe either that the individual involved has committed a crime, or that he has in his possession evidence related to a crime. Even with a warrant, police cannot typically break into a private home without first demanding entrance, unless such action is permissible under a "no-knock" statute which authorizes such entry if it is reasonable to expect the evidence will be destroyed.

The courts have ruled that in some instances it is permissible to arrest a person or conduct a search without a warrant. For example, if a felony is committed in the presence of a police officer, the officer has the right to arrest the criminal immediately, without an arrest warrant. If the police officer makes such an arrest, he may search the suspect and a limited area surrounding him to prevent the suspect from seizing a weapon or destroying evidence. Any evidence in plain view may also be seized.

The courts have permitted the police to search certain vehicles without a warrant on the grounds that the vehicle may be miles away by the time a police officer returns with a warrant.

The courts have frequently faced the problem of determining what constitutes probable cause for a search or an arrest. Generally speaking, the criterion has been common sense: On the available evidence, would a reasonable person consider there was a good basis to believe that the person to be arrested had committed a crime or that the place to be searched contained evidence of a crime?

The Supreme Court, in considering whether a police officer who "stopped and frisked" a citizen with no reason to believe the individual concerned had committed a particular crime had met this test, ruled that the Fourth Amendment did not prohibit such a search if it was reasonable on the basis of the police officer's experience and the demeanor of the individual who was frisked.

The search and seizure provisions of the Fourth Amendment are critical to law enforcement officers and will be referred to frequently throughout the rest of the book. They will be discussed in depth in Chapters 13 and 14.

Wiretappings. Listening in on a telephone conversation by mechanical or electronic means and electronic "bugging" are considered "search and seizures" under the Fourth Amendment and, therefore, they also require probable cause, reasonableness, and a warrant for their use. Congress has passed legislation which limits the use of wiretapping and bugging to the investigation of specific crimes and restricts those officials permitted to authorize them.

Evidence secured by means of an unlawful search and seizure cannot be used in either a state or federal prosecution. Thus, the phrase "innocent until proven guilty" in practice means "innocent until proven guilty by evidence obtained in accordance with constitutional guarantees."

☑ CHECK POINT

1. What four basic rights are guaranteed in the First Amendment?
2. What right is guaranteed by the Second Amendment?
3. What right is guaranteed by the Fourth Amendment?
4. Which of the first four amendments has the greatest direct significance to the law enforcement officer?

*Answers

1. The First Amendment guarantees freedom of religion, freedom of speech, freedom of the press, and freedom of assembly and petition.
2. The Second Amendment guarantees the right to bear arms.
3. The Fourth Amendment forbids unreasonable searches and seizures and requires probable cause.
4. The Fourth Amendment has the greatest direct significance to the law enforcement officer.

The Fifth Amendment

No person shall be held to answer for a capital, or otherwise infamous crime, unless on a presentment or indictment of a Grand Jury, except in cases arising in the land or naval forces, or in the Militia, when in actual service in time of War or public danger; nor shall any person be subject for the same offense to be twice put in jeopardy of life or limb; nor shall be compelled in any criminal case to be a witness against himself; nor be deprived of life, liberty, or property, without due process of law; nor shall private property be taken for public use, without just compensation.

The Fifth Amendment guarantees:
—Due process: notice of a hearing, full information regarding the charges made against him, the opportunity to present evidence in his own behalf before an impartial judge or jury, and to be presumed innocent until proven guilty by legally obtained evidence.
—Just compensation when private property is acquired for public use.
The Fifth Amendment prohibits:
—Double jeopardy.
—Self-incrimination.

Grand Jury.   The Fifth Amendment requires that before individuals are tried in federal court for an "infamous" crime, they must first be indicted by a grand jury. The grand jury's duty is to assure that there is probable cause to believe the accused person is guilty. This prevents a person from being subjected to a trial when insufficient proof exists that he has committed a crime.

An infamous crime is a felony (a crime for which a sentence of more than one year's imprisonment can be given) or a lesser offense which can be punished by confinement in a penitentiary or at hard labor.

An indictment is not required for a trial by court-martial or by other military tribunal. Also, the constitutional requirements of grand jury indictment do not apply to trials in state courts.

Double Jeopardy.   The Fifth Amendment also guarantees that citizens will not be placed in double jeopardy, that is, they will not be tried before a federal or state court more than once for the same crime. A second trial can occur, however, when the first trial results in a mistrial, for instance, when the jury cannot agree on a verdict, or when a second trial is ordered by an appellate court.

Double jeopardy does not arise when a single act violates both federal and state laws and the defendant is prosecuted in both federal and state courts. Nor does a criminal prosecution in either a state or federal court exempt the defendant from being sued for damages by anyone who is harmed by the criminal act. Further, a defendant may be prosecuted more than once for the same conduct if it involved the commission of more than one crime. For instance, if a person kills three victims at the same time and place, he can be tried separately for each slaying.

Self-incrimination.   In any criminal case, every person has the right not to be a witness against himself, that is, no one is required to provide answers to questions which might convict him of a crime. Such questions may be asked at the very earliest stages of an investigation; therefore, the Supreme Court has ruled that when an individual is interrogated in the "custody" of the police, the guarantees of the Fifth Amendment apply. "Custodial interrogation" can extend to questioning outside the police station and has even included police questioning of a defendant in his own bed.

To insure against self-incrimination, the Court has ruled in the well-known Miranda decision that citizens must be warned prior to custodial interrogation of their right to remain silent, that what they say may be used against them in court, and that they have a right to counsel which will be furnished them. If these warnings are not given, any statements obtained by the questioning are inadmissible in later criminal proceedings.

Although accused persons may waive their rights under the Fifth Amendment, they must know what they are doing and must not be forced to confess. Any confession obtained by force or threat is excluded from the evidence presented at the trial. Further, if defendants or witnesses fail to invoke the Fifth Amendment in response to a question on the witness stand, such a failure may operate as a waiver of the right, and they will not be permitted to object later to a court's admitting their statement into evidence on the basis that it was self-incriminating.

Courts have ruled that the guarantee against self-incrimination applies only to "testimonial" actions. Thus, handwriting samples, blood tests, and appearance, to include repeating words in a police line-up, do *not* violate the Fifth Amendment.

Courts have also ruled that the Fifth Amendment prohibits both federal and state prosecutors and judges from commenting on the refusal of defendants to take the witness stand in their own defense. The refusal of witnesses to testify to matters which could subject them to criminal prosecutions at a later date has also been upheld. The courts have recognized, however, a limited right of the government to question employees about the performance of official duties and have upheld the dismissals of employees who refuse to answer such questions.

Due Process. The words *due process of law* express the fundamental ideas of American justice. A due process clause is found in both the Fifth and Fourteenth Amendments as a restraint upon the federal and state governments respectively.

The clause protects against arbitrary, unfair procedures in judicial or administrative proceedings which could affect a citizen's personal and property rights. Due process requires notice of a hearing or trial which is timely and which adequately informs the accused persons of the charges against them. It also requires the opportunity to present evidence in one's own behalf before an impartial judge or jury, to be presumed innocent until proven guilty by legally obtained evidence, and to have the verdict supported by the evidence presented.

The due process clauses of the Fifth and Fourteenth Amendments provide other basic protections to prevent the state and federal governments from adopting arbitrary, unreasonable legislation or other measures which would violate individual rights. Thus, constitutional limitations are imposed on governmental interference with important individual liberties such as the freedom to enter into contracts, to engage in a lawful occupation, to marry, and to move without unnecessary restraints. Governmental restrictions placed on one's liberties must be reasonable and consistent with due process to be valid.

Just Compensation. The Fifth Amendment requires that whenever the government takes an individual's property, it must be for public use and the owner must be paid its full value. The federal government cannot take property from one person simply to give it to another. However, the Supreme Court has held that it is permissible to take private property for such purposes as urban renewal, even though ultimately the property returns to private ownership, since the taking is for the benefit of the entire community.

The property does not have to be physically taken from the owner. If governmental action leads to a lower value of private property, that may also constitute a "taking" and require payment of compensation.

The Sixth Amendment

In all criminal prosecutions, the accused shall enjoy the right to a speedy and public trial, by an impartial jury of the State and district wherein the crime shall have been committed, which district shall have been previously ascertained by law, and to be informed of the nature and cause of the accusa-

tion; to be confronted with the witnesses against him; to have compulsory process for obtaining witnesses in his favor, and to have the Assistance of Counsel for his defense.

> The Sixth Amendment establishes requirements for criminal trials. It guarantees the individual's right:
> —To have a speedy public trial by an impartial jury.
> —To be informed of the nature and cause of the accusation.
> —To be confronted with witnesses against him.
> —To subpoena witnesses for his defense.
> —To have counsel for defense.

The Sixth Amendment sets forth specific rights guaranteed to persons facing criminal prosecution.

The right to speedy and public trial requires that the accused be brought to trial without unnecessary delay and that the trial be open to the public. Intentional or negligent delay by the prosecution has been grounds for dismissal of charges. The Supreme Court has ruled that delay in prosecution is not justified by the defendant's confinement on an earlier conviction; he should be temporarily released for trial on the later charge.

Trial by an impartial jury supplements the guarantee contained in Article III of the Constitution. The requirement that the jury have twelve members and that the twelve members must reach a unanimous verdict was derived from common law, not from the Constitution. The Supreme Court has ruled that state juries need not have twelve members and has approved state statutes which require only six. Moreover, the Court has ruled that jury verdicts in state courts need not necessarily be unanimous.

The right to jury trial does not apply to trials for petty offenses, which the Supreme Court has suggested as those punishable by six months' confinement or less, for example shoplifting or some traffic violations.

In all jury trials the jury members must be impartially selected. No one can be excluded from jury service because of race, class, or sex.

The Sixth Amendment requires that accused persons must be told how it is claimed they have broken the law so they can prepare their defense. The crime must be established by statute beforehand so all persons know it is illegal before they act. The statute must clearly inform people of the exact nature of the crime.

Generally accused persons are entitled to have all witnesses against them present their evidence orally in court. Hearsay evidence cannot be used in federal criminal trials except in certain instances. Moreover, those accused are entitled to the court's aid in obtaining their witnesses. This is usually accomplished by subpoena, which orders into court as witnesses persons whose testimony is desired at the trial.

Finally, the Sixth Amendment provides a right to be represented by counsel. For many years this was interpreted to mean only that defendants had a right to be represented by a lawyer if they could afford one. However, the

Supreme Court held in 1963 in Gideon v. Wainright 372, U.S. 335 that the Amendment obligated the federal and state governments to provide legal counsel at public expense for those who could not afford it. This right extends even to cases involving "petty offenses" if a jail sentence might result. The indigent* have such a right at any "critical stage of the adjudicatory process" including the initial periods of questioning,·police line-ups, and all stages of the trial process.

In addition, indigents have the right to a free copy of their trial transcript for purposes of appeal of their conviction. Congress enacted the Criminal Justice Acts of 1964 and 1970 to implement this right to counsel by establishing a federal defender system to represent those defendants who could not afford legal counsel. Most state legislatures have enacted similar measures.

The Seventh Amendment

In suits at common law, where the value in controversy shall exceed twenty dollars, the right of trial by jury shall be preserved, and no fact tried by a jury shall be otherwise re-examined in any Court of the United States, than according to the rules of the common law.

The Eighth Amendment

Excessive bail shall not be required, nor excessive fines imposed, nor cruel and unusual punishments inflicted.

> The Eighth Amendment forbids excessive bail, excessive fines, and cruel and unusual punishments.

Bail. Bail has traditionally meant payment by the accused of an amount of money specified by the court based on the nature of the offense to insure the presence of the accused at trial. An accused who was released from custody and subsequently failed to appear for trial forfeited his bail to the court.

The Eighth Amendment does not specifically provide that all citizens have a "right" to bail, but only that bail will not be excessive. A right to bail has, however, been recognized in common law and in statute since 1791. In 1966 Congress enacted the *Bail Reform Act* to provide for pretrial release from imprisonment of indigent defendants who could not afford to post money for bail and who were, in effect, confined only because of their poverty. The Act also discouraged the traditional use of money bail by requiring the judge to seek other means as likely to insure that defendants would appear when their trial was held.

Cruel and Unusual Punishment. Whether fines or periods of confinement are "cruel and unusual" must be determined by the facts of each particular case. Clearly excessive practices such as torture would be invalid. The Supreme Court has held the death penalty itself to be cruel and unusual in certain circumstances if it is not universally applied.

---

*Poor, lacking money.

The clause also applies to punishment for a condition which the "criminal" had no power to change. For example, a law making narcotics addiction illegal was struck down by the Supreme Court as cruel and unusual since it punished a condition beyond the accused's control. Some courts have held laws punishing public drunkenness to be "cruel and unusual" when applied to homeless alcoholics since they cannot usually avoid public places.

The Ninth Amendment

The enumeration in the Constitution, of certain rights, shall not be construed to deny or disparage others retained by the people.

The Ninth Amendment emphasizes the founding fathers' view that powers of government are limited by the rights of the people and that it was *not* intended, by expressly guaranteeing in the Constitution certain rights of the people, to recognize that government had unlimited power to invade other rights of the people.

Griswold v. Connecticut (381 U.S. 479, 1965), a case involving the Ninth Amendment, involved the issue of whether the right to privacy was a constitutional right, and, if so, whether the right was reserved to the people under the Ninth Amendment or was only derived from other rights specifically mentioned in the Constitution.

Courts have long recognized particular rights to privacy which are part of the First and Fourth Amendments. Thus, freedom of expression guarantees freedom of association and the related right to be silent and free from official inquiry into such associations. It also includes the right not to be intimidated by the government for expressing one's views. The Fourth Amendment's guarantee against unreasonable search and seizure confers a right to privacy because its safeguards prohibit unauthorized entry onto one's property and tampering with a citizen's possessions or property, to include his very person.

The court in *Griswold* ruled that the Third and Fifth Amendments, in addition to the First and Fourth, created "zones of privacy" safe from governmental intrusion, and, without resting its decision upon any one of these or on the Ninth Amendment itself, simply held that the right of privacy was guaranteed by the Constitution.

The Tenth Amendment

The Powers not Delegated to the United States by the Constitution, Nor Prohibited by It to the States, Are Reserved to the States Respectively, Or to the People.

The Tenth Amendment embodies the principle of federalism which reserves for the states the residue of powers not granted to the federal government or withheld from the states.

☑ CHECK POINT

1. What rights are guaranteed by the Fifth Amendment?
2. What rights are guaranteed by the Sixth Amendment?
3. What rights are guaranteed by the Eighth Amendment?

4. What four guarantees are provided by due process?
5. Of the last six amendments, which has greatest direct significance to the law enforcement officer?

*Answers

1. The Fifth Amendment guarantees (1) persons charged with an "infamous crime" the right to a presentation of the case before a grand jury, (2) due process, (3) just compensation when private property is acquired for public use. The Fifth Amendment prohibits double jeopardy and self-incrimination.
2. The Sixth Amendment establishes the requirements for criminal trials It requires that persons accused of a crime have the right to (1) a speedy public trial by an impartial jury, (2) be informed of the nature and cause of the accusation, (3) be confronted with witnesses against them, (4) subpoena witnesses for their defense, and (5) have counsel for defense.
3. The Eighth Amendment forbids excessive bail, excessive fines, and cruel and unusual punishments.
4. Due process includes (1) notice of a hearing, (2) full information regarding the charges, (3) the opportunity to present evidence before an impartial judge or jury, and (4) presumption of innocence until proven guilty by legally obtained evidence.
5. Of the last six amendments, the Fifth Amendment prohibition of self-incrimination (*Miranda* decision) is probably of greatest significance to the law enforcement officer.

ADDITIONAL AMENDMENTS

Since the ratification of the first ten amendments (The Bill of Rights), other amendments have been passed. Of special importance to civil rights and civil liberties is the Fourteenth Amendment, passed in 1868.

The Fourteenth Amendment

Section 1. All persons born or naturalized in the United States, and subject to the jurisdiction thereof, are citizens of the United States and of the State wherein they reside. No State shall make or enforce any law which shall abridge the privileges or immunities of citizens of the United States; nor shall any State deprive any person of life, liberty or property, without due process of law; nor deny to any person within its jurisdiction the equal protection of the laws.

Section 5. The Congress shall have power to enforce, by appropriate legislation, the provisions of this article.

> The Fourteenth Amendment requires each state to abide by the Constitution and the Bill of Rights. It guarantees due process and equal protection under the law.

Due Process. The Fourteenth Amendment limits the states from infringing upon the rights of individuals. The Bill of Rights does not specifically refer to actions by states, but applies only to actions by the federal government.

Thus, state and local officers could proceed with an arrest without any concern for the rights of the accused. The Fourteenth Amendment, in essence, duplicates the Fifth Amendment, except it specifically orders state and local officers to provide the legal protections of due process.

Equal Protection. The Fourteenth Amendment also prohibits denial of the "equal protection of the laws." A state cannot make unreasonable, arbitrary distinctions between different persons as to their rights and privileges. Since "all people are created equal," no law could deny red-haired men the right to drive an automobile, although it can deny minors the right to drive. The state can make reasonable classifications; however classifications such as those based on race, religion, and national origin, have been held to be unreasonable. Thus, racial segregation in public schools and other public places, laws which prohibit sale or use of property to certain races or minority groups, and laws prohibiting interracial marriage have been struck down.

The Supreme Court has further held that purely private acts of discrimination violate the equal protection clause if such acts are customarily enforced throughout the state, whether or not there is a specific law or other explicit manifestation of action by the state.

The equal protection clause also means that citizens may not arbitrarily be deprived of their right to vote, and that every citizen's vote must be given equal weight. Therefore, state legislatures and local governments must be apportioned strictly in terms of their populations in a way that accords one person one vote.

Section 5 of the Fourteenth Amendment provides the authority for much of the civil rights legislation passed by Congress in the 1960s.

The Twenty-Sixth Amendment

The rights of citizens of the United States, who are eighteen years of age or older, to vote shall not be denied or abridged by the United States or any state on account of age. The Twenty-Sixth Amendment, adopted in 1971, lowered the voting age to eighteen.

The Proposed Twenty-Seventh Amendment

Equality of rights under the law shall not be denied or abridged by the United States or by any state on account of sex. The controversial Equal Rights Amendment (ERA), proposed by Congress on March 22, 1972, requires ratification by thirty-eight states by January, 1982.

PRINCIPLE VS. PRACTICE

There is a vast difference between stating ideals and goals and achieving them. Our forefathers wrote our Constitution and the Bill of Rights on the premise that all people would obey the law. Time has shown this is not always true. The ideals set forth in our Declaration of Independence, our Constitution, and our Bill of Rights have not been achieved automatically.

Civil rights and civil liberties must be consciously and actively sought and protected if the documents on which our government is founded are to be more than elegant words. Laws and institutions must parallel our goals and ideals of liberty, freedom, equality, justice, human dignity, individual self-determination, freedom from tyranny, and freedom of conscience.

These goals have motivated Americans since they first came to the "free" world. These same goals carried American pioneers West, looking for a new life, an El Dorado. These goals have led men and women of all races and creeds, from all parts of the country to invest tremendous energy into the civil rights movement, to risk their lives confronting violently irate traditionalists, in an effort to obtain new levels of human decency and equality, new levels of freedom and justice for millions of Americans who belong to minority groups.

In many respects the history of civil rights and civil liberties in the United States has been a fight for the attainment of the abstract values which our nation claims it is committed to achieving.

The history of civil rights and civil liberties is not simply struggle, confrontation, marching, picketing, and demanding; it is holding the government responsible for the principles which are its central purpose for existence. From the beginning, our institutions, our statutes, our legal process were means to obtain fundamental civil liberties central to the American purpose: freedom of speech, freedom of the press, freedom of assembly, freedom of religion, due process of law, the right to privacy, the right to a fair trial, the right to vote and have that vote counted fairly, the right to equal opportunity, education, housing, and employment.

The history of civil rights and civil liberties has been dynamic, reflecting constant change as new challenges emerged in the shift from a simple, homogenous, agrarian, rural society to an advanced, highly complex, industrial, urban society. Although our principles have remained the same, our institutions and laws have continually changed. Thomas Jefferson recognized the necessity for such change in a letter he wrote in the nineteenth century:

I am certainly not an advocate for frequent and untried changes in laws and constitutions. I think that moderate imperfections had better be born with because we accommodate ourselves to them and find practical means to correct their ill effects, but I know also that laws and institutions must go hand in hand with the progress of the human mind, as that becomes more developed, as more discoveries are made, new truths disclosed, and manners and opinions change with the changing circumstances, institutions must advance also, and keep pace with the times. We might as well require a man to wear still the coat which fitted him as a boy as civilized society to remain ever under the regiment of their barbarous ancestors.

Our institutions and laws must change as our society changes.

We may not think of our ancestors as "barbarous," yet our early treatment of black Americans, native Chinese-Americans, and women can hardly be considered "enlightened."

Changes have occurred. For example, at one time imprisonment was considered a constructive solution to social problems. Until recently daily devotional services in the schools were considered a way to achieve proper public values. Eighteen-year-olds were not considered mature enough to vote in most states. Progress has been made in all these areas.

Still, the history of civil liberties is not always a pleasant one, nor does it show Americans in their best light. It is painfully clear through American history at certain times and under certain circumstances individuals and groups have been deprived of their liberties and denied fundamental freedoms under the rationalization that such denial was in the public interest.

Granted, liberty is not license; if an individual abuses his freedom, takes advantage of society, corrupts justice, or poses a threat to law and order, society has the right to take action in its own behalf. The problem is to know when and where to draw that line. When have the limits of freedom been exceeded? Conversely, when have the essential social controls of free society been imposed too arbitrarily? Does the majority have the right to temporarily suspend the rights of the minority in order to preserve liberty?

Examples of attempts to suspend the rights of members of minority groups are, unfortunately, recurrent in our history. Aliens, for example, have faced this problem since the Alien and Sedition Acts of 1798. In the turbulent years of the 1840s, Catholic immigrants were often treated with intolerance as second-class citizens. The lack of equality in the treatment of Indians, slaves, free blacks following the Civil War, and women was also evident in the treatment of labor agitators and political and economic radicals with allegedly dangerous ideas. Pacifists and conscientious objectors encounter great difficulties during war years. And we have had not only arguments for, but public policy which calls for placing American Communists in a deprived legal status.

The treatment of the Japanese-Americans during World War II is an example of the complexity of civil rights and civil liberties. After the attack on Pearl Harbor many Americans honestly believed the Japanese-Americans posed a serious national threat, yet, in retrospect, we must ask ourselves if they were not victims of temporary national hysteria and if their rights were not unjustifiably sacrificed.

The Japanese began appearing on the United States West coast in the late nineteenth century and were used as cheap, reliable, highly effective labor. The Japanese, on the whole, were ambitious, aggressive, thrifty, and quick to accept the American work ethic. As they realized their importance to the system, they began to demand more wages. In 1891 the first of several strikes by Japanese agricultural workers occurred, causing considerable criticism of these "undesirable aliens," these overaggressive, insolent, money-graspers.

By World War I the Japanese had acquired nearly 75,000 acres of California land and were leasing nearly half a million acres more. Many Californians saw them as alien landlords and tried to stop their progress. But the Japanese, anxious to become part of the American system, saved their money, went to school, obtained good training, and demanded jobs commensurate with that training. However, the unions refused and few were hired, so the Japanese went into business for themselves.

Soon several thousand Japanese men were successfully operating small businesses, acquiring wealth, and seeking the benefits of American life. Many looked for property outside the Japanese ghetto. The hostile American re-action resulted in the formation of the Asiatic Exclusion League, and technical laws preventing naturalization were rigidly enforced. By this time, however, a generation of American-born Japanese with proper claim to the full rights of American citizenship had been born. As hardworking, enterprising, and thrifty as their parents, they continued to play an important but resented role in the American economy. The growing tension with Japan added to many Americans' resentment of the Japanese.

The attack on Pearl Harbor brought the situation to a climax. Some 110,000 Japanese, the majority of whom were American-born citizens, were forced by government order to sell their homes and businesses and were herded into temporary barracks (in essence, benign concentration camps).

Although at the time it was claimed that the American-Japanese were a threat to national security, if one group of citizens can be so treated during a period of national emergency, a precedent is created which should disturb every American. From the standpoint of civil liberties, the episode has long-ranging implications, for the denial of one individual's rights is a direct threat to the rights of all Americans.

In the 1930s the United States Supreme Court began to question whether justice was being attained for large numbers of Americans as a result of the federal policy of keeping "hands off" local law enforcement. After careful examination begun in 1932 and continued for forty years, it was gradually and consistently concluded that local justice was *not* always true justice. Often local courts offered no true justice for a black man in the South. Likewise, there was often little justice for a stranger accused of a crime in a community. Local standards were often biased, prejudiced, and intolerant. Therefore, the courts came to insist that uniform national standards be applied in local courts and in police procedures. The Supreme Court, charged with interpreting our laws, established Uniform National Standards to be applied to local justice.

☑ CHECK POINT

1. What rights are guaranteed by the Fourteenth Amendment?
2. How does the Fourteenth Amendment differ from the Fifth Amendment?
3. When are changes in our institutions and laws necessary?

*Answers

1. The Fourteenth Amendment guarantees due process and equal protection under the laws within each state and locality. It requires each state and local officer to abide by the Constitution and the Bill of Rights.
2. The Fourteenth Amendment is essentially the same as the Fifth Amendment except that the Fourteenth Amendment applies to state and local officers, whereas the Fifth Amendment applies to federal officers.
3. Changes in our institutions and laws are necessary as changes in our society occur.

SUMMARY

The history of civil rights and civil liberties reflects our values, national purpose, the American experience with government, and the need for flexibility within stability. If the fundamental values of our society are to be preserved and extended, citizens must understand and support those institutions and statutes which, in practice, reflect the principles set forth in the Declaration of Independence, the Constitution, and the Bill of Rights.

These documents established not only each citizen's civil liberties—freedom from government oppression, but also each citizen's civil rights—claim to affirmative assistance from the government.

Many of our basic principles relating to civil rights and civil liberties are derived from the Magna Carta. Signed in England in 1215 by King John, the Magna Carta became a model for democratic government and individual rights, laying the foundation for requiring rulers to uphold the law, forbidding taxation without representation, requiring due process of law, and providing safeguards against unfair imprisonment.

The colonists brought these ideals to America, and when they were again faced by oppression of the English king, they rebelled. Their belief in and desire for civil rights and civil liberties were stated in the Declaration of Independence which asserted that all men are created equal and are entitled to the unalienable rights of life, liberty, and the pursuit of happiness. It further asserted that governments are instituted by and derive their power from the governed.

To achieve the goals set forth in the Declaration of Independence, our forefathers drafted the United States Constitution, the basic instrument of our government and the supreme law of the land which was signed in 1789.

Some states refused to ratify the Constitution without personal guarantees. Ten amendments to the Constitution containing such guarantees were passed in 1791 and became known as the Bill of Rights. The Bill of Rights protects a person's right to "life, liberty, and the pursuit of happiness" and forbids the government to violate these rights:

The First Amendment guarantees freedom of religion, freedom of speech, freedom of the press, and freedom of assembly and petition.

The Second Amendment guarantees the right to bear arms.

The Fourth Amendment forbids unreasonable searches and seizures and requires probable cause.

The Fifth Amendment guarantees due process and just compensation when private property is acquired for public use; it prohibits double jeopardy and self-incrimination.

The Sixth Amendment guarantees the individual's rights in a criminal trial.

The Eighth Amendment forbids excessive bail, excessive fines, and cruel and unusual punishments.

Since the Fifth Amendment was directed to federal officials, an additional amendment was later ratified, the Fourteenth Amendment, which requires each state and locality to abide by the Constitution and the Bill of Rights.

The amendment process illustrates the ability of our institutions and laws to change as our needs change. Although the principles of civil rights and civil liberties do not always prevail in practice, they remain the cornerstone of our democracy, our American creed. These principles directly affect how law enforcement officers fulfill their responsibilities.

APPLICATION

Read the following case studies and answer the questions following each.

A. Liberty Jones was standing on the corner of Mytown, USA, speaking to a crowd that had gathered. Incensed about violence on television, he was advocating the destruction of all television sets. The crowd began to chant remarks as Jones accelerated his feelings about violence. Jones then led the crowd down Main Street, demonstrating peacefully with banners and shouts of "Down with television violence." As they passed a television service store, Liberty picked up a rock and threw it at the display window, shattering it. Others followed, and considerable damage was done to the store and its merchandise. Liberty was arrested and charged by the police. His defense in court was the First Amendment to the Constitution.
   1. Would the First Amendment protect Liberty in this case?
   2. What would be the arguments for and against whether Liberty was guilty of breach of peace?

B. Herman Remington was sitting in his car in his driveway, looking over a pistol he had just purchased from a local gun store. As Officer Willie Ketcham drove by, he observed Herman's actions and arrested him for possessing a firearm. When in court, Herman pleaded not guilty and stated that his arrest was a constitutional violation.
   1. Does Remington have a justifiable defense? Why or why not?

C. Detective Mary O'Brien saw Sam Newstart walking down the street and remembered that she had arrested Sam a month ago for possession of narcotics. Detective O'Brien felt very strongly that Sam would have narcotics in his possession again and decided to stop and search him. She found heroin in Sam's possession and charged him. In court Sam pleaded not guilty and claimed that his constitutional rights had been violated.
   1. What amendment would apply to this case?
   2. Will Sam's contention of violation of this amendment be upheld in court?
   3. What are the issues?

D. Officer James Strongbow arrested fourteen-year-old Billie Akerson who was riding a stolen bicycle. At the stationhouse, Officer Strongbow advised Billie that if he wanted to relieve his conscience, he should give a written statement admitting the theft. Billie did so. At the court hearing, the judge stated that he would handle the case as a moral issue and that, in view of the confession, Billie didn't need a lawyer. The parents agreed, and Billie was sent to the home school for boys for six months. While there he met Rodney Harcourt, a public defender who felt Billie was a victim of a miscarriage of justice. He appealed the case to a higher court.

1. What amendment(s) would the lawyer base his case on?
2. What are the issues?
3. Do you think the appeal should be granted?

*Answers

A. 1. The First Amendment would protect Liberty's right to express his opinions publicly. It would not protect his right to incite the crowd to violence nor his own violent act.

2. Liberty was not guilty of breaching the peace when he spoke to the crowd, nor when he led the peaceful demonstration, provided they were not obstructing traffic and there was no ordinance against peaceful street marches. (A license is required in many cities.) Liberty was guilty of breaching the peace when he threw the rock through the television service store window and when he incited others to follow suit.

B. 1. Remington has a justifiable defense under the Second Amendment which guarantees the right to bear arms.

C. 1. The Fourth Amendment applies to the case of Sam Newstart.

2. The contention of violation of constitutional rights will probably be upheld.

3. The issues are: (1) Did the officer have probable cause to suspect that a crime had been committed and that the individual stopped and searched had committed the crime? (2) Was a warrant issued? In both instances, the answer is *no*. The officer had no probable cause to believe that a crime had been committed, and she had no warrant.

D. 1. The lawyer would base his case on the Fifth Amendment which guarantees due process of law and on the Sixth Amendment which governs criminal prosecutions.

2. The issues are: (1) Was Billie informed of his right to remain silent, to refrain from self-incrimination? (2) Was Billie provided with counsel for his defense?

3. The appeal should be granted since Billie was *not* informed of his right to remain silent nor was he provided with counsel for his defense.

DISCUSSION QUESTIONS

1. What specific restrictions are placed on the police officer by the Bill of Rights?
2. Why has the Supreme Court said that state and federal governments can pass laws against carrying weapons when the Second Amendment specifically guarantees the right to bear arms?
3. Why were blacks considered "unequal" until Lincoln was President? The Constitution existed; why did it not apply to blacks?
4. What is the basic difference between civil rights and civil liberties?
5. In what well-known cases has the Fifth Amendment been repeatedly used?
6. Recall the request of the Nazi Party which wanted to gather and march through Skokie, Illinois, a basically Jewish community. The community wanted to stop them any way they legally could, as they claimed the Nazi march would bring back memories and inflict emotional pain. The Nazi Party was supported by The American Civil Liberties Union. Did the Nazi Party have the right to conduct this march?

REFERENCES

Brant, I. *The Bill of Rights: It's origin and meaning.* Indianapolis: Bobbs-Merrill Co., 1965.

Daniels, R. *The politics of prejudice.* Gloucester, MA: Peter Smith, 1966 (Copyright 1962, the Regents of the University of California).

Felkenes, G. T. *Constitutional law for criminal justice.* Englewood Cliffs, N.J.: Prentice-Hall, 1978.

Frankel, L. H. *Law, power and personal freedom.* St. Paul: West Publishing Company, 1975.

Hosokawa, B. *Nisei: The quiet Americans.* New York: Wm. Morrow and Company, 1969.

The layman's guide to individual rights under the United States Constitution. Subcommittee on the Constitution, Washington, D.C.: U.S. Printing Office.

Magna carta. *The world book encyclopedia.* World Book-Childcraft International, 1978.

Myrdal, G. *The American dilemma.* New York: Harper and Brothers, 1944.

Pritchett, C. H. *The American Constitution.* New York: Mc Graw-Hill, 1977.

Weglyn, M. *Years of infamy.* New York: Wm. Morrow and Company, 1976.

Criminal behavior frequently has its beginning during a person's youth. Juvenile delinquency is a severe problem in the United States, with youth being responsible for a substantial and disproportionate part of our crime problem.

Crime in the United States
Some Categories and Causes

3

DO YOU KNOW □ □ □

□ How crimes and punishments are determined in the United States?

□ What the characteristics of a crime are?

□ How to define the crimes of murder, assault, rape, robbery, burglary, larceny/theft, and motor vehicle theft?

□ What is meant by white-collar crime and what specific types of crimes are included in this general classification?

□ How to define narcotics and dangerous drugs? What the three general classifications of dangerous drugs are?

□ What restrictions are placed on the possession, sale, and use of narcotics and dangerous drugs?

□ What physical and psychological effects are characteristically associated with misuse of narcotics, depressants, stimulants, and hallucinogens?

□ What appear to be major causes of crime?

□ What the legal definition of a juvenile delinquent is?

□ How severe the problem of juvenile delinquency is in the United States?

□ What some major causes of juvenile delinquency seem to be?

□ How parents, school, and society can help prevent children from becoming delinquent?

□ The three most frequently formed types of juvenile gangs and the purpose of each?

□ How drug abusers have been classified?

□ What hazards are involved in labeling an individual as a delinquent or a criminal?

There is no man so good, who, were he to
submit all his thoughts and actions to the
laws would not deserve hanging ten times
in his life.   *—Montaigne*

INTRODUCTION

To assure to each United States citizen the right to "life, liberty, and the pursuit of happiness," society has established laws which all are expected to obey. It is up to individuals in law enforcement to assure that the laws *are* obeyed. To do so effectively, it is important to know what constitutes crime in the United States, what actions are illegal and under what circumstances. It is also important to understand the causes for these crimes when possible. Such understanding not only assists in dealing with individuals involved in criminal actions, it also assists in determining what preventive steps might be effective in reducing the major societal problem of crime.

Some Categories of Crimes

Crimes have been categorized in many different ways. Our discussion will focus on three broad categories: (1) Index crimes, (2) white-collar crimes, and (3) crimes related to narcotics and dangerous drugs.

> Crimes are made so by law. State and federal statutes define each crime, the elements involved, and the penalty attached to each.

Sutherland and Cressey (1978, pp. 12-14) have summarized seven interrelated and overlapping characteristics of crime delineated by Jerome Hall (1960, pp. 14-26):

1. A crime has certain external consequences called *a harm*. Crime has a harmful impact on social interests; mere intention without resulting in such a harm is not a crime.

2. The harm must be *specifically outlawed in advance*.

3. *Conduct* must occur, either intentional or reckless action or inaction, to bring about the harmful consequences.

4. *Criminal intent* must be present. Criminal intent must not be confused with motivation. The motive might be "good," but if the intention is to perform an act specifically outlawed, it is still a crime. For example, if a person steals from the rich to give to the poor, his motives are "good," but his intention is still wrong.

5. The criminal *intent* and *conduct* must be *related*. For example, a salesman who enters a home on business and then decides to steal something cannot be charged with breaking and entering.

6. A *causal relation* must exist between the outlawed harm and the intentional act. For example, if a person shoots someone and the victim suffocates while in the hospital recovering from the wound, the causal relation is not clear-cut.

7. The *punishment* must be *legally prescribed*; the action must be punishable by law.

> A crime is an intentional action which is prohibited by law and for which punishment is legally prescribed that directly causes an actual harm.

INDEX CRIME

The crimes most frequently reported to local police departments or to the FBI are listed in an *Index of Uniform Crime Reports*, issued yearly by the FBI. How much crime is unreported, is not known, however.

As noted by Nettler (1978, p. 55), "The most popular measure of crime is official statistics of offenses 'known to the police.'... Crimes known to the police are themselves a result of social processing.... Complaints to the police are subject to errors that result from mistakes and from lies." In addition, "Official statistics on crime are imperfect not only because of what is and is not included but also because of imperfections in those who do the counting"

Figure 3-1. From *Crime in the United States—1977.* Uniform Crime Reports. Reprinted by permission.

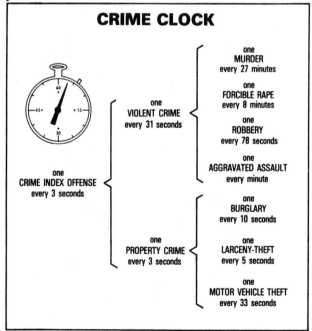

CRIME CLOCK

one
CRIME INDEX OFFENSE
every 3 seconds

one
VIOLENT CRIME
every 31 seconds

one
MURDER
every 27 minutes

one
FORCIBLE RAPE
every 8 minutes

one
ROBBERY
every 78 seconds

one
AGGRAVATED ASSAULT
every minute

one
PROPERTY CRIME
every 3 seconds

one
BURGLARY
every 10 seconds

one
LARCENY-THEFT
every 5 seconds

one
MOTOR VEHICLE THEFT
every 33 seconds

The crime clock should be viewed with care. Being the most aggregate representation of UCR data, it is designed to convey the annual reported crime experience by showing the relative frequency of occurrence of the Index Offenses. This mode of display should not be taken to imply a regularity in the commission of the Part I Offenses; rather, it represents the annual ratio of crime to fixed time intervals.

(Nettler, 1978, p. 63). In spite of these difficulties, police departments do make frequent use of the information from the Uniform Crime Reports.

The seven crimes listed in Part I of this Index are the serious crimes of the nation: (1) murder, (2) aggravated assault with a deadly weapon, (3) forcible rape, (4) robbery, (5) burglary, (6) larceny/theft of $50.00 and over, and (7) motor vehicle theft.

Although states differ in their laws and their definitions of crimes, some generalizations may be made about the various types of crime. Exceptions to what is said here may exist in individual states. The definitions and statistics in the following discussion of Index Crimes are from the 1977 *Index of Uniform Crime Reports*.

Murder (Homicide)

Murder is defined in the Uniform Crime Reporting Program as the willful killing of another person. Deaths caused by negligence, suicide, accident, justifiable homicide, attempts to murder, or assaults to murder are *not* included.

> Murder (homicide) is the killing of a human by another human.

The generally recognized levels of homicide are: (1) first-degree murder, (2) second-degree murder, (3) manslaughter (or non-negligent manslaughter), and (4) negligent homicide. The first three categories, considered to be willful acts, are classified as felonies. Negligent homicide, however, is usually considered as a misdemeanor.

First-degree murder is willful, deliberate, and *premeditated* (planned) taking of another person's life. A homicide which occurs during the commission or attempted commission of arson, robbery, rape, or burglary is also usually classified as first-degree murder, even though it was not willful, deliberate, or premeditated. The question of premeditation is always left up to the jury.

Second-degree murder is one which is *not* premeditated but the intent to kill is present. The charge of murder in the second degree or manslaughter often results from killings which do not involve weapons but rather which occur during a fight.

Manslaughter is differentiated from murder in that the element of malice is absent, that is, the death was accidental; there was no original intent, hatred, ill-will, or disregard for the lives of others. In many states manslaughter is classified as either voluntary or involuntary. *Involuntary* manslaughter involves killing someone while doing some lawful act negligently or while negligently failing to perform some legal duty. Many deaths resulting from automobile accidents are classified as involuntary manslaughter. If there is no malice or intent to harm, and if the activity engaged in which led to the death is not a felony and would not usually cause bodily harm, most state statutes define it as involuntary manslaughter. In contrast, *voluntary* manslaughter is intentionally killing someone without previous malice, but in the sudden heat of passion due to adequate provocation. For example, a man who kills another man who he found in bed with his wife would probably be found guilty of voluntary manslaughter. If a store owner kills a robber in his store, his act and many other instances of self-defense, are often defined as voluntary manslaughter.

Negligent homicide refers to an accidental death which results from the reckless operation of a motor vehicle, boat, plane, or firearm.

In 1977 an estimated 19,120 murders were committed, 48% with the use of a handgun. Seventy-five percent of the total reported murders were solved. Of all individuals processed for murder, 10% were juveniles.

Aggravated Assault

Aggravated assault is the unlawful attack by one person upon another for the purpose of inflicting severe bodily injury and is usually accompanied by the use of a weapon or other means likely to produce serious bodily harm or death. Attempts are included since it is not necessary that an injury result when a gun, knife, or other weapon is used which could and probably would result in serious personal injury if the crime were successfully completed.

> Assault is attacking a person. It may be aggravated or simple assault.

Whether an assault is aggravated or simple is determined by the prosecuting attorney and is based on the intent of the attacker. Some states include the term *battery* in their statutes; others omit the term and allow the term *assault* to refer to both the blow and threats of attack. Assaults are frequently committed in conjunction with rape, burglary, and robbery.

Aggravated assault is an unlawful attack upon a person for the purpose of inflicting severe bodily injury or death. Assault can safely be classified as *aggravated* if a gun, knife, or other weapon is used and serious personal injury is inflicted. In most states aggravated assault is a felony and carries severe penalties because it would have been murder if the victim died. The intent of the act "appears" to be murder and not simply injury.

Simple assault, the most frequent type of assault, has no intent of serious injury. It may or may not be accompanied by a threat. Hands, fists, or feet are the most frequently used weapons. Most simple assaults result from emotional conflicts and are classified as misdemeanors. The mere pointing of a gun at a person or threatening a person with bodily harm may constitute simple assault in certain situations.

In 1977 an estimated 522,510 aggravated assaults occurred, 23% with the use of firearms. Of the total aggravated assaults reported, 62% were solved; of these, 10% involved persons under age 18.

Rape

Forcible rape, as defined in the Index Program, is the carnal knowledge of a female through the use of force or the threat of force. Assaults to commit forcible rape are also included; however, statutory rape (without force) is not included.

> Rape is having sexual intercourse with a female through the use or threat of force. Rape may be aggravated or simple.

Aggravated rape involves using force, threats of immediate use of force, or taking advantage of an unconscious or helpless woman or a woman incapable of consent because of mental illness or a defect reasonably known to the attacker.

Simple rape involves misleading a victim about the nature of the act being performed; for example, having intercourse under the guise of a medical examination or treatment or knowingly destroying the victim's will to resist by use of a drug or intoxicant.

Of the 63,020 rapes reported in 1977, 74% were by force. Rape is a violent crime against the person, yet it is probably one of the most underreported crimes because the victim fears her assailant or is extremely embarrassed. Of the total forcible rapes reported, 51% were cleared by arrest; 10% of the cases cleared involved persons under age 18.

Robbery

Robbery is stealing or taking anything of value from the care, custody, or control of a person in his presence, by force or by threat of force. Assault to commit robbery and attempts are included. This violent crime frequently results in injury to the victim.

> Robbery is stealing anything of value from the control, care, or custody of a person by force or threat of force.

In 50% of the cases, robbery is accompanied by an assault upon the victim. Sometimes labeled as the most brutal and vicious of all crimes, robberies occur in all parts of the country; its victims are people of all ages, incomes, and backgrounds.

Robbers may shoot, assault, or torture their victims to find where their valuables are located. Many victims who have refused to cooperate, and even some who have, have been ruthlessly killed. Further, robbery calls are the third ranking cause of police fatalities.

The favorite weapon of most robbers is the handgun. Other weapons used include knives, acids, baseball bats, and explosives. Armed robbers frequently attack drug stores (often for narcotics), supermarkets, liquor stores, jewelry stores, gas stations, banks, residential homes, cab drivers, and pedestrians.

The classic image of a robber is a masked man pointing a gun at a lone pedestrian on a city street or in a small grocery store at night. Frequently the victims are old people who are robbed of a small amount of money and are knocked to the ground, sometimes suffering permanent injuries or even death.

Robbery produces millions of dollars for criminals and is the most frequently reported crime. Approximately 10 percent of all willful homicides are the result of robbery attempts. But statistics do not reflect the human loss and tragedy often involved in robbery. The viciousness of armed robbery can be seen from actual cases throughout the country. Consider, for example, the following case. On December 28, 1977, at 2:30 P.M., a man wearing a maroon ski mask entered the walk-up portion of an auto bank in Minneapolis, Minnesota, pointed a gun at a teller, and demanded money. While the teller was reacting to the demand, a sixty-five-year-old security guard appeared from behind a door. The robber immediately shot him, striking him in the chest and head, wounding him critically.

Not all robberies are aggravated, however. Some states have a category of *simple* robbery where no force or threat is used. A usual element of the crime of robbery is force and fear, not stealth. If a thief jostles a victim in a crowd to divert attention and picks his pocket, the crime is robbery. A normal pickpocket operation or purse-snatching is larceny, not robbery, unless there is resistance or bodily contact.

Nationally about 50% of the robberies committed are street robberies. Large cities commonly have twenty to thirty robberies reported in a twenty-four-hour period on Fridays and Saturdays.

An estimated 404,850 robbery offenses were committed in 1977, 42% with the use of firearms. Of the 27% cleared, 84% involved adults. Of the strong-arm robberies cleared, 25% involved persons under age 18. Six percent of all persons arrested for robbery were women.

Burglary

The Uniform Crime Reporting Program defines burglary as the unlawful entry of a structure to commit a felony or theft. The use of force to gain entry is not required to classify the crime as a burglary. Burglary has three sub-classifications: forcible entry, unlawful entry where no force is used, and attempted forcible entry.

> Burglary is unlawful entrance into a building to commit theft or a felony.

Many dictionaries have as their first (most common) definition of burglary, "the act of breaking into a house at night to commit theft or other felony." This definition reflects what burglary was historically (under common law)—breaking and entering a dwelling of another in the night. Modern-day statutes reflect numerous changes in that definition, broadening its scope considerably.

Some states, for example, have eliminated the word *breaking* and require only a trespass. Burglaries can occur by forcible or attempted forcible entry, unlawful entry, or without force as when a burglar opens an unlocked door or window, or remains in a building without the consent of the person in charge with the intention of committing a crime. Department stores often have been the victims of burglars who hide in the store at closing time and wait until everyone else has left, take what they want, and then break out of the store to escape.

State statutes usually define *building* as a dwelling or other structure suitable for human shelter or connected to such a structure. Warehouses, barns, garages, and some types of shelters have also been defined by the courts as "buildings." For example, California defines burglary as the entry of a structure for the specific purpose of committing theft or some other felony. A structure is anything having continuous walls, a floor and roof, windows and doors included.

State statutes also vary as to whether the crime must occur at night to be a burglary. Some states say it may occur at any time of the day or night. If entry occurs during the night, breaking may not be an essential element of the crime.

Punishments are usually most severe if the burglar has an explosive or tool in his possession, if the building entered is a dwelling and the burglar has a dangerous weapon when entering, or if he assaults someone while committing the burglary.

Some states have a modified charge of "Breaking and Entering" which is a lesser charge than burglary. The intricacies in defining burglary are interesting. For instance, if a salesperson pockets a diamond ring while making a sales call in a home, it is not burglary. However, if a person poses as a salesperson to get into a home and then steals a diamond ring, it is burglary.

An estimated 3,052,200 burglaries occurred during 1977, 73% by forcible entry, 19% by unlawful entry (without force), and the remainder by forcible entry attempts. Of the 16% cleared, 67% involved persons over age 18.

Larceny/Theft

Larceny/theft is the unlawful taking or stealing of property or articles *without* the use of force, violence, or fraud. It includes shoplifting, pocketpicking, purse-snatching, thefts from motor vehicles, thefts of motor vehicle parts and accessories, and bicycle thefts. The category does *not* include embezzlement, "con" games, forgery, and worthless checks, to be discussed shortly under white-collar crimes. It also does not include motor vehicle theft which is a separate Crime Index offense.

> Larceny/theft is unlawfully taking and removing another's personal property with the intent of permanently depriving the owner of the property.

This crime, accounting for over 50% of reported crime committed in the United States in 1977, may be classified as either a misdemeanor or a felony. It differs from robbery in that it does not involve threats of force, force, or violence. The severity of punishment usually depends on the value and type of property taken, whether it was taken from a building or a person, and the specific circumstances of the case.

Most theft statutes indicate situations where the value of the article is

Figure 3-2. Larceny Analysis—1977. From *Crime in the United States—1977 Uniform Crime Reports.* Reprinted by permission.

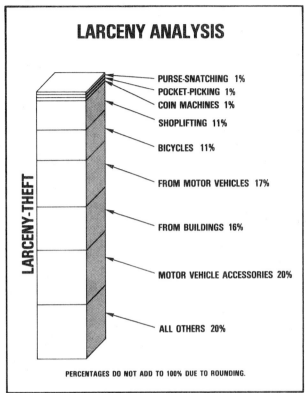

immaterial in determining whether the offense is a felony or misdemeanor. These situations include stealing from the person of another or a grave or a corpse, stealing public records or public funds, looting, and stealing articles representing trade secrets.

Some states categorize larceny into degrees. Grand and petty larceny are common identifications for value of property taken and punishment. First-, second-, and third-degree larceny also indicate a certain minimum value of the property taken and various degrees of punishment.

The most common type of theft is the theft of items from motor vehicles and motor vehicle parts and accessories. The files of police departments throughout the country are filled with reports of losses such as CB radios, stereo-tape decks, clothing, and photographic equipment taken from motor vehicles.

Other common forms of larceny are thefts from buildings such as underground garages where maintenance equipment such as lawnmowers, snowblowers, lawn hoses, and fertilizers are the target. Bicycles are also a common target for thieves. Because they are easily removed and lack serial number markings, bicycle theft has become big business for many criminals. Police departments find that in some cities dealers specialize in the sale of stolen bicycles.

Thefts from coin-operated vending machines, pocket-picking, purse-snatching, and shoplifting are other common forms of larceny/theft.

Figure 3-3.   % up and % down in types of thefts. From *Crime in the United States —1977 Uniform Crime Reports*. Reprinted by permission.

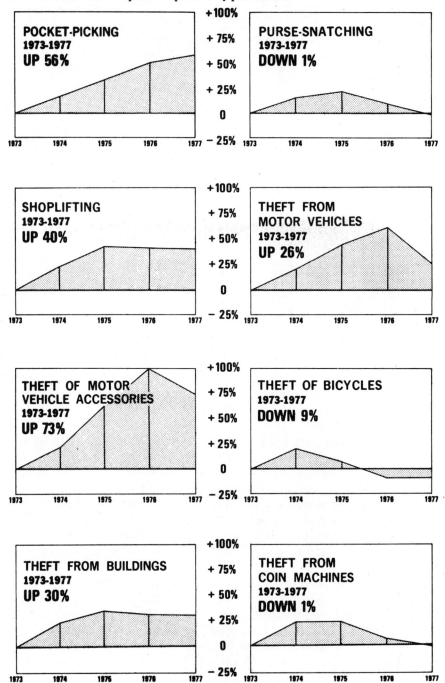

Shoplifting accounts for an estimated two billion dollars lost each year. Shoplifters range in age from five to eighty-five. The great majority are amateurs, but there are professional shoplifters (called "boosters") as well as itinerant schools for professionals. The vast majority of shoplifters apprehended are not prosecuted because merchants do not want to alienate good customers, and they do not want to spend the time involved in prosecution, so the customers pay for the shoplifting losses in higher prices.

In 1977 5,905,700 offenses of larceny/theft were reported; 37% of the thefts were motor vehicle parts, and accessories, and other thefts from motor vehicles. Twenty percent of all larceny/theft offenses reported were solved, of which 33% involved the arrest of persons under age 18. The average value of property stolen per larceny/theft was $192.

Motor Vehicle Theft

In Uniform Crime reporting, motor vehicle theft is defined as the unlawful taking or stealing of a motor vehicle, including attempts. This definition excludes taking for temporary use by those persons having lawful access to the vehicle.

> Motor vehicle theft is the unlawful taking or stealing of a motor vehicle without the authority or permission of the owner.

Motor vehicle theft rates show this crime to be primarily a large city problem; the highest rates appear in the most heavily populated sections of the country.

It is difficult to obtain a conviction for auto theft unless witnesses see the person drive the vehicle away and make positive identification later. It is also difficult to prove if the suspect intended to permanently deprive the rightful owner of its use. Therefore, another category of auto theft has been created called "Unlawful Use of a Motor Vehicle" which applies to suspects who merely have possession of a vehicle reported stolen.

Auto thefts represent the greatest monetary property loss—greater than the combined total of all other offenses. The police are not only charged with the recovery of stolen vehicles, but with the apprehension of the guilty parties.

Of the many motives for auto theft, joy-riding leads the list. Young people steal a car, take it for a ride, and then abandon it. Autos are also stolen for revenge, for transportation, for commercial use, and for use in committing other crimes such as kidnapping, burglary, and bank robbery. Autos are stolen and stripped for such parts as transmissions, engines, and seats. Sale of stolen auto parts is one of the fastest growing businesses today because of the high cost of replacement parts and the unavailability of parts for foreign-made cars. Automobiles are also stolen, modified, and given altered serial numbers, fraudulent titles, and sold to an unsuspecting public.

With the increased number of foreign students attending our universities, a relatively new scheme has caused millions of dollars of losses to American banks. The fraudulent car scheme has accelerated to a new high under the guise of car loans from banks. Foreign students buy new cars, obtain loans on them, and then ship them to foreign countries which require no proof of ownership. In addition, many vehicles reported as stolen are actually driven into lakes and rivers or buried by their owners to defraud insurance companies.

In 1977 968,400 motor vehicles were reported stolen, an estimated 1 out of every 143 registered motor vehicles. Of all motor vehicle thefts reported, 80% were automobiles, 9% were trucks or buses, and 10% were other types of motor vehicles, including motorcycles, motorized boats, and aircraft. Fifteen percent of motor vehicle thefts were cleared by arrest, of which 53% involved the arrest of individuals under age 18.

☑ CHECK POINT

1. How are crimes and punishments determined in the United States?
2. List five characteristics of crime.
3. Define: murder, assault, rape, robbery, burglary, larceny/theft, and motor vehicle theft.

*Answers

1. Crimes are made so by law. State and federal statutes define each crime, the elements involved, and the penalty attached to each.
2. A crime is an (1) intentional (2) action (3) which is prohibited by law and (4) for which punishment is legally prescribed, (5) that directly (6) causes (7) an actual harm.
3. (a) Murder (homicide) is the killing of a human by another human.
   (b) Assault is attacking a person. It may be aggravated or simple assault.
   (c) Rape is having sexual intercourse with a female through the use or threat of force. It may be aggravated or simple.
   (d) Robbery is stealing anything of value from the control, care, or custody of a person by force or threat of force.
   (e) Burglary is unlawful entrance into a building to commit theft or a felony.
   (f) Larceny/theft is unlawfully taking and removing another's personal property with the intent of permanently depriving the owner of the property.
   (g) Motor vehicle theft is the unlawful taking or stealing of a motor vehicle without the authority or permission of the owner.

Without looking back, can you name the seven Index Crimes (Part One)?

WHITE-COLLAR CRIME

Most of the crimes we have talked about so far involve violence or have the potential for violence. Other crimes, often involving billions of dollars annually, may receive less attention yet pose an extremely difficult challenge to law enforcement officers. These are the white-collar crimes.

> White-collar crime is occupational or business-related crime.

In a large southern city recently, a grand jury brought indictments on thirty-two counts against a vice-president of a bank for embezzling funds. Outstanding community leader, father of several children—a respectable individual in the community was suddenly disgraced. At the same time in a western city, a grand jury brought indictments on twelve counts against a warehouse employee who had taken merchandise from his employer's warehouse, loaded it on a friend's truck, sold it, and divided the profits. The warehouse employee, a family man who attended church regularly, was shunned by his friends and fired by his employer.

Although most people in business are honest, corruption does exist. Security abuses, tax frauds, embezzlements, bribes, and kickbacks frequently occur, often the result of a "look the other way" attitude of co-workers and employers. Not only do employees and employers frequently ignore dishonesty within their businesses, they frequently engage in such practices themselves, rationalizing their actions as acquiring something they really were entitled to. For example, the employee who makes long-distance calls on his employer's phone or who pads his expense account may tell himself that since he is underpaid, this is simply one way of getting what he has coming to him.

When stealing from the boss (company, firm, business), most employees do not consider what they are doing as theft but merely a fringe benefit of the job. Going across the street and taking the same thing from another firm would be considered dishonest—but not when taken from one's own employer.

The Chamber of Commerce of the United States (1974) has identified nine categories of white-collar crime.

White-collar crime includes: (1) securities theft and fraud, (2) insurance fraud, (3) credit card and check fraud, (4) consumer fraud, illegal competition, and deceptive practices, (5) bankruptcy fraud, (6) computer-related fraud, (7) embezzlement and pilferage, (8) bribes, kickbacks, and payoffs, and (9) receiving stolen property.

Eldefonso (1976, p.2) notes that the existence of white-collar crime has an extremely demoralizing effect upon those who lack material possessions. Such individuals, while not having the opportunity to engage in white-collar crime, may follow the example of illegal means to obtain material gain.

Criminals involved in fraudulent schemes of all types are usually extremely mobile, moving from city to city and state to state, ruining individuals and small businesses.

Securities Theft and Fraud

Securities theft and fraud may be perpetrated by clerks acting independently, by individuals who rob messengers and steal from the mails, or by well-organized rings, one of which was reported as stealing approximately five million dollars worth of stocks monthly.* The total value of all outstanding

---

*The statistics in this section are from *White Collar Crime: Everyone's Problem, Everyone's Loss.* Chamber of Commerce of the United States, 1974.

lost, stolen, or missing securities has been placed at $50 billion. Most security thefts involve cooperation of dishonest employees ("inside" people) and may involve counterfeit and bogus securities as well.

Insurance Fraud

Insurance fraud losses are approximately $1.5 billion yearly, leading to higher premiums for consumers. Since insurance is important to businesses and individuals, false claims for life, health, and accident benefits affect almost everyone.

Especially prevalent are fraudulent auto-accident claims seeking compensation for treatments for personal injury, time lost from work, and automobile repairs.

Credit Card and Check Fraud

The approximately 26 billion checks and 300 million credit cards in circulation each year present limitless opportunity for crime. Unauthorized use of credit cards (found, stolen, or counterfeited) results in an estimated loss of $100 million annually.

Check fraud, including checks passed with insufficient funds or with no account, forged checks, counterfeit checks, stolen travelers' checks, money orders, and payroll checks costs an estimated $1 billion annually.

Consumer Fraud, Illegal Competition, and Deceptive Practices

Thousands of different schemes have been reported to defraud the public, including offers for "free" articles, advice, vacations, mailing of unordered merchandise, phony contests, recommendations for unneeded repairs, "going-out-of-business" sales, unqualified correspondence schools, and price-fixing. Hundreds of other schemes undoubtedly exist but have not been reported because although the victims may realize the swindle, they do not want to admit having been "taken in."

Bankruptcy Fraud

Bankruptcy fraud, also called planned bankruptcy, scam, or bust-out, accounts for estimated annual losses of $80 million. This white-collar crime involves purchasing merchandise on credit from many different suppliers, selling the merchandise for cash which is "hidden," and then claiming bankruptcy, not paying the creditors. A small business which has extended a large amount of credit to a company that declares bankruptcy (legitimately or not) may be forced out of business. Such an owner may then decide to use the same tactic himself, rationalizing the fraud as a justified effort to save his debt-ridden business.

Computer-Related Crime

Computer-related crime is a relatively new, yet highly profitable, type of white-collar crime. As noted in the *Washington Post*, December 6, 1976:

The federal government is becoming increasingly concerned with the growing misuse of computers to steal, defraud, embezzle, sabotage and blackmail people in private and public agencies. According to a study by the General Accounting Office, 69 *computer crimes defrauded federal agencies of $2 million over the last two years. In addition, more than 400 crimes-by-computer cases have been documented over the last eight years with victims losing $200 million.*

Computer fraud may involve the input data, the output data, the program itself, or computer time.

Input data may be altered, for example fictitious suppliers may be entered, figures may be changed, or data may be removed. Some universities have experienced difficulties with student grades being illegally changed on computer cards.

Output data may be obtained by unauthorized persons through such means as wiretapping, electromagnetic pickup, or theft of data sheets.

The computer program itself might be tampered with to add costs to purchased items or to establish a double set of records.

Computer time may be used for personal use, an example of pilferage to be discussed shortly. Some employees have even used their employer's hardware and company time to set up their own computer services for personal profit.

Embezzlement and Pilferage

Many businessmen consider embezzlement and pilferage to be their most serious problem. Both are, in effect, theft. *To embezzle* is to steal or use for oneself money or property entrusted to the person. *To pilfer* is basically the same, but on a much smaller scale. The pilferer usually takes such things as office supplies, spare parts, and materials rather than money, but the result is the same. Cumulatively, the losses from pilferage may be much greater than what some other dishonest employee might embezzle. Equally dishonest is unauthorized use of company equipment, personnel, and time.

Bribes, Kickbacks, and Payoffs

Bribes, kickbacks, and payoffs are pervasive in the business world and are frequently used to obtain new clients, to keep old clients, to influence decisions, or to obtain favors. They can involve anyone from the custodian to the company president, and they can occur in any aspect of a company's operation.

Receiving Stolen Property

Although classified as a white-collar crime, receiving stolen property frequently occurs in conjunction with Index Crimes such as robbery and burglary. The individual who buys and sells stolen property is of vital importance to the success of most burglars, robbers, and hijackers. Criminals depend upon a "fence" (a professional receiver and seller of stolen property) to convert what they have stolen to cash.

☑ CHECK POINT

1. What are white-collar crimes? How do they differ from Index Crimes?
2. List at least five different types of crimes which fall under the classification of white-collar.

*Answers

1. White-collar crimes are occupational or business-related crimes. They differ from Index Crimes in that they usually do not involve violence or the potential for violence.
2. Included within white-collar crime are: (1) securities theft and fraud, (2) insurance fraud, (3) credit card and check fraud, (4) consumer fraud, illegal competition, and deceptive practices, (5) bankruptcy fraud, (6) computer-related fraud, (7) embezzlement and pilferage, (8) bribes, kickbacks, and payoffs, and (9) receiving stolen property.

ILLEGAL POSSESSION, SALE, OR DISTRIBUTION OF NARCOTICS AND DANGEROUS DRUGS

Narcotics are drugs that produce sleep, lethargy, or relief of pain, including heroin, cocaine, and marijuana. Dangerous drugs are addicting, mind-altering drugs such as depressants, stimulants, and hallucinogens.

It is a crime in most states to use or sell narcotics and dangerous drugs without a prescription. Additionally, the abuse of these substances is often closely connected to other types of crime. Homicide, rape, burglary, armed robbery, and shoplifting have been connected with the use of narcotics and dangerous drugs and with the drug abuser's need for money to support his habit.

The misuse and abuse of drugs and their illegal sale and disposition have become a national problem not limited to slum areas or to the use of hard narcotics. Consequently, new amendments by Congress, laws by state legislatures, and ordinances by local political subdivisions provide stronger regulation of the manufacture, distribution, delivery, and possession of many narcotics, depressants, stimulants, and hallucinogens.

In most states narcotics and dangerous drugs may not be used or sold without a prescription. Federal law prohibits sale or distribution not covered by prescription, but it does *not* prohibit possession for personal use.

Calculations based upon the excess of legitimate production over estimated medical need and illegal production, coupled with direct evidence of misuse and abuse, suggest a level of total abuse of an estimated 5% of the United States population or nearly 10 million people (*Fact Sheet*).

The seriousness of the problem can be better understood if the extremely negative effects of these substances are clearly understood. Although most of the narcotics and drugs to be discussed do have some legitimate medical uses, misuse can have serious, even fatal consequences.*

*The following information on narcotics and dangerous drugs is adapted from *Fact Sheet*, Drug Enforcement Administration, U.S. Dept. of Justice (no date).

Narcotics

Prohibited narcotics include heroin, cocaine, and marijuana.

Heroin is the most commonly abused narcotic. Commonly referred to as caballo, doojee, "H," Harry, horse, joy powder, scag, smack, sugar, white lady, and white stuff, it is synthesized from morphine and is up ten times more potent in its effects. Pure heroin is "cut" or diluted with nine or more parts of substances such as milk sugar, quinine, or both.

Heroin may be sniffed (snorting), smoked, injected under the skin (joy popping) or into a vein (mainlining). The first reaction is usually an easing of fears and relief from worry, followed by an intense euphoria and then, frequently, by inactivity bordering on stupor (on the nod). As with all narcotics, tolerance develops rapidly, so the heroin abuser must take increasingly larger quantities to feel its effects.

Heroin is physically addictive and expensive. It causes an easing of fears, followed by euphoria, and finally stupor.

Heroin is considered a major factor in contributing to crime because of its street cost and its continuous necessity to be used; therefore, law enforcement narcotics divisions frequently concentrate their efforts on apprehending the suppliers and pushers of heroin.

Cocaine, once widely used as a local anesthetic in surgery, has been replaced by newer drugs. It is a white or colorless crystalline powder that is inhaled or injected, producing euphoria, excitation, anxiety, a sense of increased muscular strength, talkativeness, and a reduction in feelings of fatigue. The pupils frequently become dilated, and the heart rate and blood pressure usually increase.

In large doses cocaine may produce fever, vomiting, convulsions, hallucinations, and paranoid delusions. Overdoses may so depress breathing and heart functions that death results.

The intense stimulation experienced from use of cocaine often causes its users to voluntarily seek sedation, combining depressant drugs with the cocaine. A cocaine-heroin combination is called a "speedball." Cocaine often creates a strong psychological dependence; however, physical dependence does not develop.

Marijuana is probably the most "socially acceptable" of the illegal drugs; legislation lessening penalties for its use has frequently been proposed. Although it has been known for nearly 5,000 years, it is one of the least understood of all natural drugs, yet one of the most versatile. Derived from the cannabis plant which still grows wild in many parts of the United States, its fibers have been used in twine, rope, bags, clothing, and paper. Its seeds have been used in feed mixtures. And it has been used in the treatment of a variety of clinical disorders, as an anesthetic during surgery, as an analgesic, and as a poultice for corns.

Marijuana is frequently used in the form of cigarettes, commonly referred to as reefers or goof butts. When smoked, marijuana enters the bloodstream quickly, causing rapid onset of symptoms. The effects of the drug on the user's mood and thinking vary widely, depending on the amount and strength of the marijuana as well as the social setting and the effects anticipated. The drug usually takes effect in about fifteen minutes and lasts from two to four hours. "Social" doses of one or two cigarettes may cause an increased sense of well being; initial restlessness and hilarity followed by a dreamy, carefree state of relaxation; alteration of sensory perceptions including expansion of space and time; and/or a more vivid sense of touch, sight, smell, taste, and sound; a feeling of hunger, especially craving for sweets; and subtle changes in thought formation and expression.

> Large doses of marijuana may cause distortions of body image, loss of personal identity, fantasies, hallucinations, and toxic psychoses as well as receptivity to suggestions, no matter how absurd or dangerous.

Overuse of marijuana affects an individual's ability to make decisions and renders him highly susceptible to the suggestions of others. In addition, overuse affects tasks requiring good reflexes and logic; therefore, it is very dangerous to drive a car while under the influence of this drug.

Depressants—Barbiturates

Depressants or barbiturates, commonly referred to as barbs, blue heavens, downs, goofballs, red-birds, and yellowjackets, are sedatives taken orally as a small tablet or capsule to induce sleep or to relieve tension. Housewives are the most common abusers of barbiturates. All of the 1,500 types of barbiturates available are legally restricted to prescription use only.

Small amounts of barbiturates make the user relaxed, sociable, and good-humored. Heavy doses cause sluggishness, depression, deep sleep, or coma. A barbiturate addict usually takes ten to twenty pills a day and often shows symptoms of drunkenness: speech becomes slurred and indistinct, physical coordination is impaired, and mental and emotional instability occurs. Many barbiturate addicts are quarrelsome and have a "short fuse." The risks involved in habitual use of such depressants are numerous.

> Depressants (barbiturates) are physically addictive. Withdrawal is painful and dangerous. The barbiturate addict frequently appears to be "drunk." Overdoses are common and frequently cause intentional or accidental death.

A nonlethal dose of barbiturates impairs the user's mental and emotional stability and sensitivity to pain; therefore, serious accidents may occur. Overdosage is common because users often forget how much they have already taken. When used with alcohol, barbiturates can lead to coma and death.

Barbituric acid, the ingredient of the barbiturates, is a poison. Addiction or heavy usage requires hospitalization. If the addict goes "cold turkey" with the barbs, he may very well die. Hospitalization requires three to four weeks to reduce the level of poison for recovery.

Stimulants (Amphetamines)

Amphetamines are commonly referred to as Bennies, co-pilots, crossroads, crystal, dexis, drivers, footballs, hearts, pep pills, speed, and uppers, names derived from the shape of the pill or its effect. Amphetamines are stimulants taken orally as a tablet or capsule, or intravenously, to reduce appetite and/or to relieve mental depression. They are often taken by truck drivers, salesmen, college students, and businessmen who want to stay awake for long periods and by housewives who want to lose weight.

Normal doses produce wakefulness, increased alertness and initiative, and hyperactivity. Large doses produce exaggerted feelings of confidence, power, and well-being.

Habitual users may take amphetamines for three or four days, eat nothing, and drive themselves until they black out from exhaustion. Heavy users may exhibit restlessness, nervousness, hand tremors, pupil dilation, dryness of mouth, and excessive perspiration. They may be talkative and experience delusions and/or hallucinations. Although small doses may produce cheerfulness and unusual increase in activity, heavy and prolonged use may produce symptoms resembling paranoid schizophrenia. Handling this deviant behavior has always been a source of concern and danger for law enforcement officers.

> Stimulants (amphetamines) may be emotionally and psychologically addictive. Hyperactivity, nervousness, hand tremor, dilated pupils, and excessive perspiration may indicate use of amphetamines. Users are inclined to be violent, are susceptible to serious illnesses, and can develop heart problems and/or permanent brain damage.

The expression "speed kills" underscores the dangers of misuse of amphetamines. While not physically addictive, the drugs may be emotionally and psychologically addictive. Because the body builds up a tolerance to them, heavier and more frequent doses are needed. The three greatest dangers in misuse of amphetamines are: (1) users are inclined to be violent, especially if they become paranoid; (2) they are very susceptible to ailments such as pneumonia, malnutrition, and exhaustion—results of going without food and sleep for prolonged periods; (3) they can develop high blood pressure, abnormal heart rhythms, heart attacks, and permanent brain damage.

Hallucinogens

Hallucinogens are commonly known as acid, angel dust, big D, cubes, DMT, LSD, and PCP. Probably the best known hallucinogen is LSD, which gets its name from the colorless, odorless substance lysergic acid diethylamide from which it is made.

Although hallucinogens are usually taken orally as a tablet or capsule, their physical characteristics allow them to be disguised as various commonly used powders or liquids. LSD has been found on chewing gum, hard candy, crackers, vitamin pills, aspirin, blotting paper, and postage stamps.

Other hallucinogens include DMT (dimethyltryptamine), a powerful drug similar to LSD; mescaline, a chemical derived from the peyote cactus; and psilocybin, a natural ingredient in a species of Mexican mushroom.

Hallucinogens may produce distortion, intensify sensory perception, and lessen the ability to discriminate between fact and fantasy. The unpredictable mental effects include illusions, panic, psychotic or antisocial behavior, and impulses toward violence and self-destruction. As little as one hundred-millionth of a gram of LSD can produce hallucinations lasting for hours.

Use of hallucinogens may cause serious accidents, suicides, and homicides. Indications of misuse of hallucinogens include noticeable dilation of the pupils, extreme emotionalism, shifting of moods, violence, and attempts at self-destruction.

An LSD user may become extremely emotional, shifting moods, laughing and crying uncontrollably. Or he may be unresponsive to the environment and to any attempts at communication. Many LSD users wear dark glasses, even at night, because the hallucinogens cause their pupils to dilate to the extent that light is painful.

The hallucinogen user's actions while under the influence of the drug often present an enforcement problem in terms of homicides, suicides, and accidents. A recent tragedy graphically illustrates the dangers associated with hallucinogens. A nineteen-year-old youth and a roommate had taken LSD. The youth became violent shortly after taking the drugs and wanted to fly. After a struggle with his roommate who was trying to control him, he leaped through the window, plunging twenty stories to his death and narrowly missing passing pedestrians.

Deliriants

Deliriants, volatile chemicals commonly referred to as hi-flite and laughing gas, include airplane glue, gasoline, lighter fluid, paint thinner, freon, carbon tetrachloride, and other volatile commercial products. Although technically neither narcotics nor dangerous drugs, deliriants may be a prime cause of psychological dependency among young people.

Deliriants may be sniffed or inhaled either directly from a container or from a paper or plastic bag or cloth. Redness or irritation commonly occurs around the nostrils and lips. Other reactions vary according to the deliriant

used and the amount inhaled. However, deliriants generally produce a "hi
similar to that produced by alcohol.

> Deliriants may cause brain damage and even death. Indicators of the...
> use include mental confusion, hallucinations, and black-outs.

The inhalation of deliriant type substances in large amounts over a long
period may cause permanent cell damage. The inhalation of freon (a product
used for refrigeration) can kill its users by freezing the larynx and other
parts of the respiratory tract. Still another danger is the inhalation of deliriants
from plastic bags as the user may pass out and suffocate within the plastic bag.

Figure 3-4. Spectrum and continuum of drug action. All drugs can be placed on a
continuum of stimulation-depression according to their effect on the central nervous
system. (Robert W. Earle, Ph.D., Senior Lecturer, Department of Medical Pharma-
cology and Therapeutics, University of California at Irvine, California College of
Medicine.)

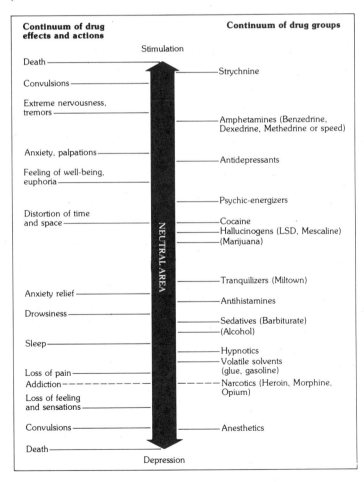

Table 3-1.   Facts about Drugs.

Name	Slang name	Chemical or trade name	Source	Classification	Medical use	How taken
Heroin	H., Horse, Scat, Junk, Smack, Scag, Stuff	Diacetyl-morphine	Semi-synthetic (from morphine)	Narcotic	Pain relief	Injected or sniffed
Morphine	White stuff, M.	Morphine sulphate	Natural (from opium)	Narcotic	Pain relief	Swallowed or injected
Codeine	Schoolboy	Methyl-morphine	Natural (from opium), semi-synthetic (from morphine)	Narcotic	Ease pain and coughing	Swallowed
Methadone	Dolly	Dolophine, Amidone	Synthetic	Narcotic	Pain relief	Swallowed or injected
Cocaine	Corrine, Gold dust, Coke, Bernice, Flake, Star dust, Snow	Methylester of benzoyl-leogonine	Natural (from coca, NOT cacao)	Stimulant, local anesthesia	Local anesthesia	Sniffed, injected, or swallowed
Marijuana	Pot, Grass, Tea, Hashish, Gage, Reefers	Cannabis sativa	Natural	Relaxant, euphoriant; in high doses, hallucinogen	None in U.S.	Smoked, swallowed, or sniffed
Barbiturates	Barbs, Blue devils, Candy, Yellow jackets, Phennies, Peanuts, Blue heavens	Phenobarbital, Nembutal, Seconal, Amytal	Synthetic	Sedative-hypnotic	Sedation, relief of high blood pressure, hy-perthyroidism	Swallowed or injected
Ampheta-mines	Bennies, Dexies, Speed, Wake-ups, Lid poppers, Hearts, Pep pills	Benzedrine, Dexedrine, Desoxyn, Methamphet-amine, Meth-adrine	Synthetic	Sympatho-mimetic	Relief of mild depression, control of ap-petite and narcolepsy	Swallowed or injected
LSD	Acid, Sugar, Big D, Cubes, Trips	D-lysergic Acid diethylamide	Semi-synthetic (from ergot alkaloids)	Hallucinogen	Experimental study of mental function, alcoholism	Swallowed
DMT	AMT, Business-man's high	Dimethyl-triptamine	Synthetic	Hallucinogen	None	Injected
Mescaline	Mesc.	3, 4, 5-tri-methoxyphen-ethylamine	Natural (from peyote)	Hallucinogen	None	Swallowed
Psilocybin		3(2-dimethyl-amino) ethylin-dol-4-oldihy-drogen phos-phate	Natural (from psilocybe)	Hallucinogen	None	Swallowed
Alcohol	Booze, Juice, etc.	Ethanol, Ethyl-alcohol	Natural (from grapes, grains, etc., via fer-mentation)	Sedative-hypnotic	Solvent, antiseptic	Swallowed
Tobacco	Fag, Coffin nail, etc.	Nicotiana tabacum	Natural	Stimulant-sedative	Sedative, emetic (nicotine)	Smoked, sniffed, or chewed

(Question marks indicate conflict of opinion. It should be noted that illicit drugs are frequently adulterated and thus pose unknown hazards to the user.)

SOURCE: *Resource Book for Drug Abuse Education,* developed as a part of the Drug Abuse Education Project of the American Association for Health, Physical Education, and Recreation, and the National Science Teachers Association (NEA), 1969.

Usual dose	Duration of effect	Effects sought	Long-term symptoms	Physical dependence potential	Mental dependence potential	Organic damage potential
Varies	4 hr	Euphoria, prevent withdrawal discomfort	Addiction, constipation, loss of appetite	Yes	Yes	No*
15 milligrams	6 hr	Euphoria, prevent withdrawal discomfort	Addiction, constipation, loss of appetite	Yes	Yes	No*
30 milligrams	4 hr	Euphoria, prevent withdrawal discomfort	Addiction, constipation, loss of appetite	Yes	Yes	No
10 milligrams	4-6 hr	Prevent withdrawal discomfort	Addiction, constipation, loss of appetite	Yes	Yes	No
Varies	Varied, brief periods	Excitation, talkativeness	Depression, convulsions	No	Yes	Yes?
1-2 cigarettes	4 hr	Relaxation, increased euphoria, perceptions, sociability	Usually none	No	Yes?	No
50-100 milligrams	4 hr	Anxiety reduction, euphoria	Addiction with severe withdrawal symptoms, possible convulsions, toxic psychosis	Yes	Yes	Yes
2.5-5 milligrams	4 hr	Alertness, activeness	Loss of appetite, delusions, hallucinations, toxic psychosis	No?	Yes	Yes?
100-500 micrograms	10 hr	Insightful experiences, exhilaration, distortion of senses	May intensify existing psychosis, panic reactions	No	No?	No?
1-3 milligrams	Less than 1 hr	Insightful experiences, exhilaration, distortion of senses	?	No	No?	No?
350 micrograms	12 hr	Insightful experiences, exhilaration, distortion of senses	?	No	No?	No?
25 milligrams	6-8 hr	Insightful experiences, exhilaration, distortion of senses	?	No	No?	No?
Varies	1-4 hr	Sense alteration, anxiety reduction, sociability	Cirrhosis, toxic psychosis, neurologic damage, addiction	Yes	Yes	Yes
Varies	Varies	Calmness, sociability	Emphysema, lung cancer, mouth and throat cancer, cardiovascular damage, loss of appetite	Yes?	Yes	Yes

*Persons who inject drugs under nonsterile conditions run a high risk of contracting hepatitis, abcesses, or circulatory disorders.

Common Factors

In spite of numerous differences produced by use of various kinds of narcotics and dangerous drugs, certain common factors occur, the most important of which are (1) they are mind-altering, (2) they may become addicting —either physically or psychologically, and (3) overdosage may result in convulsions and death.

Societal Effects

Although the drug abuser may claim that it is his "right" to ingest, smoke, sniff, or inject whatever he wants into his own body, the results of such actions do have serious implications for society as the user is no longer in control of what he thinks, says, or does, and often poses a threat to other members of society.

The occasional user of marijuana may argue that no harm is being done to anyone, but researchers point out that a person predisposed to the abuse of one drug may be likely to abuse other, stronger drugs (*Fact Sheet*). Also users of one drug may be exposed to a variety of other drug users and sellers and, through this association, may be encouraged to experiment with more potent drugs. More importantly, however, is the expense involved in supporting a drug habit. Frequently this expense causes the addict to turn to crime to obtain money with which to purchase the needed drugs.

☑ CHECK POINT

1. What restrictions are placed on the possession, sale, and use of narcotics and dangerous drugs?

2. What is a narcotic? A dangerous drug? What three classifications are usually made of dangerous drugs?

3. Match the physical and psychological effects listed on the left with the substances listed on the right:

_____ a. Slurred, indistinct speech, impaired physical coordination, sluggishness. Physically addictive.

_____ b. Hyperactivity, nervousness, hand tremor, dilated pupils, excessive perspiration. Displays of violence. Psychologically addictive.

_____ c. Noticeable dilation of pupils, extreme emotionalism, shifting of moods, violence, attempts at self-destruction.

_____ d. Redness and irritation around nose and lips. Mental confusion, hallucinations, blackouts.

_____ e. Easing of fears, intense euphoria, stupor.

_____ f. Intense stimulation, excitation, sense of increased muscular strength.

_____ g. Dreamy, carefree state of relaxation, alteration of sensory perceptions, subtle changes in thought formation.

1. amphetamines
2. barbiturates
3. cocaine
4. deliriants
5. hallucinogens
6. heroin
7. marijuana

4. Using the substances listed on the right, indicate those classified as stimulants, as depressants, and as narcotics.

*Answers

1. In most states narcotics and dangerous drugs may not be used or sold without a prescription. Federal law prohibits sale or distribution not covered by prescription, but it does not prohibit possession for personal use.
2. A narcotic is a drug which produces sleep, lethargy, or relief of pain. Dangerous drugs are addicting and mind altering. The three general classifications are depressants (barbiturates), stimulants (amphetamines), and hallucinogens.
3. a. 2   b. 1   c. 5   d. 4   e. 6   f. 3   g. 7.
4. Amphetamines are stimulants; barbiturates are depressants; and cocaine, heroin, and marijuana are narcotics. (Marijuana is also sometimes classified as a hallucinogen.)

Some Major Causes of Crime

INTRODUCTION

Criminals, like everyone else, are the product of their environment and heredity. A close-up look at one criminal may provide insight into the complex factors which interact to create a criminal as well as the complexity of the "criminal" himself.

Benjamin "Benny" McNeil, age sixty-five, stood at the booking counter of a midwestern police department laughing, joking, and seemingly indifferent to the fact that he had just been picked up for shoplifting two small drills, a a paperback book, a bottle of after-shave lotion, and a tube of toothpaste—total value: $9.85. For "Benny" who at one time had the reputation of being the most successful and artistic safe-cracker in the country, this was quite a come down.

According to "Benny's" "rap sheet," he had spent thirty-eight of his sixty-five years in detention homes. foster homes, reformatories, and prisons. "Benny" took pride in his criminal career and in the fact that he had never resorted to violence or hurt anyone. He felt strongly that his life of crime was his way to get back at society for the injustices it had heaped upon him.

"Benny," who came from a middle-income family and had one brother and one sister, began his life of crime at thirteen, breaking into school lockers, stealing billfolds from football players' pants' pockets, and shoplifting at the local shopping center. In his late teens he engaged in more shoplifting, stealing bicycles and automobiles, and stealing money from purses. With the exception of a few interruptions at the city detention home and a foster home, his criminal career progressed into other areas. From armed robbery to burglary to swindling and embezzlement, "Benny" always seemed to be successful. But he had one thing going against him. He eventually was apprehended. How many of the crimes in which he was involved are reflected in his record, only he knows. When asked by the booking officer what he was going to do when he served time on the latest shoplifting charge, "Benny" replied, "Probably go steal some more; I don't know how to do anything else very well."

How did this sixty-five-year-old handsome man who, despite his hard-boiled manner, is friendly and outgoing, come to be a criminal?

There is no simple answer. His environment disguised his crimes; he came from a law-abiding family to whom he exhibited scorn and defiance. He was no more acceptable to them as a law-abiding teen-ager than as a criminal. He never possessed the "pleasant" qualities of his brother and sister and was constantly reminded that he should be like them. When his parents conveyed kindness to him, he interpreted it as weakness. He did poorly in school, dropping out when he was sixteen. He was considered a "loner"; his only friends were younger boys with whom he felt more secure and could exert his cunning leadership abilities. The result: almost half a century of criminal activity. Scientists would have a hard time explaining "Benny's" criminal career since many different motives and behavior patterns characterize those who decide on a career of crime.

MULTIPLE CAUSES OF CRIMINAL BEHAVIOR

Criminal behavior results from the individual's basic personality and environment. To a major degree, social and economic conditions cause crime.

Rainwater (1974, p.7) has identified five different perspectives on the causation of crime:

For the social pathologist, the problem is the defective character of individuals in society ... For the sociologist who focuses on social disorganization, the problem is the ineffectiveness of rules for organizing constructive social processes. For the value conflict theorist, the problem can be understood only as a result either of conflicts among groups in society or of conflicting interests held by a single individual. For the deviance theorist, the problem lies in the instigations to rule violation created by the unequal distribution of opportunities for self-realization in society. For the labeling theorist, the problem is very much in the eye of the beholder, and in the process by which society separates its members into the moral and the immoral, the conforming and the deviant.

Each perspective offers some insight into the complexity of the causations of crime, and each illustrates that there is no single factor responsible for the existence of crime, a fact long accepted by criminologists.

Further support for the multiplicity of causes for crime is presented by Hood and Sparks (1970) who note that numerous comparisons of groups of criminals with groups of noncriminals have failed to produce any single characteristic or "factor" which absolutely distinguishes the two groups. Further, since the concepts of crime, delinquency, deviant behavior, and the like apply to such a wide range of different kinds of behavior, having in common only the fact that they have been declared contrary to legal rules in various times and places, no single causal explanation can possibly cover this wide range of behaviors.

Many Americans have come to accept the existence of crime as a part of life, a price paid by a democratic society for its high standard of living where those who "have not" seek to get their fair share in any way possible.

Crime has always been a local problem and responsibility, yet it is a social problem which concerns the entire country. Its causative factors and effects have been studied by scientists and researchers for over a century. Its increase in the last quarter-century has so alarmed the country and cities that the sixties and seventies often dictated a "law and order" platform for politicians.

Many of the causative factors of crime are well beyond the control of the law enforcement officer. Included among these are the population, its density and size, that is, how many people live in a square mile; economics; the legal policies of prosecutors; the educational system of the community; the recreational areas and facilities available; and the religious characteristics of some communities. With a breakdown in discipline in many schools with open, permissive policies and a breakdown in the family value system, crime has become one of America's gravest social problems.

The high level of unemployment, especially among the young, increases the problem. With teen-age unemployment in some large cities running 40%, attitudes and values may change considerably. The "free enterprise" system may appear to have little to offer a young person who cannot gain access to the system because no jobs are available. For some the logical alternative is to engage in crime. When frustration, emotional conflict, and desperation overcome individuals because of social and economic conditions, they frequently resort to a crime against property or persons. The result is that those individuals who have been able to cope with the stresses of the free enterprise system and are law-abiding find themselves victimized by those who have turned to crime.

Most criminal behavior is learned.

Criminologist Edwin H. Sutherland (1937) has postulated a theory concerning the genesis of criminal behavior called *differential association*. He explains the beginning of criminal behavior in the group-based learning experiences of the individual based on the following assumptions (Vetter and Silverman, 1978, p.325):

Criminal behavior is learned.

Criminal behavior is learned in interaction with other persons in a process of communication.

The principal part of the learning of criminal behavior occurs within intimate personal groups.

When criminal behavior is learned, the learning includes: (a) techniques of committing the crime ... and (b) the specific direction of motives, drives, rationalizations, and attitudes.

The specific direction of motives and drives is learned from definitions of the legal codes as favorable or unfavorable.

A person becomes delinquent because of an excess of definitions favorable to violation of the law over definitions unfavorable to violation of the law.

Differential associations may vary in frequency, duration, priority, and intensity.

The process of learning criminal behavior by association with criminal and anticriminal patterns involves all the mechanisms that are involved in any other kind of learning.

While criminal behavior is an expression of general needs and values, it is not explained by those general needs and values since noncriminal behavior is an expression of the same needs and values.

Everyone at one time or another is exposed to criminal behavior; some learn and acquire criminal actions; some do not. Why? Again, no simple reason can be given. Often a large part of the answer is found in what happens to individuals in their early years. Some children cause no problems for parents, school, and the community; others are incorrigible, creating a serious problem not only for their parents, teachers, and neighbors, but for law enforcement officers.

JUVENILE DELINQUENCY

States vary as to the age of a juvenile, but most state statutes specify an individual under the age of sixteen or eighteen. A delinquent child is usually defined as one who has violated a federal, state, or local law or ordinance, is habitually truant from school, or who is uncontrolled by his parent, guardian, or other custodian by being wayward or habitually disobedient, or who habitually conducts himself in a manner injurious or dangerous to himself or others.

> A juvenile delinquent is an individual not of legal age who fails to obey a law or ordinance.

Juvenile delinquency presents a serious problem with an enormous number of youngsters involved. Self-report studies indicate that approximately 90% of all young people have committed at least one act for which they could be brought to juvenile court (*The Challenge of Crime in a Free Society*, 1967, p. 55). However, many of these offenses are minor (for example, fighting, truancy, and running away from home), and state statutes often define juvenile delinquency so broadly that virtually all youngsters could be classified as delinquent.

Even though many offenses are minor, and even though many juvenile offenders are never arrested or referred to juvenile court, alarming numbers are. The Children's Bureau estimates that one in every nine youths and one in every six male youths will be referred to juvenile court for a delinquent act (excluding traffic offenses) before his eighteenth birthday (*The Challenge of Crime*, p. 56).

Youth is responsible for a substantial and disproportionate part of the national crime problem.

Arrest statistics point out the severity of the problem, although such statistics may be somewhat exaggerated as juveniles are often more easily caught than adults, and they often act in groups when committing the crimes, thereby producing a greater number of arrests than crimes committed.

The following table from the 1977 Uniform Crime Reports indicates the type and extent of crimes in which youth are involved (p. 189):

Table 3-2.   City Arrests by Age, 1977   [8,047 agencies; 1977 estimated population 139,416,000]

Offense charged	Grand total all ages	Ages under 15	Ages under 18	Ages 18 and over	Age 10 and under	11–12	13–14	15	16	17
TOTAL	7,008,237	620,667	1,793,884	5,214,353	67,929	135,920	416,818	350,482	412,705	410,030
Percent distribution [1]	100.0	8.9	25.6	74.4	1.0	1.9	5.9	5.0	5.9	5.9
Criminal homicide:										
(a) Murder and nonnegligent manslaughter	12,487	163	1,318	11,169	11	18	134	205	409	541
(b) Manslaughter by negligence	1,597	29	207	1,390	4	6	19	26	72	80
Forcible rape	18,916	890	3,362	15,554	45	150	695	605	901	966
Robbery	104,570	9,594	35,041	69,529	466	1,884	7,244	6,831	9,067	9,549
Aggravated assault	163,582	8,742	29,204	134,378	885	1,899	5,958	5,324	7,286	7,852
Burglary	340,726	69,698	180,421	160,305	7,512	15,713	46,473	36,307	40,114	34,302
Larceny-theft	849,851	168,199	375,891	473,960	20,753	44,281	103,165	68,328	73,309	66,055
Motor vehicle theft	104,791	15,041	56,818	47,973	381	1,771	12,889	14,432	15,207	12,138
Violent crime [2]	299,555	19,389	68,925	230,630	1,407	3,951	14,031	12,965	17,663	18,908
Percent distribution [1]	100.0	6.5	23.0	77.0	.5	1.3	4.7	4.3	5.9	6.3
Property crime [3]	1,295,368	252,938	613,130	682,238	28,646	61,765	162,527	119,067	128,630	112,495
Percent distribution [1]	100.0	19.5	47.3	52.7	2.2	4.8	12.5	9.2	9.9	8.7
Subtotal for above offenses	1,596,520	272,356	682,262	914,258	30,057	65,722	176,577	132,058	146,365	131,483
Percent distribution [1]	100.0	17.1	42.7	57.3	1.9	4.1	11.1	8.3	9.2	8.2
Other assaults	316,565	23,936	65,154	251,411	2,813	5,708	15,415	11,742	14,410	15,066
Arson	12,010	4,090	6,492	5,518	1,223	1,079	1,788	983	815	604
Forgery and counterfeiting	47,194	1,213	6,725	40,469	64	209	940	1,168	1,865	2,479
Fraud	127,423	10,161	21,091	106,332	390	1,934	7,837	7,175	1,519	2,236
Embezzlement	4,550	114	670	3,880	12	23	79	82	175	299
Stolen property; buying, receiving, possessing	81,351	8,853	28,788	52,563	527	1,726	6,600	5,750	7,150	7,035
Vandalism	159,490	54,352	97,906	61,584	11,321	15,027	28,004	15,827	15,182	12,545
Weapons; carrying, possessing, etc.	112,658	4,429	18,754	93,904	251	808	3,370	3,536	4,964	5,825
Prostitution and commercialized vice	74,216	354	3,197	71,019	26	61	267	397	820	1,626
Sex offenses (except forcible rape and prostitution)	48,129	3,473	9,127	39,002	365	741	2,367	1,809	1,904	1,941
Drug abuse violations	428,583	15,317	104,628	323,955	236	1,340	13,741	19,780	31,505	38,026
Gambling	47,048	288	2,039	45,009	7	40	241	403	533	815
Offenses against family and children	22,915	1,237	2,388	20,527	699	142	396	362	402	387
Driving under the influence	706,690	278	16,725	689,965	56	23	199	612	4,428	11,407
Liquor laws	259,156	8,035	96,669	162,487	173	552	7,310	14,723	31,379	42,532
Drunkenness	1,000,279	4,155	39,901	960,378	187	364	3,604	5,898	11,120	18,728
Disorderly conduct	554,832	34,032	110,193	444,639	3,669	7,720	22,643	19,427	25,298	31,436
Vagrancy	40,912	1,185	4,745	36,167	82	182	921	1,011	1,231	1,318
All other offenses (except traffic)	1,131,692	92,149	255,001	876,691	11,253	19,384	61,512	51,982	56,030	54,840
Suspicion	19,718	1,686	5,123	14,595	228	332	1,126	961	1,244	1,232
Curfew and loitering law violations	81,141	23,027	81,141	---------	1,146	3,965	17,916	17,908	24,119	16,087
Runaways	135,165	55,947	135,165	---------	3,144	8,838	43,965	36,888	30,247	12,083

From *Crime In The United States*, 1977. Reprinted by permission.

[1]Because of rounding, the percentages may not add to total.

[2]*Violent crime* is offenses of murder, forcible rape, robbery, and aggravated assault.

[3]*Property crime* is offenses of burglary, larceny, theft, and motor vehicle theft.

The seriousness of the problem is evident in the amount of relatively serious property crimes: burglary, larceny, and motor vehicle thefts. In addition, although juveniles account for more than their share of arrests for several serious crimes, such arrests are only a small part of all juvenile arrests. Juveniles are most often arrested for petty larceny, fighting, disorderly conduct, liquor-related offenses, and noncriminal conduct such as curfew violations, truancy, incorrigibility, or running away from home.

Factors Related to Juvenile Delinquency

Delinquents often come from backgrounds of social and economic deprivation, that is, their families have lower than average incomes and social status. Equally or perhaps even more important, however, is the area in which the youth lives. One study showed that lower-class youths will seldom be classified as delinquents if they live in upper-class neighborhoods, and numerous other studies have established the relationship between certain deprived areas, especially the slums of large cities, and delinquency (*The Challenge of Crime*, p. 189).

As with most crime, arrest rates for delinquents are highest in the cities, particularly the larger cities, next highest in the suburbs, and lowest in rural areas. The delinquency rate is high among children from broken homes as well as among children who have several brothers and/or sisters. Delinquents often do poorly in school, are below their normal grade level, and have dropped classes or have dropped out of school completely when they are old enough to do so.

According to a press clipping, a fourteen-year-old boy was brought into court on charges of robbing and assaulting a sixty-five-year-old woman with a knife. Sitting in the closed session court room was a woman to whom the judge pointed and asked the boy if he knew. The youngster antagonistically stated, "No." The judge then informed the boy that she was his mother whom he had not seen since she had left him at the age of four months on the steps of the city general hospital because "she did not like the child or child's father." The boy had subsequently lived in ten orphanages and foster homes. Following his sentence to a state training school, the boy bitterly stated to the judge, "The world has done me wrong, and it will have to pay me back. If it doesn't give me what I have coming, I'll take it."

This is not a unique situation. The question is how to deal with such attitudes. Constructive prevention and correction of such attitudes and behaviors is desperately needed. However, to attempt to prevent or correct juvenile antisocial behavior without an understanding of the underlying causes is futile. What accounts for the juvenile brutalities that too frequently capture the headlines, the gang beatings of people, the torturing to death of elderly people "for fun," the deadly juvenile gang wars, the vandalism in schools and churches? Society must give reasonable answers to such questions rather than blaming all delinquency on crime comics, movies, sparing the rod, or mollycoddling young offenders.

The societal focus on the causes of delinquent behavior in children is justifiable because juvenile delinquents commit a disturbing proportion of serious offenses and because many of them grow up to be habitual offenders.

Consequently, the prevention and correction of juvenile delinquent behavior offers one potential means of reducing our nation's high adult crime rate.

Historical Assumptions

Historically simplistic answers have been sought for complex, baffling problems. For example, for centuries the western world operated on the belief that everyone knew the difference between right and wrong, and that if anyone did wrong and broke the law, it was because he willfully chose to do so. This belief underlies our system of criminal law and its reliance on punishment.

Closely related to this concept was the idea that delinquents and criminals differed from the rest of the population in being "born bad." Over the last two decades people have explained all the misbehavior of the age on one factor or another: feeblemindedness, poverty, slums, gangs, drinking, broken homes, lack of playgrounds, failure to punish children, nutrition, divorce, depression, inflation, and on and on. Today crime and horror comics, pornography, violence on television and in the movies, and parental permissiveness are bearing the brunt of the blame for juvenile delinquency. It has even been said that there are no delinquent children, only delinquent parents!

Rarely does a simple explanation exist for a serious or chronic misbehavior by a particular child except in the infrequent cases of brain damage, disease, or accident. Children grow into chronic behavior given certain combinations of situations and their own unique personalities.

Children are directly influenced by their own basic individuality, their home, their school, and their community (society).

Basic Individuality

Babies start life as self-centered, dependent beings who, although they have absolutely no control over themselves or their environment, have an urge for self-preservation, aggressive drives, emotions such as love, anger, and fear, and basic needs which must be met. If their wants are denied, they cry, scream, and sometimes show aggression that might be murderous if they were not so helpless. If permitted to continue in this self-centered world of infancy and given free rein to their impulsive actions to satisfy their wants, *any* child could grow up to be a thief, killer, or rapist.

In the growing-up process it is normal for a child to be dirty, to fight, to grab, to steal, to tear things apart, to talk back, to disobey, and to lie. As noted by Ilg and Ames (1955, p. 137):

Finding a 6-year-old who lies or steals, who has moments of nearly ungovernable rage and who thinks the world ought to revolve around him is not much of a surprise to a psychologist, however hard it may be, temporarily, on parents, relatives, and the neighborhood. But finding the same behavior in a 14- or 15-year-old can be frightening. The whole question of why growth went wrong is a tremendously complicated one....

The parent, the school, and society must teach youth self-discipline, adherence to societal expectation, and must, at the same time, provide for meeting the child's basic needs.

To teach its youth self-discipline and conformity to societal expectations, most societies depend largely on authority expressed through various pressures. It depends on the pressures of physical realities such as the hazards imposed by fire, knives, and stairways, which children must learn to respect if they do not want to get hurt. It depends on the pressures of the competing needs of brothers and sisters, neighbors, and peers. It depends upon the rules and sanctions imposed by parents, schools, custom, laws, police, and the courts.

From infancy on, every child needs the continuous but reasonable discipline of adults. However, intense authority, strict regimentation, or harsh and frequent whippings may build resentment, hate, and a sense of guilt. Dr. Haim G. Ginott (1965, p. 72) warns: "Parents who are in the midst of a declared or undeclared war with their children...should recognize the fact that this war cannot be won....Even if we win a battle and succeed in enforcing our will, they may retaliate by becoming spiritless and neurotic, or rebellious and delinquent."

In addition to reasonable discipline, children must have their basic emotional needs satisfied. Haskell and Yablonsky (1970) cite four basic needs which must be met. First and most important is the need for emotional security, the assurance that one belongs, is loved, and wanted. Infants get this from their parents. As they grow older this sense of security is nurtured by belonging to the family, the neighborhood, the gang, the club, the union, etc. Few people seek or tolerate isolation or ostracism.

A second basic need is for a sense of adequacy or worthiness, the feeling of being competent in at least one activity for which the child gets recognition and praise and gains the crucial sense of being useful. A third need is for new experiences, for adventure and excitement. And a fourth need is an increasing desire for independence as the child advances toward manhood or womanhood.

It is largely through satisfying these basic emotional needs for security, self-worth, excitement, and independence that parents, the school, and the community persuade youth to give up immediate satisfaction of their desires, to exercise self-control, to conform to society's standards, and to avoid delinquent behavior. With some children this is easier than with others. Ilg and Ames (1955, pp. 317-319) have identified three general groups of children: (1) those made of basically sturdy "stuff," who are stable and able to rise above the most adverse circumstances; (2) those who are susceptible to their surroundings and need good upbringing and positive influences to become good citizens; and (3) those who have an inadequacy in their basic individuality. It is from the third group which the majority of delinquents come.

Ilg and Ames contend that these children are not "born criminals," but that the task of growing up to accept and follow society's rules is hard for them, sometimes impossible. Some are lacking in intelligence. Some never develop emotionally. Some lack inhibition and restraint or the ability to foresee the end result of their actions. They caution: "Here as elsewhere the best that parents and society can do for our children may not be too good. And here as elsewhere it is not all up to the parents or to society. Even though there is much that they can do, we must always remember that at least a part of the answer—sometimes most of it—lies in the organism itself" (p. 319).

Parental Influence

The mechanisms at work in good parent-child relationships can be seen all around us. Although there is no one way to be a "good" parent, certain principles recur in the literature on child development. The child's need to belong, to be loved and approved is just as insistent as the need for food. In effect, parents might offer their children this love and approval in exchange for giving up infantile habits and sources of pleasure. Gradually children accept the frustrations, nonaggressions, and the endless "don'ts" and "nos" of their early years. Soon they develop their own control mechanism, their conscience, to govern their behavior according to the beliefs, values, and attitudes they have adopted from those they love and admire.

We can also see the failure of these mechanisms, where instead of love, approval, consistent discipline, and respect for their individuality, children experience from their parents excessively harsh discipline, constant criticism, indifference, or unpredictable swings between harshness and laxness. Such children with no incentive to control their aggressions, are likely to be cruel, quarrelsome, destructive, defiant, selfish, jealous, and to show little feelings of remorse or guilt. If brutality in their early years clamped down on their every effort to let out some of their hostility, the hostility may, in time, explode in torturing a dog or cat, in hurting other children, in setting fire to the school building, in theft, murder, and other hienous crimes. Such is the background of some of the children whose atrocious behavior makes the headlines.

Influence of the School

Children spend a great deal of time in school; consequently, its influence is often profound. According to some, the school is *the* most important influence on a child's development. Dr. William Glasser (1969, pp. 2-4) states: "If school failure does not exist, other handicaps [poverty, color, broken home, poor relationship with parents] can be more easily overcome." Dr. Glasser places highest emphasis on *success:* "I do not accept the rationalization of failure commonly accepted today, that these young people are products of a social situation that precludes success. Blaming their failure upon their homes, their communities, their culture, their background, their race, or their poverty is a dead end for two reasons: (1) it removes personal responsibility for failure, and (2) it does not recognize that school success is potentially open to all young people...." (pp. 4-5). According to Dr. Glasser, the most critical years are ages five to ten, but failure at any stage in a student's education can greatly diminish chances for success in life:

Very few children come to school failures, none come labeled failures; it is school and school alone which pins the label of failure on children...If, however, the child experienced failure in school during these five years [ages five to ten], by the age of ten his confidence will be shattered, his motivation will be destroyed, and he will have begun to identify with failure. Convinced that he is unable to fulfill his needs through the logical use of his brain, he will return to behavior directed by his emotions...He will abandon the pathways of love and self-worth and grope blindly toward what seem to him to be the only paths left open, those of delinquency and withdrawal (pp. 26-27).

Influence of Society

The social aspects of an individual's environment, his neighborhood, associates, customs, beliefs, attitudes, also shape the individual's personality. Just as some place emphasis on the parents' influence and others emphasize the schools' influence, many such as Ramsey Clark (1970, p. 17) stress societal influences: "Crime reflects more than the character of the pitiful few who commit it. It reflects the character of the entire society....What they are and what they experienced came largely from society—for its influence on them and on their forebearers."

Among most primitive people the basic emotional needs of children were met automatically by the group or tribe as well as by the parents. The tribe or village was small and everyone knew everyone else. All shared the same activities in work, education, and recreation; all shared the same beliefs and superstitions. The adaptations demanded of children were comparatively few and simple, with practically no choice of beliefs or behavior patterns to create conflicts within the child. Consequently, although the group's behavioral standards were often primitive, nonconformity to those standards (delinquency) was almost unknown. As society progressed, however, this was no longer true:

Our youth now love luxury—they have bad manners and contempt for authority. They show disrespect for their elders and love idle chatter in place of exercise.... Children are now tyrants—not the servants of their households. They no longer rise when elders enter the room. They contradict their parents, chatter before company, gobble up their food, and tyrannize their teachers. (Socrates, Fifth Century B.C.)

Upon first reading, the above statement might seem to apply to today's youth as well. It is obvious that the problem of juvenile behavior has been of concern for centuries.

Records going back to colonial times indicate that a considerable amount of juvenile delinquency has always existed in this country. Nevertheless, the lifestyle of earlier days was less conducive to delinquent behavior. Before the automobile, life centered in the home, the church, and the school, in relatively stable neighborhoods. A child might grow to adulthood without going ten miles from his birthplace. The family was likely to be a clan of many members. Children whose parents were missing, brutal, indifferent, or failed to meet the children's emotional needs, might get satisfaction and guidance from a grandmother, an aunt, the woman next door, the minister, the priest, or the teacher. The self-contained neighborhood and the self-contained classrooms, like the tribe, gave children support and imposed powerful controls on their behavior.

Crime In The United States   **99**

As for the other basic needs, the typical youngster was from early years a useful hand on the farm, in the family shop, or in the home, obtaining a sense of competence, usefulness, and growing independence while learning a vocation. Youths fit into life by living and sharing. Untamed country surrounding even the big cities provided excitement and new experiences. The rebels and the violent could always escape to the frontier and not influence less rebellious and violent youth.

Today, however, industrialization, mechanization, mobility, urbanization, and teeming populations have transformed the conditions of life and multiplied the problems of adjustment for children. The clan family with its helpful grandparents and maiden aunts has disappeared. The automobile has obliterated the self-contained neighborhood and, by enabling youth on the farms as well as in the cities to seek recreation in the anonymity of distance, has practically ended the neighborhood's control over youths' behavior. At the same time the car invites delinquency over a large geographical area and vastly increases its dangers. In addition, boys and girls seldom grow into a vocation in the family business, and modern technology has almost eliminated daily chores like carrying out the trash, beating the rugs, picking vegetables, and even mowing the lawn. In too many homes, today's youngsters feel unneeded, superfluous, almost a kind of toy.

Simultaneously mechanical inventions take children farther from nature, its satisfactions, and its lessons. The house is too small for recreation; the streets are dangerous. Today's youth often have no permissible readily available outlet for their energies. It is understandable that our streets are clogged with souped-up cars, children breaking school windows and street lights, experimenting with liquor, narcotics, and drugs.

Seriously and chronically delinquent children are produced in rural areas and in well-to-do neighborhoods, but the majority come from slums which magnify all the modern social conditions, making it difficult for today's children to grow up as well-adjusted adults.

Slums are a major causative factor in juvenile delinquency.

In blighted neighborhoods, with run-down, overcrowded housing, few churches, poor schools, and no playgrounds, with constantly changing populations and without neighborhood consciousness, pride or leadership, where vice flourishes and derelicts, crooks, and gangs seek refuge, children from emotionally impoverished homes have a far greater chance of becoming serious delinquents than if they lived in a more favorable neighborhood. Slums contribute disproportionately to the load of the juvenile courts and are a prime factor in precipitating delinquent behavior in children whose family relationships have predisposed them towards it.

When gangs dominate the social life of adolescents in blighted areas, they may even enlist some emotionally well-adjusted youngsters in delinquency. In today's society of interdependent, fragmented families, few homes can satisfy all the economic, vocational, social, and recreational needs of its children. The family and child depend upon the community as never before.

If the needs of children for constructive citizenship are to be satisfied in this age of machines and technology, the home, the schools, the community, and individuals in law enforcement will have to shoulder a large part of the job. If they do not, the danger of high juvenile-crime rates and the formation of juvenile gangs is great.

☑ CHECK POINT

1. What are some major causes of crime?
2. What is the legal definition of a juvenile delinquent?
3. How severe is the problem of juvenile delinquency in the United States?
4. What are some major causes of juvenile delinquency?
5. How can parents, school, and society help prevent children from becoming delinquent?

*Answers

1. Criminal behavior results from the individual's basic personality and environment. To a major degree, social and economic conditions cause crime. There is no single causative factor.
2. A juvenile delinquent is an individual not of legal age (usually 18) who fails to obey a law or ordinance.
3. The problem of juvenile delinquency is severe; youth is responsible for a substantial and disproportionate part of the national crime problem.
4. Juvenile delinquency has the same diversity of causes as adult criminal behavior; it is influenced by children's basic individuality, their home, their school, and their community. Education, race, poverty, home environment, and numerous other factors may influence delinquent behavior.
5. The parent, the school, and society must teach youth self-discipline and adherence to societal expectations, and must, at the same time, meet the child's basic needs.

JUVENILE GANGS

Haskill and Lewis (1970) have classified juvenile gangs into three basic types: (1) the social gang, (2) the delinquent gang, and (3) the violent gang. Overlap exists between the groups with some social gangs engaging in delinquent behavior, some delinquent gangs engaging in violent behavior, and some violent gangs engaging in social or delinquent behavior. Overlap also occurs among members; some youths belong to more than one type of gang.

Social Gangs

Social gangs consist of youth who band together for friendship and a feeling of belonging.

"Tough" slum youths may form a social gang as a means of obtaining security. The gang is a relatively permanent organization which often centers around a specific location such as a malt shop, roller rink, or bowling alley. The members know each other well, have a deep sense of comradeship and loyalty, and consider themselves to be the "in" group; everyone else is "out of it." Social gang members often wear jackets or sweaters with insignia or writing to identify themselves. Their activities are usually social, including such functions as athletics and dances. Membership is based primarily on feelings of mutual attraction, with members allowing their individual preferences to be overridden by the wishes of the gang. The leader is usually the most sociable, with the rest of the members trying to imitate his actions.

Delinquent Gangs

A delinquent gang usually consists of youth who have joined together to obtain material profit illegally.

Unlike the social gang, the delinquent gang is not interested in having "fun"; its primary objective is materialistic. They believe in acquiring material possessions (the capitalistic philosophy), but they reject the socially acceptable means of acquiring it.

The delinquent gang frequently "raises" money by engaging in burglary, petty thievery, shoplifting, car prowling, mugging, and assault for profit. The delinquent gang is usually a very close, closed, small, mobile group which can commit crimes and escape with minimum risk. Membership is hard to obtain since each member depends on the other. Therefore, a new member must be approved by all existing members. The membership seldom changes, as risks of someone becoming an informant are high. Usually new members are taken in only to replace members who have been arrested or imprisoned.

The leader of the delinquent gang is the best "criminal," best organizer, and best planner. Although members of the delinquent gang may belong to social or violent gangs also, their basic loyalty is to the delinquent gang because of its opportunity for profit.

Most delinquent gang members are emotionally stable youths who have learned criminal ways by association with other delinquent youths, usually in slum settings. Most emotionally disturbed delinquents do not have the social skills required to fit in with a gang of any type and are forced to steal on their own.

Violent Gangs

Violent gangs usually consist of sociopathic youths who engage in violence for "kicks" and for prestige.

Violent gang members find pleasure in creating fear in others; this gang is organized for emotional gratification, and all activities center around violence or talk of violence. Sometimes membership is initially based on self-protection and then broadens into aggressive violence.

Membership changes frequently, since the club members are themselves very unstable and changing. They often exaggerate the size of the gang to intimidate rival gangs and to make themselves feel more powerful. They also often accumulate small arsenals including switchblades, hunting knives, zip guns, regular guns, pipes, chains, blackjacks, hand grenades, bayonets, and machetes.

Territorial rivalries between violent gangs frequently lead to bloody gang wars that often have no clear purpose. Many start over insignificant events such as one member inadvertently entering a rival gang's territory, or saying something "smart," or dating a rival gang member's girl. Such minor incidents provide disturbed youth a rationale to vent their hostilities toward school, family, neighborhood, another person, or any other target. Emotions are easily aroused and violent actions become contagious. In a typical gang war most participants have little or no idea what the cause of the war is or what they are expected to do except fight. Yet such wars may result in serious, permanent injury and death for the members involved and sometimes for innocent by-standers as well. Therefore, citizens and law enforcement react strongly to gang wars and their destructiveness. Ironically, the more citizens and law enforcement agencies clamp down on a violent gang, the more prestige it is likely to assume with other gangs; therefore, they may welcome or even seek direct confrontations with police.

The following true account of a gang leader illustrates the temperament, outlook, and background of a youth who, although not from the slums, grew up on his own and became a chronic juvenile delinquent.

PORTRAIT OF A GANG LEADER

His small, round badge of courage is on his back: the puckered scar left by a bullet wound. He is proud of the scar, and prouder still that he can shrug it off as an accepted part of his life-style. "Almost everybody's been shot," smiles the 19-year-old black youth known as "Bartender," a leader of one of the street gangs that flourish in the Los Angeles area.

Bartender is known as Lyle Joseph Thomas on police records and his dossier is full. He has been arrested eleven times on charges that include assault on a police officer, simple assault, strong-armed robbery and possession of a carbine. But, thanks to the vagaries of juvenile justice, he has never served time in jail.

With both of his parents working, Bartender grew up on his own in suburban Compton, gradually drifting into trouble. "They hate me," he says of his mother and father, who had just kicked him out of the house when *Time* Correspondent Joseph N. Boyce came past to talk. "They take turns getting on my ass."

A high school graduate, Bartender is intelligent and knows it ("I used to see the brothers writing graffiti on the walls—spelling names wrong. I decided I wanted to help them"). He makes $121 a week as a porter at Kaiser Foundation Hospital, but his real life belongs to the Piru, the street gang of about 150 members who hang around Compton's Leuders Park taking drugs, playing basketball and planning robberies and burglaries. "I do my share," acknowledges Bartender, explaining: "People be broke." But mainly the Piru plots, attacks and defends itself against its hated enemies, the local chapter of the Crips, which is perhaps the most vicious and largest street gang in the area. (The Crips got its name when its leader was shot in the leg and thereafter strutted around his turf with a cane.)

The rivalry between the two gangs started with fistfights four years ago in the high school cafeteria. Then someone brought his mother's gun to school, and the killing started. Now the battles are called "gang-bangs," and they are often settled by blasts from sawed-off shotguns and .38s. Police estimate that about ten members of the Piru and the Crips have been killed to date. "People get high and just don't care sometimes," Bartender explains. "Somebody says go do something, and everybody is game for it because they don't want to look like they're scared. At the beginning, when you first start banging, you're scared. But after a while, you can't be. Like myself—I got a lot of people looking for me, and if I clinched up, I wouldn't last at all."

Bartender's courage often came from marijuana, cocaine, acid, "whites" (amphetamines) and "reds" (Seconal). They are still easy to get and so are guns. "You can get any kind of a 'roscoe'—twelve-gauge shotguns, four-ten shotguns, 9-mm. pistols, 38s, .357-cal. Magnums. I remember one person outside the gang even had a flamethrower."

Asked what he thinks of the juvenile justice system, Bartender laughs and responds, "I wish I were still a juvenile." Now that he is 19 and for the first time answerable for his crimes as an adult, Bartender some-

times talks about quitting the Piru. "This year I have a job. Next year I'll have a car and a pad." But in the next breath, he talks of his loyalty to the gang, the fact that if he were to quit, "there's more chance of those left getting downed [killed] quick. Besides, I live in Crip neighborhood—I'd still get messed with when I got to my pad. The only way to stop is to get out of Compton, and that's something that's not easy to do."

"Reprinted by permission from TIME, The Weekly Newsmagazine; Copyright Time Inc. 1975."

TYPES OF DRUG ABUSERS

Just as juveniles have specific reasons for joining gangs, so most drug abusers have specific reasons for their actions, reasons which should be understood by individuals in law enforcement if they are to do their job effectively.

> Narcotics and dangerous drugs are used by all classes of people, sometimes legally, sometimes illegally.

The Drug Enforcement Administration of the United States Department of Justice *(Fact Sheet)* has identified four main types of drug abusers: situational, spree, hard-core, and nonconformist.

> Situational users take drugs for a specific purpose and usually only periodically.

Situational users include individuals such as salesmen who take pills to keep awake during a long drive, athletes who take pills to give them extra energy and stamina, and housewives who take "fat" pills to lose weight. These people may or may not exhibit psychological dependence; they rarely have physical dependence. Frequently their drugs are legally obtained, and they seldom encounter legal difficulties as a result of their misuse of drugs.

> Spree users take drugs for "kicks."

This group usually consists of college or high school age individuals who use drugs simply for the excitement and/or the experience. Although some degree of psychological dependence may develop, little or no physical dependence usually occurs because of the sporadic and mixed pattern of use. Some spree users try drugs only a few times to show defiance of convention, to participate in a daring experience, or simply as a means of being "one of the gang." Frequently spree users take drugs in groups and/or at social functions.

> Hard-core users are "addicts" who are psychologically and/or physically dependent on drugs.

Hard-core addicts' activities revolve almost entirely around the drug experience and center on securing drugs. They usually exhibit strong psychological dependence on the drug, often reinforced by physical dependence when certain drugs are used. Frequently hard-core addicts begin as spree users and become increasingly dependent on the use of drugs to feel "good." This group poses the greatest problem for law enforcement officers.

> Nonconformist users are middle- or upper-middle-income individuals rebelling against society.

Nonconformist users tend to believe that our society's laws and customs are antiquated or wrong and that a new way of life must be found. Since drugs are an integral part of their "culture," they might be classified as hard-core abusers. The major difference is that most nonconformist users do not come from slum areas but from middle- or upper-middle-income families, have higher educational levels, and are less apt to become involved in criminal activities to support their habit.

These four types of users have considerable overlap. A spree or situational user may deteriorate into a hard-core user or may become an advocate of the nonconformist philosophy. The transition occurs when the interaction between drug effects and a personality causes a loss of control over drug use. To the user the drug becomes a means of solving or avoiding the problems of daily existence.

THE HAZARDS OF LABELING

We have just talked about crimes, criminals, juvenile delinquents, and drug addicts. Such labels are helpful in discussing and in academic situations, but they should be avoided as much as possible when actually dealing with individuals. The following observations by D. F. Duncan (1969, pp. 41-45), although referring specifically to delinquency, apply equally to all other types of labels which we often thoughtlessly apply to individuals.

The delinquent label accomplishes four major changes in the life of the child to whom it is attached. First, as a self-fulfilling prophecy, it encourages the child to identify himself as a delinquent and bad. He organizes his behavior, attitudes, and ambitions accordingly.

Secondly, the label acts to strip the youth's community of the positive means of control it normally employs to hold the behavior of its youth in line with its values. By rejecting the child who has acquired a delinquent label, society withdraws its recognition and affirmation.

Third, the label serves effectively to cut off legitimate opportunities for success and recognition. The most significant people in a child's life—his peers, family, neighbors and authority figures react to the child labeled delinquent with mistrust, suspicion and caution.

The fourth and most critical result of the delinquent label is that it opens the door to illegitimate opportunities to the child. If a youth accepts its delinquent label and seeks out friends who have also been labeled, his behavior will tend to conform to the standards of those friends from whom he is forced to seek recognition and approval.

Labels are dangerous because they may become "self-fulfilling," they may impair society's control mechanism, cut off legitimate opportunities for success and recognition, and cause the person so labeled to seek out others who have been similarly labeled.

Although individuals may engage in criminal acts, they should still be regarded as a person, not a criminal per se. In addition, people's behavior can change. As noted by Driscoll (1978, pp. 76-77), although studies of the careers of adult "criminals" demonstrate the importance of delinquency as a harbinger of criminality, they also show that the great majority of delinquents never reach criminal maturity and do not move into adult criminality. Conversely, some adult "criminals" have no history of delinquency because such a history would preclude their appointment to positions of trust; this is particularly true of those who commit white-collar crimes. Driscoll notes that an older embezzler may never attain "criminal maturity" because he does not incorporate criminal attitudes into his personality and does not have the self-concept of a criminal. He sees himself as a normal person caught in a unique circumstance that permits no alternative except the violation of a financial trust.

☑ CHECK POINT

1. What are the three most frequently formed types of juvenile gangs and what is the primary purpose of each?
2. What are the four categories of drug abusers?
3. What dangers are involved in labeling people?

*Answers

1. Social gangs—youth band together for friendship and a feeling of belonging. Delinquent gangs—youth join together to obtain material profit illegally. Violent gangs—sociopathic youth engage in violence for "kicks" and prestige.
2. Situational users—take drugs for a specific purpose and usually only periodically. Spree users—take drugs for "kicks." Hard-core users—"addicts," psychologically and/or physically dependent on drugs. Nonconformist users—middle- or upper-middle-income individuals rebelling against society.
3. Labels may become self-fulfilling, may impair society's control mechanism, may cut off legitimate opportunities for success and recognition, and may cause the person so labeled to seek out others who have been similarly labeled.

SUMMARY

The law enforcement officer functions in a society where the citizens enjoy great freedom. Sometimes, however, this freedom is viewed by citizens as license to do as they please, to ignore the laws of society. State and federal statutes have defined actions which are not to be tolerated—crimes—and have set specified penalties for each. Although state statutes vary in their definitions of and penalties for crimes, certain generalizations can be made. Generally, a crime is an intentional action which is prohibited by law and for which punishment is legally prescribed, which directly causes an actual harm.

The crimes most frequently reported to police, the most serious crimes in the nation, are called Part One Index Crimes. They include murder, assault, rape, robbery, burglary, larceny/theft, and motor vehicle theft.

A second category of crime, although receiving less attention and involving less violence, is white-collar crime which involves billions of dollars annually. White-collar crime—occupational or business-related crime—includes fraud involving securities, insurance, credit cards, checks, bankruptcy, and computers, as well as illegal competition, deceptive practices, embezzlement and pilferage, bribes, kickbacks, and payoffs, and receiving stolen property.

A third category of crime which frequently poses a problem for individuals in law enforcement is the illegal possession, sale, or distribution of narcotics and dangerous drugs. (Narcotics are drugs that produce sleep, lethargy, or relief of pain, including heroin, cocaine, and marijuana; dangerous drugs are addicting, mind-altering drugs including depressants, stimulants, and hallucinogens.) In most states narcotics and dangerous drugs may not be used or sold without a prescription. Federal law also prohibits sale or distribution not covered by prescription, but it does not prohibit possession for personal use. In spite of numerous differences among the narcotics and dangerous drugs, they share the common dangers of being mind-altering, potentially addicting, and possibly lethal. In addition, since the drug habit is very expensive, addicts frequently engage in other types of crimes to support the habit. Further, drug addicts frequently have no control over what they do, thereby posing a threat to others.

Given the diversity of the crimes committed, it is not surprising that no single factor or cause can be identified for criminal behavior. Such behavior, most of which is learned, results from the individual's basic personality and environment. Social and economic conditions are major factors in the existence of crime.

Frequently criminal behavior has its beginning during a person's youth. Juvenile delinquency is a severe problem in the United States, with youth being responsible for a substantial and disproportionate part of our crime problem. The same social and economic conditions operate in the youth's development as operated in the development of adult criminal behavior. Children are directly influenced by their own basic individuality, their home, their school, and their community. All must share in teaching youth self-discipline and adherence to societal expectation, and all must assist in meeting the child's basic needs.

In addition to understanding the numerous possible causes for criminal behavior, law enforcement officers should be familiar with the reasons juveniles form gangs and the reasons individuals abuse drugs, as they will be expected to deal with both.

The reasons underlying gang formation affect whether the gang will pose a serious problem for law enforcement especially in slum areas. Juvenile gangs may be classified as social, delinquent, or violent, with overlap sometimes occurring. The social gang, consisting of youth who band together for friendship, usually poses no problem for the law enforcement officer and may, in fact, be of assistance in dealing with the other types of gangs. The delinquent gang, consisting of youth who cooperate in stealing and robbing, often poses a problem for law enforcement officers, as does the violent gang, consisting of sociopathic youths who engage in violence for "kicks" and prestige. Their gang wars may lead to serious injury and death not only for the members involved, but for innocent bystanders as well.

The reasons underlying drug abuse also influence whether the drug user will become a serious legal problem. Situational users who take drugs only periodically for a specific purpose, spree users who take drugs for "kicks," and nonconformist users who take drugs to rebel against society seldom pose serious problems for the law enforcement officer. In contrast, hard-core users, addicts who are physically and/or psychologically dependent on drugs, often engage in crime to secure drugs or money to buy drugs and do present a serious problem to law enforcement.

In spite of the necessity of labels such as criminal, juvenile delinquent, and drug addict, the dangers of such labels should be recognized. Although crime does exist, by law, criminal behavior is engaged in by individuals who, in spite of their actions, are entitled by law to their civil rights and civil liberties.

APPLICATION

1. Ask ten people to define crime. See how much agreement there is.

2. Suzie Brown worked as a waitress in the Mytown Cafe. She was pleasant and well-liked, so she received many tips. Suzie was one of those fortunate individuals who never seemed to gain weight, so she constantly snacked on food from the kitchen. When her friends came in, she often cut their bill in half for them, making sure that the bill did cover her boss's costs for the food. Since she was planning on being married in two months and had few items for her kitchen, she began taking glasses, plates, and silverware home with her, an item at a time.

   a. Which of Suzie's actions are crimes?
   b. How would these crimes be classified?

3. Bill and Joe were close friends who had known each other for years. One evening while they were sitting around drinking beer, Bill got out a gun he wanted to sell to Joe. Jokingly he pointed it at Joe and said, "You'd better give me a good price for this little beauty, or I'll plug you," and he pulled the trigger. The gun was loaded, and Joe was killed instantly.
   a. Was Bill guilty of a crime?
   b. What if Joe were only wounded? Would the situation be altered?

4. Jack had a 1976 Firebird Trans-Am for which he paid $5900. He paid $800 a year for insurance. In February, Jack lost his job and could no longer make

his car payments nor keep up his insurance. Late one Saturday night his car was "stolen." He reported it to the police Sunday morning and to his insurance company on Monday. The car was found Monday afternoon in an open field with the windows smashed and the interior incinerated. Jack collected full price on his car and he paid his friend, Tom, $100 for doing a good job.

a. Was Jack guilty of a crime?

b. Was his friend guilty of a crime?

*Answers

1. You will probably get ten different definitions from the ten people.
2. a. Eating food which she didn't pay for is pilfering.
   Cutting her friends' bills is theft or embezzlement.
   Taking glasses, plates, and silverware is pilfering (theft).
   b. These are classified as white-collar crimes.
3. a. Bill would probably be found guilty of negligent homicide.
   b. Yes.
4. a. Jack was guilty of insurance fraud.
   b. His friend is an accessory after the fact.

DISCUSSION QUESTIONS

1. Why is motor vehicle theft in a different category than larceny/theft?
2. Why are some crimes divided into categories or degrees?
3. When is check fraud considered a crime? If a person wrote a check for ten dollars more than he had in his checking account, would this be a crime?
4. Where does alcohol fall in the categories of drugs and crimes?
5. How does our city rank in the United States as far as occurrence of Index Crimes? Drug abuse?
6. Which drugs pose the greatest problem for law enforcement?
7. What problems can arise in the legal definition of a juvenile delinquent and serious crimes such as murder?
8. Are there any delinquent or violent gangs in our city?

REFERENCES

Barlow, H. D. *Introduction to criminology.* Boston: Little, Brown and Company, 1978.

Brandstatter, A. F. and Hyman, A. A. *Fundamentals of law enforcement.* Beverly Hills: Glencoe Press, 1971.

The challenge of crime in a free society. President's Commission on Law Enforcement and Administration of Justice. Washington, D.C.: U.S. Government Printing Office, February 1967.

Children in custody (Advance report on the juvenile detention and correctional facility census of 1972-1973). U.S. Department of Justice, Law Enforcement Assistance Administration, Washington, D.C.: National Criminal Justice Information and Statistics Service, May, 1975.

Clark, R. *Crime in America.* New York: Simon and Schuster, 1970.

Crime in the United States, 1977. Uniform Crime Reports, Washington, D.C.: United States Department of Justice, October 18, 1978.

Driscoll, J. P. *Criminology—instructor's guide.* Philadelphia: Lippincott, 1978.

Duncan, F. "Stigma and delinquency," *Cornell journal of social relations*, Vol. 4 (1969), pp.41-45.

Eldefonso, E. and Hartinger, W. *Control, treatment, and rehabilitation of juvenile offenders*. Beverly Hills: Glencoe Press, 1976.

Fact sheet. Washington, D.C.: Drug Enforcement Administration, United States Department of Justice (no date).

Ginott, H.G. *Between parent and child*. New York: Macmillan, 1965.

Glasser, W. *Schools without failure*. New York: Harper and Row, 1969.

Hall, J. *General principles of criminal law*. (2nd ed.) Indianapolis: Bobbs-Merrill, 1960.

Haskell, M.R. and Yablonsky, L. *Crime and delinquency*. Chicago: Rand McNally and Company, 1970.

Hood, R. and Sparks, R. *Key issues in criminology*. New York: McGraw-Hill, 1970.

Ilg. F.L. and Ames, L.B. *Child behavior*. Gesell Institute. New York: Dell Publishing, 1955.

Nettler, G. *Explaining crime*. (2nd Ed.) New York: McGraw-Hill, 1978.

"Portrait of a gang leader," *Time*, June 20, 1975, p.12.

Rainwater, L. *Inequality and justice*. Chicago: Adline Publishing Company, 1974.

Sutherland, E.H. *The professional thief*. Chicago: University of Chicago Press, 1937.

Sutherland, E.H. and Cressey, D.R. *Criminology*. (10th ed.) Philadelphia: Lippincott, 1978.

Sutherland. E.H. and Cressey, D.R. *Principles of criminology*. (5th ed.) Philadelphia: Lippincott, 1955.

Vetter, H.J. and Silverman, I.J. *The nature of crime*. Philadelphia: W.B. Saunders Company, 1978.

White collar crime: Everyone's problem, everyone's loss. Washington, D.C.: Chamber of Commerce of the United States, 1974.

Organized crime is heavily involved in gambling, drugs, prostitution, pornography, loansharking and infiltration of legitimate businesses. The photo shows $50,000 worth of illegal drugs seized by the police. If they could be traced back to their ultimate source, it would most probably be an organized crime family.

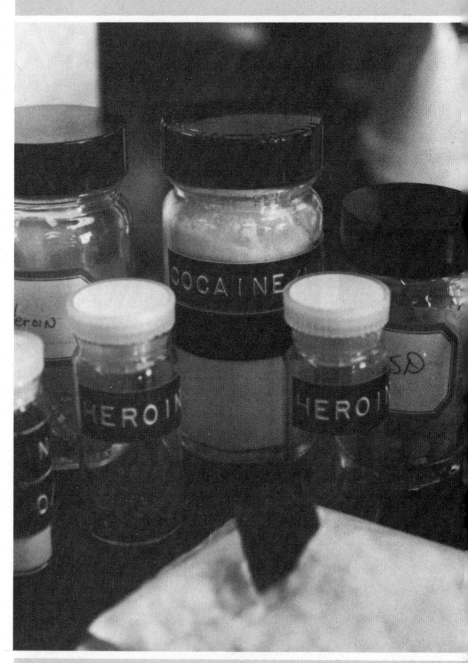

Organized Crime in the United States

A National Threat

4

> Organized crime will put a man in the
> White House some day, and he won't
> know it until they hand him the bill.
> —Ralph Salerno

INTRODUCTION

According to the Report of the Task Force on Organized Crime (1976, p.7):

Organized crime exists in both urban and rural areas, ... Organized crime income is presently invested in a variety of businesses, including liquor establishments, night-clubs, health spas, travel agencies, massage parlors, motels, real estate agencies, nursing homes, and pornographic book stores and films. There are no "safe" enterprises, for organized crime may choose to infiltrate and take over wherever there is potential profit. Tactics adopted by organized crime include homicide, arson, and intimidation.

ORGANIZED CRIME DEFINED

Definitions of organized crime vary, from lengthy, detailed statements to simple eleven word definitions. California's definition of organized crime is one of the more detailed (Organized Crime, 1976, p.214):

Organized crime consists of two or more persons who, with continuity of purpose, engage in one or more of the following activities:
1. *The supplying of illegal goods and services, i.e., vice, loansharking, etc. ...*
2. *Predatory crime, i.e., theft, assault, etc. ...*

Several distinct types of criminal activity fall within this definition of organized crime. The types may be grouped into five general categories:
1. *Racketeering.*
2. *Vice Operations (narcotics, prostitution, loansharking, gambling).*
3. *Theft/fence rings (fraud, bunco schemes, fraudulent document passers, burglary rings, car thieves, truck hijackers).*
4. *Gangs (youth gangs, outlaw motorcycle gangs, prison gangs).*
5. *Terrorists.*

In contrast, Delaware has an eleven-word definition: "A group of individuals working outside the law for economic gain."

Although definitions vary, all definitions have certain features in common.

> Organized crime is two or more persons working together outside the law for personal gain.

Organized crime is *conspiratorial* crime, sometimes involving a hierarchy of persons who coordinate planning and executing illegal acts. It usually involves continued commitment by key members, although some persons with specialized skills may participate briefly in the ongoing conspiracies.

Figure 4-1.   The Classic Pattern of Organized Crime.

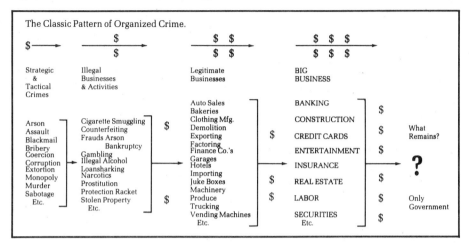

From *The Crime Confederation* by Ralph Salerno and John Tompkins. Copyright ©1969 by Ralph Salerno and John S. Tompkins. Used by permission of Doubleday & Company, Inc.

The Task Force on Organized Crime (*Organized Crime*, p. 7) notes:

In nonlegal terms, organized crime has been called everything from nonexistent to a vast conspiracy. As one observer of the organized crime scene noted, "For most purposes the term 'organized crime' has no precise legal configuration, although some specific attributes of syndicated criminal operations can be accurately defined."

Another problem encountered in discussing the problem of organized crime and possible solutions to it is the fact that organized crime itself is not illegal. According to Cressey (1969, p.229):

It is not against the law for an individual or group of individuals rationally to plan, establish, develop, and administer an organization designed for the perpetration of crime. Neither is it against the law for a person to participate in such an organization. What is against the law is bet-taking, usury, smuggling and selling narcotics and un-taxed liquor, extortion, murder, and conspiracy to commit these and other specific crimes. Because "organized crime" is merely a social category, rather than a legal category, police and other governmental agencies cannot even routinely compile information on it as they do for other categories of crime.

> Organized crime has many names including the mob, the syndicate, the rackets, the Mafia, and Cosa Nostra.

The preceding terms, especially the Mafia and Cosa Nostra, probably make you think of organized crime as much more than our previous definition of "two or more persons working together outside the law for personal gain."

Organized crime does usually refer to a type of crime which is very distinct from other types of crime, even when they are engaged in by a group of individuals. For example, five people in a community may set up a bike-stealing ring and become very proficient at it. The local authorities may consider this group of five to be "organized crime," but most persons in law enforcement would not.

DISTINCTIVE CHARACTERISTICS OF ORGANIZED CRIME

All crime is a threat to our country, but organized crime poses a unique threat. Two features of organized crime set it apart from other types of crime and make it especially threatening, not only to police officers, but to our entire democratic process.

> Organized crime is distinct from other forms of crime in that it is characterized by corruption and "enforcement" tactics.

Corruption

Our bike-ring thieves, while organized, would probably not seek to buy political favors or police protection. In contrast, true organized crime would. In their quest for material and personal wealth and power, organized crime figures corrupt not only their victims, but individuals within the criminal justice system as well.

The President's Commission on Law Enforcement and Administration (*Challenge of Crime*, 1967, p. 241) drew the following conclusions about organized crime in the United States.

In many ways organized crime is the most sinister kind of crime in America. The men who control it have become rich and powerful by encouraging the needy to gamble, by luring the troubled to destroy themselves with drugs, by extorting profits from honest and hardworking businessmen, by collecting usury from those in financial plight, by maiming or murdering those who oppose them, by bribing those sworn to destroy them. Organized crime is not merely a few preying on a few. In a very real sense, it is dedicated to subverting not only American institutions, but the very decency and integrity that are the most cherished attributes of a free society. As the leaders of Cosa Nostra and their racketeering allies pursue their conspiracy unmolested, in open and continuous defiance of the law, they preach a sermon that all too many Americans heed: The government is for sale; lawlessness is the road to wealth; honesty is a pitfall and morality a trap for suckers.

The types of corruption connected with organized crime are graphically illustrated in Figure 4-2.

Enforcement Tactics

A second unique characteristic of organized crime is the use of enforcement tactics. Our bike-ring thieves may take punitive action against someone who attempts to move in on their territory, but they would not have a full-time "enforcer" to protect their interests. Organized crime, on the other hand, usually has one or more fixed positions for "enforcers" who maintain organizational integrity by arranging for the maiming and killing of recalcitrant members and those who oppose them.

Unfortunately, organized crime's violent tactics seem to have caught the

Figure 4-2.   A Typology of Organized Crime Payoffs.

Participants	How Obligations Are Incurred	How the Debts Are Paid
Elected Officials (Federal)	Support in political campaigns. Trips, vacations on company expense accounts, cash through foundations, and cash bribes through lobbyists, etc.	Political appointments Contracts Personal favors Paroles, pardons
Appointed Staff	Campaign workers Liaison with revenue sources Cash payoffs	Hired as staff worker Retains contact with revenue sources Conducts business for elected official
The Elected Official	**State** Campaign contributions Trips on private accounts Cash through lobbyists Tips on investments, i.e., public franchises and licenses **Local** Campaign contributions Promise to self interest groups—gamblers, etc. Money to citizens' committees during preelection campaign Cash payoffs through lobbyists	Contracts Allocations of franchises Granting licenses such as liquor Contracts for local service— garbage, ambulance, towing, etc. Abstain from enforcing certain type of laws
The Judge	**All Levels** Campaign contributions Cash payoffs	Favorable decisions Probation, parole and select court assignment
The Lawyer	Client contacts and referrals Campaign workers Liaison with business and criminal clientele Cash payoffs (fees)	Appointments to positions to keep contacts with proper clients Consultants on contracts, crime commissions, etc.
The Police	**All Levels** Political patronage Campaign contributions to elected offices Budget manipulation Cash payoffs	Select enforcement methods Preferential treatment in the degree of enforcement Lack of enforcement

Denny F. Pace, Jimmie C. Styles, *Organized Crime: Concepts and Control* © 1975, p. 31. Reprinted by permission of Prentice-Hall, Inc., Englewood Cliffs, New Jersey.

public's fancy, as evidenced by the tremendous success of books and movies such as *The Godfather, Honor Thy Father,* and *The Valachi Papers.* The public interest in gangsters' activities implies an element of voyeurism in participating vicariously in something illegal, yet exotic and tacitly approved. Because of the popularity of books and movies concerning organized crime, many Americans are much more aware of its existence than was formerly true, but few realize the true threat it poses to our society.

☑ CHECK POINT

1. How would you define organized crime?
2. What names are commonly used by organized crime?
3. What two characteristics of organized crime set it apart from other crimes committed by a group of individuals?

*Answers

1. Organized crime is two or more persons working together outside the law for personal gain.
2. Organized crime has been called the mob, the syndicate, the rackets, the Mafia, and Cosa Nostra.
3. Organized crime is distinct from other forms of crime in that it is characterized by (1) corruption and (2) enforcement tactics.

Before looking at the structure of organized crime and the types of activities in which it engages, let us look briefly at the history of organized crime—how it came to America and how powerful it has become.

A BRIEF HISTORY OF ORGANIZED CRIME

Organized crime in America is almost synonymous with the Mafia or Cosa Nostra. Therefore, we begin our mini-history of organized crime with the origins of the Mafia.

Mafia is an Italian word which refers to the lawless, violent bands of criminals who engaged in cattle-stealing, kidnapping, and extortion in Sicily in the nineteenth and early twentieth century. Members of the Mafia were bound by a rigid ethical code, the *omerta*, which required any member who suffered an injustice to take personal vengeance without contacting the law. The Mafia was not a centralized organization; it had no official hierarchy, but rather it consisted of many small groups, each autonomous in its own district.

The Mafia used terrorist methods against the peasant electorate to obtain political office in many communities, giving them influence with the police force and legal access to weapons.

Late in the nineteenth century the Italian government's efforts to suppress the Mafia caused many of its leaders to leave the country. Many came to the United States and maintained their organizations here. They found ample opportunity for their traditional occupation. The new immigrants, bewildered by America's language and customs and gathered together in "Little Italys" in New York, Chicago, New Orleans, and other cities, were easy prey for the Mafia who had brought all their talents and philosophy with them. Word of their success quickly reached Sicily, and many more Mafia members came to America.

Prosperous Italian farmers and merchants who understood the Mafia's capabilities were among the first targets of the "brotherhood." A truck farmer, for example, might receive a notice to leave a hundred dollars in a shed "or else." The note would be written in the unmistakable Mafia dialect and signed with the Black Hand. If the farmer did not do as he was instructed, he would find a black hand stenciled on his fence, shed, or house—the final warning. The truck farmer would pay; he would not go to the police, for he knew that even in Italy the police were helpless against the Mafia. In America the police could not possibly know their power, and they were not especially friendly to the new immigrants. The Italian immigrants believed they must pay or be killed. The police were, for the most part, completely unaware of the situation.

Toward the end of the nineteenth century, however, the situation changed. The first American policeman to openly oppose the Mafia was Chief David Hennessey of New Orleans. A group of mafiosi (Mafia members) headed by Antonio and Carlo Matranga controlled New Orleans docks, the center of the country's rapidly growing fruit trade from Latin America. No freighter could unload until the importer paid them a fee. No longshoreman would work without orders from a Mafia boss. Since dock racketeering was common all along the seaboard, the importers did not complain.

Then, in 1890, a series of brutal murders shook the city (Gage, 1972, p.73): "One Italian had his throat cut and was dumped into a canal. Another, almost decapitated, was found with what was left of his head stuffed into his own roaring fireplace. Shotguns, bombs and daggers—the traditional Mafia methods—were accounting for several murders a week."

Chief Hennessey, an honest, intelligent, imaginative policeman personally conducted a thorough investigation and came up against the system created by the New Orleans Mafia. Suddenly he lost all support. His own police officers, many Italian, would not assist, nor would members of the Italian colony, even though most of them were being extorted by the Mafia.

Hennessey persisted despite numerous warnings and offers of bribes. He continued to piece together the network through which the Matranga family ruled the New Orleans docks. He discovered that the brutal murders resulted from a feud between the Matrangas and the Provenzano brothers who had tried to move in on their territory. Hennessey was able to build a case and was ready to present it to the grand jury. However:

> The brotherhood decided that he had moved in too close and knew too much. A few days before he was to testify, as he was walking home from police headquarters one evening, a salvo of shotgun blasts cut him down. He was terribly wounded, but he managed as he staggered and fell, to pull his service revolver from its holster. Heaving himself up in a last gesture of defiance, he emptied his gun. A detective who happened to be nearby and heard the shooting dashed up and found the chief sitting on the stoop of a house, gun still clutched in his fingers…A few hours later, after a number of violent struggles in the hospital against the paralysis that prevented him from speaking, he was dead (Gage, 1972, p. 74).

Public pressure forced the police to seek out and prosecute those responsible for Chief Hennessey's death. Several Mafia members were captured and brought to trial. However, the Mafia hired the best legal talent available and also bribed and intimidated the jury. The result was that the jury could not decide on the guilt of three of the men, and they found all the rest innocent.

Citizens of New Orleans called a protest meeting which began peacefully, but which erupted into a roaring, bloodthirsty mob of several thousand citizens who marched on the jail, battered down the gates, and dragged the Mafia members out into the street. (The Mafia members had been taken back to the Parish Prison following the trial to complete various legal formalities.) The violent mob hung two Mafia members from the city's lamp post and riddled them with bullets. They lined up nine other mafiosi in front of the prison wall and shot them to pieces.

Counteractions against the Mafia did not destroy them; they simply made them more secretive, more prone to use terrorist tactics.

A few years later, another wave of Mafia immigration began as the result of Mussolini's decision to make Sicily the political and intellectual center of his Mediterranean Fascist empire. To do this, he realized he must break the brotherhood's rule of the island. He selected Colonel Cesare Mori, a professional policeman who hated the Mafia, to do the job. He gave him extraordinary powers and over a thousand hand-picked policemen. Mori instituted a ruthless campaign of arrests and prosecutions which resulted in another wave of Mafia immigrants to the United States. In Sicily, many of the Mafia members simply stopped operations for a while, waiting for the time when they could again function. Although Mori believed he had crushed the Mafia, he was mistaken.

The new Mafia immigrants joined friends and relatives already established in the United States. Sondern reports that: "By 1925 the Mafia in the United States was reaching new and undreamed of heights of wealth and power as a result of Prohibition and the organizing genius of Al Capone in Chicago and Charlie 'Lucky' Luciano in New York" (Gage, 1972, p. 79).

> The Mafia probably originated with the lawless, violent criminal bands who dominated nineteenth century Sicily. They came to the United States in 1880 and continued their terrorism and extortion. By 1925 they were a wealthy, powerful, highly organized operation.

During Prohibition, the Italian, German, Irish, and Jewish groups competed with each other in racket operations. The Italian groups were successful in switching their enterprises from prostitution and bootlegging to gambling, extortion, and other illegal activities. They consolidated their power through murder and violence.

According to Cressey (1969, p. 9):

Near the end of Prohibition, the basic framework of the current structure of American organized crime...was established as the final product of a series of "gangland wars" in which an alliance of Italians and Sicilians first conquered other groups and then fought each other. During these conflicts the Italian-Sicilian alliance was called the "Mafia," among other things.... The Italian-Sicilian apparatus set up as a result of a 1930-1931 war between Italian and Sicilian criminals continues to dominate organized crime in America, and it is still called "The Mafia" in many quarters.

Organized criminal activities in the United States are characterized by secrecy, gang wars, violence, and occasional prison sentences. From the early days of the Matrangas and the Provenzano brothers in New Orleans to the present time, constant gang wars and assassinations to control the illicit activities in this country have occurred. There was open warfare in Chicago in 1929 when Al Capone and Bugs Moran fought constantly for control of the underworld traffic in liquor. Finally Capone's gunmen invaded Moran's headquarters, herded seven men into a garage, lined them up against a wall, and killed them in the infamous St. Valentine's Day Massacre.

In 1936 Charles "Lucky" Luciano was sentenced to fifty years in prison on prostitution charges and was subsequently deported to Italy. In 1947 Benjamin "Bugsy" Segal was murdered in his Beverly Hills home. In 1957 Albert Anastasia was gunned down in a barber shop as he was getting a haircut; his assassins were never apprehended. In 1971 Joseph Colombo, Sr. was gunned down in a New York Italian Day Rally; he survived but was totally disabled. He ultimately died from the injuries in 1978. In 1972 Joey Gallo was shot to death in Umberto's Clam House in New York's Little Italy section, perhaps in retaliation for the assassination attempt on Joseph Colombo, Sr.

In addition to violence, leaders of the various organized crime families obtain and maintain their positions of power through a code of conduct similar to, and just as effective as, the Sicilian Mafia's code. The code requires underlings not to seek police protection, but to be "standup guys," going to prison for the boss if necessary. The code gives the leaders complete power over everyone in the organization. Loyalty, honor, respect, and absolute obedience are ingrained in family members through ritualistic initiations and customs, through monetary rewards, and, when necessary, through violence.

Although no one is to "inform" to the outside world, if such an event occurs, the organization has its own elaborate system of internal informants. Therefore, the code not only protects leadership, it makes it very difficult for law enforcement to cultivate and maintain informants within the organization. Despite prescribed mechanisms for peaceful settlement of disputes between family members, the boss may order the execution of any family member for any reason.

One of the best known Mafia members, Joseph Valachi, a narcotic trafficker and organized crime baron, was the first man to violate the oath of silence. Valachi was the first to say that the members of the Mafia actually called their organization the Cosa Nostra, which means "our thing." In 1963 Valachi testified before the McClellan committee in Washington, for the first time exposing the innermost secrets of the Cosa Nostra, naming those responsible for gangland killings, and describing the structure of the organization.

A member of the Mafia for thirty years, Valachi spent a week on the witness stand outlining for national television his life story from his first burglary in 1921 to 1962 when he killed a man in an Atlanta prison yard. Valachi described routine business deals and matter-of-fact murders. He identified hundreds of Cosa Nostra members and described the organization in great detail. It was the first time law enforcement officials in the United States had corroboration that organized crime had a structure.

THE STRUCTURE OF ORGANIZED CRIME

The President's Commission on Law Enforcement and the Administration of Justice (*Challenge of Crime,* 1967, pp. 192-193) described the basic structure of organized crime:

> Today the core of organized crime in the United States consists of 24 groups operating as criminal cartels in large cities across the Nation. Their membership is exclusively Italian, they are in frequent communication with each other, and their smooth functioning is insured by a national body of overseers....
>
> These 24 groups work with and control other racket groups, whose leaders are of various ethnic derivations. In addition, the thousands of employees who perform the street-level functions of organized crime's gambling, usury, and other illegal activities represent a cross-section of the Nation's population groups....
>
> The scope and effect of their criminal operations and penetration of legitimate businesses vary from area to area. The wealthiest and most influential core groups operate in New York, New Jersey, Illinois, Florida, Louisiana, Nevada, Michigan, and Rhode Island.

Figure 4-3.   Organized Crime Cartels.

From *The Crime Confederation* by Ralph Salerno and John Tompkins. Copyright©1969 by Ralph Salerno and John S. Tompkins. Used by permission of Doubleday & Company, Inc.

Each of the twenty-four groups is known as a *family* with membership varying from as many as seven hundred men to as few as twenty (*Challenge of Crime,* p. 193): "Each family can participate in the full range of activities in which organized crime generally is known to engage. Family organization is rationally designed with an integrated set of positions geared to maximize profits. Like any large corporation, the organization functions regardless of personnel changes, and no individual—not even the leader—is indispensable. If he dies or goes to jail, business goes on."

The hierarchial structure of the families resembles that of the Mafia groups that have operated for almost a century on the island of Sicily. *Theft of the Nation* (Cressey, 1972) describes in detail the national structure as well as the intricate structure of the family itself.

> The *Commission* is the highest ruling body of Cosa Nostra.

The Commission, also called the "High Commission," the "Grand Council," the "Administration," the "Roundtable," and the "Inner Circle," is a combination board of business directors, legislators, supreme court justices, and arbitrators, but its primary function is judicial.

The ultimate authority on organizational disagreements, the Commission is made up of nine to twelve bosses of the most powerful families in the country. Some families do not have members on the Commission, but they usually have a specified Commission member to look after their interests. Commissioners are not equal in power and authority; informal understandings give one member authority over another.

Within the family itself, an intricate structure has been established.

> An organized crime *family* consists of a boss, an underboss, a consigliere, caporegime, and soldiers.

Each family is headed by one man, a *boss*, who maintains order and maximizes profits. He is subject only to the national advisory group, the Commission; his authority in all family matters is absolute.

Each boss has an *underboss*, a vice-president or deputy-director, who collects information, relays messages, passes instructions down to his own underlings, and acts for the boss in his absence.

The boss also has a *consigliere* (counselor or advisor) who is on the same level as the underboss, but who operates in a staff capacity. He is often an elder member of the family, partially retired from a criminal career, who gives advice to family members including the boss and underboss; therefore, he has great influence and power.

Below the underboss are the *caporegime* (lieutenants), lower-echelon personnel. Some caporegime serve as buffers between the top members of the family and the law. To maintain their insulation from the police, the boss will usually insist that all commands, information, complaints, and money flow through a trusted go-between. A caporegima does not make decisions or assume any of the boss's authority.

Other caporegime are chiefs of operating units which vary with the size and activities of particular families. The caporegima often has one or two associates who work closely with him, carrying orders, information, and money to the men in his unit. The caporegima is similar to a plant supervisor or sales manager.

The lowest level members of the family are the *soldiers* or "button men" who report to the caporegima. Soldiers may operate illicit enterprises such as loan-sharking operations, dice games, bookmaking operations, smuggling operations, or vending machine businesses on a commission basis. Or they may "own" the business and pay a percentage to the organization for the right to operate. Frequently soldiers form partnerships with one another or with capo-regime. Some soldiers and most upper-echelon family members are involved in more than one enterprise.

The soldiers oversee a large number of *employees*, not family members and not necessarily Italian. Employees do most of the actual work, but they have no buffers or insulation from the law. They take bets, answer phones, sell drugs, make book, and work in legitimate businesses. For example, in a major lottery business which operated in black neighborhoods in Chicago, the workers were blacks, the bankers for the lottery were Japanese-Americans, but the game, including the banking operation, was licensed for a fee by a "family" member.

The Chain of Command

The hierarchy or chain of command within a family is illustrated in Figure 4-4. Notice that the soldiers are responsible for corruption of police and public officials as well as for exercising control (enforcing). Notice also the illegal activities as well as the legitimate businesses in which organized crime is involved.

Figure 4-4. An Organized Crime Family.

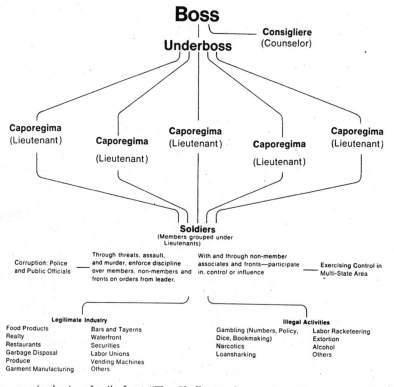

An organized crime family from "The Challenge of Crime in a Free Society," 1967, p. 194, President's Commission on Law Enforcement and Administration of Justice.

☑ CHECK POINT

1. Briefly explain how the Mafia originated.
2. How is the Mafia organized, beginning with the Commission and going down to the employees who are not actually part of the Mafia but who do most of the actual work?

*Answers

1. The Mafia probably originated with the lawless, violent criminal bands who dominated nineteenth-century Sicily. They came to the United States in 1880 and continued their terrorism and extortion. By 1925 they were a wealthy, powerful, highly organized operation.
2. The Commission is the highest ruling body of organized crime. It dictates to families. An organized crime family is headed by a boss, assisted by a consigliere (counselor) and an underboss. The underboss has under him caporegime (lieutenants), and they have under them soldiers. Under the soldiers are the employees, part of the organized crime network, but not part of the family. They do most of the work and take most of the risks.

THE NATURE AND EXTENT OF ORGANIZED CRIME ACTIVITIES IN THE UNITED STATES

The diversified yet interrelated nature of organized crime activities is evident in the Report of the Task Force on Organized Crime (*Organized Crime*, pp. 10-12):

Gambling has long been a traditional arena for organized crime, and is one area law enforcement officials fear that there may be attempts by organized crime elements to take over any gambling operations that may be legalized in the future. As for other activities, the drug business (notably cocaine trafficking) is growing; pornography also is showing astronomical distribution profits. Loansharking is found to be tied into several other activities, including gambling, and arson and fraud are tied into insurance irregularities.

There are also large, organized hijacking rings, armed robbery groups, and increasing vehicle losses, including heavy equipment. Untaxed cigarettes are another major problem. Credit card and stock frauds, sale of stolen and counterfeit securities, and the manufacture and distribution of counterfeit money are among prevalent white-collar crimes.

There apparently is a link between organized crime and street crime where drug operations, fencing, gambling, and certain burglaries are concerned.

Drug addicts pose a major problem in terms of burglaries. Some law enforcement people believe that most established crime figures began their careers in street crime operations. They also point to ties between organized crime and thefts of credit cards, airline tickets, securities, and money. They believe that channels controlled by organized crime are used to launder stolen money and to distribute stolen credit cards.

The relationship between corruption and street crime also is important, with elements creating a subculture in which certain people believe they are above the law. In some communities their impact is so strong that they in fact become the law, maintaining a well-insulated position and buying official protection.

Legitimate businesses are not only infiltrated or manipulated, but also are taken over by organized crime. For example, the liquor industry is a primary arena for organized crime operations—one often ignored in crime reports and one that benefits from weaknesses in law enforcement. Alcoholic beverage outlets are the underworld's retail market for all its goods and activities, and tax fraud is a frequent occurrence in connection with liquor operations.

Another vulnerable area is the vending machine industry—whether the machines are operated for services, entertainment, or other purposes. Because they involve large cash flows, these machines are a growing operational area for organized crime.

Organized crime figures are believed to have influence over the banking industries, grand juries, and some members of the legal profession.

> Organized crime is heavily involved in gambling, drugs, prostitution, pornography, loansharking, and infiltration of legitimate businesses.

Gambling

Illegal gambling (placing bets with bookmakers) is a billion-dollar business in the United States. It occurs throughout the country with organized crime maintaining control by violence and by providing services including protection, sharing of financial risks (layoffs), legal assistance, and financial aid.

> Sports betting, supported by millions of American citizens, is organized crime's largest source of revenue.

Wagers on football are most popular. Organized crime often either controls gambling operations or takes a cut of someone else's operation. The "street people" (bookies) are part of the organized crime network, but they are not part of organized crime itself, and they know little about it.

Organized crime is also involved in legal gambling, such as the casinos in Las Vegas, race tracks throughout the country, and even legal charity games. Only lotteries seem to have escaped the infiltration of organized crime.

Without participation of "law-abiding" citizens, organized crime would lose billions of dollars and much of its power. Unfortunately, countless millions of citizens contribute to the wealth and power of organized crime by making illegal bets. The benefits to the bettor are numerous, even when legitimate games are available. Illegal games offer greater variety, better odds, regular service, and a fast, guaranteed payoff. The bettor can phone in bets, charge them, preserve anonymity, and avoid having to pay taxes on winnings. These advantages offset the risks of getting caught or becoming indebted to organized crime.

Betting on Sports. Most bets are made on football, baseball, and basketball, both professional and college. Although the majority of bets are made between acquaintances, the vast majority of money wagered is bet through bookmakers. The bookie handles larger bets which cannot comfortably be made between friends. He acts as a "broker" for those who want to bet large amounts of money on a given team.

Many bookmakers subscribe to a national handicapping service which provides detailed information about the teams playing and a list of point spreads. The bookmaker begins his day on a telephone, with a call to the biggest book in town, getting the opening odds or point spreads on the day's games. In exchange for this service, he bets approximately $1,000 a month with the "big man" who himself has obtained the line from a syndicate in a distant city and who places at least $5,000 a month with the syndicate in exchange for its expertly calculated line.

The bookmaker often makes his calls from public phone booths as federal authorities frequently check telephone bills to see who is being called and where they are located.

When the bettors call in, the bookie writes down the wagers on a single sheet of paper which he can stuff under a floor board or into a slit in a door if raided. Some bookies use combustible paper treated chemically to vanish in a puff of smoke when touched with a cigarette or match, leaving no ashes. Other bookies use water-soluble paper which disintegrates when dropped into a toilet or sink, leaving no evidence.

The Numbers Game. Betting on numbers is legal in a few states, but operating a numbers game is *not* legal. The most popular form of the numbers game consists of a player choosing any three-digit number from 0 to 999. The player has one in a thousand chances to win. The winning number is determined by betting totals or payoff odds on selected races at horse racing tracks. The two most common systems are the Brooklyn System and the New York System.

The Brooklyn number is the last three digits of the track's total pari-mutual handle for the day. The New York number is more complicated, combining the payoff odds for win, place, and show horses in the first seven races. Because the first digit is calculated after the third race, the second digit after the fifth race, and the last digit after the seventh race, the New York number is often referred to as playing 3-5-7.

Numbers are played in offices, factories, and residential areas. The numbers organization has three layers. At the bottom are many runners and collectors who report to a smaller number of controllers, the agents or associates of a relative handful of bankers at the top. The runner, controller, and banker are somewhat comparable to salesman, district manager, and president in a legitimate business. Figure 4-5 illustrates the structure of the illegal numbers game.

Illegal numbers game operators require several illicit services, including access to large amounts of money in case they are heavily hit and protection from the law. Organized crime's capital and contacts put it in a position to provide the money and the protection. Since the numbers game is the most visible of organized crime's activities, it is peculiarly susceptible to police interference and requires an extensive network of contacts with public officials at many levels. Therefore, it provides an entry point to the law enforcement structure. Corruption related to the numbers game is pervasive, affecting arrests, investigations, prosecutions, and sentencing.

Besides having an elaborate structure, gambling also has its own terminology which should be understood by individuals in law enforcement.

Figure 4-5.   Illegal Numbers Game Structure.

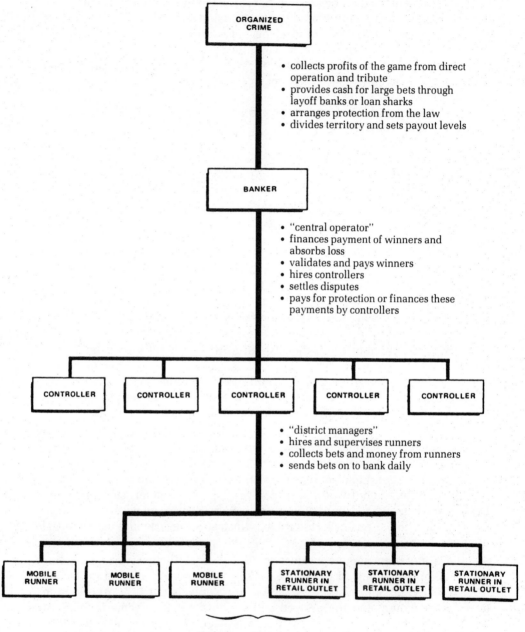

ORGANIZED CRIME
- collects profits of the game from direct operation and tribute
- provides cash for large bets through layoff banks or loan sharks
- arranges protection from the law
- divides territory and sets payout levels

BANKER
- "central operator"
- finances payment of winners and absorbs loss
- validates and pays winners
- hires controllers
- settles disputes
- pays for protection or finances these payments by controllers

CONTROLLER   CONTROLLER   CONTROLLER   CONTROLLER   CONTROLLER
- "district managers"
- hires and supervises runners
- collects bets and money from runners
- sends bets on to bank daily

MOBILE RUNNER   MOBILE RUNNER   MOBILE RUNNER   STATIONARY RUNNER IN RETAIL OUTLET   STATIONARY RUNNER IN RETAIL OUTLET   STATIONARY RUNNER IN RETAIL OUTLET
- "sales team"
- collects bets and money from players and transfers them to controllers
- formally pays winners

"Legal Gambling in New York," p. 47. Reprinted by permission of the Fund for the City of New York, 342 Madison Avenue, N.Y.

Gambling Terminology (*Legal Gambling in New York,* 1972):

Across the board—a bet on a horse. The same amount for win, place, or show.

Action—betting or wagering in any form.

Agent—a collector for the bookmaker.

Bagman—one who collects the money for the powers who afford the protection.

Banker—one who finances an illegal gambling operation.

Bolita—a variation of the numbers game.

Bookie—one who accepts a wager.

Bookie odds—limitations set on the odds that will be paid off.

Bunco—to cheat or swindle.

"C"—when appearing on a policy slip, indicates that the bettor is playing a number in combination.

Cash room—a set location where bets can be placed and results determined.

Collector—one who accepts bets from players.

Controller—boss of the collectors, to whom they turn in their policy slips.

Creep joint—a gambling operation held in a different location every night.

Daily double—a two horse parlay, on the first and second races only.

Handle—the total amount bet at a race track in a given day.

Horse degenerate—a person who has a compulsion to bet on the horses.

Ice—protection money.

Juice—payment for protection.

Line—refers to the odds to be paid by the bookie or the point spread in some sports.

On juice—person taking payment for providing protection.

Parlay—a combination bet, two or more races.

Pool selling—selling gambling tickets on the outcome of a sporting event.

Protection—money paid to insure continued operation.

Route man—usually a trusted employee of a lottery.

Runner—agent or bookmaker.

Scratch sheet—daily publication of racing information.

Shaving points—in sports betting, a player, in collusion with the gambler, attempts to have his team win by a certain number of points.

Shill—a person who hustles action for the gambler.

Slip—record of a wager made with a bookie.

Super dropper—a wealthy gambler or sucker who habitually loses heavily.

Tout—one who gives information on horse races.

Track odds—odds established at the track by parimutuel machines.

Wheel—owner or backer of a numbers operation.

Writer—employee of the bookie, one who writes the numbers.

Drugs

Organized crime's involvement in drugs concentrates on heroin, a trade made to order because of its large demand, substantial profit, and need for an efficient organization with a good deal of capital as well as street-level protection.

The sale of narcotics is usually organized like a legitimate import business. Organized crime purchases large quantities of drugs from Europe, Asia, or Mexico and then distributes it in smaller lots to middle-level wholesalers who cut and package it. They distribute it to lower-level wholesalers who cut it further and sell it to dealers on the street.

Organized crime figures usually do not become directly involved beyond the middle level, thus protecting themselves from the authorities. They are primarily financiers, putting up capital for large-scale purchases. Frequently even import and distribution is taken over by others.

Marijuana, perhaps the most widely used drug today, also appears to be a money-maker for organized crime. In the southeastern part of the United States, the Coast Guard and Drug Enforcement Administration, assisted by local officers, seized 1.5 million pounds of marijuana worth $500 million. Probably two to three times that amount may have slipped by law enforcement officials. Most of the marijuana has been transported by boat or airplane from Columbia, South America. In fact, more marijuana is shipped from Columbia than coffee, a major export. The street value of marijuana has risen to an all-time high of $500 a pound.

Organized crime may also be involved in the illegal production or distribution of prescription drugs. In the early 1970s the New Jersey State Commission on Investigation found evidence that organized crime and some newer black groups were financing illegal laboratories to produce "speed" in Newark, Atlantic City, Philadelphia, Detroit, and Canada.

Prostitution

Prostitution, one of organized crime's rackets since the turn of the twentieth century, reached its peak during the Depression, but since that time has declined. The Organized Crime Task Force of the President's Commission on Law Enforcement (*Organized Crime*, 1976) quoted from the 1952 Second Interim Report of the United States Senate's Kefauver Committee which investigated organized crime:

> Before the First World War, the major profits of organized criminals were obtained from prostitution. The passage of the Mann White Slave Act, the changing sexual mores, and public opinion combined to make commercialized prostitution a less profitable and more hazardous enterprise.... Prostitution is difficult to organize and discipline is hard to maintain.

One form of prostitution—streetwalking—was probably too conspicuous and hard to regulate for organized crime. Not only do streetwalkers get arrested frequently, they also may be involved in prostitution-related crimes (robbery of customers, assault), and they frequently have pimps, individuals regarded with contempt by most organized crime members. When organized crime is involved in prostitution, it is usually in such forms as call girls, brothel trade, massage parlors, and encounter joints. Although organized crime takes a large share of the profits derived from prostitution and limits the prostitutes' independence, it also provides valuable services: housing, clients, and protection from the law.

Pornography

The pornography industry consists of films, magazines, books, sexual devices, and various "service" establishments. A number of recent studies indicate that pornography is organized crime's latest business. As with gambling and the drug trade, pornography is a prohibited product with a large market, requiring good organization, money, muscle, and lax law enforcement.

It is not known when organized crime became involved in pornography, but the Supreme Court decision in 1967, *Redrup v. N.Y.*, may have been a contributing factor. This case left unclear what constitutes pornography, making it difficult for law enforcement officers to build cases. Although organized crime's links to the porno industry are documented as early as the 1950s, it did not become heavily involved until the late 1960s. By 1969 it is estimated that organized crime controlled 60% of the porno movies in New York.

The Task Force Report on Organized Crime (p. 227) notes that organized crime's pornographic operations cover the country, and that although no accurate figures exist on what profits organized crime receives, it must be good money or organized crime would not be involved. One source put the gross from peepshows in Baltimore alone at about $10 million a year in 1973.

Supreme Court decisions related to pornography have complicated the problem of law enforcement officers when dealing with the porno industry. The Court has not extended First Amendment protections to pornography, so it is not automatically legal, but the Court's decisions have left unclear what constitutes pornography. At present three somewhat vague criteria exist:*

1. The dominant theme of the material must appeal to "prurient" interests;
2. The material must be utterly without redeeming social, political, literary, or scientific value; and
3. The material must be patently offensive in its depiction of sexual matters, in terms of contemporary standards.

Each state must pass its own legislation defining the standards, but a jury representing the community decides on individual cases.

The pornography issue was further complicated by a 1969 Supreme Court ruling† which held that pornography for private use in one's home is legal.

Some pornography laws have successfully withstood legal challenge. However, public display of pornography, mailing unsolicited material, and sale or distribution to minors are banned nationally. Additionally, the federal government bans using the mails or interstate commerce facilities for conveying pornographic material.

The focus of attention in this relatively new area for organized crime has been on defining what is pornographic and how to control it; therefore, little attention has been paid to means of specifically controlling organized crime's involvement.

Loan Sharking

Loan sharking, lending money at higher than legally prescribed rates, is the second largest source of revenue for organized crime. Gambling profits often provide the initial capital for loan shark operations. Many types of individuals become involved with loan sharks: gamblers to pay off gambling debts, drug addicts to obtain needed drugs, businessmen to buy goods or to close deals.

Interest rates may vary from 1% to 150% a week, depending on the relationship between the lender and the borrower, the intended use of the money, and the size of the loan. A common rate for the small borrower is 20% a week.

*U.S. Supreme Court, Miller v. California, 413 U.S. 15, 37 L.Ed. 2d 419, 93 S. Ct. 2607 (1973).

†Stanley v. Georgia, 394 U.S. 557, 89 S. Ct. 1243, 22 L.Ed. 2d 542 (1969).

The payments are usually due at a certain hour on a certain day, and failure to make payment may result in a rise in interest rate and/or physical brutality.

According to the President's Commission on Law Enforcement and Administration of Justice (*Challenge of Crime*, p. 189): "No reliable estimates exist of the gross revenue from organized loan sharking; but profit margins are higher than for gambling operations, and many officials classify the business in the multi-billion dollar range."

Infiltration of Legitimate Business

Organized crime invests much of its money in legitimate business, thereby establishing a source of legal funds. Because business ownership is easily concealed, it is difficult to determine all the types of businesses which organized crime has penetrated. Control of businesses is usually acquired through one of four methods (*Challenge of Crime*, p. 190):

1. Investing concealed profits acquired from gambling and other illegal activities.
2. Accepting business interests in payment of the owner's gambling debts.
3. Foreclosing on usurious loans.
4. Using various forms of extortion.

The ordinary businessman can seldom compete with organized crime which has large amounts of ready cash, union connections, and "enforcers" to assure "cooperation."

According to the Task Force Report:

Organized crime tends to engage in those legitimate businesses that can profit from political influence. Its profits are made possible, to a large extent, by its corruption of the public officials charged with regulating those businesses. The opportunity for corruption exists in every instance where government regulates business. The public officials charged with such regulatory activities are open to bribery in exchange for disregarding, for example, character requirements in the area of liquor licensing, zoning laws in the issuance of construction permits, and fire and health violations in building inspection. (Organized Crime, p. 25).

☑ CHECK POINT

1. List six crimes which are frequently engaged in by members of organized crime.
2. What is organized crime's largest source of revenue? Can you name its second largest source of revenue also?

*Answers

1. Organized crime is involved in gambling, drugs, prostitution, pornography, loan sharking, and infiltration of legitimate businesses.
2. Gambling on sports (especially football) is organized crime's largest source of revenue. Loan sharking is its second largest source of revenue.

THE THREAT OF ORGANIZED CRIME

The primary goals of organized crime, whether through illegal enterprises such as gambling or legitimate businesses, are making money and maximizing profit. Organized crime has found it expedient to invest large amounts of money in corrupting political figures from the local level to the federal level as well as figures within the law enforcement field. Cressey has stated that the goal of organized crime is "the nullfication of government." Organized crime can flourish only if it can control police investigations, prosecutions, judicial proceedings, and the corrections process.

> The direct national threat is that organized crime seeks to corrupt and control police officers, prosecutors, judicial proceedings, and the corrections process.

Police Corruption

Police officers' discretionary powers make them prime targets for corruption. (We will be discussing police discretion in depth later.) They can decide what laws to enforce, and organized crime may pay them handsomely not to enforce certain laws. Failure to arrest and prosecute those whom officers know have violated the law is only one form of police corruption. Goldstein (pp. 16-18) lists several other forms of corruption:

—Agreeing to drop an investigation prematurely.

—Agreeing not to inspect various locations where a violation may be occurring.

—Reducing the seriousness of a charge against an offender.

—Agreeing to alter testimony at a trial.

—Influencing departmental recommendations regarding the granting of licenses.

—Agreeing to alter departmental records of arrested persons.

When police officers are corrupt, the entire department becomes less effective and honest police officers do not know who they can trust within the department. Police corruption also erodes the public's confidence in them.

Corruption in the Judicial System

A study done in cooperation with the New York City Police Department during 1960-1970 (*Organized Crime*, p. 25) covered 71 raids resulting in the positive identification of 99 persons who had a total of 356 arrests among them. Of these arrests, 198 were dismissed, 63 were acquitted, 12 were found guilty and given suspended sentences, 77 were fined, and 5 served jail sentences. The average fine was $113; the average jail sentence was 17 days. Although it is obvious from the preceding statistics that some judicial corruption exists, it is seldom proven.

Corruption in the Correction System

Salerno and Tompkins (1969, p. 183) present convincing evidence that when organized crime figures do go to prison, they are usually quite comfortable:

> *Sam Giancana, for instance, frequently used the warden's office in the Cook County jail for business conferences, was permitted out of his cell after "lights out," and had easy access to liquor, special foods, and expensive cigars. And 3 weeks after Sam deStefano was moved by court order from Illinois Stateville Prison to a Chicago hospital for surgery, it was discovered that he was operating a loansharking business from his hospital room and enjoying fine foods, vintage wines, card games with underworld friends, and visits from women. Harold Koenigsberg, an enforcer and loan shark collector for Costa Nostra figures, was a Federal prisoner in Hudson County jail. Tracking down rumors, Federal authorities found that Koenigsberg lived in a special room with a telephone and women and food sent in. At one point in the ensuing flap, Koenigsberg sent his lawyer to court to try and recover $1,000 he had lent the warden.*

THE PATTERN OF ORGANIZED CRIME— THE REALITY OF THE THREAT

Return to p. 113 and study the chart depicting the classic pattern of organized crime which highlights the seriousness of the threat organized crime presents to our society. The testimony of Joseph (The Baron) Barboza, syndicate crime enforcer, in hearings before the Select Committee on Crime graphically demonstrates the seriousness of the threat posed by organized crime.* After several of his friends and associates were killed, Mr. Barboza broke with the mob and testified against a number of racketeers. As a result of his testimony, four men were convicted of first degree murder and sentenced to death. While associated with the mob, Mr. Barboza was reported to be the most feared rackets enforcer in New England.

Mr. Nolde: Mr. Barboza. Will you please describe your first connection with the New England mob?

Mr. Barboza: It was around 1962, when I bundled a man that was running from the bakers union in Boston. I was given a thousand-dollar contract on him to bundle him. We got him during the hurricane, everybody was off the street and we hit him with sash weights. A Greek man, we popped his roots in, dislocated his shoulder blade, gave him 16 stitches in his knee, and he got thumped about the head with a sash weight from a window. It was about a 20-pound lead weight. I refused the $1,000 that was offered to me when it was over. It subsequently led to about $70,000 by refusing that thousand dollars through other channels.

Mr. Brasco: Okay. That $70,000 you made, was that for bundling people also?

Mr. Barboza: No. Primarily shylocking and shakedown and so forth.

Mr. Nolde: You mentioned shylocking or loan sharking. Would you describe the shylocking or loan sharking operation?

Mr. Barboza: Yes. I would take a hundred dollars and give it to a person and he would pay me $5 a week interest on this $100 that I would give him. In other

---

*Excerpted from *Organized Crime in Sports (Racing)*, Hearings before the Select Committee on Crime, House of Representatives, 1972.

words, I would say, "Give me $105 back next week. And the person would say, "Here's $5, I want to carry the $100 over till next week." As long as he paid that $5 interest every week he could hold on to that hundred dollars. Some guys hold on to it maybe 3 or 4 years and just pay $5, and $10 on $200, $15 on $300, $25 on $500, $50 on a thousand. So that in one year's time, with $2,000 I turned $2000 into $25,000. And a couple of years later I had $5,500 coming in every week in the way of interest.

Mr. Nolde: How much money did you have on the street at that point?

Mr. Barboza: I had about $70,000.

Mr. Nolde: And you were getting a return on it every week?

Mr. Barboza: $5,500 a week....

Mr. Brasco: Can we go back to the point as to why these men were killed?...

Mr. Barboza: Yes sir. At the time, anyway, the boss in the office was afraid of independent operators. They were making moves that the office wasn't used to. They were killing people at bus stops, walking into their houses, and killing them, walking in night clubs and killing them. People were found in backs of trunks with their heads sawed off. People were found in suitcases, dissected. Guys were found floating in the river. There was a lot of hits in Boston and all different types of hits that put a lot of fear into these people that were connected with the office.

Mr. Phillips: You say there were other factors which led you to break with the office as you put it?

Mr. Barboza: Right.

Mr. Phillips: Was one of these factors the fact that they bombed your attorney?

Mr. Barboza: Well, they blew up my attorney's car and he lost his leg. He lost his right leg, and he lost chunks out of his left leg, and today he still picks pieces of steel that come out of his face and body.

Mr. Phillips: In addition to the lawyer and shooting up the fellows who worked with you, did they make a move on your wife or family?

Mr. Barboza: Crot went down to my house, where I lived at the time, took off the back screen window, and they terrified the family there.

Mr. Phillips: Congressman Brasco asked you what caused you to break with the mob. One of the factors that caused you to break with the mob was that while you were in prison, someone took over your rackets; is that correct?

Mr. Barboza: And stepped into my shylocking deal.

Mr. Phillips: And your nightclub operation?

Mr. Barboza: Yes, Ralph wound up getting his family taken care of from my efforts.

Chr. Pepper: Mr. Barboza, you have told us a lot of lurid and dramatic details about some of the methods of gang operations. How many people have you known of who were, according to your best knowledge, killed on account of gang action?...

Mr. Barboza: I would say from 1960 to 1966, maybe 75, and during, well more than that. It is pretty rough to estimate, Mr. Pepper.

Chr. Pepper: Roughly in a period of 10 years, maybe a hundred people?

Mr. Barboza: Yes.

Chr. Pepper: Has it been your observation that when people who are members of gangs, who derive their money from illegal operations by what is called a legitimate business, they generally carry over into the operation of the legitimate business the tactics they used in the illegal operation they carried on?

Mr. Barboza: Yes.

Chr. Pepper: So if gang members did infiltrate into horse racing, the chances are they would carry over into that operation some illegal activity; is that correct?

Mr. Barboza: Yes, sir.

Chr. Pepper: From having been on the other side of the table as it were, in your past operations, and now from the point of view of the public, would you think it desirable if we could set up more of the strike forces like they now have in New York where the federal, state, and local officials are all working in close integration together?

Mr. Barboza: Very much so.

Chr. Pepper: It would be helpful in fighting organized crime?

Mr. Barboza: Yes, sir. Mr. Pepper, organized crime is probably the worst threat to the United States. The Mafia in this country is the biggest. The trouble is, nobody wants to get involved with the politicians. And then at a certain point everybody lets it slide. So my concern is this: As I was on the other side of the fence, and right now I am doing everything in my power to try and do something for my children, because I don't want to leave it for their children, and they are leaving something for their generations. Would you want your great-grandchildren to be part of the mob, as far as working in an office? That is what it is coming to, because little by little, they are swallowing everything in legitimate business. And those they can get, they brutalize and intimidate and front for them. So that it is up to people like you, and it is up to the news media, to make the public aware of the threat the Mafia is, and to keep it in the public's eye all of the time, not just now and then.

Chr. Pepper: Another question: We hear so much about gang operation and the mobs. To what extent is there gang operation or are there mobs in the United States today?

Mr. Barboza: To what extent?

Chr. Pepper: To your knowledge. Pick out any city.

Mr. Barboza: New York is the stronghold of the Mafia. And Chicago is very strong, and Las Vegas....

Chr. Pepper: Just one other question. Do you know anything about the participation of the gangs in the heroin trade?

Mr. Barboza: I know it was coming in...packed in sardine cans, in cases of sardine cans coming into this country...and it was coming out of New York. In fact, New York is noted as the biggest, the strongest dope that you can buy in the country as far as heroin.

Mr. Nolde: How did Romeo Martin get killed?

Mr. Barboza: He got five .38 dumdums in his right side. One bullet went through his neck and out through his arm, one bullet was hit here, one bullet was hit here, and the last one was right here (indicating).

Mr. Nolde: Why was he killed?

Mr. Barboza: He was killed because he was running his mouth about chauffeuring Ray around, which he wasn't. He was killed because he lied...because of the beef he had with Ralph...because he took $10,000 he was supposed to give to a lawyer...because he threatened to kidnap a man's son and the man was a nephew of Louie's...

Mr. Nolde: Why was Carl Eaton killed?

Mr. Barboza: Because he was the postman in the football cards.

Mr. Nolde: Against the office?

Mr. Barboza: Yes. He was shot with two .38-type bullets, in the head.

Mr. Nolde: What about Connie Hughes?

Mr. Barboza: Connie Hughes was killed because of what—involved especially was his last move when he killed Buddy. He was a wheelman when his broad shot him.

Mr. Nolde: And Benny Christopher?

Mr. Barboza: He was killed because he was told at least seven times to close down a barbudi game.

Mr. Brasco: In terms of the fight against organized crime, it seems to me in any event, what you are dealing with is a combination of racketeers knowing or being rather astute in the basic weaknesses of individuals: money, cars, women. And also in some of the problems that we have in society. Take loan sharking. I am curious. Did many of the people you lent money to qualify for bank loans? I am talking about business people now.

Mr. Barboza: Yes, but some of them did, some of them didn't. But the ones that did, needed the money right away, and couldn't get it right away.

Mr. Brasco: So it is fair to say they take, and you took, advantage of all the weaknesses you could see in society and in human nature?

Mr. Barboza: Yes. In regard to infiltration, in other words, like Al Capone started the scheme of investing illegitimate money into legitimate enterprises. Well, he pioneered it, but he looks like a nothing compared to the vast sums that are stuck in now by the mob. Now, where the people make the mistake is that they will find out that the Mafia came into a factory. They bought a piece of the joint, so they say as long as I do my work, I don't have nothing to do with him. All of a sudden, months later, somebody comes flying down the stairs with his neck broken, and that person is there and all of a sudden he is involved, because if he says anything he is going to get killed....

Chr. Pepper: Mr. Barboza, without excusing any illegal acts you may have committed in the past, I want to commend you for now doing what you can to break up this shocking menace of organized crime in this country. It is an almost unbelievable fact that such a thing could exist in this great free country. You can be very helpful to those in authority who are trying to do something about it. We appreciate your coming here, giving your testimony to the committee.

NOTE: On February 11, 1976, while a protected witness of the U.S. Marshal's Office and using a new identification furnished to him by the federal government, Joseph (The Baron) Barboza, age 40, was gunned down and killed on the streets of San Francisco—a victim of an enforcer for organized crime.

THE POLICE OFFICER AND ORGANIZED CRIME

The problem of organized crime is everyone's problem. Unfortunately, many people believe that sole responsibility rests with law enforcement—that it is up to the police officer to apprehend those involved in organized crime. Here, more than in any other area of law enforcement, the police officer needs the help of the citizen and a judicial and political system free of corruption.

> Among the special problems the law enforcement officer encounters when dealing with organized crime are:
> —The lack of citizen cooperation.
> —The code of ethics of organized crime members which prevents them from giving information.
> —The tremendous wealth, power, and organization behind them.
> —The corruption of other police officers, politicians, judges, jury members, and corrections officers.

Perhaps one of the most serious of the problems is lack of citizen cooperation. Citizens not only do not want to get involved; many actually promote organized crime by engaging in illegal activities from which organized crime obtains its working capital, for example illegal betting, buying stolen goods from fences, buying drugs, and so on.

The challenge is clear; however, it is also clear that law enforcement cannot do the job alone. A large part of the challenge rests in enlisting public support.

☑ CHECK POINT

1. What specific threats do organized crime pose to the United States?
2. What special problems does organized crime present to law enforcement?

*Answers

1. Organized crime poses a threat in that it seeks to corrupt and control police officers, prosecutors, judicial proceedings, and the corrections system.
2. Among the special problems the law enforcement officer encounters when dealing with organized crime are (1) lack of citizen cooperation, (2) the code of ethics of organized crime members which prevents them from giving information, (3) the tremendous wealth, power, and organization behind them, and (4) the corruption of other law enforcement officers, politicians, judges, jury members, and corrections officers.

SUMMARY

Organized crime is a threat not only to its victims but to our entire society. Its two unique characteristics, use of corruption and strong-arm tactics, can destroy respectable citizens and eventually the country if allowed to go unchecked. Unfortunately, the severity of the threat is seldom recognized by the public and is sometimes not recognized by individuals within law enforcement. Until the elimination of organized crime becomes a priority for police departments and communities, it poses a direct threat to each of us and to our society.

Organized crime goes by many names including the mob, the syndicate, the rackets, the Mafia, and Cosa Nostra. It probably originated with the lawless, violent criminal bands who dominated nineteenth-century Sicily. They came to the United States in 1880 and continued their terrorism and extortion. By 1925 they were a wealthy, powerful, highly organized operation.

The structure of organized crime consists of a ruling body, the Commission, which oversees the activities of each "family" within the organization. Each organized crime family consists of a boss, an underboss, a consigliere, caporegime, and soldiers.

Organized crime is heavily involved in gambling, drugs, prostitution, pornography, loan sharking, and infiltration of legitimate businesses. Its largest source of revenue is sports betting, particularly wagers on football games. Loan sharking is its second largest source of revenue.

Not only does organized crime cost the nation billions of dollars annually and ruin hundreds of lives, it also poses a direct national threat because it seeks to corrupt and control police officers, prosecutors, judicial proceedings, and the corrections process. Nonetheless, many citizens actually promote organized crime by engaging in their illegal activities, for example, buying stolen property, placing bets with bookies, and the like. Among the difficult problems the law enforcement officer encounters when dealing with organized crime are (1) lack of citizen cooperation, (2) the code of silence of family members, (3) their tremendous wealth, power and organization, and (4) the corruption of other police officers, politicians, judges, jury members, and corrections officers.

Although not a crime in itself, organized crime is truly a serious problem to be dealt with by law enforcement agencies.

APPLICATION

Many of the activities engaged in by organized crime are classified as *victimless crimes,* that is, all persons engaged in the activity are voluntary participants. Victimless crimes include such activities as gambling, viewing pornography, and prostitution. Many people argue that such activities should not be crimes; they should be legalized or decriminalized.

Read the following summaries* on the arguments for and against general reform and reform to combat organized crime. Formulate your own opinion on this topic.

General Arguments for Reform

It is not the proper function of government or the criminal justice system to regulate private morality or behavior through criminal laws; that is the role of nonlegal institutions.

The laws are ineffective. They do not deter involvement in the proscribed activities, either by organized crime or the public. Neither fines or jail rehabilitate or alter the behavior of offenders.

---

*From *Organized Crime: Report of the Task Force on Organized Crime,* National Advisory Committee on Criminal Justice Standards and Goals, 1976, pp. 230-232.

The laws are unenforceable. The volume of activity is too great, public support is lacking, and criminal justice systems resources are inadequate.

There is no evidence that legalization/decriminalization will lead to a harmful increase in immoral behavior. The activities are already easily accessible to anyone who wants them.

The rights of individuals to live as they want, so long as they do not harm others, is a fundamental principle on which this Nation was founded.

There is no proof that the moral standards of the country are declining, or that the Nation as a whole is being negatively affected by victimless crimes.

The burden of proof that harm results from these crimes should rest with those wishing to impose sanctions, not with participants in the activities.

Society cannot morally declare persons to be victims when they do not see themselves as such.

Even if the law's function is to provide symbolic guidance for a correct standard of behavior, it is questionable that the laws against victimless crimes guide people in the right direction. Instead, they may engender cynicism and disrespect for the criminal justice and legal systems and for government in general.

The laws are hypocritical. They allow some activities while proscribing others that are comparable; they penalize some people involved in an activity, but not others.

More realistic and well-founded policies must be developed. Current policies are based on emotion, outdated moral norms and values, and inaccurate information. Using up-to-date information on the effects of an activity, and bearing in mind the many priorities to be met, policymakers must weigh the costs of an activity against the costs of ineffective laws. Goals and effective approaches must then be developed.

The laws have many hidden costs: creation of a class of criminals who would not otherwise be considered criminals; discriminatory, arbitrary, and selective application of the laws; unsavory and often degrading tactics employed by the police to obtain evidence or make arrests; increase in crime associated with victimless crimes; creation of subcultures of criminals who reinforce one another's behavior; overburdening the criminal justice system; creation of antagonism among minority youth toward police as a result of enforcement that hits the inner city hardest; and failure to afford constitutional rights to the accused because of efforts to process cases quickly.

There is a lack of public support for the laws.

Overemphasis on the law blunts efforts to find other solutions to abuses of the proscribed activities.

The basis on which the laws were originally promulgated no longer apply; social mores and values have changed, and new information on the effects of the activities contradicts previously held theories and assumptions.

General Arguments Against Reform

The activities known as victimless crimes are antithetical to Christian beliefs and the principles on which the Nation was founded.

Modification of the sanctions against these activities will result in a disastrous increase in their occurrence. This in turn will lead to a moral decline of society. The Nation will become a second class power. Both the Greek and Roman civilizations were destroyed by the decadence of their citizenry.

Because morality affects the viability of a nation, it is a proper function of government to regulate morality by the use of criminal laws.

Laws are a reflection of social values and should be used, even symbolically, as a guide to proper behavior.

There has never been a serious, sustained effort to enforce the laws, so it is inaccurate to say the statutes are ineffective. A reform government backed by the public can wipe out organized crime, vice, and corruption.

Better law enforcement in terms of other crimes will not necessarily result from freeing resources by modifying the victimless crime laws, for "There is no empirical evidence that the police do a better job of protecting persons and property."* Perhaps there is a limit to the amount of resources a police department can effectively spend.

There are better ways to combat corruption than eliminating the victimless crime laws. Legalization will not eliminate the temptation to corrupt, because it will involve new regulations.

It is traditional in this country for government to protect individuals from themselves. For example, the state requires motorcycle drivers and riders to wear helmets.

The fact that a law seems unenforceable is no reason to abolish it. For example, murder and theft laws are not 100 percent enforceable but are nevertheless needed. A preferable alternative to abolishing the victimless crime laws is providing more resources to implement them.

The laws do not serve as deterrents because they are not strictly enforced and the sanctions are not strong enough.

If the criminal justice system is overburdened, the answer is not to eliminate certain laws. It is to increase the resources available to it.

If the laws result in more related crime, enforcement efforts should be stepped up.

There are not enough hard facts on the impact of victimless crimes to justify modifying the laws.

Arguments for Reform to Combat Organized Crime

Laws create the conditions under which organized crime can thrive—namely, prohibition of a good or service for which there is large demand and whose supply requires capital, expertise, and continuous organization. The laws should be changed in order to deprive organized crime of these conditions.

Capital essential to organized crime's survival derives largely from its operations in victimless crimes. This capital is used to finance other illegal activities that are clearly detrimental to the public interest.

Given the unenforceability of the laws, criminal justice officials are too often cooperative targets for corruption. The source of temptation must be removed.

Reform of the laws would free valuable resources for a more concerted and effective attack on the upper levels of organized crime.

Arguments Against Reform to Combat Organized Crime

Decriminalization or legalization would allow organized crime to continue in the victimless crime activities, but on a legal basis. Because of its prior experience, organized crime would have an advantage over the competition. Even in legal games, organized crime can still find ways to increase its profits illegally.

Legalizing only selected activities or aspects of them will not affect organized crime overall. That element of society will still have other illegal and legal businesses and will in all likelihood find other activities to move into, as at the end of Prohibition.

Legalization, because it involves regulations and licenses, offers ample opportunity for corruption.

It will be difficult to establish legal activities that can compete with the services and advantages organized crime operations offer. Competitive legal activities may not

---

*Goldberg,William I.,"Victimless Crimes: Should Police Preserve Community Morals." *Tennessee Law Enforcement Journal*, p. 56, reprinted from *Police Law Quarterly*, 1 (April 1972).

be possible unless some Federal laws are changed, such as the tax on gambling winnings.

It is not certain that either private interests or the government will want to provide all goods and services—for example, prostitution and heroin.

1. Which position do you support and why?

2. As a citizen, what is your responsibility in supporting this view?

3. As a law enforcement officer, what is your responsibility?

4. Who is responsible for interpreting the laws regarding victimless crimes?

*Answers

1. Answers will vary here. You should be familiar with both sides of the controversy.
2. As a citizen, you should make your views known to your *legislators*, the persons responsible for making the laws.
3. As a law enforcement officer, your responsibility, as an agent of the executive branch of government, is to enforce the existing laws, whether you personally agree with them or not.
4. Judges are responsible for interpreting the laws regarding victimless crimes.

DISCUSSION QUESTIONS

1. Why would or could you blame a person for not testifying against organized crime?
2. A recent article described witnesses testifying against organized crime. After testifying they had their names changed and were moved with their families to a different location. After several moves and a promise of protection from the federal government, the witnesses were informed that due to lack of funds, they couldn't be protected any longer. How do you view this decision?
3. Why is it so difficult for the police to deal with organized crime on a local level?
4. Why is it dangerous to have the mob infiltrate legitimate businesses?
5. What are some ways the average citizen can help stop or slow down organized crime?
6. Should we fear organized crime? Is it truly a dangerous threat to our society?
7. Why isn't more being done to curb organized crime? What is being done?
8. Does our area have organized crime? If so, in what activities do they engage?
9. Is the disappearance of Jimmy Hoffa connected with organized crime?

REFERENCES

The challenge of crime in a free society. President's Commission on Law Enforcement and Administration of Justice. Washington, D.C.: U.S. Government Printing Office, 1967.

Conklin, J. E. (Ed.) *The crime establishment: Organized crime and American society.* Englewood Cliffs, New York: Prentice-Hall, 1973.

Cressey, D. R. *Theft of the nation: The structure and operations of organized crime in America.* New York: Harper and Row, 1969.

Gage, N. (Ed.) *Mafia, USA.* Chicago: Playboy Press, 1972.

Goldstein, H. *Police corruption.* New York: Police Foundation, 1975.

Legal gambling in New York: A discussion of numbers and sports betting. New York: Fund for the City of New York, 1972.

"Maffia or Mafia." *Universal standard encyclopedia, vol. 15.* New York: Unicorn Publishers, 1954.

Maas, P. *The Valachi papers.* New York: G. P. Putnam's Sons, 1968.

Organized crime: Report of the task force on organized crime. National Advisory Committee on Criminal Justice Standards and Goals. Washington, D.C.: 1976.

Organized crime in sports (racing). Hearings before the Select Committee on Crime. House of Representatives. 92nd Congress, 2nd session, Part 2 of 4 parts (May through July, 1972), Washington, D.C.: U.S. Government Printing Office, 1973.

Salerno, R. and Tompkins, J. S. *The crime confederation. Cosa Nostra and allied operations in organized crime.* New York: Doubleday and Company, 1969.

Sondern, F. J. *Brotherhood of evil: The Mafia.* New York: Manor Books, 1972.

Vetter, H. J. and Silverman, I. A. *The nature of crime.* Philadelphia: W. B. Saunders Company, 1978.

Section Two
Law Enforcement: The Total Context

Police officers not only function within the context presented in Section One, they are part of a vast network of law enforcement agencies encompassing federal, state, county, local, public, and private agencies (Chapter 5). The structure of their specific law enforcement agency and its specific goals prescribe to a large extent their responsibilities (Chapter 6). The complex role they are expected to fulfill in meeting these goals is challenging, sometimes frustrating, and always vital to the welfare of our citizens and our country (Chapter 7). In addition, the image established by preceding law enforcement officers directly affects present law enforcement officers. An image of the law enforcement officer as a positive, constructive, valuable force in the community is of direct benefit to the effectiveness of law enforcement efforts as well as to the job satisfaction and positive self-concept of the individual law enforcement officers (Chapter 8).

The law enforcement network, the independent department structure and goals, the role to be fulfilled, and the image of this role complete the context in which the modern law enforcement officer functions.

A law enforcement seminar. Law enforcement is a cooperative effort among local, county, state, federal and private law enforcement officers.

Law Enforcement Agencies

A Mutual Effort

DO YOU KNOW □ □ □

- □ Who the chief law enforcement officer at the federal and state level is?
- □ What the difference is between intelligence agents and investigative agents?
- □ What agencies and bureaus are related to law enforcement in the
- □ Department of Justice? The Department of the Treasury?
- □ What primary functions are performed by the Federal Bureau of Investigation? The Drug Enforcement Administration? The U.S. Marshals? The Bureau of Customs? The Internal Revenue Service? The Secret Service? The Bureau of Alcohol, Tobacco, and Firearms Tax? The Immigration and Naturalization Service? The Bureau of Prisons? Postal Inspectors? The armed forces military police?
- □ What services the FBI provides to state and local law enforcement agencies?
- □ What legislation created the Law Enforcement Assistance Administration (LEAA)?
- □ What the primary function of LEAA is?
- □ What the LEAA has accomplished in the past ten years?
- □ What problems have faced the LEAA?
- □ What state agencies are involved in or offer assistance to law enforcement?
- □ What the two main types of county law enforcement are?
- □ What major differences exist between public and private law enforcement officers?

INTRODUCTION

Chapter 1 described the evolution of law enforcement into our complex, five-level system of federal, state, county, municipal, and township and special district police, some having numerous departments and agencies, but all working toward common goals.

Although law enforcement is primarily a local responsibility, criminal activities frequently do not remain localized; they may extend throughout a county, a state, or across the country. This is particularly true of organized crime. In such instances local authorities benefit from the assistance of other law enforcement agencies. Conversely, since the actual crimes are committed in a specific place, federal and state officials rely upon the cooperation of local law enforcement officers. Each can provide valuable assistance to the other.

This chapter focuses on the numerous federal and state agencies which not only play a major role in the fight against crime and the protection of all citizens but which also provide vital information and assistance to local law enforcement agencies. County agencies and private security agencies' role in law enforcement are also discussed briefly.

Federal Agencies

Federal law enforcement agencies were created by Congress to meet the needs of a dynamic, rapidly growing democracy. Federal agents fulfill important responsibilities.

Intelligence agents produce and disseminate information on foreign and domestic areas which affect national security. *Investigative agents* conduct investigations to determine compliance with federal laws. They carry guns, make arrests, and are usually enforcement-oriented.

Of the numerous federal agencies, many are established within the Department of Justice and the Department of the Treasury.

THE DEPARTMENT OF JUSTICE

The Department of Justice is the largest law firm in the country, representing the citizens in enforcing the law. It plays a significant role in protecting citizens through its efforts for effective law enforcement, crime prevention, crime detection, and prosecution and rehabilitation of offenders. It also conducts all suits in the Supreme Court which concern the United States.

The Attorney General is head of the Department of Justice and the chief law officer of the federal government.

The department has several divisions including the Antitrust Division, the Civil Division, the Land and Natural Resources Division, the Civil Rights Division, the Criminal Division, and the Tax Division.

The *Civil Rights Division*, established in 1957 to secure effective federal enforcement of civil rights, is responsible for enforcing federal civil rights laws prohibiting discrimination on the basis of race, color, religion, or national origin in the areas of voting, education, employment, and housing, in the use of public facilities and public accommodations, and in the administration of federally assisted programs (*U.S. Government Manual*, p. 333).

The *Criminal Division* is responsible for approximately nine hundred federal statutes, including statutes relating to bank robbery; bank violations; kidnapping; extortion; loan sharking; illegal gambling; labor racketeering; aircraft hijacking; fraud against the government; mail fraud; bankruptcy fraud; election fraud; bribery of public officials; perjury; obstruction of justice; conflict of interest; theft and larceny of public property; counterfeiting; forgery; interstate transportation of stolen motor vehicles, securities, and other property; illegal interception of private communications; illegal trafficking in narcotics and other controlled substances; distribution of obscene materials; illegal transportation of firearms and explosives; crimes on the high seas and government reservations, and other territorial jurisdiction offenses (*U.S. Government Manual*, pp. 333-334).

The *Tax Division* prosecutes taxpayers under the criminal laws of the United States and has played an important role in curbing organized crime through such tax prosecutions.

Given these numerous responsibilities, the Department of Justice has organized investigative and intelligence branches directly involved in law enforcement.

The Department of Justice's law enforcement agencies include the Federal Bureau of Investigation, the Drug Enforcement Administration, United States Marshals, the Immigration and Naturalization Service, and the Bureau of Prisons.

The Federal Bureau of Investigation (FBI)

One of the best known federal agencies is the Federal Bureau of Investigation—the FBI. The FBI is an investigative branch of the U.S. Department of Justice whose responsibilities are set by federal statutes. Created in 1908 as the Bureau of Investigation, it was renamed the Federal Bureau of Investigation in 1935. Its national headquarters in Washington, D.C., maintains Field Divisions in strategic cities in the United States and its possessions.

The FBI is the primary investigative agency of the federal government. Its special agents have jurisdiction over more than 170 federal crimes. They are responsible for general investigations, both criminal and civil, and for domestic intelligence dealing with the internal security of the nation. FBI agents are very different from municipal police officers; they often must enforce laws against quite dangerous criminals. They are not subjected to the same demands for service that local police officers are; they don't handle drunks, answer domestic calls, respond to medical emergencies, or deal with deviant persons, which are the most frequent local problems of the community.

> The Federal Bureau of Investigation's responsibilities include: espionage; interstate transportation of stolen property; kidnapping; unlawful flight to avoid prosecution, confinement, or giving testimony; sabotage; piracy of aircraft and other crimes aboard aircraft; bank robbery and embezzlement; and enforcement of the Civil Rights Acts.

Espionage includes illegally obtaining or disclosing information affecting the national security, either for the benefit of a foreign power or to the detriment of the country.

Interstate transportation of stolen property includes transportation of stolen automobiles as well as counterfeit, altered, or forged securities with the intent to defraud.

Kidnapping includes the unlawful abduction of a person, transporting the person across a state line, and holding him or her for ransom, reward, or favors.

Unlawful flight to avoid prosecution, confinement, or giving testimony includes the interstate flight of a person to avoid giving testimony in any felony proceedings. Fugitives apprehended are usually released to local authorities for extradition and prosecution or confinement.

Sabotage generally includes the willful destruction or attempted destruction of national defense materials, premises, or utilities, or the manufacture or construction of the preceding in a defective manner.

Piracy (hijacking) of aircraft and other crimes aboard an aircraft includes assault, intimidation, or interference with aircraft personnel, the commission of various crimes such as murder, assault, rape, or robbery aboard an aircraft, or the false reporting of any such activities.

Bank robbery and embezzlement include robbery, burglary, larceny, embezzlement, or misapplication of funds by an officer or employee and the false entry in the books or records from any member bank of the Federal Reserve System or federal programs such as urban development funds, grants, and the like.

Enforcement of the Civil Rights Acts of 1960 and 1964 requires that the FBI deter anyone who seeks to obstruct federal court orders. They must also see that no discrimination occurs in public accommodations, public facilities, or public education institutions.

In addition to these numerous responsibilities, the FBI provides valuable services to law enforcement agencies throughout the country.

The FBI has an Identification Division, a crime laboratory, and a National Crime Information Center (NCIC) which may be used by any law enforcement agency in the country. The FBI also compiles statistics and releases Uniform Crime Reports annually.

The *Identification Division* was established in 1924 as a result of the tremendous value of fingerprint identification data. The FBI is the central repository for fingerprint information; all police agencies in the country contribute to and may obtain information from it.

Data from the identification records are furnished to law enforcement and governmental agencies at the federal, state, county, and local levels for official use only. Wanted notices, periodically distributed by the FBI at the request of other law enforcement agencies, frequently result in the apprehension of dangerous criminals. However, the Identification Division is not restricted to criminal matters; many missing persons have been located, and victims of amnesia and homicides have been identified.

The Identification Division also maintains a disaster squad to assist in identifying victims of disasters such as explosions, storms, and plane crashes in which fingerprints are often the only means of identifying victims.

The *Crime Laboratory*, established in 1932, is the largest, most effective criminal laboratory in the world. Its facilities are available without cost to any city, county, state, or federal law enforcement agency in the country. Physical evidence obtained in a criminal investigation is examined not only to support evidence against a suspect, but also to establish the innocence of accused persons. Included in the laboratory's services are identification of firearms, shoe prints, and tire prints; mineral analyses; and examination of blood, documents, hairs, fibers, and poisons.

The *National Crime Information Center (NCIC)*, established in 1967, is a complex, computerized, electronic data-exchange network developed to complement computerized systems already in existence and those planned by local and state law enforcement agencies.

The numerous law enforcement agencies serving as terminals in the system are directly linked to the control center of the NCIC at FBI headquarters. The system is adjusted so that each terminal can communicate directly and immediately with the control center.

Records on file in the NCIC concern wanted persons, stolen vehicles, vehicles used in the commission of felonies, stolen or missing license plates, stolen guns and other items of stolen property which are serially identifiable such as television sets, boat motors, and so on. The reservoir of scientifically stored data on criminal activities gathered by federal, state, and local law enforcement agencies gives the street officer of any law enforcement agency in any part of the country up-to-the-minute information upon request in a matter of seconds.

Uniform Crime Reports are another service provided by the FBI. Since 1930, by an act of Congress, the FBI has served as a national clearing-house for United States crime statistics. States report their monthly crime statistics to the FBI, which in turn releases information quarterly and annually regarding all crimes reported to them.

Crimes are categorized by their seriousness and their frequency. Part One crimes consists of homicide, rape, assault, robbery, burglary, larceny/theft, and motor vehicle theft. Part Two crimes consist of arson, forgery, prostitution, narcotics, and the like. Uniform Crime Reports give law enforcement administrators valuable information related to crime rates in similar communities, felony and misdemeanor arrests, and the clearances for crimes. The FBI reports are valuable in assessing needed manpower, equipment, and budget increases.

The FBI Uniform Crime Reports seek to: (1) measure the trends of serious crime, (2) record the volume of all crime, and (3) determine significant police matters related to crime such as number of employees per thousand capita, the number of officers assaulted each year, the number of officers killed each year, and the types of action which caused the assaults or deaths.

☑ CHECK POINT

1. Who is the chief law enforcement officer at the federal level?
2. What is the difference between intelligence agents and investigative agents?
3. Under what department is the FBI organized?
4. What are three areas of responsibility of the FBI?
5. Name three services provided by the FBI to law enforcement agencies throughout the country.

*Answers

1. The United States Attorney General is the chief law enforcement officer at the federal level.
2. Intelligence agents produce and disseminate information on foreign and domestic areas which affect national security. Investigative agents conduct investigations to determine compliance with federal laws; they are enforcement-oriented.
3. The FBI is organized under the Department of Justice.
4. The FBI's responsibilities include espionage; interstate transportation of stolen property; kidnapping; unlawful flight to avoid prosecution, confinement, or giving testimony; sabotage; piracy of aircraft and other crimes aboard aircraft; bank robbery and embezzlement; and enforcement of the Civil Rights Acts.
5. The FBI provides assistances to other law enforcement agencies throughout the country through its Identification Division, its crime laboratory, the National Crime Information Center, and its Uniform Crime Reports.

Federal Drug Enforcement Administration (FDEA)

Prior to 1973, many fragmented government agencies pursued various courses of action in combatting dangerous drugs. In 1973 the Bureau of Narcotics and Dangerous Drugs (BNDD), the Office for Drug Abuse Law Enforcement, the Office of National Narcotics Intelligence, and the drug and investigative and intelligence units of the Bureau of Customs were merged into the Federal Drug Enforcement Administration.

> The primary emphasis of the Federal Drug Enforcement Administration (FDEA) is on apprehending the suppliers and distributors of illicit drugs rather than on arresting drug abusers.

Narcotics agents seek to stop the flow of drugs at their sources, both domestic and foreign, to assist state and local police in preventing illegal drugs from reaching local communities. They become involved in surveillance, raids, interviewing witnesses and suspects, searching for evidence, and seizure of contraband goods.

To accomplish their goals, the FDEA has developed an overall federal drug strategy that includes planning, workable programs, evaluation, and intelligence. Charged with the full responsibility of the prosecution of suspected violators of federal drug laws, they have liaison with law enforcement officials of foreign governments. They have highly trained agents stationed in all major United States cities and in thirty countries throughout the world.

The FDEA is also responsible for the regulation of the legal manufacture of drugs and other controlled substances under the Controlled Substances Act of 1970. Since intelligence is an essential element in the success of any enforcement agency, FDEA has an Office of Intelligence staffed by experienced criminal investigators and intelligence analysts. An important facet of this intelligence program is the continued exchange of information with other federal, state, local, and foreign law enforcement agencies.

FDEA maintains six regional laboratories throughout the country to accumulate up-to-date information regarding drugs under its jurisdiction. This information is distributed to law enforcement agencies, allowing them to better cope with drug abuse problems and their related effects.

Since successful prosecution of controlled substances cases requires physical evidence, the laboratories provide definitive identification of such substances as well as expert testimony in court. The laboratories also have the capability of fingerprint processing and photographic printing and development.

The federal government recognized the existence of a drug problem in this country nearly sixty-five years ago. Early government response embodied in the Harrison Narcotic Act of 1914 was directed exclusively at controlling the supply of dangerous drugs. The Harrison Act established federal control over the supply, distribution, and use of narcotics. But almost no attention was given at the federal level to the treatment and rehabilitation of drug users until the early 1930s when the United States Public Health Service Hospitals at Lexington, Kentucky, and Fort Worth, Texas, were established to treat drug addicts.

The Special Action Office for Drug Abuse Prevention, established in 1971, placed further emphasis on treatment and rehabilitation of drug addicts. The mission of this office is twofold: (1) to reduce drug abuse in the United States and (2) to develop a comprehensive, long-term federal strategy to combat drug abuse.

The Special Action Office covers all federal programs or activities related to drug abuse education, training, treatment, rehabilitation, and research. It was the Special Action Office which assisted in a nationwide review of all methadone maintenance programs, and its recommendations were instrumental in changing the status of the drug to a recognized form of medical treatment, under strict governmental controls.

The United States Marshals

In 1789 Congress created the office of United States Marshal. The U.S. Marshals are appointed by the President with the approval of the Senate, as recommended by the Attorney General, for a period of four years.

The U.S. Marshal's Office is responsible for arresting persons for whom warrants are issued charging a federal crime, providing physical security for U.S. courtrooms and personal protection for federal judges, jurors, and attorneys, for transporting prisoners, and for protecting witnesses.

Each Marshal's Office has a staff of deputy marshals to carry out the functions and responsibilities. The functions of most deputy marshals are more enforcement than investigative. They are responsible for (1) seizing property in both criminal and civil matters to satisfy judgments issued by a federal court, (2) providing physical security for United States courtrooms and protection for federal judges, jurors, and attorneys, (3) transporting federal prisoners to federal institutions when transferred or sentenced by a federal court, and (4) protecting government witnesses whose testimony might jeopardize their safety. Such witnesses are protected by the government by being salaried, relocated in other cities, and provided with new identities.

Immigration and Naturalization Service (INS)

The Immigration and Naturalization Service has Border Patrol Agents who serve throughout the U.S., Canada, Mexico, Bermuda, Nassau, Puerto Rico, the Philippines, and Europe. They conduct investigations, detect violations of immigrant and nationality laws, and determine whether aliens may enter or remain in the U.S. It also has Immigration Inspectors who are responsible for detecting people who are in violation of immigration and nationality laws. They work with Border Patrol Agents and other investigators in determining whether an applicant may enter the U.S.

The service administers a variety of federal laws that pertain to the admission, exclusion, or deportation of aliens who have unlawfully come into the country and taken up residence. They are also responsible for the registration of all aliens in this country and make recommendations to the courts regarding persons applying for citizenship or citizens for whom the service is requesting deportation.

> The Immigration and Naturalization Service conducts investigations, detects violations of immigration and nationality laws, and determines whether aliens may enter or remain in the United States.

The extensive activities of the Border Patrol have resulted in many arrests for smuggling contraband and aliens into the United States. Searches for smuggled aliens are often made of automobiles, airplanes, and boats. The Border Patrol primarily uses airplanes, boats, and vehicles to deter illegal smuggling. Air-to-ground operations and searches of freight trains traveling between the United States and Mexico are common.

The Bureau of Prisons

Correctional Officers are responsible for supervising, safeguarding, and training inmates of federal prisons, reformatories, and camps. They act as foremen of work assignments, enforce rules and regulations within the institutions, and carry out plans developed for correctional treatment and modification of attitudes of the inmates.

> The Correctional Officers of the Bureau of Prisons supervise, safeguard, and train inmates of federal prisons, reformatories, and camps.

The Bureau of Prisons is an integral part of the federal criminal justice system. It is responsible for the care and custody of persons convicted of federal crimes and sentenced to federal penal institutions. The Bureau operates a nationwide system of maximum, medium, and minimum security prisons, halfway houses, and community program offices.

☑ CHECK POINT

1. What is the primary emphasis of the Federal Drug Enforcement Administration?
2. Name three responsibilities of the U.S. Marshal's Office.
3. Name two responsibilities of the Immigration and Naturalization Service.
4. Name two responsibilities of the Bureau of Prisons.
5. Without looking back, can you name the five agencies organized within the Department of Justice which are heavily involved in law enforcement?

*Answers

1. The primary emphasis of the Federal Drug Enforcement Administration is apprehending the suppliers and distributors of illicit drugs rather than arresting drug abusers.
2. The U.S. Marshal's Office is responsible for arresting persons for whom warrants are issued charging a federal crime, providing physical security for U.S. courtrooms and personal protection for federal judges, jurors, and attorneys, for transporting prisoners, and for protecting witnesses.

3. The Immigration and Naturalization Service conducts investigations, detects violations of immigration and nationality laws, and determines whether aliens may enter or remain in the United States.
4. The Bureau of Prisons supervises, safeguards, and trains inmates of federal prisons, reformatories, and camps.
5. The Department of Justice's law enforcement agencies include the Federal Bureau of Investigation, the Federal Drug Enforcement Administration, the United States Marshal's Office, the Immigration and Naturalization Service (Border Patrol), and the Bureau of Prisons.

THE DEPARTMENT OF THE TREASURY

The Department of the Treasury also has several agencies directly involved in law enforcement activities.

> Law enforcement agencies under the jurisdiction of the Department of the Treasury include the Bureau of Customs, the Internal Revenue Service, the Secret Service, and the Bureau of Alcohol, Tobacco, and Firearms Tax.

The Bureau of Customs

The Bureau of Customs has agents stationed primarily at ports of entry to the United States, places where people and/or goods enter and leave, either by boat, plane, or car. Customs Agents conduct investigations concerning the prevention and detection of frauds on the Customs revenue and the smuggling of merchandise and contraband into or out of the United States.

> Bureau of Customs Special Agents assure that property duty is paid on goods coming into the country and that narcotics, drugs, and defense materials do not enter or leave the country illegally.

Bureau of Customs Agents enforce the Tariff Act, the Mutual Security Act, and the Narcotic Drug Import and Export Act. They have authority to conduct investigations and searches on all ships registered under U.S. laws.

Customs is active in suppressing the traffic in illegal narcotics and works in close cooperation with the Federal Drug Enforcement Administration. Customs Patrol Officers maintain uniformed and plainclothes surveillance at docks and airports.

The Internal Revenue Service (IRS)

The Internal Revenue Service, established in 1862, is responsible for the enforcement of all internal revenue laws. Special Agents obtain facts in tax fraud cases, particularly for income tax, excise tax, and coin-operated gaming devices

> Internal Revenue Service Agents investigate willful tax evasion, tax fraud, and the activities of gamblers and drug peddlers.

The service has responsibility in the areas of social security taxes, federal stamp taxes, estate taxes, excise taxes, the filing of income tax reports, and the willful evasion by citizens to pay their taxes. The Intelligence Division has been actively engaged in the prosecution of gamblers, drug peddlers, and others committing fraud against the government and citizens through illegal stock transactions, nondisclosure of income, and the transfer of money out of the country.

Among the functions of its many offices throughout the country, the IRS assists the general public in preparing tax returns, collects internal revenue taxes, and determines delinquent and additional tax liability.

Internal Security Inspectors investigate charges against IRS employees involving criminal violations of the Internal Revenue Code or violations of the Criminal Code.

The United States Secret Service (SS)

The Secret Service was established in 1865 to fight currency counterfeiters. In 1901 they were given the responsibility of protecting the President of the United States, members of his family, the President-elect, and the Vice-President.

> Secret Service Special Agents guard the President and Vice-President and their families, the President-elect and the Vice-President-elect, and former Presidents upon request. They also investigate counterfeiting of U.S. currency and forged government checks and bonds.

The Secret Service is also responsible for the investigation of threats against the President, either by mail or verbally. In 1976 the Secret Service became responsible for the protection of Presidential candidates as a result of threats against several of them and the actual shooting of a Presidential candidate, Governor George Wallace of Alabama.

In addition to its protective duties, the Secret Service has two major law enforcement functions: the suppression of counterfeiting and the suppression of forgery of government checks and bonds.

It has other duties, too, such as the investigations of U.S. financial institutions. In their efforts to suppress counterfeiting and forgery, agents rely heavily on scientific investigation. To aid the agents, the Bureau of Engraving and Printing in Washington maintains a laboratory with modern scientific crime detection equipment. From the examinations conducted at the laboratory, the Secret Service gets valuable information which often leads its agents to the successful conclusion of cases.

In addition to Secret Service Special Agents, two uniformed groups are under the control and direction of the Service: the White House Police and the Treasury Guard Force.

The *White House Police* protect the Executive Mansion and its grounds. Officers assigned to the White House Police are highly trained in subversive activities, techniques of identifying potential threats to the President, and in self-defense tactics.

The *Treasury Guard Force* protects the Treasury Building and the Treasury Annex in Washington. The Treasury Building has 475 rooms and covers the greater part of two city blocks. Beneath this building are safety vaults where the nation's money and valuable papers are kept. The Treasury Guard Force is assigned to the continuous protection of the immense sums in the U.S. Treasury.

The Bureau of Alcohol, Tobacco, and Firearms Tax (BAFT)

This Bureau was made famous by the television stories of Eliott Ness, *The Untouchables*. Their responsibility is to control the licenses issued to persons in the manufacture, sale, and distribution of alcohol. They inherited the firearms problem during Prohibition when the gangs sawed off shotguns and rifles so they could be carried under their clothes and carried machine guns in violin cases so as to be ready for gang warfare on the streets.

The Bureau, an enforcement arm of the Department of the Treasury, is primarily a licensing and investigative agency involved in federal tax violations.

> Alcohol, Tobacco, and Firearms Tax Inspectors enforce federal laws dealing with the manufacture, sale, and distribution of illegal alcoholic beverages, cigarettes, and firearms.

The Firearms Division is responsible for enforcing the Gun Control Act of 1968 which deals with the manufacture, sale, transfer, and possession of restricted firearms in the United States including the illegal possession of automatic weapons, machine guns, and sub-machine guns by persons other than antique collectors.

The Bureau also regulates commerce in all types of guns interstate and to or from foreign countries. In addition, they collect the taxes of U.S. importers, manufacturers, and dealers of firearms. The Bureau maintains a close relationship with other federal, state, and local law enforcement agencies so that gun control laws are rigidly enforced.

The objectives of their criminal enforcement activity are to eliminate illegal possession and use of firearms, destructive devices, and explosives; to suppress the traffic in illicit distilled spirits; to enforce the criminal violation and forfeiture aspects of the federal wagering laws; and to cooperate with state and local law enforcement agencies to reduce crime and violence (*U.S. Government Manual*, p. 437).

OTHER FEDERAL LAW ENFORCEMENT AGENCIES

Although the majority of federal law enforcement agencies are within the Department of Justice and the Department of the Treasury, other federal agencies are also directly involved in law enforcement activities.

> Other federal law enforcement agencies include the U.S. Postal Inspectors, the Coast Guard, the military police of the armed forces, and investigators and intelligence agents and security officers for numerous federal units.

U.S. Postal Inspectors enforce federal laws pertaining to the mailing of prohibited items such as explosives, obscene matter, and articles likely to injure or cause damage. Any mail that may prove to be libelous, defamatory, or threatening can be excluded from being transported by the Postal Service. The Postal Inspectors are responsible for protecting the mails and the recipients of mail. They also investigate any frauds perpetrated through the mails such as chain letters, gift enterprises, and similar schemes. The Postmaster General is also authorized to prevent the delivery of mail to persons who might be using the mails to conduct a fraudulent business.

The *U.S. Coast Guard*, under the jurisdiction of the Department of Transportation, assists local and state agencies which border the oceans, lakes, and national waterways. They have been actively involved in preventing the smuggling of narcotics into this country.

The *armed forces* also have law enforcement responsibilities. The uniformed divisions are known as the Military Police in the Army, the Shore Patrol in the Navy, and the Security Police in the Marine Corps and Air Force. The military police in each service are primarily concerned with the physical security of the various bases under their control. Within each operation, the security forces control criminal activity, court martials, discipline, desertions, and the confinement of prisoners. In the time of war they are responsible for prisoner-of-war activity as well as custodial care and movement of refugees.

☑ CHECK POINT

1. What are the law enforcement responsibilities of the Bureau of Customs?
2. What are the law enforcement responsibilities of the Internal Revenue Service?
3. What are the law enforcement responsibilities of the United States Secret Service?
4. What are the law enforcement responsibilities of the Bureau of Alcohol, Tobacco, and Firearms Tax?
5. Without looking at the preceding questions, can you name the four agencies with direct law enforcement responsibility within the Department of the Treasury?
6. Name at least four other federal law enforcement agencies, not in either the Department of Justice or the Department of the Treasury.

*Answers

1. Bureau of Customs Special Agents assure that proper duty is paid on goods coming

into the country and narcotics, drugs, and defense materials do not enter or leave the country illegally.

2. Internal Revenue Service Agents investigate willful tax evasion, tax fraud, and the activities of gamblers and drug peddlers.

3. Secret Service Agents guard the President and Vice-President and their families, the President-elect and the Vice-President-elect, and former Presidents upon request. They also investigate counterfeiting of U.S. currency and forged government checks and bonds.

4. Alcohol, Tobacco, and Firearms Tax Inspectors enforce federal laws dealing with the manufacture, sale, and distribution of illegal alcoholic beverages, cigarettes, and firearms.

5. Law enforcement agencies under the jurisdiction of the Department of the Treasury incude the Bureau of Customs, the Internal Revenue Service, the Secret Service, and the Bureau of Alcohol, Tobacco, and Firearms Tax.

6. Other federal law enforcement agencies include the U.S. Postal Inspectors, the Coast Guard, the military police of the armed forces, and investigators and intelligence agents and security officers for numerous federal units.

The importance of federal assistance to state and local law enforcement agencies was stressed in the President's Crime Commission Report (*Challenge of Crime*, 1967, p. 284):

> *Most local communities today are hard-pressed just to improve their agencies of justice and other facilities at a rate that will meet the increase in population and crime. They cannot spare funds for experimental programs or plan beyond the emergencies of the day. Federal collaboration gives state and local agencies an opportunity to gain on crime rather than barely stay abreast of it by making funds, research, and technical assistance available and thereby encouraging changes that, in time, may make criminal administration more effective and fair.*

Traditionally the federal government has been deeply involved in law enforcement assistance by providing local and state agencies with training, identification, and laboratory services. The Immigration and Naturalization Service, the Federal Drug Enforcement Agency, and the Federal Bureau of Investigation, as well as other federal agencies with law enforcement responsibilities, have contributed to law enforcement technology and training. However, the type of federal "collaboration" described in the preceding statement referred specifically to an important, influential, yet sometimes controversial federal agency within the Department of Justice—the Law Enforcement Assistance Administration.

THE LAW ENFORCEMENT ASSISTANCE ADMINISTRATION (LEAA)*

In 1968 Congress enacted the Omnibus Crime Control and Safe Streets Act; Title 1 of this Act established the Law Enforcement Assistance Administration. The Act was amended in 1970 and the LEAA program expanded. The Crime Control Act of 1973 further strengthened the Agency and extended its authorization through 1976. The Crime Control Act of 1976 extended the program through September of 1979.

*Adapted from *The Law Enforcement Assistance Administration: A Partnership for Crime Control.* LEAA, U.S. Department of Justice, Washington, 1976. Reprinted with permission.

In 1974 the Congress gave LEAA greater responsibility for juvenile delinquency prevention and control, consolidating programs previously under the Agency and the Department of Health, Education, and Welfare. The Juvenile Justice and Delinquency Prevention Act of 1974 authorized a three-year juvenile delinquency program to support innovative projects developed by state and local government. The program was extended through September 1979 by the Juvenile Justice Amendments of 1977.

Created by the Omnibus Crime Control and Safe Streets Act of 1968, The Law Enforcement Assistance Administration (LEAA) provides financial resources, technical advice, and leadership to state and local law enforcement agencies. States and localities set their crime control priorities, devise specific action programs, and allocate LEAA funds according to their approved plans.

LEAA works in partnership with state and local governments, which have historically assumed the prime responsibility for crime reduction and law enforcement. Congress affirmed this historical responsibility in the Omnibus Crime Control and Safe Streets Act: "Crime is essentially a local problem that must be dealt with by state and local governments if it is to be controlled effectively."

On the other hand, as noted by Richard W. Velde, former LEAA Administrator: "Crime control is everyone's business. It is not just the business of the criminal justice system—of police, courts, and corrections—but of all citizens who want to live in harmony and peace."

Realizing the national significance of the crime problem, Congress created the LEAA to join state and local law enforcement agencies in their efforts to combat crime. Under the anticrime partnership, the federal government supplies financial resources, technical advice and leadership. However, states and localities set their own crime control priorities, devise specific action programs, and allocate LEAA funds according to their carefully developed plans.

Federal Funds

In ten years LEAA has awarded more than $6 billion to state and local governments to improve police, courts, and correctional systems; to combat juvenile delinquency; and to finance innovative crime-fighting projects. In addition, LEAA conducts activities such as the following:

—Sponsors comprehensive state planning to reduce crime and improve criminal justice.

—Stimulates the creation of new ways to attack specific nationwide problems such as organized crime and drug abuse.

—Addresses issues such as protecting the privacy and security of criminal history information and promoting the employment of minority-group members and women in criminal justice agencies.

—Conducts research to increase knowledge about the causes of criminal behavior, develops innovative techniques to prevent and control crime, and evaluates the effectiveness of criminal justice programs.

—Adapts and uses advanced technology to make police agencies, courts, and correction systems more effective.

—Advises state and local governments and their agencies about technical matters, for example, the use of television technology in court proceedings.

—Develops reliable statistics on crime victims, offenders, and the operations of the criminal justice system.

—Helps train and educate criminal justice personnel and sponsors the improvement of criminal justice curricula in colleges and universities.

Planning for Crime Control

A key element of the LEAA program is planning—the cornerstone of successful crime control. Although states and localities need federal help, they must assess their criminal justice needs, set their own priorities, and plan their own programs. To assure state-local responsibility and control, Congress awards the bulk of LEAA funds in the form of *block grants* based on state populations. LEAA controls are restricted to maintaining the integrity of the program and assuring that states and localities adhere to legislative mandates. This ensures that states and localities take the initiative, with LEAA providing leadership and guidance from its Washington headquarters.

State Planning Agencies, commonly known as *SPA's*, are responsible for preparing and revising comprehensive crime control plans. State Planning Agency board members are appointed by governors and chief executives of eligible jurisdictions. Members represent the criminal justice field, local and state government, urban-renewal interests, and citizen, professional, and community organizations. Under the Safe Streets Act, LEAA finances planning grants and then awards action grants to finance the planned improvements.

The LEAA planning budget is distributed according to state populations. To insure local involvement in the planning process, each state must make at least 40% of its planning grant available to local government units. LEAA may waive this requirement in states which have the bulk of responsibility for law enforcement and criminal justice or where adherence to the 40% formula would not contribute to the efficient development of the state plan. For example, the police in Baltimore, St. Louis, and Kansas City are formally under the state government; the city has no direct authority. Consequently, Maryland and Missouri may not have to allocate 40% of their planning grants to cities.

The State Plan must be comprehensive—a total, integrated analysis of the state's law enforcement and criminal justice problems. It must include goals, priorities, and standards, and it must address methods and resources required for crime prevention; for identification, detection, and apprehension of suspects; for adjudication; for custodial treatment of suspects and offenders; and for offender rehabilitation.

Block Action Grants

Once a plan is approved, LEAA awards the state a block action grant to carry out specific improvement projects. Block grants are allocated according to population to fifty-five eligible jurisdictions: the fifty states, Washington, D.C., Puerto Rico, American Samoa, Guam, and the Virgin Islands. The State Planning Agency then subgrants these funds to cities, counties, and state agencies.

Subgrants and matching funds are required. States must subgrant to local governments the percentage of action funds that correspond to state and local expenditures for law enforcement in the preceding fiscal year. For example, if all nonfederal spending for law enforcement in a state consists of 30% in state funds and 70% in funds spent by localities, then the block action grant must be earmarked the same way; the state would retain up to 30% of the money for statewide programs and pass the other 70% on to local governments.

These grants require a 10% nonfederal match. Half of that match for local projects must be from state funds.

Major Achievements

Every state and locality has felt the impact of LEAA's nationwide anti-crime program. Tens of thousands of programs and projects have been supported with LEAA funds, and millions of hours have been applied to identify effective, efficient, economical ways to reduce crime and improve criminal justice. Projects have been developed to reduce crime and improve criminal justice, to improve the management and administration of courts, to deploy police officers more effectively, to find jobs for ex-offenders, to sharpen the skills of criminal justice personnel, to give prosecutors better tools to fight crime, and to break the jail-street-crime-jail cycle of the drug addict. In addition, LEAA has other major accomplishments.

LEAA has supported: victimization surveys; establishment of standards and goals; high-impact programs; surveys of jails, courts, private security industry, and juvenile correctional facilities; development of new equipment; in-service and preservice educational grants and loans (LEEP), as well as hundreds of state and local anticrime projects.

LEAA's National Crime Panel provides a wealth of valuable information to help law enforcement officials and criminal justice planners create better programs to control crime. The program uses scientific sampling methods to obtain statistical data about the amount, trends, and nature of crime; its costs; the characteristics of crime victims; and the relationships between victims and offenders.

Standards and goals for crime control were developed by the National Advisory Commission on Criminal Justice Standards and Goals with the support of LEAA.

High Impact Anticrime Programs were financed by LEAA ($160 million) in eight cities: Atlanta, Baltimore, Cleveland, Dallas, Denver, Newark, St. Louis, and Portland. The program goal was to reduce burglary and stranger-to-stranger street crime (homicide, rape, aggravated assault, and robbery) by 5% in two years and by 20% in five years. An additional objective was to demonstrate the effectiveness of crime-specific planning as a means of reducing crime.

Although the programs varied from city to city, common components included:

—Public education projects to inform citizens how to protect themselves and their property.

—Expanded police patrols, better trained, with improved equipment, including modern communications systems enabling police officers to arrive more quickly at crime scenes.

—Projects to process street crime and burglary cases faster and more efficiently in courts.

—Rehabilitation of target offenders, particularly juveniles and narcotics addicts.

Evaluations of the program show that crime-oriented planning is essential to good programs. In addition, a number of individual projects had a high success rate. Through a program in which residents marked their valuables with identification numbers, Denver reduced burglary 25% in a high crime area. A St. Louis foot patrol project helped reduce residential burglary 35% in a target area.

Surveys have also been conducted by LEAA. It has studied the nation's jails—finding enormous deficiencies—the nation's courts, juvenile correctional facilities, and the private security industry. LEAA formed a Private Security Advisory Council to recommend improvements and needed legislation.

New equipment has also been developed by LEAA. For example, LEAA's National Institute of Law Enforcement and Criminal Justice has developed a reasonably-priced, lightweight, bulletproof vest. The vest, made of a synthetic fiber, weighs only two or three pounds more than an ordinary sport coat and will stop a bullet fired by most handguns. It is credited with saving more than twenty police lives in two years.

Aid to Police

Police officers today must be highly professional, skilled, well-educated, and extensively trained in law enforcement techniques. They must have superior equipment; outstanding command and control systems; and excellent management, information, and communications systems. In recent years LEAA has given extensive help to police and sheriff's agencies in meeting these needs.

LEAA funds have been used for special street crime patrols, mobile cruising units, storefront police projects, special police units for high-rise apartments, team policing, police training, special crime prevention campaigns, community relations efforts that bring police into contact with the poor and the young, and new efforts to deal effectively and responsibly with juvenile crime.

The criminal justice system critically needs well-educated personnel. LEAA's manpower development program is helping to build the necessary reservoir of skilled employees through the *Law Enforcement Education Program (LEEP)* which has given grants and loans totaling more than $150 million to 200,000 men and women employed in criminal justice agencies, enabling them to enroll in college courses to upgrade their criminal justice capabilities. Grants cover tuition, fees, and books up to $250 per academic quarter or $400 per semester. Grant recipients are not required to repay the grant if they continue to work, full time, in a criminal justice agency for two years after completing a LEEP-financed course.

In addition, LEEP makes loans to a limited number of preservice students preparing for future criminal justice employment and to criminal justice practitioners and in-service students who attend school full-time. Loans pay for direct education costs up to $2,200 per academic year. Loan recipients receive a 25% cancellation of LEEP indebtedness for each year of full-time employment with a criminal justice agency after they complete full-time study. More than 80% of these are police employees.*

Evaluation of LEAA

The LEAA program has been controversial since its inception. From the beginning, some community groups and local bodies of governments have opposed the states' administration of the program in the belief that states are not familiar with or responsive to the needs of the cities. Whether LEAA programs will have a significant effect on crime has never been determined.

> Problems encountered by the LEAA include community groups and local bodies of governments opposed to state administration of the program, unrealistic expectations and goals, unstable management, delays in publication of planning guidelines, and excessive requirements for paperwork in completing plans.

An evaluation of LEAA was presented at the 1977 National Conference of State Criminal Justice Planning Administrators by Richard D. Lamm, Governor of Colorado. Lamm (1978), noted that LEAA has "endured a very troubled history," due in part to extremely unrealistic and high expectations which led to inevitable excesses and failures. In the program's early years, the Nixon "law and order" administration exerted great pressure to get money out into the field without allowing states sufficient time to properly plan for use of the funds. In addition, LEAA's management has been unstable; it has had five administrators in seven years, each with his own philosophy. Finally, frequent delays in publishing the guidelines for the annual planning cycle have hampered the states' ability to plan properly.

---

*End of adaptation from: The LEAA: A Partnership for Crime Control.

In spite of these difficulties, however, the LEAA has several proven accomplishments:

> *State, regional, and local officials agree that block grants have had some effect in slowing the rise in crime. Available evidence indicates that Safe Streets monies have not only upgraded traditional criminal justice activities, but also have initiated new and innovative approaches to old problems. The program has provided fresh resources to an area too long under-financed and has focused public attention on a system too long neglected. . . .*
>
> *Of 440 long term projects that were initiated with LEAA funds, 64% were continually operated, expanded or maintained at about the same level with other sources of funds after termination of LEAA funds. . . . Given the rather severe budgetary constraints all units of government have suffered in the last few years, this rate of assumption of LEAA projects is astounding and in itself should be a good indicator that persons at the state and local level consider these projects to be valuable (Lamm, 1978, pp. 33-35, 66).*

Lamm, while noting the apparent success of LEAA efforts, finds the agency has room for improvement. He notes that the present LEAA planning guidelines are excessive, more a burden than a benefit to many states attempting to implement them. He cites as an example that Georgia's FY1977 Criminal Justice Plan was 1,400 pages long concerning $9 million in LEAA funds, while their plan for Title XX(HEW) funds was under 100 pages yet concerned over $60 million in federal funds. In light of this, LEAA should streamline the planning process and minimize the guidelines.

The future of the LEAA is still undecided. If it can continue to demonstrate successful programs, Congress will probably continue it.

☑ CHECK POINT

1. What legislation created the Law Enforcement Assistance Administration (LEAA) and approximately when?
2. What is the primary function of LEAA?
3. List five accomplishments of the LEAA.
4. List three problems which have faced the LEAA.

*Answers

1. The LEAA was created by Title I of the 1968 Omnibus Crime Control and Safe Streets Act.
2. The primary function of LEAA, as the name implies, is to provide assistance to state and local law enforcement agencies, including financial resources, technical advice, and leadership.
3. Accomplishments of the LEAA include: victimization surveys; establishment of standards and goals; high-impact programs; surveys of jails, courts, private security industry, and juvenile correctional facilities; development of new equipment; inservice and preservice educational grants and loans (LEEP); as well as hundreds of state and local anticrime projects.
4. Problems encountered include: community groups and local bodies of governments opposed to state administration of the program, unrealistic expectations and goals, unstable management, delays in publication of planning guidelines, and excessive paperwork in completing plans.

State Law Enforcement Agencies

Many of the federal agencies have state counterparts.

> State agencies with law enforcement responsibilities include State Bureaus of Investigation and Apprehension and State Fire Marshal Divisions as well as Departments of Natural Resources, Driver and Vehicle Services Divisions, and Departments of Human Rights.

OFFICE OF THE STATE ATTORNEY GENERAL

> The State Attorney General is the chief law enforcement officer at the state level. His office usually includes an Antitrust Division, a Consumer Protection Division, a Criminal Division, and an Opinions Office.

The Attorney General is the chief legal counsel for the state. His office provides representation and advice to agencies in the executive branch of state government. The Attorney General proposes and drafts legislation on a variety of subjects and assures that all state laws are adequately and uniformly enforced. His office also supervises district attorneys and sheriffs.

In addition to an Antitrust Division and a Consumer Protection Division, the Attorney General's office has a *Criminal Division* which conducts criminal appeals, advises local prosecutors on the conduct of criminal trials, and helps develop and prosecute certain criminal cases, particularly those of organized crime and white-collar crime.

The Attorney General's Opinions Office provides information to state and local officials on effects and requirements of state laws when laws either appear to conflict or are unclear in their application.

STATE BUREAU OF INVESTIGATION AND APPREHENSION

States vary in their organizations and functions of agencies that offer support to other law enforcement agencies in the state. They usually are organized to assist local law enforcement officials. The Bureau places investigators throughout the state to assist in investigations of major crimes and organized criminal activities; aids in investigating the illegal sale or possession of narcotics and prohibited drugs; conducts police science training courses for peace officers; provides scientific examination of crime scenes and laboratory analysis of evidence; and maintains a criminal justice information and telecommunications system. The Bureau also provides statistical information on crimes and crime trends in the state.

STATE FIRE MARSHAL DIVISION

Designated State Fire Marshals investigate suspicious and incendiary fire origins, fire fatalities, and large-loss fires; tabulate fire statistics; and provide education, inspection, and training programs for fire prevention.

The *Fire Prevention Section* provides information on the state's Uniform Fire Code, removal of combustible materials, correction of fire hazards, fire prevention, and general information on smoke/heat detectors, fire alarms, fire extinguishers, and other fire protection appliances.

The *Inspection and Investigation Section* organizes investigation of all fires of suspicious and incendiary origin, large-loss fires, and fire fatalities. The Section also conducts on-going inspection of public and private schools, state hospitals, convalescent and other special purpose homes, hotels, rooming houses and other multiple dwellings, dry-cleaning establishments, motion picture theaters, places of assembly, and all installations where petroleum products, liquified petroleum gas and natural gas are manufactured, stored or distributed.

The *Fire Prevention Awareness Section* identifies problem fire areas, inspects fires and buildings to guarantee fire safety standards, conducts public awareness programs, and maintains contact with local fire departments.

STATE DEPARTMENT OF NATURAL RESOURCES (FISH, GAME, AND WATERCRAFT)

Some states combine fish, game, and watercraft under one division, a Department of Natural Resources which enforces all laws and rules under its jurisdiction including hunting, fishing, and trapping laws and licenses, and laws on the operation of watercraft. In some states the department is responsible for the Firearms Training laws. The Division may hold auction sales to dispose of furs, firearms, and hunting, fishing, and trapping equipment confiscated from violators of fish and game laws.

Conservation officers investigate complaints about nuisance wildlife, misuse of public lands and waters, violations of state park rules, and unlawful appropriation of state-owned timber. Conservation officers also dispose of big game animals struck by motor vehicles, assist state game managers on wildlife census projects, enforce wild-rice harvesting rules, and assist in identifying needed sites for public access to lakes and streams.

The department also issues resident and nonresident boat licenses and licenses for hunting, fishing, and trapping.

DRIVER AND VEHICLE SERVICES DIVISION

The *Motor Vehicle Section* registers motor vehicles, issues ownership certificates, answers inquiries, returns defective applications received through the mail, licenses motor vehicle dealers, supplies record information to the public, and, in some states, registers bicycles.

The *Drivers' License Section* tests, evaluates, and licenses all drivers throughout the state; maintains accurate records of each individual driver including all violations and accidents occurring anywhere in the United States and Canada; interviews drivers whose record warrants possible revocation, suspension or cancellation; records the location of every reported accident; assists in driver education efforts; and administers written and road tests to applicants.

THE DEPARTMENT OF HUMAN RIGHTS

The Department of Human Rights enforces the Human Rights Act which prohibits discrimination on the basis of race, color, creed, religion, national origin, sex, marital status, status with regard to public assistance or disability in employment, housing, public accomodations, public service, and education. It is also responsible for current affirmative action laws. It investigates and conciliates discrimination complaints. When conciliation is not possible, it settles the complaint through legal proceedings.

CRIME VICTIMS' REPARATIONS BOARD

Some states have a Crime Victims' Reparations Board which allows innocent victims of crime to recover their medical costs and loss of wages. If death results from a criminal act, the funeral expenses of the victim and the dependent's loss of support may be paid by the state.

To qualify for reparations, a person must be an innocent victim of a crime (or a legal dependent of a deceased victim), must report the crime to local law enforcement agencies within five days, and must cooperate completely with the law enforcement agency. No reparations for property damage or loss are paid. Generally the first $100 of a claim is deductible, with a maximum claim of $25,000 paid to each victim.

Some government indemnity programs for victims of crime exist in a few states. This new form of needed social legislation focuses on the plight of the victim rather than on the criminal offender. Examples of recent reparations include a minor male victim who was assaulted by three juveniles for no apparent reason and suffered dental damages in excess of $1,200. He was awarded $1,118. A twenty-three-year-old female victim was shot by a former boy friend incurring over $2,000 in medical bills which were not covered by any insurance. She was awarded $1,959.

STATE POLICE AND STATE HIGHWAY PATROL

The most visible form of state law enforcement are the state police who often have general police powers and enforce all state laws, and state highway patrols who focus their attention upon the operation of motor vehicles on public highways and freeways.

> Some state police enforce all state laws; others enforce only traffic laws on highways and freeways and are usually designated as state highway patrol.

The Michigan State Police and the Pennsylvania State Police are examples of agencies which have general police powers. In contrast, Florida's Highway

Patrol deals with traffic while the Florida Department of Law Enforcement conducts investigations. Similarly, the Minnesota Highway Patrol directs its primary attention to enforcement of traffic laws while the Minnesota Bureau of Criminal Apprehension limits its function to investigative and enforcement functions at the state level.

In California, the Department of the California Highway Patrol is responsible for enforcing the traffic laws, investigating traffic accidents, and rendering aid to motorists on the state and interstate highways. The California State Police are responsible for protecting only state property. They protect the state capital and grounds as well as other state government buildings located throughout the state.

Some state highway patrol organizations maintain a traffic safety section that coordinates traffic safety programs throughout the state to assure uniformity in adherence to the many traffic laws. They assist all organizations, both public and private, in planning and operating effective safety programs. They may assist local agencies by providing intensive enforcement training for traffic personnel. They may also maintain auto theft records more efficiently because of their statewide jurisdiction. They may also provide laboratory and investigative personnel to assist local agencies in the investigation of hit-and-run cases and auto theft.

In addition, some highway patrol agencies coordinate the activity and maintain records on commercial vehicle enforcement, maintain public scales on the highways, inspect all school buses, and investigate accidents involving school buses throughout the state. Licensing or registration of official smog-control devices or headlights and other safety equipment installations as well as inspection stations may also be functions performed by state highway patrol.

☑ CHECK POINT

1. Who is the chief law enforcement officer at the state level?
2. List four other state agencies involved in law enforcement.

*Answers

1. The State Attorney General is the chief law enforcement officer at the state level.
2. Other state agencies involved in law enforcement include: State Fire Marshal Divisions, State Bureaus of Investigation and Apprehension, Departments of Natural Resources, Driver and Vehicle Services Divisions, Departments of Human Rights, State Police, and State Highway Patrol.

County Law Enforcement Agencies

County law enforcement agencies account for approximately 3000 of the 40,000 law enforcement agencies in the United States (Vetter and Simonsen, 1976, p. 100).

The two main types of county law enforcement agencies are the county sheriff and the county police.

THE COUNTY SHERIFF

The county sheriff is usually the principal law enforcement officer of a county. The position is established by state constitution. The sheriff, usually an elected official, may or may not be well-qualified for performing the complex duties assigned to him.

He appoints deputy sheriffs to assist him in fulfilling his responsibilities. The hundreds of sheriffs' departments vary greatly in organization and function. In some states the sheriff is primarily an officer of the court; criminal investigation and traffic enforcement are delegated to state or local agencies. In other states, notably the south and west, the sheriff and his deputies perform both traffic and criminal duties.

The sheriff's staff ranges in size from one (the sheriff himself) to several hundreds, including sworn deputies as well as civilian personnel. Likewise, a wide range of technical proficiency and expertise also occurs among sheriff's personnel. Some departments have little equipment; others have fleets of patrol vehicles, airplanes, helicopters, and lavishly equipped crime laboratories.

Many state constitutions have designated the sheriff as the chief law enforcement officer of the county.

THE COUNTY POLICE

The county police, not to be confused with the county sheriff and his deputies, are found in areas where city and county governments have been merged, such as in Florida. County police departments are headed by a chief of police, usually an administrator appointed from within the department, who is accountable to a county commissioner, prosecutor, manager, or director of public safety.

Private Security Forces

Private security forces include watchmen, guards, and patrolmen. These private security officers perform many of the same functions as public law officers: controlling entrances and exits to facilities; preventing or reporting fires; promoting safety; safeguarding equipment, valuables, and confidential material; and patrolling restricted areas. Businesses, educational, industrial, and commercial organizations frequently hire private security guards to protect their premises and investments.

There are, however, important differences between private and public security forces.

Private security forces differ from public security forces in several ways:
—They are salaried with private funds.
—They are responsible to an employer.
—They have a specific shift.
—They have limited authority and then only on the premises which they were hired to guard.

—They have no authority to make arrests except as a citizen's arrest.
—They have no authority to carry a concealed weapon.
—Their uniform and badge must not closely resemble that of the regular police officer.

In contrast to private security forces, "public" police officers are salaried with public funds. They are responsible to a chief of police and ultimately to the citizens of the community. Technically they are on-duty twenty-four hours a day and have full authority to uphold the law, including the authority to make arrests and to carry a concealed weapon.

Still, the public police officer cannot be everywhere at the same time. Therefore, many businesses and organizations have elected to hire special "protection." Basically, two different types of private security may be hired: private patrolmen and private watchmen.

As the name implies, private patrolmen operate both on and off the premises of their employer and may have several customers to check periodically during a specified time period. However, private watchmen stay on the property to safeguard the premises at all times.

A further distinction exists between the security officer employed by a large industrial concern and the night watchman employed by a small firm. The former are usually carefully screened, well paid, and trained to perform specific duties. In contrast, the night watchman is frequently retired from a regular job (sometimes as a "public" police officer), needs only temporary work, or is simply supplementing his regular income by taking on a second job.

☑ CHECK POINT

1. What are the two main types of county law enforcement?
2. List five major differences between public and private law enforcement officers.

∗ Answers

1. The two main types of county law enforcement agencies are the county sheriff and the county police.
2. Private security officers are salaried with private funds, are responsible to an employer, have a specific shift, have limited authority and then only on the premises which they were hired to guard, have no authority to make arrests except as a citizen's arrest, have no authority to carry a concealed weapon, and must not wear a uniform or badge which closely resembles that of a regular police officer.

SUMMARY

Law enforcement in the United States is a cooperative effort among local, county, state, federal, and private law enforcement officers. Each has something to offer and to gain from the other.

At the federal level several law enforcement agencies are under the jurisdiction of the Departments of Justice and the Treasury. The U.S. Attorney General, as head of the Department of Justice, is the chief federal law enforcement officer. Within his department are the Federal Bureau of Investigation, the Federal Drug Enforcement Administration, United States Marshals, the Immigration and Naturalization Service, and the Bureau of Prisons.

The FBI, in addition to its numerous investigative responsibilities, provides assistance to law enforcement agencies throughout the country through its Identification Division, its crime laboratory, its National Crime Information Center, and its Uniform Crime Reports.

Law enforcement agencies within the Department of the Treasury include the Bureau of Customs, the Internal Revenue Service, the Secret Service, and the Bureau of Alcohol, Tobacco, and Firearms Tax.

Other federal law enforcement agencies include the U.S. Postal Inspectors, the Coast Guard, and the military police of the armed forces.

Although not itself a law enforcement agency, the Law Enforcement Assistance Administration (LEAA) provides financial resources, technical advice, and leadership to state and local law enforcement agencies. In spite of several problems, the LEAA has had some effect on almost every law enforcement agency in the country and has seemed to have some effect in slowing the rise in crime.

State law enforcement agencies include State Bureaus of Investigation and Apprehension, State Fire Marshals Divisions, State Depatments of Natural Resources, Driver and Vehicle Services Divisions, Departments of Human Rights, State Police, and State Highway Patrol.

At the county level, the two main types of law enforcement agencies are the county sheriff and the county police.

In addition, private security officers provide special protection for businesses and educational, industrial, and commercial organizations. They perform many of the same functions as public law officers, but they also differ in several important ways.

You may rightly be wondering, what about *local law enforcement*? This is the focus of the remainder of the book.

APPLICATION

1. For each of the agencies listed below, indicate whether they are a part of the Department of Justice (J), the Department of the Treasury (T), or some other governmental agency (O):

____ a. Bureau of Alcohol, Tobacco, and Firearms Tax (BATF)
____ b. Bureau of Customs
____ c. Sheriff's Office
____ d. Federal Drug Enforcement Administration (FDEA)
____ e. Federal Bureau of Investigation (FBI)
____ f. Immigration and Naturalization Services (INS)
____ g. Internal Revenue Service (IRS)
____ h. Postal Inspectors
____ i. Secret Service (SS)
____ j. State Police
____ k. United States Marshal
____ l. United States Attorney General
____ m. United States military police

2. Using the preceding agencies, state which agency would have the responsibility for the problems and activities which follow:

___ a. Piracy of an aircraft
___ b. Kidnapping
___ c. Distributing illegal drugs
___ d. Protecting witnesses in federal court cases
___ e. Arresting persons charged with federal crimes
___ f. Apprehending smuggled aliens
___ g. Protecting the President and his family
___ h. Assuring payment of duty on goods coming into the country
___ i. Investigating tax fraud
___ j. Investigating counterfeiting of U.S. currency
___ k. Espionage
___ l. Regulating interstate commerce in firearms
___ m. Enforcing traffic laws on highways and freeways
___ n. Sabotage
___ o. Bank robbery

3. Check the characteristics below which are typical of a *private* security officer (in contrast to a public peace officer):

___ a. Has full authority to make arrests
___ b. May wear a uniform and a badge
___ c. Is on duty twenty-four hours a day
___ d. Works for an employer
___ e. Has authority to carry a concealed weapon
___ f. Salaried from private funds

*Answers

1. a. T   d. J   g. T   j. O   m. O
   b. T   e. J   h. O   k. J
   c. O   f. J   i. T   l. J
2. a. FBI   f. INS   k. FBI
   b. FBI   g. SS   l. BATF
   c. FDEA   h. Bureau of Customs   m. State Police (Highway Patrol)
   d. FBI   i. IRS   n. FBI
   e. FBI   j. SS   o. FBI
3. b, d, f should have been checked.

DISCUSSION QUESTIONS

1. How do different law enforcement agencies relate to each other?
2. Which departments have jurisdiction over other departments?
3. Why aren't all the federal law enforcement agencies under the Department of Justice?
4. What major differences are there between a private security officer and a public law enforcement officer?

5. What state law enforcement agencies do we have? Which are of most importance in assisting our local law enforcement agency?
6. What form of county law enforcement do we have?
7. Where is our regional FBI office? What facilities and services does it offer?

REFERENCES

The challenge of crime in a free society. President's Commission on Law Enforcement and Administration of Justice. Washington, D.C.: U.S. Government Printing Office, February, 1967.

Lamm, R. D. Evaluating LEAA—is it worth continuing? *Security management,* 22:1, January, 1978, pp. 33-35, 66.

Law enforcement and related jobs with federal agencies. Washington, D.C.: U.S. Civil Service Commission, December, 1975.

The law enforcement assistance administration: A partnership for crime control. Washington, D.C.: LEAA, U.S. Department of Justice, 1976.

Sullivan, J. L. *Introduction to police science.* New York: McGraw-Hill, 1966, 1971.

U.S. government manual: 1976-77 (revised 5-1-76). Washington, D.C.: Office of the Federal Register, National Archives and Records Service, General Services Administration.

Vetter, J. S. and Simonsen, C. E. *Criminal justice in America.* Philadelphia: W. B. Saunders Company, 1976.

Common goals of police departments include: preserving the peace, protecting civil rights and civil liberties, enforcing the law, preventing crime and providing services.

Local Law Enforcement

Goals and Organization to Meet
the Community's Needs

DO YOU KNOW □ □ □

- □ What is the difference between a goal, an objective, and a task?
- □ What the basic goals of most local law enforcement agencies are?
- □ How objectives are instrumental in achieving goals?
- □ How routine tasks can gain in significance when goals and objectives are stated?
- □ What two basic organizational categories in a typical police department are?
- □ Who is the chief law enforcement officer at the local level?
- □ What major functions are undertaken in field service? In administrative service?
- □ What primary tasks are performed in routine patrol? In a traffic division? In investigation? In community relations programs?
- □ What specialized officers may exist within a local police department?
- □ Why accurate records and communications are important in law enforcement?
- □ Why centralization of records is encouraged?
- □ How officers receive their information?
- □ What is the primary method of receiving and sending information between headquarters and units in the field?
- □ What type of reports are required in law enforcement?
- □ What the NCIC is?
- □ What is required by the Data Privacy Act?

The will of the people is the best law.
—Ulysses S. Grant.

INTRODUCTION

Crimes are committed in a specific place; therefore, they have most immediate impact upon local law enforcement. Although local law enforcement agencies vary greatly depending on their size, resources, and problems, most police departments work toward similar goals and within basically similar organizational structures.

The most important individual within the police department is the law enforcement officer whose basic function is to protect and assist the public. The officer's effectiveness depends on the goals and objectives of the police department and upon its organizational structure.

Goals, Objectives, and Tasks

An effective police department needs clearly specified goals, objectives, and tasks to fulfill its responsibilities to the community.

> A *goal* is a broad, general, desired outcome.
> An *objective* is a specific, measureable means of achieving the goal.
> A *task* is a specific activity which contributes to reaching the objective.

Goals, objectives, and tasks are interdependent; each alone can accomplish little, but in combination they can provide the needed direction to achieve whatever ends are sought by the department.

GOALS

A goal is a general statement of direction, purpose, or intent. It is a desired outcome or end to be achieved.

> Common goals of police departments include:
> —To preserve the peace.
> —To protect civil rights and civil liberties.
> —To enforce the law.
> —To prevent crime.
> —To provide services.

The goals of a police department often depend, in large degree, upon community attitudes and desires. Some communities feel that the primary function of the police is to prevent crime and to maintain order. Police intervention in family quarrels, racial disputes, threatened gang wars, or any situation which may lead to criminal acts is expected and supported. In other communities the emphasis is on law enforcement. A police officer who intervenes in a family quarrel may be criticized for not being "out catching criminals."

The suggestion has even been made that two separate types of police officers are needed: peace officers and law enforcement officers. However, such a separation seems neither realistic nor efficient. What is required is an "all-purpose" police officer who can perform both functions effectively.

It is usually quite easy to reach agreement on goals. For example, few people would argue with the value of the preceding goals. However, placing goals into a priority ranking and finding means to accomplish these goals is more difficult. Effective progress toward goal achievement depends on a plan, and that plan must include clearly stated objectives for meeting each goal.

OBJECTIVES

An objective is a statement of a specific activity which can be measured within a given time frame and under specifiable conditions.

> Objectives facilitate planning, assignment of responsibility, and evaluation of progress toward goals.

For example, given the goal "preventing crime," we need to ask, how can it be accomplished? Opinions will vary, as will reasonable options. Budgetary constraints often limit what objectives might be set for reaching a specific goal. In spite of such constraints, however, specific objectives should be set for each department goal.

Returning to the goal of "preventing crime," objectives for achieving this goal might include: to educate the public, to institute operation identification procedures, to make police officers highly visible, to increase the number of police officers on patrol at a given time, or to assist offenders who are returning to society.

Figure 6-1.

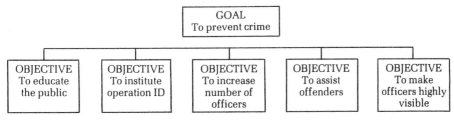

Although it is difficult to measure "prevented crime," it is less difficult to measure implementation of public education, institution of operation ID, visibility of officers, and the like. The accomplishment of broad goals can be evaluated by the successful accomplishment of objectives set for reaching the goal.

The advantages of clearly stated objectives are numerous. They help to establish priorities; they provide direction for present activities and the assignment of responsibility; they assist in the evaluation of completed activities and in planning for the future; they enhance communication between the police department and the public—citizens can be informed of precisely what the department is trying to accomplish—and, perhaps most important, clearly stated objectives enhance communication within the police department. They make possible the precise specification of tasks to be accomplished to achieve the objectives. Police officers, supervisors, administrators, support personnel, all know what is expected and what outcomes are desired.

TASKS

Once the objectives have been stated, ways to achieve them must be determined. These are the tasks or activities which must be performed to meet the objective which will contribute to reaching the desired goal.

> When tasks are seen as ways of achieving objectives which lead toward realization of a department goal, they become more significant.

Some tasks may seem unimportant, but if each task is looked upon as contributing to accomplishing an objective which in turn contributes to achieving a goal, each routine task becomes important in itself.

Figure 6-2.

For example, while asking police officers "to educate the public" provides more direction than asking them "to prevent crime," the directive is still too general to be of much assistance. Specification of the tasks involved in "educating the public" is needed. Tasks identified might include talking to elementary school children about the seriousness of shoplifting, giving a speech to a community group about the importance of locking car doors, and so on.

If goals, objectives, and tasks are clearly stated, each person knows what is expected and can make a full contribution to the department's efforts to reach its goals. All police officers should be familiar with the goals and objectives of their department, with their role in working toward these goals (the focus of the next chapter), and with the specific tasks they are expected to perform to successfully fulfill their complex role (the focus of Section Three).

☑ CHECK POINT

1. What is the difference between a goal, an objective, and a task?
2. What are some basic goals of most local law enforcement agencies?

3. How are objectives instrumental in achieving goals?
4. How can routine tasks be given significance?

*Answers

1. A goal is a broad, general, desired outcome. An objective is a specific, measurable means of achieving the goal. A task is a specific activity which contributes to reaching the objective. Goals, objectives, and tasks differ in their specificity, but all seek to accomplish the same general purpose.
2. Among the common goals of most police departments are (1) to preserve the peace, (2) to protect civil rights and civil liberties, (3) to enforce the law, (4) to prevent crime, and (5) to provide services.
3. Objectives facilitate planning, assignment of responsibility, and evaluation of progress toward goals.
4. Routine tasks can be given significance by perceiving them as ways of achieving objectives which lead toward realization of a department goal.

ORGANIZATION OF THE DEPARTMENT— TASKS AND PERSONNEL

For efficient operation, personnel and tasks must be logically organized. The two basic organizational units within most police departments are *field services* (also called operations or on-line services) and *administrative services* (also called staff or support services).

> Most police departments are organized into two basic units: field services and administrative services. Tasks and personnel are assigned to one or the other.

Field services include patrol, traffic control, community services, and investigation. Administrative services include recruitment and training, planning and research, records and communications, crime laboratories, and facilities including the police headquarters and jail. Teamwork is essential within and between field services and administrative services.

> The chief law enforcement officer at the local level is the chief of police.

The chief of police oversees the operation of the entire department and coordinates the efforts of field and administrative services. Under him, depending on the size of the department, are captains, lieutenants, sergeants, and police officers.

You might compare the chief of police to the coach of an athletic team— both plan the strategy and "call the shots" which the "team captain" and the "players" put into action. Unlike in sports, however, the chief of police can actually "get into the game" and often does, especially in smaller departments. We can carry the analogy further and compare the citizens of a community with the fans at a sporting event—both let the "team" know what they think of them—often very vocally, and both may influence decision-making. Their support generally makes for a much better showing by the team.

A typical department might be organized something like the following:

Figure 6-3.

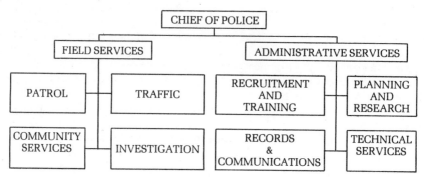

The specific organization within a police department is influenced by the department's size, location, and the extent and type of crime with which it must deal. For example, a small police department often combines patrol, traffic, community services, and investigative tasks in a single division; a large police department usually has separate divisions for each. A community with a major freeway running through its business section faces different problems than a community located on a coast or on a border between the United States and Canada or Mexico. Communities with large groups of minorities face different problems than those which are homogeneous. For some communities, traffic control is a major problem; for others gambling, smuggling, or racial unrest may be priorities.

No matter what the organization of the department, its primary responsibilitiy is to provide field services to the citizens of the community.

FIELD SERVICES

Movies and television have made the public aware of police operations and the type of services provided, yet this view is often a distorted, unrealistic picture of what actually happens "on the street."

> Field services include patrol, traffic, community services, and investigation.

Sometimes these functions are performed by one division; sometimes they are performed by separate divisions. They may be further *specialized* by the type of individual involved: juveniles, gamblers, prostitutes, burglars, dope peddlers, and so on; by specific geographic areas (beats); or by specific times when the demand for service is highest, for example, holiday traffic or abnormal conditions such as strikes and protests.

Traditionally, however, police departments have been *generalist* organizations; that is, most of their personnel is assigned to routine patrol and each officer is responsible for providing basic law enforcement services of all types to a specified geographic area. This routine patrol has been and is the backbone of police work in smaller departments. Larger departments tend to be more specialist-oriented.

Patrol

Usually 60-70% of a department's police officers are assigned to patrol operations. Although other divisions may have more prestige, patrol officers are the first and primary contact between the public and the criminal justice system. They not only initiate the criminal justice system, they strongly influence the public's perception of this system.

Patrol is responsible for providing continuous police service and high visibility of law enforcement. Tasks include crime prevention, response to calls for service, self-initiated activity, and completing administrative functions.

Patrol accounts for a major portion of most departments' expenditures, activities, personnel, and visibility. Whether measured by the number of police officers involved, the number of dollars spent, or by the reality that the uniformed police officer is the most visible part of our law enforcement system, patrol is the most vital component of police work. All other units are supplemental to this basic unit.

Patrol provides both crime- and noncrime-related services including preventing or deterring crime, apprehending criminals, recovering stolen property, providing emergency assistance, and giving citizens a sense of community security and confidence in the police.

Patrol is normally performed by uniformed officers in marked vehicles, although some larger departments assign uniformed officers to motorcycle and foot patrol in heavily populated or congested areas. This visibility, in itself, is one way to deter and repress crime. In addition, because the officers are in their vehicle and already moving, patrol allows the officers to respond quickly to calls for crime- and noncrime-related service; for example, to apprehend suspects or to assist in medical emergencies. Specific activities and responsibilities within the patrol function are the focus of Chapter 9.

Traffic

Traffic may be a responsibility of patrol, or it may be a separate function. A well-rounded traffic program involves many activities designed to maintain order and safety on streets and highways.

Traffic officers are usually responsible for enforcing traffic laws, directing and controlling traffic, providing directions and assistance to motorists, investigating motor vehicle accidents, providing emergency assistance at the scene of an accident, gathering information related to traffic, and writing reports.

Although the traffic responsibilities of a police officer may not have the glamour of a criminal investigation, they are critical not only to the safety of the citizens in a community but also to the police image.

The primary objectives of most traffic programs are to obtain the best possible movement of vehicles and pedestrians consistent with safety and to reduce losses from accidents. Chapter 10 describes the functions performed by the traffic officer in more detail.

Community Service/Community Relations

In essence, every action of a police officer has an effect on community relations—either positive or negative. Many larger departments have established separate community relations division or community service divisions to strengthen communication channels between the public and their police department and/or to stress public education programs and crime prevention programs.

> Every action of a police officer is, in effect, a part of community relations. Specific community relations or community service divisions seek to improve communications between the police and the public and/or to promote public education and crime prevention programs.

The importance of community relations and community service will be seen throughout the remainder of the book. Chapter 8 focuses on community relations; Chapter 11 focuses on community service programs and approaches.

Investigation

Although some investigations are carried out by patrol officers, the investigation services division (also sometimes known as the detective bureau) has the responsibility for follow-up investigation. The success of any criminal investigation relies on the cooperative, coordinated efforts of both the patrol and the investigative functions.

> The primary responsibilities of the investigator are to make certain the crime scene is secure, interview witnesses and interrogate suspects, photograph and sketch the crime scene, obtain and identify evidence, and record all facts related to the case for future reference and testimony in court.

To accomplish a successful investigation, police officers must (1) take their time, (2) use an organized approach that is efficient and methodical, as this may be their only chance to observe the scene, (3) recognize the issues and find facts to settle these issues, and (4) determine if a crime has been committed, and, if so, by whom and how. These topics are the focus of Chapter 12.

☑ CHECK POINT

1. What are the two basic organizational categories in a typical police department?
2. Who is the chief law enforcement officer at the local level?
3. What major functions are undertaken in field services?
4. What are the primary tasks performed under patrol?
5. What are the primary tasks performed under traffic?
6. What are the primary tasks performed under community relations/services?
7. What are the primary tasks performed under investigation?

*Answers

1. The two basic organizational categories in a typical police department are field services and administrative services.
2. The chief of police is the chief law enforcement officer at the local level.
3. The major functions undertaken in field services are patrol, traffic, community relations/services, and investigation.
4. Patrol is responsible for providing continuous police service and high visibility of law enforcement. Tasks include crime prevention, response to calls for service, self-initiated activity, and completing administrative functions.
5. Traffic officers are usually responsible for enforcing traffic laws, directing and controlling traffic, providing directions and assistance to motorists, investigating motor vehicle accidents, providing emergency assistance at the scene of an accident, gathering information related to traffic, and writing reports.
6. Although every action of a police officer is, in effect, a part of community relations, specific community relations/services divisions seek to improve communications between the police and the public and to promote public education and crime prevention programs.
7. The primary responsibilities of the investigator are to make certain the crime scene is secure, interview witnesses and interrogate suspects, photograph and sketch the crime scene, obtain and identify evidence, and record all facts related to the case for future reference and testimony in court.

Specialized Officers

In addition to the basic divisions which may exist within a police department, larger departments frequently train officers to perform highly specialized tasks.

> Specialized officers may include evidence technicians, intelligence officers, juvenile officers, vice officers, K-9 officers, tactical forces officers, and reserve officers.

Evidence Technicians. Some police agencies, such as suburban police departments with a complement of forty or more officers, have established the position of evidence technician. The evidence technician is usually a patrol officer who has received extensive classroom and laboratory training in crime scene investigation. In departments which have small detective bureaus and relatively inexperienced officers, this position fills a notable void. The officer has not been relieved of regular patrol duties, but may be called upon to conduct a crime scene investigation. Use of evidence technicians provides better coordination of the preliminary investigation of crimes and increases the probability that the investigation will be successful during the preliminary stage because other patrol officers work with the evidence technician as a team.

Figure 6-4.   Members of an Underwater Recovery Unit, marking for evidence a weapon which was recovered from the bottom of a lake. The gun, sunk beneath the water in mud, weeds, and slime, eluded divers for a full day. It was used in a homicide and discarded in the lake. Reprinted with permission of Capt. Bob Mack, Minneapolis Police Reserve Underwater Recovery Unit.

It is the evidence technician's responsibility to photograph the scene, take all necessary measurements, search the scene for physical evidence, and interview any suspects or witnesses still at the scene.

Evidence technicians carry tools to collect, mark, and identify evidence found at the scene, including cameras, fingerprint equipment, recorders, sketching equipment, and casting or impression material. They may have a vacuum cleaner in the equipment van for gathering evidence from a carpet or the inside of a car.

Through their laboratory training, evidence technicians know precisely what the laboratory can determine from the evidence submitted. They do not have the type of equipment a full-scale crime laboratory possesses, but they do have some equipment to conduct preliminary tests for blood and certain types of narcotics and to identify the classifications of fingerprints.

Their classroom and laboratory training make them valuable assets to the patrol force because when not busy investigating crime scenes, they do regular patrol work.

Intelligence Officers. Most large cities have an intelligence division whose top officer reports directly to the chief of police and whose activities are kept secret from the rest of the police department.

Intelligence units work in two areas. The first area is long-term, ongoing investigations into such criminal activity as illegal sale of guns, payoffs to police officers or politicians, major drug cases, and activities of organized crime. They often work on the same case in cooperation with county, state, and federal investigators.

The second area of intelligence work is investigation of their fellow police officers in the department. For example, the intelligence unit may investigate a complaint of an officer drinking on duty, corruption, or other activities considered "conduct unbecoming a police officer."

Intelligence officers obtain information, buy information, infiltrate criminal groups, solicit data, conduct surveillances, and develop sources of information to keep themselves updated on criminal activity in the community. Any factual information that could lead to an arrest is given to the chief of police who assigns it to another division of the police department for action.

Intelligence officers do not wear uniforms or drive marked cars. They may even use assumed names and fictitious identities. To avoid identification problems, some large police agencies use officers who have just graduated from rookie school, as they are less known on the street.

Intelligence files are separate from regular police records. Persons who are selected as intelligence officers must be highly skilled in investigations, interpersonal relationships, and communications. They must be loyal and have a high degree of integrity and interest in the job.

Juvenile Officers. The police officer is often the first contact a child has when he is in legal trouble. Therefore, it is justifiable and logical to have juvenile police specialists to work primarily with juvenile offenders.

Because most juvenile work is informal and includes powers to release, refer, or detain, juvenile officers must be chosen from the most qualified officers in the department. Specialists in handling juveniles should know the goals and functioning of the juvenile justice system because, in reality, they sit as judges of a youngster's actions and also serve the functions of social workers. Officers who work primarily with juveniles should be highly concerned for the welfare of the child, highly trained in the law, and able to recognize the difference between a neglected, dependent juvenile, and a juvenile delinquent.

Juvenile officers can provide assistance to all other departments within their own agency when juveniles are involved. They are the training officer of the patrol division when it comes to juvenile procedures. Since juveniles commit more than 50% of the local crimes, all officers are juvenile officers much of the time, and it is the uniformed patrol division which has the most contact with these juvenile offenders.

Juvenile officers can also represent the police department in the juvenile's home, school, church, and the juvenile courtroom. Since prevention and control of juvenile delinquency are usually among the objectives of a police department, juvenile officers are a definite asset. They can plan and implement programs through the various service organizations within the community.

The role of the juvenile officer in the community is that of a highly visible specialist who probably has more influence upon the juveniles in the community than any other single person in law enforcement.

Vice Officers.   Vice problems vary from community to community; for example, some sections of the country allow legal prostitution, but many sections of the country do not. Vice officers usually concentrate their efforts on illegal gambling, prostitution, pornography, narcotics, and liquor violations. Sometimes their work is coordinated with intelligence officers.

Vice officers often maintain an unconventional lifestyle, frequently assuming an appearance that does not identify them with the police department. Therefore, these officers frequently are isolated. For example, street "narcs," because of the dangerous atmosphere in which they work, cannot afford to call or be seen with other police officers. Their activities are completely removed from the mainstream of the police department.

In large departments vice, intelligence, and organized crime are often separate units with a staff of officers. In small departments these responsibilities may be handled by a single officer. No matter what the size of the department, vice officers must possess knowledge, courage, integrity, education in city ordinances and state and federal laws, as well as continuous, intensive training on investigative techniques.

Many communities tolerate gambling, but few tolerate prostitution or narcotics; consequently, many vice officers concentrate on removing pimps from circulation and arresting narcotics peddlers. A major problem is discovering who is "behind the scenes" or the organizer of these operations. The narcotic peddler, pimp, and prostitute are highly visible and, therefore, more susceptible to arrest than the "brains" or "boss" of the operation. Because of this situation, vice officers may allow narcotics peddlers, pimps, and prostitutes to operate—to the anger of many citizens—in the hopes of discovering who is responsible for the organization.

Once vice becomes established in a community, more criminals are frequently attracted to the community. They may either believe that the law enforcement is ineffective in the community or that the police already have so many problems with vice that their operations will go unnoticed. If left uncontrolled, vice operations can create other police problems such as embezzlement, burglary, robbery, and murder. A community that allows vice to flourish is often politically corrupt and frequently has corruption within the police department as well.

K-9 Officers.   Man has used dogs in a variety of ways for thousands of years. Dogs have been used in police work in the United States, Europe, and throughout the world for more than fifty years. Today K-9 units exist in more than three hundred towns and cities in the United States.

Today's police dog has had intensive schooling with one officer—his partner. Both spend many weeks under a special trainer. The dog works with only one partner and will respond to only his commands. The police dog's use in most cities falls into five categories: search, attack and capture, drug detection, bomb detection, and as a crime deterrent.

Few cities in the United States use their K-9 corps to control crowds. The police want people to regard the big police dogs not as vicious threats, but as friends who can protect them and help to prevent crime.

Search dogs are specialists, almost like precision instruments. Their highly developed sense of smell can be used for tracing or searching by direct scent. Good results have been obtained in searching large buildings and open areas either in daylight or darkness.

In the summer of 1970 the U.S. Customs Service began an experimental program using drug detection dogs in a drive against narcotics smuggling across the nation's borders. The experiment proved so immediately successful that it was increased as rapidly as the dogs could be trained at the U.S. Customs Dog Training Center in San Antonio, Texas.

The value of these dogs has been demonstrated on many occasions. In San Francisco, an anonymous phone call sent patrolman W. D. Langlois and his "partner," Bourbon, rushing into the main branch of the Crocker Bank where a live bomb cached in a safe-deposit box might detonate at any moment. Ignoring scores of other boxes, the dog dashed straight to the one which contained the explosives. Minutes later the bomb was safely removed.

Tactical Forces Officers.   Special crime tactical forces are immediately available, flexible, and mobile officers used for deployment against any emergency or crime problem. Tactical units supplement the patrol force and may operate selectively in high frequency crime areas. They may suppress burglaries, robberies, or auto thefts. They may be used in hostage situations and where persons have barricaded themselves. They are frequently deployed in sniper situations to protect police officers. In addition, they may perform rescue missions, provide security for visiting dignitaries, and rescue hostages.

They are deployed when the regularly assigned patrol forces cannot effectively cope with an emergency situation, on the basis of current crime pattern analyses, or on information received regarding expected crime activity.

Chicago has been operating a special street crime force since 1956 to reduce crime in certain parts of the city. The Detroit Police Department has two distinct tactical forces, one a crime prevention unit, the other a low-visibility unit designed to reduce street robbery and other violent street crimes. The latter unit specializes in decoy techniques. The Seattle Police Department also has a "decoy squad," a flexible group of officers operating primarily during nighttime hours in high-crime areas or in areas where certain types of specialized crimes are occurring.

The Kansas City, Missouri, Police Department uses its tactical force to provide investigative support. Its squads operate in various counties and cities. Los Angeles has a Special Weapons and Tactics Section (SWAT), which maintains a manpower pool available for activities ranging from directing traffic to suppressing riots.

Tactical force officers receive special training in numerous areas including crowd control, patrol maneuvers, investigative techniques, and stakeout tactics. SWAT team members are highly trained in marksmanship, guerrilla tactics, patrolling, night operations, camouflage and concealment, and the use of chemical agents. They frequently have field exercises to develop discipline and teamwork.

Figure 6-5. Philadelphia Police Department SWAT team in field exercises. Source: Sutor, *Police Operations,*© West Publishing Co., 1976.

Reserve Officers. Some police departments have reserve units to help achieve the department's goals. The reserve officers patrol in uniform and are visible symbols of law enforcement although they cannot write citations. The reserve officers also help in public education programs, informing the public about such things as Operation Identification, drugs, and bike safety. When a crime does occur, the reserves can guard the crime scene while the regular officers continue with their routine or specialized patrol.

☑ CHECK POINT

1. What specialized officers may be used by a police department?

*Answer

1. Specialized officers may include evidence technicians, intelligence officers, vice officers, K-9 officers, tactical forces officers, and reserve officers.

ADMINISTRATIVE SERVICES

Adminstrative services include records and communications, recruitment and training, and provision of special facilities and services.

The two areas which most directly affect the efficient provision of field services are *communications* and *records*.

> Centralized, integrated systems of communications and records increase the effectiveness and efficiency of field services.

Communications

To properly serve the community, police officers must be kept currently and completely informed. They must know how much of each type of crime occurs, such as burglaries, car prowls, malicious destruction of property, and auto thefts. They also have to know where the crimes are occurring. Are they residential burglaries? Shopping center car prowls? What type of property is being vandalized? Is there a pattern? What time are the residential burglaries occurring? What time are car prowls occurring? Nighttime or daytime? From garages or shopping centers? What types of cars are most frequently stolen?

> Current information is usually provided at roll call and by means of radio.

Roll Call.   One of the most important functions of the administrative division in their support of the other units of the police department is keeping members informed of daily police operations and providing administrative instructions and special assignments and tasks to be performed. This is usually done at a roll call session before the officers on the next shift go out into the street.

Up-to-date information is usually contained in a daily bulletin which contains brief summaries of what has transpired in the previous twenty-four hours. Officers are given a short resume of each complaint received and acted upon as well as descriptions of missing and/or wanted persons, descriptions of stolen personal property, and stolen autos.

Radio Communication.   The information provided at roll call is continuously up-dated by radio. Data is available to officers in patrol cars or carrying portable radios. This immediate communication has improved the safety of law enforcement officers and has provided for better allocation of resources.

> Radio is the primary method of transmitting and seeking information between headquarters and units in the field.

The introduction of the small hand-carried portable police radio and the beeper have extended the communications system so that officers on foot may be reached to assist mobile patrol units.

Many police departments operate on several radio frequencies assigned by the Federal Communications Commission (FCC). Police radio frequencies

Figure 6-6.   Typical Daily Bulletin.

MYTOWN U.S.A. POLICE DEPARTMENT   ROLL CALL NFORMATION

DAILY BULLETIN—FROM: 0801 12/17/79 to 0800 12/18/79

Because of inclement weather, officers are cautioned to drive their patrol vehicles carefully.
The accident rate for the police department has increased, and officers are reminded that they will be held responsible for accidents caused by the careless operation of their patrol cars.
The following incidents were reported in the past 24 hours:

Time	Complaint Number	Reported As	Squad	Written Report	Summary and Action Taken
0830	76026953	Radar	555	yes	70 & Sunnydale. No tags issued.
0931	76026954	Medical	802	yes	Mytown Nursing Home, ambulance, heart attack.
1049	76026955	Adm. Detail	850	no	Hq. training rookies.
1142	76026956	Shoplifter	627	yes	Arko Stores, juveniles. Citations issued.
1236	76026957	Bank run	556	no	City Hall.
1345	76026958	Vandalism	802	yes	76 & Heritage Hill, Car window $75.00.
1402	76026959	Accident	555	yes	Emerson & Broadway. PI-ambulance.
1530	76026960	Burglary	627	yes	5124 Grove. TV set. $400.00
1722	76026961	Vandalism	850	yes	9001 Poplar Bridge, Broken window-$50.00.
1852	76026962	Bomb threat	556	yes	St. Henry's Church. Evacuated. No bomb found.
1931	76026963	Found property	555	yes	9700 France. Box of insulation. Placed in property room.
2015	76026964	Accident	575	no	Mytown Shopping Center. Minor damage.
2127	76026965	Theft under $50	802	yes	From car. Clothing-$15.00.
2242	76026966	Public safety	555	no	Kids in construction. Dispersed.
2323	76026967	General assist.	850	no	98 & James. Escort wide load.
0015	76026968	Alarm	555/575	no	Mytown Fabrics. False. Malfunction.
0117	76026969	Gate open	802		Mytown Cemetary. Closed gate.
1245	76026970	Armed robbery	556/627	yes	Mytown Stop & Shop. $40.00 2 males, white, 20-22, blue '77 Vega.
0322	76026971	Window peeper	802/850	no	Unfounded. Mannequin placed in front of window.
0459	76026972	Security check	555	no	Mytown Drugs. Lights on. Swampers.
0639	76026973	Medical	556/802	yes	Officer Mortiki, appendicitis attack. Ambulance.
0740	76026974	Speeders	850	no	85 & Burnham Rd. Gone on arrival.

Officer Mortiki had his appendix removed today. Don't send flowers as he's allergic to pollen. Send money.

attempt to assure the dissemination of information to only the police officer and to maintain the confidentiality of that information. However, a large number of police monitors are sold to the general public, and many retail electronics stores publish lists of police radio frequencies. Therefore, some police jurisdictions have adopted a code transmitting message system which not only helps preserve confidentiality of information but which also conserves airtime and allows emergency calls to be transmitted without undue delay.

The dependability of radio transmissions has improved steadily over the years and has resulted in a great reduction in response time to calls for service or criminal activity.

A typical radio system has four channels providing the capability of (1) contacting car to car in its own jurisdiction, (2) contacting their own dispatchers, (3) contacting another officer patrolling in a different political subdivision through a repeater system, and (4) placing emergency calls. The fourth channel is reserved for such emergencies as roadblocks, disasters, and civil defense messages.

Communications is the lifeline of the police department. The police *dispatcher,* or in some cases the telephone operator, receives all citizens' requests for police service. In some instances the calls come directly to the dispatcher who must act upon them and determine their priority. Some agencies have telephone operators screen the calls prior to giving them to the dispatcher to segregate informational calls from service calls.

Dispatchers have the responsibility for dispatching patrol vehicles to requests for service and knowing what patrol vehicles are ready for assignment. They may also have some records responsibility, for example, making out the original incident complaint report (ICR), noting the time the call was received, the time the patrol vehicle was dispatched, the time it arrived, the time it cleared, and the disposition of the call.

In addition dispatchers may have to handle any walk-in complaints. Some dispatchers also have the added responsibility of monitoring their jails through a closed-circuit television hookup. Such a system exists in many smaller and medium-sized departments today.

In larger agencies several dispatchers handle the incoming calls and give them priority according to their seriousness and the availability of officers to respond. Larger agencies may also have direct and complete integration of police radio with regular telephone service. In this system any call to the police emergency number is automatically channeled to the dispatcher who controls squad cars assigned to the area from which the caller is telephoning.

Some cities have what is called the *911 system*. A person who wishes to call the police dials 911 on the telephone, and a central dispatching office receives the call directly. The 911 system has been implemented in many cities in the United States. The eventual goal is to have this number as the emergency number to call for police service in any city in the United States.

Dispatchers must be dependable, accurate when disseminating information, and efficient so that a quick response can be made to police situations. They must be highly trained in the use of the radio system and the computer as well as familiar with emergency plans, the geographic areas the officers work in, disruptions in communications, and good public relations practices.

☑ CHECK POINT

1. What services are provided by administration?
2. Why are accurate records and communication important to a police department?
3. How do officers receive their current information?
4. What is the primary method of receiving and sending information between headquarters and units in the field?

*Answers

1. Administrative services include records and communications, recruitment and training, and provision of special facilities and services. Of these, records and communications are of most importance to the officer in the field.
2. Accurate records and communication increase the effectiveness and efficiency of field services.
3. Officers receive their current information from roll call and by radio.
4. Radio is the primary method of transmitting and seeking information between headquarters and units in the field. This is done by a radio dispatcher.

Records

The quality of records maintained is directly related to the quality of communications and field services provided. To give proper direction, a police agency must have a sound record system as well as an efficient communication system. Police departments throughout the country vary in their reporting systems and their needs in management control and effective operational control.

The activities of a police department require keeping records, not only of criminal activity, but of all essential activities of the department. As noted by John Griffin (1958, p. 31): "These activities might be regarded as comparable to production or sales reports in a business organization in the sense that they tell what the department has done in a given period of time. Both internal and external data...can be used by the administrative heads of the departments in the measurement of accomplishment and efficiency. These data also keep the public informed of police activity and may do much to create a favorable climate of public opinion."

The complexity of each department's records system is dictated by its needs and problems. Many different types of short transactions that police agencies must handle are continuously in process. Most of the information used to find the perpetrator of a crime would be useless unless it is integrated into a system of records. Unless the data received is recorded logically and systematically, it is impossible to coordinate the facts, especially when they are gathered by a number of persons. For example, uniform patrol may handle a preliminary investigation of a case while the investigative services division may follow up on the report.

Centralization. Services divisions generally should *not* maintain separate records, as the tendency to operate independently makes coordination difficult.

Centralization of records allows the various line functions to be coordinated.

Situations may exist where space limitations do not allow complete centralization of records. However, normally records should be located near the point where complaints are received, radio squads controlled, and prisoners booked.

In a small agency where a dispatcher or desk officer may handle all such duties alone, these functions can readily be observed and their close relationship noted. In a larger organization, the duties may be handled by a major division, with numerous employees performing specialized functions. For example, a radio dispatcher may handle only radio messages, another officer may handle only telephone complaints, and still another may handle over-the-counter information and complaints.

As smaller departments grow, the patterns remain the same, but with an increasing refinement of duties. Centralization fixes record-keeping responsibility and relieves the line-operating units from the responsibility of these administrative functions.

Types of Records.

Police records may be categorized as (1) administrative records, (2) arrest records, (3) identification records, and (4) complaint records.

Administrative records include inventories of police equipment, department memorandums, personnel records, evaluation reports, and all general

Figure 6-7. Typical Offense Report.

ANYTOWN, U.S.A. POLICE DEPT. AN 0272100	Supervisor Approved: S/A 316A Date & Time Report Made:	**OFFENSE REPORT** FOR ALL CRIMES, ATTEMPTS, INVESTIGATIONS & INCIDENTS Page of

Offense or Incident | UOC | Grid No. | Complaint No.

Date & Time Occurred | Address of Occurrence | Name of Firm (if not victim)

Victim (if Firm, Name of Firm & Prop.) | If victim is a person: Sex, Age | Business Address | Business Phone | Home Address | Home Phone

Person Reporting Offense to Police | Business Address | Business Phone | Home Address | Home Phone

Date / Time of Complaint | Reporting Officer (R/O) | Assisting Officer(s) A/O

How Complaint Received: Found by Police ☐ Radio ☐ Citizen ☐ Station ☐ Letter ☐ Phone ☐

If Vehicle Involved, Make, Year, Model | Color | State | License

Name: Owner ☐ Driver ☐ | Address

Quantity | Loss / Suspect: Complete & Detailed Description | Value

Offense Cleared By: Arrest ☐ Exceptionally ☐ Case Unfounded ☐ Inactive (Not Cleared) ☐ Other ☐

PERSONS ARRESTED, SUSPECTS, WITNESSES & ADDITIONAL DETAILED REPORT ON SUPPLEMENTARY information which reflects correspondence or services rendered.

Arrest records contain information obtained from arrested persons when they are booked as well as information about the control and/or release of prisoners and court procedures.

Identification records contain fingerprints, photographs, and other descriptive data obtained from arrested persons.

Complaint records usually contain information related to complaints and reports received by the police from citizens or other agencies as well as any actions initiated by the police. Since police work is public business, it requires accurate records of complaints received and the action taken by the police. Complaints may be criminal or noncriminal in nature; they may involve lost property, damaged property, traffic accidents, medical emergencies, or a missing person. Requests for police assistance may also involve robberies, murders, burglaries, vandalism, or children playing in the streets or cats up in trees. Although most complaints are minor, each must be treated with personal concern to the complainant and as a matter of importance to the police.

Most police agencies have a procedure for recording complaint information either on sheets or data processing cards. Initial complaint records (ICRs) are filled out on all complaints or requests for service received by the dispatcher or a police officer.

Information on the ICR normally shows the complainant, victim, address of each, type of complaint, time of day, day of week, the officer handling the complaint or request, the area of the community where it occurred, the disposition, whether there was an arrest, and whether further follow-up reports or further investigation is justified by the investigative services division.

Initial complaint reports may be numbered sequentially and coded for filing or for placing into a computer for later retrieval. For example, a street robbery may be coded 005, a nighttime burglary coded 023, and shoplifting coded 047, etc.

In the case of auto thefts, missing persons, recovered property, or an arrest, further reports will be made separately such as missing persons report, property recovered report, or the fingerprinting and booking of an arrested suspect report.

To minimize records work, some police departments use a combined complaint form containing a variety of information such as the initial complaint report, a missing-persons report, a stolen property report, an arrest report, a juvenile report, a case report sheet, an auto theft report, and so on. The disadvantages of the combined complaint form far outweigh the advantages. The retrieval of one category of information is difficult. In addition, a combined report tends to limit the amount of information an officer puts in the report.

An efficient reporting system requires separate reports for the initial and the follow-up investigation as well as separate reports for accidents, missing persons, wanted persons, auto thefts, stolen and recovered property, arrests, juveniles involved in any type of incident, photographic files, fingerprint files, and reports of the confiscation of property from prisoners. These reports will be disucssed in greater detail in Chapter 9.

Benefits of Efficient Records System. Efficient records systems are a vital management tool which aid in assessing department accomplishments, in developing budget justifications, in determining additional manpower needs, and in evaluating the performance of officers as well as the attainment of objectives and goals.

Evaluation of carefully kept records will generally reflect needs in training, recruitment, public relations, allocation of resources, and general effectiveness. The periodic evaluation of records by management in planning and research has allowed police agencies to provide better service to the public and, in turn, they have gained public support.

Computerized Information (NCIC). Many informational tools available to police agencies today are the result of the introduction of random-access storage and retrieval systems and computers into the police field. Although only a few large police agencies currently have access to their own computer information, in the future such information will connect all law enforcement agencies in the country in a vast communications network.

A step in this direction was taken in 1967 when the FBI implemented its computerized crime information storage system, the National Crime Information Center (NCIC).

> The National Crime Information Center allows all police agencies in the country to have access to the computerized files of the FBI.

Under this sytem, each state has a number of computer terminals which interface with the FBI master computer in Washington D.C. The computer contains records of stolen property such as guns, stolen autos, and office machines, and, in some cases, persons who are wanted on warrants.

The NCIC computer receives its information from other federal law enforcement agencies and from state and local law enforcement agencies. The NCIC makes it possible for a law enforcement officer in Texas who stops a suspicious person or car from California, to contact the dispatcher by radio or teleprinter requesting information. The dispatcher can make an inquiry to the computer in Texas which, in a matter of seconds, makes an inquiry on the status of the individual and/or the car to the NCIC terminal in Washington. The police officer can be quickly informed if the car has been stolen or if an arrest warrant is outstanding on the individual in the car.

The great volume of information contained in various state and federal computers is another aid given to police officers in maintaining up-to-date records systems.

Privacy of Records. The most sensitive aspect of computerized or manual records on persons arrested and related information about them is the possibility of including in the file unsubstantiated information which might contain derogatory, incomplete, or incorrect information—information which disseminated to the wrong person could prove damaging and provide cause for a civil action against the police agency. In addition, police agencies often tend to retain information longer than necessary.

As a result, by authority of the Omnibus Crime Control and Safe Streets

Act of 1968 which was amended by the Crime Control Act of 1973, the Department of Justice has issued regulations to assure that criminal history record information, wherever it appears, is collected, stored, and disseminated in a way that insures the completeness, integrity, accuracy, and security of such information and that protects individual privacy.

> A Data Privacy Act regulates the use of confidential and private information on individuals in the records, files, and processes of a state and its political subdivisions.

The regulations apply to all state and local agencies and individuals collecting, storing, or disseminating criminal history information processed either manually or automated.

The LEAA has required each state to submit to them operational procedures to assure completeness and accuracy of records, the limitations on dissemination, the general policies on use and dissemination, with emphasis on security and audits, and verification of their adherence to these regulations.

Some law enforcement agencies have expressed dissatisfaction with provisions relating to law enforcement records and with the dissemination of criminal history information, particularly for employment purposes.

Because states have been slow in passing Privacy Act Legislation, a certain amount of confusion often occurs among those who try to abide by the Department of Justice regulations. The effect of some state legislation has been that in the absence of an emergency classification, almost all information or data a police agency has kept on individuals legally must be made available to anyone requesting it. This unfortunate situation has been avoided in other states.

Minnesota, a progressive state in handling private data, passed legislation in 1974 and 1976* to regulate the use of confidential and private information on individuals in the records, files, and processes of the state and its political subdivisions. The law provides three categories of information (termed *data* in the law): private, confidential, and public. Various regulations have been set for each type of data.

Private data is data which by state or federal law or emergency classification of the State Commissioner of Administration is *not* public but is accessible to the person who is the subject of the information. The term *private data* (and *confidential data* as well), does not include arrest information that is reasonably contemporaneous with an arrest or incarceration (except data made private, confidential, or nonpublic under the law relating to juveniles or any other statute). Police probation records of juveniles are in this category and may not be disclosed to the public except by order of the juvenile court. The social security number of employees is also classified as private data. The law does not provide for making data private by charter or ordinance.

---

*Data Privacy Act (Laws 1974), Ch. 479 as amended by Laws 1975, Ch. 401 and Laws 1976, Ch. 283, coded as Minnesota Statute 15.162 to 15.169.

Confidential data includes data collected by a civil or criminal investigative agency as part of an active investigation for the purpose of commencing a legal action.

Public data includes all information which is accessible to the public in accordance with the public records law. In effect, the term means all information excluded from the private and confidential data categories including (1) the name, age, and address of the arrested persons, (2) the nature of the charge, (3) the time and place of the arrest, (4) the identity of the arresting agency, and (5) information as to whether an individual has been jailed and the location of the jail.

Emergency classifications are also provided for by the law. Any police agency may apply to the Commissioner of Administration for permission to classify particular data or types of data (except arrest information) as private or confidential. An application may cover all types of confidential or private data. The application itself, however, is classed as public data. To receive an emergency classification as private or confidential, the information must meet three standards:

—No statute either allows or forbids classification of the data as private or confidential.

—The data has been treated as either private or confidential by custom and is recognized by other similar state agencies or other similar political subdivisions and by the public.

—A compelling need exists for immediate emergency classification which, if not granted, could adversely affect the public interest or the health, safety, well-being, or reputation of the subject of the data.

A police agency or a city violating the data privacy act is liable, in Minnesota, to a person who suffers any resulting damage. The person damaged may bring an action against the police agency or the responsible authority to cover any damages sustained, plus costs and reasonable attorney's fees. If the violation is willful, the city is also liable for exemplary damages of not less than $100 nor more than $1,000 for each violation. (M.S.466.03).

The gathering of information by law enforcement personnel facilitates the formulation of effective strategies against criminals whose operations often go interstate. However, both privacy and freedom of information legislation can severely restrict the flow of free information between law enforcement agencies. The Privacy Act of 1974, for example, requires the purging and sealing of records, thereby preventing different governmental agencies from collecting an inclusive criminal history on any one individual.

In addition, the Federal Privacy Act restricts government surveillance activities and prevents the public, the actual victims of criminals, from knowing what the actual threats are. Freedom of information legislation also can impede law enforcement. Unless law enforcement data are specifically exempted, law enforcement files can be examined by persons under investigation who could then destroy evidence or otherwise neutralize an investigation.

Where law enforcement data is not specifically exempted by law, a request for emergency classification of certain information should be made either to the courts or the state's Administration Department. Emergency classification could be requested in the accumulation of evidence on organized crime, prostitution, or other related law violations prior to prosecution.

☑ CHECK POINT

1. Why is centralization of records encouraged in police departments?
2. What types of reports are used in most police departments?
3. What is the NCIC and how is it of value to the police officer in the field?
4. What is required by the Data Privacy Act?

*Answers

1. Centralization of records allows the various line functions to be coordinated.
2. The types of reports used in most police departments may be categorized as administrative, arrest, identification, or complaint records.
3. The NCIC is the National Crime Information Center which allows all police agencies in the country to have access to the computerized files of the FBI.
4. A Data Privacy Act regulates the use of confidential and private information on individuals in the records, files, and processes of a state and its political subdivisions.

COORDINATION OF ADMINISTRATIVE AND FIELD SERVICES

The importance of accurate, complete records and an efficient communication system used in conjunction with effective field services may be seen in the following case.

Police in Mytown were faced with a rash of automobile thefts. After interviewing the victims of stolen autos, including shoppers, employees, and salespersons of a shopping center, investigators determined that the vehicles were being stolen between the hours of eight and ten A.M. on Mondays, Wednesdays, and Fridays and that they were being recovered in the parking lots of the Mytown University.

A team of investigators with portable radios and unmarked vehicles began a surveillance at 7:30 A.M. on a Monday. Noting a suspicious young girl in her twenties looking into vehicles at 8:30 A.M., the surveillance team was alerted. One of the investigators, with a portable radio carried in a shopping bag, followed the girl into the shopping center. She went into several stores, exited each quickly, went up one escalator, down another, and back out into the parking lot where she looked into several other cars. She then went back into the shopping center and repeated her previous actions. When she returned to the parking lot a second time, still followed by the investigator, she went directly to a 1977 Buick, started the vehicle, and drove away.

The investigator immediately radioed the surveillance team and gave them the car's license number, description, and direction of travel. The vehicle and suspect were stopped at a road block on the perimeter of the shopping center. A vehicle registration of the license number indicated that she was not the owner of the car. Further, she had not been given permission by the lawful owner to use it.

After being taken to the police station, she stated that she stole the vehicle to get to school. She confessed to stealing eleven cars, all with keys left in them. She went up and down the isles of the parked vehicles until she found a car with the keys in it. Then she went into the shopping center to avoid suspicion before returning to drive the car away.

The information contained in an efficient record system and an effective communications system allowed the Mytown Police Department to place the best available manpower in the most strategic area at the most opportune time, thus making an arrest and preventing further auto thefts, at least by one college student taking advantage of a free ride to school every day.

SUMMARY

Although numerous federal and state agencies are directly involved in law enforcement, the ultimate responsibility is usually at the local level. It is here that the goals of law enforcement are initiated, based on what the citizens of the individual community perceive to be their most pressing needs.

Goals are the broad, general, desired outcome of a program—what the ultimate aim of the program is. Objectives are specific, measurable means of achieving the goals. Tasks are specific activities which contribute to reaching the objectives, and, therefore, the goal.

Among the common goals of police departments are a commitment to preserve the peace, to protect civil rights and civil liberties, to enforce the law, to prevent crime, and to provide services. To accomplish these goals, the police department states objectives—the means for accomplishing them. These objectives facilitate planning, assignment of responsibility, and evaluation of progress toward goals. After objectives have been stated, the specific tasks or steps which must be taken to accomplish the objective are defined. When specific tasks are directly tied to objectives which lead to achievement of the desired goals of the department, even the most seemingly insignificant task can take on importance and meaning.

Police officers work within the context of the goals, objectives, and tasks defined by their department. They also work within the basic organizational structure of their department which, most often, is divided into two sections: field services and administrative services. Tasks and personnel to accomplish them are assigned to one of these two sections.

Overseeing the entire police department is the chief of police, the primary law enforcement officer at the local level, who coordinates both the field services and the administrative services.

Within the field services provided in a police department are patrol, traffic, community service, and investigation. Sometimes these are specialized departments; sometimes the services are provided by a single department. In addition, many police departments, particularly the larger departments, have specialized officers such as vice officers and juvenile officers.

Administrative services provide support for field services, including records and communications, recruitment and training, and special facilities and services. Most current information is conveyed to police officers at roll call or by radio, the primary method of transmitting and seeking information between headquarters and units in the field.

In addition to direct communication, police officers also rely upon information contained in the department's records. Centralization of these records allows the various line functions to be coordinated. Among the types of records the police officer may use are administrative, arrest, identification, and complaint records. Further, the NCIC provides all police agencies in the country access to the computerized files of the FBI.

Access to information is not always unlimited, however. A Data Privacy Act regulates the use of confidential and private information on individuals in the records, files, and processes of a state and its political subdivisions.

APPLICATION

A. Identify each of the following as to whether it is a goal, objective, or task:

1. The chief of police issues a statement that traffic accidents must be reduced the following year.
2. Officers execute a search warrant.
3. Officer Sigafoos meets secretly with a narcotics informant.
4. The mayor of Mytown makes a public statement that the police department will clear the streets of prostitutes.
5. Officer Hoffman is instructed by his supervisor to clock speeders on Highway 101 and 96th Street.
6. The Research and Planning officer presents a plan to reduce traffic accidents.
7. Patrol officers conduct surveillances on known burglars in their areas.
8. The chief of police requests two additional officers in his budget to reduce the crime rate.
9. The Research and Planning officer evaluates crime statistics over a six-month period.
10. The Mytown special crime detail uses a decoy plan for two weeks to entice pursesnatchers to reduce these crimes.

B. Specify which field service personnel in a large police department would be assigned in the following instances (patrol, traffic, community relations/services, investigation, or specialized officers):

1. Search a crime scene
2. Conduct an Operation Identification Program
3. Search a warehouse with a dog
4. Conduct a police department open house
5. Conduct an accident investigation
6. Direct traffic at a sporting event
7. Classify fingerprints
8. Answer a medical emergency call
9. Interview a witness
10. Answer a burglary call

*Answers

A. 1. Goal 3. Task 5. Task 7. Task 9. Objective
    2. Task 4. Goal 6. Objective 8. Objective 10. Objective

B. 1. Investigation (patrol) 5. Traffic 8. Patrol
    2. Community relations/service 6. Traffic 9. Investigation
    3. Specialized officer 7. Specialized officer 10. Patrol
    4. Community relations/service

DISCUSSION QUESTIONS

1. What are the goals of our police department? What objectives have they stated for reaching these goals?
2. Does our police department have a computerized record-keeping system? If not, what is the closest link with the National Crime Information Center?
3. Which is more important: field services or administrative services?
4. How has communication between the officer in the field and headquarters changed in the last hundred years?
5. What affect does the Data Privacy Act have on investigations of individuals involved in organized crime?
6. What does the listing of activities in the sample roll call indicate about the "typical" day of a police officer?

REFERENCES

The challenge of crime in a free society. President's Commission on Law Enforcement and Administration of Justice. Washington, D.C.: U.S. Government Printing Office, February, 1967.

Chapman, S. G. and Johnston, Col. T. E. *The police heritage in England and America.* Institute for Community Development and Services, Continuing Education Service, Michigan State University, 1962.

Folley, V. L. *American law enforcement.* Boston: Holbrook Press, 1973.

Gay, W. G. and Schack, S. *Prescriptive package: Improving patrol productivity. Volume 1 Routine patrol.* Washington, D.C.: Office of Technology Transfer, National Institute of Law Enforcement and Criminal Justice, Law Enforcement Assistance Adminsitration, U.S. Department of Justice (Grant Number 76-NI-00-0055, July, 1977).

Griffin, J. *Statistics essential for police efficiency.* Springfield, IL: Charles C. Thomas Company, 1958.

Iannone, N. F. *Principles of police patrol.* New York: McGraw Hill, 1975.

Koehler, W. R. *Koehler method of guard dog training.* New York: Howell Book House, 1967.

Martin, T. C. Seattle Police Department's "decoy squad," *FBI law enforcement bulletin,* February 1978, pp. 17-20.

More, H. W. Jr. *Texting and readings: The American police.* Criminal Justice Series, St. Paul: West Publishing Company, 1976.

Orbann, A. *Dogs against crime.* New York: The John Day Company, 1968.

Schack, S. and Gay, W. G. *Prescriptive package. Improving patrol productivity. Volume II Specialized patrol.* Washington, D.C.: Office of Technology Transfer, National Institute of Law Enforcement and Criminal Justice, Law Enforcement Assistance Administration, U.S. Department of Justice (Grant Number 76-NI-00-0055, July, 1977).

Sutor, A. P. *Police operations.* St. Paul: West Publishing Company, 1976.

Wilson, O. W. and McLaren, R. C. *Police administration.* (4th ed.) New York: McGraw-Hill, 1977.

As our society has developed and expanded, so has to the role of the police officer. Today's law enforcement officer needs numerous mental, physical, personal and professional skills.

The Modern
Law Enforcement Officer 7
A Complex Role

DO YOU KNOW□ □ □

- ☐ How the police officer's roles relate to the "people"?
- ☐ What five basic roles the police officer must play?
- ☐ What services can reasonably be expected from a police officer?
- ☐ What demands are placed upon a police officer in fulfilling these roles?
- ☐ What special physical, intellectual, and emotional skills are required to fulfill the roles professionally?
- ☐ How to explain to a lay person the complex role of the modern police officer?

*Public officers are the servants of the
people to execute the laws which
people have made.*
—Grover Cleveland

INTRODUCTION

Most people have a general idea of what a police officer is and does.
Many people also have very specific ideas about what a police officer should
be and do. The clearly defined roles of enforcing the laws and preserving the
peace, established centuries ago, have become more complex, and additional
roles have been added to the traditionally accepted roles.

The "Law Enforcement Code of Ethics" sets forth the currently accepted
roles of the police officer as well as how these roles are to be carried out—the
dual focus of this chapter.

THE POLICE OFFICER AND THE PEOPLE

You learned earlier that police authority comes from the people—their
laws and institutions. Police officers are ultimately responsible to the public
they serve, and they usually recruit their officers from among them.

Although the Tenth Amendment reserves police power for state and local
governments, these governments must adhere to the principles of the Constitution and the Bill of Rights as well as to federal and state statutes. Police
officers are not only a part of their community, they are also part of the state
and federal government that provides their formal base of authority as well as
a part of the state and federal criminal justice system that determines society's
course in deterring lawbreakers and rehabilitating offenders.

Figure 7-1. Sources of Police Authority.

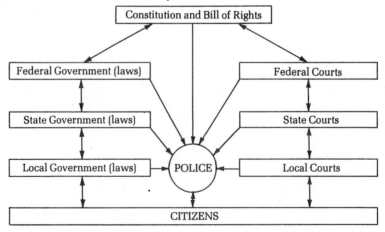

Note that between the citizens, governments, and courts, the arrows go
two ways. Not only are the people ultimately responsible for the establishment of governments and courts, they also elect the representatives who serve

there. The citizens also directly influence the police. To a large extent, the specific goals and priorities of the police are established by what the community wants. For example, a community might want more patrols at night, stricter enforcement of traffic regulations during rush hour, or reduced enforcement for certain "crimes" such as speeding.

Priorities are often more influenced by the desires of the policed than by any other consideration. Because the success of the police depends heavily upon public support, the wishes of the citizens must be listened to and considered.

> The people largely determine the role of the police and give them their authority to fulfill this role. Their support is vital.

In addition, because the police are highly visible representatives of local government and are on duty twenty-four hours a day, people often call upon them for services which they are not, specifically, required to perform. Other agencies might be providing these services, but people do not know of them. For example, if a woman seeks help in dealing with a drunk husband (he is not abusing her; he is just drunk), a drug counselor, minister, or social worker might be the appropriate person to call. The woman, however, often doesn't know this. Since the police officers' reactions to requests for help affect the amount of respect received and promote a cooperative relationship with the public, police officers usually respond as helpfully as possible, even when the matter is technically civil and outside their responsibility (and sometimes their expertise).

BASIC ROLES OF THE POLICE OFFICER

Since the citizens of a community have such a great influence on the role of the police within the community, many differences exist in roles performed by police officers in different geographic localities. Generally, however, five basic roles are performed.

> Five basic roles of most police officers are:
>   To enforce laws.
>   To preserve the peace.
>   To prevent crimes.
>   To protect civil rights and civil liberties.
>   To provide services.

These roles often overlap. For example, officers intervening in a barroom fight may not only enforce a law by arresting a suspect for assault, they may maintain order, prevent others from becoming involved in the fight, protect the civil rights and civil liberties of the suspect, the victim, and the bystanders, and provide emergency service to an injured victim.

Success or·failure in fulfilling each role directly affects the success or failure of fulfilling the other roles. Although we have listed five "roles" normally performed by police officers, in reality, it is a single role comprised of numerous responsibilities.

Law Enforcement—Crime Repression

The term *law enforcement officer* underscores the central importance of this long-accepted responsibility as does the quotation at the beginning of the chapter. Historically, enforcement of laws has been the prime responsibility of police officers. However, this long-accepted role has become increasingly complex. Not only must decisions be made as to what laws to enforce, but also the police have become an integral part of the criminal justice system, responsible not only for apprehending offenders, but for assisting in their prosecution as well.

> Police officers are responsible for enforcing laws and for assisting in the prosecution of offenders.

The stereotype of the police officer emphasizes the role of "crime fighter," often to the exclusion of all others, perhaps because it is the most active and dangerous role a police officer performs.

In enforcing laws, police officers perform many functions: investigating offenses, interrogating suspects, interviewing witnesses, conducting searches, acting upon leads, participating in stake-outs, apprehending suspects, recovering stolen property, testifying in court, suppressing riots, combatting organized crime, and patrolling to discover crimes in progress.

The patrol function is central to law enforcement. Not only may law enforcement officers encounter crimes in progress, they may also encounter "suspicious" circumstances which may be crime-related. Questioning of a suspicious person might lead to arrests for outstanding warrants, possession of narcotics or concealed weapons, burglary, and other serious crimes.

Because each community and each state have numerous statutes to be enforced and limited resources, full enforcement of all laws is never possible. Even if it were, it is questionable whether full enforcement would be in keeping with legislative intent or the people's wishes. The police can, do, and must exercise *discretion* in which laws to enforce; that they cannot enforce all laws at all times must be accepted by both the police officer and the public. More on discretion in a few pages.

Each police department must decide which reported crimes to actively investigate and to what degree, as well as which unreported crimes to seek out and to what degree. The law does not set priorities; it simply defines crimes, classifies them as felonies or misdemeanors, and assesses penalties for them. The police department sets its own priorities, based on citizen's needs.

Usually police departments concentrate the majority of their resources on "serious" crimes—those which pose the greatest threat to public safety and/or cause the greatest economic losses (the Index Crimes). From that point on, priorities are usually determined by past police experience, the wishes and expectations of the citizens, and the resources available.

Engaging in law enforcement activities such as arresting armed robbers and using force when needed are sanctioned by statute and public opinion. On the other hand, if police become involved in conflicts which do not involve a "crime," such as loud domestic arguments, their action may be viewed as interference. Even within the traditional role of enforcing laws, decisions must be made as to what is proper and what is not.

Further, the police officer's responsibility does not end with the enforcement of a law and the apprehension of a suspect. In effect, when the police arrest an offender, they have initiated the criminal justice process. The offender's guilt must then be determined in court. The police officer plays a key role in assisting the prosecutor in preparing the case and often is called upon to present evidence in court (the focus of Chapter 15). Unfortunately, since police are in the closest contact with the public, they are often blamed for failures in the criminal justice system. For example, an assault victim whose attacker is found innocent in court may feel resentment not only against the court, but against the police.

The release of a suspect from custody for lack of sufficient evidence, the failure of a prosecutor to take a case to trial, or the failure of the corrections system to reform a convict prior to parole or release, all directly affect the role police officers must play as well as their public image. And the public image of the police officer is critical when you consider that a large percent of police work is in direct response to citizen complaints or reports. In fact, members of the community may be the single most important factor in the total law enforcement effort.

Preserving the Peace

The role of preserving the peace has also long been traditionally accepted by law enforcement officers. They have the legal authority to arrest individuals for disturbing the peace or for disorderly conduct.

> Police are responsible for preserving the peace.

Police are often called upon to intervene in noncriminal conduct such as that which occurs at public events (crowd control), in social relations (domestic disputes), and in traffic control (parking, pedestrians) to maintain "law and order." They frequently help people solve problems that they can't cope with alone.

Often such problems, if unresolved, could result in crime. For example, loud parties, unruly crowds, or disputes between members of a family, business partners, a landlord and tenant, or a businessman and his customer might result in bodily harm—assault. Studies indicate that domestic violence frequently leads to homicide. In Detroit, one-half of all homicides in 1974 resulted from domestic disputes. In New York City, as many people have been killed each year for the last three years by family members as have been killed in Northern Ireland (King, 1977).

The police officer's effectiveness in actually preserving the peace will largely be determined by public acceptance of this role. Often if a police officer simply asks a landlord to allow a tenant access to his apartment or asks the host of a loud party to turn down his stereo, this is enough. Mere police presence may reduce the possibility of a crime—at least temporarily.

If the citizens respect the police and accept their suggestions, it is likely that police officers will be successful in preserving the peace. On the other hand, if the citizens do not accept this function and do not respect the police, the presence of police may provoke crime and violence. Here, as in the enforcement of laws, public support is vital.

Crime Prevention

Crime prevention is closely related to law enforcement and preservation of the peace. If the "peace" has been kept, crime has, in effect, been prevented. Crime prevention differs from peace-keeping and law-enforcing in that it attempts to eliminate potentially dangerous or criminal situations.

A routine patrol might not only discover a crime in progress, it might also deter or prevent crimes from being committed. If the police are very visible in a community, it is likely that many crimes will be prevented. However, this is extremely difficult to prove since we don't know what crimes might have been committed if the police were not present. Even the best patrol system will have little effect on preventing crimes of passion or crimes committed in private homes.

> Police officers are responsible for attempting to prevent a crime.

Notice the word *attempting*. These efforts will often be unsuccessful. Just as police officers cannot be expected to enforce all the laws at all times, they cannot be expected to prevent all crimes from occurring.

Crime prevention activities frequently undertaken by police officers include working with juveniles, cooperating with probation and parole personnel, educating the public, instigating "Operation Identification" programs, and providing visible evidence of police authority. In addition, many of the community services often provided by police departments (discussed in Chapter 11) aid considerably in crime prevention.

Protection of Constitutional Rights

The first paragraph of the "Law Enforcement Code of Ethics" concludes with the statement that a law enforcement officer has a fundamental duty "to respect the Constitutional rights of all men to liberty, equality, and justice," the rights and liberties described in Chapter 2. Civil rights and civil liberties have gained increasing recognition within the last decade.

As noted by the National Advisory Commission on Criminal Justice Standards and Goals (*The Police* 1973, p. 9): "Any definition of the police role must acknowledge that the Constitution imposes restrictions on the power of the

Figure 7-2. Law Enforcement Code of Ethics. Reprinted by permission of the International Association Chiefs of Police.

SECTION VI
LAW ENFORCEMENT PERSONNEL

Law Enforcement Code of Ethics

As a Law Enforcement Officer, my fundamental duty is to serve mankind; to safeguard lives and property; to protect the innocent against deception, the weak against oppression or intimidation, and the peaceful against violence or disorder; and to respect the Constitutional rights of all men to liberty, equality and justice.

I will keep my private life unsullied as an example to all; maintain courageous calm in the face of danger, scorn, or ridicule; develop self-restraint; and be constantly mindful of the welfare of others. Honest in thought and deed in both my personal and official life, I will be exemplary in obeying the laws of the land and the regulations of my department. Whatever I see or hear of a confidential nature or that is confided to me in my official capacity will be kept ever secret unless revelation is necessary in the performance of my duty.

I will never act officiously or permit personal feelings, prejudices, animosities or friendships to influence my decisions. With no compromise for crime and with relentless prosecution of criminals, I will enforce the law courteously and appropriately without fear or favor, malice or ill will, never employing unnecessary force or violence and never accepting gratuities.

I recognize the badge of my office as a symbol of public faith, and I accept it as a public trust to be held so long as I am true to the ethics of the police service. I will constantly strive to achieve these objectives and ideals, dedicating myself before God to my chosen profession . . . law enforcement.

legislatures to prohibit protected conduct, and to some extent defines the limits of police authority in the enforcement of established laws."

> Police are responsible for protecting citizens' constitutional rights.

The Commission goes on to state, however, that (1973, p. 9): "concern for the constitutional rights of accused persons processed by the police has tended to obscure the fact that the police have an affirmative obligation to protect all persons in the free exercise of their rights. The police must provide safety for persons exercising their constitutional right to assemble, to speak freely, and to petition for redress of their grievances."

Many citizens are angered when a suspect's rights prevent prosecution of the case. They begin to have doubts about the criminal justice system. However, should these same individuals find themselves in the position of being suspected of a crime, they, doubtless, would expect their rights to be fully protected. (Recall the Magna Carta and how these rights began.) It was Sir John Fortescue who said, "Indeed, one would rather twenty guilty persons should escape the punishment of death than one innocent person should be executed." "Civilized" countries must guarantee all citizens, even those perceived as unworthy of such protection, their constitutional rights or there is danger of a "police state."

The authority, goals, and methods of the police must promote individual liberty, public safety, and social justice. The role of protecting civil rights and civil liberties is perceived by some as the single most important role of the police officer. As a case in point, the National Advisory Commission on Criminal Justice Standards and Goals states (1973, p. 9): "If the overall purposes of the police service in today's society were narrowed to a single objective, that objective would be to preserve the peace in a manner consistent with the freedoms secured by the Constitution."

Provide Services

In addition to enforcing laws, preserving the peace, assisting in preventing crime, and protecting civil rights and liberties, the police are often called upon to provide additional services to their community.

This role is acknowledged in the first sentence of the "Law Enforcement Code of Ethics": "As a law enforcement officer, my fundamental duty is to serve mankind...." Many police departments have as their motto: "Serve and Protect."

However, as society has become more complex, so have the types of "service" requested. Many new requests (often demands) are made upon the police because of their authority. Included among the numerous functions the police may perform in providing services are giving information, directions, and advice; counseling and referring; licensing and registering vehicles; intervening in domestic arguments; working with neglected children; rendering emergency medical or rescue services; dealing with alcoholics and the mentally ill; finding lost children; dealing with stray animals; and controlling traffic and crowds. In addition, many police departments provide community education programs regarding crime, drugs, safety, and the like.

> Police may be responsible for providing services.

Notice the word *may* in the above role definition. Considerable disagreement exists regarding what type and amount of services the police should provide.

On one hand, individuals like Bernard Garmire (1972, pp. 3-7) feel that this role should *not* be performed by police officers. He contends that to expect police to perform the two conflicting roles of law enforcement and community service is wrong:

> *Even if the numbers of policemen were vastly increased, even if their training were improved, and even if their resources were expanded, I still submit that they could not perform both roles—so sharply do they conflict and so different are the skills required. One person simply cannot reasonably be expected to master both roles intellectually and jump psychologically from one to another in an instant's notice....If we are to restore any semblance of faith in the police by the public—and the police themselves— we must begin first by defining the police role very carefully so that it does not distort reality ... by fostering the belief that police ... could function as a gigantic surrogate service agency to the community handling all the needs of the people all the time.*

Garmire critizes sharply the view that the police department is a "social agency of last resort—particularly after 5:00 P.M. and on weekends."

On the other hand, many contend that provision of social services is critical to effectively perform the other functions expected of police officers, a position supported in the Task Force Report of the President's Commission of Law Enforcement and Administration of Justice (1967, p. 14):

> *Proposals to relieve the police of what are essentially social services have also been lacking in their consideration of the relationship of such services to the incidence of more serious crimes. Domestic disturbances, for example, often culminate in a serious assault or a homicide. The down-and-out drunk is almost a certain victim of a theft if he is left to lie on the street and has any article of value on him. The streetwalking prostitute may, in one sense, be primarily a social problem, but many streetwalkers engage regularly in arranging the robbery of their patrons as a supplement to their income.*
>
> *It might be desirable for agencies other than the police to provide community services that bear no relationship to crime or potential crime situations. But the failure of such agencies to develop and the relationship between the social problems in question and the incidence of crime suggest that the police are likely to remain, for some time, as the only 24-hour-a-day, 7-day-a-week agency that is spread over an entire city.*

In between these two positions regarding the social service function of the police is that of the National Advisory Commission on Criminal Justice Standards and Goals (1973, pp. 14-15). They recognize that police are often inappropriately asked to perform functions which might better be performed by another agency of the government—usually because they are the only government representatives available around the clock and because they have the resources and the authority to use force if necessary. They also note, however, that in many small cities and towns, the police services provided (even though considered by some to be inappropriate "social services") could *not* be provided by any other agencies. They conclude:

> The concept of a flexible police role, adjustable to local conditions, does not require police agencies to accept submissively the imposition of duties basically unrelated to their essential purpose. On the contrary, effective and efficient policing requires that police agencies restrict themselves as far as possible to the provision of services that directly or indirectly serve to achieve their basic objectives of preserving the peace and protecting constitutional guarantees.
>
> Thus, while it may be appropriate in certain instances for a police agency to perform a nonpolice function, such as providing ambulance service or collecting stray animals, it must be undertaken only after a full public examination of its effect on other and more basic services provided by the agency....Services have to be placed into perspective with all other services provided by the police, and considered as part of the local police role in determining objectives and priorities for the delivery of all police services.

Many police agencies have provided personnel with information to refer persons in need to the proper agency. For example, since New York City began using a citywide "911" emergency number, telephone calls for nonpolice municipal services have decreased dramatically. Police officers in Washington, D.C. use the *Referral Handbook of Social Services*, which indexes available governmental and private services by problem and agency. Police in Milwaukee, Wisconsin, have a comprehensive directory of almost five hundred community agencies and organizations.

What is of primary importance is that people who need help receive it; who provides the help is secondary. However, since many people are likely to first turn to the police for help, the police officer must be prepared to either provide the help or to refer the person to an agency which can provide it.

☑ CHECK POINT

1. How do the roles of a police officer relate to the "people"?
2. What are the five basic roles usually performed by police officers?
3. State what services you feel can reasonably be expected from a police officer.

*Answers

1. The people largely determine the role of the police and give them their authority to fulfill this role. Their support is vital.
2. The five basic roles most often performed by police officers are to enforce laws, preserve the peace, prevent crime, protect civil rights and civil liberties, and provide services.
3. Answers to this question will depend upon your own opinion as to what type of services the police should provide. You should be able to give reasons for your answer.

HOW THE ROLES ARE PERFORMED

Look again at the two middle paragraphs of the "Law Enforcement Code of Ethics":

I will keep my private life unsullied as an example to all; maintain courageous calm in the face of danger, scorn, or ridicule; develop self-restraint; and be constantly mindful of the welfare of others. Honest in thought and deed in both my personal and official life, I will be exemplary in obeying the laws of the land and the regulations of my department. Whatever I see or hear of a confidential nature or that is confided to me in my official capacity will be kept ever secret unless revelation is necessary in the performance of my duty.

I will never act officiously or permit personal feelings, prejudices, animosities or friendships to influence my decisions. With no compromise for crime and with relentless prosecution of criminals, I will enforce the law courteously and appropriately without fear or favor, malice or ill will, never employing unnecessary force or violence and never accepting gratuities.

Not only are police officers expected to enforce laws, preserve the peace, prevent crimes, protect constitutional rights, and perform community services, they are expected to do so in an impeccable, professional manner. As noted by Dwight Dalbey of the FBI (James, 1968, p.104):

We expect of a police officer the wisdom of Solomon in understanding the law, the strength of Sampson in arresting a criminal, the gentleness of St. Francis of Assisi in repelling a riot, the patience of Job in dealing with each of us, and the moral purity of Caesar's wife in a nation whose public and private morals in areas outside police work are sometimes open to legitimate questions.

In spite of these expectations, police officers are human, with emotions, biases, and weaknesses. Their work is sometimes dangerous. They see suffering, injustice, cruelty. They see people at their best and their worst. They are under constant pressure, even when things are momentarily calm. They must make rapid decisions, often without any guidelines. They frequently lack the necessary equipment and/or training. Their work is further complicated by people's conflicting expectations of them. And, they are often forced into situations where they may come off "looking bad," for example, being forced into shooting a crazed, gun-firing teenager.

> The roles must be carried out skillfully and professionally. This requires mental, intellectual, physical, and personal proficiencies.

To perform in the manner expected by the department and the community, the police officer needs numerous proficiencies. The following listing summarizes the results of a University of Chicago study of the behavioral requirements needed to perform police patrol duties.*

Mental. Police officers must:

Endure a long period of monotony in routine patrol yet react quickly (almost simultaneously) and effectively to problem situations observed on the street or to orders issued by the radio dispatcher (in much the

---

*Saunders, Charles B., Jr. *Upgrading the American Police.* Brookings Institution, 1970, pp. 17-18. Reprinted with permission of the publisher.

same way that a combat pilot must react to interception or a target opportunity).

Have the facility to act effectively in extremely divergent interpersonal situations. A police officer constantly confronts persons who are acting in violation of the law, ranging from curfew violators to felons.

Endure verbal and physical abuse from citizens and offenders (as when placing a person under arrest or facing day in and day out race prejudice) while using only necessary force in the performance of their functions.

Tolerate stress in a multitude of forms, such as meeting the violent behavior of a mob, arousing people in a burning building, coping with the pressures of a high-speed chase or a weapon being fired at them, or dealing with a woman bearing a child.

Personal.   Police officers must:

Relate to the people of their beat—businessmen, residents, school officials, visitors, etc. Their interpersonal relations must range up and down a continuum defined by friendliness and persuasion on one end, and firmness and force at the other.

Exhibit a professional, self-assured presence and a self-confident manner in their conduct when dealing with offenders, the public, and the court.

Take charge of situations, e.g., a crime or accident scene, yet not unduly alienate participants or by-standers.

Be flexible enough to work under loose supervision in most of their day-to-day patrol activities and also under the direct supervision of superiors in situations where large numbers of officers are required.

Exhibit personal courage in the face of dangerous situations which may result in serious injury or death.

Maintain objectivity while dealing with a host of "special interest" groups, ranging from relatives of offenders to members of the press.

Maintain a balanced perspective in the face of constant conflict, e.g., refrain from accepting bribes or "favors," provide impartial law enforcement, etc.

Intellectual.   Police officers must:

Exhibit initiative, problem-solving capacity, effective judgment, and imagination in coping with the numerous complex situations they are called upon to face, e.g., a family disturbance, a potential suicide, a robbery in progress, an accident, or a disaster. Police officers themselves clearly recognize this requirement and refer to it as "showing street sense."

Make prompt and effective decisions, sometimes in life-and-death situations, and be able to size up a situation quickly and take appropriate action.

Demonstrate mature judgment, as in deciding whether an arrest is warranted by the circumstances or a warning is sufficient, or in assessing a situation where the use of force may be needed.

Demonstrate critical awareness in discerning signs of out-of-the ordinary conditions or circumstances which indicate trouble or a crime in progress.

Adequately perform the communication and record-keeping functions of the job, including oral reports, preparation of formal case reports, and the completion of departmental and force forms.

Be capable of restoring equilibrium to social groups, e.g., restoring order in a family fight, in a disagreement between neighbors, or in a clash between rival youth gangs.

Be skillful in questioning suspected offenders, victims, and witnesses of crimes.

Gain knowledge of their patrol area, not only of its physical characteristics but also of its normal routine of events and the usual behavior patterns of its residents.

Physical. Police officers must:

Exhibit a number of complex psycho-motor skills, such as driving a vehicle in normal and emergency situations, firing a weapon accurately under extremely varied conditions, maintaining agility, endurance, and strength, and showing facility in self-defense and apprehension, as in taking a person into custody with a minimum of force.

Few roles in modern society are as demanding as that of the police officer.

A CAUTION

Police officers deal with crisis on a daily basis, usually that of someone else. Sometimes, however, the demands of the roles and how they are expected to be performed create enough stress to put police officers, themselves, into a crisis situation.

> A police officer's job is highly stressful and may result in a personal crisis for the officer.

Bennett-Sandler and Ubell (1977, pp.47-51) state that some modern departments have hired phychologists or counselors to help their members deal with the symptoms of job-related stress: alcoholism, suicide attempts, and the like. When faced with severe or prolonged stress, many police officers become what has been called "burned-out samaritans" (Maslach, 1976, pp. 16-22).

According to Ellison and Genz (1978, p.3): "A situation is more likely to be stressful and result in crisis reactions if it is unpredictable and if the individual has, or feels he has, little or no control over it." When stress results in "burnout," the individual tends to place himself at a great distance from the situation in which he is involved; he tends to go by the book rather than by the specific situation; a major symptom of burnout is "the transformation of a person with original thought and creativity on the job into a mechanical bureaucrat" (Maslach, 1976, p. 18).

Maslach (1976, p.18) also describes symptoms which indicate when a person is burning out: "He becomes cynical and develops negative feelings about his clients. He may begin to talk of them as other than human, and to withdraw from contact with them."

According to Ellison and Genz (1978, p.3): "The reactions described by Maslach are seen all too frequently in police officers." Niederhoffer (1967), too, describes the increasing alienation and cynicism in urban police officers which are similar to Maslach's example of burnout. In fact, he asserts that the kind of cynicism that is directed against life, the world, and people in general is endemic to police officers of all ranks and persuasion.

Ellison and Genz examine some of the specific factors which might account for burnout. They first identify two specific types of particularly stressful situations: the first is the wounding or death of a fellow officer, especially one's partner; the second is the maiming or sexual assault of a child. They note that as long as only one kind of basic skill is required in a job, problems are minimal, but that when assignments require different, contradictory skills, problems do arise: "When the necessity for interaction and sensitivity to human feelings and behavior is combined in an assignment with the necessity for dealing with situations which demand distancing because they (police officers) deal with basic human fears of mutilation, trauma, and death, the officer must attempt to perform the almost impossible balancing act of working appropriately with 'clients' who are undergoing ego-threatening crisis and protecting his own ego" (1978, pp. 4-5).

Ellison and Genz feel that burnout is more of a problem when officers are required to handle large numbers of serious calls and/or when they are not equipped or trained to handle them. Further, they believed that "job-related stress is exacerbated, and indeed, may be caused by certain traditional police practices. One of the most devastating of these is the indiscriminate use of a military model. This model sees police skills as technological ones. It assumes that every assignment involves skills that do not vary greatly from individual to individual or with the setting. It views discretion as unimportant and inappropriate for all but top brass" (1978, pp. 4-5).

Unfortunately, this model simply does not work in many situations. As noted by Reiss (1971, p.45), discretion is an integral part of policing:

> It is incumbent upon a police officer to enter upon a variety of social stages, encounter the actors, determine their roles, and figure out the plot. Often, before they can act, the police must uncover the "plot" and identify the roles and behavior of the actors. This is true even in emergency situations where an officer is expected to assess the situation almost immediately and make judgments as to what he must do.

A commonly held, but unjustifiable view of discretion is presented by Klein (1963):

> American police officers are in a difficult position, for in order to do their work efficiently they must use more power than the law seems to give them. They are re-

sponsible for maintaining order and for catching and arresting people suspected of violating the criminal law, but they cannot meet these responsibilities under the power and authority granted them. At the same time, if they exceed their authority when dealing with certain suspects and offenders, they are subject to severe public criticism.

> Police officers must use discretion to fulfill their responsibilities, but every time they do so they leave themselves open for criticism.

Sutherland and Cressey (1978, p.389) call attention to the fact that "although police officers are expected to help make crime dangerous for all, they are to use discretion and to exercise certain judicial functions as they do so. They must decide whether a certain act is in violation of the law, and also whether it probably can be proved that the law has been violated."

Police officers, even those assigned to patrol duties in a large city, are typically confronted with, at most, a few serious crimes in the course of a single tour of duty. They tend to view such involvement, particularly if there is some degree of danger, as constituting "real" police work. However, it is apparent that they spend considerably more time keeping order, settling disputes, finding missing children, and helping with medical emergencies than they do in responding to criminal conduct which is serious enough to call for arrest, prosecution, and conviction.

This does not mean that "serious" crime is unimportant to police officers. Quite the contrary is true. But it does mean that they perform a wide range of other functions which are of a highly complex nature and which often involve difficult social, behavioral, and political problems rather than major crimes.

Today's law enforcement officers need a broad background as well as broadening experiences to meet the complex challenges of a modern, changing, multiethnic and multiracial society. On that point there is near-unanimous agreement.

☑ CHECK POINT

1. List as many special physical, intellectual, personal, and mental skills as you can which are required to fulfill the roles of a police officer professionally.
2. What emotional dangers are involved in police work?
3. How does "discretion" present a problem for the police officer?
4. Write an explanation of or describe the complex role of the modern police officer which would be understood by a lay person.

*Answers

1. Answers to this question will vary considerably. Reread pp. 213-215 to evaluate your response.
2. A police officer's job is highly stressful and may result in a personal crisis for the officer.
3. The military model, upon which many police departments are based, does not encourage discretion, nor does it prepare the officer for it; yet police officers must use

discretion to fulfill their responsibilities. However, every time they do so, they leave themselves open for criticism.

4. Your answer should contain references to the five basic functions usually performed by the police, the skills and dangers involved, and the importance of the public in successfully fulfilling these roles. It should avoid use of technical language. You might evaluate your answer by comparing it to the following chapter summary.

SUMMARY

The people largely determine the role of the police and give them their authority to fulfill this role. Their support is vital in assisting the police officer to fulfill five basic roles.

Police officers must *enforce laws*, federal, state, and municipal, to protect the health and welfare of the community. For example, they enforce highway laws to make the streets safe for driving; they arrest people who violate the privacy of another person's home, who unlawfully sell narcotics, or who otherwise break the law.

They *preserve the peace* in a professional manner by patrolling troubled areas, intervening in domestic disturbances, and advising people in community disputes, such as landlord and tenant disagreements.

They *prevent crime* by being highly visible in the community, by personally contacting people to show the police department's concern for them, by educating the public about crime and crime prevention, and by involving them in programs such as Operation ID, in which valuables are marked for later identification in case of theft.

They *protect civil rights and civil liberties* by living and enforcing the principles contained in the Bill of Rights, such as respect for free speech, the right of privacy, and the right to due process under the law.

They also *provide necessary services* such as rendering first aid in medical emergencies, investigating traffic accidents, watching homes when people are on vacation, and assisting in community programs.

These roles must be carried out skillfully and professionally, and require numerous mental, intellectual, physical, and personal proficiencies. A police officer's job is highly stressful and may result in a personal crisis for police officers, especially if they are lacking public support. They must use discretion to fulfill their responsibilities, but they are often criticized for their decisions.

APPLICATION

Read the following description of a hypothetical work-shift of a police officer. Identify the various roles performed and the skills needed to perform these roles professionally.

8:00 A.M. Officer McGuire stops at the Woodway Elementary School and gives the second-graders a talk on the role of the police officer in the community.

9:00 A.M. Officer McGuire leaves the school and notices a group of shouting, screaming children congregating in a circle on the playground. Upon investigation, Officer McGuire finds that two youngsters are scuffling on the ground. He stops the fight, lectures them about the evils of fighting, and then warns and releases them after they shake hands with each other.

9:25 A.M.   Officer McGuire checks back in his squad car and receives a description over the radio of a car which has just been stolen. As he is patrolling Highway 1, he notices the car reported as stolen being driven by a juvenile. He puts on his red lights and siren and pulls the car over. He gives the youngster the Miranda rights and after interviewing him he determines that the youngster has, indeed, taken the car. He has the vehicle towed and takes the youngster to the station to be further interviewed by a juvenile officer for a disposition.

11:15 A.M.   Back on patrol, Officer McGuire receives a call to an automobile accident at 10th and Moore street. Upon arriving, he notices that the arm of one of the victims is bleeding profusely. He immediately obtains some sterile bandages from his first-aid kit and applies pressure to the cut. He calls for an emergency squad to take the person to the hospital. After this, he continues his investigation of the accident; he comes back into service at 12:10 P.M.

12:15 P.M.   Officer McGuire stops at Mabel's Restaurant to eat lunch. While there he notices two customers who are arguing vehemently. They get up and start to push each other around, but Officer McGuire intervenes and restores order.

12:40 P.M.   Back on patrol, Officer McGuire checks a house whose occupants are on vacation. He notices the back door is ajar, so he calls for assistance. When another officer arrives, he and Officer McGuire conduct a thorough search of the house. Finding everything in order, the officers close the door securely and Officer McGuire continues on his patrol.

1:05 P.M.   Officer McGuire is sitting with his radar unit on Interstate 1 in a 55 mph zone. He clocks the third car through the radar at 70 mph. He pursues the violator and issues a citation.

1:18 P.M.   While working radar on the same highway, Officer McGuire is dispatched to Oak and Main for a possible disturbance. When he arrives, he notices a small group of people standing around shouting obscenities at a person who is standing on a chair voicing his disapproval about how the government is handling our foreign affairs. After considerable discussion with the people involved, Officer McGuire successfully disperses the crowd. Although the man on the chair continues to berate the government, he draws considerably less attention.

2:15 P.M.   Officer McGuire is dispatched to the Mytown Shopping Center on a call that a person has passed out. After checking the person, Officer McGuire calls the emergency rescue unit and then begins mouth-to-mouth resuscitation.

3:00 P.M.   Officer McGuire is dispatched to 1215 Acorn Avenue where a home has been burglarized. He requests the dispatcher to send the Mobile Crime Laboratory to assist in the investigation.

4:00 P.M.   Off duty.

*Answers

Time of Call	Role Performed	Skill/Knowledge Required
8:00 A.M.	Provide services	Knowledge of the laws and those which children are most likely to violate
	Prevent crime by encouraging children to obey the law	
		Effective public relations skills
9:00 A.M.	Preserve the peace	Skill in handling juveniles
9:25 A.M.	Enforce laws	Knowledge of laws of arrest, how to stop a motor vehicle
		Knowledge of Bill of Rights, particularly advising a person of his rights (5th Amendment)
11:15 A.M.	Provide services	Skill in driving defensively to an emergency situation
		Knowledge of first aid and accident investigation
12:15 P.M.	Preserve the peace	Skill in dealing with people in an emotionally-charged situation
12:40 P.M.	Prevent crime	Skill in observing situations which are suspicious
	Provide services	
		Knowledge of how to search a house thoroughly and sensibly in case the burglar is still on the premises.
1:05 P.M.	Enforce laws	Knowledge of traffic laws
		Skill in operating radar, stopping a vehicle, and approaching a violator
1:18 P.M.	Protect civil rights and civil liberties	Knowledge of and skill in crowd control and protection of individual rights
2:15 P.M.	Provide services	Skill in rendering first aid
3:00 P.M.	Enforce laws	Knowledge of crime scene investigation, preservation of evidence, and criminalistics.
	Provide services	Skill in crime scene investigation.

DISCUSSION QUESTIONS

1. When and why was the Code of Ethics begun? Has it ever been reviewed?
2. How do police relate to their community?
3. How have the roles of a police officer changed over time?

4. Which of the roles are most important?
5. What services *should* police officers provide? Which are provided in our community?
6. How do the basic roles overlap?
7. Why is the support of the people vital to the successful accomplishment of the responsibilities of the modern police officer?
8. Why does Garmire believe it is hard for an officer to change roles? Don't we all play many different roles in our lives? Isn't it harder to be the same all the time?
9. What aspects of the Code of Ethics seem most relevant to the 1980s?
10. Should there be more or less use of police discretion?
11. What might a police department do to lessen the stress involved in being a police officer?
12. Why is Klein's view of discretion on pp. 216-217 described as "unjustifiable"? Do you agree?

REFERENCES

Bennett-Sandler, G. and Ubell, E. Time bombs in blue, *New York magazine*, March 21, 1977, pp. 47-51.

Ellison, K. W. and Genz, J. L. The police officer as burned-out samaritan, *FBI law enforcement bulletin*, March 1978, pp. 2-7.

Garmire, B. L. The police role in an urban society, in *The police and the community* Robert F. Steadman (ed.). Baltimore: The Johns Hopkins University Press, 1972, pp. 3-7. (Copyright by the Committee for Economic Development.)

Germann, A., Day, F. and Gallati, R. *Introduction to law enforcement and criminal justice.* Springfield, IL: Charles C. Thomas Publishers, 1966, pp. 26-27.

James, H. *Crisis in the courts.* New York: David McKay Company, 1968, p. 104. Copyright by the Christian Science Publishing Society. Based on a series of weekly articles in *The Christian Science Monitor*, April to July, 1967.

King, W. *New York Times*, December 3, 1977.

Klein, H. T. *The police: Damned if they do, damned if they don't.* New York: Crown, 1963.

MacDonald, W. F. Administratively choosing the drug criminal: Police discretion in the enforcement of drug laws, *Journal of drug issues*, 3:1973, pp. 123-134.

Maslach, C. Burned-out, *Human behavior*, September, 1976, pp. 16-22.

Munro, J. L. *Administratrative behavior and police organization.* Cincinnati: W. H. Anderson, 1974.

Nierderhoffer, A. *Behind the shield.* New York: Anchor, 1967.

The police. National Advisory Commission on Criminal Justice Standards and Goals. Washington, D.C.: U.S. Government Printing Office, 1973. (LEAA Grant #72-DF-99-0002, and NI 72-0200.)

Reiss, A. J. Jr. *The police and the public.* New Haven, CT: Yale University Press, 1971.

Saunders, Charles B., Jr. *Upgrading the American police.* Washington, D.C.: The Brookings Institution, 1970.

Smith, B. *Police systems in the United States*, New York: Harper & Row, 1940.

Sutherland, E. H. and Cressey, D. R. *Criminology.* (10th ed.) Philadelphia: J. B. Lippincott, 1978.

Task force report: The police. President's Commission on Law Enforcement and Administration of Justice. Washington, D.C.: U.S. Government Printing Office. 1967.

Good community relations and a positive police image formed through daily contacts between police and citizens are necessary if officers are to fulfill their assigned responsibilities. The photo shows an officer distributing basketball cards containing crime prevention tips to school children.

Police Image and Community Relations

A Critical Factor

DO YOU KNOW □ □ □

- ☐ How the police image originates?
- ☐ What factors influence this image?
- ☐ What negative character traits are sometimes part of the police image?
- ☐ Why police image and community relations are important?
- ☐ What most public relations programs emphasize?
- ☐ What most community relations programs emphasize?
- ☐ What factors interfere with good community relations and two-way communication?
- ☐ What single element is critical for any successful community relations program?

*No one means all he says, and yet very
few say all they mean for words are
slippery and thought is viscous.*
—Henry Brooks Adams

INTRODUCTION

This was graduation day for Rookie Officer Stephen Marston—the final day of sixteen weeks' training at the Police Academy. He had been looking forward to this for years, and it was finally here.

He sat in the auditorium listening intently to the final speaker who was emphasizing that the police image was of utmost importance to any police agency and the image depended on each individual officer. "Be professional looking," said the speaker. "Watch your weight, keep your clothes immaculate, your shoes shined; you are a highly visible individual in your community. Be meticulous about your conduct; avoid rudeness, discourtesy, and dishonesty. Be fair with everyone. When you handle a situation on the street, keep your private views to yourself. Stifle your emotions. Don't let your own feelings out."

Officer Marston believed what the speaker said, but in the back of his mind many questions remained unanswered. He understood from talking with other officers that the police image consisted of much more than stifling feelings and looking like a well-dressed model. Police officers were supposed to be super-human beings.

"Are they?" Officer Marston asked himself. "What about police work in general? What affects the image of a police officer over a period of years? What about these things they refer to as discretion, the police personality, and the authoritarian attitude that one seems to acquire over time? As a new officer, who am I? Am I going to have identity problems? What am I going to be like ten years from now? What's this thing called 'police culture' I hear so much about?"

Officer Marston was already familiar with the name given to the macho behavior of some new police officers—"The John Wayne Syndrome"—which basically meant that they usually enforced the letter of the law, forgetting about the spirit of the law. He was going to try to avoid that, but what about the rest of his questions? Only time would tell.

As Officer Marston shook his head to clear the fog that had suddenly come over him, he heard the speaker conclude: "And, above all, don't forget your image."

Officer Marston mumbled to himself, "I won't."

Officer Marston's questions could be multiplied over and over in every rookie class in the country. Little do most rookies know that someday, perhaps soon, as they gain experience, they, too, may become the victims of many external and internal controls of the police department and society that will affect their behavior and their personality.

This chapter has combined police image and community relations because the two subjects are inseparable and interdependent. It is the community for whom the police image is projected, and it is the community which establishes what that image is. Unfortunately, what the police department seeks to project and what the community actually perceives are sometimes worlds apart.

Before getting into the discussion of police image, we must first recognize that each police officer is an individual. Police officers are fathers, mothers, sons, daughters, uncles, aunts, coaches of Little League teams, church members, and neighbors. As people, they like to be liked, but often their profession requires that they take negative actions against those who break the law. As a result, they are often criticized and berated for simply doing their job.

Although police officers are individuals just like those in the community they have sworn to "serve and protect," their behavior is very public. As noted by More (1976, p.126): "Policemen may simply be very ordinary people who happen to be extraordinarily visible."

Still, the public's image of the police varies greatly. Some see police officers as saviors; others see them as militaristic harassers. The sight of a police officer arouses feelings of respect, confidence, and security in some citizens; fear, hostility, and hatred in others; and indifference in yet others.

The image of the police officer frequently portrayed on television has not been very helpful. The "Starsky and Hutch" tactics, with much violence and disregard for civil rights, is often presented as *the* way a police officer should behave. It would be unfortunate if citizens came to accept (or expect) such behavior from their police officers in real life.

> The police image results from everyday contacts between individual police officers and citizens.

In spite of what is written in books or portrayed on television and in movies, the abstraction we call the "police image" is primarily the result of day-to-day contacts between police and citizens. It is the behavior of police officers at the patrol level rather than at the command level that is of greatest importance in establishing the police image. In turn, the individual behavior of the police officer who creates the police image is the result of several factors including length of service, the community served (ghetto or exclusive suburb), training, and experience.

FACTORS INFLUENCING POLICE BEHAVIOR AND IMAGE

In addition to easily identifiable and predictable factors such as experience, training, and locality served, numerous subtle factors influence police behavior and image, including the nature of police work itself, a confusion of identity, the police officer's unique relation to the criminal justice system, the democratic nature of our society, and the individual officer's personality.

> Police behavior and image are influenced by the nature of police work.

The preceding chapter introduced the numerous demands placed upon the police officer. Police officers are under constant pressure and faced with rapidly changing conditions, sometimes life-threatening situations, with few guidelines and little supervision; they frequently must "play it by ear." Skolnick (1967) describes two principle variables of the policeman on the beat—danger and authority. He cautions that these variables must be interpreted in the light of constant pressure to appear efficient.

The stressfulness of the situation in which police officers are placed is described by More (1976, p.33):

It is obviously difficult and often impossible for police officers to respond in an appropriate manner to the numerous incidents called to their attention. They are under constant pressure, especially in highly congested areas, to handle a volume of cases that is beyond their capacity—forcing them to develop short-cut responses to run-of-the-mill situations. They lack adequate training with respect to some of the more complex social problems. And there has been little effort to provide individual officers with the guidelines which they require if they are expected to make more effective and judicious decisions in disposing of the incidents which come to their attention. In the absence of adequate resources, training, and guidance, the tendency is for individual police officers to attempt to meet largely by improvisation the varied demands made upon them.

Police officers cannot be expected to perform expertly in every situation; it is not humanly possible. Such expectations are as unrealistic as those expressed by a man who had just hired a new secretary and told her: "What do you mean you can't type; you have ten fingers don't you?" Simply because a person is a police officer does not mean that he can handle every situation which arises. The observation of Lord Wavell, a British Army field marshal, might apply equally to an American police officer (Tanner, 1960, p.4):

Stupidity in (army) generals shouldn't excite or surprise one since they were selected from an extremely small class of human beings who were tough enough to be generals at all. The essential quality was not that they should be extremely clever or sensitive, but that they should continue to function even if not particularly well, in situations in which a more sensitive and less stable organism would have stopped functioning altogether.

In addition to having to improvise in many situations, police officers must deal with people from all walks of life who are involved in criminal and non-criminal activities and must use broad discretion in a wide variety of situations with little supervision. They deal with crimes already committed, with people who are hurt, confused, angry, and upset; yet they must remain neutral, calm, objective. They may appear indifferent or unsympathetic, but, much like physicians, they cannot become personally involved and still do a professional job. They must remain detached and objective.

Police work also requires constant decision-making by the law officer. In fact, law enforcement has been described as a sequence of discretionary decisions. This discretion may lead to wide variations and inconsistencies in how the law is enforced, which citizens rightly criticize. Just as children need consistent discipline, adults in a community need and expect consistent enforcement of the laws—fairness and impartiality.

Police officers must also decide whether to give priority to a situation or not. They may encounter a cat in a tree, a downed power line, people locked out of cars or houses, noisy teenagers, and family disputes. If the officer does respond to such situations, there is often little to do other than give support, advice, and/or assistance.

Frequently police officers are called to make someone who is not breaking the law stop doing something which someone else views as "bad"; for example, noisy kids playing ball in a vacant lot next door to a woman who is trying to sleep. Formerly the family, the church, or the school usually kept people "in line," but more and more often people see the police as their only chance to force someone who is misbehaving to "straighten up." However, in such situations, police officers cannot do much. In fact, they may add to the problem. Trying to make someone "be good" when they don't want to is a thankless task which is usually doomed to failure. When citizens see such failure, they have a reduced opinion of the effectiveness of law enforcement, without realizing that in such instances the "law" has no authority.

The image resulting from the nature of police work might easily be compared to the image of a football referee. It is readily accepted that referees are necessary to the game. Without them chaos would reign, and the team with the strongest, "dirtiest" players would always win. Despite their criticality, however, their image is frequently negative. No matter what call they make, a great many people are unhappy with them. They are usually perceived as being on the opponent's side. Defeats are frequently blamed on referees; however, seldom is a referee given credit for a team's victory. It is often a thankless, sometimes dangerous job. Fans have thrown pop bottles and attempted to physically assault referees. Likewise, abusive names are frequently hurled at the referee. If often makes one wonder what type of individual could continue to work under such pressures.

> Police behavior and image are influenced by a confusion of identity.

Police officers are sworn to "serve and protect" the people in their community and at the same time to enforce the laws. We talked earlier about the controversy regarding how much service police departments should provide to the community. In reality, most police officers spend as much as 80% of their time being "helpful" rather than making arrests. Frequently, however, the public does not see them as helpful. Help that is not asked for is very often interpreted as interference; "When I want help, I'll ask for it" is a common and natural response to an unsolicited offer of "assistance."

A case in point is the domestic call. Neighbors may call the police to report a wife, husband, or child beating. (Surprisingly, a recent survey reports that over two million husbands per year are severely beaten up by their wives.) The police response to such calls is frequently fraught with danger to the officer; 22% of all police fatalities occur during response to "domestics." These unglamorous, potentially highly dangerous calls are not technically within the the police officer's realm of responsibility, but when a service call comes in, the officer must respond.

The role conflict faced by many police officers has a direct influence on the image projected (More, 1976, p.180):

He wants to function as a crime fighter, but does not. He is not trained or rewarded for being a peace keeper or community service agent. His quasi-judicial role is poorly differentiated. He works on the one hand in an autonomous situation on the street, but on the other hand is supposed to be highly responsive to a chain of command. All these issues engender role conflict in the police officer.

Most police officers feel they are law enforcement officers, not social workers. They didn't create nor can they control the social problems which exist and which prompt numerous service calls. When they do respond to such calls, their help is often perceived as interference; they may be berated or even assaulted.

> Police behavior and image are influenced by their unique relation to the criminal justice system.

Another factor influencing the police image is the officers' relationship to the law. Although police officers frequently initiate the criminal justice system by investigating and apprehending criminals, they often feel like outsiders in the judicial system. They may feel their investigation and apprehension of criminals is hampered by legal restrictions and that the suspect has more rights than the victim of the crime.

Although police officers are frequently blamed for rising crime rates, their participation in the legal system is often minimized. They may be made to feel is if they were on trial during the court proceedings as the defense attorney cross-examines them. They are seldom included in any plea bargaining. And frequently defendants are found "not guilty" because of loopholes or legal technicalities. When a confessed robber is acquitted on a technicality or a known rapist is not brought to trial by the prosecutor, police officers may take this as a personal affront, as a criticism of their investigative expertise. In addition, citizens of the community may also blame the police officers for the unsuccessful prosecution of the suspect. Further, legal technicalities may even result in the police officer being sued for false arrest.

Another difficulty in the police officer's relation to the law is the frequent confusion of identity. Although police represent the law, they are *not* the law. However, some police officers, consciously or subconsciously, feel they have a very special relationship to the law. And, indeed, they do. Obviously, police officers cannot and do not arrest all the offenders they encounter. Because of their discretionary powers, the individual police officer, in effect, makes law enforcement policy on a daily basis.

Police behavior and image are influenced by the democratic nature of our society.

It is extremely difficult to be a law officer in a diverse, democratic society. Civil rights and civil liberties are stressed so heavily that often police officers feel they cannot function effectively; they perceive that the criminals have all the breaks on their side. However, herein lies the special challenge which, faced squarely, can make police work the highly challenging and rewarding profession that it is to many police officers. At an Annual Meeting of the International Association of Chiefs of Police, Quinn Tamm stressed that (Germann, Day, and Gallati, 1966, pp. 112-113):

The theme that must run beneath every police training program is that the rule of law is the very heart and soul of American police action. It must be the golden thread which ties together all the varied subjects that constitute the curricula of our schools. ...No matter how carefully we teach our young officers and no matter how skilled they become at such techniques as interviewing, patrol, sketching, plaster casting, photography, and the like, they will not be real officers until the conviction has become part of their very being that everything they do must be done in a reasonable and constitutional manner. This is the true mark of a professional officer. In the final analysis we are not so much interested in developing good photographers and good interviewers as we are in sending into the community officers truly knowledgeable of their role in a free country who are incidentally good photographers and good inter-viewers.

☑ CHECK POINT

1. **How does the police image originate?**
2. **List four factors that influence police behavior and image.**

✳ Answers

1. The police image results from everyday contacts between individual police officers and citizens.
2. Factors influencing police behavior and image include: (1) the nature of police work itself, (2) a confusion of identity—help people vs. arrest people, (3) the police officer's unique relation to the law, and (4) the democratic nature of our society. In addition, officers' personalities have a direct influence on their behavior and image as the following pargraphs illustrate.

THE POLICE PERSONALITY

Popular and scientific literature related to the police image often identifies several personality traits of the "typical" police officer.

Police officers are frequently described as being suspicious, cynical, bigoted, indifferent, authoritarian, and brutal.

Suspicious

Police work requires a police officer to be wary of situations which are out of the ordinary, for example, a person with an umbrella on a sunny day or a person wearing sunglasses at midnight. Not only is keen observation critical to effective investigation and crime prevention, it is critical to self-defense. Danger is always possible in any situation. In fact, police work is one of the most dangerous occupations in the country. A police officer can be killed while writing out a simple traffic ticket. Skolnick (1974, pp. 45-46) believes that the policeman "develops a perceptual shorthand to identify certain kinds of people as symbolic assailants, that is, as persons who use gesture, language, and attire that the policeman has come to recognize as a prelude to violence. This does not mean that violence by the symbolic assailant is necessarily predictable. On the contrary, the policeman responds to the vague indication of danger suggested by appearance."

Cynical

Because police officers deal with criminals, they are constantly on-guard against human faults. Police officers see people at their worst. They know that people lie, cheat, steal, torture, kill. They deal with people who don't like police, who even hate them, and they feel the hatred. Additionally, they may see persons they firmly believe to be guilty of a heinous crime be freed by a legal technicality. Recall Niederhoffer's (1967) assertion that "the kind of cynicism that is directed against life, the world, and people in general...is endemic to policemen of all ranks and persuasions." This cynicism may also lead to paranoia.

Bigoted

Police are frequently victims of problems they have nothing to do with and over which they have no control. They are not to blame for the injustices suffered by members of minority groups: housing, educational, and employment discrimination. Yet often members of minority groups perceive the police officers as a symbol of the society which has denied them its privileges and benefits. Tension between minority-group members and any representatives of "authority" has become almost a way of life in many parts of large cities. The minority-group members vent their anger and frustration on the police, and some police, understandably, come to feel anger and dislike for them.

Indifferent

When police officers are called to the scene of a homicide, they are expected to conduct a thorough, impartial investigation. Their objectivity may be perceived by grieving relatives of the victim as indifference or coldness. However, police officers must remain detached; one of the grieving relatives might well be the murderer. Further, a certain amount of "distancing" is required to work with difficult situations. Ellison and Genz (1978, p. 4) state that officers who must deal with assignments involving mutilation and death develop coping mechanisms: "These defenses, which permit one to do an important job well, often prevent him from doing the work which involves interacting with others."

Authoritarian

Effective law enforcement requires authority; authoritarianism "comes with the job." Without authority and respect, the police officer could not effectively compel citizens of the community to obey the law. As noted by Pascal: "Justice without force is powerless; force without justice is tyrannical." The physical appearance of the police officer adds to this authoritarian image. The uniform, gun, club, and handcuffs project an image to which most people respond with uneasiness or even fear. Yet this image projects the right of the police to exercise the lawful force of the state in serving and protecting as well as in enforcing laws. The difficulty arises when the power that comes with the position is transferred to "personal power." Perhaps Henry Brooks Adams was correct in 1907 when he said, "The effect of power and publicity on all men is the aggravation of self, a sort of tumor that ends by killing the victim's sympathies."

Brutal

Sometimes force is required to subdue suspects. Unfortunately, the crime-related aspects of a police officer's job are what frequently draw public attention. When police officers have to physically subdue a suspect, people notice. When they help someone get into a car they've locked their keys into, few notice. Sometimes, however, more force is used than is required. This, too, is easier to understand if one thinks of the other personality traits which often become part of the police "personality," particularly cynicism and authoritarianism. Police officers may use excessive force with a rapist if they believe that the probability is great that the rapist will never be brought to trial because of the prosecutor's policies on rape cases. They may also erroneously believe that violence is necessary to obtain respect from individuals who seem to respect nothing but force and power.

Significance of the Negative Personality Traits

The purpose of the preceding discussion was not to excuse the negative traits frequently found in some police officers. It was intended to provide some insight into the possible causes for such negative traits in the hope that police officers new to the field will be aware of and avoid these common pitfalls in logic. Even though understandable, such negative traits are *not* excusable. Sometimes, however, the fault is not in the behavior but in the *perception* of the behavior.

> Although negative personality traits may be understandable, they are not excusable. Sometimes, however, the fault is not in the behavior but in the way it is perceived.

The eyes of the beholder determine how a police officer's actions will be interpreted or described. A person who dislikes police officers will probably perceive a specific behavior negatively, while the same behavior might be perceived positively by an individual who has a high regard for police officers. Consider, for example, the following actions and the way each is described by an individual who feels negatively about the police and one who feels positively about the police.

Action by Officer	Negative Person	Positive Person
Steps in to stop a fight in a bar.	Interference.	Preserving the peace.
Questions a rape victim.	Indifferent, cold.	Objective.
Uses a baton to break up a violent mob.	Brutal.	Commanding respect.
Steadily watches three youths on a corner.	Suspicious.	Observant.

Given the fact that the police have numerous encounters with people who do not like them, that they must frequently take action against lawbreakers which elicits highly negative reactions, and that they are often presented on television and in the movies and newspapers in mob-control situations where public dislike of the police is most strongly displayed, it is small wonder that most police officers believe the public is against them. According to W. Westley (1970), 73% of policemen interviewed believed the average citizen disliked police officers. Evidence from field surveys, however, suggests the opposite— that attitudes are predominantly positive and supportive of police (*Law and Society Review*, 1973, pp. 135-152).

Student Survey of Image of Police Officer

In the spring of 1978 the authors conducted a survey of 192 students and their perception of police officers. Of the 192 students, 60 were from law enforcement classes, 62 from psychology classes, and 70 from sociology classes. Each student was asked to write five words to describe a police officer. The responses were categorized as positive (e.g. friend), negative (e.g. borderline gunman), or neutral (e.g. law enforcement officer). The results indicated that over half the students surveyed had a positive image of the police officer and that less than one-fourth had a negative image.

Table 8-1.   Summary of Students' Responses to their perception of a police officer:

Responses	L.E.	Psych.	Soc.	Total
Positive	74.5%	63.4%	37.7%	58.1%
Neutral	13.8%	16.8%	30.8%	20.9%
Negative	11.7%	19.8%	31.5%	21.0%

As might be expected, the students in law enforcement were most positive in their responses. Also of interest was the great diversity of responses—a total of 343 different descriptors of police officers! Of these 148 were positive, 87 were neutral, and 108 were negative.

Eight terms, all positive, were used by over ten students. These terms were, in order of decreasing frequency of occurrence: Honest (12%), helpful (11.5%), friendly (11%), intelligent (8%), strong (7.5%), authoritative—taken in a positive way since the other terms in the students' listings were positive (7%), understanding (6%), and responsible (5%). Positive terms listed by 4% of the students were: alert, brave, caring, courageous, courteous, dedicated, fair, kind, professional, protective, quick thinking, respectable, and smart.

The neutral terms most frequently described a role played by the police officer. These roles included such diverse functions as: actor, advisor, civil (community) servant, counselor, enforcer of the law, example, father image, judge, law officer, lawyer, manager, minister, paramedic, politician, public servant, supervisor, and worker. The most commonly used term classified as neutral by the authors was human (8%). The only other neutral term used by over ten students was *tough*.

The negative characteristics frequently attributed to police officers in the literature were not frequently given by students, except for "authoritarian" which was the most frequently given negative response (6%). The other terms cited in the literature were seldom used by the students surveyed:

Bigoted	3 students	Indifferent	1 student
Brutal	0 students	Suspicious	0 students
Cynical	2 students		

Unfortunately, the students' negative terms were *much* more negative than the above, including such terms as: corrupt, dictator, enemy, gestapo, ignorant, irresponsible, killer, mean, mentally unstable, nerd, paranoid, power hungry, rude, stupid, and untouchable. Although such perceptions were indicated by only a small number of students, the fact that they occurred at all is cause for concern.

☑ CHECK POINT

1. What negative characteristics are frequently attributed to police officers?
2. How might these negative characteristics be explained?
3. Does explaining the reason for a negative characteristic excuse it?
4. Why might two different people view the same police behavior in opposite ways?

*Answers

1. Negative personality characteristics frequently attributed to police officers include: suspicious, cynical, bigoted, indifferent, authoritarian, and brutal.
2. Each of the characteristics can be explained by the nature of police work, the conflict of identity, our democratic society, and the fact that the policeman is human.
3. Explaining the reasons for negative characteristics does not excuse them.
4. Police behavior might be viewed by two different people in opposite ways if one had a positive image of the police and the other had a negative image of the police. This was demonstrated in the student survey in which "authoritarian" was perceived as both negative and positive by many students.

THE POLICE CULTURE

Police officers work nights and weekends; they deal with highly confidential material which cannot be shared with friends; they must enforce the law impartially, whether it is a friend or a stranger who violates a law; and they frequently face public hostility, abuse, name-calling, and biased reporting in the media. A combination of the preceding factors largely accounts for the existence of a "police culture."

> The dominant characteristic of the police culture is isolationism. It may result in a "them" vs. "us" situation.

Individuals who become police officers frequently find that they lose their nonpolice friends within a few years. They work different hours—nights and weekends, and they may make some of their friends uneasy, especially their friends who drink and drive or who habitually speed. Recall the quotation at the beginning of Chapter 3; everyone breaks the law at one time or another. Police officers' friends often do not understand some of the actions they are forced to take in fulfilling their responsibilities.

Police officers not only frequently lose their nonpolice friends, they may come to realize that they are now a part of a group which is isolated from the rest of society. Although they are highly visible, they are set apart. They may be feared, disliked, hated, or even assaulted by citizens, making them close ranks for protection and security. The closer they become, the greater the suspicion and fear on the part of the citizens, leading to even tighter ranks, and so the cycle goes. Police officers are expected to take the place of mother, father, church, and school—to be "family"—to those who will not accept them.

The police become the "in" group and everyone else is the "outgroup." As noted by Skolnick (1967, p. 52) social isolation produces a we-they view of the world. To a police officer the world consists of cops and civilians, or perhaps better phrased as cops versus civilians.

This "them" vs. "us" leads to defensiveness exhibited in such ways as reluctance to give up traditional police responsibilities (for example, traffic control on state highways), or reluctance to explain their actions to citizens. Official police silence is sometimes necessary to protect the rights of others or to safeguard an investigation, but sometimes it is, in reality, a defensive response.

Police officers who isolate themselves from the community and from their nonpolice friends frequently develop a "one-track" life with the central focus being law enforcement. They may have few outside interests, devoting their attention to reading articles and watching programs related to law enforcement and socializing only with other individuals in the law enforcement field.

The result of such isolation from the rest of society is frequently a paranoia similar to that typically seen in some members of minority groups. But there is an important difference between the isolation of a minority-group member and that of police officers. Police officers have physical powers—guns and clubs—and the authority to use them to preserve law and order for the very individuals who they feel have rejected them. This can pose a highly inflammatory situation and may partially account for the extensive riots of the 1960s.

Whether it did or not, the riots of the sixties highlighted the dire need for better relations between the police and the citizens they serve. Often, however, efforts are directed only at changing the public's attitude, not at changing police behavior as well. It must always be remembered that the public responds to what is presented to them.

☑ CHECK POINT

1. What is the dominant characteristic of the "police culture"?
2. What is the frequent result of this culture?

*Answers

1. The dominant characteristic of the "police culture" is isolation.
2. This isolation frequently results in a "them" vs. "us" view of the world.

IMAGE BUILDING: PUBLIC AND COMMUNITY RELATIONS

The current relationship between police officers and citizens is not always good. Some citizens don't want to get involved or are apathetic. Other citizens are suspicious of the police and of the entire criminal justice system. Still others have no regard for laws or police officers.

The Importance of Police-Community Relations

The criticality of good police-community relations is well illustrated by looking at what happens when relations are poor. As noted by the President's Commission on Law Enforcement and the Administration of Justice in their task force report (*The Police*, 1967, p. 144):

Hostility, or even a lack of confidence of a significant portion of the public has extremely serious implications for the police. These attitudes interfere with recruiting, since able young men generally seek occupations which are not inordinately dangerous and which have the respect and support of their relatives and friends.

Public hostility affects morale and makes police officers less enthusiastic about doing their job well. It may lead some officers to leave the force, to accept more prestigious or less demanding employment.

In addition, poor police-community relations has a direct effect on law enforcement. You learned earlier how important citizen cooperation was in preventing crime and detecting those responsible for crime committed.

> Good police-community relations are important not only to recruit and retain high-caliber individuals as police officers, but to effectively fulfill the responsibilities assigned to police officers.

Public Relations Programs

Public relations programs frequently seek to enhance the image of the police officer, to gain understanding and acceptance of their role in the community. The programs are directed to groups or the entire community. The police officer may be portrayed as the friend of the young and the old, may appear at school and church programs, sponsor Little League teams or Law Enforcement Days, or hand out bumper stickers encouraging people to "support their local police."

> The primary emphasis of most public relations programs is to raise the image of the police officer.

Such programs are usually geared to the needs of the police. Sometimes they are only cosmetic or token efforts to gain community approval.

However, public relations is an accepted and healthy form of propaganda used very successfully by major corporations and by many law enforcement agencies. For example, the Minnesota Highway Department distributes a Minnesota Highway Patrol Coloring Book that portrays the patrol officer in a very positive, helping way.

Figure 8-1.   Minnesota Highway Patrol Coloring Book. Reprinted with permission.

There is nothing wrong with a police department employing such tactics. The problem arises when a department institutes a special unit to "take care of the public image" and assumes that this is all that is required. No amount of bumper stickers or sponsorships will counteract negative actions by police officers. Respect must be earned; it cannot be bought or commanded. It must always be remembered that the police image is primarily the result of daily contacts between the police officer and citizens of the community.

The President's Task Force Report (1967) outlines three types of community-relations training being conducted in several police agencies. Most programs concentrated on public relations, attempting to teach the police officers how to improve the image of the police and how to conduct themselves so as not to alienate the public—how to talk courteously to citizens, and how and why to avoid physical or verbal abuse and discrimination. A second type of training gave police officers an understanding of the various kinds of individuals with whom they would come in contact and the various neighborhoods of the city. The third type of training was aimed at changing attitudes and prejudices of recruits and police officers. Role-playing and small discussion groups helped the officers to think through their own emotions and beliefs to see how these might influence their actions as police officers.

Any public relations program should be realistic in the image it hopes to convey to the public. As Garmire (1972, p. 11) puts it:

I do not believe that police officers and the police service can become objects of love and endearment; it is not in the nature of men, particularly Americans, to give such affection to those representatives of authority who directly control their lives. And, no matter how we describe the activities of the police, the business of police is policing. The most we can hope for, public-community relations or public relations notwithstanding, is respect for the police as professionals, confidence in their integrity, and public conviction that the police will perform their mission.

Conveyance of such an understanding requires more than public relations programs. *It requires, first and foremost, appropriate actions by police officers,* and second, sound community relations programs.

Police-Community Relations Programs

While public relations programs are a one-way effort directed at raising the image of the police, police-community relations programs seek to provide means for police and citizens to work together to achieve their mutual goal of law and order.

> The primary emphasis of police-community relations programs is to provide two-way communication between police and citizens to work toward achieving law and order in the community.

Many people are concerned about the relationship between the police and the citizens. Many people think they know the answer to the problem. Police officers feel that if citizens would only understand the responsibilities of law enforcement officers and would obey the law themselves, there would be no problem. Citizens, on the other hand, frequently believe that if the police would be more human and understanding, the problem would be solved. Both sides are partly right and partly wrong; however, their attitudes toward one another frequently interfere with working together to find answers to their mutual problems.

Factors Interfering with Communication*

Several factors interfere with two-way communication between police officers and citizens.

> Important factors limiting two-way communication between police and community are negative attitudes toward each other and unwillingness to listen to the other's side.

The following comments are indicative of attitudes which block two-way communication:

From the Police

People just don't respect the police any more.

We can't get cooperation. People just don't care.

Yeah, you walk into the kind of situations I face, and have people call you obscene names and threaten you, and then see if you can keep your temper.

Talk about police brutality. What about citizen brutality against the police? We're in danger of attack every minute of the day.

You hear some mother tell her kid that if he isn't good she'll turn him over to a cop. Just a little kid. Man, that really chills you.

Folks these days think they can choose the laws they want to obey or disobey. That's the real problem.

Even when you want to make a legitimate arrest, for disorderly conduct or DWI or anything, first thing you know you're surrounded by an angry mob wanting to fight.

With all the new court decisions and departmental policies an ordinary police officer is expected to be a constitutional lawyer. One little mistake and the judge turns a criminal loose, and a conscientious police officer gets a reprimand. How can we do our job under those conditions?

One police officer gets out of line and its smeared all over the newspapers for a week. A hundred guys do a good job and nobody notices. Sure, we have some bad apples on the force, but I resent all of us being condemned just because of those few.

People sweep floors and make more money than I do. If the public wants professional police, they're going to have to pay for them. I like police work, but I'm getting out if they don't do something about salaries, and quick.

You can say that again. I know guys on welfare driving newer cars than I can afford.

*Adapted from *Police and Community Relations ... is a Two-Way Street*; National Conference of Christians and Jews, 1969. Written by Don McEvay for the National Conference of Christians and Jews. Reprinted by permission of the author.

From the Community

> Don't ask me to cooperate with the fuzz, baby. They never done nothing for me except push me around.

> Why do they have to be so arrogant? A little common courtesy would go a long way.

> We haven't got a chance. The police act like it was a federal crime to be a teenager.

> A bunch of guys are just hanging around the corner, not doing nothing wrong, and they come along and yell, "Okay, you guys, move along."

> They act like we don't belong in America just because we speak Spanish. We're just as much citizens as anybody else.

> I know I should cooperate more. But it just doesn't pay to get involved.

> They expect us to obey the law. Let's see them start doing it themselves. They know every pusher and prostitute on the street, but they don't do a thing as long as they get their kickback.

> I heard a cop call my daddy "Boy." They're not going to get by with that stuff with me.

> A police officer raps you around real good. Then you make a complaint and that's the end of it. They never investigate those things, so what's the use? Just because we don't dress like people on Madison Avenue or wear our hair to suit them, they treat us like animals. It's not brutality so much as constant harassment.

> The thing that bugs me is that if you run a red light, the police officer will drag you out of the car and throw you across the hood and frisk you. There ain't no cause for that.

> Why can't a cop explain to you what he is detaining you for? If you ask "What for?" they threaten you with resisting arrest.

> The police in my town are supposed to wear identification badges, but the names are never in sight when you want to see one. They must put them in their pockets every time things get a little rough.

> Just try and find one when you need him. They're all up at the diner drinking coffee ... and then walk out without paying for it, too.

You've probably heard many of the comments, or similar ones, before. You may even have made some of them yourself. When the two lists are placed side by side, several interesting similarities are evident. Whether the sentiments of a hostile citizen or an embittered police officer, the pride, fear and isolation, the need for understanding, and the demand for respect are strikingly similar.

> Stereotypes interfere with communication and good relations.

Police resent being the targets for obscene epitaphs. They don't like being called *the fuzz, flatfoot, honkie cop, fascist pig* any more than private citizens like being referred to as *animals, young punks, scum, niggers, spikes, dorks,* and an endless variety of other racial and ethnic slur words. Words have the power to inflame and incite to violence. Classifying all members of a group into one negative category is immature and ignorant. Each group has good and bad individuals within it. It is individuals who should be considered, not the group to which they happen to belong.

> Group protectiveness interferes with communication and good relations.

People tend to think in terms of the "in-group"—the group to which they belong—and the "out-group." The out-group is everyone else and usually is perceived as being "bad." If citizens perceive police as members of the "out-group," they will be uncooperative and perhaps even hostile. Nobody wants to tell on a friend or sometimes even a total stranger who is a private citizen like himself. Similarly, group protectiveness may make it difficult for a police officer to "blow the whistle" on a fellow officer.

> Societal factors interfere with communication and good relations.

Today it is more difficult to get a case through court, more dangerous to walk the streets at night, and more of a strain to get along with neighbors crowded in on all sides. Living in this generation requires more skill, knowledge, patience, and good will.

Police work also requires better training and more self-discipline than ever before. Law enforcement is no longer a job. It is a profession. Likewise, the citizen must be willing to pay the price for living in this generation. One of the costs is personal involvement. To stand aside and expect others to carry the load is to default in one of the primary obligations of citizenship. As Seneca (Troades) noted: "He who does not prevent a crime when he can, encourages it."

The police and public are bound together in a common destiny. What is good for one is inevitably good for the other. What is bad for one, is bad for the other. If police work for low salaries, with inadequate training, in hostile communities that provide little cooperation and frequent danger, they are not going to operate effectively. Citizens can do something to alleviate these conditions and thereby assure themselves of better and more professional police services.

As long as citizens live in fear of the police, believing them to be unfriendly mercenaries at best and brutal oppressors at worst, they will not provide the environment essential for effective law enforcement. R. F. Kennedy once said: "Every society gets the kind of criminal it deserves. What is equally true is that every community gets the kind of law enforcement it insists upon."

Approaches to Police-Community Relations

Several approaches have been taken to police-community relations programs. Bureaus have been established within police agencies. Community-wide citizen groups have been formed. Civilian review boards or advisory committees have worked with police agencies in establishing goals and priorities. Large scale educational programs have been successful when they have promoted dialogue rather than simply conveying information (public relations). As noted by the President's Commission on Law Enforcement and the Administration of Justice (*The Police*, p.159):

Citizens who distrust the police will not easily be converted by information programs they consider to come from a tainted source. However, even for these groups, long-term education based upon honest and free DIALOGUE between the police and the public can have an effect. Indeed, this is one of the basic goals of the citizen advisory committees. On the other hand, citizens who are neutral or supportive can benefit from increased understanding of the complicated problems and tasks of the police. Informational programs can also generate support for more personnel, salary increases, sufficient equipment, and other resources to improve the efficiency of police work. It can help the cooperative citizen to avoid becoming a victim of crime and show him how to work more effectively with the police. And, to the extent that the police department is genuinely working at improved community relations, dissemination of this information to the press and other media does have a positive effect on community relations.

> The police officer on the street is ultimately responsible for the success of police-community relations programs.

The police officer on the street is *the* community-relations officer of the department. The officer's actions, demeanor, appearance, and empathy for people are all accountable for positive or negative community relations.

Community acceptance of crime prevention programs initiated depends on the overall effectiveness of all police operations. Hundreds of programs have aided the police in their efforts toward not only community relations, but improved law enforcement, as you will see in Chapter 11. As police officers' knowledge of the community and its citizens increases, so does their effectiveness as law enforcement officers. Their street contacts and sources of information are also vastly improved.

Community relations is a responsibility of both the police and the citizen. The police may contribute to improving two-way communication by:

—Understanding the problems of the citizen and keeping an open mind, using good judgment.
—Paying attention rather than displaying a casual attitude. Police officers should listen attentively. If they disagree on a point, they should do so politely. They should show consideration rather than ignoring the citizen. The problem the citizen conveys to the police officer may be of utmost importance to him or her.
—Using courteous words. Sarcasm in either words or attitude is readily apparent to the citizen and hampers communication. Tone of voice can be as important as the words used. Tone can incite anger or instill confidence.
—Being patient. Police officers must exercise self-command and self-discipline. Although patience and kindness may be misperceived by some as a sign of weakness, this is not true.

—Giving time. Give citizens time to air their problems. Do not rush them.

—Showing enthusiasm. Officers should approach each contact with enthusiasm, believing in themselves and their communities. A lackadaisical attitude will thwart the objectives of any contact.

—Being helpful instead of hindering. Officers should be responsible to the ideas of citizens. Being helpful or rendering aid is one of the most important functions of a police officer.

—Showing sincerity. Mere words, in themselves, are not proof of sincerity. Police officers must be honest and straightforward in their citizen contacts.

—Being polite and friendly. A smile at the opportune moment is an asset to a police officer. It is hard for anyone to ignore a friendly smile. In fact, an effective public relations program would be to have all police officers simply smile and say "hello" to people they meet during the day.

☑ CHECK POINT

1. **State two reasons for the importance of good police-community relations.**
2. **What is the primary emphasis of most public relations programs?**
3. **What is the primary emphasis of most police-community relations programs?**
4. **List two factors that interfere with meaningful two-way communication between the police and the community.**
5. **What is the critical element required for any successful police-community relations program?**

*Answers

1. Good police-community relations are important in recruiting and retaining high-caliber individuals as police officers and in effectively fulfilling the responsibilities assigned to police officers.
2. The primary emphasis of most public relations programs is to raise the image of the police officer (a one-way type of communication).
3. The primary emphasis of police-community relations programs is to provide two-way communication between police and citizens to work toward achieving law and order in the community. (This will be the focus of Chapter 11.)
4. Important factors limiting two-way communication between police and the community are negative attitudes toward each other and unwillingness to listen to the other's side.
5. The critical element required for any successful police-community relations program is an effective, professional police officer's daily contacts with the citizens of the community.

SUMMARY

The police and the citizens of a community are dependent on each other. How each views the other and how effectively they can communicate together will have a vital influence on the effectiveness of police officers in fulfilling their responsibilities.

The police image results largely from everyday contacts between individual citizens and individual police officers. The police officer's behavior and the resulting image conveyed are influenced by the nature of police work, by the frequent confusion of identity and role conflict, by the police officer's unique relation to the criminal justice system, by the democratic nature of our society with its emphasis on civil rights and civil liberties, and by the police officer's personality.

Police officers are frequently described as being suspicious, cynical, bigoted, indifferent, authoritarian, and brutal. Although these negative personality traits may be explained by the factors previously enumerated, they may not be excused. Sometimes, however, the fault is not in the behavior of the police officer, but in the way it is perceived by the citizen.

The dominant characteristic of the "police culture" is isolationism which may result in a "them" vs. "us" orientation which does little to further good community relations.

Good community relations are important not only to recruit and retain high-caliber individuals as police officers, but to effectively fulfill the responsibilities assigned to police officers. Some police departments attempt to improve their image by instituting public relations programs—programs which emphasize raising the image of the police officer rather than opening channels of communications. Other departments concentrate on community-relations programs to provide two-way communication between police and citizens to work toward achieving law and order in the community.

This communication may be limited by such factors as negative attitudes toward each other and unwillingness to listen to the other's side.

No matter what type of program is instituted, however, the fact remains that the police officer on the street is ultimately responsible for the success of the police-community relations program and for the image of the police held by the citizens of the community.

APPLICATION

A. While answering a minor call, Officer Sheila O'Connor is flagged down by a nine-year-old girl who wants to talk to a police officer. Officer O'Connor tells her that she is on a call at the present time and cannot talk. She explains to the girl that as soon as she has finished her call, she will come back and talk to her. She asks the girl's name and address so she can contact her.
   1. Will the little girl have a favorable or unfavorable image of the police? Why?
   2. Is there anything Officer O'Connor might have done differently?

B. The Mytown chief of police has directed his officers to canvass their respective residential patrol areas and notify the residents that there have been a series of burglaries and that the police would like the residents who see any suspicious activities to call the police immediately.
   1. Would this approach cause a favorable reaction from the residents or might it make them afraid to leave their homes at night?
   2. From the standpoint of public relations, how would you view this type of operation?

C. While at a fire, it is Officer Applequist's job to control the crowd so that flying debris does not injure any spectators. Because of the large amount of activity, Officer Applequist becomes irritated and orders the crowd to go home, telling them, "You are all just nosey neighbors looking for a thrill; go home and let us do our job."

1. Was Officer Applequist right in telling them to go home?
2. How would you evaluate his actions from a public relations standpoint?
3. How would you have handled the situation?

*Answers

A. 1. She will probably have a favorable impression of the officer because the officer took the time to take her name and address, intending to talk to her later. However, if the officer failed to follow-up, the little girl's favorable impression would be destroyed.
   2. Yes. Since the call was a minor matter, it could have been delayed. Officer O'Connor could have stopped and talked with the little girl at the time. Five minutes would have probably satisfied the little girl.

B. 1. It could create a favorable reaction because it would indicate personal concern by the police for the residents. It might also make a few of the residents fearful of leaving their homes, but the increased alertness of the citizens for each other would probably cause the majority to have a favorable and appreciative attitude toward the police.
   2. It is a constructive form of public relations.

C. 1. Yes, they should be instructed to go home, but not in the manner used by Officer Applequist.
   2. He should not have lost his professional objectivity.
   3. He should have explained that leaving was for their own protection as well as to assist the fire fighting efforts.

DISCUSSION QUESTIONS

1. How do police officers deal with their own lives when they spend so much time with the worst of people?
2. How can police get away from the superhuman image?
3. What are some societal factors interfering with police work?
4. Why is the police officer on the street responsible for the success of police-community relations programs and the police image?
5. What is the dominant characteristic of the police culture?
6. What are some ways the police can get the public on their side?
7. Whose problem is it when the police and the community don't get along?
8. Has the police image changed in the past ten years? The past hundred years?
9. What do you feel is the police image?
10. What do you think is the general image of the police in our community?

REFERENCES

Bent, A. E. and Rossum, R. A. *Police, criminal justice, and the community.* New York: Harper and Row, 1976.

Cohn, A. W. and Viano, E. C. *Police community relations: Images, roles, realities.* Philadelphia: J. B. Lippincott Company, 1976.

Ellison, W. K. and Genz, J. L. The police officer as burned-out samaritan. *FBI law enforcement bulletin,* March 1978, pp. 2-7.

Garmire, B. L. The police role in an urban society. In *The police and the community* (R. F. Steadman, ed.). Baltimore: Johns Hopkins University Press, 1972.

Genz, J. L. and Lester, D. Authoritarianism in policemen as a function of experience, *Journal of police science and administration*, 4:1, 1976, pp. 9-13.

Germann, A., Day, F. and Gallati, R. *Introduction to law enforcement and criminal justice*. Springfield, IL: Charles C. Thomas Publishers, 1966.

Law and society review, 8:1, fall, 1973, pp. 135-152.

More, H. W. Jr. *The American police* (text and readings), Criminal Justice Series, St. Paul: West Publishing Company, 1976.

McNamara, R. Uncertainties in police work: The relevance of police recruits' backgrounds and training, *The police: Six Sociological essays*, (D. Bordua, ed.), New York: John Wiley & Sons, 1967.

Munro, J. L. *Administrative behavior and police organization*. Cincinnati: W. H. Anderson Company, 1974.

Niederhoffer, A. *Behind the shield*. New York: Anchor, 1967.

The police. The President's Commission on Law Enforcement and Administration of Justice. Task Force Report, Washington, D.C.: U.S. Government Printing Office, 1967.

Police and community relations . . . is a two-way street! New York: National Conference of Christians and Jews, 1969.

Skolnick, J. H. *Justice without trial: Law enforcement in a democratic society*. New York: John Wiley and Sons, 1967.

Stang, D. P. The police and their problems: *Law and order reconsidered*, Washington, D.C.: U.S. Government Printing Office, 1969.

Tanner, J. M. *Stress and psychiatric disorder*. Oxford: Blackwell Scientific Publications, 1960.

Westley, W. A. *Violence and the police: A sociological study of law, custom, and morality*. Cambridge: M.I.T. Press, 1970.

Section Three

Police Operations:
Getting the Job Done

By this point you should have a good understanding of the importance and complexity of being a law enforcement officer. The concepts from the preceding two sections should be kept in mind as you read about the day-to-day operations of the police officer. The citizens' civil rights and civil liberties, the laws to be enforced, the crimes to be dealt with, the other agencies that can lend assistance, the structure and goals of the individual police agency, the roles to be fulfilled, and the image of the police in the community all directly affect daily operations.

Despite a common conception that the police officer's routine is one of high-speed chases, shoot-outs, and close calls with dangerous criminals, this is only a small part of a police officer's job. Some officers never draw their gun in twenty years of service. A great part of their time is spent in preventing crime and in providing services to the community.

Operations can be divided into four basic categories: patrol—the backbone of police operations (Chapter 9), traffic (Chapter 10), community service (Chapter 11), and investigation (Chapter 12). You have already been briefly introduced to each of these; in this section you will get a close-up view of each. Although discussed separately, the four categories have considerable overlap. In some smaller agencies all four functions are performed by a single field-services division. In very small agencies they may be performed by a single police officer. Larger agencies, on the other hand, may have divisions within each of these four categories.

Patrol is a vital part of
police work,
responsible for
providing continuous
police services and
high visibility law
enforcement.

Patrol

The Backbone of Police Work

DO YOU KNOW□ □ □

- □ What primary tasks are performed by patrol?
- □ How specialized patrol differs from routine patrol?
- □ What methods of patrol may be used?
- □ What the central features of team policing are?
- □ What specific organizational change is common to all team policing programs?
- □ What the three primary goals of team policing are?
- □ How the police officers' role and image may be altered when team policing is instituted?
- □ What four basic types of team policing have been developed?
- □ What advantages and disadvantages accompany team policing programs?

*The execution of the laws is more
important than the making of them.*
—Thomas Jefferson

INTRODUCTION

Andrew Sutor (1976, pp. 84-87) vividly depicts what happened in Montreal,
Canada, in October, 1969, when the police went on strike and the city was
without police:*

*Rioting, arson, and looting broke out. In parts of Montreal there were piles of
broken glass, blocks of looted stores and burned-out vehicles.*

*During the day there were twenty-three major holdups, including ten bank rob-
beries. Armed men made off with $28,000 from the City and District Savings Bank on
St. Denis Street. Four men with machine guns held up a finance company. Conditions
became so bad that in a radio address Lucien Saulnier, Chairman of the Executive
Committee of the City, advised citizens to stay home and protect their property. One
householder who did, shot a burglar dead.*

*Around 8 p.m. scores of taxis pulled up at the Murray Hill Limousine Company
garage. Taxi drivers had long held a grudge against the company. Molotov cocktails
were thrown, and buses and cars were set afire. Employees opened fire on the mob
with shotguns. A provincial policeman was shot dead; other persons were wounded
by gunfire.*

*Passersby were caught up in the violence, and a mob, two to three hundred strong,
left the Murray Hill garage and proceeded toward Montreal's main shopping and hotel
district. With clubs, baseball bats and rocks the mob commenced an orgy of senseless
destruction and looting....*

*So extensive was the damage that a glass expert estimated that it would cost
$2,000,000 merely to replace the broken windows. The total damage from fires, destruc-
tion and theft has been placed at millions more.*

*...The extent of the lawlessness was amazing. One man reported: "I don't mean
hoodlums and habitual lawbreakers, I mean just plain people committed offenses they
would not dream of trying if there was a policeman standing on the corner. I saw cars
driven through red lights. Drivers shot up the wrong side of the street because they
realized no one would catch them. You wouldn't believe the number of car accidents I
saw, because drivers took chances cutting corners and crossing traffic lanes against
regulations. They knew there was no cop around to make a record of it."*

In his summary Sutor concludes: "You have often heard that crime prevention
by police is hard to measure. For one long day Montreal had the scale and it
measured 'anarchy.' " (p. 88)

> Patrol is responsible for providing continuous police service and high
> visibility of law enforcement.

Patrol is the most vital component of police work. All other units are supplemental to this basic unit. Patrol can contribute to each of the common goals

*Reproduced by permission from *Police Operations* by Andrew P. Sutor, Copyright © 1976, West
Publishing Company. All rights reserved.

of police departments, including preserving the peace, protecting civil rights and civil liberties, enforcing the law, preventing crime, and providing services.

TYPES OF PATROL

Patrol is frequently categorized as being either *routine* or *specialized*. Both routine and specialized patrol seek to deter crime and apprehend criminals as well as to provide community satisfaction with the services provided by the police department. Routine patrol does so by providing rapid response to calls for service; specialized patrol by focusing its efforts on already identified problems. Whether routine or specialized patrol is used depends on the nature of the problem and the tactics required to deal with it most effectively.

Routine Patrol

There is nothing "routine" about routine patrol. Its demands and challenges change constantly; the patrol officer may be pursuing an armed bank robber in the morning and rescuing a cat from a tree in the afternoon. As noted previously, routine patrol is the most basic unit of the police department. It is the primary means by which the police department fulfills its responsibility to the community.

Officers on routine patrol perform four major tasks:
—Crime prevention.
—Calls for service.
—Self-initiated activity.
—Administrative functions.

The workload of routine patrol can be summarized as follows:

Figure 9-1.

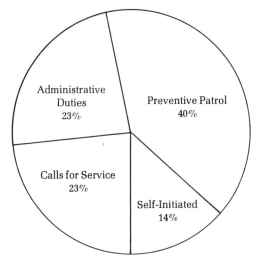

From: *Improving Patrol Productivity. Volume I. Routine Patrol*, National Institute of Law Enforcement and Criminal Justice, 1977, p. 3.

Crime Prevention.   The theory behind preventive patrol is that the presence of highly visible mobile patrol units will help prevent crime. As noted by the President's Commission on Law Enforcement and Administration of Criminal Justice (*Challenge of Crime*, 1967): "Preventive patrol, the continued scrutiny of the community by visible and mobile policemen, is universally thought of as the best method of controlling crime that is available to the police." The Montreal experience would seem to support this contention.

Preventive patrol is generally accomplished by uniformed officers moving at random through an assigned area. Since officers usually decide for themselves what they will do while on preventive patrol, this time is sometimes referred to as "noncommitted" time. It comprises between thirty to forty percent of patrol time, but it is often broken into small segments due to interruptions by self-initiated activities, service calls, and administrative duties.

Sometimes priorities for preventive patrol are identified and/or assigned during roll call. For example, patrol officers may be alerted to the presence of a known escaped criminal sighted in the area to watch for while on patrol.

Self-Initiated Tasks.   Officer-initiated activities usually result from officers' observations while on preventive patrol; that is, they encounter situations which require their intervention. For example, an officer may see a crime in progress and arrest the suspect. Usually, however, officer-initiated activities involve community relations or crime prevention activities such as citizen contacts or automobile and building checks. Officers may see a large crowd gathered and decide to break it up, thereby preventing a possible disturbance or even a riot. Or they may see a break in a store's security, take steps to correct it, and thus prevent a possible burglary later.

Such self-initiated activities occupy about 14% of an officer's patrol time. Officers are sometimes hesitant to get involved in community services and preventive activities because such duties make the officers unavailable for radio dispatches and interfere with their ability to respond rapidly to service calls. Hand-held radios and beepers have allowed patrol officers more freedom of movement and allowed them to initiate more activity.

Calls for Service.   The two-way radio has made the service call *the single most important element of patrol*. A radio dispatch almost always takes precedence over other patrol activities. For example, if an officer has stopped a traffic violator (a self-initiated activity) and receives a service call, most department's policy requires the officer to discontinue the contact with the motorist and answer the service call.

Too often little attention is paid to the officer's use of noncommitted time, which is often regarded as having no function other than to ensure the availability of officers to quickly respond to service calls. Frequently noncrime service calls interrupt a patrol officer's self-initiated activity that could prevent or deter crime. Emphasis on rapid response to *all* service calls has sometimes retarded the development of productive patrol services.

Calls for service account for approximately one-fourth of the officer's workload. An example of the type of incidents, in order of frequency, is given in the following table:

TABLE 9-1. Incidents in the 20th precinct, New York City Police Department, ranked in order of frequency of occurrence, 1967-68.

Incident type	Number of incidents	Total time (in minutes)	Average time (in minutes)
1. Other	5,629	162,310	28.8
2. Unfounded	5,132	102,881	20.0
3. Sick	4,552	202,143	44.4
4. Dispute	3,582	106,016	29.6
5. Burglary	2,518	104,881	41.7
6. Disorderly groups	1,693	37.780	22.3
7. Intoxicated person	1,555	41,830	25.9
8. Other misdemeanors	1,190	106,034	89.1
9. Injured	1,170	46,063	41.1
10. Alarm of fire	1,013	30,483	30.0
11. Auto accident	547	32,943	60.2
12. Larceny from auto	514	17,579	34.2
13. Robbery	512	33,476	65.4
14. Malicious mischief	435	16,261	37.4
15. Dead on arrival	402	60,216	149.8
16. Utility trouble	378	14,502	38.4
17. Felonious assault	309	26,982	87.3
18. Auto accident injury	286	25,334	88.6
19. Traffic violation	270	7,201	27.1
20. Accidental alarm	264	6,873	26.0
21. Grand larceny	235	11,598	49.4
22. Vehicle mechanical trouble	201	7,201	35.8
23. Grand larceny—pocketbook snatch	130	6,366	48.9
24. Auto safety check	126	4,175	33.1
25. Prowler	121	3,549	29.3
26. Auto larceny	104	12,556	120.7
27. False alarm of fire	86	1,865	21.7
28. Arrest—serving summons	81	2,480	30.6
29. Dangerous condition	81	3,510	43.0
30. Motor vehicle recovered	73	7,211	98.8
31. Other felonies	64	9,559	149.4
32. Narcotics	59	13,582	230.2
33. Found person	46	2,802	60.9
34. Traffic warrants	40	713	17.8
35. Property recovered	35	1,848	52.8
36. Rape	29	1,622	55.9
37. Missing persons	24	1,096	45.7
38. Auto accident—serious injury or death	13	2,587	199.0
39. Attempted suicide	13	1,056	81.2
40. Weapons	9	1,298	144.2
41. Prostitution	7	1,090	155.7
42. Gambling	7	813	116.1
43. Homicide	6	1,744	290.6
44. Suicide	6	607	101.2
45. ABC violation	5	160	32.0

Source: From the report of the President's Commission on Law Enforcement and the Administration of Justice. (*Challenge of Crime in a Free Society*) 1967.

Administrative Duties.   Accounting for another one-fourth of patrol time is administrative work, including preparing and maintaining the patrol vehicle, transporting prisoners and documents, writing reports, and testifying in court. Efforts to make patrol more cost-effective have often been aimed at cutting time spent on administrative duties. Some departments have greatly reduced the time officers spend maintaining their vehicles. Other departments have drastically reduced the amount of paperwork required of the patrol officers by allowing them to dictate reports which secretaries then transcribe.

The types of reports police officers frequently use include: Motor Vehicle Report, Vehicle Recovery Report, Offense Report, Continuation Report, Juvenile Report, Juvenile Report Summary, Persons Report, Arrest/Violation Report, and Record Check.

Specialized Patrol

Specialized patrol is designed to handle problems and situations that require concentrated, coordinated efforts. Such problems frequently involve a need for covert surveillance and decoys, tactics which cannot be used by uniformed patrol officers.

> Specialized patrol officers concentrate on specific problems and are relieved of routine service calls.

Usually a department requires at least thirty officers to assign some of them to standing specialized patrols. Smaller departments usually have specialized patrols only as needed. Assignments of specialized patrol may include hostage and sniper situations, VIP protection, riot- or crowd-control, and rescue operations.

Since these special problems are usually infrequent, the primary purpose of specialized patrol is to deter suppressible crime and to apprehend on-site offenders. *Suppressible crimes* are crimes which commonly occur in locations and under circumstances which provide police officers a reasonable opportunity to deter or apprehend offenders. Included in the category of suppressible crimes are robbery, burglary, car theft, assault, and sex crimes.

Specialized patrol operations are often used to saturate particular areas or to stake out suspects and possible crime locations. Countermeasures to combat street crimes have included police decoys to catch criminals—one of the most cost-effective and productive apprehension methods available. Officers have posed as cab drivers, old women, truck drivers, money couriers, nuns, and priests. They have infiltrated drug circles with undercover agents. Usually operating in high-crime areas, decoy officers are vulnerable to violence and injury. However, the results are considered worth the risk; an attack upon a decoy almost always results in a conviction of the attacker. Large police departments may use as many as twelve different decoy teams working at the same time in their high-crime areas.

In addition, the LEAA has assisted in setting up "sting" programs in many large metropolitan areas. Law enforcement personnel rent warehouses, set up videotape cameras and recording equipment, and, through authorized law enforcement procedures, buy stolen items from criminals. This type of operation has succeeded in eliminating a great deal of crime in metropolitan areas and has resulted in the conviction and sentencing of some master fences and master criminals.

When routine or specialized patrol are unable to prevent the commission of crimes or to apprehend a suspect in a crime, it often becomes the responsibility of the investigative services division.

☑ CHECK POINT

1. What are the four primary tasks performed by an officer on patrol?
2. How does routine patrol differ from specialized patrol?

*Answers

1. The four primary tasks usually performed during routine patrol are crime prevention, calls for service, self-initiated activity, and administrative duties.
2. Specialized patrol officers concentrate on specific problems and are relieved of routine service calls. They may or may not wear uniforms.

METHODS OF PATROL

Numerous methods of patrol have been used, often in combination, including foot, automobile, motorcycle, bicycle, mounted, aircraft, and boat as well as canine patrol.

> Patrol may be accomplished via foot, automobile, motorcycle, bicycle, horseback, aircraft, and boat. The most commonly used and most effective patrol is usually a combination of automobile and foot patrol.

Foot Patrol. Foot patrol, the oldest form of patrol, has the advantage of close citizen contact. Most effective in highly congested areas, it may help to deter burglary, robbery, purse-snatching, and muggings. Although the use of foot patrol has declined over the years, many large cities still use it extensively. Foot patrol is relatively expensive and does limit the officer's ability to pursue suspects in vehicles and to get from one area to another rapidly. Used in conjunction with motorized patrol, foot patrol is highly effective.

Automobile Patrol. Automobile patrol offers the greatest mobility and flexibility and is usually the most cost-effective method of patrol. It allows wide coverage and rapid response to calls—the vehicle provides instant communications with headquarters. The automobile also provides a means of transporting special equipment and prisoners or suspects. The obvious disadvantage of automobile patrol is that access to certain locations is restricted, for example, inside buildings. Therefore, officers may have to leave their vehicles to pursue suspects on foot.

Motorcycle Patrol. Motorcycle patrol is similar to automobile patrol; however, it foregoes the advantage of transporting special equipment and prisoners to overcome the disadvantage of limited access presented to automobiles. The motorcycle is also better suited to maneuver easily through heavy traffic or narrow alleys.

Bicycle Patrol.   Bicycle patrol is sometimes used in parks and on beaches, or in conjunction with stake-outs and surveillance. Although used infrequently, it adds another dimension of patrol available in special circumstances.

Mounted Patrol.   Like foot patrol, mounted patrol is decreasing in the United States, but it is still used effectively in larger cities such as New York to quell civil disorders and riots and to patrol bridle paths and parks. Although expensive, this method of patrol has a unique advantage—the size and mobility of the horse is more effective in an unruly crowd than an officer on foot or in a vehicle.

Air Patrol.   Air patrol is another expensive yet highly effective form of patrol, especially when large geographic areas are involved, for example a widespread search for a lost person, a downed plane, or an escaped convict. Helicopters and small aircraft are generally used in conjunction with police vehicles on the ground in criminal surveillance and in traffic control, not only to report tie-ups, but to clock speeds and radio to ground units. Helicopters have also been used to rescue persons from tall buildings on fire. In addition, aircraft is a cost-effective means of transporting prisoners over long distances.

Boat Patrol.   Boat patrol is used extensively on our coasts to apprehend gun and narcotics smugglers. Inland, boat patrols are often used to control river and lake traffic.

Figure 9-2.   Sheriff's water patrol submersing a water pump preparatory to fighting a fire on a launch.

Canine Patrol. Canine patrol is a specialized method of patrol usually found only in larger departments. It has been used in crowd control, in searching out burglars in warehouses, and in identifying hidden narcotics. Dogs have also been trained and used extensively in major airports to locate bombs and/or narcotics on planes.

Combination Patrol. Combination patrol provides the most versatile approach to preventing or deterring crime and apprehending criminals. The combination used will depend not only on the size of the police department but upon the circumstances which arise.

Table 9-2. Summary of patrol methods.

METHOD	USES	ADVANTAGES	DISADVANTAGES
Foot	Highly congested areas Burglary, robbery, theft, purse snatching, mugging	Close citizen contact High visibility Develop informants	Relatively expensive Limited mobility
Automobile	Respond to service calls Provide traffic control Transport individuals and documents	Most economical Greatest mobility and flexibility Offer means of communication Provides means of transporting people and documents	Limited access to certain areas Limited citizen contact
Motorcycle	Same as automobile except for transporting individuals	Maneuverability in congested areas and areas restricted to automobiles	Inability to transport much equipment Not used during bad weather
Bicycle	Stake-outs Parks and beaches	Quiet and unobtrusive	Limited speed
Mounted	Parks and bridle paths Crowd control	Size and maneuverability of horse	Expensive
Aircraft	Surveillance Traffic control Searches and rescues	Covers large areas easily	Expensive
Boat	Deter smuggling Water traffic control Rescues	Access to activities occurring on water	Expensive
Canine	Locating bombs, drugs, and burglars	Minimizes officers' risks	Expensive

☑ CHECK POINT

1. List as many methods of patrol as you can.
2. Which is usually the most effective method of patrol?

*Answers

1. Methods of patrol include foot, automobile, motorcycle, bicycle, mounted, aircraft, boat, and canine.
2. A combination of automobile and foot patrol is usually the most effective method.

TEAM POLICING

The team approach is not restricted to law enforcement. There are health-care teams in our medical clinics and team teaching in our schools. Logically, a team approach, the pooling of special talents into one coordinated effort, should be efficient and effective. Although the concept is simple and seemingly reasonable, implementation is complex, involving not only changes in organization but in the roles and functions of the police officer.

Characteristics of Team Policing

Team policing in the United States, patterned after a unique patrol experiment in Aberdeen, Scotland, in 1948, is designed to deliver patrol, investigative, and community services on a more informal basis. In other words, neighborhood team policing combines the specialized services and equipment of large urban departments with the more personal community contact of small departments.

Police services are decentralized with a team of officers assigned around-the-clock responsibility for crime control and police services in a specific area.

> Central features of team policing include:
> —Combining patrol, investigative, and community relation services.
> —Decentralization.
> —Cooperative decision making.
> —Permanent assignment to a team and a geographic area.

In many programs the officer's responsibilities are expanded to include investigative work as well as community relations services. Departments become decentralized, and as a result, decision-making is a product of teamwork, giving officers a voice in planning actions and policies which directly affect them. These features not only increase officer job satisfaction, they also frequently improve the quality and quantity of police services delivered to the community.

Some see team policing as a return to the golden age of police work typified by a friendly, well-known corner police officer who helped the residents manage their problems and who learned a great deal about them in the process. However, these friendly neighborhood police officers were very susceptible to corruption because of their familiarity with local residents, so they were transferred frequently to prevent them from getting to know people well enough to be corrupted. In addition, because they were on foot, they were slow to respond to calls for service. This was rectified by putting them into patrol cars for faster response over a large area.

The removal of the "beat" cop from the streets created new problems: lack of community contact between the police and the citizens. As a result, the President's Commission on Crime urged that officers in patrol cars should be considered foot officers who use cars for transportation from one point to another. Many officers, however, did not see it that way.

Many officers resist getting out of their cars to talk to citizens; some even feel it is a degrading type of appeasement. In addition, the practice contradicts the tactical principle of preventive patrol which requires the continual presence of moving, motorized street patrol. Some departments stress this principle to the extent that department regulations forbid unnecessary or unofficial conversations with citizens.

However, recent research on the effectiveness of preventive patrol indicates that a crime prevented by a passing patrol vehicle can, and usually is, committed as soon as the police are gone. In effect, police presence only prevents street crime if the police can be everywhere at once.

Lack of community contact is not the only criticism which has been made of the traditional police organization. It has also been criticized as being militaristic, centralized, stifling, task-oriented (specialized), and nonchallenging professionally. Police officers are not encouraged to communicate their ideas, to improve their skills, or to work with other officers in the department. They are likely to become bored or apathetic. If they do, the public can sense this attitude and may respond the same way.

Because of the inherent problems in the traditional police organization and the job dissatisfaction of many police officers, the President's Commission on Law Enforcement and the Administration of Justice (*Challenge of Crime*, 1967) recommended that:

Police departments should commence experimentation with a team policing concept that envisions those officers with patrol and investigative duties combining under unified command with flexible assignments to deal with the crime problem in a defined sector.

Organizational Changes

The features common to most team policing programs require several organizational changes within a police department.

> The most critical organizational change, common to all team policing programs, is *decentralization* of services.

This decentralization is often accomplished by shifting decision-making downward, increasing the management and operational responsibility of team leaders and first-line supervisors. Communications are enhanced not only by scheduled conferences and meetings, but by informal meetings as well. In some instances, roll call is replaced by informal meetings.

Decentralization also usually includes assigning a team to a clearly defined, relatively small geographic area.

Although team policing means different things to different departments, a 1973 study of team policing suggests that most programs have three basic operational elements (Sherman et al, 1973, pp. 3-5):

Geographic stability of patrol.

Maximum interaction among team members.

Maximum communication among team members and the community.

The authors identify the most basic operational element as geographic stability of patrol. This same study identified common organizational supports in addition to the three basic operational elements: unity of supervision, lower-level flexibility in policy making, unified delivery of services, and combined investigative and patrol functions.

The teams have been organized in two different ways: shift teams and area teams. A *shift team* usually has no formal coordination of the various shifts serving a single area. The supervisor of the shift team reports to a watch commander who is responsible for only a single shift within a twenty-four-hour period. This approach provides less continuity of service.

Area teams, usually headed by a lieutenant, provide law enforcement services twenty-four hours. This around-the-clock responsibility allows a single team leader to coordinate all patrol activities in the same area and provides considerable flexibility in deploying officers to meet changing levels of service demands throughout the day.

Area teams have three distinct advantages over shift teams. First, they provide continuity of service to citizens; second, they allow for alteration of schedule; and third, they have a larger manpower pool from which to draw.

Goals of Team Policing

Team policing is intended to accomplish several things (Olmos, 1977, p. 32):

Decentralize police operations.

Promote participatory management in problem solving and decision-making.

Encourage police officers to feel commitment and responsibility toward their clientele.

Increase the effectiveness of the police in combatting crime through increased information flow.

Produce an atmosphere of cooperation between the police and public.

Provide job-enriching experiences to line officers by developing their skills as well-rounded professional officers (generalists).

Promote accountability for the quality of police service within given areas or communities.

These several purposes are frequently combined into meeting three goals most often stated by team policing programs.

> The primary goals of most team policing programs are to:
> Reduce crime.
> Enhance police-community relations.
> Enhance the officer's role and image.

Reducing Crime.   The traditional role of the law enforcement officer was to seek out and apprehend individuals who committed crimes. This role is still important and is one of the primary goals of most team policing programs.

One approach to reducing crime is combining the patrol and investigative functions, thus improving coordination of efforts. Another aspect of team policing which has the potential for reducing crime is the more effective and efficient management of patrol workload with improved manpower allocations, increased number of dispatch calls serviced, and decreased response time.

A third aspect of team policing, and perhaps the most important in crime reduction, is close citizen contact. Many believe that the most effective way to reduce crime is through citizen cooperation. Citizens can report crimes in progress. After a crime is committed, the tactical emphasis switches from prevention to interception. Again the police greatly depend on information from the public to increase their chances of intercepting a criminal. If prevention and interception fail, the police turn to investigation. As with prevention and interception, investigation requires citizen cooperation not only in apprehending a suspect, but also in providing testimony in court proceedings.

A team policing program's success in reducing crime is difficult to evaluate. First, law enforcement efforts are not the only factor influencing crime trends; social and economic factors are also very influential. In addition, evaluation of crime rates relies on victimization studies which do not adequately reveal how many and what types of crimes are being committed; they only describe reported crimes. However, in spite of the shortcomings in evaluation, most departments which have implemented team policing programs that have proven to be successful in other areas also feel that they have been successful in reducing crime, even though hard data is not available to support this claim.

Police-Community Relations. Improved police-community relations is not only a goal of team policing, it is also a means of accomplishing the goal of reducing crime. In most team policing programs, the patrol officer is responsible for initiating police-citizen contacts and carrying out activities designed to reduce police-citizen conflicts. Community relations objectives include initiation of crime preventive programs, improvement of police-citizen cooperation, encouragement of citizen involvement in and concern for public safety issues, and neighborhood assistance officer programs, to be discussed more fully in Chapter 11.

Enhanced Officer Roles, Responsibilities, and Image. Team policing, with its decentralization and its downward shifting of decision-making, expands the role of police officers, making them professionals who perform a variety of tasks, often without supervision. Most programs stress the development of *generalist* officers.

> Police officers' roles are expanded to include investigation and community relations work. They are also more actively involved in decision-making.

Although responding to calls for service may still be their primary responsibility, they also perform work traditionally assigned to specialists:

follow-up on investigations, develop community relations contacts, and assist supervisors in coordinating team activities.

The expanded patrol officers' role and additional responsibility frequently increases job satisfaction as well as efficiency.

In addition to changing the role of the police officer, some departments have attempted to change the image of their officers. Albany, Dayton, and Los Angeles have used special vehicle marking and coloring schemes. Albany, Dayton, Holyoke, Menlo Park, and St. Petersburg have also adopted civilian-style blazer uniforms.

> The police officers' image is sometimes changed to suggest that they are friendly, helpful members of the neighborhood. Some departments have substituted blazers for uniforms.

Most of the experiments rested on the assumption that informal clothing would make citizens more comfortable around the police, would increase citizen identification with them, would decrease citizen-police isolation, and would increase communication between citizens and police.

Such changes were not without their problems, however, as illustrated in the experience of Menlo Park.

In 1970 Menlo Park, a San Francisco suburb, established a new image, a new philosophy, and a new uniform which eliminated the military blue matching shirt and trousers, the badge, and the nightstick, and replaced them with slacks, a tie, an emblem, and a double-knit blazer which hid the officer's gun. The change was not an attempt to look dashing or modern; it was an attempt to show the public that the police were there in the community to help.

The new image created problems, however, for both the citizens and for the officers. Neither citizens nor other uniformed police officers from other areas were able to recognize the blazer-clad individuals as police officers. In 1978, in keeping with the team policing emphasis on cooperative decision making, the Menlo Park police officers voted to revert to their traditional police uniform, indicating that the blazer did not carry enough authority to perform their jobs effectively. An important, though not openly admitted, factor in the decision may also have been peer pressure—reaction from police in other departments.

☑ CHECK POINT

1. What are the central features of team policing?
2. What is the most critical organizational change common to all team policing programs?
3. What are the three primary goals of most team policing programs?
4. How are the police officer's role and image often affected by implementation of team policing programs?

*Answers

1. Central features of team policing include combining patrol, investigative, and community relations services; decentralization; cooperative decision-making; and permanent assignment to a team and a geographic area.
2. Decentralization of services is the most critical organizational change common to all team policing programs.
3. The primary goals of team policing are to reduce crime, enhance police-community relations, and enhance the officer's role and image.
4. Police officers' roles are expanded to include investigation and community relations work. They are also more actively involved in decision-making. The police officers' image is sometimes changed to suggest that they are friendly, helpful members of the neighborhood. Some departments have substituted blazers for uniforms.

Categories of Team Policing

Team policing is found in small, medium, and large cities in equal numbers, not just in the big cities. It is found in both urban and suburban communities and in all parts of the country. Most team programs have replaced random roving patrol with objective-based patrol activities. Teams are assigned crime prevention, investigative, and community relations activities to perform when not responding to calls. Some departments place more emphasis on one of these activities than the others, and hence can be classified by their primary focus.

Four basic categories of team policing are:
—Basic patrol teams.
—Patrol-investigative teams.
—Patrol-community service teams.
—Full-service teams.

Basic patrol teams are synonymous with routine patrol in most respects. In routine patrol, the simplest form of team policing, the department is organized into teams responsible for basic preventive patrol, radio dispatch service, and traffic duties. The officers do not have investigative or community relations responsibilities, and specialists such as evidence technicians are not usually assigned to the team. The primary objectives of basic patrol teams are improved manpower allocation, reduced response time, and the clearance of service calls.

The *patrol-investigative team* combines the basic patrol and follow-up investigative responsibilities. Some departments have transferred almost half of their detectives to the team. Although the detectives perform most of the follow-up investigations, patrol officers are responsible for conducting more complete preliminary investigations and are occasionally assigned to investigative follow-ups. According to a national evaluation of the investigative effectiveness of teams (Gay, Day, and Woodward, 1977, pp. 23-27), "at the very least, teams with investigative functions have performed as well as, and in some cases, better than, non-team control units." This same evaluation suggested two advantages of combining patrol and investigative functions: (1) team policing contributes to the breakdown of officer-investigator isolation and hostility existing in many traditionally organized departments and provides an organizational context in which officers and investigators can coordinate their activities; and (2) since most crime is committed locally, it is natural for officers and investigators who are permanently assigned to a small number of beats to acquire knowledge of the assigned area and its people, thus increasing their investigative effectiveness.

The *patrol-community service team* combines basic patrol and community relations responsibilities. It may also include traffic responsibilities. The assignment of community responsibilities to team officers is hoped to increase both the level and kinds of service delivered to the community. Many patrol-community service teams have increased their attention to noncrime services such as interpersonal disturbances, auto accidents, missing persons, and referrals to social agencies for assistance.

Full-service teams are the most complex team policing programs, combining patrol, investigative, and community relations responsibilities. They also sometimes include traffic responsibilities. The decentralization of these functions usually involves transfer of detectives, community relations, and traffic personnel. Frequently three to four detectives are assigned to each team, thereby having a significant impact on the detective bureau of most departments. Most full-service teams are organized as area teams.

Full-service teams may be classified further as either multispecialist or generalist. *A multispecialist team*, as the name implies, combines patrol officers and specialists (detectives and community relations officers) under the direction of a team leader. The patrol officers participate in investigative and community relations activities, but the team specialists have primary responsibility.

In contrast, *generalist teams* expect each team officer to perform both basic patrol and specialist duties. The generalist approach severely reduces the number of personnel and functions assigned to centralized bureaus within a police department.

☑ CHECK POINT

1. What are the four basic categories of team policing programs?

＊Answer

1. The four basic categories of team policing are basic patrol teams, patrol-investigative teams, patrol-community service teams, and full-service teams.

Team Policing Across the Country

Each department using team policing has a slightly different organization, slightly different goals, and slightly different achievements. Yet each shares common goals with other police departments: perserving the peace, preventing crime, enforcing laws, preserving civil rights and civil liberties, and providing community services. A brief review of some team policing programs in various parts of the country illustrates the variety of approaches taken in implementing team policing.

Syracuse: Crime Control Team. Syracuse, N.Y., was the first to combine patrol and investigative functions into a single unit with geographic responsibility for crime control. The Crime Control Team consisted of eight police officers; a deputy leader; and a team leader, a lieutenant with considerable discretion in directing the team's activities and operations. The team was relieved of routine, noncriminal duties and given responsibility for controlling serious crime, apprehending offenders, and conducting investigations in a small area of the city. The decentralized Crime Control Team operated independently of the rest of the agency and achieved considerable success in reducing crime and increasing crime clearance rates. The team concept has been extended to other agency operations.

Los Angeles: Basic Car Plan. The objectives of the Basic Car Plan are to prevent crime by improving community attitudes toward the police, to provide stability of assignment for street police officers, and to give each team a proprietary interest in its assigned area. The plan was first tested in two divisions and then expanded city-wide in 1970. Each police division has geographic areas of varying size determined by workload and crime frequency data. A team consists of nine officers per shift assigned to a specific area and responsible for providing police service twenty-four hours a day. Specialized personnel are not assigned to the Basic Car Teams. Each team is headed by a senior lead officer. The patrol watch commander's and field sergeant's supervisory responsibilities remain unchanged. The team and citizens in each area hold formal meetings monthly. Informal meetings occur more frequently.

Detroit: Beat Commander System. This system began in 1970 in two scout car areas in Detroit's 10th Precinct. The beat commander, a sergeant, commands approximately twenty men, including three detectives who investigate only cases originating in the beat command area. Two additional sergeants provide around-the-clock supervision. The primary element of the system is stability of the team's assignment to a specified neighborhood. The goals are to improve police-community understanding, cooperation in crime control, police efficiency, and job satisfaction.

New York City: Neighborhood Police Team. New York City began operations in one radio motor patrol sector with a team consisting of a sergeant and eighteen officers. The system was later expanded throughout the department. Although similar in structure to the Detroit system, Neighborhood Team Policing police officers have greater investigative responsibilities because detectives are not directly involved in the program. The principal goals of the project are crime control and improved community relations. Benefits resulting from the program include improved supervision and motivation, resulting in increased productivity and efficiency as well as substantial reductions in response time to calls.

Dayton: Team Policing. Dayton decentralized authority and functions and concentrated upon community participation. The system used a generalist team approach to produce a community-based police structure, changing the traditional military structure of the police organization to a neighborhood-oriented professional organization. The experiment began in a district comprising one-sixth of the city. The personnel included thirty-five to forty officers, twelve community service officers, four sergeants who acted as leaders for teams of ten to twelve men, and a lieutenant in charge, selected by the chief of police and approved by neighborhood groups. Team leaders were selected from a slate of sergeants by vote of the officers. Team members made most decisions democratically.

Advantages and Disadvantages of Team Policing

Team policing in any form attempts to strengthen cooperation and coordination of effort between the police and the public to prevent crime and to maintain order. The decision to institute team policing depends on officer expectations, department expectations, community expectations, manpower, budget, and numerous other factors. Ironically, many citizens want their police officers to be friendly, warm, and "caring," but they also expect them to "keep the streets safe" and "crack down" on lawbreakers. Fulfilling both expectations simultaneously is no easy task.

Unfortunately, no hard data supports or discredits team policing. Since departments vary so greatly in their approach, the data that does exist is inconclusive. However, certain advantages and disadvantages or potential hazards have been tentatively identified.

Possible *advantages* of team policing:
—Improves police-community relations.
—Improves job satisfaction.
—Reduces crime.
Possible *disadvantages* of team policing:
—More costly.
—Places great demands upon supervisory personnel.
—Requires intensive retraining of officers.
—Added opportunity for graft and corruption.

According to Ralph Olmos (1977, p. 33): "While team policing appears to present a viable alternative to the traditional staff and line organization, it does entail certain risks. One drawback is that it is substantially more costly than line patrol due to increased manpower requirements. Additionally, it places great demands upon supervisory personnel and requires intensive retraining of patrol officers and specialists as well. There is also the included risk of added opportunity for graft." However, he goes on to state that evidence strongly indicates that properly implemented neighborhood team policing greatly improves police-community relations, employee job satisfaction, and causes reduction in crime as well.

The advantages and disadvantages must be carefully weighed in arriving at a decision regarding implementation of team policing. If the decision is made to implement, precautions must be taken to assure success.

Factors Contributing to Success or Failure of Team Policing

A study supported by the Police Foundation (Sherman, et al, 1973, pp. 107-108), examined seven programs in depth. The study identified three principle reasons team policing either failed or reached only partial success:

1. Middle-managers in the departments, seeing team policing as a threat to their power, subverted and, in some cases, actively sabotaged the plans.
2. Teams were dispatched by radio too often to permit their stay in a particular neighborhood.
3. The patrols never received a sufficiently clear definition of how their behavior and role should differ from that of a regular patrol; at the same time, they were considered an elite group by their peers, who often resented not having been chosen for the project.

According to the authors of this study, "whether a specific community should adopt team policing...depends first on that community's goals, and second on that community's judgment of team policing's effectiveness within its own situation. Most of all, it depends on both the commitment and the available resources to manage a complex process of institutional and community change."

☑ CHECK POINT

1. What are two possible advantages of team policing?
2. What are two possible disadvantages of team policing?

*Answers

1. Possible advantages of team policing include: improvement of police-community relations, improvement of job satisfaction, and reduction in crime.
2. Possible disadvantages of team policing include: cost, greater demand upon supervisory personnel, need for intensive retraining of officers, and risk of added opportunity for graft and corruption.

SUMMARY

Of all the operations performed by the police, *patrol* is the most vital. Patrol is responsible for providing continuous police service and high visibility of law enforcement. The four major tasks which are performed by officers on *routine patrol* are crime prevention, responding to calls for service, engaging in self-initiated activities, and performing administrative functions. Other patrol officers may be assigned to *specialized patrol* where they can concentrate on specific problems because they are relieved of routine service calls.

Patrol may be accomplished by foot, automobile, motorcycle, bicycle, horseback, aircraft, and boat. Canine patrol is often used in special instances. The most commonly used and generally most effective patrol is a combination of automobile and foot patrol.

In recent years several police departments have been experimenting with *team policing* which involves combining patrol, investigative, and/or community-relations services; decentralization; cooperative decision-making; and permanent assignment to a team and a geographic area. The most critical organizational change involved in implementing team policing is decentralization of services.

The primary goals of most team policing programs are to reduce crime, enhance police-community relations, and enhance the officer's role and image. The officer's role is often expanded to include investigation and/or community relations work. The image is sometimes changed to suggest that the police officer is a friendly, helpful member of the neighborhood. Some departments have abandoned the traditional police uniform in favor of blazers, but this change is not without its problems. The primary problem is one of identification.

When team policing is implemented, it is generally one of four types: basic patrol team, patrol-investigative team, patrol-community service team, or full-service team. Full-service teams may be either multispecialist teams or generalist teams.

Team policing has been tried in several parts of the country, meeting with some successes and some failures. The advantages and disadvantages of this approach to patrol must be carefully weighed by any police department considering implementing a team policing program.

APPLICATION

A. Mytown, USA, with a complement of thirty officers, has a burglary problem in a neighborhood that encompasses six square blocks. The Mytown chief of police decides to decentralize his police department and assign a neighborhood team policing unit to combat the crime. He assigns eight patrol officers and two detectives to the area and waits for some favorable results.

1. Should Mytown have team policing for this problem? Do you predict that it will be successful?
2. Should Mytown have team policing on a regular basis?

B. Downtown, USA, population 450,000 has a complement of 500 police officers. It is faced with a potentially volatile situation. A dissident group has obtained a permit to hold a meeting in one of the local parks. People are aroused and the police department must maintain order.

1. What patrol methods would you suggest the police use to maintain order?

C. The Mytown Police Department has a dignitary coming to town who will have his own personal security unit with him. However, additional protection is needed. Mytown has been requested to furnish it. (Recall that they have a department consisting of thirty officers.)

1. How can the Mytown Police Department best provide the requested security—or should they deny the request?

*Answers

A. 1. No. In a thirty-officer police department, the special assignment of ten officers to a team would deny adequate protection to the rest of the community.
   2. Mytown should *not* have team policing on a regular basis because the department is too small.

B. 1. Because the police want to avoid confrontation between the two groups, foot patrol would be the most effective. In this type of patrol, the police could form a cordon to keep the two groups apart. If horse patrol were available, it could be used because the size and mobility of the horses are highly effective with unruly crowds.

C. 1. Because Mytown is a small department, an ad hoc (as needed) specialized patrol could be set up to work in cooperation with the security group. The specialized patrol could cover the outside perimeters of the security area while the dignitary's security unit handled his close-in, personal protection.

DISCUSSION QUESTIONS

1. What type of patrol is used in our community?
2. What would happen if our police officers went on strike?
3. Why doesn't patrol have as much prestige as investigation?
4. Why is patrol considered a hazardous assignment by some and a "drag" by others?
5. What is the reason for team policing? How did it come about?
6. What are the advantages of team policing *to the officer*? What are the disadvantages?
7. Who decides whether team policing will be implemented?
8. Is team policing used anywhere in our state? If so, has it been successful? If not, what were the problems?
9. How do the majority of police officers feel about team policing?
10. What problems are involved in informal dress? Would these problems be likely to arise in our police department?

REFERENCES

The challenge of crime in a free society. U.S. President's Commission on Law Enforcement and Administration of Justice. Washington, D.C.: U.S. Government Printing Office, 1967.

Gay, W. G., Day, H. T., and Woodward, J. P. *Neighborhood team policing.* National Evaluation Program, Phase 1 Summary Report, National Institute of Law Enforcement and Criminal Justice, Law Enforcement Assistance Administration, U.S. Department of Justice, February, 1977.

Gay, W. G. and Schack, S. *Prescriptive package: Improving patrol productivity—Volume 1, Routine patrol.* Office of Technology Transfer, National Institute of Law Enforcement and Criminal Justice, Law Enforcement Assistance Administration, U.S. Department of Justice (Grant Number 76-NI-00-0055), July 1977.

Iannone, N. F. *Principles of police patrol.* New York: McGraw Hill, 1975.

More, H. W., Jr. *The American police. Text and readings.* Criminal Justice Series, St. Paul: West Publishing Company, 1976.

Olmos, R. A. Team policing, *Minnesota police journal,* October 1977, pp. 32-33.

Schack, S. and Gay, W. G. *Prescriptive package: Improving patrol productivity—Volume II, Specialized patrol.* Office of Technology Transfer, National Institute of Law Enforcement and Criminal Justice, Law Enforcement Assistance Administration, U.S. Department of Justice (Grant Number 76-NI-00-0055), July 1977.

Sherman, L. W., Milton, C. H., and Kelly, T. V. *Team policing: Seven case studies.* Mineola, New York: Police Foundation, 1973.

Sutor, A. P. *Police operations: Tactical approaches to crimes in progress.* St. Paul: West Publishing Company, 1976.

Wilson, O.W. and McLaren, R. C. *Police administration.* (4th ed.) New York: McGraw-Hill, 1977.

The traffic officer does not have a glamorous job, but it is a job that is critical to the safety of citizens in the community.

Traffic
Law Enforcement in a Mobile Society

DO YOU KNOW □ □ □

□ What the responsibilities of the traffic officer are?
□ What five actions are included in effective traffic law enforcement?
□ What the Enforcement Index is and how it is used?
□ What selective enforcement is and what purpose it serves?
□ What specific tasks are performed by the police officer when responding to a traffic accident?
□ What should be included in a traffic accident report?
□ What the most frequent cause of motor-vehicle accidents is?
□ What purposes are served by traffic reports? Who makes use of them?

*Motor-vehicle accidents are the leading
cause of death for people between the ages
of one and forty-four!*
—Accident Facts

INTRODUCTION

Officer Mortiki was on his second day with the Mytown Police Department patrolling in a one-man patrol car down the main street of Mytown, USA, a medium-sized city adjacent to a large metropolitan area. Mytown police officers were generalists, as the department was not large enough to have separate, specialized divisions. Officer Mortiki, extremely proud of his new profession, vowed he would be the best police officer in Mytown. He was enthusiastic about putting into practice all the elements of police work he had been taught in rookie school the past twelve weeks. As he wondered what it would be like, the dispatcher suddenly began broadcasting a call to Mortiki—his first call: a traffic accident.

Dispatcher: Car 555.

Officer Mortiki: Go ahead.

Dispatcher: A personal injury accident at the corner of G and L Streets. That's at the corner of George and Lincoln.

Officer Mortiki recognized the use of the phonetic alphabet when transmitting broadcasts where letters are used. It avoided any misunderstanding.

Standard Phonetic Alphabet

A—Adam	J—John	S—Sam
B—Baker	K—King	T—Tom
C—Charles	L—Lincoln	U—Union
D—David	M—Mary	V—Victor
E—Edward	N—Nora	W—William
F—Frank	O—Ocean	X—Xray
G—George	P—Paul	Y—Yellow
H—Henry	Q—Queen	Z—Zebra
I—Ida	R—Robert	

Officer Mortiki: Corner of George and Lincoln, personal injury accident. On the way with lights and siren.

He repeated the information to make certain there was no mistake in what he had received. As Officer Mortiki turned on the red lights and siren to respond to the emergency accident call, he vividly remembered what the instructor had taught him about responding to emergency calls:

Proceed to the scene promptly and safely. This means that you get there as rapidly as possible, but that you obey all traffic laws; reckless driving not only endangers others but decreases your chance of arriving at the scene safely.

Upon arriving at the scene, park the patrol car safely and conveniently. Leave the red lights on to warn approaching traffic of the accident and to prevent passersby who might be looking at the accident scene from running into the patrol car.

Upon arrival at the scene, Officer Mortiki did just that. He noticed that two vehicles had collided at the intersection and were a hazard to other cars traveling in the area. He immediately called the radio dispatcher for assistance before he left his vehicle.

As he approached the accident scene, Officer Mortiki noticed that one of the victims was bleeding profusely from his head. Having his first-aid kit handy, he applied a compress to stop the bleeding. He did not see any other injured persons. Since the victim was conscious and ambulatory, he escorted him to the patrol car. There he requested an ambulance and two tow trucks to clear the intersection.

Assuring himself that he had done everything possible to attend to the victim, he left his car as assistance arrived. Officer Donnely would handle the details of clearing the intersection while Officer Mortiki would interview the drivers and any witnesses who may have seen the accident happen.

Officer Mortiki knew from his instruction at the police academy that the thorough investigation of a traffic accident was probably the most important investigation an officer could make. Traffic, a major concern of every community in the nation, involved many nonpolice agencies which are seeking solutions to traffic problems—the problems of moving a very mobile society whose principal mode of transportation is the motor vehicle.

As Officer Mortiki interviewed the injured driver, the ambulance arrived and the victim was transported to the hospital. Officer Mortiki would interview him again when his treatment was completed. Mortiki interviewed the other driver and then sought out the names of witnesses who might give him details about the cause(s) of the accident.

Mr. Barney, who lived on the corner, told Officer Mortiki that the hedges along the property lines of a specific house obstructed drivers' views. Officer Mortiki recorded that observation and made a notation to give the information to the traffic engineer who might inspect the hazard.

Another witness stated that the cars never slowed down as they entered the intersection. In Officer Mortiki's mind this was an education problem. Another person who lived in the block stated that there should be a traffic control sign at the intersection to slow down speeding cars. Probably a traffic engineering problem and an enforcement problem, thought Officer Mortiki. A little selective enforcement might be in order. Officer Mortiki completed his interviewing of the witnesses and those in the residential area who were concerned about the accident.

He then proceeded to make careful observations of and to photograph the accident scene. He measured distances, drew a diagram, and recorded the vehicles' direction of travel, the time of day, weather conditions, and road conditions. These notes would be useful in reconstructing the scene should the case end up in court.

As he completed his notes, he saw that Officer Donnely was having the cars towed away and was cleaning the intersection of debris so it would be safe for other cars.

The preceding account illustrates one important facet of the police officer's traffic responsibility. It also illustrates the complexity of this responsibility, involving not only investigation, but service and the interrelation with other agencies such as traffic engineering.

THE RESPONSIBILITIES OF THE TRAFFIC OFFICER

A well-rounded traffic program involves many activities designed to maintain order and safety on streets and highways.

> Traffic officers are usually responsible for:
> —Enforcing traffic laws.
> —Directing and controlling traffic.
> —Providing directions and assistance to motorists.
> —Investigating motor-vehicle accidents.
> —Providing emergency assistance at the scene of an accident.
> —Gathering information related to traffic and writing reports.

Although the traffic responsibilities of a police officer may not have the glamour of a criminal investigation, they are critical not only to the safety of the citizens in a community but also to the police image.

The primary objectives of most traffic programs are to obtain the best possible movement of vehicles and pedestrians consistent with safety and to reduce losses from accidents.

Enforcing Traffic Laws. Police officers seek to obtain the compliance of motorists and pedestrians with traffic laws and ordinances as well as driver license regulations and orders. They issue warnings or citations to violators. Traffic officers provide law enforcement action related to operating and parking vehicles, pedestrian actions, and vehicle equipment safety.

Directing and Controlling Traffic. Police officers frequently are called upon to direct traffic flow, to control parking, to provide escorts, and to remove abandoned vehicles. They frequently are asked to assist in crowd control at major sporting events. They also are responsible for planning traffic routing, removal of traffic hazards, and emergency vehicle access for predictable emergencies.

Providing Directions and Assistance to Motorists. Police officers provide information and assistance to motorists and pedestrians by patrolling, maintaining surveillance of traffic and the environment, conducting driver-vehicle road checks, and being available when needed.

Investigating Motor-Vehicle Accidents. Police officers obtain and report the facts about accident occurrence as a basis for preventing accidents and providing objective evidence for citizens involved in civil settlements of accident losses. Police officers investigate accidents, including gathering facts at the scene and reconstructing the accident. They may also prepare cases for court and appear as prosecution witnesses when there has been a violation such as drunk driving (DWI).

Providing Emergency Assistance at the Scene of an Accident. At an accident scene the police officer may assist accident victims by administering first aid, transporting injured persons, protecting property in the vehicle, and towing disabled vehicles or helping the owner to obtain towing service.

Gathering Information Related to Traffic and Writing Reports. The police officer reports on accidents, violations, citations and arrests, disposition of court actions, drivers' cumulative records, roadway and environmental defects, and exceptional traffic congestion. The reports assist the traffic engineer and traffic-safety education agencies by providing information useful in their accident prevention programs as well as in planning for traffic movement or vehicle parking.

Sometimes police officers serve unofficially as the city's road inspectors as they discover problems in either road conditions or traffic flow. They may propose corrections to achieve safer, more effective motor vehicle and pedestrian travel and vehicle parking.

☑ CHECK POINT

1. Name at least five major responsibilities of the traffic officer.

*Answer

1. Traffic officers are usually responsible for (1) enforcing traffic laws, (2) directing and controlling traffic, (3) providing directions and assistance to motorists, (4) investigating motor-vehicle accidents, (5) providing emergency assistance at the scene of an accident, (6) gathering information related to traffic, and (7) writing reports.

TRAFFIC LAW ENFORCEMENT

A properly administered and executed police traffic law enforcement procedure is probably the most important component of the overall traffic program. If people obey the traffic laws, traffic is likely to flow more smoothly and safely, with fewer tie-ups and accidents. Effective traffic law enforcement usually consists of at least five major actions.

> Traffic law enforcement may take the form of:
> —On-the-spot instructions to drivers and pedestrians.
> —Verbal warnings.
> —Written warnings with proper follow up.
> —Citations or summonses.
> —Arrests.

Each of these actions has importance to traffic law enforcement. The circumstances of each individual incident will determine which action is most appropriate. It is up to the traffic officers to decide which action to take, but their decisions will be more impartial and consistent if they have guidelines on which to base them.

The question inevitably arises as to how much enforcement is needed to control traffic and reduce accidents. How many traffic citations will constitute the right amount to meet enforcement requirements and still retain public support for the police department?

This is a local issue which must be determined for each individual city and municipality. However, a nationally-approved guide, called the *Enforcement Index*, has been developed to assist in this determination.

The Enforcement Index

The Enforcement Index is calculated by dividing the number of convictions with penalty for hazardous moving traffic violations during a given period by the number of fatal and personal injury accidents occurring during the same period.

Enforcement Index = $\dfrac{\text{number of convictions for hazardous } \textit{moving traffic violations}}{\text{number of fatal and personal injury accidents.}}$

Recommended Index Figure: 20 to 25

For example, if during January a city had 25 fatal or personal injury accidents and the police department had 300 convictions for hazardous moving traffic violations, you would divide 300 by 25 and arrive at an index figure of 14—below the recommended level. This city should have from 500 to 625 convictions for hazardous moving violations rather than 300.

While not conclusive, this index provides one means of measuring the *quantity* of enforcement. The International Association of Chiefs of Police and the National Safety Council, through statistical research, have suggested that an index of 20 to 25 is both obtainable and effective for most cities. In other words, for each fatal and personal injury accident there should be twenty to twenty-five convictions for hazardous moving traffic violations.

To attain an effective traffic program, the index value may have to be raised in some cities and lowered in others. The index is simply a management tool designed to measure general compliance of the motorists in the community.

Quantity of enforcement alone is not sufficient. The public becomes aroused when there are too many citations. Good enforcement must also be of high *quality*.

Selective Traffic Law Enforcement

Because an astronomical amount of traffic violations occur every hour of every day, police departments cannot enforce all traffic regulations at all times. It is impossible to achieve 100% enforcement and almost always unwise to try to do so.

Selective enforcement is proportioned to traffic accidents with respect to time, place, and type of violations. It emphasizes hazardous violations which cause serious accidents.

Selective enforcement is not only logical, it is practical, since most police departments' limited manpower requires them to spend time on violations that contribute to accidents. Enforcement personnel, such as officers on solo motorcycles or assigned to a radar unit, are usually the officers assigned to selective traffic enforcement. The officer's activity is directed to certain high-accident areas, during certain days of the week and certain hours of the day or night.

Studies in city after city have proven a definite relationship between accidents and enforcement. In analyzing accident reports, one finds at the top of the list year after year the same traffic violations contributing to accidents and the same group of drivers being involved. Accidents will be discussed in greater detail in a few pages.

Selective enforcement is based upon thorough investigation of accidents, summarization, and careful analysis of the records. Adequate records are essential to the overall effectiveness of the selective enforcement program.

Quantity and quality of traffic law enforcement go hand in hand in any community. Many police departments have found that without quality, selectivity, or direction, their desired objectives in traffic supervision programs simply will not work. The public resents quantity goals that cause a police officer to issue many traffic citations and the court dockets to become overloaded with "not guilty" pleas. In departments where quality is emphasized, the public usually complies with safe driving techniques and acknowledges and supports safety programs.

Almost everyone has heard in exhaustive detail a friend's version of getting an "unfair" speeding ticket. They will tell several people about it. In terms of quality and selective enforcement, this has the effect of informing the general public that the police are doing their job. It may also prevent others from speeding.

High-quality enforcement is not only supported by the public, it has an important effect on the would-be traffic violator. When the public is informed of the police department's enforcement program and it is understood and believed to be reasonable and fair, the public will usually accept and support it.

☑ CHECK POINT

1. What five actions are usually included in effective traffic law enforcement?
2. What is the Enforcement Index and how is it used?
3. If a city has 8 serious traffic injuries or fatalities in a given month and there have been 300 convictions on hazardous moving traffic violations, what is this city's Enforcement Index Figure? Evaluate the quantity of their traffic law enforcement for that month.
4. What is selective enforcement and what purpose does it serve?

∗Answers

1. Traffic law enforcement may take the form of (1) on-the-spot instructions to drivers and pedestrians, (2) verbal warnings, (3) written warnings with proper follow-up, (4) citations or summonses, and (5) arrests.
2. The Enforcement Index measures quantity of traffic law enforcement. It is deter-

mined by dividing the number of convictions for hazardous moving traffic violations by the number of fatal and personal injury accidents in a given period. The
recommended index figure is 20 to 25.

3. Three hundred divided by eight equals 37.5. This index figure is much higher than
the recommended level. Too many convictions may be occurring.

4. Selective enforcement is proportioned to traffic accidents with respect to time,
place, and type of violation. It emphasizes enforcing hazardous violations which
cause accidents. The purpose of selective enforcement is to make the best possible
use of manpower and to reduce accidents.

TRAFFIC AND PATROL

Detecting traffic violations is no different for a patrol officer than detecting vandalism, auto theft, burglary, or trespassing. The officers know general
police methods, they appreciate the functions they have to perform while on
patrol, and they know traffic laws and the department's traffic policies. A
thorough knowledge of the department's overall traffic program, its objectives
and operations, will make the patrol officers assigned to traffic responsibilities
more effective.

While on patrol, police officers may also inspect facilities, detect hazardous road situations, and note locations where traffic control signs may be
needed. In addition, they are readily available to respond to accident calls.

TRAFFIC ACCIDENTS

As noted at the beginning of this chapter, motor-vehicle accidents are a
leading cause of death for people ages one to forty-four. During the hour in

Figure 10-1.   Motor-vehicle deaths per registered vehicles.

Between 1912 and 1976, motor-vehicle deaths per 10,000 registered vehicles were
reduced 91 per cent, from 33 to 3. (Mileage data were not available in 1912.) In 1912,
there were 3,100 fatalities when the number of registered vehicles totalled only
950,000. In 1976, there were 46,700 fatalities, but registrations soared to 142 million.

Deaths 46,700

Disabling injuries..1,800,000

Costs ....$24.7 billion

Motor-vehicle mileage ....1,412 billion

Death rate per 100,000,000 vehicle miles 3.31

Registered vehicles in the U.S. 142,400,000

Licensed drivers in the U.S. 133,800,000

ACCIDENT TOTALS	Number of Accidents	Drivers (Vehicles) Involved
Fatal	40,600	59,000
Disabling injury	1,200,000	2,000,000
Property damage and nondisabling injury	15,600,000	26,400,000
Total (rounded)...	16,800,000	26,400,000

From *Accident Facts*, 1977 Edition, National Safety Council, Chicago, p. 40.

which you are reading this chapter there have probably been two hundred traffic accidents resulting in injury and five resulting in death. Billions of dollars are lost annually through motor-vehicle accidents, and the cost in human suffering and loss is impossible to estimate.

In 1976, 46,700 persons died in traffic accidents. Alcohol was a factor in at least half of these fatal accidents. Although we have twenty-four times as many traffic deaths now as in 1910, there are three hundred times as many cars on the road (*Accident Facts*, p. 40). Traffic law enforcement and highway improvements seem to have had some positive impact.

Figure 10-2.   Principal Classes of Motor-Vehicle Deaths.

About two out of three deaths in 1976 occurred in places classified as rural. In urban areas, more than one-third of the victims were pedestrians; in rural areas, the victims were mostly occupants of motor vehicles. Over half of all deaths occurred in night accidents, with the proportion somewhat higher in urban areas.

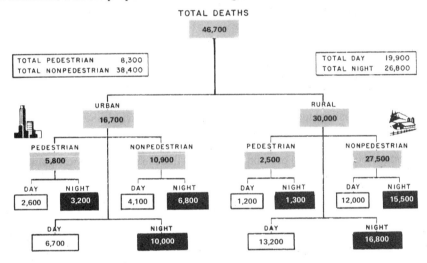

From *Accident Facts*, 1977 Edition, National Safety Council, Chicago, p. 41.

Causes of Motor-Vehicle Accidents

Motor-vehicle accidents result from numerous causes, but by far the *most important single cause is wrong driver attitude.*

Good driving attitudes are more important than driving skills or knowledge, a fact frequently overlooked in driver education programs. Drivers who jump lanes, try to beat out others as they merge from cloverleafs, race, follow too closely, or become angry and aggressive account for many of our serious motor-vehicle accidents. Driver behavior such as illegal and unsafe speed, failure to yield the right of way, crossing over the center line, driving in the wrong lane, and driving while under the influence of alcohol make the traffic statistics rise year after year.

And, year after year the same group of drivers cause the most frequent accidents: male drivers ages 20 to 29. Although males are involved in more accidents than females, males also do more driving.

The three basic causes of motor-vehicle accidents are:
—Human faults, errors, violations, and ATTITUDES.
—Road defects.
—Car defects.

Figure 10-3. Relative importance of three basic elements in accidents.

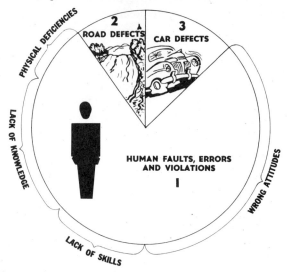

Federal Bureau of Investigation. Reprinted by permission.

Responsibilities of the Officer Called to the Scene of an Accident

You were introduced to several of the responsibilities of the officer called to the scene of an accident when you read the account of Officer Mortiki at the beginning of this chapter.

The officer called to the scene of an auto accident should:
—Proceed to the scene rapidly but safely.
—Park safely and conveniently.
—Administer emergency first-aid if required.
—Interview all persons involved as well as all witnesses.
—Provide needed assistance to victims.
—Accurately observe and record all facts related to the accident.
—Clear the scene as soon as possible to restore traffic flow.

You may want to reread the account of Officer Mortiki's response to the accident call (pp. 272-273).

It is important that all facts related to the accident are accurately observed and recorded. The time of day should be noted, as a setting or rising sun might have temporarily blinded one of the drivers. All marks on the road

Figure 10-4. Accident rates per age and per sex.

Age of driver

There were about 133,800,000 drivers in the nation in 1976. The approximate number in each age group is shown in the table below, along with each group's accident experience for the year. The figures in the last two columns at the right indicate the frequency of accident involvement; the higher the number, the higher the involvement in each age group.

Age of Drivers—Total Number and Number in Accidents, 1976

| Age Group | All Drivers | | Drivers in Accidents | | | | | |
| | Number | % | Fatal | | All | | Per No. of Drivers | |
			Number	%	Number	%	Fatal*	All**
Total	133,800,000	100.0%	59,000	100.0%	28,400,000	100.0%	44	21
Under 20	13,600,000	10.2	9,800	16.6	5,100,000	18.0	72	38
20-24	15,700,000	11.7	12,300	20.9	5,600,000	19.7	78	36
25-29	16,100,000	12.0	7,400	12.5	3,800,000	13.4	50	24
30-34	14,300,000	10.7	6,300	10.7	3,000,000	10.6	44	21
35-39	12,000,000	9.0	3,900	6.6	2,000,000	7.0	33	17
40-44	11,300,000	8.4	3,900	6.6	1,700,000	6.0	35	15
45-49	11,800,000	8.8	3,500	5.9	1,700,000	6.0	30	14
50-54	11,200,000	8.4	2,800	4.8	1,400,000	4.9	25	13
55-59	9,000,000	6.7	2,400	4.1	1,300,000	4.6	27	14
60-64	6,800,000	5.1	2,100	3.5	1,000,000	3.5	31	15
65-69	5,700,000	4.3	1,600	2.7	900,000	3.2	28	16
70-74	3,700,000	2.8	1,200	2.0	300,000	1.0	32	8
75 and over	2,600,000	1.9	1,800	3.1	600,000	2.1	69	23

Source: Drivers in accidents based on reports from 25 state traffic authorities. Number of drivers by age are NSC estimates based on reports from state traffic authorities and research groups.
*Drivers in Fatal Accidents per 100,000 drivers in each age group.
**Drivers in All Accidents per 100 drivers in each age group.

Sex of driver

Of the estimated 133,800,000 drivers in 1976, about 72,800,000 are males and 61,000,000 are females. Males are involved in more accidents than are females, as shown in the table below, but the difference is due at least partly to differences in the amount of driving done by the members of each sex, and to differences in the time, place, and circumstance of the driving.

Sex of Driver Involved in Accidents, 1961-1976

| Year | Drivers in Fatal Accidents | | | | Drivers in All Accidents | | | |
| | Male | | Female | | Male | | Female | |
	No.	Rate†	No.	Rate†	No.	Rate††	No.	Rate††
1961	40,000	75	6,000	30	14,900,000	278	3,600,000	180
1962	43,000	77	7,000	34	15,000,000	268	4,000,000	193
1963	46,200	79	7,800	36	15,700,000	267	4,300,000	198
1964	48,900	79	8,600	38	16,700,000	270	4,800,000	210
1965	50,300	78	8,900	37	18,300,000	282	5,300,000	221
1966	54,600	81	9,700	37	18,600,000	276	5,700,000	218
1967	54,600	80	9,900	35	18,500,000	272	5,800,000	205
1968	59,500	84	10,500	35	19,600,000	275	6,400,000	211
1969	59,800	80	10,900	33	20,000,000	268	6,800,000	209
1970	57,800	75	10,700	31	20,500,000	265	7,200,000	209
1971	56,700	70	11,100	30	20,900,000	256	7,400,000	199
1972	59,000	68	11,900	28	21,000,000	243	8,100,000	201
1973	55,900	63	11,400	27	20,200,000	227	7,900,000	189
1974	48,000	55	9,800	24	17,800,000	205	7,300,000	177
1975	46,500	52	9,600	22	19,100,000	212	8,400,000	195
1976	48,100	51	10,900	24	19,600,000	206	8,800,000	191

Source: Accidents and Drivers—NSC estimates based on reports from state motor-vehicle departments and Federal Highway Administration. Mileage—NSC estimates based on survey data from National Family Opinions, Inc.
†Number of drivers in fatal accidents per 1,000,000,000 miles driven.
††Number of drivers in all accidents per 10,000,000 miles driven.

Reprinted from *Accident Facts*, p. 41, 1977 Edition with permission of the National Safety Council, Chicago, Illinois.

should be measured and recorded. The condition of the road should be noted: wet or dry; muddy, dusty, or sandy; dirt, asphalt, or cement. The width of the street and any obstructions to vision should also be noted. The comprehensive traffic accident report which follows illustrates the amount of detail required for an effective traffic accident report.

Figure 10-5. Comprehensive Traffic Report Form.

TRAFFIC ACCIDENT REPORT
POLICE DEPARTMENT

VEHICLE NO. 1
CIRCLE OWNER (LAST) (FIRST) (MIDDLE)
DRIVER
2 ADDRESS (NO AND STREET)
(CITY) (STATE)
3 SEX | RACE | DATE OF BIRTH | 4 DRIVER'S LICENSE NO ST
5 VEHICLE MAKE | YEAR | TYPE | 6 CIRCLE DAMAGED AREAS
7 VEHICLE LICENSE NO | STATE | YEAR
MOVING / STOPPED / PARKED } 8 DIRECTION FACING:
(INDICATE STREET)

9 CENTRAL CASE NUMBER
10 DATE OF ACCIDENT MONTH | DAY | YEAR
TIME ☐ A M ☐ P M | DAY OF WEEK
11 ACCIDENT LOCATION
N S E W ☐ ☐ ☐ ☐ SIDE OF
(STREET)
___ FT N S E W ☐ ☐ ☐ ☐ OF/AT
INTERSECTING STREET OR HOUSE NO
1 AT INTERSECTION | 3 ON PUBLIC PROPERTY
2 NOT AT INTERSECTION | 4 ON PRIVATE PROPERTY } OFF STREET

VEHICLE NO. 2
1 CIRCLE OWNER (LAST) (FIRST) (MIDDLE)
DRIVER
2 ADDRESS (NO AND STREET)
(CITY) (STATE)
3 SEX | RACE | DATE OF BIRTH | 4 DRIVER'S LICENSE NO ST
5 VEHICLE MAKE | YEAR | TYPE | 6 CIRCLE DAMAGED AREAS
7 VEHICLE LICENSE NO | STATE | YEAR
MOVING / STOPPED / PARKED } 8 DIRECTION FACING:
(INDICATE STREET)

12 CLASSIFICATION OF ACCIDENT
☐ PROPERTY DAMAGE ONLY
☐ INJURED OR FATAL MOTORIST
☐ INJURED OR FATAL PEDESTRIAN
☐ OTHER ____________
☐ HIT & RUN
☐ POLICE VEH INV
☐ OTHER CITY VEH INVOLVED
☐ CITY PROP DAMAGE

13 DATE NOTIFIED OF ACCIDENT MONTH | DAY | YEAR | TIME ☐ A M ☐ P M
14 INVESTIGATION MADE ☐ AT SCENE ☐ ____________

15 CHECK IF APPLICABLE ☐ PHOTOS TAKEN ☐ STATEMENT TAKEN ☐ BRAKE TEST MADE ☐ MEASUREMENTS TAKEN
16 SEAT BELTS INSTALLED ☐ YES ☐ NO | IN USE ☐ YES ☐ NO

17 DAMAGE TO OTHER PROPERTY: (IDENTIFY PROPERTY – AMOUNT OF DAMAGE – OWNER'S NAME AND ADDRESS)

18 TYPE OF ACCIDENT ("X" ONE ONLY)
COLLISION OF MOTOR VEHICLE WITH:
1 PEDESTRIAN
2 MOTOR VEHICLE IN TRAFFIC
3 PARKED MOTOR VEHICLE
4 RAILROAD TRAIN
5 BICYCLIST
6 ANIMAL
7 FIXED OBJECT
8 OTHER OBJECT
9 RAN OFF ROAD
10 OVERTURNED IN ROAD
11 OTHER NON-COLLISION
12 OTHER: ____________

19 MANNER OF COLLISION ("X" ONE ONLY)
1 ANGLE
2 MERGING
3 CUTTING IN
4 SIDESWIPE, VEHICLE IN SAME DIRECTION
5 SIDESWIPE, VEHICLE IN OPP DIRECTION
6 HEAD ON
7 REAR END
8 TURNING MANEUVER
9 PARKING MANEUVER
10 OTHER: ____________

DRIVER 1 2 3 — 20 WHAT DRIVERS WERE DOING IMMEDIATELY BEFORE ACC
1 GOING STRAIGHT AHEAD
2 CHANGING LANES
3 MAKING RIGHT TURN
4 MAKING LEFT TURN
5 MAKING U TURN
6 SLOWING OR STOPPING
7 STARTING IN TRAFFIC
8 LEAVING PARKING PLACE
9 STOPPED IN TRAFFIC
10 PARKED
11 BACKING
12 DRIVERLESS MOVING VEH
13 OTHER: ____________

DRIVER 1 2 3 — 21 APPARENT VIOLATIONS
1 SPEED TOO FAST
2 FAILED TO YIELD RIGHT OF WAY
3 ON WRONG SIDE OF ROAD
4 OVERTOOK IMPROPERLY
5 PASSED STOP SIGN
6 DISOBEYED TRAFFIC SIGNAL
7 FOLLOWED TOO CLOSELY
8 MADE IMPROPER TURN
9 OTHER: ____________
10 BRAKES INADEQUATE
11 LIGHTS IMPROPER
12 NO IMPROPER DRIVING

DRIVER 1 2 3 — 22 PHYSICAL CONDITION
1 HAD NOT BEEN DRINKING
HAD BEEN DRINKING AND:
2 OBVIOUSLY DRUNK
ABILITY IMPAIRED
ABILITY NOT IMPAIRED
IMPAIRMENT NOT KNOWN
ALCOHOL TEST ADMINISTERED
3 PHYSICAL HANDICAP
4 ILL
5 SLEEPY, TIRED, ETC
6 APPARENTLY DRUGGED
7 APPARENTLY NORMAL

VEHICLES 1 2 3 — 23 TYPE OF STREET
1 EXPRESSWAY
2 EXPRESSWAY ENT., EXIT RAMP
3 BLVD., DRIVE, PARKWAY
4 BUSINESS, MFG
5 LOCAL RESIDENTIAL STREET
6 ALLEY
7 DRIVEWAY
8 OTHER ____________

24 WEATHER
1 CLEAR
2 RAINING
3 SNOWING
4 FOG OR MIST

27 LIGHT CONDITION
1 DAYLIGHT
2 DAWN, DUSK
3 DARKNESS

25 ROAD CONDITION
1 DRY
2 WET
3 SNOWY, ICY
4 CONST., REPAIR

28 STREET LIGHTS
1 ON
2 OFF
3 NONE

26 TRAFFIC CONTROL
1 STOP SIGN
2 TRAFFIC SIGNAL
3 OFFICER
4 R R X-ING GATES
5 R R X-ING SIGNAL
6 OTHER: ____________
7 NO CONTROL

30 ARRESTS
DRIVER NO | SUMMONS NO
CHARGES
COURT RM | COURT DATE | TIME ☐ A M ☐ P M
DRIVER NO | SUMMONS NO
CHARGES
COURT RM | COURT DATE | TIME ☐ A M ☐ P M

29 WITNESSES (INCLUDING OCCUPANTS):
NAME | ADDRESS (NO AND STREET) | (CITY) | (STATE)

REPORTING OFFICER(S) | NO | DIST/UNIT | BEAT NO OF ASSIGNMENT | BEAT NO OF OCCURRENCE | 32 SUPERVISOR APPROVING

Traffic accident reports should include all relevant details, including information about the drivers, their actions, their vehicles, the type of accident, the manner of collision, the type of street, weather conditions, road conditions, light conditions, and existing traffic control.

Look again at the comprehensive traffic report form on pp. 282-283 and find where each of the details are recorded.

Figure 10-5. Continued.

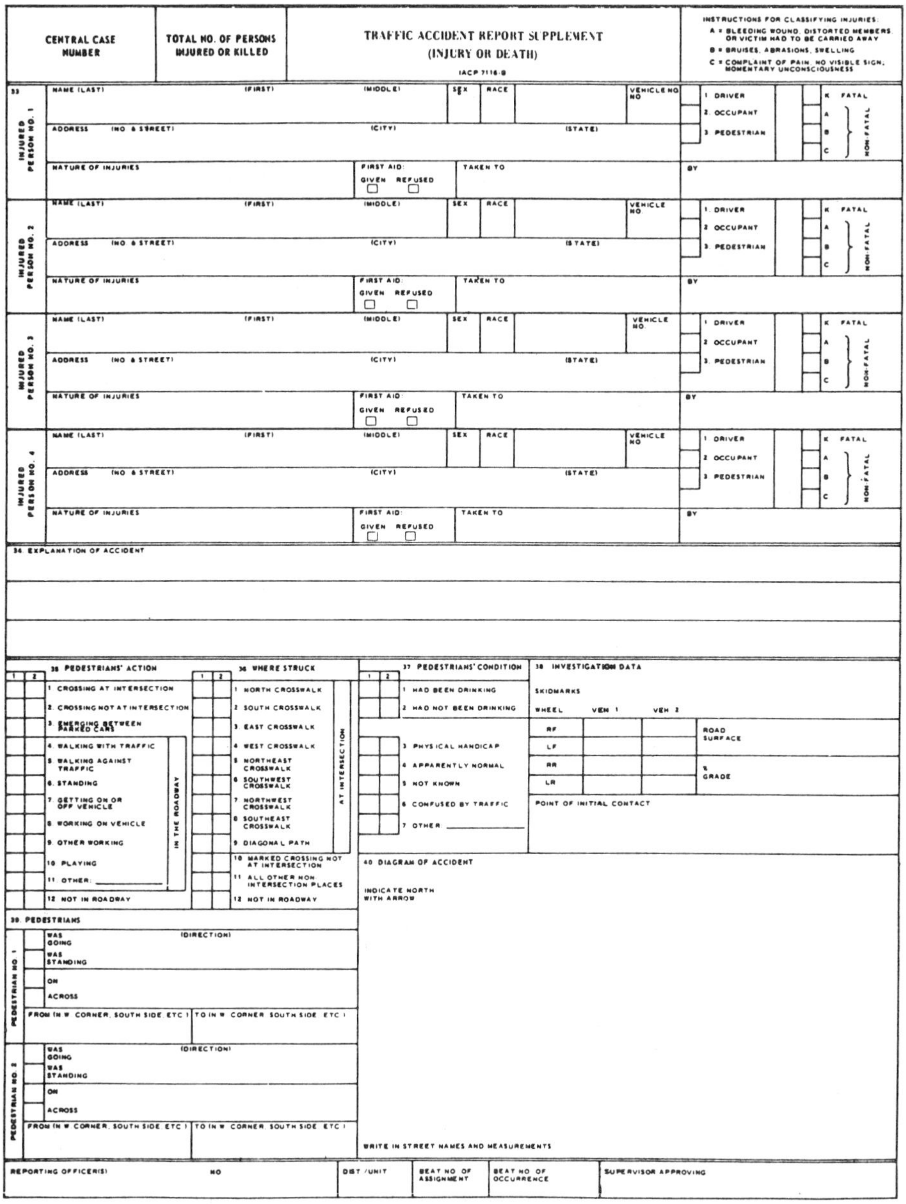

CENTRAL CASE NUMBER

TOTAL NO. OF PERSONS INJURED OR KILLED

TRAFFIC ACCIDENT REPORT SUPPLEMENT
(INJURY OR DEATH)
IACP 7116-B

INSTRUCTIONS FOR CLASSIFYING INJURIES:
A = BLEEDING WOUND, DISTORTED MEMBERS OR VICTIM HAD TO BE CARRIED AWAY
B = BRUISES, ABRASIONS, SWELLING
C = COMPLAINT OF PAIN, NO VISIBLE SIGN; MOMENTARY UNCONSCIOUSNESS

33 INJURED PERSON NO. 1
NAME (LAST) (FIRST) (MIDDLE) SEX RACE VEHICLE NO.
ADDRESS (NO. & STREET) (CITY) (STATE)
NATURE OF INJURIES FIRST AID: GIVEN REFUSED TAKEN TO BY
1. DRIVER 2. OCCUPANT 3. PEDESTRIAN
K FATAL A B C NON-FATAL

INJURED PERSON NO. 2
NAME (LAST) (FIRST) (MIDDLE) SEX RACE VEHICLE NO.
ADDRESS (NO. & STREET) (CITY) (STATE)
NATURE OF INJURIES FIRST AID: GIVEN REFUSED TAKEN TO BY
1. DRIVER 2. OCCUPANT 3. PEDESTRIAN
K FATAL A B C NON-FATAL

INJURED PERSON NO. 3
NAME (LAST) (FIRST) (MIDDLE) SEX RACE VEHICLE NO.
ADDRESS (NO. & STREET) (CITY) (STATE)
NATURE OF INJURIES FIRST AID: GIVEN REFUSED TAKEN TO BY
1. DRIVER 2. OCCUPANT 3. PEDESTRIAN
K FATAL A B C NON-FATAL

INJURED PERSON NO. 4
NAME (LAST) (FIRST) (MIDDLE) SEX RACE VEHICLE NO.
ADDRESS (NO. & STREET) (CITY) (STATE)
NATURE OF INJURIES FIRST AID: GIVEN REFUSED TAKEN TO BY
1. DRIVER 2. OCCUPANT 3. PEDESTRIAN
K FATAL A B C NON-FATAL

34 EXPLANATION OF ACCIDENT

35 PEDESTRIANS' ACTION (1, 2)
1. CROSSING AT INTERSECTION
2. CROSSING NOT AT INTERSECTION
3. EMERGING BETWEEN PARKED CARS
IN THE ROADWAY:
4. WALKING WITH TRAFFIC
5. WALKING AGAINST TRAFFIC
6. STANDING
7. GETTING ON OR OFF VEHICLE
8. WORKING ON VEHICLE
9. OTHER WORKING
10. PLAYING
11. OTHER: ______
12. NOT IN ROADWAY

36 WHERE STRUCK (1, 2)
AT INTERSECTION:
1. NORTH CROSSWALK
2. SOUTH CROSSWALK
3. EAST CROSSWALK
4. WEST CROSSWALK
5. NORTHEAST CROSSWALK
6. SOUTHWEST CROSSWALK
7. NORTHWEST CROSSWALK
8. SOUTHEAST CROSSWALK
9. DIAGONAL PATH
10. MARKED CROSSING NOT AT INTERSECTION
11. ALL OTHER NON-INTERSECTION PLACES
12. NOT IN ROADWAY

37 PEDESTRIANS' CONDITION (1, 2)
1. HAD BEEN DRINKING
2. HAD NOT BEEN DRINKING
3. PHYSICAL HANDICAP
4. APPARENTLY NORMAL
5. NOT KNOWN
6. CONFUSED BY TRAFFIC
7. OTHER: ______

38 INVESTIGATION DATA
SKIDMARKS
WHEEL VEH 1 VEH 2
RF
LF
RR
LR
ROAD SURFACE
% GRADE
POINT OF INITIAL CONTACT

39. PEDESTRIANS
PEDESTRIAN NO. 1
WAS GOING (DIRECTION)
WAS STANDING
ON
ACROSS
FROM (N.W. CORNER, SOUTH SIDE, ETC.) TO (N.W. CORNER, SOUTH SIDE, ETC.)

PEDESTRIAN NO. 2
WAS GOING (DIRECTION)
WAS STANDING
ON
ACROSS
FROM (N.W. CORNER, SOUTH SIDE, ETC.) TO (N.W. CORNER, SOUTH SIDE, ETC.)

40 DIAGRAM OF ACCIDENT
INDICATE NORTH WITH ARROW
WRITE IN STREET NAMES AND MEASUREMENTS

REPORTING OFFICER(S) NO. DIST./UNIT BEAT NO. OF ASSIGNMENT BEAT NO. OF OCCURRENCE SUPERVISOR APPROVING

☑ CHECK POINT

1. **List at least five specific tasks which might be performed by a police officer who responds to a traffic accident service call.**

2. What are the three basic causes of motor-vehicle accidents?
3. What is the single most important factor in motor-vehicle accidents?
4. List at least six items which should be included in a traffic accident report.

*Answers

1. A police officer who responds to a traffic accident call should: (1) proceed to the scene rapidly but safely, (2) park safely and conveniently, (3) administer emergency first-aid, (4) interview all persons involved as well as all witnesses, (5) provide needed assistance to victims, (6) accurately observe and record all facts related to the accident, and (7) clear the scene.
2. The three basic causes of motor-vehicle accidents are (1) human faults, errors, violations, and attitudes, (2) road defects, and (3) car defects.
3. Driver *attitude* is the single most important factor in motor-vehicle accidents.
4. Traffic reports should include information about the drivers, their actions, their vehicles, the type of accident, the manner of collision, the type of street, weather conditions, road conditions, light conditions, and existing traffic control.

Importance of Accident Reports

Accident reports by police officers provide a guide for many other department activities as well as a guide for other agencies involved in traffic and safety.

> Accident reports provide important information for:
> —Enforcement of laws.
> —Traffic engineering.
> —Educational activities.

In addition, a host of other agencies involved in traffic make use of the information contained in traffic accident reports. Public information agencies such as newspapers, television, and radio disseminate information about traffic, traffic conditions, road conditions, and traffic accidents. Attorneys and the courts use traffic accident reports in determining the facts in traffic accidents which result in law suits. The state motor-vehicle department or state department of public safety, which has the power to suspend or revoke drivers' licenses, also uses information contained in these reports. Legislative bodies in each state may rely on traffic accident reports when they plan for providing funds, equipment and personnel to effectively enforce traffic safety programs and when they determine what laws must be passed to control traffic.

Traffic accident reports may be used by engineers, both federal and state, who research ways to improve highway systems and by the National Safety Council and state safety councils which compile statistics related to accidents: Who is having them? Where? When? How? The reports may be used by insurance companies which base their automobile insurance rates upon the accident record of the community.

Clearly, traffic accident reports have a multitude of purposes.

> Traffic accident reports may serve as the basis of traffic law enforcement policy, accident prevention programs, traffic education, legislative reform of traffic laws, traffic engineering decisions, and motor-vehicle administration decisions.

In some smaller police departments, a police officer might be assigned to work with public works departments or city engineers in traffic engineering. Although not involved in the technical design, construction, or maintenance decisions and problems, the officer contributes information beneficial to mechanical operations such as routine maintenance by calling in hazardous road situations encountered while on routine patrol; inspecting facilities and making recommendations for the erection of traffic control signs, needed painting of street lines, crosswalks, and curbs; and performing similar activities of a non-technical nature.

Although large cities usually have special traffic engineers, police officers still contribute expertise to those who make the final decisions. Police officers' most important contribution to traffic engineering is the research they compile related to accidents and congested streets. They further report hazardous conditions which need attention. In return, traffic engineers often furnish the police with advice and information to further their traffic supervision policies. This relationship can result in increased accident prevention and attainment of traffic control goals and objectives.

PUBLIC EDUCATION PROGRAMS

The police also seek to educate the public in traffic safety. Although it is not one of their primary functions, they often participate in local school programs, private safety organizations, local service clubs, and state safety councils, as we will discuss in more depth in Chapter 11. The police are in a position to know why these programs are important and how they can contribute to the good of the community.

Traffic safety education also has high public relations value. An officer on the school grounds supervising the school crossing guards (patrols) or teaching youngsters bicycle safety contributes much to the police officers' image. It reflects their concern for the safety and welfare of the community's youth. However, since safety education is a community responsibility, community agencies should assume their share of work and not rely solely upon the police department for the entire effort.

☑ CHECK POINT

1. What purposes are served by traffic reports?
2. List at least three agencies who might make use of police traffic reports.

*Answers

1. Accident reports provide important information for enforcement of laws, traffic engineering, and educational activities.

2. Traffic accident reports may be used by the police department, public information agencies, attorneys and courts, state motor-vehicle departments or state departments of public safety, legislative bodies, engineers, insurance companies, and traffic groups.

SUMMARY

Traffic is a major problem in most cities. Many manhours are spent in traffic-related police work. Traffic officers have numerous responsibilities to fulfill and specific tasks to perform including enforcing traffic laws, directing and controlling traffic, providing directions and assistance to motorists, investigating motor-vehicle accidents, providing emergency assistance at the scene of an accident, gathering information related to traffic, and writing reports.

The laws the officers enforce, the services they provide, and the information they compile are important to the total police department traffic program as well as to the image conveyed to the public.

Traffic law enforcement may take the form of on-the-spot instructions to drivers and pedestrians, verbal warnings, written warnings with follow-up, citations or summonses, or arrests. The type of enforcement may be guided by the Enforcement Index and by use of selective enforcement principles.

In spite of a highly effective traffic program, motor-vehicle accidents will occur. The three basic causes of such accidents are (1) human faults, errors, violations, and *attitudes*, (2) road defects, and (3) car defects. An officer called to the scene of an accident must proceed to the scene rapidly but safely, park safely and conveniently, administer emergency first-aid if required, interview all persons involved as well as all witnesses, provide needed assistance to victims, accurately observe and record all facts related to the accident, and then clear the scene as soon as possible to restore normal traffic flow. The accident report should include all relevant details including information about the drivers, their actions, their vehicles, the type of accident, the manner of collision, the type of street, weather conditions, road conditions, light conditions, and existing traffic conditions.

It is important that accident reports be accurate and complete as they provide information for enforcement of laws, traffic engineering, and educational activities. They may also serve as the basis of traffic law enforcement policy, accident prevention programs, traffic education, legislative reform of traffic laws, traffic engineering decisions, and motor-vehicle administration decisions.

The responsibilities of the traffic officer in a mobile society are numerous, demanding, and vital.

APPLICATION

The Mytown Police Department has just released its statistics on accidents for the year. There appears to be a 20% increase in personal injury accidents and a 10% increase in property damage accidents. The chief of police has instructed all officers to report any ideas they have to reduce the accident rate. Officer Daryl Olson, after two months on patrol, has made the following observations and recommendations for reducing the traffic accident rate.

He has noted that accidents involving drinking drivers are happening late Friday night, early Saturday morning, late Saturday night, and early Sunday morning. He suggests that liquor lounges in Mytown set up breathalyzer tests so patrons may test themselves before leaving to see if they are under the allowable blood alcohol level to legally drive a motor vehicle.

He has observed many drivers disobeying the 55 mph speed limit and recommends establishing some tolerance and guidelines and then issuing citations. To do this, he recommends that a speed survey be made on the major highways.

Officer Olson also has observed that a large number of accidents are caused by drivers of all ages when they make improper or erratic lane changes. He suggests selective enforcement to cope with this problem.

Although not directly involved in any bicycle accident investigations, Officer Olson has observed an increasing proportion of young adults and adults riding bicycles improperly and causing hazardous conditions for both pedestrians and automobile drivers. He recommends that the Mytown Police Department establish a bicycle safety program, that bicycle patrols be used to educate bicyclists, and that citations be issued to bicyclists who disobey the law.

1. Which of the above recommendations has the most potential for reducing the accident rate in Mytown? Why?
2. What type of traffic enforcement is more productive, general or selective? Why?

*Answers

1. Officer Olson's recommendation that tolerances and guidelines be used in issuing citations to enforce the 55 mph speed limit is the best recommendation for reducing the accident rate because excessive speed is the major cause of personal injury accidents.
2. Selective enforcement is most productive because it most directly affects the citizens who are given citations. Good selective enforcement is usually supported by the public (except those who get the citations).

DISCUSSION QUESTIONS

1. How should an officer approach an accident scene and what should be done first?
2. Have you ever been involved in a traffic accident? How would you evaluate the performance of the officer(s) responding to the call?
3. What can the public do to make the traffic officer's job easier?
4. Does our police department use an Enforcement Index?
5. How does an officer determine who gets a verbal or written warning and who gets a ticket (citation)?
6. Is the idea of selective enforcement a good one? When and where should it be used?

REFERENCES

Accident facts, 1977 ed. Chicago: National Safety Council, 1977.

Baker, J. S. *Traffic accident investigator's manual for police.* (4th ed.) Evanston, IL: Traffic Institute, Northwestern University, 1963.

Eastman, G. D. (Ed.) *Municipal police administration.* Washington, D.C.: International City Management Associations, 1971.

O'Connor, G. W. and Venderbusch, C. G. *The patrol operation.* (2nd ed.) Washington, D.C.: International Association of Chiefs of Police, 1967.

The patrol operation. Washington, D. C.: International Association of Chiefs of Police, 1970.

President's Committee for Traffic Safety. *The action program.* Washington, D.C.: U.S. Government Printing Office, 1964.

Waters, J. R. and McGrath, S. A. *Introduction to law enforcement.* Columbus: Charles E. Merrill Publishing Company, 1974.

Police community service programs emphasize helping citizens to learn to help themselves in preventing crime and preserving individual safety and well-being.

Community Service
Helping Citizens Help Themselves

11

DO YOU KNOW □ □ □

- □ What community services the police department may provide its citizens?
- □ What the difference is between public relations, community relations, and community service?
- □ What types of community service programs have been instituted to deter crime?
- □ What types of community service programs have been instituted to promote the general safety and welfare of citizens?
- □ What factors related to juvenile delinquency a police officer should learn to recognize?
- □ What a school-liaison program is and how effective it has been?

*The vocation of every man and woman is
to serve other people.—Leo Tolstoi (1886)*

*The highest and best form of efficiency is
the spontaneous cooperation of a free
people.—Woodrow Wilson (1921)*

INTRODUCTION

"Police...and the communities they serve need to be reminded that police are people dealing with people, that it is people who commit crimes, and it is people who need police assistance" (Radlet, 1970, p. 62).

The types of assistance provided by the police take a variety of forms. We discussed earlier (Chapter 7) the types of service which might be expected from a police department and the controversy as to how much and what types of service are justified.

> Police departments provide a wide variety of services including giving information, directions, and advice; counseling and referring; licensing and registering vehicles; intervening in domestic arguments; working with neglected children; rendering emergency medical or rescue services; dealing with alcoholics and the mentally ill; finding lost children; dealing with stray animals; controlling crowds; and providing community education programs on crime prevention, drug abuse, safety, and the like.

Although some police departments have a separate division assigned the responsibilities of community service and some have made community service a responsibility of a patrol team, in reality, community service is a vital part of every police officer's job.

Before looking at specific community service programs, the distinction should be made between public relations, community relations, and community service.

> *Public relations* is one-way communication aimed at improving the police image.
> *Community relations* most often refers to efforts to improve two-way communication between citizens and the police.
> *Community service* usually refers not to image-building but to actual service and efforts to help citizens learn to help themselves in preventing crime and accidents.

Often these three categories are combined in a single event or activity. For example, a police department might sponsor a "Police Pride Month." Publicity related to the accomplishments of the police department would constitute public relations. The department might hold public demonstrations of their capabilities followed by a tour of the police department and an open exchange between citizens and police officers—community relations. They might also include in their plans educational displays and programs dealing with safe use of firearms or how to recognize a youngster with a drug problem and what to do about it—community service.

Community service efforts may be individual acts such as finding a lost child, or they may be formal programs such as police-school liaison programs which we will discuss later in the chapter. They may concentrate on providing information, or they may provide information and require specific action by the citizen.

COMMUNITY SERVICE PROGRAMS TO DETER CRIME

Many police departments have instituted programs aimed at preventing crime in the community.

> Crime prevention programs include store security, home security, car security, operation identification, and neighborhood or block watch programs.

Store Security

Police departments may assist store owners in their efforts to reduce losses from shoplifting by studying their stores and then recommending action, such as hiring store detectives, implementing educational campaigns, installing convex wide-angle-mirrors in isolated areas, installing closed-circuit television cameras to watch shoppers from observation booths, and/or installing electronic systems using special magnetic or microwave-sensitive tags. The tags require a deactivating device or a special tool to be removed without damaging the merchandise. If a customer leaves an area of the store before a salesperson removes the tag or deactivates it, a sensor sounds an alarm and store security personnel take over.

Home Security

Police departments may also provide home security inspections in which an officer goes to a citizen's home, evaluates its security, and suggests methods for making the home a less inviting target for crime. Recommendations may be made to install deadbolt locks, improve lighting, and so on. In some communities a subsidy is available for half the cost of making recommended changes.

Automobile Security

Because of the vulnerability of autos to theft, many anti-theft programs and devices have been introduced to make it more difficult for a person to steal a car and more difficult for that person to use or sell it without its stolen nature being detected.

Automobile manufacturers have contributed by making the mechanism of the ignition switch lock the steering wheel and by having a separate steering post lock key and door lock key. Some police agencies have placed on every parking meter a sticker stating: "Have you locked your car?" and provided dashboard stickers which remind motorists: "Have you taken your keys and locked your car?"

Some cities have encouraged their used-car dealers to fence in their lots or chain their entrances and exits. Public education campaigns have also been instituted using newspaper, radio, television, and placard publicity as well as bumper stickers with slogans reminding motorists to lock their cars.

Because 72% of the autos stolen are taken by persons under the age of twenty-one, extensive educational campaigns have been launched to educate youth about the seriousness of car theft and its consequences. Law enforcement agencies have also taken stronger measures to assure the immediate processing of persons apprehended.

Law enforcement agencies constantly have stressed the need for a uniform title law throughout the country. It is possible in some states for an applicant to appear before a licensing agent and obtain a title for a car without the agent seeing the car for which the title is being issued. However, many states are considering legislation requiring that before a vehicle is licensed, it must be taken before a commissioned officer who would personally check the motor and verify the serial numbers.

Operation Identification Programs

Police have also implemented "operation identification" programs in which citizens are provided tools and markers to identify their property with a permanent I.D. number. If these items are lost or stolen and recovered by the police, the I.D. number provides a positive method of identifying the rightful owner. If the items are found in the possession of a burglar or thief, the number can aid the police in prosecuting and convicting the suspect.

Stickers and decals are furnished those citizens participating so that they can place a warning on their doors and windows.

Figure 11-1. Operation I.D. Sticker.

Courtesy of Minnesota Crime Watch—Department of Public Safety.

The warning labels and the marking of personal property with a permanent I.D. number are positive approaches to deter a burglar or thief from attempting to steal that property.

Neighborhood or Block Watch Programs

Block watch programs have been initiated, instructing homeowners to form cooperative block groups to deter burglaries and thefts during the absence of homeowners and to provide places of safety for children who might be threatened on their way to or from school. Such neighborhood watch programs bring neighbors together in an effort to reduce the incidence of crime in their neighborhood. The program involves being aware of who your neighbors are, what their daily routines are, and being aware of suspicious activities or persons in the neighborhood and reporting anything unusual to the police.

With cooperation and involvement of all citizens, such as sharing the responsibility of checking each other's homes when they are on vacation, the neighborhood is a safer place to live. Most programs emphasize that residents should *not* try to apprehend suspects, so the program should not be in danger of creating "vigilante" actions.

Ironically, the more successful a block watch program is, the greater the number of crimes reported is. When the statistics are evaluated, however, in spite in a rise in number of crimes reported, the number of crimes committed should go down.

Other Programs

Programs in the schools, such as lectures and video aids in "Children and the Law" have aided police in their fight against vandalism and shoplifting. They reach a segment of society that represents the future citizens, informing the children of the problem of crime in our society and how they might help reduce this problem.

☑ CHECK POINT

1. What community services might a police department provide its citizens?
2. What is the difference between public relations, community relations, and community service?
3. What types of community service programs have been instituted to deter crime?

*Answers

1. Police departments provide a wide variety of community services including giving information, directions, and advice; counseling and referring; licensing and registering vehicles; intervening in domestic arguments; working with neglected children; rendering emergency medical or rescue services; dealing with alcoholics and the mentally ill; finding lost children; dealing with stray animals; controlling crowds; and providing community education programs on crime prevention, drug abuse, safety, and the like.
2. Public relations is one-way communication aimed at improving the police image. Community relations most often refers to efforts to improve two-way communication between citizens and the police. Community service usually refers to actual service

performed by the police or to efforts to help citizens learn to help themselves in preventing crime and accidents.

3. Crime prevention programs have included store security, home security, car security, operation identification, and neighborhood or block watch programs.

PROGRAMS TO PROMOTE
SAFETY AND GENERAL WELFARE

In addition to programs which seek citizen cooperation in deterring crime, many police departments have implemented community service programs to provide citizens with information and guidance in protecting their general safety and welfare.

> Community service programs may emphasize drug abuse prevention, bike safety, or general safety.

Drug Abuse Prevention

Drug abuse prevention is a responsibility of local law enforcement agencies. They have attacked the problem of drug abuse and narcotics by attempting to apprehend the illegal distributor, by educating and seeking voluntary compliance by industries producing and distributing narcotics and dangerous drugs, and by educating the public on the hazards of drugs and narcotics.

Through various programs with civic groups and the schools, law enforcement officers can make citizens aware of the hazards of narcotics and dangerous drugs. By presenting factual information through pamphlets, speeches, films, and displays to a variety of organizations, especially the schools, law enforcement personnel may heighten the local citizens' concern and instill cooperation in combatting the problem of drug abuse in the community.

Bike Safety

Bike safety programs are found throughout the country. The Minnesota Highway Department, for example, has a "talking" bike that presents safety rules to the children through a tape-recorded message.

Mike the Talking Bike has all the necessary safety features for a bike to be used in traffic: reflectors on the spokes and the sidewalls of the tires are a luminous white, the new pedal reflects, and a tall yellow flag is on the rear. Throughout the presentation the children are reminded to be visible when riding bicycles, to ride on the proper side of the road, and to stop and yield the right-of-way before crossing streets. They are cautioned to always be careful—to watch for traffic and to drive defensively. Even if the bike rider is in the right, he usually is the loser if an accident occurs.

An earlier version of the Minnesota Highway Patrol talking bike was Spike, an old battered-up bike that told the children all the bad things he did to get into trouble. He also told them about the little boy who was riding him when he was hit by a car and killed. A combination of these two bikes might make a very effective presentation for the youngsters.

Other bike safety programs include police officers going into grade schools, conducting safety inspections of the children's bicycles, licensing them, and sponsoring bike rodeos which concentrate on both knowledge about bike safety and demonstration of safe bike-riding skills.

General Safety

Some community service programs emphasize general safety and welfare. An example of one such program is Eden Prairie, Minnesota's, Safety City program.

Safety City is a scaled-down city with houses, businesses, church, school, park, movie theater, fire station, and police station. Twice a year Safety City is set up for one week to give area school children age five to nine a controlled, realistic environment in which to learn or review community safety rules. The cost of materials and labor are furnished by Homart Company, a local firm. Staffing consists of public safety officers, community service officers, reserves, and Homart employees. The program is administered by the Shopping Center and Juvenile Division of the Eden Prairie Crime Prevention Unit.

The purpose of Safety City is to teach area children how to be safe within their own environment. In addition to the buildings, this miniature city includes streets, sidewalks, stop signs, street semaphores, and a railroad crossing, each constructed so they are easily recognizable to children.

Figure 11-2.   Safety City.

The children enter the gates of Safety City and follow a specific route. They can be led by a community service officer, but a public safety officer is in Safety City at all times to handle difficult questions and to oversee the entire operation. The City has two public safety officers, four community service officers or reserves, and one or two firemen. The community service officers lead groups and miniclasses at the individual stops. One public safety officer from the patrol unit conducts the pedestrian and bike safety classes. He takes individual children through a series of learning exercises to increase their skills in pedestrian and bicycle safety, specifically sidewalks, sign knowledge, stoplights, railroad tracks, and the use of school crossings.

At the first stop, the City Park, safety in the park is explained. An animated figure of a stranger handing out candy teaches children what to do in such situations, that is, the do's and dont's with strangers. Safety on playground apparatus is also briefly explained. Beginning with this stop and continuing throughout the tour, the merits of vandalism prevention are explained.

The next stop is a nondenominational church used to demonstrate that when crisis erupts in the family, there is always a place to seek help. This counseling help can also be found in police, school, and county agencies. As the tour proceeds through the first intersection, children learn to cross a semaphore-controlled intersection safely.

The police station (public safety building) is the next stop on the tour. Here children learn the purpose of police and laws, who police officers are, and what they do. This stop also includes a reminder to all children that they should know their telephone number and address. The whens and hows of calling on the telephone are included. A crime prevention display in the rear of the public safety building is geared to the younger set and includes such things as bicycle theft prevention.

The next stop on the tour is the retail shopping center where children are told the impact of shoplifting and its effect on their lives. The tour is then assisted by a patrol officer who instructs the children in how to cross the railroad tracks safely. After crossing the tracks, the patrol officer instructs the children in pedestrian safety. The children then use the school crossing aided by the school patrol.

The next stop is the fire department where a fireman explains to the children fire prevention and what to do in case of a fire. Behind the fire station is a display on fire prevention set up by the Fire Prevention Bureau.

Next the children pass a house and are reminded that they can call the police from their homes when they are frightened or when an accident occurs. They are also instructed on the proper respect for other people's property.

The last stop in Safety City is the movie theater where short crime-prevention films are shown—one movie per group, less than five minutes each. Upon leaving the gates of Safety City, each child receives a "Safety City Certificate" showing that he or she has visited Safety City.

DETERRING JUVENILE DELINQUENCY

Traditionally the police officer's role was clearly defined: arrest lawbreakers and preserve the peace. Although historically the police have been viewed as punitive and authoritarian, this view is changing. Rather than simply apprehending and punishing offenders, police officers now also seek to educate and to promote prevention of crime. Modern approaches to juvenile delinquency take several forms, but all have in common a goal of *preventing* juvenile delinquency.

Knowledge of Indicators of Potential for Delinquent Behavior by Juveniles

Certain factors may indicate that a youngster has the potential for or actually is involved in delinquent behavior. Police should learn to recognize these factors and take appropriate actions, considering community resources and school and police department policies.

Police officers are in a unique position to help juveniles because they are usually the first persons of authority to confront the juvenile offender during or following a delinquent act. Additionally, police officers are often familiar with the youngsters in their patrol area whose behavior marks them as potential delinquents, and they have the authority to reprimand, release, or refer youngsters to court.

> The police officer can learn to recognize the environmental and personal factors contributing to or indicative of delinquency.

Environmental factors potentially contributing to delinquency include broken homes, criminal parents, incompetent parents, erratic discipline, economic insecurity, impoverished neighborhoods, transient populations, and racial and other tensions.

Personal factors or behavior indicating potential delinquency include unsociability, cheating, lying, fighting, temper tantrums, anxiety, guilt feelings, hostility and aggression, laziness, truancy, running away from home, and a rebellious attitude.

The environmental and personal factors may be complicated by misuses of alcohol, narcotics and drugs, by economic factors, by physical disabilities, by sexual problems, or by numerous other factors. The result is frequently youths who show overwhelming symptoms of weakness and inadequacy. They cannot accept life as it is, cannot conform, cannot get along, cannot compete, and/or cannot exercise self-control.

The sooner a police officer recognizes such youngsters and attempts to work with them, the greater the chance that the juveniles will not become delinquents.

Police-School Liaison Programs

Prevention programs in juvenile delinquency began in the early twentieth century when a wave of social reform swept through the western world. The earliest documented program, established in 1905 in Portland, Oregon, was designed to protect young girls. In 1918 New York City assigned "welfare officers" to each precinct, the beginning of a program which expanded into a comprehensive community program called "The Juvenile Aid Bureau," a forerunner of the more modern police-school liaison programs.

> A police-school liaison program places a police officer within the school.

The purpose of such police-school liaison programs is well stated by the program in Tucson, Arizona (*School Resource Manual*, 1967):

> *The School Resource Officer Program is a cooperative effort of the public schools and law enforcement agencies to develop an understanding of law enforcement functions and to prevent juvenile delinquency and crime.*

Although police participate in many different types of school programs, such programs do not exist in a large number of police jurisdictions. Where they do exist, they have evolved gradually in response to community requests. Formal programs frequently result from surveys conducted by forward-looking police departments.

The need for specialized training of juvenile officers in understanding children and their problems has also been recognized. The importance of special training for officers appointed to juvenile units and the need for close police-school relationships is supported by the Flint, Michigan Program, the first publicized, comprehensive, formalized police-school liaison effort in the United States (Morrison, 1968, p.62). Cooperatively developed between 1958 and 1960 by school, police, court, social agency, and community personnel interested in decreasing juvenile delinquency in Flint, the program has been a model for many police-school programs.

The police officer (called police counselor) is assigned to a junior or senior high school and is also responsible for the feeder elementary school(s). The officer does not wear a uniform and is not responsible for enforcing school rules and regulations; rather, he deals with predelinquent or actual delinquent behavior problems around the school, keeps records of student contacts, and uses this information for counseling the students.

A counseling team composed of a Dean of Counseling, Dean of Students, Visiting Teacher, Police Counselor, and Nurse Counselor may recommend that a student be referred to other individuals or agencies for help. The functions of the counseling team include the following (Flint Public Schools, 1965, p. 2):

—Identifying pupils with specific problems.
—Collecting, studying, and evaluating data.
—Relating and interpreting information.
—Planning a course of action.
—Serving as a resource person in the area of specialization.

—Accepting responsibility for analysis and treatment in the area of specialization.

—Cooperating and communicating with other team members, school personnel, and outside agencies.

—Conducting in-service education for staff, parents, and community agencies.

—Making progress reports when specific responsibilities have been assigned.

Before this program, one in every thirty-six children in a certain area of Flint were involved in delinquency. One year later the ratio had dropped to one in every two hundred eighty (Grandstatter and Brennan, 1967, p. 200) The Flint Program was so successful that it was instituted as a permanent part of the police department's public services.

Another program which has achieved nation-wide prominence is the Tucson Arizona Police Department School Resource Officer Program whose purpose statement you read earlier. Patterned after the Flint Program, the Tucson Program has made several modifications, the most noticeable and perhaps most important being that the officer wears full police uniform. The rationale for this change is that students learn to see that the uniformed police officer's primary function is to help. This fosters the traditional "beat cop" personalized approach where the police officer was a familiar and welcome part of a neighborhood, knowledgeable of the residents and their problems. Like the Flint Program, the Tucson Program uses the team approach, but the police officer makes the final decisions about referrals (*School Resource Manual*).

Almost all programs in the United States today started with placement of an officer in a junior high school who was also responsible for the feeder elementary school(s). Most police school liaison programs are similar to the Flint and Tucson Programs.

Evidence of the success of such programs is most convincing from outside the United States, from the Liverpool City Police Juvenile Liaison Officer Scheme, initiated in 1951, and similar to present United States programs (Morrison, 1968, pp.62-64). Documentation of the program's success is possible because of the British Isles' homogeneous population and the consistency with which they apply sanctions against juvenile delinquents. Juvenile delinquency trends in Liverpool were compared with all of England and Wales from 1954 to 1960. Between 1956 and 1960 Liverpool's delinquency rates fluctuated, but never reached the higher rates of the comparative areas. In 1960 the Liverpool rate was approximately 41 points lower than the rate for all of England and Wales, suggestive of the success of the Liverpool Program. However, the program met strong criticism on the grounds that the police lacked training in social group work and that they fostered punitive and inflexible attitudes in the treatment of children.

These same criticisms have been made against programs in the United States.

In spite of some documentation of the success of police-school liaison programs in decreasing juvenile delinquency, serious criticisms are frequently made of the programs.

. Although school administrators are usually enthusiastic about police-school liaison programs and believe the programs help to reduce delinquency, many citizen groups are strongly opposed to such programs. The Southern Chapter of the Arizona Civil Liberties Union (1966) has listed eight objections to the police-school liaison program.

1. The invasion of the privacy of the home.
2. The indiscriminate interrogation of students who are neither suspects nor offenders concerning offenses committed both inside and outside the school precincts, related and unrelated to school activities.
3. The interrogation of students without the supervision or presence of school authorities or parents.
4. The establishment of a network of informers among junior high and elementary students.
5. The use of police officers, rather than trained school personnel, as disciplinarians.
6. The use of unprotected minors as a source for data regarding the activities and opinions of parents, neighbors, and other adults in the community.
7. The harassment of juveniles with a history of delinquency, through continual surveillance and frequent questioning, a harassment which has led to drop-outs.
8. The misuse of the educational process for police purposes.

Objections have also been raised by individuals within law enforcement (Shephard and James, 1967, pp. 2-3):

1. The primary objective of police-school liaison programs is to change the attitudes of the students toward police. It is believed that even highly-trained and skilled professionals may not be effective in changing attitudes. Further, since attitudes can be positive or negative, the end results of such efforts by police may be self-defeating.
2. Few officers have the training or experience to prevent delinquency in a school setting.
3. These programs take manpower from regular police efforts. There is a serious shortage of police manpower in the cities, and police departments can ill afford to assign officers to a police-school program.
4. Possible legal complications that result from the school authorities, who stand *in loco parentis* (in place of the parents) to the child, delegating the right to inspect and interrogate students in the school.
5. The possibility that some stigma might be attached to the school that is chosen for an experimental program.

6. The possibility that the police officer may be used as a school disciplinarian.

These objections were raised over a decade ago, and many of them have since been eliminated by changes in the program. The ultimate decision as to whether such programs will be implemented rests with the citizens of each community, for without their support, there is little chance of success. Where community support has existed, however, such programs have made a significant impact not only on prevention of juvenile delinquency but also on attitudes toward police officers and our system of law enforcement.

☑ CHECK POINT

1. What types of community service programs have been instituted to promote the general safety and welfare of citizens?
2. What factors related to juvenile delinquency should a police officer learn to recognize?
3. What is a police-school liaison program?
4. How effective have police-school liaison programs been?

*Answers

1. Community service programs have emphasized drug abuse prevention, bike safety, and general safety such as the Safety City project.
2. The police officer can learn to recognize the environmental and personal factors contributing to or indicative of delinquency.
3. A police-school liaison program places a police officer within the school.
4. When the citizens have been cooperative, the police-school program has generally been effective not only in reducing juvenile delinquency but also in strengthening the police officer's image. Serious objections have been made to such programs, however.

SUMMARY

Although the type and amount of community service provided by a police department varies from city to city, a certain level of community service is expected everywhere. The services provided include giving information, directions, and advice; counseling and referring; licensing and registering vehicles; intervening in domestic arguments; working with neglected children; rendering emergency medical or rescue services; dealing with alcoholics and the mentally ill; finding lost children; dealing with stray animals; controlling crowds; and providing community education programs on crime prevention, drug abuse, safety, and the like.

Community service should be differentiated from public relations and community relations. Public relations emphasizes building a positive image of the law enforcement officer. Community relations emphasizes improving two-way communication between citizens and the police, with the raising of image being an anticipated side-effect. Community service, in contrast, emphasizes actual police assistance or efforts to help citizens learn to help themselves in preventing crime and preserving individual safety and well-being.

Several community service programs focus on crime prevention, including store security, home security, car security, operation identification, and neighborhood or block watch programs.

Other community service programs emphasize drug abuse prevention, bike safety, and the general public safety such as the Safety City project.

The majority of police departments also have as a department goal to reduce juvenile delinquency in their city. They encourage the police officer to learn to recognize the environmental and personal factors that contribute to or are indicative of delinquency. Some departments have become involved in police-school liaison programs which place a police officer within the school, working directly with the students. When the community is supportive of such programs, they are usually successful in lowering the incidence of juvenile delinquency as well as raising the community's opinion of the police. However, several serious criticisms have been made of the police-school liaison program. Each community must decide whether such a program might be effective in its specific situation.

APPLICATION

The following activities are engaged in by the Mytown Police Department. Identify each as being primarily public relations, community relations, or community service oriented. Then select one activity from each category which you feel has the most potential benefit for the community and the department.

A. Informational pamphlets
   1. How to make your home secure
   2. What to do before going on vacation
   3. Know your police department

B. Speeches on drug abuse to service organizations, schools, and businesses

C. Press releases
   1. Release of local crime statistics
   2. Interviews with local police officers
   3. Public warnings of fraud schemes, stolen checks, and so on

D. Operation Smile (distribute buttons with the slogan and actually "smile")

E. Law Enforcement Week
   1. Public display of police equipment
   2. Slide show on burglary prevention
   3. Demonstration of life-saving techniques

F. School activities
   1. Distribute "Schools open, drive carefully" bumper stickers
   2. Assist school crossing guards
   3. Instruct children in safe street crossing

G. Operation Identification
   1. Assist public in marking their valuables
   2. Distribute decals for doors

H. Business and residential security checks

I. Public tours of the police department
   1. Demonstrate facilities and equipment
   2. Coffee and cookies and an informal interchange between police officers and citizens

J. Neighborhood meetings
   1. Discuss problems common to the neighborhood and the police
   2. Formulate a plan with cooperation of citizens
   3. Implement the plan of action

K. Minority group relations
   1. Set up meetings with leaders of minority community
   2. Work with leaders on mutually agreed upon programs
   3. Implement a ride-along program

L. Bicycle Safety Program
   1. Inspect bicycles for safety at parks, playgrounds, and schools
   2. Distribute reflectorized safety materials for bicycles
   3. Demonstrate bicycle safety throughout the community

M. Sponsorship of Little League teams

*Answers

A. 1. Community service
   2. Community service
   3. Community relations
B. Community service
C. 1. Community relations
   2. Public or community relations
   3. Community service
D. Community relations
E. 1. Public relations
   2. Community service
   3. Community service
F. 1. Community service
   2. Community service
   3. Community service
G. 1. Community service
   2. Community service

H. Community service
I. 1. Public relations
   2. Community relations
J. 1. Community relations
   2. Community relations
   3. Community service
K. 1. Community relations
   2. Community relations
   3. Community relations
L. 1. Community service
   2. Community service
   3. Community service
M. Public relations

DISCUSSION QUESTIONS

1. What community services are available in our community? Which are most important? Which might be frivolous? Are any necessary services *not* provided?
2. What types of crime prevention programs are used in our community?
3. What types of safety promotion programs are used in our community?
4. Does our community have a police-school liaison program? If not, why? If so, how effective does it seem to be?
5. Which of the criticisms of the police-school liaison program seem most valid?

6. Which is the most important: public relations programs, community relations programs, or community service programs? Why?

7. Can you imagine a situation in which a police department placed so much emphasis on public relations that it had the opposite effect than intended, that is, the image of the police was lowered rather than raised?

8. Have you ever personally received service from a police officer? What were the circumstances? How would you evaluate the officer's performance? Have you ever needed a service which was not provided?

REFERENCES

Arizona Civil Liberties Union, Southern Chapter, Tucson, Arizona, release dated June 2, 1966. (Mimeographed.)

The challenge of crime in a free society. A report by the President's Commission on Law Enforcement and the Administration of Justice. Washington: D.C.: U.S. Government Printing Office, February 1967.

Children in custody. U.S. Department of Justice, Law Enforcement Assistance Administration, National Criminal Justice Information and Statistics Service, May 1975. (Advance Report on the Juvenile Detention and Correctional Facility Census of 1972-1973.)

Flint public schools regional counseling teams, October 1965 (Mimeographed.)

Grandstatter, A. F. and Brennan, J. J. Prevention through the police. *Delinquency prevention,* W. E. Amos and C. F. Wellford, (Eds.). Englewood Cliffs: Prentice-Hall, 1967.

Haskell, M. R. and Yablonsky, L. *Crime and delinquency.* Chicago: Rand-McNally, 1970.

Morrison, J. The controversial police-school liaison programs. *Police,* November-December, 1968, pp. 60-64.

Radlet, L. A. Who's in charge of law and order? *Police-community relations: An anthology and bibliography,* W. H. Hewitt and C. L. Newman (Eds.). Mineola, N.Y.: Foundation Press, 1970.

School resource manual. Adopted by Tucson District #1 School Board, June 21, 1966. Revised and accepted February 21, 1967.

Shephard, G. H. and James J. Police—do they belong in the schools? *American education,* September 1967, pp. 2-3.

Officers investigating the scene of a hit-and-run traffic fatality involving a stolen car. Note the danger that curious witnesses may disturb valuable evidence at a crime scene unless it is secured.

Investigation

An Objective Quest for Truth

12

DO YOU KNOW☐ ☐ ☐

☐ What the primary characteristic of an effective investigator is?

☐ What the primary responsibilities of the investigator are?

☐ Who is usually responsible for the preliminary investigation? The follow-up investigation?

☐ Why both sketches and photographs of a crime scene are usually needed?

☐ What questions the investigator must seek answers to?

☐ How the investigator must deal with evidence?

☐ What types of evidence are likely to be found at the scene of a crime?

☐ Who may be a witness to a crime?

☐ What the Miranda warning is?

☐ Why two people may see the same event yet report it differently?

☐ How witnesses may be aided in making an identification?

☐ Why some witnesses may be perceived as uncooperative?

☐ What the three basic types of identification are? When each is appropriate?

☐ What the critical element in a field identification is?

☐ What rights the suspect has during the identification process?

☐ What instructions and precautions should be taken to assure the legality and admissibility of an identification in court?

☐ What relevance the Wade decision has to identification of a suspect?

☐ What precautions must be taken if both photo and line-up identification are used?

☐ What should be done if a suspect refuses to participate in a line-up?

When you have eliminated the impossible,
whatever remains, however improbable,
must be the truth.
—Sir Arthur Conan Doyle (1890)

Every fact that is learned becomes a key
to other facts.
—E. L. Youmans

INTRODUCTION

On January 2, Detective Molly O'Brien was sent to the Lakeside Super Market on Front Street to investigate a burglary. Using the pattern for a crime scene search for crimes against property, including protecting the scene from contamination and a methodical approach, she proceeded to photograph the scene and to collect and mark evidence. She noticed that the rear window of the supermarket had been broken and that entry had been gained through this window. She carefully took a generous amount of glass from the floor and marked it as evidence. She also found a sledge hammer and a crowbar apparently used to pry open the steel cabinets containing receipts. She noticed fireproof insulation on the crowbar and metal fragments and paint similar to the cabinets on the sledge hammer. She took separate samples of the paint and the fireproof insulation from the cabinet. Upon further investigation, Detective O'Brien found toolmarks on several doors outside where entry had been attempted. Using a mold, she made a casting for future comparison with similar burglaries in the area. Upon completion of the investigation, she submitted the evidence to the crime laboratory for analysis and comparison.

On January 10, while on patrol, Officers James and Fisher received a call to a silent burglary alarm at the Kwik Stop Super Market. As they approached the building, they saw two burglary suspects entering the back door. James and Fisher called for a back-up unit and then entered the supermarket. They found the two suspects hiding in the office and took them into custody. They then searched their vehicle where they found a large screwdriver which they submitted to the crime laboratory. At headquarters the suspects' clothing was taken as evidence and submitted to the crime laboratory for comparison purposes as they were suspects in other burglaries in the area.

The suspects were charged with burglary of the Kwik Stop Super Market. Several days later, the crime laboratory report of analysis and comparison of evidence seized from the suspects showed the following:

—The casting of the identifications found on the doors at the Lakeside Super Market indicated that they were made by the same size screwdriver found in the burglar's vehicle on January 10.

—The metal and paint samples matched those on the sledge hammer and the crowbar found at the scene of the Lakeside Super Market.

—The insulation on the pry bar also matched the insulation of the steel cabinets at the Lakeside Super Market.

—Samplings of metal, paint, glass, and insulation found in the two suspects' pants cuffs were identical in composition to those submitted to the crime laboratory by Detective O'Brien.

Faced with this evidence, the suspects confessed to the burglary of the Lakeside Super Market and to several others in the area.

This case was successfully solved because the officers understood their functions at the crime scene and performed them skillfully. They knew that both in science and law they must observe strict rules of procedure for physical-evidence integrity. They took adequate samplings of the evidence representative of the crime as well as samples for control purposes.

A large part of an investigator's role centers around obtaining information and evidence. The successful investigator obtains proof that a crime has been committed as well as proof that a particular person (the suspect) committed the crime. In the preceding case, the suspects confessed because of the sufficient evidence against them. However, the investigators did *not* determine the suspects to be guilty; they remained objective in their investigation.

> A primary characteristic of an effective investigator is *objectivity.*

The investigator seeks to find the truth, not simply to prove suspects guilty. As stated in Article 10 of the *Canons of Police Ethics:*

The law enforcement officer shall be concerned equally in the prosecution of the wrong-doer and the defense of the innocent. He shall ascertain what constitutes evidence and shall present such evidence impartially and without malice. In so doing, he will ignore social, political, and all other distinctions among the persons involved, strengthening the tradition of the reliability and integrity of an officer's word.

The law enforcement officer shall take special pains to increase his perception and skill of observation, mindful that in many situations his is the sole impartial testimony to the facts of a case.

RESPONSIBILITIES OF THE INVESTIGATOR

To accomplish a successful investigation, police officers must (1) take their time, (2) use an organized approach which is efficient and methodical, because this may be their only chance to observe the scene, (3) recognize the issues and find facts to settle these issues, and (4) determine if a crime has been committed, and, if so, by whom and how.

> The primary responsibilities of the investigator are to:
> —Assure that the crime scene is secure.
> —Record all facts related to the case for further reference.
> —Photograph and sketch the crime scene.
> —Obtain and identify evidence.
> —Interview witnesses and interrogate suspects.
> —Assist in the identification of suspects.

Each of these responsibilities will be discussed in a few pages, but first a distinction should be made between the preliminary investigation and the follow-up investigation.

The *preliminary investigation* consists of actions performed immediately upon receiving a call to respond to the scene of a crime. This preliminary investigation is usually conducted by patrol officers. When patrol officers receive a call to proceed to a crime scene, they must proceed to the scene promptly and safely; render assistance to anyone who is injured; arrest the suspect if he is still at the scene; secure the crime scene and protect any evidence; interview complainants, witnesses, and suspects; collect evidence; and make careful notes of all facts related to the case. The patrol officers' responsibility for the preliminary investigation terminates after they have completed all they can accomplish to the point where a delay in additional action will not substantially affect the successful outcome of the investigation.

The *follow-up investigation* is usually conducted by the investigative services division, sometimes also known as the detective bureau. Therefore, the success of any criminal investigation relies on the cooperative, coordinated efforts of both the patrol and the investigative functions. In some smaller departments, however, the same officer may handle both the preliminary and the follow-up investigations.

> Patrol usually conducts the preliminary investigation; investigators or detectives usually conduct the follow-up investigation.

Investigators

The manner in which investigators are used varies from agency to agency. The investigator assists the patrol force in combatting crime and aids in gathering evidence and preparing cases against persons arrested for serious crimes. The investigator is responsible for the investigation of crimes that the patrol division cannot complete because of restrictions in time and area.

Investigators must be suspicious, inquisitive, patient, persevering, thorough, objective, and must have knowledge of investigative procedures. Investigators are specialists who were selected for certain required traits, some of which are obtainable only through training and experience. The knowledge of how criminals react and their experience of actual or simulated crimes are of great value since most investigators deal with all categories of crimes. They must be able to interact with many types of people and must learn to play various roles from time to time. They will solve most crimes through intelligence, hard work, and information. They must develop useful sources of information—informants who know what is going on in the community. Their skill at their job is reflected in the outcomes of their investigations. As noted by O. W. Wilson (1962, p.112):

In no branch of police service may the accomplishment of the unit and of its individual members, be so accurately evaluated as in the detective division. Rates of clearances by arrest, of property recovered and of convictions, serve as a measure of the level of performance. ... A detective division built of members retained on this selective basis is most likely to contain the best investigators on the force.

Although most investigators handle all categories of crimes, in large cities specialization may occur within investigative units. Some officers specialize in the investigation of crimes against the person, such as murder, forcible rape, robbery, and assault. Others may concentrate on crimes against property, such as burglaries, larcenies, and auto theft. Other investigative units, most frequently in our largest cities, handle only organized crime and white-collar crime cases such as check fraud and embezzlement.

The advantage of working with only one type of crime is that the investigators become increasingly expert in looking for clues and evidence in that particular class of offense. They develop informants and become familiar with the method of operation (modus operandi or m.o.) of habitual criminals. Further, their working relationship with the prosecutor is enhanced, as both understand the problems of the other in bringing a case to court.

Whether specialized detective, general investigator, or patrol officer, each law enforcement officer must know the basics of effective investigation to perform effectively.

☑ CHECK POINT

1. What is the primary characteristic of an effective investigator?
2. What are the primary responsibilities of an investigator?
3. Who is usually responsible for the preliminary investigation? The follow-up investigation?

*Answers

1. The primary characteristic of an effective investigator is objectivity.
2. The primary responsibilities of an investigator are to: (1) assure that the crime scene is secure, (2) record all facts related to the case for future reference (3) photograph and sketch the crime scene, (4) obtain and identify evidence, (5) interview witnesses and interrogate suspects, and (6) assist in the identification of suspects.
3. Patrol usually conducts the preliminary investigation; investigators or detectives usually conduct the follow-up investigation.

SECURING THE CRIME SCENE

The crime scene area must first be secured to minimize contamination of the scene and outlying areas. The investigator in charge should limit the number of officers assigned to the crime scene, using only those required to do the work. Although some crimes do not have identifiable scenes, (for example, embezzlement) or known scenes, the majority of crimes do, for example bank robberies, burglaries, homicides, assaults, and bombings.

> Any surrounding that contains evidence of criminal activity is considered a crime scene, and it must be secured.

The suspect may have left evidence such as fingerprints, blood, footprints, a weapon, a tool, strands of hair, fibers from clothing, or some personal item, such as a billfold which may contain identification. No evidence should be touched or moved until photographing and sketching of the scene are complete.

RECORDING ALL RELEVANT INFORMATION

Investigators do not rely upon memory; they record all necessary information by photographing, sketching, and taking notes to be used later in a written report of the investigation. Photographs, sketches, and notes are a permanent aid to memory and may be helpful not only in investigating the case and writing the report, but also in testifying in court.

The notes should be written in a notebook, not on scraps of paper that might be lost or misplaced. They should be written in ink because they are a permanent record and also because pencil may smear and become unreadable over time. The notes should be written legibly and be identified by the investigator's name, the date, and the case number. They should contain *all* relevant facts, especially the names and addresses of victims, witnesses, and possible suspects.

> The investigator must obtain answers to the questions: who? what? where? when? how? and why?

Although each specific type of crime requires somewhat different information, most investigations require answers to such questions as the following (Hess and Wrobleski, 1978, pp.22-24):*

When: did the incident happen? was it discovered? was it reported? did the police arrive on the scene? were suspects arrested? will the case be heard in court?

Where: did the incident happen? was evidence found? stored? do victims, witnesses, and suspects live? do suspects frequent most often? were suspects arrested?

Who: are suspects? accomplices?
        Complete descriptions would include the following information: sex, race, coloring, age, height, weight, hair (color, style, condition), eyes (color, size, glasses), nose (size, shape), ears (close to head or protruding), distinctive features (birthmarks, scars, beard), clothing, voice (high or low, accent), other distinctive characteristics such as walk.

Who: were the victims? associates? was talked to? were witnesses? saw or heard something of importance? discovered the crime? reported the incident? made the complaint? investigated the incident? worked on the case? marked and received the evidence? was notified? had a motive?

What: type of crime was committed? was the amount of damage or value of the property involved? happened (narrative of the actions of suspects, victims, and witnesses; combines information included under "how")? evidence was found? preventive measures had been taken (safes, locks, alarms, etc.)? knowledge, skill, or strength was needed to commit the crime? was said? did the police officers do? further information is needed? further action is needed?

---

*Hess and Wrobleski. *For the Record: Report Writing in Law Enforcement,* John Wiley and Sons, Inc., 1978. Reprinted by permission.

How: was the crime discovered? does this crime relate to other crimes? did the crime occur? was evidence found? was information obtained?

Why: was the crime committed (was there intent? consent? motive?) was certain property stolen? was a particular time selected?

Answers to these questions are obtained by observation and by talking to witnesses, complainants, and suspects. They are recorded in notes, photographs, sketches, or are in the form of actual physical evidence.

PHOTOGRAPHING AND SKETCHING THE CRIME SCENE

In addition to taking notes, the investigator or crime-scene technician should photograph and sketch the crime scene. Photographic coverage of the scene must be done carefully. In addition to being technically competent and well equipped, the photographer must photograph objects which are related to the case and in such a way that no distortion occurs. The photographs should show the scene as it was found. They are usually taken in a series and "tell a story." In addition, they usually are taken from general to specific, that is, first an entire room, then one area of the room, then specific items within that area.

The evidence and location should be shown in their proper relationship and in a sequence that will orient a person unfamiliar with the scene. If a photograph is intended to show dimensional relationships, a suitable scale should be included. Photographs of evidence such as shoeprints, tire tracks, and toolmarks must be done using close-up photography.

In addition to photographs, a sketch should also be made of the crime scene before any evidence is moved.

> Both photographs and sketches are usually needed. The photographs include all detail and can show items close up. Sketches can be selective and can show much larger areas.

Sketches supplement photographs. They can be selective, and they can also show entire areas, for example, an entire layout of a home or business. The sketch need not be an artistic masterpiece as long as it includes all relevant details and is accurate and clear. The sketch should show the locations of all important evidence found during the crime-scene search.

☑ CHECK POINT

1. What general questions must the investigator find answers to?
2. Why are both sketches and photographs of a crime scene usually needed?

*Answers

1. The investigator must find answers to the questions of who, what, where, when, why, and how.

2. Both sketches and photographs are usually needed of a crime scene because although the photograph can include all detail and can show items close-up, only sketches can be selective and show large areas such as layouts of buildings.

OBTAINING AND IDENTIFYING EVIDENCE

A primary responsibility of the investigator is to obtain and identify evidence. All important decisions will revolve around the available evidence and how is was obtained.

> The investigator must recognize, collect, mark, preserve, and transport physical evidence in sufficient quantity for analysis and without contamination.

Effective investigators understand their function as a finder of facts and the supplier of proof which has both a scientific and a legal basis for presentation in court. Items of evidence found at the crime scene are usually routinely taken and held pending apprehension of a suspect. Frequently evidence is sent to a crime laboratory for analysis and comparison.

> Among the more common types of evidence found at the crime scene are: blood, hair, fingerprints, fibers, documents, footprints or tire prints, tool fragments, toolmarks, broken glass, paint, insulation from safes, firearms, and explosives.

Physical evidence is often categorized into two areas: crimes against persons and crimes against property. The kind of evidence to be anticipated is often directly related to the type of crime committed.

Crimes against the person include homicide, forcible rape, robbery, assault, kidnapping, and sex crimes. These crime scenes frequently contain evidence such as blood, hair, fibers, fingerprints, footprints, and weapons.

Crimes against property include burglary, larceny, arson, and auto theft. These crime scenes are commonly characterized by forcible entry with tools leaving marks on doors, windows, safes, money chests, cash registers, and desk drawers. Evidence often includes tool fragments, toolmarks, disturbance of paint, wood, broken glass, insulation from safes, and other types of building materials.

Specific Evidence and Scientific Aids

Blood can be classified as having come from humans or animals. Human bloodstains can be classified into one of the four international blood groups: A, B, AB, or O. Bloodstains may be valuable as evidence in assaults, homicides, burglaries, hit-and-run, and rape. Although blood cannot be identified as having come from a particular individual, race, or sex, it can be helpful in eliminating suspects.

Hair can also be classified as having come from humans or animals. It is not possible except in very unusual cases to determine definitely that a questioned hair sample came from a particular person. It can be determined, however, that the hair of unknown sources matches a known hair sample from a certain individual in all microscopic characteristics and, accordingly, could have originated from the same source. It can be established that the hair was pulled out forcibly if the root end is present. In addition, the region of the body from which the hair was removed can be determined with considerable accuracy from the length, size, color, stiffness, and general appearance. Hair from the scalp, beard, eyebrows, eyelid, nose, ear, trunk, and limbs all have different characteristics. Hair from each racial group can be identified by its shape. The sex and age of a person cannot be determined from a hair examination with any degree of certainty except in the case of infant hair.

The possibility of hair evidence in any crime should never be overlooked. Hair is often valuable as a means of personal identification or as an investigative aid in cases such as hit-and-run, unusual death, and rape. Hair may be found from both the victim and the suspect on clothing, weapons, undergarments, blankets, sheets, seat covers, and the undercarriage of vehicles.

Fibers are excellent aids to·investigators. It is possible to identify fibers as to type, such as wool, cotton, rayon, nylon, and so on. Sometimes it is possible to determine the type of garment from which the fibers came. In assault and homicide cases some contact usually occurs between the victim and the suspect causing clothing fibers to be interchanged. Fingernail scrapings and weapons may also contain fiber evidence. In burglaries, clothing fibers are frequently found where the burglar crawled through a window or opening. In hit-and-run cases, clothing fibers are often found adhering to the fenders, grill, door handle, or parts of the undercarriage of the automobile.

Document examination consists of a side-by-side comparison of handwriting, typewriting, or other written or printed matter. Age, sex, and race cannot be determined with certainty. However, in cases such as check forgery and alteration of wills, stocks, and bonds, conclusions based on examinations conducted by competent experts are positive and reliable. Such handwriting testimony has been accepted in our courts for many years. Typewriter samples may also identify the manufacturer, make, model, and age of a typewriter.

Fingerprints are often found at crime scenes. Fingerprint identification is currently the most positive form of identification because the ridge arrangement on every finger of every person is different and unchanging, although as a person grows, the patterns enlarge slightly. Experts in fingerprints look for nine basic patterns which can occur in any combination.

Latent fingerprints are made by sweat or grease which oozes out of the pores from little wells situated under the ridges at the ends of the fingers. When a person grasps an item with reasonable pressure, this grease takes the pattern of the person's fingerprints. This usually happens if the item grasped has a highly polished surface such as glass, polished metalware, highly glazed fabrics, or paper. It usually will not occur if the item grasped is soft, spongy, or has a rough surface.

Fingerprints may be found in an infinite number of places and under varied circumstances. Most crime scenes contain fingerprints of the suspect.

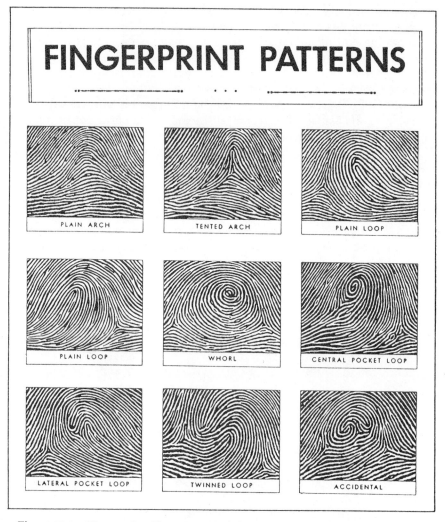

FINGERPRINT PATTERNS

PLAIN ARCH

TENTED ARCH

PLAIN LOOP

PLAIN LOOP

WHORL

CENTRAL POCKET LOOP

LATERAL POCKET LOOP

TWINNED LOOP

ACCIDENTAL

Figure 12-1.   Fingerprint Chart, courtesy of Faurot, Inc., 229 Broadway, New York, N.Y., 10007.

Usually articles such as weapons, tools, documents, glass, metal, or any other objects which could have been touched or handled by the perpetrators may have latent fingerprints on them.

Finding fingerprints is only half the job; they must be matched with the actual (inked) fingerprints of a suspect to be valuable as evidence. For example, consider the following situation. Three men checked into a motel at 11:00 P.M. Shortly after midnight when a new desk clerk came on duty, the men went to the office and committed an armed robbery. Police investigating the scene went to the room occupied by the three men and found a latent fingerprint on an ashtray. This print was later matched up to one of the suspects whose fingerprints were on file with the police department. This evidence placed the suspect at the motel which he had denied ever having been to.

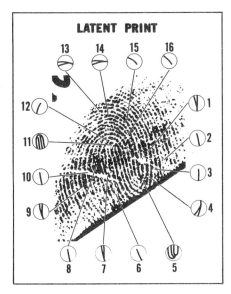 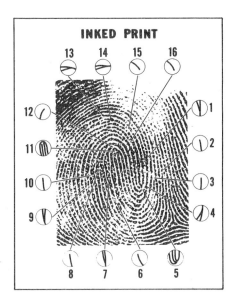

Figure 12-2. Positive identification of a fingertip. Three men checked into a motel at 11:00 p.m. Shortly after midnight when a new desk clerk came on duty, the men went to the office and committed an armed robbery. Police investigating the scene went to the room occupied by the three men and found the latent fingerprint on an ash tray. This print was later matched up to one of the suspects whose fingerprints were on file with the police department.

A shoe or tire impression can be a "material witness" in locating a criminal and placing him at the scene of a crime. Such evidence is sometimes more reliable than an eyewitness. Impressions from shoes or tires are often found where the perpetrator of the crime hastily entered or left the scene of the crime and overlooked the impressions. Investigators carefully preserve such evidence by making a plaster cast of it. It often serves as a vital link to a criminal.

Tool fragments may also be found at the crime scene. These pieces may later be matched to a broken tool in the possession of a suspect.

Toolmarks may be left where windows have been forced with screwdrivers, or pry bars, locks snipped with bolt cutters, or safes attacked with hammers, chisels, and/or punches. All these tools leave marks which, under favorable conditions, can be identified as definitely as fingerprints. Toolmarks are most commonly found in the crimes of burglary and malicious destruction of property. They may be found on windowsills, frames, doors, door frames, cash register drawers, file cabinets, or cash boxes.

Glass is also an aid to the laboratory crime investigator. Glass is an excellent source of positive identification because two pieces of glass rarely contain the same proportions of sand, metal, oxides, or carbonates. Police officers frequently encounter glass from windows, automobiles, bottles, and other objects as evidence in burglaries, murders, assaults, and a large variety of other crimes.

ITEM #3   ITEM #2
ITEM #4

L-667455

Figure 12-3. This pry tool was used to pry open the rear door of a hardware store. Items 2 and 4 were found at the scene of the burglary. Item #3 was found in a tool box in the suspect's car. This evidence led to his conviction for burglary.

When a criminal breaks a window, minute pieces of glass are usually found in his clothing, for example in his pant cuffs, breast pockets, or, to a lesser extent, on the surface of his clothing. Since these fragments are minute, they should be removed with a vacuum sweeper. Larger fragments should be carefully collected. The area adjacent to the actual break in a glass is critical in the examination. Fragments should not be overlooked.

Microscopic examination of glass fragments by an expert can determine:

—Whether a minute glass fragment probably or definitely came from a particular broken glass object.

—If a large fragment came from a particular glass object which was broken.

—If a fragment came from a particular kind of glass object such as a window pane, a spectacle lens, a bottle, etc.

—The origin of a fracture, its direction, and the direction of the force producing it.

—The order of occurrence of multiple fractures.

An investigator can determine whether glass was broken from the inside of a building by noticing where the fragments are.

Paint frequently is transferred from one object to another during the commission of a crime. Paint is often smeared on tools during unlawful entry. It

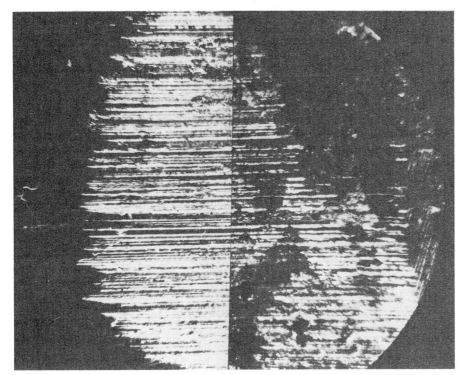

Figure 12-4. Striation pattern of a sledge hammer used to open a safe. Note fine vertical line dividing the photograph. Left half is evidence obtained at the scene of the crime. The white marks are safe insulation. The right photograph shows the actual hammer when it was seized from the suspect. The white marks are also safe insulation. This was matched up under a comparison microscope and magnified.

may be chipped off surfaces during burglaries. It may flake off automobiles during hasty getaways following impacts. Paint has often proved to be a strong link in the chain of circumstantial evidence. It may have sufficient individual and distinct characteristics for significant examination or comparison. It often associates an individual with the crime scene, or it may eliminate innocent suspects.

Insulation from safes may also prove valuable as evidence. Microscopically insulation can be identified by composition, color, mineral content, and physical charcteristics. Since few laymen normally come into contact with this type of material, particles of safe or fireproof insulation material on the clothing or shoes of a suspect are a strong indication of guilt.

Firearms left at a crime scene may be traced to their owner through the serial number, the manufacturer's identification, or the dealer who sold the gun. The firearm might also contain the suspect's fingerprints or other marks which could lead to his identification.

The make of the weapon is usually determined by the riflings in the barrel, spiral grooves cut into the barrel of a gun in its manufacture. The riflings vary considerably from manufacturer to manufacturer.

In addition, the entry of a bullet can be determined by the hole it makes; the bullet produces a cone-shaped hole, entering from the small point of the hole and emerging through the large end.

Explosives may be of value as evidence in burglary; malicious destruction of property such as school buildings, churches, or public buildings; murder; or murder attempted by an explosive placed in an automobile or a home. The area around an explosion may contain such items as blasting caps, cap fragments, detonating wire, safety fuse, dynamite paper, cotton, soap, masking tape, primacord, or steel fragments. In some cases it is possible to find samples of unexploded materials.

☑ CHECK POINT

1. How must the investigator deal with the physical evidence found at a crime scene?
2. What types of evidence are likely to be found at the crime scene?

*Answers

1. The investigator must recognize, collect, mark, preserve, and transport physical evidence in sufficient quantity for analysis and without contamination.
2. Among the more common types of evidence found at the crime scene are: blood, hair, fingerprints, fibers, documents, footprints or tire prints, tool fragments, toolmarks, broken glass, paint, insulation from safes, firearms, and explosives.

INTERVIEWING WITNESSES AND INTERROGATING SUSPECTS

The investigator must gain information by talking with victims, witnesses, friends, coworkers, neighbors, or immediate members of the family, as well as by talking with suspects in the case.

Witnesses

A witness is a person other than a suspect who has helpful information about a specific incident or a suspect.

> A witness may be a complainant, an accuser, a victim, an observer of the incident, a source of information, or a scientific examiner of physical evidence.

Most evidence at a trial is presented through witnesses. A person who is a qualified witness, who can perceive what was seen first-hand and can relate this experience, is an invaluable aid in the prosecution of a defendant.

Witnesses are valuable because they may have seen:

—The suspect actually committing the crime.

—A tool, gun, or instrument used in the commission of the crime in the suspect's possession subsequent or prior to the crime's commission.

—Property that was stolen in the suspect's possession subsequent to the crime's commission.

—The suspect making preparations to commit the crime, or heard him threatening to commit the crime, or knew that he had a motive for committing it.

—The suspect going to or leaving the scene of the crime about the time the crime was committeed.

In cases such as robbery, assault, or rape, the eyewitness testimony of the victim or a witness may be all that is necessary for a conviction.

Suspects

Before interrogating any suspect, the police officer must give the *Miranda warning*, as established in Miranda v. Arizona, 384 U.S. 436, 86 S.Ct. 1602 (1966) when the United States Supreme Court asserted that suspects must be informed of their right to remain silent, to have counsel present, a state appointed counsel if they cannot afford one, and warned that anything they say might be used against them in a court of law. Many investigators carry a card which contains the Miranda Warning to be read before interrogating a suspect:

Figure 12-5. Miranda Warning Card

MIRANDA WARNING

1. YOU HAVE THE RIGHT TO REMAIN SILENT.
2. IF YOU GIVE UP THE RIGHT TO REMAIN SILENT, ANYTHING YOU SAY CAN AND WILL BE USED AGAINST YOU IN A COURT OF LAW.
3. YOU HAVE THE RIGHT TO SPEAK WITH AN ATTORNEY AND TO HAVE THE ATTORNEY PRESENT DURING QUESTIONING.
4. IF YOU SO DESIRE AND CANNOT AFFORD ONE, AN ATTORNEY WILL BE APPOINTED FOR YOU WITHOUT CHARGE BEFORE QUESTIONING.

WAIVER

1. DO YOU UNDERSTAND EACH OF THESE RIGHTS I HAVE READ TO YOU?
2. HAVING THESE RIGHTS IN MIND, DO YOU WISH TO GIVE UP YOUR RIGHTS AS I HAVE EXPLAINED TO YOU AND TALK TO ME NOW?

On the evening of March 3, 1963, an eighteen-year-old girl was abducted and raped in Phoenix, Arizona. Ten days after the incident, Ernesto Miranda was arrested by Phoenix police, taken to police headquarters, and put in a line-up. He was identified by the victim and shortly thereafter signed a confession admitting the offenses. Despite objections to the statement by the defense attorney, the trial court admitted the confession. Miranda was convicted and sentenced to from twenty to thirty years on each count.

Miranda appealed on the grounds that he had not been advised of his constitutional rights under the Fifth Amendment. The Arizona Supreme Court ruled in 1965 that because Miranda had been previously arrested in California and Tennessee, he knowingly waived his rights under the Fifth and Sixth Amendments when he gave his confession to the Phoenix police. Justice McFarland of the Arizona Supreme Court ruled that because of Miranda's previous arrests, he was familiar with legal proceedings and individual rights and made an intelligent waiver.

In 1966, upon appeal, the U.S. Supreme Court reversed the Supreme Court of Arizona in a 5-4 decision and set up precedent rules for police custodial interrogation. Chief Justice Warren stated: "The mere fact that he signed a statement which contained a typed-in clause stating that he had 'full knowledge of his "legal rights"' does not approach the knowing and intelligent waiver required to relinquish constitutional rights."

The U.S. Supreme Court mandated that any time a person was in police custody police officers must give the Miranda warning so that persons being questioned can intelligently waive their right not to incriminate themselves as provided by the Fifth Amendment. If the warnings are not given, the prosecution cannot prove an intelligent waiver against self-incrimination, and any statement or confession will not be admissible against the suspect.

The Miranda rule applies not only to in-custody situations, but to any instance in which a suspect is questioned and the questioning results in the individual being deprived of a substantial portion of his liberty. When police officers attempt to obtain a statement or confession from a suspect, they must first advise that person of the Miranda warning. This applies whether a suspect is questioned in the police station, in a police car, or on a street corner.

When the probable cause builds to such a point that no reasonable person could deny that an arrest would be imminent, the police officer must, at that point, give the Miranda warning to the suspect if it has not already been given.

When the Miranda decision was handed down in 1966, there was much controversy. Many police officers and citizens complained that the court was "handcuffing the police," hampering them in their duties. However, the Federal Bureau of Investigation had been advising suspects of their constitutional rights for several years before the Miranda decision. These fears and objections over the years have proven unfounded.

Interviewing and Interrogating Techniques

Witnesses who are pressured to give information may become antagonized and refuse to cooperate. Suspects very often are uncooperative. The following simple procedures may help make an interview with a witness or an interrogation of a suspect more productive*:

—Prepare for each interview in advance if time permits. Know what questions you need to have answered.

---

*From *For The Record: Report Writing In Law Enforcement*, pp.51-52. Hess and Wrobleski, John Wiley and Sons, Inc., 1978, Reprinted by permission.

—Obtain your information as soon after the incident as possible. A delay may result in the subject's not remembering important details.

—Be considerate of the subject's feelings. If someone has just been robbed, or seen an assault, or been attacked, the individual may be understandably upset and emotional. Allow time for the person to calm down before asking too many questions. Remember that when emotions increase, memory decreases.

—Be friendly. Try to establish rapport with the subject before asking questions. Use the person's name; look at the person as you ask question; respond to the answers.

—Use a private setting if possible. Eliminate as many distractions as you can, so that the subject can devote full attention to the questions you ask.

—Eliminate physical barriers. Talking across a desk or counter, or through a car window, does not encourage conversation.

—Sit rather than stand. This will make the subject more comfortable and probably more willing to engage in conversation.

—Encourage conversation. Keep the subject talking by:
  Keeping your own talking to a minimum.
  Using open-ended questions, such as "Tell me what you saw."
  Avoiding questions that call for only a "yes" or "no" answer.
  Allowing long pauses. Pauses in the conversation should not be un-
    comfortable. Remember that the subject needs time to think and
    organize his thoughts. Give the subject all the time needed.

—Ask simple questions. Do not use law enforcement terminology when you ask your questions. Keep your language simple and direct.

—Ask one question at a time. Allow the subject to answer one question completely before going to the next question.

—Listen to what is said, and how it is said.

—Watch for indications of tension, nervousness, surprise, embarrassment, anger, fear, or guilt.

—Establish the reliability of the subject by asking some questions to which you already know the answers.

—Be objective and controlled. Recognize that many persons are reluctant to give information to the police. Among the several reasons for this reluctance are fear or hatred of police, fear of reprisal, lack of memory, or unwillingness to become involved. Keep control of yourself and your situation. Do not antagonize the subject, use profanity or obscenity, lose your temper, or use physical force. Remain calm, objective, and professional.

The basic objective of an interview is to get the facts from a witness to eventually prove to the court that the suspect in question did, in fact, commit the crime. The interview itself must be carefully planned by the officer, with only relevant questions asked. In addition to seeking facts and evidence, the investigator is looking for honest witnesses, witnesses who demonstrate concern and cooperativeness.

Some witnesses are fearful, disinterested, or unwilling to get involved. With such witnesses, investigators must develop a rapport: be tolerant of the witness's position and thinking; eliminate misunderstanding, mistrust, and suspicion; and induce confidence. They must recognize that each individual will have a somewhat different view of the same incident.

Witness Perception

Experience has illustrated time and again that no two people will view the same situation in exactly the same way.

> Perception of an incident is affected by the viewer's accuracy of observation, interpretation of what is seen, and attention paid to the incident.

When F. Lee Bailey, a noted criminal attorney, appeared on "The Tonight Show" he staged what was thought to be a purse-snatching. (Nobody knew in advance this was happening.) Afterwards Bailey interviewed people who thought they saw what had happened. Each person saw something completely different. In reality, a man had come out and simulated stabbing someone and to cover up that act he stole a purse on his way out and a lady screamed. This caught everybody's attention and people immediately believed the crime was simply purse-snatching. Nobody told the same story, and nobody gave a good description of the man who ran out.

How a witness describes what has happened is affected by many factors, some subjective (within the individual) and some objective (inherent to the situation). Because these factors vary from person to person, two people looking at the same thing may see something different. Take, for example, the following illustration:

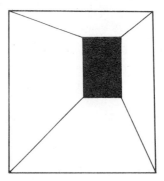

Whether the black surface projects toward the viewer or away depends completely upon the viewer's perception. In fact, the same person may see the black surface as projecting on first viewing, yet as receding on a second viewing.

Context, too, can alter how an object or event is perceived. For example, how do you "interpret" the following: 13

Now how do you interpret it?   A 13 C   12 13 14

Another factor affecting perception is the amount of attention which is focused on an incident. When an incident barely catches the attention of a witness (as on "The Tonight Show" incident), perception is liable to be faulty. One reason for this is the human tendency to complete comprehension of a situation to make it meaningful. That is, people tend to organize their observations into a complete, meaningful picture. A witness may see a man with a mask on and his right hand extended *as if* holding a gun, and the witness may mentally *add* the gun in his perception of the incident, even though it did not actually exist. To overcome this tendency and obtain valid information, police officers must be aware of how and why people think and act in given situations. In other words, they should try to put themselves in the other person's position and use what is called "street sense" and empathy.

The Noncooperative Witness

A recent Witness Cooperation Study (Witness Responses...1976) of almost 3,000 randomly selected witnesses indicated that many citizens are incorrectly perceived as noncooperative. According to this study (p. 6): "Prosecutors were apparently unable to cut through to the true intentions of 23% or more of those regarded as noncooperative and recorded the existence of witness problems when this was a premature judgment at best and an incorrect decision at worst." The primary cause for this problem was attributed to faulty communication between police, prosecutor, and witness.

> Problems arise when witnesses are not contacted, when their role is not explained, when they are not told when and where to appear, when their participation is discouraged, and when they are given vague instructions.

The study showed that the police did not obtain the correct addresses for 23% of the witnesses at the time of the crime, that the prosecutors often did not ensure that witnesses knew when and where to appear, that police sometimes asked for witness identification within hearing of suspects, and that witnesses often had no understanding of their role in the judicial process.

☑ CHECK POINT

1. Who may be a witness to a crime?
2. What is the Miranda warning?
3. Why may two people see the same event yet report it differently?
4. Why are some witnesses incorrectly perceived as uncooperative?

*Answers

1. A witness may be a complainant, an accuser, a victim, an observer of the incident, a source of information, or a scientific examiner of physical evidence.

2. The Miranda warning is a statement to be given to suspects before they are inter-rogated. It informs them of their right to remain silent and their right to have a lawyer present if they elect to talk.

3. Two people may see the same event yet report it differently because perception of an incident is affected by the viewer's accuracy of observation, interpretation of what is seen, and attention paid to the incident.

4. Witnesses may be incorrectly perceived as uncooperative when problems arise be-cause witnesses are not contacted, their role is not explained, they are not told when and where to appear, their participation is discouraged, or they are given vague instructions.

OBTAINING IDENTIFICATION OF A SUSPECT

If police officers do not actually witness the commission of the crime, eye-witness identification plays an important part in the arrest as well as in the trial proceedings.

Aids to Witness Identification of Suspects

> Very specific questions and use of an identification diagram may aid witnesses in their identification of suspects.

Rather than simply asking a witness to describe a suspect, it is often helpful if the investigator asks specifically about such items as the following:

Sex
Color
Age
Height
Weight
Build—stout, medium, slim, stooped, square-shouldered
Complexion—flushed, sallow, pale, fair, dark
Hair—color, thick or thin, bald or partly bald, straight, kinky, wavy, style
Eyes—color, close or far apart, bulgy or small
Eyebrows—bushy or normal
Nose—small, large, broad, hooked, straight, short, long, broken
Beard—color, straight, rounded, chin whiskers only, goatee, long sideburns
Mustache—color, short, stubby, long, pointed ends, turned-up ends
Chin—square, broad, long, narrow, double and sagging
Face—long, round, square, fat, thin, distinctive pimples or acne
Neck—long, short, thick, thin
Lips—thick, thin
Mouth—large, small, drooping or upturned
Teeth—missing, broken, prominent, gold, conspicuous dental work
Ears—small, large, close to head or extended outward, pierced
Forehead—high, low, sloping, bulging, straight
Distinctive marks—scars, moles, amputations, tattoo marks, peculiar walk or talk
Peculiarities—twitching of features, rapid or slow gait, eyeglasses or sunglasses, stutter, foreign accent, gruff or feminine voice, nervous or calm
Clothing—mask: if so, color; did it have eye slits, ear openings, mouth openings? Did it cover the whole face, have any designs on it? Did the suspect wear a hat

or cap (baseball, golf, etc.)? Any markings on the hat? Shirt and tie, sport shirt only, scarf, coat or jacket? Gloves, color of trousers, shoes, stockings, dressed well or shabbily, dressed neatly or carelessly? Any monogram on shirt or jacket?

Weapon used (if any)—shotgun, rifle, automatic weapon, hand gun. Was weapon readily shown or concealed? Taken with or left at scene?

Jewelry—any noticeable rings, bracelets, or necklaces, earrings, watch?

Figure 12-6.   Witness Identification Diagram.

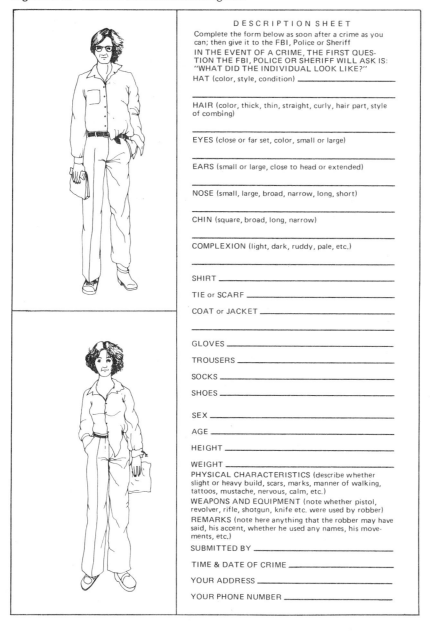

DESCRIPTION SHEET

Complete the form below as soon after a crime as you can; then give it to the FBI, Police or Sheriff

IN THE EVENT OF A CRIME, THE FIRST QUESTION THE FBI, POLICE OR SHERIFF WILL ASK IS: "WHAT DID THE INDIVIDUAL LOOK LIKE?"

HAT (color, style, condition) _____

HAIR (color, thick, thin, straight, curly, hair part, style of combing) _____

EYES (close or far set, color, small or large) _____

EARS (small or large, close to head or extended) _____

NOSE (small, large, broad, narrow, long, short) _____

CHIN (square, broad, long, narrow) _____

COMPLEXION (light, dark, ruddy, pale, etc.) _____

SHIRT _____

TIE or SCARF _____

COAT or JACKET _____

GLOVES _____

TROUSERS _____

SOCKS _____

SHOES _____

SEX _____

AGE _____

HEIGHT _____

WEIGHT _____

PHYSICAL CHARACTERISTICS (describe whether slight or heavy build, scars, marks, manner of walking, tattoos, mustache, nervous, calm, etc.)

WEAPONS AND EQUIPMENT (note whether pistol, revolver, rifle, shotgun, knife etc. were used by robber)

REMARKS (note here anything that the robber may have said, his accent, whether he used any names, his movements, etc.)

SUBMITTED BY _____

TIME & DATE OF CRIME _____

YOUR ADDRESS _____

YOUR PHONE NUMBER _____

In addition to questions related to the suspect's appearance, the investigator might also assist the witness by using a description sheet such as the one in Figure 12-6.

Other information related to the suspect must also be obtained by the investigator. It is important to know how the suspect left the scene—running, walking, in a vehicle—and in what direction.

If the suspect escaped in a vehicle, the investigator should obtain information about the license number, make of the vehicle, number of passengers, direction of travel, the color and size of the car, as well as any other identifiable features such as racing stripes, hood ornaments, customized features, broken taillights or headlights, body damage, and so on. The car, if identified, may lead the investigator to the suspect.

If the witness knows the suspect, the investigator should ask about the suspect's personal associates, his habits, and where he is likely to be found.

Usually, however, the witness does not know the suspect. If investigators can identify a suspect based on information given by the witness or on their own intuition as to who might be responsible for the crime, they must follow strict procedures in establishing that the individual is identified by the witness.

> The three basic types of identification are:
> —Field identification.
> —Photographic identification.
> —Line-up identification.

Each type of identification is used in specific circumstances, and each must meet certain legal requirements to be admissible in court. Frequently more than one type of identification is used.

Field Identification

> Field identification is used when a suspect is temporarily detained or arrested. It is "at-the-scene" identification.

Generally the suspect is returned to the crime scene for possible identification, or the witness may be taken to where the suspect is being held. In either case, field identification is generally used when a suspect matches the description given by a witness and is apprehended close to the scene of the crime.

> Field identification is based on a *totality of circumstances* in which a witness identifies a suspect as being the person who committed a crime. The suspect does *not* have the right to have counsel present at a field identification.*

---

*United States v. Ash Jr., 413 U.S. 300, 93, S.Ct. 2568 (1973).

Totality of circumstances takes into consideration the concentration a witness had upon the suspect at the time the crime was committed, the accuracy of the witness's description of the suspect, the certainty of the witness at the time of the confrontation, and the length of time between commission of the crime and the field identification.

Justifiable use of field identification is illustrated in the following incident. On January 1 at 11:30 A.M., the Mytown Stop and Shop Delicatessen was robbed by a single gunman. Officers Webster and Kleven responded immediately to the call and obtained a description of the gunman as well as another man waiting outside in a getaway car. Other units were notified and a description of the gunman, driver, and car was given over the radio. Shortly after the broadcast, Officers Wilson and Bryant spotted a car fitting the description of the getaway car and chased it into a dead-end alley. The suspects fit the descriptions broadcast. They attempted to flee, but were apprehended by the officers. Officers Wilson and Bryant were almost certain they had the right men because the original descriptions matched those of the men in custody and they had attempted to escape.

The quick capture of the suspects justified the fairness of a field identification. There was a need for such immediate identification, so Officers Wilson and Bryant took the suspects back to the scene of the armed robbery, taking advantage of the freshness of the incident in the memory of the victim and the other witnesses. They were also eliminating innocent persons who, for one reason or another, might come under suspicion. The suspects were identified by the victim and the witnesses as being the armed robber and driver. The totality of circumstances made such field identification fair and legal.

> The critical element in a field identification is *time*.

Studies have shown a 60% probability of arrest if response time to crime calls was within one minute. However, the probability of arrest was considerably less when response time was longer. Rapid response greatly improves the officer's chances of apprehending suspects still at the scene. In such cases field identification is obviously justified. Even when the suspects have left the scene, however, if they are apprehended within a reasonable time (up to approximately 15 minutes) after commission of the crime, immediate identification is justified. A reasonable basis for believing that immediate identification is needed must exist before using field identification.

Photographic Identification

In a large eastern city police department, Jill McTaggart was brought into police headquarters as a suspect in an armed robbery of a service station which occurred several days ago. She was sitting in the photo-identification area, facing the front of the camera. The camera clicked, and a *mug shot* of Jill McTaggart was ready for the files.

> If a suspect is *not* known, witnesses may make identification through mug shots.

Most people are familiar with the procedure of having victims and witnesses go through mug books in hopes of finding a picture of the person they saw commit a particular crime. This type of identification is time-consuming and is only profitable if the suspect has a record.

Mug shots are not the only types of photographs used in suspect identification. Frequently officers know, or have a strong suspicion about, who committed a given crime. In such instances, they may present photographs to victims and/or witnesses who may identify the suspect from among the photographs.

> Photographic identification is reserved for times when the suspect is *not* in custody or it is *not* possible to conduct a fair line-up. Photographic identification should use a minimum of six people of comparable race, height, weight, and general description.
>
> Witnesses should be instructed that they are not obliged to identify anyone from the photographs.

Photographs used for suspect identification should not contain labels which reveal that a certain suspect has a criminal record. The identification is to be impartial, based on the witness's view of the suspect, and untainted by the suspect's past record.

Both the United States Supreme Court and several state supreme courts have issued decisions recognizing the hazards in identification from photographs. However, each has stated that every case must be considered on its own facts. Admissibility in court is more probable if the witness was shown the photographs when he was alone and had had no communications with any other witnesses.

A typical identification by photograph session might go something like this: Officer Bryce McCloud has eight photographs in his hand, approaches the witnesses, and says, "You will be asked to look at these photographs. You should not assume that the photographs contain the picture of the person who committed the crime. You do not have to identify anyone. It is just as important that innocent persons are freed from suspicion as it is to identify guilty parties. Please do not discuss the case with other witnesses or indicate in any way that you have identified anyone."

☑ CHECK POINT

1. How may witnesses be aided in making an identification?
2. What are the three basic types of identification?
3. What is field identification?

4. Upon what is field identification based?
5. Does the suspect have the right to an attorney during field identification?
6. What is the critical element in field identification?
7. When is it appropriate to use a mug shot for identification?
8. When is it appropriate to use regular photographs in identification?
9. What precautions should be taken and what instructions should be given when using photographic identification to assure the legality and admissibility of the identification in court?

*Answers

1. Very specific questions and use of an identification diagram may aid witnesses in their identification of suspects.
2. The three basic types of identification are field identification, photographic identification, and line-up identification.
3. Field identification is used when a suspect is temporarily detained or arrested. It is "at-the-scene" identification.
4. Field identification is based on a totality of circumstances in which a witness identifies a suspect as being the person who committed a crime.
5. The suspect does *not* have the right to an attorney during field identification.
6. The critical element in field identification is time.
7. Mug shots may be used for identification when the suspect is not known.
8. Photographic identification is used when the suspect is not in custody or it is not possible to conduct a fair line-up.
9. Photographic identification should use a minimum of six people of comparable race, height, weight, and general description. Witnesses should be instructed that they are not obliged to identify anyone from the photographs.

Line-Up Identification

A line-up is generally used when a suspect is in custody. The basic idea of the line-up is to provide the opportunity for witnesses to observe several individuals, one of whom is the suspect, to see if he can be identified.

> A line-up is used when a suspect is in custody. It should contain a minimum of six persons of similar race, height, weight, and general description. Witnesses must be instructed that no identification need be made.

The witnesses not only can see the persons in the line-up, they also can hear them speak. A suspect may be asked to speak, walk, turn, assume a stance or a gesture, or put on clothing. If witnesses have described the suspect's clothing, then all persons in the line-up or none should wear that type of clothing. Obviously if only one dressed the way witnesses described, the tendency would be to pick him. Some police departments have a small inventory of clothing and personal effects such as sunglasses, masks, scarves, gloves, and coats which they have the participants in a line-up wear, depending upon the description of the witness(es).

A number of important court decisions have been made regarding line-up identification. One of the most important is the Wade decision.

> The *Wade* decision* states that "prior to having a suspect participate in a line-up, the officer must advise the suspect of his constitutional right to have his lawyer present during the line-up." Requesting a suspect to participate in the line-up is *not* a violation of the person's civil rights.

Although requesting participation is not considered a form of self-incrimination under the Fifth Amendment, the line-up is considered a "critical stage" in the legal process. The Wade decision was based on a case in which Wade was convicted of robbing a Texas bank. His case went to the United States Supreme Court, which reviewed the proceedings and then sent the case back to an appeals court. In its review, the high court said: "The Sixth Amendment of the Constitution guarantees that every citizen shall have the right of counsel in criminal prosecution. When a citizen is suspected of a crime and required to participate in a line-up where witnesses attempt to identify him, then he has a constitutional right to have his lawyer present." The U.S. Supreme Court stated that "a line-up is just as critical a stage of the prosecution as the trial itself." It should be noted, however, that this particular constitutional right does *not* apply to field identification or to photographic identification.

When using line-up identification, the officer must know the legal requirements accompanying such an identification as well as the composition of the line-up itself. A legal line-up should assure that:

—The suspect has been advised of his right to a lawyer.

—A lawyer has been secured if requested.

—The witnesses have been given impartial pre-line-up advice.

—The line-up is conducted fairly.

—The individuals in the line-up meet the requirements previously specified.

The following description illustrates the sequence of a typical line-up identification as well as complications which might arise.

Background.   On December 24th the Mytown State Bank was robbed by three armed gunmen. Several witnesses obtained a good look at the robbers, and the men apparently knew it. When the officer sought out one of the suspects, the neighbors said that he hadn't been out of his apartment for three days. The robbery had occurred four days prior. The suspect was taken into custody without a struggle. Since the robbery had occurred four days ago, field identification was not justified. And, since the suspect was in custody, photographic identification was not justified. A line-up was called for.

Constitutional Rights.   At headquarters, Officer James Fisher sat across the desk from the suspect and said, "We are preparing a line-up in which you will take part. Witnesses will observe you and decide if you were involved in

---

*United States v. Wade, 388 U.S. 218, 87 S. Ct. 1926 (1967).

the crime of armed robbery or not. You have a right to have your attorney present at the line-up to observe. If you do not have an attorney and are unable to afford one, we will obtain one for you at no cost to be at the line-up. If you wish, you do not need to have an attorney present at the line-up. Do you understand?"

Generally when an officer talks about "reading a suspect his rights," he means the Miranda rights protecting the suspect from self-incrimination. For a line-up, however, the officer is talking about the suspect's Sixth Amendment right to have a lawyer present as specified in the Wade decision. The Miranda decision is not relevant.

The suspect may waive his right to have an attorney present at the line-up. If this occurs and as a result of the line-up witnesses pick him out as one of the armed robbers, Officer Fisher would have to satisfy the court that the suspect "knowingly and intelligently" waived his right to counsel in the line-up. Since none of the United States Supreme Court cases on line-ups gives a clear indication of what kind of evidence would support such a waiver, Officer Fisher must document his conversation with the suspect either by a signed statement, a tape recording, or a signed waiver. Generally this is not a problem, as most suspects ask for a lawyer.

Officer Fisher continues, "What do you want me to do? Do you want to have an attorney present at the line-up?" The suspect responds, "You better get me a lawyer. I don't know any."

Obtaining a Lawyer. It is now up to Officer Fisher to obtain a lawyer for the suspect. In some instances the lawyer called may refuse to represent the suspect, or he may say he will come and then fail to do so. If the lawyer refuses to come, the officer must either try to change his mind or find another lawyer. If the lawyer says he will come, but then fails to do so, color photographs can be taken of the line-up and used following the procedures for photographic identification. The photographs must be marked with the time, date, and place, and made available to the prosecutor. This will assist the prosecutor in admitting the photographs as evidence of identification if the suspect is brought to trial.

In most instances the lawyer will agree to appear at the line-up and does so. In Officer Fisher's case, the lawyer agrees to appear at 3:00 P.M. Officer Fisher informs the suspect, "Your lawyer has agreed to be present for the line-up. Until then you will be returned to confinement until three o'clock when you will participate in the line-up." Officer Fisher directs Officer MacAloon to take the suspect to the holding area until it is time for the line-up.

When the suspect's counsel arrives prior to the line-up, Officer Fisher allows them a few minutes together in private. If the lawyer advises his client not to participate in the line-up, the suspect's refusal to participate can be used against him in court. The line-up should proceed as scheduled.

If for any reason a suspect refuses to cooperate in a line-up, photographic identification may be used. The suspect's refusal to participate may be used against him in court.

In our case, however, the suspect and his lawyer agree that the suspect will participate in the line-up.

Pre-line-up Advice.   The first contact of the individuals in the line-up with the witnesses should be fair. Therefore, the witnesses are instructed that there will be several persons in the line-up. To determine which, if any, of these persons were involved in the particular armed robbery, the witnesses will be asked to observe each person carefully. Officer Fisher explains to the witnesses that he is just as interested in eliminating suspects as implicating them. He asks the witnesses not to discuss identification with friends, family, or anyone else prior to the line-up, since this might jeopardize the fairness of the line-up or a subsequent trial. He also advises them not to make a statement or give any outward recognition if an identification is made.

It is now time. The drama begins in the line-up room. There are five people, all witnesses, spaced far enough back in the room to be considered beyond the sight of those in the line-up. Two officers are available to answer questions. Officer Bryce McCloud, positioned at the front of the room, reads the instructions: "Ladies and Gentlemen. In a few moments several men will appear on the stage. You will be able to see them, but they will not be able to see you. Each man will be asked to do certain things, such as turning, speaking. When the entire line has completed this process, I will ask whether anyone desires one or more of the suspects to repeat something. If you do, please raise your hand and an officer will talk with you. If one suspect is asked to repeat, we will ask the entire line to repeat. Please do not talk with each other at any time. Communicate only with the officers, and then do so in private. When the line-up is completed, please fill out the card we have given you, whether you have made an identification or not, and hand it to the officer. If you cannot identify anyone, please indicate this. If you can identify a suspect, mark the card with his number in the line."

In the Wade decision, the United States Supreme Court pointed out that once a witness picks a suspect from a line-up, the witness is not likely to change his identification in a courtroom. Therefore, if the defense counsel can prove that Officer Fisher did not take adequate precautions to avoid misidentification at the line-up, a judge would probably disallow any identification of that suspect by Officer Fisher's witnesses, including courtroom identification.

Therefore Officer Fisher avoids any actions that might coach the witnesses into identifications or give them the impression that someone in the line-up had to be identified. One reason a lawyer has a right to be at the line-up is to observe its fairness. Another reason is to listen to the witnesses' identification and perhaps even to speak to them after the line-up, thereby preparing a better cross-examination of these witnesses.

A Fair Line-Up.   The line-up begins. The door opens and six men come in, each approximately the same height, none bearded, and all casually dressed. Each carries a number and sign. One officer comes in ahead of them and one behind them. The suspect's attorney enters carrying a legal pad and sits among the witnesses, merely an observer. He has a right to be in the room, but has no authority to interfere with the conduct of the line-up. At the conclusion of the line-up he may talk to the witnesses, but they are not obliged to talk to him. If at all possible when the defense counsel is present, a prosecutor should also be present. Any objections the suspect's counsel may have can be given to the prosecutor.

Officer Fisher is aware that mismatches have occurred in line-ups—with only one person coming close to fitting the witnesses' description. In some instances, witnesses have described Indian or black suspects who are put in a line-up with whites. This unfairly narrows the choices and may lead the witnesses into a false identification. Officer Fisher avoided this mistake by selecting the minimum of six persons and having them of comparable race, height, weight, and general appearance.

Officer McCloud addresses the men in the line-up, "I will ask each of you to say the following words: 'Stay where you are. Don't move. This is a stick-up.' All right, Number One, say those words."

After the first man in the line-up says the phrases, Officer McCloud asks the others in turn to repeat the same words. As he continues down the line of suspects to repeat his initial instruction of phrases, he comes to Number Five. He repeats, "Number Five, the words are: 'Stay where you are. Don't move. This is a stick-up.'"

Number Five refuses to repeat the phrase, whereupon Officer McCloud states, "I will remind you that although you need not answer any questions, your refusal to repeat these words will be used as evidence against you in court." Reluctantly, Number Five repeats the phrase after drawing considerable attention to himself.

After Number Six repeats the words, each man is asked to step forward, present his left profile toward the witnesses, and bring his left hand up to his face as if the hand were covering his mouth. Each does this. Number Five does not. As a result of Number Five's actions, the defense counsel and the prosecutor lean across their chairs and confer in low voices.

Although Officers Fisher and McCloud are trying to conduct the line-up fairly, the suspect is obviously calling attention to himself. He had been told previously that he would not have to make incriminating statements, but that he would be required to repeat certain words or phrases. If the officers try to compel him to follow their instructions, they may suggest to the witnesses that this man must do so in order that they might identify him.

Suppose we had a different situation and the suspect indicated he wouldn't even participate in the line-up. That would give Officer Fisher a different opening to the line-up and, unfortunately, by using force to compel him to participate, Officer Fisher might suggest to the witnesses that this "guilty" man must be up there so they could identify him. His lawyer would see it that way, and so might a judge in a court of law. The lawyer would have a valid objection because any violence that might ensue from his client's refusal to participate in the line-up could be construed as prejudicing the witnesses. In a situation such as this, the prosecutor would advise that identification by photograph be used.

When a suspect is in custody, a line-up should be used as long as it can be done without force and in a "fair" manner. If these conditions cannot be satisfied, photographic identification should be used.

> Witnesses should not make photographic identification and then line-up identification within a short period of time.

If a line-up can be held, there is no reason to show pictures. If both are done in a short period of time, the officer destroys any doubt the witness might have that the person in the picture is the guilty party. A recent midwest supreme court ruling reversed a guilty decision because a photo identification and line-up were held within minutes of each other.

☑ CHECK POINT

1. When is a line-up used?
2. What precautions should be taken and what instructions should be given to assure the legality and admissibility of a line-up identification in court?
3. What relevance does the Wade decision have to identification of a suspect?
4. Does the Fifth Amendment (forbidding self-incrimination) have any relevance in any of the three types of identification? If so, which one, and why?
5. What should be done if a suspect refuses to participate in a line-up?
6. What precautions must be taken if both photographic and line-up identification are used?

*Answers

1. A line-up is used when a suspect is in custody.
2. A line-up should contain a minimum of six persons of similar race, height, weight, and general description. Witnesses must be instructed that no identification need be made.
3. The Wade decision states that "prior to having a suspect participate in a line-up, the officer must advise the suspect of his constitutional right to have his lawyer present during the line-up."
4. The Fifth Amendment does *not* have relevance for any of the three types of identification. Requesting a suspect to participate in a line-up is *not* a violation of his civil rights.
5. If for any reason a suspect refuses to cooperate in a line-up, photographic identification may be used. The suspect's refusal to participate may be used against him in court.
6. Witnesses should not make photographic identification and then line-up identification within a short period of time.

SUMMARY

A large part of an investigator's role centers around *objectively* obtaining and presenting information and evidence. The primary responsibilities of the investigator are to (1) assure that the crime scene is secure, (2) record all facts related to the case for future reference, (3) photograph and sketch the crime scene, (4) obtain and identify evidence, (5) interview witnesses and interrogate suspects, and (6) assist in the identification of suspects.

Although patrol usually conducts the preliminary investigation of a crime, investigators or detectives usually conduct the follow-up investigation. Cooperation between patrol and investigative functions is essential for success-ful resolution of cases.

Investigators, be they patrol officers or detectives, are responsible for securing the crime scene, which includes any surrounding area that contains evidence of criminal activity. They must obtain answers to the questions: who? what? where? when? how? why? Usually they must obtain both photo-graphs and sketches because although photographs include all details and can show items close up, sketches can be selective and can show much larger areas.

A primary responsibility of investigators is to recognize, collect, mark, preserve, and transport physical evidence without contamination in sufficient quantity for analysis. Such evidence may consist of blood, hair, fingerprints, documents, footprints or tire prints, tool fragments, toolmarks, broken glass, paint, insulation from safes, firearms, and explosives.

In addition, investigators must interview witnesses and interrogate sus-pects. A witness may be a complainant, an accuser, a victim, an observer of the incident, a source of information, or a scientific examiner of physical evi-dence. A suspect, the person believed to have committed the crime, should not be interrogated without first being given the Miranda warning which advises him that he has the "right to remain silent...the right to speak with an attorney and to have the attorney present during questioning."

Information obtained from witnesses is usually critical to resolution of a case. Unfortunately, witnesses' perception of what happened often varies be-cause the perception is affected by the viewer's accuracy of observation, inter-pretation of what is seen, and attention paid to the incident. In addition, prob-lems may arise when witnesses are not contacted, when their role is not explained, when they are not told when and where to appear, when their par-ticipation is discouraged, or when they are given vague instructions. In such instances, the witness may incorrectly be perceived to be "noncooperative."

In addition to physical evidence, eyewitness identification plays an im-portant part in the arrest and in the trial proceedings. Very specific questions and use of an identification diagram may aid witnesses in their identification of suspects. Once this information has been obtained, the investigator may use three basic types of identification: (1) field identification, (2) photographic identification, or (3) line-up identification. Sometimes more than one type of identification is used.

Field identification is used when a suspect is temporarily detained or arrested. It is usually "at-the-scene" identification. Field identification is based on totality of circumstances in which a witness identifies a suspect as being the person who committed the crime. The suspect does *not* have the right to have a counsel present at a field identification. The critical element in a field identification is time—it should usually occur within approximately fifteen minutes of the commission of the crime to be legally admissible.

Photographic identification may be of two types—mug shots or "ordinary" photographs. Mug shots are usually used when the suspect is not known to the witness or the police. "Ordinary" photographic identification is used when the police have a fairly good idea of who is involved in the crime and the suspect is not in custody or it is not possible to conduct a fair line-up. Photographic identification should use a minimum of six people of comparable race, height, weight, and general description. Witnesses should be instructed that they are not obliged to identify anyone from the photographs.

A line-up is used when a suspect is in custody. The same legal requirements exist as for photographic identification: the line-up should contain a minimum of six persons of similar race, height, weight, and general description. Witnesses must be instructed that no identification need be made.

The Wade decision states that "prior to having a suspect participate in a line-up, the officer must advise the suspect of his constitutional right to have his lawyer present during the lineup." Requesting a suspect to participate in a line-up is *not* a violation of the person's civil rights. However, if for any reason the suspect refuses to cooperate in a line-up, photographic identification may be used and the suspect's refusal to participate may be used against him in court. If both photographic identification and line-up identification are used, they should *not* be done within a short period of time.

APPLICATION

A. Officer Clancy Morgan was dispatched to the scene of a homicide at 1012 Abbott Avenue, Mytown, USA. Upon arriving at the scene, he noticed a man sitting in a chair holding his head in his hands. Officer Morgan also noticed a gun on the table and the body of a woman lying nearby. Officer Morgan immediately telephoned for crime laboratory personnel and for detectives to come to the scene. While awaiting their arrival, Officer Morgan asked the man what happened. The man stated that he was the husband of the deceased woman lying on the floor. "I killed her," he explained. "We were drinking for the past several hours, when she made some nasty remarks about my mother. I became angry, grabbed the gun out of the drawer in the living room, and shot her." Officer Morgan continued to question him about details of the shooting and made several notes in his notebook. The detectives and the crime laboratory personnel arrived, and he turned the investigation over to them.

   1. Did Officer Morgan do the right thing in listening to the man's conversation?
   2. Would Officer Morgan's testimony be admitted into court if he had to testify?
   3. Would any of the testimony or conversation be admissible?

B. While on patrol at 2:00 A.M., Officer Angela Willey noticed a juvenile carrying a portable television set in the business district of Mytown, USA. She stopped the juvenile to make inquiry. The youngster gave Officer Willey evasive answers which aroused her suspicions. Suddenly the juvenile blurted out, "You've got me; I burglarized the TV shop down the street." At this point Officer Willey advised the juvenile of his rights, placed him under arrest, and took him to the juvenile bureau.

   1. Should Officer Willey have advised the suspect of his rights prior to when she did?
   2. Did she handle the situation properly?
   3. Will Officer Willey's statement of the suspect's admission of burglary be admitted into court?

Answers

A. 1. Yes. However, when the man stated, "I killed her," he should have stopped the man from talking and advised him of his rights under the Miranda decision. Then if the suspect wanted to continue to talk, Officer Morgan could have continued questioning him.
   2. No, because he did not advise the suspect of his rights.
   3. Yes. Only the portion where the man stated, "I killed her," because that was a spontaneous statement which the officer could not have prevented.
B. 1. No, because she was merely making inquiry into a suspicious activity.
   2. Yes. The circumstances required an inquiry, and she advised him at the proper point.
   3. Yes, because it was a spontaneous statement the officer couldn't have prevented.

DISCUSSION QUESTIONS

1. In a large city with much crime, how might team policing be used to improve investigating efficiency of the department? What disadvantages are there?
2. If patrol officers apprehend a suspect, do they conduct the line-up?
3. If there was a crime and the suspect was unusually tall or was a member of a minority group not common in the area, how could you hold a fair line-up?
4. In what crimes is eyewitness testimony all that is required for conviction?
5. Why wouldn't people want to help put a stop to crime by being witnesses?
6. How do you convince witnesses to get involved when they really don't want to?
7. Can you force a witness to answer questions?
8. If two witnesses disagree on an identification, what happens?
9. If five witnesses are to identify a suspect in a line-up and four of them pick one person and one picks another, is it assumed that the majority are right, or is the line-up inconclusive?
10. How are participants in a line-up chosen?
11. Is it legal to put other suspects in a line-up with the prime suspect?
12. Why does the suspect *not* have the right to counsel at a field identification?
13. According to Plautus, "One eye-witness is of more weight than ten hearsays." Would you agree?
14. Disraeli has said, "Time is precious, but truth is more precious than time." How might you relate this to field identification?

REFERENCES

Bloch, P. B., and Weidman, D. R. *Managing criminal investigation.* Washington, DC: U.S. Government Printing Office (LEAA Grant #72-TA-99-1077), 1975.

Busch, F. X. *Law and tactics in jury trials.* Indianapolis: Bobbs-Merrill Company, 1949.

Bushnell's Case, 6 How. St. Tr. 999.

Gerber, S. R., and Schroeder, O., Jr. *Criminal investigation and interrogation.* Cincinnati: W. H. Anderson Company, 1962.

Hess, K. M., and Wrobleski, H. M. *For the record: Report writing in law enforcement.* New York: John Wiley and Sons, 1978.

Perkins, R. M. *Criminal law and procedure.* (3rd ed.) Brooklyn: Foundation Press, 1966.

The prosecution function and defense function. New York: Standards for the Administration of Criminal Justice, American Bar Association, 1971.

Soderman, H., and O'Connell, J. *Modern criminal investigation.* (5th ed.) New York: Funk and Wagnalls, 1962.

Waddington, L. C. *Criminal evidence.* Encino, CA: Glencoe Publishing Company, 1978.

Wilson, O. W. *Police planning.* Springfield, IL: Charles C. Thomas Company, 1962.

Witness responses misunderstood by prosecutors, *Target,* (LEAA Newsletter), 5:1, January 1976, p. 6.

Section Four

In Search of Justice: The Police Officer's Role in the Criminal Justice System

Having looked at the day-to-day operations in which law enforcement officers become involved, we return full circle to our initial discussion of civil rights and civil liberties, the Bill of Rights, and constitutional safeguards.

In this section the police officer's function within the criminal justice system is examined—what constitutes a lawful arrest (Chapter 13), a lawful search (Chapter 14), and the police officer's role in the judicial system from the issuance of a warrant through the court trial (Chapter 15).

The Fourth
Amendment requires
that an arrest be
reasonable and based
upon probable cause.

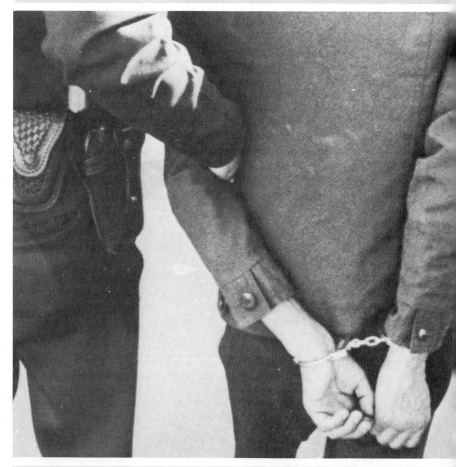

Lawful Arrest

Reliance Upon Reason and Probable Cause

13

DO YOU KNOW □ □ □

- ☐ The major provisions of the Fourth Amendment?
- ☐ How to define seizure, reasonable, arrest, and "stop and frisk"?
- ☐ On what major sources probable cause can be based?
- ☐ What the major categories of informational probable cause are?
- ☐ What the authorities for lawful arrest without a warrant are?
- ☐ How to analyze a hypothetical arrest situation and determine whether the arrest is lawful?
- ☐ What basic principles underlie "stop and frisk"?
- ☐ What the differences are between an arrest and "stop and frisk"?
- ☐ What significance the Terry case has in relation to the Fourth Amendment?
- ☐ How to analyze a hypothetical "stop and frisk" situation and determine whether it is lawful?

Reason never has failed men. Only force and oppression have made the wrecks in the world.—William Allen White

Common sense is instinct and enough of it is genius.—W. H. Shaw

INTRODUCTION

On June 5th the Swingers' Club in Mytown was robbed of $100 by a Caucasian male, approximately six feet tall, weighing 160 pounds, with dark brown eyes. The man was wearing a green jacket and a scarf which masked part of his face. He carried a sawed-off .410 gauge shotgun which was discharged into the ceiling of the premises during the robbery. The ejected shell was later found and turned over to the police. The Mytown sheriff sent out a teletype message regarding the armed robbery and describing the suspect. The message was received by the Uptown Police Department in a neighboring suburb.

On June 6th Denise Watson took a sawed-off .410 gauge shotgun and clip and a partially filled box of .410 gauge shotgun shells to the rectory of St. Henry's Church in Uptown. In response to a call from a priest, two detectives from the Uptown Police Department went to the rectory and talked with Mrs. Watson. She told them that the shotgun and shells belonged to her husband, that he was at home, and that he had committed the Mytown robbery.

The two detectives, both having seen the teletype message, took the shotgun and shells from Mrs. Watson and went to the Watson home where she voluntarily gave them a gray satchel containing, among other things, money and .410 gauge shotgun shells. Watson was arrested for armed robbery and taken into custody. No search was ever made of the Watson residence.

The questions in the prosecutor's mind when presented with the facts were: "Was there probable cause for the suspect's arrest?" and "Was there a constitutional seizure of evidence?" The test the prosecutor must use before issuing a complaint is, does he, himself, believe the suspect guilty *beyond a reasonable doubt* and does he believe all the evidence is legally admissible?

In this case his answers to the questions were "Yes," and the case went to trial. Watson was found guilty of armed robbery in a superior court and sentenced to ten years in the penitentiary.

REASONABLE SEIZURES—LAWFUL ARRESTS—AND THE FOURTH AMENDMENT

The constitutional standards for searches and seizures are contained in the Fourth Amendment:

The right of the people to be secure in their persons, houses, papers, and effects, against unreasonable searches and seizures, shall not be violated, and no warrant shall issue but upon probable cause, supported by oath or affirmation, and particularly describing the place to be searched and the persons or things to be seized.

The Fourth Amendment requires that seizures be reasonable and based on probable cause. These requirements apply not only to seizure of property but also to the "seizure" or arrest of persons. Arbitrary arrests have no place in a democratic society. In fact, colonial grievances against unreasonable searches and seizures, in part, led to the revolt against English authority. The Constitution, formulated after the revolution, guaranteed the right to be secure from "unreasonable seizure."

Statutes throughout the United States generally define *arrest* as the taking of a person into custody by the actual restraint of the person or by his submission to the custody of the officer that he may be held to answer for a public offense.

The courts have held that before citizens can be deprived of their liberty there must be justification for the seizure. To assure that justification exists, officers are required to clearly establish a basis for the arrest.

The rules for determining what constitutes a reasonable search and/or seizure result from interpretation of the first part of the Fourth Amendment, called the "reasonable search and seizure clause," which states: "The right of the people to be secure in their persons, houses, papers, and effects, against unreasonable searches and seizures shall not be violated."

Reasonable means sensible, justifiable, logical, based on reason.

The word *reason* means "possessing good sound judgment"; "well balanced." "Possessing good judgment" implies making decisions. Each case and situation is different from other cases and other situations; therefore, police officers must use their personal judgment as to what action to take. "Well balanced" applies to a built-in stability for justice. On the one hand there is the justification for an action, whether it be an arrest based on probable cause or an arrest warrant or stopping and frisking someone. On the other hand, the justification for the actions must be balanced by observing the limitations on each action. When the limitations for any action are exceeded, we have gone beyond the reasonableness that made the action legal. Justification and limitation must always be considered together.

PROBABLE CAUSE—LAWFUL ARREST— AND THE FOURTH AMENDMENT

The terms *reasonable* and *probable cause* provide a very fine, but significant, weight to balance the scales of justice which measure the conduct of all people. Without what is referred to as probable cause, the laws that govern us might easily become unbalanced, that is, too permissive or too restrictive.

The second part of the Fourth Amendment, called the "Warrant Clause," states: "No warrant shall issue but upon probable cause..." In other words, all warrants (search and arrest warrants) must be based on probable cause.

> *Probable cause* is defined in the Fourth Amendment as "a state of facts that lead a man of ordinary care and prudence to believe and conscientiously entertain an honest and strong suspicion that the person is guilty of a crime."

An unlimited number of factors can contribute to an officer's decision to seek the issuance of an arrest warrant, or to arrest without a warrant. Every case is unique; therefore, the officer must determine probable cause based on the sum total of the facts of a particular case.

☑ CHECK POINT

1. Which amendment establishes the citizen's right to be free from unreasonable searches and seizures?
2. What are the major provisions of this amendment?
3. Define the terms *arrest, reasonable, and probable cause.*

* Answers

1. The Fourth Amendment establishes the citizen's right to be free from unreasonable searches and seizures.
2. The Fourth Amendment assures all United States citizens that they will not be arrested (seized) without a good reason and that any warrant to arrest will be based on probable cause. (These same guarantees apply to searches as will be discussed in Chapter 14.)
3. *Arrest* is generally defined as the taking of a person into custody by the actual restraint of the person or by his submission to the custody of the officer that he may be held to answer for a public offense.

   Reasonable is defined as sensible, justifiable, logical, based on reason.

   Probable cause is defined in the Fourth Amendment as "a state of facts that lead a man of ordinary care and prudence to believe and conscientiously entertain an honest and strong suspicion that the person is guilty of a crime."

ARREST WITHOUT A WARRANT

Usually an officer should have an arrest warrant issued by a magistrate. However, an officer has the authority to make a lawful arrest *without* an arrest warrant.

> Police officers may make lawful arrests without a warrant for felonies or misdemeanors committed in their presence or for felonies not committed in their presence if they have probable cause.

Specifically, the four authorities for arrest *without* a warrant are:

1. When a public offense is committed or attempted in an officer's presence.
2. When a person arrested has committed a felony, although not in an officer's presence, for example, an all-points bulletin on a bank robber before a warrant is issued.
3. When a felony has in fact been committed, and the officer has reasonable cause to believe that the person has committed it; for example, an officer answers a shooting call and the suspect is still at the scene.
4. On a charge made upon probable cause of the commission of a felony by the person arrested; for example, a woman accuses her boyfriend of stealing $500 from her; the officer searches the boyfriend and finds the money.

The first authority allows for an arrest for a public offense committed or attempted in the presence of an officer. "Public offense" includes both felonies and misdemeanors. To determine whether a public offense has been committed, ask this question: "Would you be justified in seeking a complaint upon which an arrest warrant would be issued, and could you testify to all the elements of the crime?"

"Committed or attempted in the presence of an officer" means the crime was apparent to the officer's senses, including sight, hearing, and smelling. A conversation over the telephone is within the officer's presence; therefore, a conversation lawfully overheard that might be indicative of criminal conduct is in the officer's presence. The odor of marijuana is evidence that a crime is being committed in the officer's presence and may constitute probable cause to affect an arrest. In most cases, however, the officer will actually see the crime committed, and this is where the first authority generally applies. A suspect can be arrested without a warrant for a misdemeanor *only* if the offense is committed in the officer's presence.

The remaining authorities allow an officer to arrest a suspect for a *felony* which was not committed in his presence. Any lawful arrest, with or without an arrest warrant, requires probable cause. Without an arrest warrant, police officers can arrest a suspect for a felony only if they have probable cause based on their own observations or on information provided to them. They cannot make this same type of arrest for a misdemeanor.

Citizen's Arrest

If an officer does not see a misdemeanor committed, but a citizen does see the act, the citizen may make an arrest and then turn the suspect over to the police officer.

> If a citizen sees a suspect commit a misdemeanor but the police officer does not see the act, the citizen may make the arrest.

Figure 13-1. Citizen's Arrest Form.

```
                    DEPARTMENT OF POLICE

                   CITY OF ANYWHERE, U.S.A.

      CERTIFICATE AND DECLARATION OF ARREST BY PRIVATE PERSON

        AND DELIVERY OF PERSON SO ARRESTED TO PEACE OFFICER


                                  DATE _____

                                  TIME _____

                                  PLACE _____

I, _____, hereby declare and certify that I have arrested

(Name) _____

(Address) _____

for the following reasons:

_____

_____

_____

_____

_____

and I do hereby request and demand that you _____
a peace officer, take and conduct this person whom I have arrested to the nearest magis-
trate, to be dealt with according to law; and if no magistrate can be contacted before
tomorrow morning, then to conduct this person to jail for safekeeping until the required
appearance can be arranged before such magistrate, at which time I shall be present, and
I will then and there sign, under oath, the appropriate complaint against this person for
the offense which this person has committed, and for which I made this arrest; and I will
then and there, or thereafter as soon as this criminal action or cause can be heard,
testify under oath of and concerning the facts and circumstances involved herein. I will
save said officer harmless from any and all claim for damage of any kind, nature, and
description arising out of his acts at my direction.

                        Name of private person
                        making this arrest: _____

                        Address _____

Peace Officer Witness to this statement:

_____

_____
```

SOURCES OF PROBABLE CAUSE

You recall that probable cause is "a state of facts that lead a man of ordinary care and prudence to believe and conscientiously entertain an honest and strong suspicion that the person is guilty of a crime." That strong suspicion may be founded on several sources.

> Probable cause may be based on:
> —Observation by officers.
> —Expertise of officers.
> —Circumstantial factors.
> —Information communicated to officers.

More often than not, observational probable cause will be supplemented by expertise, circumstantial and/or informational probable cause. In general, the officer has reason to believe a person is involved in a specific crime. For example, the officer sees a car weaving down the highway at 55 mph, the posted speed limit. Although the driver is not speeding, a car weaving from lane to lane would lead any reasonable person to entertain a strong suspicion that the driver was under the influence of alcohol or drugs. The officer has not only a right but an obligation to stop the driver because he jeopardizes his own life as well as the lives of other people on the highway.

When he stops the weaving driver, he discovers that the driver is suffering from a sneezing attack caused by a gust of wind blowing a cloud of dust into the car. Obviously an arrest would not be justified even though the probable cause strongly suggested the driver was drunk. On the other hand, if the driver had shown signs of having been drinking, such as the odor of alcohol on his breath, red eyes, slurred speech, or incoordination, the officer would need additional corroboration by administering a sobriety test at the scene and further evidence such as a breath or urine test at the time of booking.

Police officers first have to justify an arrest by proving to themselves that a crime has been committed and that sufficient evidence exists to convince a jury "beyond a reasonable doubt" that the suspect was involved in the crime. Probable cause to stop a person in reference to a specific crime does not always mean that an arrest will occur.

Observational Probable Cause

Observational probable cause is what the officer sees, hears, and/or smells, that is, evidence which is presented directly to the officer's senses. This is similar to eyewitness testimony, and it is the strongest form of probable cause. The courts have generally recognized certain types of events as being significant in determining probable cause.

Suspicious activities are generally regarded as contributing to probable cause. For example, a car being driven slowly can be a suspicious activity when (1) the car has circled a block several times, (2) the men in the car are carefully observing a building, (3) the building is closed, and (4) the building is located in a high-crime area. All four factors contribute to probable cause.

Familiar criminal patterns are also generally recognized as contributing to probable cause. The conduct of a person can be indicative of a familiar pattern associated with the sale of stolen property or narcotics or of someone who is casing a building.

Officers assemble factors that contribute to probable cause for arrest. Any one factor, by itself, may not be sufficient to establish probable cause, but collectively they provide justification—probable cause.

Expertise and Circumstantial Probable Cause

Expertise and circumstantial probable cause are often tied to observational probable cause. Police officers' knowledge of criminal traits and their ability to "put the pieces together" may also contribute to probable cause. For example, two police officers questioned two men seen driving from an alley at 2 A.M. The officers noted the license number of the car, the occupants' names, and questioned the driver and passenger. The two men were allowed to continue, but a short time later, when the officers learned there had been a burglary in a nearby town, they forwarded the description of the car and its occupants to the local law enforcement officers. The suspects were apprehended, and a search of the vehicle revealed burglary tools as well as the property taken in two burglaries.

In the original confrontation with the suspects, the two officers were not satisfied with the suspects' explanation of why they were there at such an early hour, and even though they did not have sufficient evidence for an arrest or could not establish probable cause for an arrest, their investigation of the suspicious circumstances eventually led to the arrest and conviction of the suspects, who later pleaded guilty to seven prior offenses, all felonies.

Arrest and conviction in this case were based on the officers' decision as to when there was sufficient reason to act on probable cause. To arrest without a warrant when a felony has been committed, the officers must have reasonable cause to believe that the person(s) arrested committed the crime.

Informational Probable Cause

Informational probable cause covers a wide range of sources. In the case previously described, the information about the two suspects forwarded by the police officers to the police in the nearby town constituted informational probable cause.

> The major categories of reliable informational probable cause are: (1) official sources, (2) victims of crimes, and (3) citizen informants.

Official sources include police bulletins, police broadcasts, and roll-call information. This information can be relied upon because it is received through official police channels. Information coming from official sources is, in itself, generally sufficient to justify arrest. Although the police officer may arrest on the basis of information received through official channels, this does not relieve the prosecution from establishing that the *original* source of information was reliable, that is, the original source of information was sufficient to establish probable cause to arrest.

It is the source, not the manner of transmission, that will be considered at a trial. Police officers may testify that the information on which they acted was sent over the police radio, but the defendant has the right to demand to know where the information originated and who passed it on to the dispatcher. In other words, as in any other case, the original source of the information must be reliable. For instance, if police officers make an arrest based on information obtained directly from other police officers, the original officers may be required to testify at the trial as to their source of information, and it is that source which must establish probable cause to arrest. The source may be a victim of a crime, a witness to a crime, or an informant.

Victims of crimes are also usually a reliable source of informational probable cause. Officers can and are entitled to rely on the information supplied by victims of crimes committed against their person or property and to use this information in making the decision to arrest suspects. Their statements to police officers can be the source of the officers' belief that they have probable cause to look for a person or persons involved in the commission of a crime.

An example of this comes from the case of Chambers v. Maroney Supreme Court of the U.S. 1970. 399 U.S. 42, 90 S. Ct. 1975 (1970) which involved the armed robbery of a Pennsylvania service station and which later went to the Supreme Court on the question of admissibility of evidence, as will be discussed in Chapter 14. From the attendant at the service station (the victim), police received a description of the two men who had robbed the station. The attendant said one man wore a green sweater and the other a trench coat. The attendant's statement was sufficient for the officers to establish probable cause that the two men described had committed the crime.

Apprehension of the robbers came within an hour because two teenagers had become suspicious of a blue station wagon that had circled the service station block several times. They told the officers that four men were in the vehicle and they had seen it speed out of a parking lot shortly after the robbery. The boys described the man in the green sweater as being one of the four occupants of the station wagon. The information from the boys pinpointed the robbers' method of escape and established that four men were in the vehicle instead of two. The information from the victim of the crime gave police probable cause to arrest the two men; the information from the boys aided in locating them.

Into which category of informational probable cause does the information supplied by the boys fit? They weren't an official source, a victim, or an informant. They had only witnessed suspicious actions, not an adequate basis for arrest. The information does *not* constitute informational probable cause; it was helpful, but far from sufficient to establish probable cause for an arrest. As a matter of fact, what the boys saw was actually just one of those small pieces of a puzzle assembled to create justification for an arrest—what has already been defined as circumstantial factors.

Citizen informants quite often provide probable cause. Included in this category are citizens who actually witness a crime and openly aid in the apprehension of the suspect. Eyewitnesses are persons who have observed a crime, who expect no favors from the police, and who do not exchange information for protection or act out of motives for revenge. If complete and otherwise credible, information from a citizen informant, based on his personal knowledge that a felony has been committed, is generally sufficient probable cause to justify a felony arrest or to obtain an arrest or search warrant.

Even though information from citizen informants, witnesses to the commission of a crime, is evidence to establish informational probable cause, it is not necessarily absolute evidence. With time permitting, police officers must evaluate as thoroughly as they can that they are, in fact, dealing with an actual witness to a crime.

There would be little doubt if a customer was in a store when it was robbed, and the owner was shot and killed, and the customer gave police a description of the assailant. The customer would still be at the scene of the crime when the police arrived.

But compare the authenticity of this witness to the one which follows. A man walked into a police station and identified himself as a serviceman on leave. He gave his address and telephone number and then informed the officers that he had just seen marijuana in the possession of and smoked by a number of people at a given address. The information proved to be accurate; the police went to the address, found people in possession of marijuana, arrested them, and charged them with possession. The judge ruled that the arrest was *not* justified because the officers had not established probable cause to arrest prior to going into the dwelling and finding the marijuana.

Why? Because they had not established the witness as a "reliable informant," nor had they any reason to believe his information was reliable. The serviceman was unknown to them; in fact, the officers didn't even check his identity further than what he had provided. There were no other circumstances, no additional evidence that would corroborate his information and thus make it reliable.

In the case of the grocery store robbery, in contrast, the officers already had independent evidence that a crime had been committed—a man was killed, and the customer was still at the scene of the crime when they questioned him. The customer was an eyewitness and could be accepted as such. The serviceman had to be considered an "untested informant" unless additional evidence proved he was a reliable source of information.

☑ CHECK POINT

1. When may police officers make a lawful arrest without an arrest warrant?
2. What can be done if a citizen sees a misdemeanor committed but a police officer does not see the act?
3. On what major sources can probable cause be based?
4. What are the major categories of informational probable cause?

*Answers

1. Officers may make a lawful arrest without a warrant for a felony or a misdemeanor committed in their presence or for a felony not committed in their presence if they have probable cause.
2. If a citizen sees a suspect commit a misdemeanor but a police officer does not see the act, the citizen may make the arrest.
3. Probable cause may be based on (1) observation by officers, (2) expertise of officers, (3) circumstantial factors, and (4) information communicated to officers.
4. The major categories of reliable informational probable cause are (1) official sources, (2) victims of crimes, and (3) citizen informants.

"STOP AND FRISK"

The courts have stated that suspicious circumstances impose upon police officers the *duty* to investigate, that is, to stop and question suspects. The procedure of stopping and questioning suspects is directly regulated by the justifications and limitations associated with lawful searches and seizures.

Although we associate a thoroughness to the terms "search and seizure" that does not seem to apply to the terms "stop and frisk," the United States Supreme Court (Terry v. Ohio, Supreme Court 1968. 392 U.S. 1, 88 S. Ct. 1868 [1968]) says there *is* a *seizure* whenever a police officer restrains an individual's freedom to walk away; and there *is* a *search* when an officer makes an exploration of an individual's clothing even though it may be called a "pat down" or a "frisk."

> A stop is a seizure if physical force or a show of authority is used. A frisk is a search.

Although stopping and frisking fall short of being a technical arrest and a full-blown search, they *are* definitely forms of search and seizure. Police officers stop citizens of their communities as part of their duties. This is daily practice, but most encounters cannot be considered "seizure of the person" because the officer doesn't restrain the individual's liberty. So, an officer can stop a citizen without the action being considered a seizure of the person. Defining the term *frisk*, however, leaves no other alternative than to consider it a search.

The United States Supreme Court (*Terry*) had definite opinions about the type of search called a frisk: "It is simply fantastic," the court stated, "to urge that such a procedure, performed in public by a police officer, while the citizen stands helpless, perhaps facing a wall with his hands raised, is a 'petty indignity'. ... It is a serious intrusion upon the sanctity of the person, which may inflict great indignity and arouse strong resentment, and it is not to be undertaken lightly." The Supreme Court gave its own definition of "stop and frisk" by calling it a "protective search for weapons." As always, where there is a justification for taking specific action, there are also limitations. According to the Supreme Court, a protective seizure and search for weapons carries these limitations.

> "Stop and frisk" is a "protective search for weapons" in which the "intrusion" must be "confined to a scope reasonably designed to discover guns, knives, clubs and other hidden instruments for the assault of a police officer or others."

Since some states do not have "stop and frisk" laws, when this type of protective search and seizure for weapons is referred to, it is on the basis of the opinion of the United States Supreme Court.

The Supreme Court's opinion on "stop and frisk" and the rights and limitations for this type of action are illustrated in the case of Henry v. United States, 361 U.S. 98, 80 S. Ct. 168, 4 L.Ed. 2d 134 (1959), which involved an arrest made by officers who had observed Henry and another man stop twice in an alley and load cartons into a car. When the officers saw the two men driving off, they waved Henry's car to stop, searched it, took the cartons, and later made the formal arrest. The men were convicted in Illinois courts of unlawful possession of stolen radios. The Supreme Court overruled the Illinois verdict saying that an actual arrest had taken place when the officers stopped the suspect's car. The problem in this case was that the officers observed the transaction from a distance of some three hundred feet and could not determine the size, number, or contents of the cartons. The suspects were formally placed under arrest some two hours after they were taken into custody.

The issue in this case was whether there was probable cause for the arrest leading to the search that produced the evidence on which the conviction rested. Since probable cause to arrest had not been established at that time, the court said the stolen merchandise could *not* be accepted as evidence. Future cases in many states were decided on this 1959 case, and the accepted opinion was that stopping a vehicle or an individual constituted an actual arrest.

The case of State of Minnesota v. Fish, 280 Minn. 163, 159 N.W. 2d 786 (1968) involved the stopping of a car in the early morning hours by two police officers. Later the officers were able to establish probable cause to arrest the driver and a passenger for the burglary of a bar. Technically this was not a "stop and frisk" situation because Minnesota statutes give law enforcement officers the right to stop any motorist and demand to see his driver's license. There was no search of the suspects or the vehicle until probable cause had been established. In upholding the conviction, the Minnesota Supreme Court made the following observation for this case and then repeated it in Minnesota v. Fox, 281 Minn. 567, 160 N.W. 2d 660 (1968). "The essential needs of public safety permit police officers to use their faculties of observation and to act thereon within proper limits. ... It is not only the right but the duty of police officers to investigate suspicious behavior, both to prevent crime and to apprehend offenders." The court explained the limitations it believed went with such action by stating, "Of course, the right of police officers to stop suspicious persons does not extend to a right of search, in the absence of probable cause." In short, the court said the police officer has the right to stop suspicious persons and that the right applies to preventing crimes and apprehending offenders.

In the first case, no search was made until after probable cause to arrest had been established. In the second case, the court was asked to rule on a search that produced marijuana which was used to convict the suspect. Here, then, the court was faced with a full search for evidence and could only return the opinion that such a search was invalid since probable cause to arrest had not been established. (Searches will be studied in depth in Chapter 14)

This leaves one important question unanswered. Do police officers have the right to frisk for weapons when they stop a suspicious person? This is, of course, assuming that the officers actually believe the person is armed or dangerous. The most definite comment on this question comes from the United States Supreme Court in the case of Terry v. Ohio, 392 U.S. 1, 88 S. Ct. (1968).

The case began in 1963 with Detective Martin McFadden of the Cleveland Police Department, who conducted his days at a casual pace. He liked to walk the streets of Cleveland, watching and meeting people. Sometimes he would just stand for a while, letting the people walk past. It wasn't his hobby; it was his job. For thirty years he had spotted criminal activity such as pickpocketing and shoplifting, and he was good at his job. McFadden's success was attributable not just to the years of experience or the knowledge of criminal activity he had gained, but to his patience. The average criminal couldn't wait the way McFadden could.

One afternoon in 1963 Detective McFadden saw two men standing near a jewelry store. For all practical purposes they just seemed to be talking to each other, but to McFadden, a man of thirty years of detective work (thirty-nine years of police experience), "they just didn't look right." He had never seen the two before and couldn't say what first drew his attention to them, but he decided to take a post in a nearby store entrance and watch for a while.

The two men repeated a ritual nearly a dozen times. One man would walk to the window, pause, look into the window for a while, and then walk toward the corner. He would come back to look into the same window and then rejoin his companion. After a short conference, the man would repeat the entire walk to the store window, up to the corner, back to the store, and then back to rejoin the first man.

Here's how the United States Supreme Court looked upon this activity. It said "the man 'hovered' for an extended period of time" and that they were having "conferences" and "peered" and "stared" into the store window.

While this was going on, Detective McFadden continued to watch the two. At one point a third man joined them, talked with them briefly, then left. When he left, the other two spent several more minutes repeating the routine.

By this time McFadden suspected they were casing the store for a "stick-up." As he made this decision, McFadden told the court, he also feared they might have a gun. He had already decided to investigate their activity further when the two men walked toward the store where the third man was waiting. At this point, the detective's knowledge was confined to what he had observed. He didn't know any of the three men by name or sight, and he had received no information on them from any other source.

McFadden approached the three, identified himself as a police officer, asked for their names, and then decided to act. He turned one man, later identified as John Terry, around, putting Terry between himself and the other two men. McFadden then made a quick "pat down" of Terry's outer clothing. He could feel a pistol in one of Terry's pockets but was unable to remove the gun. Keeping Terry between himself and the others, he ordered all three men to enter the store. As they obeyed him, McFadden removed Terry's coat and took a .38 caliber revolver from the pocket. Inside the store McFadden asked the owner to call for a police wagon while he patted the outer clothing of the others, taking another revolver from the coat of a man named Chilton. At the station Terry and Chilton were formally charged with carrying concealed weapons.

When Terry and Chilton were brought to court, their lawyers moved that the guns could not be used as evidence, claiming they were illegally seized. If the guns couldn't be used as evidence, there was no evidence and there was no charge or case.

The trial judge heard the two cases at the same time. He made two decisions which, at first, seemed to contradict each other. First, he rejected the defense motion that the evidence had been illegally seized. Then he rejected a prosecution contention that McFadden had established probable cause to arrest, and, therefore, the officer had taken the guns in a search which was incidental to a lawful arrest. If neither theory applied, what did?

The judge said that on the basis of McFadden's experience, he had reasonable cause to believe the defendants were conducting themselves suspiciously and some interrogation should be made of their actions. Purely for his own protection, the court added, McFadden had the right to frisk the men whom he believed to be armed. The judge said McFadden had stopped the suspects for the purpose of investigation, no arrest occurred at that point, and the "frisking of the outer clothing for weapons" was *not* a full search.

Both men appealed their conviction to the United States Supreme Court, but before the court's decision was handed down in 1968, Chilton had died. Therefore, their review applied only to Terry.

The court recognized Detective McFadden as a man of experience, training, and knowledge. Consider the weight the court placed on McFadden's simple statement that the two men "just didn't look right." McFadden was certainly "a man of reasonable caution." And, as a man of "ordinary care and prudence," he waited until he had strengthened his suspicions, making his move just prior to what he believed would be an armed robbery.

The United States Supreme Court upheld the Ohio court verdict; it said that McFadden had "acted reasonably" because (1) Terry's and Chilton's actions were consistent with McFadden's theory that they were contemplating a daylight robbery, (2) such a robbery would most likely involve the use of guns, and (3) nothing in the men's conduct, from the time the officer first noticed them until he confronted them, gave him any reason to doubt his theory.

The Court went on to say that McFadden had to make a quick decision when he saw the three gathered at the store and his actions were correct.

Seven principles applicable to "stop and frisk" came from the Terry case. It established that the authority to "stop and frisk" is independent of the power to arrest. A stop is *not* an arrest, but it is a "seizure" within the meaning of the Fourth Amendment and therefore requires reasonableness.

The specific principles which arose from the Terry case can be applied to most "stop and frisk" situations.

1. Police officers have the right and duty to approach and interrogate persons in order to investigate crimes.
2. Police officers may stop and make a *limited* search of a suspect if they observe unusual conduct which leads them to reasonably conclude in light of their experience that criminal activity may be afoot and that the individual whose suspicious behavior the officers are investigating at close range is armed and probably dangerous.
3. The test of the officers' action is whether a "reasonably prudent man in the same circumstances would be warranted in the belief that his safety or that of others was in danger."
4. Officers may proceed to "stop and frisk" if nothing occurs to change the officers' theory that criminal activity may occur or that the suspect is armed.
5. The type of search in "stop and frisk" must be limited. It is a "protective seizure and search for weapons and must be confined to an intrusion which is reasonably designed to discover guns, knives, clubs, or other hidden instruments of assault."
6. If these conditions (principles 1-5) are met, the "stop and frisk" does *not* constitute an arrest.
7. Since "stop and frisk" actually involves a search and seizure, it must be governed by the intent of the Fourth Amendment of the Constitution which forbids indiscriminate searches and seizures.

While it is true that both the stop and the arrest are "seizures" and both must be justified by showing of reasonableness, there are some important differences between a stop and an arrest.

Table 13-1. Stop and Arrest.

	STOP	ARREST
JUSTIFICATION	Reasonable suspicion	Probable cause
INTENT OF OFFICER	To resolve an ambiguous situation	To make a formal charge
SEARCH	Possibly a "pat-down"	Complete body search
RECORD	Minimal	Fingerprints, photographs, and booking

☑ CHECK POINT

1. When is a stop a "seizure"? When is a frisk a search?
2. How has the United States Supreme Court defined *"stop and frisk?"*
3. What Supreme Court case established important principles related to "stop and frisk?" What were the most important principles established?
4. What are three important differences between a stop and an arrest?

✳Answers

1. A stop is a seizure if physical force or a show of authority is used. A frisk is always a search, although a very limited one.
2. "Stop and frisk" is a "protective search for weapons" in which the "intrusion" must be "confined to a scope reasonably designed to discover guns, knives, clubs and other hidden instruments for the assault of a police officer or others."
3. The Terry v. Ohio case established important principles related to "stop and frisk," including the right and duty of police officers to investigate suspicious behavior and to make a limited search of a suspicious person who has been stopped. It established that the authority to "stop and frisk" is independent of the power to arrest and that a stop is *not* an arrest. However, since it is a "seizure" within the meaning of the Fourth Amendment, it does require reasonableness.
4. Justification for a stop is reasonable suspicion; for an arrest it is probable cause. The intent of the officer in a stop is to resolve an ambiguous situation; the intent of the officer in making an arrest is to make a formal charge. The search in a stop is very limited, possibly a "pat down"; in an arrest it is usually a full body search. The record made following a stop is usually minimal whereas the record made following an arrest contains fingerprints, photographs, and the booking form.

SUMMARY

Citizens of the United States are protected against unreasonable arrest (seizure) by the Fourth Amendment. An arrest is usually defined as the taking of a person into custody by the actual restraint of the person or by his submission to the custody of the officer that he may be held to answer for a public offense. Such arrests must be *reasonable*, that is, sensible, justifiable, logical, based on reason, and they must be predicated on *probable cause*, which courts have defined as "a state of facts that lead a man of ordinary care and prudence to believe and conscientiously entertain an honest and strong suspicion that the person is guilty of a crime."

The Fourth Amendment requires that arrests be made by having a magistrate issue an arrest warrant, but police officers may make an arrest without an arrest warrant for a felony or misdemeanor committed in their presence or for a felony not committed in their presence if they have probable cause. A person can be arrested for a misdemeanor only if (1) there is an arrest warrant or (2) the crime was committed in the officer's presence. A person can be arrested for a felony if (1) there is an arrest warrant, (2) the crime is committed in the presence of an officer, or (3) there is probable cause that the person committed a felony. If a citizen sees a suspect commit a misdemeanor but a police officer does not see the act, the arrest can only be made by the citizen unless a warrant is issued.

Probable cause may be founded on (1) observation, (2) expertise, (3) circumstantial factors, and (4) information conveyed to the officers, including official sources, victims of crimes, and citizen informants.

"Stop and frisk" is a form of search and seizure and, as such, is governed by the intent of the Fourth Amendment which demands that all searches and seizures be based on reason. A stop is *not* an arrest; the authority to "stop and frisk" is independent of the power to search or arrest. A frisk, however, *is a* search. The type of search allowed under "stop and frisk" is limited to a protective seizure and search for weapons, not a search for evidence of a crime.

APPLICATION

Read the following case descriptions and analyze whether the arrests in each were lawful.

A. While patrolling Highway 101, Officer Sherry MacAloon noticed a new Ford Thunderbird exceeding the speed limit by 25 mph. She used her red lights and siren to pull the car over. As she approached the car she noticed that the driver was very young and nervous and that the vent window was broken and there were no keys in the ignition. The driver was unable to produce an owner's registration card or a driver's license. He answered her questions evasively. Officer MacAloon checked the license plate through her dispatcher and learned they were stolen plates. She then checked the serial number of the vehicle and found that it, too, had been reported stolen. Officer MacAloon arrested the driver for auto theft.

1. What were the suspicious facts in this case?
2. Was it reasonable to stop the suspect?
3. Did the events following the stop lead to probable cause to arrest the suspect?
4. Was a warrantless arrest justified in this instance?

B. One afternoon while Officer Mullaney was patrolling his beat in a shopping center, a clerk from a local drug store ran out of the store and shouted that a man had just stolen a box of cigars worth $5.00. The officer interviewed the witnesses to the theft and obtained the following description: "The suspect was 6'4", weighed approximately 250 pounds, was wearing a purple jacket and red pants, and had a one-inch scar on his chin." The officer notified the radio room, and the dispatcher issued a radio broadcast for the suspect. Four hours later a patrol car spotted a man fitting that description entering a parked vehicle and placed him under arrest. Upon arresting him, the officer patted him down for weapons and found a pocketful of cigars which he seized as evidence. The suspect was taken to the station and booked for possession of stolen property.

1. Was the arrest legal?
2. Was the evidence seized in the search legal?
3. Do you think the man would be convicted?

C. The background of the case of Sibron v. New York, 392 U.S. 40, 88 S. Ct. 1889, 20 L. Ed. 2d 917 (1968) began when an officer watched Sibron for eight hours in one day. The officer had seen him talking to many known narcotic addicts, became suspicious, followed him, and finally asked him to step out of a restaurant where he could be searched. The officer found a packet of heroin on Sibron and charged him with unlawful possession of narcotics. The New York Courts, which *do* have a "stop and frisk" law, convicted Sibron, who then appealed his case to the Supreme Court.

1. Do you think the Supreme Court upheld the New York decision? Why or why not?

D. A recent district court conviction for aggravated robbery went before the state supreme court when the defendant charged that the arresting officer did not have sufficient knowledge or information to establish probable cause and, therefore, the arrest was illegal. The state admitted that the arresting officer had no personal knowledge of the facts justifying the arrest, except that there was a pickup order for the defendant. The arresting officer had obtained a photograph of the defendant at roll-call. The following circumstances surrounded the case: A woman was knocked down by two men just outside a bank. They took her purse, which contained more than $12,000. One witness told the police that as he was coming toward the bank, he passed a parked car which the two fleeing robbers entered, and he got a good look at the driver, the third man and the defendant in this appeal. He described the man to the police, including the fact the man was unshaven and wore a dark jacket. Another witness to the robbery wrote down the license number of the car and gave it to the police.

In court, two employees of a parking lot testified the defendant drove into the lot about thirty minutes after the time of the robbery, parked his car, tossed a jacket through an open window and left. The men originally identified the defendant from photographs shown to them by police. Although residents of the apartment building where the defendant was thought to be living didn't know him by the name the police gave them, they were able to identify him from pictures shown to them by a detective. Several weeks had passed since the robbery when this identification was made, and residents of the apartment building told the police that the defendant was getting ready to move. The police entered the building and arrested the suspect.

1. Was there sufficient evidence to establish probable cause?
2. Was a warrantless arrest proper? Why or why not?

*Answers

A. 1. The excessive speed was in violation of the law and was perceived by the officer.
   2. The officer was reasonable in stopping the speeding driver.
   3. The events following the stop: broken vent window, lack of keys in the ignition, lack of registration and driver's license, stolen plates, and car having been reported stolen, added up to probable cause for arrest.
   4. Yes, there was reason for the stop and probable cause for the arrest.

B. 1. The arrest was *not* legal because it was a misdemeanor and the officer did *not* witness it. The radio broadcast should not have been made unless an arrest warrant had been issued for the suspect.

2. The search was not legal since the arrest was not legal.

3. The man would not be convicted on the basis of what had transpired. He might, however, be convicted on the word of the victim of the crime if he secured an arrest warrant.

C. 1. No. The Supreme Court reversed the decision because the officer had conducted a search, not a frisk for weapons, without having probable cause to make an arrest. This case demonstrated that the courts will not tolerate the use of "stop and frisk" for full scale searches.

D. 1. There was sufficient evidence to establish probable cause. The state supreme court ruled that the police were in full possession of facts which showed that a felony had been committed and that the defendant was the driver of the get-away vehicle. Probable cause was established by the totality of the information possessed by the police as a unit.

2. A warrantless arrest was proper. Although warrantless arrests are not favored, arrest without a warrant for a felony, on probable cause, is proper when circumstances lead the arresting officer to reasonably believe that an immediate arrest is essential to prevent escape.

DISCUSSION QUESTIONS

1. In a state where "stop and frisk" is legal, can a police officer be sued for stopping and frisking someone?
2. What can be done if a misdemeanor is committed and no police officer sees it, but a citizen does see it and refuses to make a citizen's arrest?
3. Which carries greater authority: reasonableness or probable cause?
4. According to Sir Arthur Conan Doyle, author of the Sherlock Holmes mystery stories: "When you have eliminated the impossible, whatever remains, however improbable, must be the truth." Discuss this quotation in light of what you know about lawful arrest.
5. What are the most important factors in determining if and when an arrest occurred?
6. Must all elements of probable cause exist prior to a lawful arrest?

REFERENCES

Creamer, J. S. *The law of arrest, search and seizure.* Philadelphia: W. B. Saunders, 1975.

Cushman, R. E. and Cushman, R. F. *Cases in constitutional law,* (3rd ed). New York: Appleton-Century-Crofts, 1968.

Dowling, J. *Criminal procedure.* St. Paul: West Publishing Company, 1976.

Felknes, G. T. *Constitutional law for criminal justice.* Englewood Cliffs, N.J.: Prentice-Hall, 1978.

Ferdico, J. *Criminal procedure for the law enforcement officer.* St. Paul: West Publishing Company, 1976.

Fisher, D. *Laws of arrest.* Evanston, IL: Traffic Institute, Northwestern University, 1967.

Friedelbaum, S. H. *Contemporary constitutional law.* Boston: Houghton Mifflin, 1972.

Handbook of search and seizure. Washington, D.C.: U.S. Justice Department, U.S. Government Printing Office, 1971.

Inbau, F. E., Thompson, J. R. and Zagel, J. B. *Criminal law and its administration.* Mineola, N.Y.: The Foundation Press, 1974.

Kelly, A. H. and Harbison, W. *The American Constitution.* (4th ed.) N.Y.: W. W. Norton, 1970.

Lewis, P. W. and Peoples, K. D. *The supreme Court and the criminal process.* Philadelphia: W. B. Saunders, 1978.

Lockhart, W. B., Kamisar, Y. and Choper, J. H. *Constitutional rights and liberties.* (4th ed.) St. Paul: West Publishing Company, 1975.

Maddex, J. L., Jr. *Constitutional law.* St. Paul: West Publishing Company, 1974.

Mendelson, W. *The constitution and the supreme court.* (2nd ed.) New York: Dodd, Mead and Company, 1968.

Pritchett, C. H. *The American Constitution.* New York: McGraw-Hill, 1977.

Tresolini, R. J. and Shapiro, M. *American constitutional law.* (3rd ed.) New York: Macmillan, 1970.

The three basic conditions justifying a right to search are: 1. a search incident to a lawful arrest 2. if consent to the search is given 3. if a search warrant has been issued.

ALL
HAND CARRIED
ITEMS
INCLUDING
LADIES PURSES
MUST BE
INSPECTED
AT THIS POINT

Lawful Search and Seizure

Reason and Probable Cause Revisited

DO YOU KNOW □ □ □

- □ What is established by the Exclusionary Rule?
- □ What the principle justifications (preconditions) for a reasonable search are?
- □ What authorities and restrictions are provided by the following cases: Chimel, Weeks, Mapp, Carroll, Coolidge?
- □ What limitations are placed on searches?
- □ What a search warrant is and what it must contain?
- □ When forcible entry is legal?
- □ When Nighttime and No-knock warrants are justified?
- □ What challenges might be made to a warrantless search?
- □ What special conditions apply to search of automobiles?
- □ What is meant by "plain view" evidence and what qualifies an item as such?
- □ How to analyze a search situation and determine whether the search is reasonable and lawful?

*The truth is found when men are free to
pursue it.*
—*F. D. Roosevelt (1936)*
*The spirit of truth and the spirit of
freedom—they are the pillars of society.*
Henrik Ibsen (1877)

INTRODUCTION

On October 21, 1957, two police officers arrived at the home of Samuel Jameson with a warrant for his arrest on the charge of homicide. After placing Jameson under arrest and informing him of his rights, the officers searched the entire house, confiscating a sales receipt for the type of gun used in the shooting, a shirt with bloodstains on it, and a briefcase bearing the initials of the murder victim—all indicators of his guilt. However, when the case was brought to trial, the judge ruled that the material confiscated by the police officers was *not* admissible as evidence.

It often seems inappropriate when a judge refuses to admit evidence which clearly links a defendant to a crime, but the courts are bound by rules affecting the admissibility of evidence. Material can only be admitted as evidence if it is obtained according to standards set forth in the United States Constitution. Looking at the situation from a different perspective, the court cannot accept evidence which was obtained in violation of the rights guaranteed to all United States citizens.

There was a time when courts in our country did not inquire into the source of evidence as long as it was relevant to proving the guilt of the accused. In fact, in England they still adhere to this premise. For a number of years our courts upheld convictions based on evidence seized from a defendant regardless of how it was acquired. Shortly after 1900, however, the federal courts abandoned this practice and began to inquire into the methods by which evidence was obtained.

The federal courts declared that in the future "... they would require that evidence be obtained in compliance with constitutional standards"—Weeks v. United States, 232 U.S. 382, 34 S. Ct. 341 (1914)—standards set forth in the Fourth Amendment or Article Four of the Bill of Rights. By this point, you may almost know the wording from memory:

The right of the people to be secure in their persons, houses, papers, and effects, against unreasonable searches and seizures, shall not be violated, and no warrant shall issue but upon probable cause, supported by oath or affirmation, and particularly describing the place to be searched and the persons or things to be seized.

THE EXCLUSIONARY RULE

Without procedures for enforcing the provisions of the Fourth Amendment, the impressive constitutional language would be meaningless. Consequently, the procedures and the power for their enforcement were vested in the courts. They must refuse to consider evidence obtained by unreasonable search and seizure methods, regardless of how relevant the evidence is to the case.

This rule, known as the *Exclusionary Rule,* is the direct result of the Supreme Court decision in the case of Weeks v. U.S. The Exclusionary Rule, defined in the Weeks case as a matter of judicial implications, was made applicable to the *federal* courts in 1914. In 1961 the Exclusionary Rule reached maturity when the Supreme Court, in the case of Mapp v. Ohio, 367 U.S. 643, 81 S. Ct. 1684 (1961), extended the rule to every court and law enforcement officer in the nation.

> Courts uphold the Fourth Amendment by use of the *Exclusionary Rule* which demands that no evidence may be admitted in a trial unless it is obtained within the constitutional standards set forth in the Fourth Amendment. Weeks v. U.S. made the Exclusionary Rule applicable in federal courts. Mapp v. Ohio made it applicable to every court in the country.

On May 23, 1957, three Cleveland police officers arrived at Dolree Mapp's residence pursuant to information that a person wanted for questioning in connection with a recent bombing was hiding in Miss Mapp's home and that there was also a large amount of gambling paraphernalia hidden there. After telephoning her attorney, Dolree Mapp refused to admit the officers without a search warrant. Three hours later the officers returned with reinforcements and again sought entrance. When she did not come to the door, the police officers gained entry by forcibly opening one of the doors. Miss Mapp demanded to see the search warrant. When a paper claimed to be the warrant was held up by one of the officers, she grabbed it and placed it in her bra. A struggle ensued in which the officers recovered the piece of paper and handcuffed Miss Mapp. A thorough search was conducted of the entire apartment, including the basement of the building. Obscene materials, for the possession of which the defendant was ultimately convicted, were discovered as a result of that widespread search.

The state contended that even if the search were made without authority, it was not prevented from using the evidence at the trial because Wolf v. Colorado, 338 U.S. 25, 69 S. Ct. 1359, 93 L. Ed. 1782 (1949) had authorized the admission of such evidence in a state court; furthermore, Ohio did not follow the Exclusionary Rule. After a discussion of other applicable cases, the Supreme Court decreed that henceforth evidence obtained by procedures which violated Fourth Amendment standards would no longer be admissible in state courts.

Since 1961 the Exclusionary Rule applies to both the federal and state courts and evidence secured illegally by federal, state, or local officers is inadmissible in any court.

The Exclusionary Rule has great implications for the procedures followed by police officers since neither the most skillful prosecutor nor the most experienced police officer can convince a jury of a defendant's guilt without adequate and lawfully obtained evidence.

Police officers must obtain evidence which establishes that a crime has been committed, and they must obtain evidence which connects the defendant to the specific crime—usually long before the case comes to the prosecutor. Further, they must obtain such evidence without violating the rights of the defendant.

Only if police officers obtain evidence that will be acceptable in court is there a probability of conviction. But, many questions must be answered in determining acceptability of evidence. Consider the following situation.

Two officers stop a motorist driving down a street during the early morning hours. Even without knowing the reasons for stopping the motorist or whether the officers actually suspected he was guilty of a crime, we can assume that since a search was executed, it was a thorough one. In their search the officers find two packets of heroin on the man. Will the evidence be accepted in court? That depends! What was the justification for stopping the motorist and was the search reasonable? If this individual is brought to trial, the officers will have to provide the judge with justifiable reasons for suspecting the man was carrying drugs.

REASONABLE SEARCH AND SEIZURE—
PRINCIPLE JUSTIFICATIONS OR PRECONDITIONS

Guilty persons are convicted based on the facts which the court finds admissible. Police officers' reports must contain all the reasons for a search or seizure as proof of the reasonableness of their conduct. The questions most frequently asked by the prosecutor and the courts before admitting evidence are:

—Was the search reasonable?

—Was the arrest, if there was one, legal?

There are rules to guide the police officers in answering these questions on a day-to-day basis. The rules often seem contrary to what many people consider to be reasonable; however, these rules, contrary or not, *must* be considered when deciding whether a search or seizure is reasonable. The courts abide by these rules and base their decisions on them.

Since the word *unreasonable* is ambiguous, the courts have adopted guidelines to measure reasonableness and to assure law enforcement personnel that *if* certain rules are adhered to, their search and/or seizure will be acceptable—reasonable.

> The three principal justifications established by the court for the right to search are:
> 1. If the search is incidental to a *lawful arrest*.
> 2. If *consent* is given.
> 3. If a *search warrant* has been issued.

These circumstances are the *preconditions* for a reasonable, legal search.

A search which occurs under any one of these conditions is considered justified or reasonable.

☑ CHECK POINT

1. What is the Exclusionary Rule and what is its primary purpose?
2. On what case is the federal application of the Exclusionary Rule based?
3. On what case is the state application of the Exclusionary Rule based?
4. What are the three principle justifications (preconditions) for a reasonable search?

✱ Answers

1. The Exclusionary Rule demands that no evidence may be admitted in a trial unless it is obtained within the constitutional standards set forth in the Fourth Amendment. Its purpose is to assure citizens the rights guaranteed them by the Fourth Amendment.
2. The federal application of the Exclusionary Rule is based on Weeks v. U.S.
3. The state application of the Exclusionary Rule is based on Mapp v. Ohio.
4. The three principal justifications (preconditions) established by the court for the right to search are (1) if the search is incidental to a lawful arrest, (2) if consent is given, or (3) if a search warrant has been issued.

LIMITATIONS ON SEARCHES

A reasonable search involves more than justification by an arrest, consent, or a search warrant. *Limitations* on the search itself are set. After establishing the right to search, police officers must determine the limitations on that right—limitations imposed by law and interpreted by the courts.

We have already looked at one type of limitation on a search, that is the search involved in "stop and frisk." A search conducted in a "stop and frisk" situation must be limited to a search for weapons, not evidence.

> The most important limitation imposed upon any search is that the scope must be narrowed. *General searches are unconstitutional.*

Limitations on a Search Incidental to a Lawful Arrest

In a search incidental to a lawful arrest, the search must be made simultaneously with the arrest and must be confined to the immediate vicinity of the arrest.

> Limitations upon a search made incidental to an arrest are found in the *Chimel Rule* which states that the area of the search must be within the immediate control of the suspect—that is, it must be within his reach.

The Chimel case (Chimel v. California, 395 U.S. 752, 89 S. Ct. 2034, 23 L. Ed. 2d 685 [1969]) involving a search incidental to an arrest, provides a definition of search of a person and a dwelling as well as the limitations of the search. Officers went to the Chimel home with a warrant to arrest Ted Chimel on a charge of burglarizing a coin shop. Mrs. Chimel admitted the officers, who then waited ten to fifteen minutes for her husband to come home. When the arrest warrant was handed to Chimel, he was told that the officers wanted to "look around." He objected, but was informed that the officers had a right to search because it was a lawful arrest.

The officers opened kitchen cabinets, searched through hall and bedroom closets, looked behind furniture in every room, and even searched the garage. (Prior to this case, the courts had accepted fairly extensive searches incidental to an arrest.) On several occasions the officers had the wife open drawers and move the contents so they could look for items removed in the burglary. The search took nearly an hour and resulted in the officers finding numerous coins.

Chimel was convicted in a California court, but he appealed his conviction on burglary charges on the grounds that the evidence, the coins, had been unconstitutionally seized. The United States Supreme Court studied the principle of searches incidental to an arrest and determined:

When an arrest is made, it is reasonable for the arresting officer to search the person arrested in order to remove any weapons that the latter might seek to use in order to resist arrest or effect his escape.

It is entirely reasonable for the arresting officer to search for and seize any evidence on the arrestee's person in order to prevent its concealment or destruction and the area from within which the arrestee might gain possession of a weapon or destructible evidence.

The officers' justification for extending the search was based in the phrase that "It is entirely reasonable ... to search ... the area from within which the arrestee might gain possession of ... destructible evidence."

In the Chimel case, the Supreme Court specified that the area of search could include only the arrestee's person and the area within his *immediate control.* The court defined "immediate control" as being that area within the person's reach.

The Chimel case resulted in a clear definition as to what beyond the suspect himself could be searched when officers are using the authority of a search incidental to an arrest. The court pointed out that if an arrest is used as an excuse to conduct a thorough search, such as the search conducted in the Chimel case, the police would have power to conduct "general searches" which were declared unconstitutional by the Fourth Amendment over 180 years ago.

One can sympathize with the officers who had alerted Chimel's wife that they were looking for stolen coins and then felt they had to find them or face the possibility she would remove them. But the law allows only a limited search in this situation. Undoubtedly a magistrate would have issued a search warrant for the stolen coins if the officers had realized the limitations on their search and had requested the warrant.

Ironically, prior to the burglary, Chimel had wandered about the coin store, asked the owner where he kept his most valuable coins, inquired into the alarm system, and bragged that he was planning a robbery. Later he took exception to the owner's testimony that it was a "sloppy job," excitedly claiming that the burglary had been "real professional." But the Supreme Court reversed the California decision because the conviction had been based on evidence obtained in a search which was beyond reasonable limits.

An interesting sideline in the Chimel case is that three days after the initial search, officers again entered Chimel's house looking for evidence to support a separate charge of robbery. No evidence was seized on the second search, but Chimel was convicted and sentenced on the robbery charge.

Limitations on a Search with Consent

In a search where consent is given, the United States Supreme Court provides that the consent must be free and voluntary; therefore, it cannot be given in response to a claim of lawful authority by the officer to conduct the search at the moment. As with searches incidental to lawful arrest, a search with consent must be conducted only in the actual area for which the consent is given.

> Consent must be free and voluntary, and the search must be limited to the area for which the consent is given.

As noted by the Maine Supreme Court (State v. Barlow, Jr., 320 A. 2d 895, 900 [Me. 1974]): "It is a well established rule in the federal courts that a consent search is unreasonable under the Fourth Amendment if the consent was induced by deceit, trickery or misrepresentation of the officials making the search." A recognized exception to this general rule is when undercover operations are involved.

When a court is asked to determine if consent to search was "free and voluntary," it considers such things as the subject's age, background, mental condition, and education. The number of officers involved should not be a factor if no aggressiveness is displayed. As stated in People v. Reed, 393 Mich. 342, 366, 224 N.W. 2d 867, 878 (1975): "Where aggravating factors are not evident, the number of officers alone will not have an adverse effect on the consent. The presence of a large number of officers in an apartment does not present a situation which is *per se* coercive."

The time of day might also be a consideration. Officers should generally avoid seeking voluntary consent to search at night. In Monroe v. Pape 365 U.S. 167, 209-10, 81 S. Ct. 473, 495-496 (1961) Justice Frankfurter said: "Modern totalitarianisms have been a stark reminder, but did not newly teach, that the kicked-in door is the symbol of a rule of fear and violence fatal to institutions founded on respect for the integrity of man. . . . Searches of the dwelling house were the special object of this universal condemnation of official intrusion. Nighttime search was the evil in its most obnoxious form."

Perhaps most important is the way in which the request to search is made. It must, indeed, be a request, not a command.

Limitations on a Search Conducted with a Search Warrant

A search conducted with a warrant must be limited to the specific area and specific items delineated in the warrant.

Recall the provision of the Fourth Amendment that the warrant must particularly describe "the place to be searched and the persons or things to be seized."

☑ CHECK POINT

1. What is the most important limitation imposed upon any type of search?
2. What limitations are imposed upon a search incidental to a lawful arrest?
3. What case establishes these limitations on a search incidental to a lawful arrest?
4. What limitations are imposed upon a search with consent?
5. What limitations are imposed upon a search with a warrant?

∗ Answers

1. The most important limitation imposed upon any search is that the scope must be narrowed. General searches are unconstitutional.
2. A search made incidental to an arrest must be limited to the suspect and the area within his immediate control—that is, within his physical reach.
3. The Chimel v. California case established the limitations upon searches incidental to lawful arrests.
4. In a search with consent, the consent must be free and voluntary, and the search must be limited to the area for which the consent is given.
5. A search conducted with a warrant must be limited to the specific area and specific items delineated in the warrant.

SEARCH WARRANTS

We are all protected against unreasonable searches and seizures by the United States Constitution, which guarantees that probable cause, supported by oath or affirmation, shall be the basis for issuing a search warrant. Our courts have interpreted this guarantee to mean that any search or seizure other than one conducted with a warrant is technically unreasonable. The courts do, however, recognize that emergency situations will arise in which a police officer will not have the opportunity to secure a warrant.

A *search warrant* is a judicial order directing a police officer to search for specific property, seize it, and return it to the court. Probable cause is required for issuance of all warrants. Technically, all searches are to be made under the authority of a search warrant issued by a magistrate.

A search warrant is an order issued by any court of record or by a justice of the peace in a county having no municipal court other than a probate court. The court must have jurisdiction in the area where the search is to be made.

The warrant must contain the reasons for requesting the search warrant; the names of the persons presenting affidavits, for example, the officer who applied for the warrant, his colleagues, or others who have information to contribute; what specifically is being sought; and the signature of the judge issuing it.

The procedures for obtaining and executing search warrants vary from locality to locality, but the following example illustrates what is generally involved. Generally a search warrant may be issued for the following reasons:

1. The property or material was stolen or embezzled.
2. The possession of the property or material constitutes a crime, e.g., stolen property or drugs.
3. The property or material is in the possession of a person with intent to use them to commit a crime, e.g., possession of burglary tools with intent to use them.
4. The property or material was used in committing a crime, e.g., a gun, knife, or burglary tools.
5. The items or evidence tends to show that a crime has been committed or that a particular person has committed a crime, e.g., letters, clothing.

When police officers present an affidavit to a magistrate, their facts must be sufficiently detailed to enable the magistrate to determine that probable cause to search exists. The affidavit need not be as polished as an entry in an essay contest, but it should not skimp on the facts.

The Constitution does not require all necessary information to appear on the face of the complaint, as long as a sworn affidavit made at the time the warrant was issued contains those facts.

The importance of including all necessary information becomes obvious in the case of the State v. J. H. Campbell 281 Minn. 1, 161 N.W. 2d 47 (1968). The defendant was convicted of first-degree murder in the shooting death of a man in an armed supermarket robbery. It was known the robber wore a paper-bag mask over his head while committing the crime and had been stabbed in the chest by the man he fatally shot. The defendant, who lived near the supermarket, had obtained treatment for a stab wound at a local hospital. A warrant was secured to search his apartment. The search turned up bloody clothing, a gun identified as the one used in the robbery, and pieces of paper which matched the torn-out sections of the paper-bag mask.

The defense attacked the search, saying the warrant had been granted on an affidavit which was insufficient to provide the magistrate with probable cause. The Supreme Court said that, by itself, the affidavit was insufficient and repeated that the magistrate cannot rely on an officer's decision that he has sufficiently established probable cause, but must make his own judgment of probable cause based on the facts presented. However, probable cause for issuing a search warrant may be established by sworn testimony before the issuing magistrate if the testimony supplements the factual statements of the affidavit, is recorded in writing by the magistrate, and is made available for the trial. Although the affidavit was somewhat sketchy and did not provide the source of information used, the issuing judge *had* questioned the officer and elicited additional sworn statements which satisfied the magistrate that probable cause did exist. The Supreme Court agreed that the search warrant was valid and upheld both the use of the evidence and the conviction of the defendant.

Figure 14-1. Search Warrant.

INSTRUCTIONS FOR OBTAINING AND EXECUTING SEARCH WARRANTS

(Sample Worksheets Attached)

THE FOLLOWING DOCUMENTS ARE NECESSARY TO OBTAIN A SEARCH WARRANT AND COMPLETE A LAWFUL SEARCH. DOCUMENTS MUST BE PREPARED IN THE NUMBER OF COPIES TO BE FILED OR SERVED AS INDICATED:

APPLICATION FOR SEARCH WARRANT AND SUPPORTING AFFIDAVIT
(3 PAGES), COPIES FOR COURT, PROSECUTING ATTORNEY, POLICE. (PAGES 1-1, 1-2 and 1-3)

SEARCH WARRANT (1 PAGE), COPIES FOR COURT, PROSECUTING ATTORNEY, POLICE AND PERSON OR PREMISES SERVED. (PAGE 2-1)

RECEIPT, INVENTORY AND RETURN (1 PAGE), FOR COURT, PROSECUTING ATTORNEY, POLICE AND PERSON OR PREMISES SERVED. (PAGE 3-1)

THE COURT COPY SHALL BE THE ORIGINAL OF ALL DOCUMENTS AND BEAR SIGNATURES.

ONE OR MORE PEACE OFFICERS MAY APPLY AND SUBMIT AFFIDAVITS FOR A SEARCH WARRANT, BUT THE WARRANT SHALL BE ISSUED ONLY TO PEACE OFFICERS OF THE COUNTY IN WHICH THE SEARCH IS TO BE MADE.

APPLICATION FOR SEARCH WARRANT AND SUPPORTING AFFIDAVIT

THE BASIC ELEMENTS NECESSARY ARE:

1) A COMPLETE DESCRIPTION OF THE TOOLS, LOOT, WEAPONS OR OTHER EVIDENCE (FINGERPRINTS, HAIR, ETC.) OF THE CRIME, INCLUDING MODEL AND SERIAL NUMBERS AND ALL IDENTIFYING MARKS.

2) A DETAILED DESCRIPTION OF THE PLACE OR PERSON TO BE SEARCHED, FOR EXAMPLE, THE HOUSE, GARAGE AND ALL APPURTENANT STRUCTURES AND THE PREMISES AT 777 E. SEVENTH ST., YOUR CITY, YOUR STATE; OR A 1970 4-DOOR FORD, ANYWHERE VEHICLE LICENSE MV #5472, SERIAL #17HB6543; OR APT #111, AT 520 ASHLAND AVE., ALL ASSIGNED STORAGE AREAS AND GARAGE, ALL PUBLIC AREAS AND THE PREMISES AT 520 ASHLAND AVE., YOUR TOWN, YOUR STATE.

A police officer must present adequate evidence for a magistrate to determine probable cause. If sufficient facts are contained in the application and supporting affidavit or supplementary facts are presented during questioning of an officer who applies for a warrant, a magistrate will issue the search warrant.

Figure 14-1. Search Warrant Continued.

3) A DESCRIPTION OF THE CRIME, FOR WHICH EVIDENCE IS SOUGHT, AND

4) THE DETAILED REASON FOR BELIEVING THE EVIDENCE IS LOCATED IN A GIVEN PLACE, INCLUDING ESTABLISHMENT OF RELIABILITY OF INFORMANT.

AFFIANT MAY REQUEST THE SEARCH WARRANT BE ISSUED TO TWO OR MORE PEACE OFFICERS OF THE COUNTY IN WHICH SEARCH IS TO BE MADE.

THE APPLICATION AND SUPPORTING AFFIDAVIT MUST BE PRESENTED TO A JUDGE OF A COURT OF RECORD (MUNICIPAL, COUNTY, OR DISTRICT) AND SIGNED BY AFFIANT UNDER OATH ADMINISTERED BY THE COURT. THE APPLICATION NEED NOT BE TAKEN TO THE PLACE TO BE SEARCHED.

SEARCH WARRANT

THE SEARCH WARRANT SHALL BE PREPARED AND SUBMITTED WITH THE APPLICATION TO THE JUDGE.

THE PEACE OFFICERS NAMED IN THE SEARCH WARRANT MUST CONDUCT THE SEARCH AND MAY HAVE THE ASSISTANCE OF OTHER OFFICERS ACTING UNDER THEIR SUPERVISION.

AN OFFICER CONDUCTING A SEARCH MUST GIVE A COPY OF THE WARRANT, AND A RECEIPT IF PROPERTY OR THINGS ARE TAKEN, TO THE PERSON IN WHOSE POSSESSION THE PROPERTY OR THINGS ARE FOUND. IN THE ABSENCE OF ANY PERSON, HE MUST LEAVE SUCH COPY OF THE WARRANT AND RECEIPT IN THE PLACE WHERE THE THINGS ARE FOUND.

IF THE EVIDENCE SOUGHT IS OF A CRIME TO BE PROSECUTED IN ANOTHER JURISDICTION, THE WARRANT SHOULD INDICATE THE INDIVIDUAL TO WHOM THE THINGS SEIZED SHALL BE DELIVERED. OTHERWISE THE OFFICER EXECUTING THE WARRANT SHALL RETAIN CUSTODY OF THE THINGS SEIZED.

RECEIPT, INVENTORY AND RETURN

AT THE SCENE OF THE SEARCH ALL ITEMS TAKEN PURSUANT TO THE WARRANT MUST BE LISTED ON THE RECEIPT. ANY ITEMS NOT NAMED IN THE WARRANT BUT SEIZED AS EVIDENCE OR CONTRABAND SHOULD BE DESIGNATED AS SUCH AND ALSO LISTED.

THE COPY OF THE RECEIPT LEFT AT THE PLACE OF SEARCH MUST BE SIGNED BY THE OFFICER EXECUTING THE WARRANT BUT NEED NOT BE NOTARIZED.

THE OFFICER EXECUTING THE WARRANT MUST FORTHWITH RETURN THE ORIGINAL SIGNED SEARCH WARRANT, RECEIPT, NOTARIZED INVENTORY AND RETURN TO THE COURT ISSUING THE WARRANT.

TO ESTABLISH CHAIN OF POSSESSION, IT IS PREFERABLE THAT ITEMS SEIZED BE MARKED AND TAGGED AT THE PLACE WHERE FOUND'

The use of search warrants has increased since the Chimel decision which restricted the area that could be searched incidental to a lawful arrest. Prior to the Chimel case, some courts allowed extensive searches incidental to a lawful arrest. The Chimel ruling, however, makes it necessary for police officers to obtain a search warrant as well as an arrest warrant if they want to search a suspect's house incidental to the execution of the arrest warrant.

Figure 14-1. Search Warrant Continued.

APPLICATION   1-1

STATE OF ANYWHERE, COUNTY OF _____   _____ COURT

STATE OF ANYWHERE)
) SS.   **APPLICATION FOR SEARCH WARRANT AND SUPPORTING AFFIDAVIT**
COUNTY OF_____)

_____, being first duly sworn upon oath, hereby makes application to this Court for a warrant to search the (premises) (motor vehicles) (person) hereinafter described, for the property and things hereinafter described.

Affiant knows the contents of this application and supporting affidavit, and the statements herein are true of his own knowledge, save as to such as are herein stated on information and belief, and as to those, he believes them to be true.

Affiant has good reason to believe, and does believe, that the following described property and things, to wit:

(are)   (will be)
(at the premises)   (in the motor vehicle)   (on the person) described as:

located in the _____ of_____, County of_____, and State of Anywhere.

This affiant applies for issuance of a search warrant upon the following grounds: (Strike inapplicable paragraph)

1. The property above-described was stolen or embezzled.
2. The property above-described was used as means of committing a crime.
3. The possession of the property above-described constitutes a crime.
4. The property above-described is in the possession of a person with intent to use such property as a means of committing a crime.
5. The property above-described constitutes evidence which tends to show a crime has been committed, or tends to show that a particular person has committed a crime.

COURT - WHITE COPY • PROS. ATTY. - YELLOW COPY • PEACE OFFICER - PINK COPY

What May Be Seized

As stated in the Fourth Amendment, the search warrant must clearly specify or describe "the things to be seized." The prosecution or the state must accept the burden of proof when items are seized that are not specifically stated in the warrant. This does not mean such items cannot be seized. They can, if a reasonable relationship exists between the search and the seizure of materials not described or if officers discover contraband—any-

Figure 14-1.   Search Warrant Continued.

```
                                                      APPLICATION      1-2
        The facts tending to establish the foregoing grounds for issuance of a search warrant are as follows:












                                                  (attach and identify additional sheet if necessary)
        A nighttime search is necessary to prevent the loss, destruction or removal of the objects of the search because:







           An unannounced entry is necessary (to prevent the loss, destruction or removal of the objects of the search
        (and) to protect the safety of the peace officers) because:







           WHEREFORE, Affiant request a search warrant be issued, commanding_____
        _____
        _____
        (a) peace officer(s), of the State of Anywhere, (to enter without announcement of authority and purpose)
        (in the daytime only)   (in the daytime or nighttime)
        to search the hereinbefore described (premises) (motor vehicle) (person)
        for the described property and things and to seize said property and things and keep said property and things in
        custody until the same be dealt with according to law.


                                               _____
                                                Affiant

        Subscribed and sworn to before me this
        _____day of_____, 19__.         _____
                                                Judge of                        Court

              COURT - WHITE COPY  •  PROS. ATTY. - YELLOW COPY  •  PEACE OFFICER - PINK COPY
```

thing which is illegal for a person to own or have in his possession such as heroin or a machine gun.

Police may seize items not specified in the search warrant if they are similar in nature to those items described, if they are related to the particular crime described, or if they are contraband.

Figure 14-1. Search Warrant Continued.

SEARCH WARRANT   2-1

STATE OF ANYWHERE, COUNTY OF _____ _____ COURT

TO:_____

_____ (A) PEACE OFFICER(S) OF THE STATE OF ANYWHERE.

WHEREAS, _____ has this day on oath, made application to the said Court applying for issuance of a search warrant to search the following described (premises) (motor vehicle) (person):

_____

_____

located in the _____ of _____ , county of _____ STATE OF ANYWHERE

for the following described property and things: (attach and identify additional sheet if necessary)

WHEREAS, the application and supporting affidavit of_____ (was) (were) duly presented and read by the Court, and being fully advised in the premises.

NOW, THEREFORE, the Court finds that probable cause exsists for the issuance of a search warrant upon the following grounds: (Strike inapplicable paragraphs)

1. The property above-described was stolen or embezzled.

2. The property above-described was used as a means of committing a crime.

3. The possession of the property above-described constitutes a crime.

4. The property above-described is in the possession of a person with intent to use such property as a means of committing a crime.

5. The property above-described constitutes evidence which tends to show a crime has been committed, or tends to show that a particular person has committed a crime.

The Court further finds that proable cause exsists to believe that the above-described property and things (are) (will be) (at the above-described premises) (in the above-described motor vehicle) (on the person of _____).

The Court further finds that a nighttime search is necessary to prevent the loss, destruction, or removal of the objects of said search.

The Court further finds that entry without announcement of authority or purpose is necessary (to prevent the loss, destruction, or removal of the objects of said search) (and) (to protect the safety of the peace officers).

NOW, THEREFORE, YOU_____

THE PEACE OFFICER(S) AFORESAID, ARE HEREBY COMMANDED (TO ENTER WITHOUT ANNOUNCEMENT OF AUTHORITY AND PURPOSE) (IN THE DAYTIME ONLY) (IN THE DAYTIME OR NIGHTTIME)   TO SEARCH (THE DESCRIBED PREMISES) (THE DESCRIBED MOTOR VEHICLE) (THE PERSON OF_____) FOR THE ABOVE-DESCRIBED PROPERTY AND THINGS,   AND TO SEIZE SAID PROPERTY AND THINGS AND   (TO RETAIN THEM IN CUSTODY SUBJECT TO COURT ORDER AND ACCORDING TO LAW) (DELIVER CUSTODY OF SAID PROPERTY AND THINGS TO_____ _____).

BY THE COURT:

Dated_____ , 19__.   JUDGE OF _____ COURT

COURT - WHITE COPY • PROS. ATTY. - YELLOW COPY • PEACE OFFICER - PINK COPY • PREMISES/PERSON - GOLD COPY

Consider this example. On two separate occasions, officers arrived at a private dwelling with search warrants authorizing them to seize items taken from burglaries. On both occasions their knock was unanswered, so they entered through a living room window. They seized many items on the search warrants as well as other similar items not specifically mentioned in the warrants. When the case came to court, the defense challenged those items introduced as evidence of the burglaries which were not specifically mentioned in

Figure 14-1. Search Warrant Continued.

RECIEPT, INVENTORY AND RETURN   3-1

STATE OF ANYWHERE, COUNTY OF_____   _____COURT

RECEIPT, INVENTORY AND RETURN

I,_____ , received the attached search warrant

issued by the Honorable_____ , on_____ , 19____ , and have
executed it as follows:

Pursuant to said warrant, on _____ , 19___ , at _____ o'clock ___m.,   I
searched the (premises) (motor vehicle) (person) described in said warrant, and left a true and correct copy of said
warrant
(with) (in) (at)_____

I took into custody the property and things listed below: (attach and identify additional sheet if necessary)

_____

_____

_____

_____

_____

_____

_____

_____

_____

_____

_____

_____

(Strike when appropriate:)

I left a receipt for the property and things listed above with a copy of the warrant.

None of the items set forth in the search warrant were found.

I shall (retain) or (deliver) custody of said property as directed by Court order.

_____ , being first duly sworn, upon oath, deposes and says
that he has read the foregoing receipt, inventory and return and the matters stated are true and correct, except as to
such matters stated therein on information and belief, and as to those, he believes them to be true.

Subscribed and sworn to before me this
_____day of_____ , 19____

_____   _____
Notary Public,   County, Anywhere   Signature

My commission expires_____

COURT - WHITE COPY • PROS. ATTY. - **YELLOW COPY** • **PEACE OFFICER** - PINK COPY • PREMISES/PERSON - GOLD COPY the warrants. The lower court allowed the evidence to be used, and the state supreme court upheld the decision. The high court said the items seized in addition to those mentioned in the warrants were similar to items which the stores had on hand when the burglaries occurred.

In addition, contraband discovered during a search authorized by a warrant may also be seized. It is not necessary that the contraband be connected to the particular crime described in the search warrant.

Gaining Entrance

Police officers are usually required to announce their authority and purpose before entering a home. This protects the citizen's rights and avoids needless destruction of property where the owner or occupant is willing to voluntarily admit a police officer. Sometimes, however, the suspect will not allow entrance, or there may be no one home.

> Generally police officers must announce themselves. They may enter a house by force to execute a search warrant if they are denied entrance or if there is no one home.

Police officers who arrive to execute a search warrant and find the house unoccupied may forcibly enter the house to search it. If the dwelling is an apartment, they could probably get a passkey from a caretaker, but this would still be considered a forced entry. So is opening a closed but unlocked door or window.

Officers who are denied entrance to execute a search warrant may break an inner or outer door or window to gain entry.

Nighttime and No-Knock Search Warrants

> Two special types of search warrants, Nighttime and No-Knock, must be authorized by a magistrate as a special provision of a search warrant.

A search warrant will normally be issued to be served during daylight hours, that is, from sunrise to sunset. *Nighttime* searches may be justified and requested of the court by police officers. They must state the reasons, based on facts, for fearing that unless the search is conducted in the night the objects of the search might be lost, destroyed, or removed.

Similarly, unannounced entries for the purpose of executing search warrants must also receive prior judicial authorization. The *No-Knock* search warrant is reserved for situations where the judge recognizes that the "normal" cooperation of the citizen cannot be expected and that an announced entry may result in the loss, destruction, or removal of the objects of the search; for example, surprise entries are often used in searches for narcotics and gambling equipment. In either of these instances, the court will usually acknowledge that evidence can easily be destroyed during the time required to give notice, demand admittance, and accept the citizen's denial of entry.

☑ CHECK POINT

1. What is a search warrant?
2. On what must a search warrant be based?
3. Technically, who must authorize all searches?
4. During a search with a warrant, when may items which are not described in the warrant be legally seized?
5. When may forcible entrance be used?
6. What two special types of warrants may be requested if it is feared that the objects of the search might be lost, destroyed, or removed?

*Answers

1. A search warrant is a judicial order directing police officers to search for specific property, seize it, and return it to the court.
2. Probable cause is required for issuance of all warrants.
3. Technically, all searches are to be made under the authority of a search warrant issued by a magistrate.
4. Police may seize items not specified in the search warrant if they are similar in nature to those items described, if they are related to the particular crime described, or if they are contraband.
5. Generally police officers must announce themselves. They may enter a house by force to execute a search warrant (or an arrest warrant) if they are denied entrance or if there is no one home.
6. Nighttime and No-Knock search warrants may be authorized by a magistrate as a special provision when officers fear objects of the search might be lost, destroyed, or removed.

WARRANTLESS SEARCHES

When police officers follow the letter of the law and secure a search warrant, they receive an advance court decision that probable cause does exist. It was originally believed that the magistrate should be the sole judge of probable cause, but when emergency situations became apparent, the courts decided there were times when reasonable searches and seizures could be based on the decisions of police officers. In all instances where a magistrate has not made the decision of probable cause, the police officer or the prosecution must assume the task of proving that the search was reasonable.

Emergency Situations

In situations where police officers sincerely believe they have established probable cause and there is no time to secure a warrant, they can act on their own decision. But, it is here that the opportunity for a defense lawyer to challenge the legality of the search can be based. While a number of challenges can be raised, two occur most frequently.

If the defense raises one of these challenges in a case involving evidence seized as a result of a warrantless search, the burden of proof is on the officer and the prosecution. It must be proven that the officer was "reasonable and prudent" and had gathered sufficient facts to make the important decision that probable cause to search existed and that the search must be conducted immediately.

> When police officers conduct a search without a warrant, they may be challenged on the basis that:
> —A magistrate would *not* have issued a warrant had the officers presented the facts before the court (probable cause was not established).
> —The officers had ample opportunity to secure a warrant and, therefore, had no justification to act without one.

The Fourth Amendment says a great deal in only fifty-four words. It guarantees that United States citizens will not be unjustly searched or arrested and that their property will not be unlawfully seized. With added historical court decisions, most of the language of our present laws governing search and seizure is represented.

The Fourth Amendment was intended to interpose a magistrate between the police and the citizen—requiring a magistrate to study the evidence presented by the police and decide whether a warrant should be issued. The Constitution is a product of a period when authority had been badly misused, and it was presumed the magistrates would be more objective than officers.

A strict interpretation of the Constitution requires that a magistrate decide whether probable cause exists. When the officer presents the facts to a magistrate and is granted a warrant, the defense lawyer cannot attack the decision of the individual officer. When the search warrant is issued, it becomes an order from the court, as the Constitution intended it to be. It is no longer the prosecution which has to defend its actions, but the lawyer for the accused who has to prove that a magistrate erred in issuing the warrant. This is the preferable position to be in.

> A warrantless search (in the absence of a lawful arrest or consent) is justified only in emergency situations where probable cause exists and the search must be conducted immediately. The officer is acting without the authority of the magistrate and must accept the burden of proof for probable cause.

While the laws are still intended to provide protection, they are also designed to meet emergency situations not considered in the original amendment. There are rules to be observed in such situations; each must fall within the guarantees in the Fourth Amendment. The key is to protect all citizens against unreasonable searches and seizures.

The men who drafted the Constitution understood that other reasonable measures would have to be accepted to uphold the laws of the nation. The Supreme Court, therefore, surveys cases brought before it to determine whether the action taken in a particular situation was reasonable according to the Fourth Amendment. What may be reasonable in one situation may not be reasonable in another. For instance, you could justify a warrantless search of a vehicle by stating the reasons you believed it would be gone if you waited to obtain a search warrant. This same logic, however, cannot be applied to a search of a house or any other fixed object.

We have already looked at three types of warrantless searches:

—Searches connected with "stop and frisk" (limited to a search for weapons).

—Searches incidental to an arrest.

—Searches when consent has been given.

Although Supreme Court approval of warrantless searches incidental to an arrest was established in cases prior to 1920, it was the Chimel opinion in 1969 that confined the area of search to an area within the immediate control of the persons arrested. This opinion did *not* apply to automobiles, however.

As noted, searches may be conducted without a warrant even though the search is not associated with "stop and frisk," incidental to an arrest, or with consent; but when it is conducted under these circumstances, police officers must prove that an emergency existed which did not allow them to secure a search warrant. Very frequently this involves automobiles and other conveyances having *mobility*.

Warrantless Searches of Automobiles and Other Conveyances

When a vehicle is involved, the "rules of reasonableness," although within the boundaries of the Constitution, are quite different. The courts have long recognized the need for separate exemptions from the requirement of obtaining a search warrant where mobility is involved.

The precedent for a warrantless search of an automobile resulted from Carroll v. United States 267 U.S. 132, 45 S. Ct. 280, 69 L. Ed. 543, (1925) which established two basic principles justifying warrantless searches of automobiles.

> *Carroll* v. *U.S.* set the precedent for warrantless searches of automobiles provided (1) there is probable cause for the search, and (2) the automobile or other conveyance would be gone before a search warrant could be obtained.

The Carroll case did not involve a search incidental to an arrest. The concern was with probable cause for a search, not for an arrest.

During Prohibition in the 1920s, some 1500 agents pursued bootleggers, many of whom brought liquor down from Canada. In addition to the imports, there was so much local production that the 9500 stills raided in the first six months of prohibition were known to be only a small fraction of the total.

Visualize a scene in a "honky tonk" during the 1920s. Four men are sitting at a table holding a meeting; two are supposed buyers, and two are bootleggers. The "buyers" are actually federal prohibition agents. Although the meeting seems to go well, the two bootleggers, George Carroll and John Kiro, are somewhat suspicious. They indicate that the liquor has to come from the east end of Grand Rapids, Michigan. They will get it and return in about an hour. Later that day, Carroll calls and says delivery cannot be made until the next day. But the two do not return the next day.

The agents returned to their normal duty of watching a section of road between Grand Rapids and Detroit known to be used by bootleggers. Within a week after their unsuccessful attempt to make the "buy," the agents recognized Carroll and Kiro driving by. They gave chase but lost the car near East Lansing.

Two months later they again recognized Carroll's car coming from the direction of Detroit. They pursued the car and this time were successful in overtaking them. The agents were familiar with Carroll's car, they recognized Carroll and Kiro in the automobile, and they had reason to believe the automobile would contain bootleg liquor. A search of the car revealed sixty-eight bottles of whiskey and gin, most of it behind the upholstering of the seats where the padding had been removed. The contraband was seized, and the two men were arrested.

George Carroll and John Kiro were charged with transporting intoxicating liquor and were convicted in federal court. Carroll's appeal, taken to the United States Supreme Court, resulted in a landmark decision defining the rights and limitations for warrantless searches of vehicles.

> The Carroll decision established that the right to search an automobile is *not* dependent on the right to arrest the driver or an occupant, but rather it is dependent upon the probable cause the seizing officer has for believing that the contents of the automobile violate the law.

The knowledge of the two men and their operation as well as the fact that their car was believed to be used in the transportation of liquor, produced the probable cause necessary to justify a search. So the first principle establishing this as an exception to the rule requiring a search warrant was met.

Regarding the *mobility* of such a conveyance, the court amplified its opinion to include some of the key reasons why an automobile can be exempted while a house or fixed object cannot:

—A vehicle or conveyance can be quickly moved out of the jurisdiction or locality in which the warrant must be sought.

—The occupants of a vehicle are immediately alerted.

—The vehicle's contents may never be found again if a police officer has to wait to obtain a search warrant before searching the car.

The Supreme Court saw each of these possibilities in the case against George Carroll and, consequently, provided a basis for making a similar judgment in a situation where these circumstances might occur.

The requirement of mobility is also present in the case of Chambers v. Maroney Supreme Court of the U.S. 399 U.S. 42, 90 S. Ct. 1975, 26 L. Ed. 2d 419 (1970).

> The Chambers case established that a car may retain its mobility even though it is impounded.

This case involved the armed robbery of a service station. As you may recall from the earlier account of the case, the station attendant described the two men who held guns on him, and two boys provided officers with a description of a vehicle they had seen the men in, circling the block prior to the robbery and again speeding out of the area. Within an hour officers spotted the vehicle and identified the occupants as being those whom the three witnesses had described. They stopped the car and arrested the men. The evidence seized and later used to convict Chambers and the other man included two revolvers and a glove filled with change they had taken from the service station.

Chambers based an appeal on the fact that the officers took the car to the police station before searching it. The defense contended that the search was illegal because it was made incidental to rather than simultaneous with the arrest. The defense was right. As a search incidental to an arrest, it would have been illegal. But the court observed the same set of circumstances in relation to the warrantless search of a vehicle; the seizing officers did have probable cause to believe that the contents of the automobile violated the law. Therefore, it was the right to search, not the right to arrest, that provided the officers with the authority for their actions.

The Supreme Court added another opinion to the Chambers case when it said that it was not unreasonable under these circumstances to take the vehicle to the police station to be searched. In other words, the probable cause to search at the scene continued to exist at the police station. Based on the facts, the Supreme Court said there was probable cause to search, and since it was a fleeing target, the Chambers' vehicle could have been searched on the spot where it was stopped. The court reasoned that probable cause still existed at the police station, and so did the mobility of the car. The court quickly pointed out that such actions must be confined to vehicles and other conveyances having mobility.

☑ CHECK POINT

1. When is a warrantless search justified?
2. When a search is conducted without a warrant, what are the two challenges most frequently raised?
3. What constitutes an "emergency" situation justifying a warrantless search?
4. What are the two basic principles justifying warrantless searches of automobiles?
5. From what case did these two principles emerge?
6. What is the right to search an automobile dependent upon?
7. What case established that a car may retain its mobility even though it is impounded?

* Answers

1. Warrantless searches are justified in "stop and frisk," incidental to a lawful arrest, with consent, in an emergency situation, and when mobility is involved.

2. The two challenges most frequently raised for warrantless searches are (1) that a magistrate would not have issued a warrant had the officer presented the facts before the court and (2) the officer had ample time to secure a warrant and, therefore, had no justification to act without one.
3. An emergency situation exists when the officer has probable cause to search and the search must be conducted immediately.
4. The two basic principles justifying warrantless searches of automobiles are (1) there is probable cause for the search and (2) the automobile or other conveyance would be gone before a search warrant would be obtained, that is, it has mobility.
5. These principles came out of the Carroll case.
6. The right to search an automobile is dependent upon the probable cause the seizing officer has for believing the contents of the automobile violate the law—*not* on the right to arrest. (*Carroll* decision)
7. The Chambers case established that a car may retain its mobility even though it is impounded.

Yet another interpretation of mobility was provided in the case of Coolidge v. New Hampshire 403, U.S. 443, 91 S. Ct. 2022, 443, 29 L. Ed. 2d 564 (1971).

> Coolidge v. New Hampshire established that the rule of mobility cannot be applied unless there is actually a risk that the vehicle would be moved.

The Coolidge case, a homicide, tested the requirements of mobility. A fourteen-year-old girl disappeared in Manchester, New Hampshire, and her body was found eight days later. She had been shot. A number of errors were made in the case, including the fact that arrest and search warrants were drawn up and signed by the man who became the chief prosecutor.

A neighbor's tip led police to E. H. Coolidge, whom officers admitted was fully cooperative, even to the point of agreeing to a polygraph examination. The examination was conducted several days after Coolidge was first questioned. During the next two and a half weeks, evidence against Coolidge began to accumulate. The evidence included what the prosecution said was the murder weapon, which officers had obtained from Mrs. Coolidge. The arrest and search warrants were drawn up based on this evidence. The search warrant specifically designated Coolidge's car, which was in the driveway in plain view of the house at the time of the arrest. Mrs. Coolidge was told she was not allowed to use the car, and it was impounded prior to other officers dropping Mrs. Coolidge at a relative's home. During the next fourteen months the car was searched three times, and vacuum sweepings from the car were introduced as evidence.

Coolidge was convicted of the girl's murder. His appeal challenged the legality of the evidence seized from the car. Discounting the fact the warrants were invalid and the prosecution could not prove the search was incidental to an arrest, the prosecution contended the seizure of the car should be allowable based on the standards established by the Carroll and Chambers cases.

The court considered the principles of the Coolidge case and weighed them against those of the two precedent cases. Because testimony from witnesses and from Coolidge indicated that his car was at the scene of the murder, the court accepted the fact that probable cause to search had been established. But was there sufficient cause to fear the automobile might be moved?

The court said there was *not*. Coolidge could not have gained access to the automobile when the officers came to arrest him, and he had, in fact, received sufficient prior warning that he was a prime suspect to have already fled. The only other adult occupant, Mrs. Coolidge, was driven to a relative's home by other officers who were with her after the vehicle was actually taken to the station.

Neither the Carroll or Chambers opinions could apply here because of the following differences:

—There appeared to be no criminal intent to flee.

—This was not a case of a fleeting opportunity to search on an open highway after a hazardous chase.

—There was no evidence of contraband, stolen goods, or weapons.

—There was no evidence of any friends of Coolidge's waiting to move the car and the evidence therein.

—The automobile in question was secured from intrusion when it was found.

Since the Coolidge premises were guarded throughout the night, and since Mrs. Coolidge was with officers until after the car had been towed in, it had been secured all the time.

The court could not accept the prosecution's contention that the Coolidge vehicle was included in the category of mobility. The prosecution then contended that the evidence was admissible because it was in plain view. The court also rejected this contention, and rightly so, as we will discuss soon.

Instrumentalities of a Crime

The following rule applies to vehicles or other conveyances when they are used in the commission of serious crimes such as felonies.

> Such instruments of a crime may be seized and searched if the vehicle is an integral part of the defendant's apparatus for the commission of the crime.

This generally includes "get-away vehicles" as well as automobiles, trailers, or similar conveyances used to secrete or transport stolen items.

In a recent Minnesota case, one of two men involved in a holdup jumped into a get-away car. He immediately jumped out when a squad car stopped the car and was shot when he attempted to escape. The officers searched the vehicle and retrieved a revolver from under the front seat. Although the defense claimed this was an illegal search, the district and state supreme court viewed the car as "an instrumentality of the crime." The courts upheld the use of the evidence because it had been obtained in a reasonable search.

Plain View

Plain view refers to evidence which is not concealed and which is inadvertently seen by an officer engaged in a lawful activity.

Several factors determine what constitutes plain view. First, the police officer must be engaged in lawful activity prior to the discovery of plain view evidence. Such circumstances might occur while the officer is executing a warrant to search for another object, while in "hot pursuit" of a suspect, during a search incidental to a lawful arrest, during "stop and frisk," or any other legitimate reasons justifying an officer's lawful presence.

Second, the seized items must not be concealed. As the name implies, they must be in "plain view." Third, the discovery of the evidence in plain view must be inadvertent, by accident. Police officers cannot obtain a warrant to search an automobile and fail to mention a particular object they are looking for and then justify its seizure pursuant to the plain view doctrine. If they were looking for it initially, it must be mentioned in the warrant. Fourth, plain view alone is not sufficient to justify the warrantless seizure of evidence.

In the Coolidge case the court could not accept the seizure of the car as being within "plain view" limitations because the officers intended to seize the car when they came onto Coolidge's property. So the rule applied to Coolidge and to all "plain view" cases following is that the discovery of evidence in plain view must be inadvertant—by accident. The plain view doctrine applies even though the objects seized are not under the immediate control of the suspect.

In contrast to the Coolidge case is one in which local officers received information that one or two motels in their jurisdiction were to be burglarized during a particular weekend. Patrols in those areas were alerted. When one squad noticed a vehicle slowly driving around one of the motels, the activity wasn't enough to presume the existence of probable cause to arrest. But since the situation called for investigation, the car was stopped.

While talking to the driver and his passenger, the officers heard conflicting statements as to why the men were in the area. One officer could see a partially concealed television set in the back seat and could identify at least part of the word *motel* on the set. When questioned, the driver and his passenger presented differing stories as to how they happened to have the television in the car. The men were arrested, and the television set proved to be a valuable piece of evidence in their conviction.

In reviewing the case, the Supreme Court recognized that the stolen item had been seized within the limitations of the plain view rule. The officers had probable cause to stop the vehicle for investigation, and, thus, they had the right to be in a position to see the television set. The discovery of the television set was not the only fact that led to the arrest. The officers were alerted that there might be a motel burglary, and they considered the movement of this particular car to be suspicious. In addition, the men's responses to their questions were contradictory.

☑ CHECK POINT

1. When does the rule of mobility not apply to warrantless search of an automobile?
2. What case established the above precedent?
3. What is an "instrumentality of a crime" and how does it relate to warrantless searches?
4. What four factors constitute plain view evidence?

∗ Answers

1. The rule of mobility cannot be applied unless there is actually a risk that the vehicle will be moved.
2. This precedent was established in Coolidge v. New Hampshire.
3. An "instrumentality of a crime" refers to a vehicle which is an integral part of the suspect's apparatus for committing a crime (such as a get-away car). Such instruments of a crime may be seized and searched without a warrant.
4. Plain view refers to evidence (1) which is not concealed and (2) which is inadvertently seen by an officer (3) while engaged in a lawful activity, and (4) is supported by other factors. Plain view alone does not justify the warrantless seizure of evidence.

SUMMARY

Though the Fourth Amendment was intended to guarantee that law enforcement searches would be based on the issuance of warrants, it provided for exceptions. The Fourth Amendment is reasonable in protecting the rights of the people while allowing law enforcement the right to investigate crime. It is strong enough to protect citizens, but also flexible enough to enable police officers to uphold the Constitution.

The standards established by the Fourth Amendment are enforced by use of the Exclusionary Rule which states that no evidence can be admitted in a trial unless it is obtained within the standards established in the Fourth Amendment. The federal precedent for this rule is found in the case of Weeks v. United States. The state precedent is found in the case of Mapp v. Ohio.

"Reasonable" searches and seizures must meet the standards set forth in the Fourth Amendment. The three principle justifications for a search are (1) it is incidental to a lawful arrest, (2) consent is given, or (3) a search warrant is obtained.

Even when one of these conditions is met, certain limitations are placed on the search. The most important limitation imposed upon any search is that the scope must be narrowed. General searches are unconstitutional. The limitations placed on searches incidental to lawful arrest come from the case of Chimel v. United States which states that the scope of the search must be narrowed to the area within the suspect's immediate control. The limitations to a search made with consent are that the consent must be free and voluntary, not in response to an implied right to search, and the scope must be limited to the area for which consent has been given. The limitations to a search made with a warrant are stated within the warrant itself.

Most searches require a warrant. A search warrant is a judicial order directing a police officer to search for specific property, seize it, and return it to the court. Probable cause is required for issuance of all warrants. Technically, all searches are to be made under the authority of a search warrant issued by a magistrate. If a search is conducted with a warrant, the burden of proof as to admissibility of evidence seized is on the defense; if it is conducted without a warrant, the burden of proof is on the searching officer and the prosecution.

Police may seize items not specified in the search warrant if they are similar in nature to those items described, if they are related to the particular crime described, or if they are contraband.

When police officers execute a search warrant, they generally announce themselves. They may enter a home by force if they are denied entrance or if no one is home. Two special types of search warrants, Nighttime and No-Knock, may be requested if the officers fear the objects of the search might be lost, destroyed, or removed.

Warrantless searches, based on probable cause, have been justified in "stop and frisk," incidental to a lawful arrest, with consent, in an emergency situation, and when mobility is involved.

The two most frequent challenges to such warrantless searches which may be raised by the defense are that (1) there was insufficient evidence to establish probable cause, so a search warrant would not have been issued by a magistrate, and (2) there was sufficient time to obtain a search warrant.

Special provisions have been made for warrantless searches of cars and other conveyances due to their mobility. Precedents for the warrantless search of an automobile were established by the Carroll case which demonstrated that probable cause must exist along with mobility—the belief that the car and/or evidence would be gone by the time a search warrant was obtained. It also demonstrated that the right to search was not dependent on the right to arrest, but rather on probable cause. The Chambers case demonstrated that a car may retain its mobility even though it is impounded. The Coolidge case demonstrated that the rule of mobility cannot be applied unless there is actually a risk the vehicle will be moved. A car may also be searched without a warrant if it is an instrumentality of a crime.

A special instance of legal seizure of evidence without a warrant exists in the plain view situation, that is, evidence which is not concealed is inadvertently seen by an officer engaged in lawful activity and is supported by other facts and/or evidence.

APPLICATION

Read each of the following cases and then answer the questions related to the legality of the search and seizure involved.

A. A convict has escaped from a penitentiary and police officers are searching homes in the area surrounding the penetentiary in an attempt to find the escapee. They arrive at the home of a man who refuses them admittance. The police explain that a convict has escaped and that they, therefore, have a right to search the surrounding area. The man insists he has not seen the convict and begrudgingly admits the police officers. During the subsequent search, the police come across a counterfeiting press and stacks of counterfeit money. They arrest the man on charges of counterfeiting and confiscate the press and the money.

1. Was the search legal? Why or why not?
2. Will the evidence be admitted in court? Why or why not?

B. A detective is investigating a homicide and wants to search the victim's hotel room. He asks permission of the manager and is granted permission and a passkey. The detective finds several pieces of evidence which connect the victim with the suspect in custody.

1. Is the search legal? Why or why not?
2. Will the evidence be admitted in court?

C. A clerk in a neighborhood supermarket reported that a friend of hers passed a forged check two days ago in a local drugstore and that her friend had other stolen checks in his possession. The next day the officers went to the suspect's house and asked for admittance. They were denied admittance, but entered forceably. In the bedroom they found one hundred stolen checks of the kind that were being passed.

1. Was the search legal? Why or why not?
2. What might they have done differently?

D. At about 3:00 A.M., two plainclothes officers were patrolling a neighborhood that had a reputation for narcotics activity. The officers saw an individual standing on the corner looking up and down the street suspiciously. As they continued their surveillance, they saw a car pull up quickly and the individual jumped into the car. The car sped off, and the officers followed it. Neither officer knew the driver or the passenger of the car. Except for the reputation of the neighborhood, neither officer had received any information to suggest that someone might be engaged in criminal activity at this time or place. They had no arrest or search warrants, and they were not searching for a participant in a previous crime.

When the car stopped for a traffic light, approximately two miles from where the officers first observed it, the officers alighted from their car, approached opposite sides of the car on foot, and identified themselves. Suddenly the passenger opened the door and began to run. As he fled, he dropped a package which was eventually identified as heroin onto the street. The officer gave chase and apprehended the individual who tried to escape. The driver gave himself up voluntarily. Both were taken to the station and booked for possession of heroin.

1. Was it reasonable for the officers to follow this car?
2. Was it reasonable for the officers to apprehend the suspect as he attempted to flee?
3. Did the officers have probable cause to arrest the suspect?
4. Did dropping the package onto the pavement by one of the suspects make a difference in the arrest?
5. Was it a legal arrest?

E. Two officers obtained a search warrant from a magistrate in their district.

The warrant directed them to look for certain distinctively marked tools taken in a burglary. Since no one answered their knock, they entered through a window which they forced open. As they began uncovering the items they were directed to find, they came across other tools having the same markings but not specifically mentioned in the warrant. They seized them too.

1. Who had to establish that probable cause to search existed?
2. Were the officers justified in a forced entry?
3. Were the officers justified in seizing the tools which were not specifically mentioned in the warrant?
4. Would these tools be admitted as evidence?
5. Suppose that the officers had also found narcotics during their search. Would it be lawful for them to seize the narcotics?

F. At 8:00 P.M. one hot July evening, Officer O'Connor was patrolling her assigned zone in an exclusive residential area when she noticed many cars parked along the street in one block and a party going on in one of the nearby houses. Officer O'Connor began checking the cars and came to one that fit the description of a burglary suspect's car reported at the morning roll-call. The color, make, and license number matched that of the car parked among those of the partygoers.

Officer O'Connor immediately notified her supervisor, who set up a stake-out of the vehicle. About twenty minutes later, the officers noticed an individual fitting the suspect's description walking down the sidewalk toward the car, pulling off his hands something long which appeared to be made of cloth. Shortly before reaching his car he discarded the items (which later proved to be a pair of stockings belonging to the victim of the residential burglary) into the gutter. They also noticed that the suspect was carrying a fur coat over his arm. As the suspect opened the door of the car under surveillance, he flung the coat into the back seat, leaned over, and placed something under the seat on the driver's side of the car.

The officers closed in and arrested the man on suspicion of burglary. At this time they searched the suspect and found several thousand dollars' worth of jewelry and rings in his pocket and observed a mink coat in the back seat of the car. They also found a gun under the front seat of the car. After they arrested the suspect, they retrieved the pair of stockings he had thrown into the gutter. They took the suspect to the station and booked him. Other officers immediately searched the neighborhood and found that a corner house had been burglarized. Other items were stacked at the front door, as if the suspect were going to return for more loot. The crime scene was searched, but no fingerprints or other evidence was found tying the suspect to the crime. Several hours later the owner of the dwelling returned home, was informed of the situation, and went to the station to identify the property recovered from the suspect as belonging to him.

The police then went to the suspect's apartment, obtained a passkey from the manager, and searched the room. They confiscated several packets of narcotics as well as three unregistered firearms. Additional charges were filed against the suspect based on this new evidence.

1. Did Officer O'Connor have probable cause to arrest the suspect?
2. Was the search of the suspect legal?
3. Was the search of the suspect reasonable?
4. What rule of search and seizure applied to the fur coat?
5. What rule of search and seizure applied to the gun?
6. Was the search of the suspect's apartment legal?
7. What evidence would be admitted in court?
8. What should the police officers have done to assure that all relevant evidence was admissible in court?

Answers

A. 1. It is an illegal search because consent was not freely given.
   2. The evidence will not be admitted in court because of the Exclusionary Rule.
B. 1. It is a legal search as he had the consent of the building manager.
   2. The evidence will be admissible in court.
C. 1. It is an illegal search despite the positive identification of the suspect by the citizen informant and the report the police had of the stolen checks. There was sufficient time to obtain a search warrant to seize the evidence. (With sufficient evidence and identification, the suspect could be charged with forgery at the drug store, but the checks seized illegally could not be introduced as evidence.)
   2. They should have gotten a search warrant.
D. 1. Yes, it was a high-crime area, late at night, and the suspects' activities were suspicious.
   2. Yes. It was a continuation of their suspicious activities. The U.S. Supreme Court said in the Terry case that "it is the duty of officers to investigate suspicious activity."
   3. Yes. Under the plain view doctrine the officer may seize any evidence that is open to view. This does not constitute a search.
   4. Yes. Prior to that time there was no probable cause for an arrest, just reasonable suspicion that something was not right and an investigation should be undertaken.
   5. Yes. There was probable cause and the suspect had contraband in possession.
E. 1. The magistrate who issued the warrant had to establish that probable cause existed based on what the police officers told him.
   2. Yes, the officers were justified in a forced entry since their knock was not answered.
   3. Yes, the officers were justified in seizing the tools not specifically mentioned in the warrant as they were similar to items which were included.
   4. Yes, the tools would be admitted as evidence.
   5. Yes, any narcotics found during the search could also be seized, as it is legal to seize contraband discovered during a search authorized by a warrant.
F. 1. Yes, roll-call information plus reasonable justification gave probable cause.
   2. Yes, it was a search incidental to a lawful arrest.
   3. Yes, it was incidental to an arrest in addition to being an instrumentality of the crime.
   4. Plain view circumstances and probable cause to believe the coat was stolen.
   5. A search of a vehicle incidental to an arrest.
   6. No, such a search is unconstitutional.
   7. The stolen items and the gun, but not the narcotics nor the unregistered guns.
   8. They should have obtained a search warrant prior to searching the suspect's apartment.

DISCUSSION QUESTIONS

1. Compare the two quotations at the beginning of this chapter. Which seems to support the Exclusionary Rule?
2. Why aren't the police given total freedom to help stop crime? Why aren't they allowed to use evidence which clearly establishes a person's guilt, no matter how they obtained this evidence?
3. What can be done if police officers know that an individual is guilty of a crime, but they have no evidence?
4. Why isn't the presence of ten officers considered intimidation when a "request" to search is made?
5. Have you ever been involved in a search and seizure situation? How was it handled?
6. From what you have learned about search and seizure, do you feel that the restrictions placed upon police officers are reasonable?
7. Why did the Court state that the search in Coolidge v. New Hampshire was not valid?

REFERENCES

Creamer, J. S. *The law of arrest, search and seizure.* Philadelphia: W. B. Saunders, 1975.

Cushman, R. E. and Cushman, R. F. *Cases in constitutional law.* (3rd ed.) New York: Appleton-Century-Crofts Educational Division, 1968.

Dowling, J. *Criminal procedure.* St. Paul: West Publishing Company, 1976.

Felknes, G. T. *Constitutional law for criminal justice.* Englewood Cliffs, N.J.: Prentice-Hall, 1978.

Ferdico, J. *Criminal procedure for the law enforcement officer.* St. Paul: West Publishing Company, 1976.

Friedelbaum, S. H. *Contemporary constitutional law.* Boston: Houghton, Mifflin, 1972.

Handbook of search and seizure. Washington, D.C.: U.S. Justice Department, U.S. Government Printing Office, 1971.

Inbau, F. E., Thompson, J. R., and Zagel, J. B. *Criminal law and its adminstration.* Mineola, N.Y.: The Foundation Press, 1974.

Kelly, A. H., and Harbison, W. *The American Constitution.* (4th ed.) New York: W. W. Norton, 1970.

Lewis, P. W. and Peoples, K. D. *The supreme court and the criminal process.* Philadelphia: W. B. Saunders, 1978.

Lockhart, W. B., Kamisar, Y. and Choper, J. H. *Constitutional rights and liberties.* (4th ed.) St. Paul: West Publishing Company, 1975.

Maddex, J. L., Jr. *Constitutional law.* St. Paul: West Publishing Company, 1974.

Mendelson, W. *The constitution and the supreme court.* (2nd ed.) New York: Dodd, Mead and Company, 1968.

Pritchett, C. H. *The American Constitution.* New York: McGraw-Hill, 1977.

Tresolini, R. J., and Shapiro, M. *American constitutional law.* (3rd ed.) New York: McMillan, 1970.

One of the ways in
which police officers
aid the criminal justice
process is by testifying
in court.

Law Enforcement and The Judicial Process

From Complaint To Disposition

15

DO YOU KNOW□ □ □

- □ What the adversary system is?
- □ What reasonable doubt is?
- □ What role police officers play in the criminal justice system?
- □ What four functions are performed by the prosecutor?
- □ What rights the accused has?
- □ What constitutes "due process"?
- □ What landmark decision resulted from the Gideon v. Wainwright case?
- □ What role is played by the defense attorney?
- □ What plea bargaining is and what purpose(s) it serves?
- □ How juvenile court differs from adult court?
- □ The significance of the Gault decision?
- □ What types of facilities other than correctional have been provided for juvenile delinquents?
- □ What the "critical stages" in the criminal justice process are?
- □ What a complaint, an information, and an indictment are?
- □ What functions are served by a preliminary hearing? A grand jury? A coroner's jury?
- □ What the discovery process is?
- □ What types of plea may be entered at the time of arraignment?
- □ How jurors are selected and what safeguards are taken to insure against bias?
- □ How the defense attorney may attempt to discredit the testimony of a police officer?

The truth, the whole truth, and nothing
but the truth.—Legal Oath
Justice is truth in action.—Disraeli (1852)

INTRODUCTION

Numerous aspects of the criminal justice process have been referred to in preceding chapters. The criminal justice system in America is a complex topic constituting a study in itself. This chapter presents only a basic overview of the major components of this system and how police officers function within it.

THE ADVERSARY SYSTEM

Our criminal justice system is based on an *adversary system*—the accuser versus the accused. The accuser must prove that the one accused is guilty.

> The adversary criminal justice system requires that the accuser prove beyond a reasonable doubt to a judge or jury that the accused is guilty of a specified crime.

The assumption is that the one accused is innocent until proof to the contrary is clearly established. Included on the side of the accuser is the citizen (or victim), the prosecutor, and the police officer. On the side of the accused is the defendant and the defense attorney. An impartial judge or jury hears both sides of the controversy and then reaches a decision as to whether the accuser has proven the accused guilty *beyond a reasonable doubt.*

> Reasonable doubt means the juror is not morally certain of the truth of the charges.

As noted by Inbau, Thompson and Zagel (1974, p.229):

It [reasonable doubt] is a term often used, probably pretty well understood, but not easily defined. It is not mere possible doubt because everything relating to human affairs and depending on moral evidence is open to some possible or imaginary doubt. It is that state of the case which, after the entire comparisons and consideration of all evidence, leaves the minds of the jurors in that condition and they cannot say they feel an abiding conviction, to a moral certainty, of the truth of the charge. The burden of proof is upon the prosecutor. All the presumptions of law independent of evidence are in favor of innocence; and every person is presumed to be innocent until he is proved guilty. If upon such proof there is reasonable doubt remaining, the accused is entitled to the benefit of it by an acquittal. For it is not sufficient to establish a probability, though a strong one arising from the doctrine of chances, that the fact charged is more likely to be true than the contrary; but the evidence must establish the truth of the fact to a reasonable and moral certainty; a certainty that convinces and directs the understanding, and satisfies the reason and judgment of those who are bound to act con-

scientiously upon it. *This we take to be proof beyond reasonable doubt; because if the law, which mostly depends upon considerations of a moral nature, should go further than this and require absolute certainty, it would exclude circumstantial evidence altogether.*

THE ROLE OF THE POLICE OFFICER

Police officers are an integral part of the criminal justice process. The criminal codes which guide police officers in enforcing laws are not a set of specific instructions, but rather are rough maps of the territory in which police officers work and assist the criminal process. Regardless of how sketchy or complete the officers' education or experience, in reality they are interpreters of the law and may function as judge and jury at the start of every case. If the case reaches the court, the court must subsequently approve or disapprove of the police officers' actions by finding the person guilty or not guilty.

For example, police officers who stop a person for speeding make a judicial decision when they give out a ticket. They might simply warn the next offender. By shooting a fleeing felon who is likely to kill someone while attempting to escape, the police officer delivers a capital penalty for a crime which may otherwise have netted probation or a prison term. When the officer brings the youngster next door home in the squad car but holds another juvenile in jail for the same offense, the police officer, in a sense, is acting as a judge, for without holding a hearing beyond listening to or ignoring the youth's protests, the officer has "sentenced" the youngster to one or more nights in detention.

Because the police officers' decisions touch so many lives, they are often considered more important than the judge in the criminal justice process. However, officers often know very little about the complex system of justice in which they play such a critical role. Countless police officers have never seen the criminal justice processes in action; often they come into court with no experience and with limited time to prepare their testimony. Police officers must be trained to fulfill their role in the criminal justice process: to assist the prosecutor, the judge, and the jury in arriving at just decisions.

> Police officers aid the criminal justice process by (1) making legal arrests, (2) legally obtaining accurate, relevant information and evidence, (3) writing complete, accurate reports, (4) identifying suspects and witnesses, and (5) providing effective, truthful testimony in court.

Errors in any of these roles may seriously damage a case or even prevent a conviction.

Equally important to fulfilling their own role is the police officers' understanding of the total system and the other key figures within this system: the prosecutor, the suspect, the defense attorney, the judge, and the jury members. As noted in Standard 1.1. of the American Bar Association Standards Relating to the Urban Police Function:

Police effectiveness in dealing with crime is often largely dependent upon the effectiveness of other agencies both within and outside of the criminal justice system. Those in the system must work together through liaison, cooperation, and constructive joint effort. This effort is vital to the effective operation of the police and the entire criminal justice system.

In today's society it is imperative that police officers become more familiar with each step of the criminal justice process so they can intelligently bring about desired results. Of critical importance is a good working relation with the prosecutor.

THE PROSECUTOR

Prosecutors are usually officials elected to exercise leadership in the criminal justice system. They may be a city attorney, county attorney, state attorney, commonwealth attorney, district attorney, or solicitor.

> Prosecutors are elected officials who serve as the public's lawyer, the determiner of law enforcement priorities, the advisor of police officers, and the preserver of civil liberties of all persons.

Prosecutors are the legal representatives of the people and the police officers. They are responsible to the people who elected them, not to any other state or local official. They determine law enforcement priorities and are the key in determining how much, how little, and what types of crimes the public will tolerate. They serve the public interest and consider the public's need to feel secure, their sense of how justice should be carried out, and the community's attitude toward certain crimes. Sometimes a case becomes so well publicized that the prosecutor is forced to "do something about it" or face defeat in the next election.

Prosecutors not only have great responsibility, they also have a varied amount of discretion. Their own experiences and biases may cause them to be selective in the cases they seek to prosecute. They may, for example, be reluctant to bring to trial cases such as minor bad checks, domestic quarrels involving assaults, or shoplifting by first offenders because they know that juries are usually reluctant to convict these defendants, especially if the offender is a housewife or mother.

In addition, prosecutors must be sensitive to the court's wishes and try to reduce the number of cases brought before it either by referring the complaint to an agency in the community for assistance or by recommending that the case be brought into a civil court or a lower criminal court.

Since prosecutors are lawyers for the public, citizens often go directly to them rather than to the police with their grievances. These cases usually involve business fraud, unfulfilled civil contracts such as default on a financial obligation, and the like. Prosecutors may have a small staff of investigators for such cases to determine if a crime has been committed or if the complainant should pursue a civil course of action.

Prosecutors are also the legal advisors for police officers; they are elected to decide what cases should be prosecuted and how. They rely heavily on the police officers' input in determining if a case should be brought to court or rejected. Often, however, misunderstanding and even ill-will may result when a prosecutor refuses a police officer's request for a complaint because of insufficient evidence or some violation of a criminal procedure such as an illegal arrest. Plea bargaining may also cause ill-will between a prosecutor and a police officer.

Since both police officers and prosecutors are striving for the same end—justice—they should be familiar with each other's problems. Police officers, for example, should understand what the prosecutor can and cannot do, which types of cases are worth prosecuting, and the need for and advantages of plea bargaining in certain situations. Prosecutors, on the other hand, should be sensitive to the police officers' objections to numerous legal technicalities and excessive paper work and should include police officers in plea bargaining when possible, or, at the least, inform them when such bargaining has occurred.

Prosecutors perform one other critical function in the criminal justice process; they are responsible for protecting the rights of *all* involved, including the suspect. In essence they have a *dual responsibility*: on the one hand they are the leader in the law enforcement community, the elected representative of the public, and the legal advisor to the police officer; on the other hand, they are expected to protect the rights of persons accused of crimes. In Berger v. United States 295, U.S. 78, 55 S.Ct. 629 (1935), Justice Sutherland defined the prosecutor's responsibility as being: "the representative not of an ordinary party to a controversy, but of a sovereignty whose obligation to govern impartially is as compelling as its obligation to govern at all; and whose interest, therefore, in a criminal prosecution is not that it shall win a case, but that justice shall be done."

☑ CHECK POINT

1. What is the adversary system?
2. How would you define *reasonable doubt*?
3. What role do police officers play in the criminal justice system?
4. What four functions are performed by prosecutors?

＊Answers

1. The adversary system places accuser against accused and requires that the accuser prove beyond a reasonable doubt to a judge or jury that the accused is guilty of a specified crime.
2. Reasonable doubt means the juror is not morally certain of the truth of the charges.
3. Police officers aid the criminal justice process by (1) making legal arrests, (2) legally obtaining accurate, relevant information and evidence, (3) writing complete, accurate reports, (4) identifying suspects and witnesses, and (5) providing effective, truthful testimony in court.
4. Prosecutors are elected officials who serve as (1) the public's lawyer, (2) the determiner of law enforcement priorities, (3) the advisor of police officers, and (4) the preserver of civil liberties for all persons.

THE SUSPECT OR DEFENDANT

Until formally accused of a crime and brought to trial, a person accused is called a *suspect*. After formal accusation and court appearance, the person is called a *defendant*.

Everyone, including a person suspected of committing crimes, has certain rights which must be protected at all stages of the criminal justice process.

> The Fourth Amendment forbids unreasonable search and seizure and requires probable cause. The Fifth Amendment guarantees due process: notice of a hearing, full information regarding the charges made, the opportunity to present evidence before an impartial judge or jury, and the right to refrain from self-incrimination. The Sixth Amendment establishes the requirements for criminal trials including the right to speedy public trial by an impartial jury and the right to have a lawyer. The Eighth Amendment forbids excessive bail and implies the right to such bail in most instances.

Suspects have all the rights set forth in the Bill of Rights. They may waive these rights, but if they do so, the waiver should be in writing because proof of the waiver is up to the police officer or the prosecution. The police officer must be able to show that all rights have been respected and that all required procedures have been complied with.

Since our system uses an adversary process to seek out basic truths, the right to counsel is fundamental. However, in 1975 in Faretta v. California, 422 U.S. 806, 95 S. Ct. 2525, 45 L. Ed. 2d 562, the United States Supreme Court held that the Sixth Amendment guarantees self-representation in a criminal case, but before the court can allow such self-representation, defendants must intelligently and knowingly waive their right to the assistance of counsel when they formulate and conduct their own defense.

A record is usually made stating that counsel is available to the defendant to prevent subsequent claims of improper waiver of counsel or lack of counsel. It has often been said, however, that "one who defends himself has a fool for a client." The purpose of the right to counsel is to protect the accused from a conviction which may result from ignorance of legal and constitutional rights. Although defendants in all criminal cases have basic constitutional rights, often they do not know how to protect them. The right to counsel is indispensable to their understanding of their other rights under the Constitution.

Although the criminal justice system is sometimes criticized when a defendant is found "not guilty" because of a technicality, such criticism is unfounded. Even though a person confesses to a hideous crime, if he was not first told of his rights and allowed to have a lawyer present during questioning, his confession should not be considered legal. As noted by the U.S. Supreme Court in Escobedo v. Illinois, 378 U.S. 478, 84 S.Ct. 1758 (1964):

No system of criminal justice can or should survive if it comes to depend for its continued effectiveness on the citizens' abdication through unawareness of their constitutional rights. No system worth preserving should have to fear that if an accused is permitted to consult with a lawyer, he will become aware of and exercise these rights. If the exercise of constitutional rights will thwart the effectiveness of a system of law enforcement, then there is something very wrong with that system.

During the past several decades, many landmark decisions of the U.S. Supreme Court have extended the rights of individuals accused of a crime to have counsel at government expense if they cannot afford to hire their own lawyer.

In Powell v. Alabama, 287 U.S. 45, 53 S.Ct. 55 (1932) the U.S. Supreme Court ruled that in a capital case, where the defendants are indigent (without money, poor) and are incapable of presenting their own defense, the court must assign them counsel as part of the due process of the law.

Between 1932 and 1963 the U.S. Supreme Court heard a variety of "right to counsel" cases. The U.S. Supreme Court ruled in Johnson v. Zerbst, 304 U.S. 458, 58 S.Ct. 1019, 82 L.Ed. 1461 (1938) that indigent defendants charged with a federal crime had the right to be furnished with counsel. However, this case said nothing about indigents who appeared in state courts.

In Betts v. Brady, 316 U.S. 455, 62 S.Ct. 1252 (1942), the U.S. Supreme Court ruled that an indigent charged in a state court had no right to appointed counsel unless charged with a capital crime. Nineteen years later Clarence Gideon, a habitual criminal, was arrested in Florida for breaking and entering a pool room. Gideon claimed to be an indigent and asked for appointed counsel. The court refused on the grounds that Florida statutes provide for appointment of counsel only in capital cases. Gideon made his request based on the Betts case, but he was turned down and subsequently sentenced to the state prison.

Gideon, in a handwritten petition, took his case to the Supreme Court. In the famous Gideon v. Wainwright case, 372 U.S. 335, 83 S.Ct. 792 (1963), the U.S. Supreme Court overruled Betts v. Brady and unanimously held that state courts must appoint counsel for indigent defendants in noncapital as well as capital cases.

> Gideon v. Wainwright established the court's responsibility for providing counsel for any indigent person charged with a felony.

Expanding on the "fairness" doctrine in 1972 in the Argersinger v. Hamlin case, 407 U.S. 25, 92 S.Ct. 2006 (1972), the U.S. Supreme Court ruled that all defendants in court who face the possibility of a jail sentence are entitled to legal counsel, and that if the accused could not afford counsel, the state must provide one.

THE DEFENSE ATTORNEY

Lawyers who undertake to represent an accused have the same duties and obligations whether they are privately retained, serving as a legal aid in the system, or appointed by the court. They interview the client about their offenses, whether they are aware of any witnesses who might assist them, and whether they have given a confession. Lawyers investigate the circumstances of the case and explore facts relevant to the guilt or innocence of their clients. They try to uncover evidence for their clients' defense and organize the case to present in court.

> The defense attorney represents the accused in court.

Defense attorneys bring their clients professional objectivity as experts in criminal procedure. Their first goal is to establish a relationship of confidence and trust. They emphasize the confidential client-lawyer relationship and explain to the accused precisely what the complaint contains, what it means, and what the consequences are. They provide technical and professional skills in analyzing the facts of the case and explaining to their clients how a judge or a jury might view the case. They determine how the law affects their client and what steps they must take to protect their clients' legal rights.

Defense attorneys also explain to their clients the decisions they as suspects must make, for example, whether to plea bargain the case, what plea to enter, whether to waive a preliminary hearing or a jury trial, and whether to testify in their own behalf. Such decisions of the accused should be fully discussed with the lawyer.

Defense attorneys, too, have several decisions: what jurors to accept, what trial motions to make, and whether or how to conduct cross-examinations. All strategies and tactical decisions are the exclusive responsibilities of the defense lawyers, but only after consultation with their clients.

☑ CHECK POINT

1. What rights does the accused have?
2. What constitutes "due process"?
3. What landmark decision resulted from Gideon v. Wainwright?
4. What role is played by defense attorneys?

* Answers

1. The accused has the right to having probable cause established, due process, a speedy public trial by an impartial jury, a lawyer, and, in most instances, bail.
2. Due process includes notice of a hearing, full information regarding the charges made, the opportunity to present evidence before an impartial judge or jury, and the right to refrain from self-incrimination.
3. Gideon v. Wainwright established the court's responsibility for providing counsel for any indigent person charged with a felony.
4. The defense attorney represents the accused in court.

DIVERTING A CASE

Before the client and his attorney go to court, the defense attorney may explore the possibility of diverting the case from the criminal justice system by using a community agency if the circumstances warrant it; for example, in cases of mental incompetence the attorney may seek to divert the case to a mental institution.

> A case may be diverted from the criminal justice system before it comes to trial.

The National Advisory Commission on Criminal Justice Standards and Goals (Courts, 1975, p. 27) defines diversion as "halting or suspending, before conviction, formal criminal proceedings against a person on a condition or assumption that he will do something in return." This definition is an expansion of an earlier Commission statement (Corrections, 1973, p. 94):

Diversion provides society with the opportunity to begin the reordering of the justice system, by redistributing resources to achieve justice and correctional goals . . . to develop truly effective prevention, justice, control, and social restoration programs. . . . Perhaps the biggest contribution that diversion can make during the next decade is to make society more conscious and sensitive to the deficiencies in the justice system, and hence, to force radical changes within the system so that appropriate offenders are successfully diverted from the system while others are provided with programs within the system that offer social restoration instead of criminal condemnation.

PLEA BARGAINING

The client and defense lawyer may also attempt to plea bargain their case.

> Plea bargaining is a compromise between defense and prosecution which prearranges the plea and the sentence, conserving manpower and expense.

Plea bargaining is legal negotiation between the prosecutor and the defense lawyer or the client to reach an agreement that avoids a court trial. The prosecutor is seeking a conviction without going through the formality of a court trial. The defense is looking for some concessions by the prosecutor to reduce the punishment for the defendant.

Basically, plea bargaining involves promises and compromises. From the prosecutor it may mean that if a series of charges are filed, the defendant would only be charged with one; the other charges would be dismissed. Or it might mean that the prosecutor would reduce a charge if only one charge was filed; for example, a charge of burglary might be reduced to breaking and entering, which carries a lesser penalty.

For the defendant and the defense attorney, it may mean a guilty plea for the preceding concessions. Or it may mean the defendant pleads guilty to the charges as stated, provided he be placed on probation rather than being sent to a correctional institution.

Prosecutors are always in the stronger bargaining position because they have filed the charge(s) and have all the evidence. The only thing the defendants have with which to bargain is that their guilty plea can save the court both time and money. According to some, however, this explanation is often not the true reason underlying plea bargaining. For example, Rosett and Cressey (1976, pp. 110-111) state:

> *Attributing negotiated pleas to overwork is a political explanation of court practice. Voicing this explanation neutralizes important and powerful interest groups who say they want adversary procedures that would maximize the amount of punishment meted out to criminals. If the explanation is accepted, prosecutors, can go about their plea-arranging ways of doing justice without encountering too much damning criticism from community leaders who want them to be tough on criminals. They avoid losing elections or being fired.*
>
> *The successful prosecutor blurs the competing conceptions of what his mission should be. One way to do this is to reduce adversariness in the interests of justice while at the same time arguing—loudly, clearly and publicly—that he engages in informal plea bargaining practices because his office is overworked, despite careful management.*

Although plea bargaining has been in existence for many years, only recently have the courts openly accepted it, often on the basis that without plea bargaining the number of full trials would increase tremendously, requiring enormous amounts of money and manpower. Recently the court has expanded the plea bargaining powers of prosecutors. In Bordenkircher v. Hayes, 434 U.S. 357 98 S. Ct. 663 (1978) the U.S. Supreme Court told prosecutors that they may threaten criminal defendants with more serious charges in attempts to obtain guilty pleas. According to the Associated Press (1978, p. 4D):

> *The plea-bargaining ruling came in a test case from Kentucky. Paul Lewis Hayes was indicted by a Fayette County grand jury in 1973 for forging an $88.30 check. Under Kentucky law, he could have been sentenced to two to 10 years in prison if convicted.*
>
> *In pretrial meetings with a county prosecutor, Hayes and his lawyer were told the prosecution would recommend a five-year sentence if Hayes pleaded guilty, making a trial unnecessary.*
>
> *Such bargains are not uncommon and are—in the words of earlier high court decisions—"important components of this country's criminal justice system" that "can benefit all concerned" when properly administered.*
>
> *But the county prosecutor in Hayes's case introduced a new weapon, saying that if Hayes, who had two previous felony convictions, refused to plead guilty a new indictment would be sought. Conviction on a habitual-offender charge would bring a life prison term, Hayes was told.*
>
> *Hayes stuck to his innocent plea, was reindicted, convicted and sentenced to life. He is not eligible for parole until he serves 15 years.*
>
> *Overturning a ruling by the Sixth U.S. Circuit Court of Appeals that the prosecutor's "reverse plea-bargaining" violated Hayes's due-process rights, the court said yesterday the prosecutors must have broad discretionary powers.*

Although plea bargaining may seem inconsistent with our legal system, such bargains are made a part of the written record, including the terms of the agreement, the disposition, and an explanation of why a negotiated disposition was appropriate in each case.

A hazard of the plea bargaining system is that it may cause police officers to feel isolated. Throughout the criminal procedures system police officers are valued; the prosecutor, the complainants, the witnesses, and society depend upon them. But when it comes to plea bargaining sessions, they are left out. Often officers will inquire about the disposition of a case of vital interest to them only to find that it has been disposed of in plea bargaining. If officers are to be part of the total system, they should have some input into the disposition of the cases or, at the least, be informed of the disposition. As criminals are placed back into society, the police officers' problems in dealing with crime grow. If police officers are to deal with these problems, they should be consulted.

☑. CHECK POINT

1. What is meant when it is said a case has been diverted?
2. What is plea bargaining and what purpose(s) does it serve?

*Answers

1. A case may be diverted from the criminal justice system before it comes to trial; that is, it may be referred to a community agency for handling.
2. Plea bargaining is a compromise between defense and prosecution which pre-arranges the plea and the sentence, conserving manpower and expense.

JUVENILE LAWS AND COURTS

Laws relating to juvenile courts attempt to secure care and guidance for each minor under the jurisdiction of the court, preferably in the minor's own home. The laws seek to protect the spiritual, emotional, mental, and physical welfare of the minor as well as the best interests of the state. Laws related to juveniles attempt to preserve and strengthen family ties whenever possible, removing minors from parental custody only when the minor's welfare or safety and/or protection of the public cannot be adequately safeguarded without such removal. When minors are removed from their own families, the courts seek to provide them with custody, care, and discipline as nearly equivalent as possible to that usually given by competent parents.

Juvenile court also has jurisdiction over neglected and dependent children who may suffer from abuse, malnutrition, unsanitary conditions in the home, or who may have been abandoned by their parents. The court also has jurisdiction over those persons who encourage, cause, or contribute to a child's delinquency. Because of its scope and clientele, the laws relating to juveniles are frequently liberally construed.

Juveniles are subjected to a conglomerate of laws and restraints which do not apply to adults. For example, juveniles are frequently arrested for liquor law violations, curfew violations, absenting from home, truancy, smoking, suspicion, and incorrigibility (these are called status offenses). The courts in which such offenses are judged differ greatly from adult courts.

Juvenile courts are informal, private, nonadversary systems which stress rehabilitation rather than punishment of youth.

Juvenile courts are more concerned with rehabilitation of the juvenile than with punishment. These courts are informal, private, and often do not follow formal judiciary procedures. Although adult courts are based on the adversary system, juvenile courts, in contrast, are nonadversary systems, even though they do have the authority of confinement.

The court may counsel children, their parents, or guardians, or place them under the supervision of a probation officer or other suitable person in their own homes under conditions prescribed by the court. These conditions might include rules for their conduct and/or that of their parents or guardian designed for the physical, mental, and moral well-being of the children.

When it is in the child's best interests, the court can transfer legal custody of the child. It may order the child placed in a foster home or a child-placing agency, committed to a youth conservation commission, transferred to a county welfare agency, or placed in a special facility if the child requires special treatment and care for physical or mental health. As noted by Trojanowicz (1978), diversion, a popular method of solving juvenile problems in recent times, shows great promise of success.

More serious offenders have been committed to mental institutions, reformatories, prisons, and county and state schools for delinquents. Some cities such as New York and Chicago have set up youth courts which are adult courts using the philosophy of juvenile courts. These youth courts usually confine their hearings to misdemeanors. When a juvenile has committed a series of serious crimes, juvenile courts have the legal power to adjudicate (judge) anyone under their jurisdiction as an adult. The juvenile is then charged and required to appear in an adult court.

The philosophy of juvenile court is that ideally children be kept in their homes pending a hearing. If detention is required for their own welfare or the public safety, it must not be in jails or police stations but in temporary quarters such as boarding homes, protective agency homes, or specially constructed detention homes. The realization of these ideals of the juvenile court system, even in some of the largest United States cities, is far from complete. In many small towns and rural districts no such facilities exist. Although juvenile court acts as the "protector of the child," children are still subjected to adverse publicity, criminal procedure, jail detention, and ineffective treatment because of the lack of proper facilities.

One of the most important aspects of the juvenile justice system is the initial contact with the law. Trojanowicz (1978, pp.175-176) feels that:

> The intake and screening process is an important aspect of the juvenile justice system. When used properly, it can effectively curtail or interrupt much delinquent behavior before it becomes serious. The intake process can also stimulate community agencies to help parents to better understand their children's behavior and the measures needed to prevent further delinquent acts.

> If the child is released at intake and no further processing takes place, there should still be a follow-up after any referral to a community agency by either the police or the intake unit. Follow-up facilitates not only the rendering of services to the child, but also promotes closer cooperation between the agencies involved.

Carey, et. al. (1967, p.26) have diagrammed the decision points in the handling of juveniles:

Figure 15-1.

Decision Points in Probation Handling of Juveniles

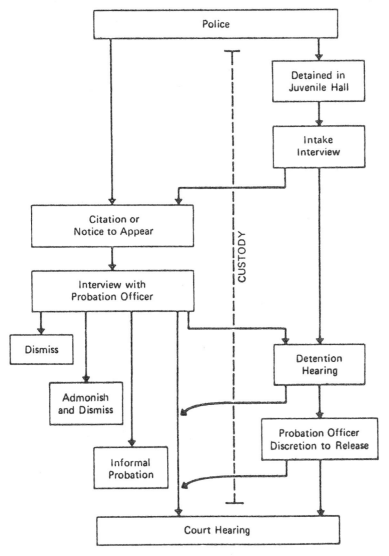

From James T. Carey, Joel Goldfarb, Michael J. Rowe, and Joseph D. Lohman, *The Handling of Juveniles from Offense to Disposition*, U.S. Department of Health, Education, and Welfare (Washington, D.C.: Government Printing Office, 1967), p. 26.

In spite of what appears to be an effective system, the informality of juvenile courts and its nonadversary structure does not always result in justice for juvenile delinquents or in protection of their civil rights.

The Gault case 387, U.S. 1, 87 S. Ct. 1428, 18L. Ed, 2d 527 (1967), which resulted in the release of thousands of juveniles from correctional institutions around the country, provides an example of how a juvenile's individual rights can be violated.

Gerald Gault was fifteen years old and on probation when he was taken into custody for allegedly making obscene phone calls to a neighbor. At 10:00 A.M. when Gerald was picked up at home, his mother and father were working. No notice was left at the home that Gerald was being taken into custody nor were any steps taken to notify his parents. Mrs. Gault arrived home about 6:00 P.M. to find Gerald missing. An older brother accidentally discovered that Gerald had been taken into custody.

Mrs. Gault went to the detention home, and the probation officer told her why Gerald was there and that a hearing would be held the next day, June 9. On June 9 the officer filed a petition with the juvenile court making only general allegations of "delinquency." No particular facts of Gerald's behavior were stated.

The hearing was held in the judge's chambers. The complaining witness was not present, no one was sworn in, no attorney was present, and no transcript of the proceedings was made. At the hearing Gerald admitted to making a less obnoxious part of the phone call in question. At the conclusion of the hearing, the judge said he would take the matter under advisement.

Gerald was returned to the detention home for another two days and then released. After the release Mrs. Gault was informed by note from the probation officer that on June 15 further hearings would be held on Gerald's delinquency. The June 15 hearing was also without benefit of complaining witnesses, sworn testimony, transcript, or counsel. The probation officer made a referral report which listed the charge as Lewd Phone Calls and filed it with the court, but it was not made available to Gerald or his parents. At the conclusion of the hearing, the judge committed Gerald as a juvenile delinquent to the State Industrial School until age 21. Gerald, only fifteen years old at the time, received a six-year sentence for an action which an adult found guilty of committing would receive a fine or a two-month imprisonment.

In a historic decision, the United States Supreme Court overruled Gerald's conviction on the grounds that:

—Neither Gerald or his parents had notice of the specific charges against him.

—No counsel was offered or provided to Gerald.

—No witnesses were present, thus denying Gerald the right of cross-examination and confrontation.

—No warning of Gerald's privilege against self-incrimination was given to him, thus no waiver of that right took place.

The Gault decision requires that the due process clause of the Fourteenth Amendment applies to proceedings in state juvenile courts.

Justice Fortas delivered the opinion of the court:

Where a person, infant or adult, can be seized by the State, charged and convicted for violating a state criminal law, and then ordered by the State to be confined for six years, I think the Constitution requires that he be tried in accordance with the guar-

antees of all the provisions of the Bill of Rights made applicable to the States by the Fourteenth Amendment. Undoubtedly this would be true of an adult defendant, and it would be a plain denial of equal protection of the laws—an invidious discrimination—to hold that others subject to heavier punishments could, because they are children, be denied these same constitutional safeguards. I consequently agree with the Court that the Arizona law as applied here denied to the parents and their son the right of notice, right to counsel, right against self-incrimination, and right to confront the witnesses against young Gault. Appellants are entitled to these rights, not because "fairness, impartiality and orderliness—in short, the essentials of due process"— require them and not because they are "the procedural rules which have been fashioned from the generality of due process," but because they are specifically and unequivocally granted by provisions of the Fifth and Sixth Amendments which the Fourteenth Amendment makes applicable to the States.

It is clear that juveniles are to be afforded all of the same rights and privileges as adults in the criminal process. The logical implications of the Gault decision require safeguards in the prehearing stage as well as use of the Miranda warning for juveniles, whether at the station house, in the squad car, or on a street corner.

NEEDED FACILITIES FOR JUVENILE CUSTODY

The disposition of juveniles and the problem of the juvenile can be partially gauged by the number of facilities existing in the United States to care for "wayward" youth.

> Facilities other than punitive correctional institutions for juveniles include reception and diagnostic centers; detention centers; training schools; shelters; ranches, forestry camps, and farms; group homes; and halfway houses.

Reception and diagnostic centers screen juvenile court commitments and assign them to appropriate treatment facilities.

Detention centers provide temporary care in a physically restrictive environment for juveniles in custody pending court disposition and often for juveniles who have been adjudicated delinquent or are awaiting return to another jurisdiction.

Training schools provide strict confinement and instruction in vocational skills. They serve delinquent juveniles committed to it by juvenile courts or placed in it by an agency with such authority.

Shelters provide temporary care similar to that of a detention center but in a physically unrestrictive environment.

Ranches, forestry camps, and farms are residential treatment facilities for juveniles who do not require strict confinement such as a training school. These ranches, camps, and farms allow juveniles greater contact with members of the community.

Group homes are residences which allow juveniles extensive contact with the community through jobs and schools. Seldom are juveniles placed in group homes on probation or aftercare/parole.

Halfway houses provide nonrestrictive residential group living where fifty percent or more of the juveniles are on probation or aftercare/parole. The juveniles are allowed extensive community contact through jobs and schools.

According to the United States Department of Justice (*Children in custody*, 1975, p. 2), in 1973 the United States operated 974 public juvenile detention and correctional facilities—367 operated under the state, 427 by local governments. Unfortunately, almost half of the correctional facilities were detention centers; shelters and halfway houses were few:

319 detention centers	59 halfway houses
187 training schools	19 shelters
103 ranches, forestry camps, and farms	17 reception and diagnostic centers
90 group homes	

Given the number of juvenile delinquents in need of facilities, the above listing shows the inadequacy of present provisions. In addition to providing facilities for juveniles who have already become delinquent, many communities are attempting to meet the problem of juvenile delinquency by programs which stress prevention rather than rehabilitation, for example police-school liaison programs as discussed earlier.

☑ CHECK POINT

1. How does juvenile court differ from adult court?
2. What landmark decision was handed down in the Gault case?
3. What types of facilities, other than correctional, have been provided for juvenile delinquents?

*Answers

1. Juvenile courts are informal, private, nonadversary systems which stress rehabilitation rather than punishment of youth.
2. The Gault decision requires that the due process clause of the Fourteenth Amendment applies to proceedings in state juvenile courts.
3. Facilities other than punitive correctional institutions for juveniles include reception and diagnostic centers; detention centers; training schools; shelters; ranches, forestry camps and farms; group homes; and halfway houses.

CRITICAL STAGES IN THE CRIMINAL JUSTICE SYSTEM

> The criminal justice system consists of several critical stages: the complaint or charge, the arrest, booking, preliminary hearing, grand jury hearing, the arraignment, and the trial.

The following diagram illustrates the complexity of the criminal justice system. Each component of the diagram will be explained in the following pages.

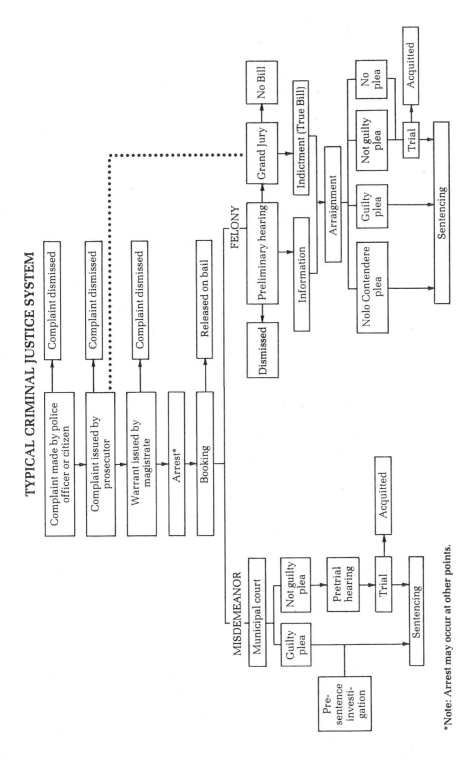

Figure 15-2. Diagram of the criminal justice system.

The Complaint or Charge

Usually the criminal justice process begins when a police officer or a citizen approaches the prosecutor to obtain a *complaint.*

A *complaint* is a legal document drawn up by a prosecutor which specifies the alleged crime and the supporting facts providing probable cause.

Figure 15-3.   Sample Complaint.

FORM 5071 Miller-Davis Co.   Complaint-Warrant for Misdemeanor

CP FORM 2.02 S. F.

STATE OF ANYWHERE

COUNTY OF __Anywhere__

_____, Plaintiff,

vs.

__Harry Megerbaum_____, Defendant.

COUNTY COURT

COMPLAINT-WARRANT
FOR
MISDEMEANOR

County Court File No.__53491___

County Attorney File No.__78-610___

_____Attorney File No._____

COMPLAINT

The Complainant being duly sworn, makes complaint to the above-named Court and states that there is probable cause to believe that the above-named Defendant committed the offense described below. The Complainant states that the following facts establish PROBABLE CAUSE:

Your complainant states that he is an Anytown police officer and while working off-duty as security at the Lyndale Grill on 31st and Lyndale within the city of Anytown, he was talking to several persons who were involved in an altercation when a person known to him as Henry Megerbaum came out of the restaurant and began to yell profanities at your complainant. Your complainant observed Megerbaum go from the restaurant to a vehicle which was parked partly on the sidewalk and partly in the restaurant parking lot. Your complainant observed Megerbaum squeal his tires as he left the parking lot and take a left turn onto Lyndale Ave. driving northbound in the southbound driving lane for a distance of three to four car lengths and continued to yell profanities at your complainant. Your complainant also observed a vehicle heading southbound on Lyndale Ave. take evasive action to avoid striking the Megerbaum vehicle.

The above-facts constitute the Complainants basis for believing that the above-named Defendant, on the __1st__ day of __May_____, 19_78_ at __Lyndale and 31st St.____

(location)

in the above-named County, committed the following described

OFFENSE

Charge: __Driving over center line_____

In violation of Section:__474.180___

Based upon the foregoing, complainant states that on the 1st day of May, 1978, within the corporate limits of the city of Anywhere, being then and there the driver of a certain motor vehicle did then and there drive and operate the aforesaid vehicle in a northernly direction on Lyndale Ave. just south of the intersection of Lyndale with 31st St. on a roadway divided by a center line, did drive said vehicle in a northernly direction on the southbound driving lane.

THEREFORE, Complainant requests that said Defendant, subject to bail or conditions of release where applicable.

(1) be arrested or that other lawful steps be taken to obtain Defendants appearance in court; or

(2) be detained, if already in custody, pending further proceedings;

and that said Defendant otherwise be dealt with according to law.

Complainant_____

(Signature of Complainant)

Being duly authorized to prosecute the offense charged, I hereby approve this Complaint.

_____

(Prosecuting Attorney)

Katherine Raze, Assistant City Attorney, 1700-A Government Center

Prosecuting Attorney Name;   Title: Address: Telephone No.

Before making a decision the prosecutor will need answers to numerous questions such as: What is the offense? Who is the suspect? What is the suspect's age? Sex? Does the suspect have a criminal record? Have a series of offenses been committed? What is the evidence? Are the elements of the crime present? Was the evidence obtained legally? Are there witnesses? Will they be cooperative? Has the suspect been arrested? Have the suspect's rights been protected?

If the facts convince the prosecutor that a crime has been committed and adequate probable cause exists that the suspect accused of the offense is

Figure 15-3. Sample Complaint Continued.

FINDING OF PROBABLE CAUSE

From the above sworn facts, and any supporting affidavits or supplemental sworn testimony, I, the Issuing Officer, have determined that probable cause exists to support, subject to bail or conditions of release where applicable, Defendant's arrest or other lawful steps to be taken to obtain Defendants appearance in Court, or detention, if already in custody, pending further proceedings. The Defendant is therefore charged with the above-stated offense.

WARRANT

TO: The Sheriff of the above-named County, or any other person authorized by law to execute this Warrant.

NOW, THEREFORE, in the name of the State of Anywhere, I hereby order that the above-named Defendant be apprehended and arrested without delay and brought promptly before the above-named Court (if in session, and if not before a Judge or Judicial Officer of such Court without unnecessary delay, and in any event not later than 36 hours after the arrest or as soon thereafter as such Judge or Judicial Officer is available) to be dealt with according to law.

TO BE COMPLETED AND SIGNED BY ISSUING OFFICER IF APPLICABLE

As the offense stated is a misdemeanor punishable by incarceration and as the following exigent circumstances exist:

I hereby direct that this warrant may be executed at any time of the day or night and on Sundays or legal holidays.

David Miller
*Issuing Officer

Conditions of Release:

Amount of Bail: _____

This Complaint-Warrant was sworn to, subscribed before, and issued by the undersigned authorized Issuing Officer this __4th__ day of __May__, 19__78__.

David Miller
*Issuing Officer Signature
Print Name __David Miller__
Title __Judge, 1st Division, Anytown__

Sworn testimony has been given before the Issuing Officer by the following witnesses:

RETURN OF SERVICE
STATE OF ANYWHERE
COUNTY OF Anyplace
I HEREBY CERTIFY and return, that I have served a copy of this COMPLAINT – WARRANT upon the defendant herein named.
Dated this 5th day of May, 19 78
Deputy Sheriff Joseph Ryan
(Person Authorized by Law to Make Service)

guilty, the prosecutor will draw up a legal form specifying the facts in the case.

If, on the other hand, the prosecutor feels insufficient evidence is presented by a police officer or a citizen, he will refuse to issue a formal accusation (complaint) against the suspect. If the suspect is in custody, he will order his release.

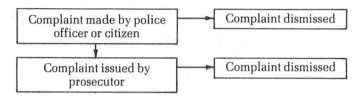

The formal complaint, which is also called the *charge,* contains all necessary evidence and facts to enable a magistrate to make an independent determination that probable cause exists for believing the offense has been committed by the accused.

The Warrant

The police officer or citizen then presents the complaint to a magistrate and, in his presence, swears to the accuracy of the content of the complaint and signs a statement to that effect. If the magistrate, after reading the complaint drawn up by the prosecuting attorney, concurs with the charge, he orders an arrest warrant (based on the probable cause established in the complaint) containing the substance of the complaint to be issued. If he does not concur, he dismisses the complaint.

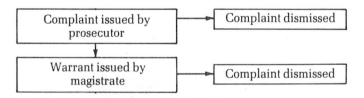

An arrest warrant directs an officer to bring the suspect before the magistrate.

The warrant is usually directed to the sheriff or constables of a county or to all police officers of the municipality within the court's jurisdiction. The officer specified then locates the suspect and arrests him if he is not already in custody. The officer may execute the warrant in any part of the county where it is issued or in any part of the state.

The Arrest

Requirements for a legal arrest have been discussed. When making the arrest, officers must inform the suspect that they are acting upon the authority of the warrant. The suspect is entitled to see it. If the officers do not have the warrant in their possession, they must show it to the suspect as soon as possible.

The arrest may occur at other points within the criminal justice process. In a misdemeanor case, it may have occurred without a complaint or warrant, provided the crime was committed in the presence of the arresting officer. Or, as will be discussed later, the prosecutor may choose to present the case to a grand jury for indictment prior to arresting a suspect.

The Booking

After a suspect is taken into custody, he is "booked" at the police station. The suspect is formally put into the police records system by the booking officer who records on the "booking" sheet the suspect's name, date, time of arrest, charge, physical description, and physical characteristics. The suspect is photographed and fingerprinted. The prints are placed on file with the FBI in Washington, D.C., and the suspect has what is known as a Police Arrest Record.

Bail and Writ of Habeas Corpus

One of the accused's rights is the right to be released from custody. Not only is this essential to his immediate freedom, but it is in keeping with the premise that a person is innocent until proven guilty. After the formal booking process is completed, the suspect is entitled to be released on bail or his own personal recognizance (R.P.R.'d) if the crime is a misdemeanor, or released on a Writ of Habeas Corpus and/or bond if the crime is a felony.

The amount of bail for each misdemeanor is determined by the judges of the municipal courts. They decide how much bail (money) is reasonable as a deposit to bring the defendant into court if he is released. However, some statutes allow a judge to set a schedule for the amount of bail required for specific offenses such as violating municipal ordinances on shoplifiting, driving under the influence of alcohol, and other violations.

In most cases the judge will set bail when the prisoner comes before the court. The elapsed time between incarceration (jailing) of a suspect and his being brought to court to answer to the charge(s) is determined either by court policy or dictated by statutory law. Therefore, a great variance often exists between jurisdictions. The Sixth Amendment guarantees a suspect a speedy trial; therefore, following an arrest, the officer must take the suspect before a magistrate without unreasonable delay. However, because some court systems do not provide round-the-clock magistrates, courts have ruled that as soon as practicable is sufficient to satisfy the law. Unreasonable delays could jeopardize a case and free a person who might otherwise be found guilty of committing a crime.

Some prisoners are discharged or released on their own personal recognizance (R.P.R.'d), meaning they are responsible for their own behavior and for appearing at their trial. This usually occurs only when the violation is minor and the suspect is in good standing in the community (for example has a family and/or steady employment) and is very likely to appear for the court appearance.

Figure 15-4.   Sample Bail Schedule

JAIL SECTION—COUNTY BAIL SCHEDULE

TRAFFIC

$100.00
DAS-DAR
DWI
UNLAWFUL ACTS—DL
   Violation instruction permit
   Fail to display DL
   Display suspended/revoked DL
   Loan DL to another
   Display DL of another
   Fail to surrender DL
   Alter/Counterfeit DL
   Violate restricted DL
   Allow prohibited person to drive
   No chauffer's license
   No Minnesota DL
   No DL in possession (NBR)
RECKLESS DRIVING
LEAVE THE SCENE OF ACCIDENT
TRUCKS OVERWEIGHT

$50.00
CARELESS DRIVING
OPEN BOTTLE

$25.00
SPEED
AUTO SEMAPHORE
STOP SIGN
PARKING OFFENSES
OBSTRUCT TRAFFIC
FAULTY EQUIPMENT
EXPIRED DL
IMPROPER ADDRESS ON DL
NO MOTORCYCLE ENDORSEMENT
HELMET REQUIRED
HITCHHIKING
OVER CENTER LINE
IMPROPER LANE CHANGE
ILLEGAL TURN
WRONG WAY-ONE WAY
FAIL TO YIELD
LITTERING
JAYWALKING

NOTE
1. *THERE IS NO BAIL ON FELONIES OR*
   GROSS MISDEMEANORS
2. When DWI and careless driving are
   charged together, combined bail is $100.00
3. On traffic warrants, bail generally follows
   the above schedule
4. On traffic warrants, fines are specified at
   the top of the warrant *if applicable.*
   (See fine forfeit procedure)

MISCELLANEOUS

$200.00
SIMPLE ASSAULT
UNLAWFUL ASSEMBLY (RIOT
   SITUATION)

$100.00
PRESENT FALSE IDENTIFICATION
"B" GIRLS
LURKING
TAMPERING
EXHIBIT OBSCENE MATERIAL
PANDERING
INDECENT CONDUCT (EXPOSING)
DISORDERLY HOUSE (OPERATE)
FALSE STATEMENT FOR RELIEF
GAMBLING
SELL FIREWORKS
WEAPONS ORDINANCE
NON-SUPPORT (MUNICIPAL WARRANT)
PETIT THEFT
DAMAGE TO PROPERTY
   (MISDEMEANOR)
POSSESSION INJECTION EQUIPMENT
LEGEND DRUG LAW
OBSTRUCT LEGAL PROCESS/
   ARREST
IMPERSONATE POLICE OFFICER
DEFRAUD INNKEEPER
ANONYMOUS/OBSCENE PHONE CALL
SELL LIQUOR WITHOUT A LICENSE
ESCAPE
INTERFERE WITH RELIGIOUS SERVICE
RECEIVE STOLEN PROPERTY
   (MISDEMEANOR)
SIMPLE ARSON
PEEPING
DISCHARGE FIREARM IN CITY

$50.00
LIQUOR REGULATIONS
   Allow minor purchase liquor/beer
   Allow minor in bar
   Furnish beer to minor
FALSE HOTEL REGISTRATION

$25.00
MINOR CONSUME/POSSESS
MINOR PURCHASE LIQUOR/BEER
MINOR IN BAR
CONSUME IN PUBLIC
DISORDERLY HOUSE (PRESENCE AT)
FAIL TO PAY CAB FARE
BREACH OF PEACE
PUBLIC NUISANCE
VAGRANCY
TRESPASSING
DISCHARGE FIREWORKS
THEFT OF GASOLINE (SIPHONING)
ILLEGAL USE OF SHORTWAVE RADIO
PARTY ORDINANCE
DISORDERLY CONDUCT
UNLAWFUL ASSEMBLY

Suspects may also post cash or some type of security to guarantee their appearance in court. If they do not have the money, they may have a bail bondsman post bond for them for a fee.

Periodically a person in jail may be released on a *Writ of Habeas Corpus* —a legal court order literally meaning "bring forth the body you have"— which commands a person holding a prisoner to bring him forth immediately.

Figure 15-5. Sample Writ of Habeas Corpus.

State of Anywhere, County of Anywhere

DISTRICT COURT, Fourth Judicial District

STATE OF ANYWHERE, To Joseph O'Brian, Warden, Anywhere State Prison

You are hereby commanded to have the body of Fred C. Smythe *by you imprisoned and detained, as it is said, together with the time and cause of said imprisonment and detention, by whatsoever name the said* Fred C. Smythe *shall be called or charged, before* Honorable Harold Milcom *the judge of the court above named at* Room 526 *in the Court House in the* City *of* Anytown *in said County and State* of Anywhere

to do and receive what shall then and there be considered concerning the said Fred C. Smythe *: and have you then and there this writ.*

WITNESS, The Honorable Harold Milcom *judge of said Court and the seal thereof at* AnyCity, *in said County and State this* 1st *day of* May *19*78

Clerk

DISTRICT COURT, Fourth *Judicial District*

County of Anywhere

STATE OF ANYWHERE U.S.A. —EX REL—

Fred Smythe

AGAINST

Joseph O'Brien, Warden

Writ of Habeas Corpus

Issued May 1 *, 1978*

, Clerk

Returned May 4 *, 1978*

, Clerk

Attorney for Relator

This means of determining whether the jailing of the suspect is legal is used primarily when the justice process moves slowly and a prisoner is detained for an unreasonable length of time before the court appearance. Habeas corpus often occurs when a person is arrested without a formal arrest warrant and the follow-up police investigation is taking an unreasonable length of time. Most states have adopted rules or guidelines as to how long a person may be jailed before either being charged, released, or making an appearance in court. These rules are somewhat flexible and range from 36 to 72 hours, taking into consideration Sundays and holidays.

Up to this point in the criminal justice process, it makes little difference as to what type of crime—misdemeanor or felony—has been committed. The process is basically the same:

TYPICAL CRIMINAL JUSTICE SYSTEM

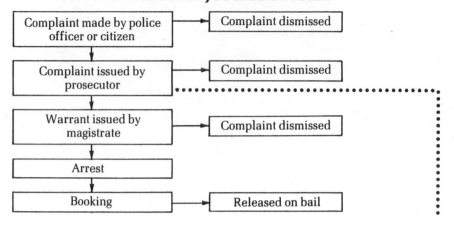

☑ CHECK POINT

1. **What are the critical stages in the criminal justice system?**
2. **What is a complaint or charge?**

*Answers

1. The critical stages in the criminal justice system include the complaint or charge, the arrest, booking, preliminary hearing, grand jury hearing, the arraignment, and the trial.
2. A complaint is a legal document drawn up by a prosecutor which specifies the alleged crime and the supporting facts providing probable cause.

Misdemeanors

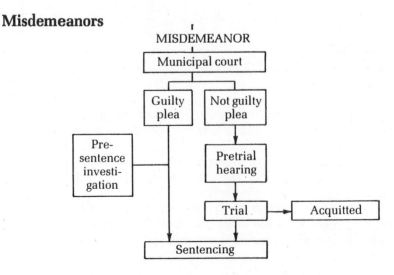

Misdemeanors are usually disposed of by ticket, tab charge, or R.P.R.'d, in which case the suspect is ordered to court. The person may plead guilty, not guilty, or have a trial, and the case is disposed of. Failure to appear results in an arrest warrant for contempt of court.

Felonies

Felony cases are more complex than misdemeanors. The complaint must be filed with the Clerk of the District or the Superior Court. Except in capital crimes, federal crimes, and those mandated by statute, the prosecutor decides whether to proceed by way of *information* or by way of *indictment.*

In a felony case the prosecutor may seek an *information* from a preliminary hearing or an *indictment* from a grand jury.

A formal written accusation, what we have thus far called the criminal complaint or charge, is also known as an information. It contains the substance of the charge against the defendant and usually is associated with a preliminary hearing. However, the United States Constitution requires an indictment by a grand jury for most crimes against federal law.

The Preliminary Hearing

The preliminary hearing is the probable cause hearing.

The magistrate first determines whether an offense has been committed and if sufficient evidence is presented to believe that the accused committed it.

If the accused is being held, it is important to both the defendant and the prosecutor to hold the hearing within a reasonable time. Most statutes and rules of criminal procedure require a preliminary hearing to be held within a "reasonable time." Some jurisdictions require a preliminary hearing to be held immediately after arrest, some within 48 to 72 hours, others within 10 to 30 days.

The preliminary hearing seeks to establish probable cause to prevent persons from being indiscriminatly brought to trial.

In a preliminary hearing, the defendant is present, with or without his counsel, and has a right to challenge what is stated against him in court. The defendant can waive counsel, but waiver of this right must be in writing. The defendant also can waive the preliminary hearing. If he does so, the case is sent to a higher court for disposition.

Preliminary hearings are generally held in a lower court or a court which has general jurisdiction such as a municipal court. In fact, 90% of all defendants appear in one of the thousands of lower courts in our country.

The magistrate in a preliminary hearing is not bound by the rules of evidence which ordinarily control a trial. Although no one rule is applicable in all parts of the country, a far broader range of evidence is usually admissible. At times the mere presentation of a signed confession is sufficient to move the case to a higher court. The evidence need only show probable cause and that the evidence reasonably and fairly tends to show the crime is as charged and that the accused committed it.

The prosecutor only has to present his evidence; he need not prove the crime was committed beyond a reasonable doubt as long as probable cause is shown. Occasionally the defense attorney or the defendant will demand a preliminary hearing if either is convinced a miscarriage of justice has occurred. Sometimes the defense will test the prosecutor's case by probing the state's potential weak areas. However, as noted, the prosecutor need release only enough evidence to establish probable cause.

The defense attorney can present evidence, cross-examine the prosecutor's witnesses, call defense witnesses, and present any types of defense.

In reality the preliminary hearing is often a minitrial where the defense obtains as much information as possible to strengthen its case should it be bound over to a higher court. Both prosecution and defense often use this stage of the criminal justice process for tactical purposes. In some instances, overwhelming evidence may lead to a guilty plea or to a request for plea bargaining.

The preliminary hearing is often a discovery tool for the defendant as he hears the evidence presented against him. If the case went to the grand jury, he would not be aware of the evidence against him, as you will learn in a few pages. Some states have eliminated this element of surprise by including the *Discovery Process* in their rules of criminal procedure.

> The Discovery Process requires that all pertinent facts on both sides be made available prior to the time of the trial.

Used properly, the Discovery Process reduces questions of probable cause and other questions normally brought out in a preliminary hearing and encourages more final dispositions before trial, thereby saving court time. Available to both the prosecution and defense attorneys, it eliminates surprise as a legitimate trial tactic.

The preliminary hearing does not determine who is going to win or lose. It merely determines whether further action should be taken. At this point the magistrate usually does not rule on complicated issues of evidence.

Theoretically, at the preliminary hearing, the magistrate determines the guilt or innocence of the accused and dismisses cases he feels the prosecutor should no longer pursue because of lack of sufficient evidence that the person committed the crime (probable cause).

The main intent of the preliminary hearing is to add to the checks and balances of the criminal justice system by preventing the prosecutor from indiscriminately bringing someone to trial. The preliminary hearing, one of the "critical stages" of due process, is a very formal proceeding insuring that all accused persons are adequately informed and that all their constitutional rights are protected.

The outcome of a preliminary hearing may be (1) to dismiss the charges, (2) present an information and bind the defendant over to a higher court, or (3) send the case to a grand jury.

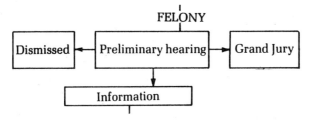

An information resulting from the preliminary hearing may look like the following:

Figure 15-6. Sample of Information.

State of Anywhere, ⎱ss.   DISTRICT COURT,

County of........Anywhere   Fourth ....*Judicial District.*

STATE OF ANYWHERE
AGAINST

Saffron Greene

I, ...William Taylor........, *County Attorney for said County,*

hereby inform the Court that on the ....10th........ *day of* ....March........ *in the year 19*78 ,

at said County........Saffron B. Greene........ *did*

willfully, unlawfully, wrongfully, knowingly, feloniously, and burglariously enter that certain garage located at that certain residence known, designated, and described as number 604 Pleasant Ave. So., in said City of Anytown, county and state aforesaid, without the consent of the person in the lawful possession thereof, said garage building being then and there the property of, in the lawful possession of, and belonging to Richard Forsythe, with intent to commit a crime therein, to-wit: of theft in said garage building, to feloniously take, steal, and carry away from said garage building and the possession of said Richard Forsythe, the chattels of the said Richard Forsythe then and there in said garage building, and to appropriate the same to the use of them, the said Saffron Greene;

contrary to the form of the statute in such case made and provided, the same being Section ..60958.. subd2
said acts constituting ....burglary........

and against the peace and dignity of the State of Anywhere.

Dated ......May 1...... *19* 78

Mary Ellen King
County Attorney.

The Grand Jury

The United States Constitution requires an indictment by a federal grand jury before trial for most crimes against federal law. It frequently hears cases involving misconduct of public officials, violations of election laws, bankruptcy fraud, criminal conduct, and the like.

> Federal, state, and county grand juries decide whether enough evidence exists to indict (bring to trial) persons in criminal cases whether they are in custody or not.

The consideration of a felony charge by a grand jury is in no sense of the word a trial. Only the prosecution's evidence is usually presented and considered. Contrary to the popular portrayal of grand juries on television and in movies, suspected offenders are usually not heard nor are their lawyers present to offer evidence in their behalf.

A grand jury is usually composed of twenty-three voting citizens of the county, selected by either the district or superior judges, jury commissioners, court officials, or some designated county supervisor. These juries may be called to duty any time the court is in session. Sixteen jurors constitute a quorum, and the votes of twelve members are usually necessary to return an indictment.

Grand juries meet in secret sessions and hear from witnesses and victims of crime. Because it meets in a secret session, it is an accusatory body and only determines whether enough evidence exists to accuse a person or persons of a crime.

The prosecutor usually has considerable foundation for believing an offense has been committed before taking a case to the grand jury. The prosecutor is authorized to subpoena witnesses before the jury. Usually only one witness appears at a time before the jury and is questioned under oath by the prosecutor.

In some states, by statute, a grand jury can hear evidence from suspects. However, in order to testify, the persons being considered for indictment must sign a waiver of immunity and agree to answer all questions posed in the grand jury session even though their testimony might be incriminating and lead to an indictment. Their testimony also may be used against them in a criminal trial. Their lawyers are not allowed to be present in the grand jury room if they are testifying.

After the grand jury receives all testimony and evidence, it begins its deliberations. No one else is allowed in the room during these deliberations. Before an indictment can be reached, the jurors must agree that all the evidence presented leads them to believe the person is guilty of a crime beyond a reasonable doubt. If the majority of the grand jurors (or a specified number) agree, they instruct the prosecutor to prepare an *indictment* which specifies all the facts of the case and the names of those who appeared before the jury.

The indictment is signed by the grand jury foreman and presented to the district or superior court judge who then orders the issuance of a bench war-

Figure 15-7. Sample of Indictment.

No. 3035—INDICTMENT.   MILLER-DAVIS COMPANY

State of Anywhere, } ss.   IN DISTRICT COURT,

County of Anywhere   Fourth *Judicial District.*

                                              Special *Term, A. D. 19* 78

THE STATE OF ANYWHERE , AGAINST

Susan Mae Hancock

ACCUSED by the Grand Jury of the County of Anywhere *and State of Anywhere,*

by this indictment of the crime of Murder in the Second Degree (Sec. dd 609.10

and Sec. 609.11, Statutes, 1974.)

                                                          committed as follows:

The said Susan Mae Hancock

on the 7th *day of* February *A. D. 19* 78 *, at the* City

of Anytown *in the County of* Anywhere *and State of Anywhere, did*

then and there, being armed with a dangerous and deadly weapon, to-wit: a gun,
commonly so-called, a more particular description of said weapon being to the
Grand Jury unknown, did then and there wilfully, unlawfully, wrongfully,
knowingly, and feloniously, without excuse or justification, without authority
of law, without premeditation, but with intent to effect the death of a human
being, to-wit: one Samuel Hancock, cause the death of the said Samuel Hancock
by then and there shooting the said Samuel Hancock, and firing the said gun
at, upon, into, and against the body and person of the said Samuel Hancock,
thereby and therewith inflicting upon the body of him, the said Samuel Hancock,
mortal wounds, of which mortal wounds, the said Samuel Hancock thereafter died
at the City of Anytown, Anywhere County, on the 7th day of February, 1978.

Contrary to the form of the Statute in such case made and provided, and against the peace and dignity
of the State of Anywhere

Dated at the City of Anytown *in the County of* Anywhere *and State*

of Anywhere , this 1st *day of* May *A. D. 19* 78

                                        _____
                                              Foreman of the Grand Jury.

The following are the names of the Witnesses duly sworn and examined before the Grand Jury
upon the findings of the above indictment:

DISTRICT COURT,

Fourth *Judicial District,*

Anywhere *County.*

The State of Anywhere ,
AGAINST

Susan Mae Hancock

INDICTMENT

For Murder in the
Second Degree

A TRUE BILL

Foreman of the Grand Jury.

Presented by the Foreman, in the pre-
sence of the Grand Jury, to the Court,
and filed in the office of the Clerk of the
District Court in and for the County of

Anywhere *, this* 1st *day of*

May 19 78

Carl Alexander *Clerk.*

By *Deputy.*

rant for the arrest of the defendant if not already in custody. If the defendant is indicted, until he is arrested or brought before the court, the fact that an indictment has been found must be kept secret; it is *not* public information.

Procedures are then implemented for the defendant's appearance in court where a trial jury may be convened to hear the case.

Grand juries may also issue what is called a *no bill*. If after hearing all the evidence presented and the witnesses, the jurors believe there is no criminal violation, the grand jury issues a *no bill*, which means they find no basis for an indictment and will no longer consider the matter unless further evidence is later presented which may warrant an indictment.

Grand juries can also take action and conduct investigations on their own initiative. This is known as a *presentment* and in some jurisdictions is sufficient to support a prosecution. Some states, however, regard a presentment as mere instructions to the prosecutor to draw up a bill of indictment. When the grand jury reviews this bill of indictment, if they agree it is a *true bill*, it becomes the basis for prosecution.

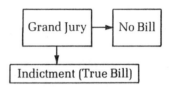

In felony cases, prosecutors sometimes avoid the preliminary hearing by going directly to the grand jury for an indictment. This presents a tactical advantage to the prosecution because grand jury hearings are not public. If the prosecution can convince a grand jury to bring about an indictment based on probable cause, the prosecution does not need a preliminary hearing. An indictment eliminates the need for such a hearing because the defendant goes straight to trial.

The defense attorney or the defendant can demand a preliminary hearing if either feels a miscarriage of justice is occurring.

The Coroner's Jury

The coroner's jury is involved in cases where the cause of death is in doubt.

Coroners investigate violent deaths where suspicion of foul play exists. By law, coroners may conduct autopsies as to the cause of death, and they may conduct inquests. The coroner's jury usually consists of six members. In some states the coroner's jury system has been abandoned and its functions performed by a professional medical examiner, usually a pathologist and a forensic expert.

☑ CHECK POINT

1. What is the difference between an indictment and an information?
2. What is the function of a preliminary hearing?
3. What is the Discovery Process?
4. What is the function of a grand jury?
5. How does a grand jury hearing differ from a preliminary hearing?
6. What is the function of a coroner's jury?

*Answers

1. An information is issued after a preliminary hearing and binds the defendant over to a higher court for trial. An indictment issues from a grand jury and binds the defendant over to court for trial.
2. A preliminary hearing is a probable cause hearing. It seeks to prevent persons from indiscriminately being brought to trial for a felony.
3. The Discovery Process requires that all pertinent facts on both sides be made available prior to the time of the trial, thus eliminating surprise as a courtroom tactic.
4. A grand jury decides whether enough evidence exists to indict (bring to trial) persons in criminal cases whether they are in custody or not.
5. It differs from a preliminary hearing in that it is private and secret.
6. A coroner's jury investigates cases where the cause of death is in doubt.

The Arraignment

When defendants are charged with a felony, whether by a preliminary hearing (information) or a grand jury (indictment), they must personally appear at an arraignment. As in the preliminary hearing, the defendants are entitled to counsel. The procedures of the arraignment vary in some states, but generally defendants appear before the court, are read the complaint, information, or indictment, and, if they have not received a copy, they are given one.

Defendants have several alternatives open when they appear for the formal arraignment.

> At the arraignment the defendant may stand mute, or plead nolo contendere, guilty, or not guilty.

Standing mute, that is, refusing to answer, is entered by the judge as a "not guilty" plea.

Nolo contendere means "no contest." The defendant, in effect, is throwing himself at the mercy of the court. This plea is often used when a person knows of some forthcoming civil action against him and does not want his plea to jeopardize his defense in the civil trial. (A guilty plea to any criminal offense could become part of the civil trial.)

Guilty means the accused admits the actual charge or a lesser charge agreed to in a plea bargaining session. A guilty plea has many consequences: possible imprisonment, being labeled a criminal, a waiver of constitutional rights, and a waiver of all defenses. Still, 90% of all criminal defendants plead guilty in the United States, but most plead guilty to reduced offenses than what they were originally charged with.

Not guilty means the accused denies the charge. He may have a valid defense for the charge such as intoxication, insanity, self-defense, or mistaken identity. Some states require defendants to automatically plead "not guilty" to capital crimes such as first-degree murder.

If the defendant pleads "guilty" or "nolo contendere," a sentencing time is set. Usually a presentence investigation is ordered to determine if probation is warranted. If the defendant makes no plea or pleads "not guilty," he has the choice of a trial by a judge or by a jury which will weigh the facts of the case and make the decision of guilt or innocence. If he wishes a jury trial, the case will be assigned to the court docket and a date set.

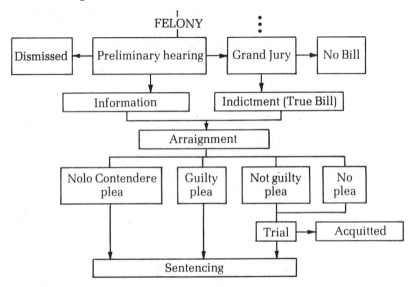

The Trial

When police officers enter the courtroom they realize that the trial is the climax in the criminal justice procedure. All previously made decisions now merge in one finality. The test of how well the police officers have investigated the case, compiled evidence and reported it, and dealt with the victim and witnesses will be weighed in the courtroom.

> The key figures are the judge, members of the jury, the defendant and defense attorney(s), and the prosecuting attorney(s), police officer(s) and witnesses.

The judge has charge of the trial and decides all matters with respect to the law. He assures that all the rules of trial procedures are followed. The jury decides all matters of fact. The advocates are the prosecuting attorney(s) and the defense attorney(s). The trial begins with the jury selection.

Jury Selection.   Safeguards built into the jury selection process not only protect the rights of the defendant but also assure the public that justice is done. Trial or *petit* jurors are selected at random by district or superior court judges or the commissioners of the county board. The judges or the commissioners randomly select a large group of prospective jurors and, when the trial is about to begin, call these people to the court and inform them of their duties in the particular case for which they may serve.

> The random selection of potential jurors and the careful questioning of each helps insure selection of six or twelve fair and impartial jurors

It is then up to the attorneys trying the case to decide which six or twelve of these individuals will be the jurors in the case. The clerk of court draws the names of six or twelve jurors from the jury list, and these individuals take their seats in the regular jury box in the order in which their names were drawn. The defense attorney and then the prosecuting attorney question each individual as to their qualifications to be a juror in this case. The judge may also question the prospective jurors.

In homicide cases or in other cases involving a great deal of publicity, the system may be altered. All the jurors except the one being questioned by the attorney are excluded from the courtroom (sequestered) to insure that neither the questions asked nor the answers provided will prejudice other jurors.

Challenges may be made to the entire panel of jurors or to individual jurors.

Challenges to the entire panel may be made if potential jurors were not separated during questioning and one potential juror made a moving speech about the guilt or innocence of the defendant. A challenge to the entire panel might also be made on the basis that the entire group was improperly selected. For example, if the names were not randomly selected, the entire panel could be excluded and a new selection of jurors made.

Challenges to individual jurors are the most frequent type of challenges. Two basic types of individual challenges can be made: challenge for cause (a reason is presented for the challenge) and peremptory challenge (no reason is presented).

Challenge for cause may take several forms. It may be based on the person's background; for example, a prospective juror with a felony record would be disqualified from sitting on any criminal case; or a prospective juror might be related to the defendant, the prosecutor, the judge, or someone involved in the case itself. Challenge for cause may also be based on the answers given during questioning. If, for example, during questioning a prospective juror blurted out, "I know the man is innocent," or, "I know that man is guilty," this would clearly indicate bias and constitute grounds for dismissal of that juror. When a prospective juror is challenged for cause, the lawyer presents a factual basis for excluding a particular person, and the judge makes the decision. Sometimes, the judge appoints three citizens to listen to the questioning and decide if a particular person should be excluded. This rather cumbersome method, called the *three triers*, is not normally used except in first-degree murder cases.

Peremptory challenges are based on an attorney's "gut reaction" or intuition that a person would be a poor juror. No specific reason is given for excluding the person; the lawyer simply does not want the person on the jury. Both the prosecution and the defense lawyers may exclude persons from the jury without a factual basis by using a limited number of peremptory challenges. Normally the defense is allowed a larger number than the prosecution. For example, in an ordinary criminal case in Minnesota, the defense has five peremptory challenges and the prosecution has three. In a first-degree murder case the defense has twenty peremptory challenges, the prosecution ten.

Opening Statements.   After the jury is selected and instructed by the judge, opening statements are presented. The prosecutor informs the jury of the state's case and how he intends to prove the charges against the defendant. The defense lawyer makes an opening statement in support of his client, or he may waive this opening statement.

Evidence and Testimony.   The prosecutor then presents evidence and the testimony of the witnesses, attempting to prove that a crime has been committed and that the defendant did it. He does so by using direct and indirect evidence, a confession, the testimony of witnesses, and/or the testimony of the police officers whose initial investigation brought the case to trial.

After each bit of evidence is presented, the defense attorney can challenge its validity, and the judge will rule on his objections. In most cases, after each witness testifies, he is subjected to cross-examination by the defense counsel, who tries to discredit the testimony.

After the prosecutor rests his case, the defense presents evidence and witnesses. One tactic frequently used by the defense attorney is to keep his client from taking the witness stand. The well-known privilege against self-incrimination is part of the Fifth Amendment. However, if the defendant takes the witness stand in his own behalf, he gives up this right of self-incrimination —the prosecutor is free to cross-examine him.

Through cross-examination, the defense attorney tries to discredit prosecution witnesses, the evidence, and the testimony of the police officers.

☑ CHECK POINT

1. What types of plea may be entered at the time of arraignment?
2. How are jurors selected?
3. What safeguards are taken to insure against bias?

*Answers

1. At the arraignment the defendant may (1) stand mute, (2) plead nolo contendere, (3) plead guilty, or (4) plead not guilty.
2. Jurors are randomly selected.
3. The random selection and the careful questioning of each potential juror helps insure selection of unbiased jurors.

The Police Officer in Court. Almost every officer has his day in court. Because of overloaded court dockets, cases usually come up well after the officers' investigation; therefore, officers must refer back to their reports and their original notes to refresh their memories. The notes may remind them that it was a cloudy day, a light rain had fallen and the streets were still wet, that it was mid-afternoon, and that clearly visible bloodstains trailed out the back door.

Police officers know the defense lawyer will probably try to convince the jury that since the sky was overcast, the officers had trouble seeing the stains clearly, but their notes say differently.

A court appearance is an important part of any police officer's duty. All elements of the investigtion are brought together at this point: the report, the statements of the witnesses, the evidence collected, and possibly even a confession from the defendant.

Although the defendant may have given the officers a bad time when he was interrogated, when he enters the court room, his lawyer will have him neatly dressed, and he will be polite—the picture of an innocent victim.

The jury will be studying not only the defendant, but the police officers as well. They should be neatly dressed and should have left any firearms out of the courtroom. As police officers walk to the witness stand and take the oath, the jury will judge them, and that judgment affects their readiness to accept the officers' testimony.

Prosecutors also judge police officers, for it is upon them that they rely for evidence with which to prosecute the case. Actually the preparation for the courtroom testimony began when the investigation began, The investigators should make accurate, complete notes and from these notes make complete reports. It is extremely difficult to take on a sharp defense lawyer six months and several investigations later unless careful notes and reports have been prepared. The police officers' functions do not end with the investigation and the solving of a criminal case; they must be prepared to testify in court regarding the case.

Before going into court, police officers should go over their notes and reports. They may revisit the crime scene to observe any changes. A review of the physical evidence collected is mandatory. They should also review any measurements made.

Even after a thorough review, when police officers enter the courtroom they may not be able to recall certain facts. In such cases they can refer to their notes or reports. Although the defense attorney may offer a challenge upon cross-examination, if officers ask to refresh their memory from their notes or reports, the challenge is unfounded because police officers have that right—provided they are *their* notes or report. If two officers on an investigation agree that one will take notes and make the report, only the officer who took the notes and wrote the report is allowed to testify from them. The other officer cannot use them to recall details.

The prosecution needs to establish the corpus delicti of the crime, which means it has to establish the elements of the crime by testimony of witnesses, physical evidence, documents, recordings, or other admissible evidence. This information usually comes from police officers, their recollections, their notes, and/or their reports. The prosecutor works with the police officers in presenting the arguments for the prosecution. On the opposing side is the defense attorney.

> The defense attorney may try to confuse or discredit a police officer by (1) rapid-fire questioning, (2) establishing that the officer wants to see the defendant found guilty, (3) accusing the officer of making assumptions, and/or (4) implying that the officer does not want anyone else to know what is in his notes.

Defense attorneys use several different techniques which police officers should be prepared for. One frequently used technique is *rapid-fire questioning*, with the intent of confusing the officer or obtaining inconsistent answers. To counter this tactic, officers should be deliberate and take their time in answering questions. They may ask the defense attorney to repeat the question to slow him down and thus thwart his efforts at rapid-fire questioning.

A typical series of questions might go something like the following:

Defense Attorney: Officer Cooley, isn't it fair to say your job is to arrest people who commit a crime?

Officer Cooley: That is only partly true. My job is to serve the public and to arrest only those whom I have a warrant for or have probable cause to arrest.

Defense Attorney: Is it fair to say you wouldn't go around arresting innocent people?

Officer Cooley: Yes. I must have probable cause to arrest a person I feel may have disobeyed the law.

Defense Attorney: Isn't it a fair assumption that when you arrest someone, you feel very strongly that she or he committed the offense?

Officer Cooley: Again, it would depend upon the probable cause that the person may have committed the offense.

Defense Attorney: Isn't part of your job to come to court and make sure the defendant is convicted?

Officer Cooley: My appearance in court is to present testimony and evidence which I've gathered related to the commission of a crime.

Defense Attorney: Isn't it true, Officer, that you may have a tendency to shade your testimony a bit to convict this defendant?

Officer Cooley: No, sir; the testimony relates only to the evidence gathered and my knowledge of the crime.

Defense Attorney: Is your principal objective in this case to see that the defendant is convicted?

Officer Cooley: No, my position in this case is to present my testimony and to serve justice to the best of my ability.

This officer has done a good job, has handled himself well in answering some extremely difficult questions.

The trial of a criminal case is a contest, a very serious contest. Someone wins and someone loses. The prosecution "wins" if it establishes the guilt of the defendant. It must prove the defendant is guilty beyond a reasonable doubt. The defendant "wins" if the prosecution fails in its obligation of proof.

Proof consists of two basic elements: the evidence itself and, equally important, presentation of this evidence. No matter how much evidence exists, if improperly presented, the prosecution will fail. Presenting evidence involves credibility, believability.

In a criminal case, the defense rarely expects to gain helpful information from police officers. The main intent is usually to discredit the officers and/or their testimony. One common approach is to *establish a motive for the officer's testimony,* to show that the officer has a personal interest in the case, to question his candor: Has he been open or holding back? Is his testimony consistent? Does it contain errors? Is the officer confident and relaxed or nervous, upset, and seemingly afraid? What is his general appearance? Does he give the appearance of a professional doing an important, serious job, or does he give the impression that he takes the trial lightly?

Let's look at how another police officer handles the questions of the defense attorney. Officer Doright has just completed his testimony upon direct examination from the prosecutor. He looks a little more confident than relaxed; in fact, he actually looks like a "slob" on the witness stand. It's difficult to imagine how he managed it, but he has brought a cup of coffee with him. If the judge doesn't stop him, the defense attorney is likely to make an issue of the cup of coffee. The defense attorney's intent is to attack the credibility of Officer Doright's testimony. He will base his arguments on the officer's motives. Although the attorney approaches Officer Doright cordially, he is definitely on the opposing side.

Defense Attorney: Is it fair to say your job is to arrest people who have committed a crime?

Officer Doright: Yup, that's right.

Defense Attorney: You don't go around arresting innocent people, do you?

Officer Doright: Never.

Defense Attorney: Do you arrest only guilty people?

Officer Doright: Yup.

Defense Attorney: Isn't it fair to say, then, that when you arrest someone, you believe he or she is guilty?

Officer Doright: Sure.

Defense Attorney: Do you believe guilty people should be punished?

Officer Doright: Sure.

Defense Attorney: Do you believe it is your job to see that they are punished?

Officer Doright: Sure do.

Defense Attorney: Do you believe you should do everything you can to see that they are punished?

Officer Doright: Yup.

Defense Attorney: Isn't part of your job to come to the courtroom and offer testimony?

Officer Doright: Sure is.

Defense Attorney: When you came into this courtroom today, did you believe that Mr. Johnson, the defendant, was guilty?

Officer Doright: Definitely.

Defense Attorney: You want Mr. Johnson convicted?

Officer Doright: Definitely.

Defense Attorney: And you want him punished?

Officer Doright: Definitely.

Defense Attorney: And you'll do everything you can to see that happen?

Officer Doright: Right.

This officer's approach indicates a personal interest in seeing the defendant convicted and punished. He says his job is to arrest people he feels are guilty and wants punished. This is not an ignoble feeling, but the defense counsel can suggest to the jury in his final arguments that Officer Doright might step beyond the bounds of fairness and honesty in his testimony since he has stated under oath he would do everything he could to see Mr. Johnson convicted. Officer Doright has made it quite clear that he has a personal objective—the conviction and punishment of the defendant.

Defense attorneys also attack a police officer's credibility by focusing on the *assumptions* or *inferences* of the officer. Assumptions and inferences are natural. We spend our whole lives making assumptions, usually reasonable ones. The law recognizes the validity of assumptions and inferences. As a matter of fact, the court will instruct the jury to make reasonable inferences. From time to time, however, a defense attorney will try to discredit police officers' testimony by asking them if they are making assumptions. If officers have, in fact, drawn inferences or made assumptions, they should not attempt to deny it, as illustrated in the following courtroom presentation.

Defense Attorney: Officer, you testified on direct examination that when you left the store, walked out the door, and found the sack, you followed a trail of bloodstains. Do you recall that specifically?

Officer Triard: Yes, sir.

Defense Attorney: Did you make a test to determine the nature of these stains?

Officer Triard: No, not me.

Defense Attorney: You made no chemical analysis?

Officer Triard: No.

Defense Attorney: Do you know if anyone else made a chemical analysis?

Officer Triard: No.

Defense Attorney: Did anyone report to you that they made a chemical analysis?

Officer Triard: No.

Defense Attorney: Then, as a matter of fact, you do *not* know now, nor did you know then, that those stains were actually blood.

Officer Triard: Well, I know what blood looks like.

Defense Attorney: What does blood look like?

Officer Triard: When it's dried, it's kind of rusty looking.

Defense Attorney: Are there other things that are rusty looking when they are dried?

Officer Triard: I suppose there are.

Defense Attorney: How about candle wax from a rust-colored candle?

Officer Triard: Could be.

Defense Attorney: We've all seen movies where the prop used is ketchup or something which resembles blood. Many substances are rusty looking when dried, aren't they?

Officer Triard: Not this; this was blood.

Defense Attorney: On what scientific basis do you draw that conclusion? I'll withdraw the question. Officer, it is fair to say that you make assumptions from time to time, isn't it?

Officer Triard: Yes.

Defense Attorney: And that in this particular case you saw a stain that looked sort of rusty and was dried, and you assumed it was blood?

Officer Triard: No. It *was* blood.

This officer has fallen into the trap of not admitting he has made an assumption. He may feel that assumptions are negative or wrong. However, in this case his assumption is legitimate and valid. The court would probably make instructions to the jury as to its legitimacy. However, the officer does not admit he has made an assumption. Therefore, the defense attorney may argue to the jury that the officer refuses to admit making an assumption, when everyone knows he did. Consequently, how reliable and believable is his testimony?

Another cross-examination tactic used by defense counsels from time to time is to present to the jury police officers' *reluctance to relinquish their notes*. The police officers' notes and their reports, as a general rule, are available to the defense counsel in making cross-examination. When police officers use their notes to testify, they are also available to the defense counsel. The following example illustrates the dangers inherent when an officer hesitates to share notes and/or reports with the defense attorney.

Defense Attorney: Officer Thomas, on direct examination you referred to some notes from time to time. May I see those notes, please?

Officer Thomas glances at the prosecuting attorney and is quite hesitant to turn the notes over. (This could easily cause suspicion in some jurors.)

Defense Attorney: Officer Thomas, is there something in those notes you don't want me to see?

Officer Thomas: Not particularly.

As the defense attorney continues to cross examine Officer Thomas, he reminds the officer that he has a right to refer to those notes. Officer Thomas turns the notes over to the defense attorney. If she should want them back to refresh her memory, she can request the notes back to testify from.

Another tactic defense attorney's often use is to inquire as to whether the officer gave the constitutional warning required according to the Miranda decision. The warning itself, if properly given, is seldom the subject of an attack by the defense counsel. The defense usually focuses on whether the defendant really understood the rights. In some cases on record the defendant has been given a Miranda card to read, waived his rights, and when the case came to trial it was found that the defendant could not read!

An attack on the officer's giving of the Miranda warning might go something like the following:

Defense Attorney: Officer Triard, what type of test did you conduct to determine whether or not the defendant understood you when you advised her of her various rights?

Officer Triard: I asked her if she understood the rights as I read them from the card to her.

Defense Attorney: And what was her response?

Officer Triard: She said she did.

Defense Attorney: Well, what tests did you make to determine whether or not she actually understood these rights?

Officer Triard: I asked if she understood what I read to her.

Defense Attorney: Do you know the defendant's I.Q.?

Officer Triard: No, but from my personal observation and conversation with her, she seemed to be reasonably intelligent.

Defense Attorney: Do you know whether or not she can read?

Officer Triard: She said she could.

Defense Attorney: Do you know whether or not she can write?

Officer Triard: She said she could.

This officer has done a good job in response to this line of questioning. Police officers are *not* expected to conduct tests to determine a suspect's I.Q. They must rely upon their own common sense.

These are only a few of the many tactics used by defense attorneys. But no matter how skilled the defense, if police officers are well prepared, well groomed, poised, and present the evidence fairly, openly, and candidly, they will be serving the interests of justice. Perhaps the most important considerations for officers testifying in court are to be composed, truthful, and impartial at all times.

Closing Statements.   After the advocates have concluded their presentation, the jury hears the closing statements, a contest in persuasion first by the prosecution stating the jury should render a guilty verdict, then by the defense attorney concluding his client is surely innocent—or at least not proven guilty beyond a reasonable doubt.

Jury Deliberation and Decision.   With the closing of the case, the judge reads the instructions to the jury. He explains the crime, what elements constitute the crime, alternate charges, and the concepts of presumption of innocence and reasonable doubt. The jury then retires behind closed doors to deliberate their findings. They can return one of three findings: guilty, not guilty, or no verdict. No verdict simply means that no agreement can be reached; this is also sometimes referred to as a "hung jury."

After the jury has come to a decision, the judge is notified and the jury returns to the courtroom. With everyone present, the jury foreman announces the verdict. Each juror is then polled as to how he voted and is asked if the verdict which the foreman has read is the verdict of the juror. If the finding is guilty, the defendant may either be sentenced immediately, or he may be given a sentencing date. If he is found not guilty, he is set free. If a hung jury results, the defendant may be re-tried at the discretion of the prosecutor.

In Review. A typical criminal justice process might be diagrammed as shown in the repeat of Figure 15-2 on page 441.

To police officers who have worked diligently to see that justice is done, the trial is the serious climax to hard work, long hours, and meticulous investigation. They must prepare for it from the time of the initial complaint to the time the jury verdict comes in.

☑ CHECK POINT

1. How might a defense attorney try to discredit or confuse police officers who are testifying in court?

*Answer

1. The defense attorney may try to confuse or discredit police officers by (1) rapid-fire questioning, (2) establishing that the officers want to see the defendant found guilty, (3) accusing the officers of making assumptions, and/or (4) implying that the officers do not want anyone else to know what is in their notes.

SUMMARY

Our criminal justice system is based on the *adversary system* which requires that the accuser prove beyond a reasonable doubt to a judge or jury that the accused is guilty of a specified crime.

Police officers aid the criminal justice process by (1) making legal arrests, (2) legally obtaining accurate, relevant information and evidence, (3) writing complete, accurate reports, (4) identifying suspects and witnesses, and (5) providing effective, truthful testimony in court.

Prosecutors are elected officials who serve as the public's lawyer, the determiner of law enforcement priorities, the advisor of police officers, and the preserver of civil liberties of all persons. They rely heavily on the support and cooperation of police officers.

Our criminal justice system has several safeguards to assure that all citizens are guaranteed their civil rights and civil liberties. The Fourth Amendment forbids unreasonable searches and seizures and requires probable cause. The Fifth Amendment guarantees due process, that is, notice of a hearing, full information regarding the charges made, the opportunity to present evidence before an impartial judge or jury, and the right to refrain from self-incrimination. The Sixth Amendment establishes the requirements for criminal trials including the right to a speedy public trial by an impartial jury and the right to have a lawyer. The Eighth Amendment forbids excessive bail and implies the right to such bail in most instances.

Defense attorneys represent the accused in court. Gideon v. Wainwright established the court's responsibility for providing counsel for any indigent person charged with a felony.

Not all criminal cases come to court. Sometimes a case is diverted to a different agency before it ever comes to trial. In other instances the case may be plea bargained. Plea bargaining is a compromise between defense and prosecution which prearranges the plea and the sentence, conserving manpower and expense.

Our judicial system for juveniles has several basic differences from the adult judicial system. Juvenile courts are informal, private, nonadversary systems which stress rehabilitation rather than punishment of youth. Nevertheless, the youth has all the rights of an adult, as indicated in the Gault decision, which requires that the due process clause of the Fourteenth Amendment apply to proceedings in state juvenile courts. In addition to numerous punitive correctional institutions for juveniles, other facilities are available including reception and diagnostic centers; detention centers; training schools; shelters; ranches, forestry camps and farms; group homes; and halfway houses. When possible, youths are allowed to remain in their homes.

The adult criminal justice system has several critical stages including the complaint or charge, the arrest, the booking, the preliminary hearing, the grand jury hearing, the arraignment, and the trial.

The complaint is a legal document drawn up by a prosecutor which specifies the alleged crime and the supporting facts providing probable cause. In a felony case the prosecutor may seek an information from a preliminary hearing or an indictment from a grand jury.

The preliminary hearing is the probable cause hearing. It seeks to prevent persons from being indiscriminately brought to trial. The Discovery Process requires that all pertinent facts on both sides be made available prior to the time of the hearing. The grand jury may decide whether enough evidence exists to indict (bring to trial) persons in criminal cases whether they are in custody or not. The coroner's jury is involved in cases where the cause of death is in doubt.

Following the preliminary hearing or the grand jury hearing, defendants appear at an arraignment where they enter their plea: they may stand mute, or plead nolo contendere, guilty, or not guilty. If they plead not guilty or stand mute, they will go to trial. They may select trial by judge or by jury. If they select jury, the jury will be randomly selected from citizens of the community and each will be carefully questioned to insure selection of six or twelve fair and impartial jurors. Police officers' testimony at the trial is of great importance. They should be aware of tactics frequently used by defense attorneys to confuse or discredit a police officer who is testifying: (1) rapid-fire questioning, (2) establishing that the officer wants to see the defendant found guilty, (3) accusing the officer of making assumptions, and/or (4) implying that the officer does not want anyone else to know what is in his notes.

Although the police officer and the prosecutor represent the accuser, in effect their ultimate responsibility is to see that justice is done—*not* that a conviction is obtained.

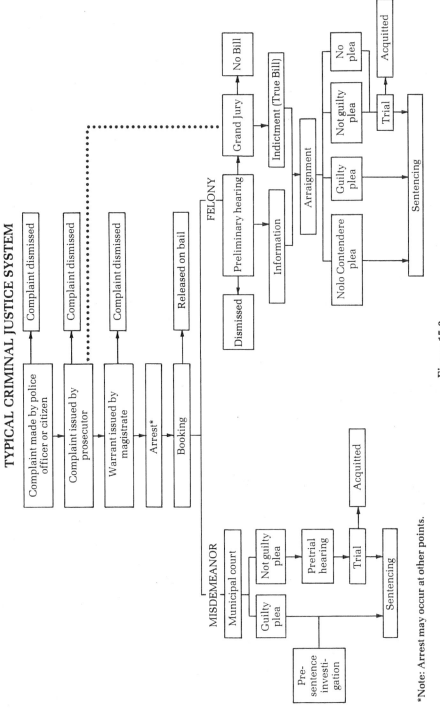

TYPICAL CRIMINAL JUSTICE SYSTEM

Figure 15-2.

*Note: Arrest may occur at other points.

APPLICATION

A. An accused is on trial for a homicide that occurred at 2 A.M., proven by the victim's broken watch. The scene of the homicide is 250 miles from Mytown, USA. The accused was given a traffic citation at 4 A.M. by a Mytown police officer. All the other circumstantial evidence points to the accused as being the guilty party.

Could the jury convict him of homicide?

B. Johnny Hardluck has been charged with the crime of burglary and has been uncooperative with the investigators. FBI Agent David Hervey hears from an informant that Johnny is innocent and covering up for his younger brother. Agent Hervey relays this information to his friend, the investigator.

Is it the officer's duty to report this to the prosecutor?

C. The prosecuting attorney has a friend whose son has been apprehended and arrested in the commission of an assault. The prosecutor refuses to issue a complaint due to his friendship.

Can the prosecutor legally do this?

D. The attorney for the defense asks that the first prospective juror being questioned be excluded without cause (peremptory challenge). The judge states that this is not reasonable, and he refuses the attorney's request.

Is this a correct procedure?

E. Diagram as completely as you can the steps in the criminal justice procedure for a felony.

*Answers

A. Possibly, but the traffic citation would create doubt. It might be physically impossible to drive 250 miles in two hours. This would create so large a "reasonable doubt" that it would pose a problem for the jury. In order to convict an accused, guilt must be "beyond a reasonable doubt."

B. Yes, because one of the duties of police officers is to keep the prosecutor informed. It is the duty of both the police officer and the prosecutor to protect the innocent. After notifying the prosecutor, the investigator should follow the prosecutor's instructions to obtain the truth of the situation.

C. Yes. He has total power over who is to be charged, what cases are bargained, and what cases go to trial. However, this example is an extreme abuse of such power.

D. No. On a peremptory challenge, lawyers do not have to give a reason. They are, however, limited in the number of such challenges. Since this was the first peremptory challenge, it was not a correct procedure for the judge to deny the request.

E. Compare your diagram with that on page 441.

DISCUSSION QUESTIONS

1. Is the jury system really fair?
2. What alternatives to the jury system are there?
3. What is the best kind of notebook for police officers to put their notes in to testify from?

4. Can the defense attorney examine the officer's entire notebook even if it contains notes on other cases?
5. Should the victim of a crime be consulted when plea bargaining is used?
6. Do juvenile courts stress rehabilitation and keeping youngsters in the home too often?
7. How can police officers be sure a person they have just arrested understands the Miranda warning?
8. Is our system truly an adversary system when the prosecutor also has to protect the accused's rights?

REFERENCES

Asch, S. H. *Police authority and the rights of the individual.* New York: Arco Publishing Company, 1971.

Associated Press, Court expands plea bargain. *Minneapolis tribune,* January 19, 1978, p. 4D.

Busch, F. X. *Law and tactics in jury trials.* Indianapolis: Bobbs-Merrill, 1949.

Carey, J. T., Goldfarb, J., Rowe, M. H., and Lohman, J. D. *The handling of juveniles from offense to disposition.* Washington, D.C.: U.S. Department of Health, Education and Welfare, 1979.

Children in custody. U.S. Department of Justice, Law Enforcement Assistance Administration, National Criminal Justice Information and Statistics Service, May, 1975. (Advance Report on the Juvenile Detention and Correctional Facility Census of 1972-1973.)

Constitutional law—attorney and client—right to counsel. *Western reserve law review,* 19, June 1968, p. 1107.

Haskell, M. R. and Yablonsky, L. *Crime and delinquency.* Chicago: Rand McNally and Company, 1970.

Inbau, F. E. and Aspen, M. *Criminal law for the police.* Radnor, PA: Chilton Book Company, 1969.

Inbau, F. E., Thompson, J. R., and Zagel, J. B. *Criminal law and its administration.* Mineola, NY: The Foundation Press, 1974.

Keeton, P. *Trial tactics and methods.* Boston: Little, Brown, and Company, 1954.

Leonard, Y. A. *The police, the judiciary and the criminal.* Springfield, IL: Charles C. Thomas Company, 1969.

Lewis, P. W. and Peoples, K. D. *The supreme court and the criminal process.* Philadelphia: W. B. Saunders, 1978.

Louisell, D. W. and Crippin, B. J. Jr. Evidentiary privileges. *Minnesota law review,* 40, March 1956, p. 413.

Markle, A. *Criminal investigation and presentation of evidence.* St. Paul: West Publishing Company, 1976.

National Advisory Commission on Criminal Justice Standards and Goals. *Corrections.* Washington, D.C.: U.S. Government Printing Office, 1973.

National Advisory Commission on Criminal Justice Standards and Goals. *Courts.* Washington, D.C.: U.S. Government Printing Office, 1975.

Rosett, A. and Cressey, D. R. *Justice by consent.* Philadelphia: J. B. Lippincott, 1976.

Sayler, R. H., Boyer, B. B., and Gooding, R. E., Jr. *The Warren court.* New York: Chelsea House, 1969.

Trojanowicz, R. C. *Juvenile delinquency, concepts and control.* (2nd ed.) Englewood Cliffs, NJ: Prentice-Hall, 1978.

Vollmer, A. *The police and modern society.* College Park, MD: McGrath Publishing Company, 1969.

Section Five

A Career in Law Enforcement:
A Challenging, Rewarding, Vital Profession

The preceding chapters demonstrate the complex and vital functions performed by law enforcement officers in the United States. The challenges and rewards of this profession should attract well-qualified, dedicated individuals to the field.

This section describes the process involved in becoming a police officer as well as what to expect upon acceptance into the field (Chapter 16). The book concludes with a brief look at what might lie ahead for those in law enforcement (Epilogue).

Police academy cadets out for a morning run. Physical fitness is not only desirable for the police officer, but also may make the difference between success and failure on the job.

The Police Career

A Challenging Profession

16

DO YOU KNOW □ □ □

- ☐ What characteristics are considered essential for an effective police officer?
- ☐ What steps are usually involved in the police officer selection process?
- ☐ What qualifications are generally required for individuals who wish to become police officers?
- ☐ What impact the Griggs v. Duke Power Company decision had on the use of tests for employment purposes?
- ☐ What most physical fitness tests are like and what they test for?
- ☐ What type of information is sought during the oral interview?
- ☐ What is of prime importance in the medical examination?
- ☐ What occurs during the background investigation?
- ☐ What the usual length and purpose of the probationary period in law enforcement are?
- ☐ What factors are important in physical fitness and which one factor is of most importance?
- ☐ What restrictions are sometimes placed on police officers' off-duty employment?
- ☐ What legal considerations in hiring practices are mandated by the Omnibus Civil Rights Law and the Equal Employment Opportunity Act?
- ☐ What benefits are derived from having a police department whose racial make-up reflects that of the community?
- ☐ What preferential hiring is? What "reverse discrimination" is?
- ☐ How women's performance on patrol has compared to that of men?
- ☐ What agencies offer careers in law enforcement and how to apply for these positions?

No one is compelled to choose the profession of a police officer, but having chosen it, everyone is obliged to perform its duties and live up to the high standards of its requirements.
—Calvin Coolidge

INTRODUCTION

For years society has sought more effective law enforcement and a criminal justice system to meet its needs. Concurrently, criminologists, psychologists, sociologists, police practitioners, and scientists have worked to solve the crime problem in America. Despite some disillusionment and cynicism, progress has been made, and the future offers encouragement.

The most visible signs of progress in the vast criminal justice system have been in the field of law enforcement, and the most notable advancement within this field has been in the *professionalization* of the police officer.

This is, in part, because 86-90% of most police agencies' budgets are allocated for personnel and, therefore, they are demanding higher quality performance from them. However, this goal is sometimes difficult to achieve because most police departments are understaffed. The attrition rate throughout the country—approximately 100,000 officers per year—compounds this problem and creates a constant demand for training.

An equally important force behind the professionalization of the police officer is the realization that to a large degree the future of law enforcement, its success or failure, is contingent on the quality and effectiveness of its police officers, their status in the community, and their ability to serve its residents. Members of minority groups and women are now perceived by most departments as necessary and valuable individuals in the department. Although members of minority groups and women have had a long, difficult battle in achieving equal employment rights, not only in the field of law enforcement, but in most other fields as well, great advancements have been made in the past decade. Today law enforcement offers excellent opportunities for *all* who are interested in a law enforcement career.

DESIRED CHARACTERISTICS OF LAW ENFORCEMENT OFFICERS

If the citizens of a community were asked what traits they felt were desirable in police officers, a compilation of their responses might read something like the following: police officers should be able to work under pressure, to accept direction, to express themselves orally and in writing; they should have self-respect and the ability to command respect from others; they should use good judgment; and they should be considerate, compassionate, dependable, enthusiastic, fair, flexible, honest, humble, industrious, intelligent, logical, motivated, neat, observant, physically fit, prompt, resourceful, self-assured, stable, tactful, warm, and willing to listen and to accept change.

Unfortunately, no one possesses all these traits, but the more of the preceding traits police officers have, the more likely they are to be effective in dealing with not only the citizens of the community, but lawbreakers as well.

An LEAA funded study conducted at Indiana University ("Indiana University Develops Police Selection Procedure," 1977, p.1) identified twelve characteristics which separated good police officers from poor ones.

Characteristics of a "good" police officer include: reliability, leadership, judgment, persuasiveness, communication skills, accuracy, initiative, integrity, honesty, ego control, intelligence, and sensitivity.

Finding individuals qualified to become police officers is no easy task. The process of recruiting and screening candidates is a continuous and critical function of all police agencies in the country. By examining personnel selection developments over the past years, police administrators can evaluate the effectiveness of their personnel selection procedures. They can assess the recommendations made by the personnel branch and whether they are implemented, and they can assess whether their procedures conform with federal guidelines and regulations.

EXAMINATION ANNOUNCEMENTS

The most common recruitment practice is to place want ads in local newspapers, including minority newspapers, to attract more minority candidates. Notices are also sent to colleges and universities inviting students to make application. The actual in-person recruiting on campuses is not as prevalent today as it was in the 1960s when the demand for police officers was at an all-time high.

Police employees are a good source of recruitment as they frequently have friends who admire them and want to become police officers too. Community bulletin boards have been used effectively by some police agencies. In addition, police professional magazines may be used when many positions are open within a single agency.

Larger cities place spot announcements on television and radio and place notices with state employment agencies. Special posters are often used in advertising on buses, in libraries, and business establishments. Notices are usually brief, stating something like the following:

• **PROTECT AND SERVE** •
BE PROUD TO BE A POLICE OFFICER
NOW HIRING

Applications may be made at Mytown Police Department
1001 Main Street, Mytown, USA

When applicants come to the designated place, they are given a fact sheet containing a brief job description, the salary range, fringe benefits, and an application to be filled out and submitted. They are also given a time and place to report for the written examination. Candidates who cannot personally appear may call or write to have the information sent to them.

Most police agencies and civil service commissions accept applications even though no openings are presently listed. The application is placed on file, and when an examination is to be conducted, the applicant is notified by mail or phone.

THE SELECTION PROCESS

Whether a formal merit system or a civil service system is used, good job selection requires sound, equitable procedures. This means that a selection system which measures the predictable success of the officer on the job must be devised if it is not already in existence.

Although procedures differ greatly from agency to agency, several procedures are common to most selection processes.

> Police officer selection usually includes:
> —A formal application.
> —A preliminary screening.
>   Written examination.
>   Psychological examination.
> —A physical agility test.
> —An oral interview.
> —A medical examination.
> —A background investigation.

Failure at any point in the selection process may disqualify a candidate.

The Formal Application—Basic Requirements to Become a Police Officer

Usually anyone who wishes to become a police officer completes a formal application.

A careful examination of this formal application shows several factors which are evaluated in a candidate: driving record, any criminal record, visual acuity, physical-emotional-mental condition, and education. Notice, too, at the bottom of the application the reference to the background check which will be conducted, as well as the other tests required. These will be discussed after the *general requirements* for becoming a police officer are outlined.

The requirements for becoming a police officer are usually clearly specified by law, as for example, in the minimum standards for peace officers prescribed in the rules of the Attorney General in Minnesota (Mn Rules Atty. Gen. 201-218).

Figure 16-1.   Preliminary Employment Application for Peace Officer.

701A
PRELIMINARY EMPLOYMENT APPLICATION FOR PEACE OFFICER

INSTRUCTIONS

1. Use a typewriter or print your answers in ink.
2. Answer all questions carefully and correctly.
3. If space provided for answer is not sufficient, use a separate sheet of paper of the same size as this application form. At the top of each separate sheet write your name, address, and position applied for.
4. Avoid all reference to religion, sex, age, race, national origin, color, membership in fraternal orders, or political affiliations.
5. Notify _____ immediately of any change of address after filing application.

DO NOT WRITE IN THIS SPACE

Physical _____

Agility _____

Psychological _____

Written _____

Veteran's preference _____

- -

1. Title of Position Applied For (Please check one or more)

   Deputy Sheriff ☐   Police Officer ☐   Highway Patrol ☐   Other ☐ _____

2. Name (First Name, Middle Initial, Last Name): _____

3. Address: _____
   Number and Street   City   State   Zip code

4. Telephone: Home (___) _____ Business (___) _____ Other (___) _____
   A/C   A/C   A/C

5. Date of Birth: _____   6. Social Security Number: ___ — ___ — ___

7. Driver's license number: _____ State: _____

   Have you ever been convicted of a crime which is a felony in State of Anywhere?   Yes ☐   No ☐

9. Visual acuity (if known): R 20/ _____ L 20/ _____

10. Is your visual acuity correctable to R 20/ _____ L 20/ _____ ?   Yes ☐   No ☐   Unsure ☐

11. Are you free from color blindness?   Yes ☐   No ☐   Unsure ☐

12. Are you aware of any physical disabilities that would prevent you from performing the duties of a peace officer? If yes, please explain.

    No ☐ Yes ☐ _____
    _____

13. Are you aware of any emotional or mental disabilities that would prevent you from performing the duties of a peace officer? If yes, please explain.

    No ☐ Yes ☐ _____
    _____

14. Are you a certified peace officer?   Yes ☐   No ☐   If yes, where? _____

15. Secondary education

    Are you a high school graduate?   Yes ☐   No ☐   If no, last year completed: _____

    Do you have a G.E.D. certificate?   Yes ☐   No ☐

16. Post-secondary education

    Total years completed: _____   Degree(s) received: _____

I hereby certify that all statements made in this application are true and complete to the best of my knowledge and ability, and I realize that any misstatement or omission of material facts may subject me to disqualification, dismissal or criminal prosecution.

_____   _____ , 19 _____
Signature (Full Name of Applicant)   Date

All applicants shall be subject to a thorough background investigation including fingerprinting. Employment of any applicant shall depend upon his or her successful completion of a written test, a physical (medical) examination, a test of physical strength and agility, a psychological evaluation, and an oral interview.

RULES AND REGULATIONS

AttyGen 207   New Peace Officers

(a) All appointing agencies, when requested, shall furnish the name, address, date of appointment, and other pertinent information concerning a newly appointed peace officer to the Executive Director.

(b) No appointing agency shall appoint any new peace officer who does not comply with the minimum selection standards hereinafter enumerated; provided, that these standards shall not be construed to restrict an appointing agency from promulgating more rigid standards in the areas enumerated.

(1) The applicant must be a citizen of the United States.

(2) The applicant must possess or be eligible for a valid State of Minnesota driver's license.

(3) The applicant must successfully pass a written examination demonstrating the possession of all mental skills necessary for the accomplishment of the duties and functions of a peace officer.

(4) The applicant shall be required to complete and submit to the appointing agency a preliminary application form before testing and a comprehensive application form after testing and just prior to hiring. The prospective employee shall be fingerprinted, and a thorough background search shall be made through the resources of local, state and Federal agencies in order to disclose the existence of any criminal record or the existence of unacceptable standards of conduct which would adversely affect the performance by the individual of his duties as a peace officer.

(5) The applicant shall not have been convicted of a felony in this state or in any other state or in any Federal jurisdiction, or of any offense in any other state or in any Federal jurisdiction, which would have been a felony if committed in this state.

(6) A licensed physician or surgeon shall make a thorough medical examination of the applicant to determine that he or she is free from any physical condition which might adversely affect the performance by the individual of his duties as a peace officer.

(7) An evaluation shall be made by a licensed psychologist to determine that the applicant is free from any emotional or mental condition which might adversely affect the performance by the individual of his or her duties as a peace officer.

(8) The applicant must successfully pass a job-related examination of his or her physical strength and agility demonstrating the possession of physical skills necessary to the accomplishment of the duties and functions of a peace officer.

(9) The applicant must successfully complete an oral examination conducted by or for the appointing agency to demonstrate the possession of communication skills necessary to the accomplishment of the duties and functions of a peace officer.

Although several of the regulations pertain to procedures the applicant must complete, some general qualifications are also cited.

Most agencies require that a police officer:
—Be a citizen of the United States.
—Have or be eligible for a driver's license in the state.
—Not have been convicted of a felony.

Requirements related to height, weight, age, education, and residency are also frequently stated.

Height, Weight, and Age Requirements. The most common minimum height requirement for police candidates has been 5'7" and the maximum 6'6". No "ideal" height or weight is specified; the requirements have been based purely on psychological reactions. It is generally thought that larger officers have less trouble handling situations that might result in violence, and it would be less necessary for them to undertake force because of their size. Height restrictions have posed problems for women and members of some minorities as will be discussed later.

> Height requirements are usually from 5'7" to 6'6".
> Weight should be in favorable ratio to height.
> Age requirements are usually from 21-35.

Weight has become a more important consideration than in the past. Recent emphasis on physical fitness has resulted in the discouragement of obesity and the encouragement of a favorable height-weight ratio. Overweight candidates generally have a difficult time passing the required physical agility tests.

Insurance companies' tables are normally used as a guide for weight requirements. For example, height-weight requirements might be as follows:

Height	Minimum Weight	Maximum Weight
5'8"	145 lbs.	175 lbs.
6'0"	165 lbs.	195 lbs.
6'4"	186 lbs.	225 lbs.

An obese candidate could be disqualified immediately, a decision usually made by an examining physician. However, in smaller cities, the chief of police may make the determination.

Depending on the supply and demand for police officers, age is generally restricted to ages twenty-one to thirty-five. However, several factors are considered when defining age requirements. The voting age is eighteen, and most large cities allow eighteen-year-olds to be tested, but keep them on an eligibility list until they are twenty-one. Age is usually waived for patrol officers who want to move laterally from one department to another. This common practice does not affect the promotional opportunities of those who might already be in the department.

Police agencies prefer younger officers because they are easily educable, have fewer firmly entrenched bad habits, are generally in better physical condition, and can more easily adapt their attitudes. They also have a tendency to show more esprit de corps and are more likely to make the police department their career.

Education. Opinions differ as to how much education a candidate for police officer should have. Most police agencies require a minimum of a high-school education or equivalency certificate. Some municipal and state agencies require no formal education, and a few require only an eighth-grade education. Smaller police departments appear to have more liberal selection educational standards.

On the other hand, some jurisdictions require at least two years of college and some a four-year degree. One recommendation of the President's Commission on Law Enforcement and Administration of Justice (*The Police* 1967, p. 123) is that educational requirements should be increased to two years of college for police officer candidates.

> Most police agencies require a minimum of a high-school education.

Some administrators use set educational standards to attain professionalism and upgrade the service. However, police chiefs are at odds as to whether education contributes significantly to the fight against crime. Unquestionably, a college-educated police officer contributes significantly to the quality of police service. On the other hand, some police chiefs feel that too much education makes social service officers of personnel who ought to be fighting crime in the streets. Some surveys indicate that the more education police officers have, the less likely they are to become involved in physical confrontations. Other police chiefs feel that to require a degreed officer to perform such mundane tasks as issuing traffic tickets and parking tickets, making money runs, and carding juveniles in liquor stores is demeaning and that such routine tasks soon diminish the highly educated officer's interest in law enforcement. Besides, they argue, most police officers see themselves as crime fighters, not social engineers.

Still, some police agencies (usually in large cities) seek to attract college-educated recruits by offering better career and promotional opportunities, higher salaries, and further educational opportunities. Often such agencies also offer incentive programs for completed education.

Residency Requirements.   Over the years, cities and municipalities have reluctantly waived residency requirements to obtain better candidates. Though generally not required, cities are again beginning to accept only candidates who reside in their cities.

> It is always preferred and sometimes required that police officers live in the community they serve.

Sometimes compromises have been made whereby candidates are given one year to move into the community they serve. City and municipal politicians feel that by living in the community, a police officer becomes more closely identified with that community, more sensitive to its crime problems, and more readily participates in community activities.

The value of living in the community served cannot be disputed. Police officers are better able to understand the problems and needs of the community. They also develop relationships with the professional groups in the community and can better understand the life style of the citizens. Additionally, politicians self-interests dictate that their police officers live in their communities so they can contribute their fair share of taxes. However, it may be economically unfeasible for police officers to afford to live in the community they serve.

The issue of pre-employment residency raises controversial legal questions. In a Minnesota case, Carter v. Gallagher, 452 F. 2d 315 (1971), the legitimacy of the state's Veteran's Preference Law was challenged. The law gave preference for government jobs to those who had lived in Minnesota before entering military service or who had lived in Minnesota for at least five years after completing their military service. The challenge was made that the requirement discriminated against veterans who, although fully qualified, had not lived in Minnesota for the required time. The Minnesota Supreme Court ruled that the state had no interest in the residency requirement and further found that the requirement was inconsistent with the equal protection clause of the Fourteenth Amendment. The court ordered the practice discontinued.

☑ CHECK POINT

1. What general characteristics are desirable in a police officer?
2. What steps usually occur during police officer selection?
3. What general qualifications are usually required for individuals who wish to become police officers?
4. What are the normal height, weight, and age requirements?
5. What are the normal educational requirements?
6. What are the usual residence requirements?

*Answers

1. Characteristics of a "good" police officer include: reliability, leadership, judgment, persuasiveness, communication skills, accuracy, initiative, integrity, honesty, ego control, intelligence, and sensitivity.
2. Police officer selection usually includes: (1) a formal application, (2) a preliminary screening consisting of a written examination and a psychological examination, (3) a physical agility test, (4) an oral interview, (5) a medical examination, and (6) a background investigation. Do not worry if you didn't remember these items; they will be easier to recall after you have read more fully about each.
3. Most agencies require that a police officer (1) be a United States citizen, (2) have or be eligible for a driver's license in the state, and (3) not have been convicted of a felony.
4. Height requirements usually range from 5'7" to 6'6"; weight should be in favorable ratio to height; age requirements are usually from 21 to 35.
5. Most police agencies require a minimum of a high-school education.
6. It is always preferred and sometimes required that police officers live in the community they serve.

Preliminary Screening Tests

The demands upon police officers are great. Not only are they subjected to emotional and physical stress, they also are placed in positions of trust and responsibility. Effective screening tests are, therefore, a necessity.

> Most candidates are required to complete a preliminary screening consisting of a written examination and a psychological examination. Standardized tests may be used.

The written examination has assumed a critical importance with the advent of civil rights legislation and the introduction of women into uniformed patrol work. Many unsuccessful applicants have challenged certain written examinations as being arbitrary and/or discriminatory. Their efforts have led to a reappraisal of the tests.

The use of specific standardized tests and their purpose must be carefully considered and justified, or the agency may run into legal difficulties. For example, in 1971 a class action suit charged the Duke Power Company for discrimination against a group of black employees by using standardized tests to determine promotion. In Griggs v. Duke Power Co. 401 U.S. 424 91 S. Ct. 849 (1971), the United States Supreme Court ruled that the Civil Rights Act of 1964 was concerned with the *consequences* of testing, not the employer's good intent or lack of intentional discrimination. The Court upheld the Equal Employment Opportunity Commission (EEOC) guidelines of 1966.

> Griggs v. Duke Power Company established that all tests used for employment purposes must measure a tested person's capability to perform a specific job. Additionally, all requirements and standards established must be business or job related.

Neither the courts nor the EEOC have drawn a distinction between the requirements for entrance examinations and those for promotional examinations. Consequently, law enforcement agencies have taken a greater interest in the content of written tests, and today's written examinations are generally of a high quality.

Some critics are opposed to any examination of candidates for employment because certain tests have been declared to be arbitrary or discriminatory. However, not all challenges come from members of minority groups. Successful challenges, whatever their origin, have been founded upon evidence that the tests in question were not job related, that is, they were invalid. A *valid test* measures what it purports to measure: in the case of law enforcement, potential success in law enforcement. The importance of validated tests is twofold. First, a validated test helps an agency discover the best candidates available. Second, it helps avoid time-consuming and costly legal challenges.

Test validation is a difficult procedure, beyond the resources of many agencies; therefore, most law enforcement agencies find it more economical to use standardized tests. Seldom, however, does an agency rely upon these tests alone. They also consider physical agility tests, oral interview results, medical examinations, and background check information.

Some police departments have supplemented their preliminary screening procedures with examinations that determine police adaptability, memory retention, reading comprehension, spelling, and potential of the candidate to fit into the present organization.

Those candidates who survive the original preliminary testing or screening procedures of the police agency go on to other testing procedures including physical agility tests, oral interviews, medical examinations, and a thorough background check.

Physical Agility Tests

Physical fitness tests are usually administered to determine a candidate's coordination and muscular strength and to predict whether the candidate is in good or poor physical condition. The type of test varies with police agencies throughout the country.

> Physical agility tests evaluate a candidate's coordination, speed of movement, and strength. The most common physical agility tests are similar to a military obstacle course which must be completed in a designated time.

A candidate may be required to run a designated number of yards and while doing so, hurdle a three-foot barrier, crawl under a twenty-four inch bar, climb over a four or six foot wall with both hands on the top of the wall, and sprint the remaining distance—all within a designated time period monitored by a police officer with a stopwatch.

Candidates may also be required to climb ropes or fire ladders, do chin-ups (grasp a bar and pull up a required number of times), or push-ups (from a front leaning rest position, hands flat on the floor with the chest barely touching the floor, push up a required number of times).

Other variations of the physical agility test may be required, but usually only a minimum of strenuous activity is required.

Physical agility tests are necessary because they simulate what an officer may have to do on the street—jumping over a fence, climbing a wall, or chasing someone through back yards or streets. Candidates who are considerably overweight rarely pass the physical agility test.

Usually a candidate unable to pass the test the first time is given a second chance. A second failure results in disqualification.

A candidate can prepare for the physical agility test through a regular system of workouts. Running is an excellent general conditioner because it develops endurance and strengthens the legs. Sit-ups, leg-lift exercises, push-ups, and lifting light weights are also helpful in preparing for the physical agility test. Like knowledge, physical fitness does not develop overnight; it develops gradually over an extended period.

The Oral Interview

Oral boards usually consist of three to five skilled interviewers, knowledgeable in their fields. They may be staff officers from the agency doing the hiring or from other agencies, psychologists, sociologists, or representatives of a community service organization. The entire interviewing board may consist of members of a police or civil service commission. In smaller jurisdictions, oral boards are sometimes replaced by an interview with the mayor, a councilman, or the chief of police.

> The oral interview seeks information about the candidate's personality and suitability for police work.

The interview, whether structured or unstructured, is designed to elicit answers revealing the candidates' personalities and suitability for police work, *not* to determine their technical knowledge in the police field.

The candidate should be prepared to answer questions such as the following:

—Why do you want to be a police officer?

—What have you done to prepare for a career in law enforcement?

—What do you feel are the causes of crime?

—What are your favorite hobbies?

—Have you talked to your wife/husband about this position of police officer?

—What does she/he think about it?

—What is the last book you have read?

—What was your favorite subject in school?

—When did you last get drunk?

The oral interview will also test the candidate's ability to use good judgment in specific situations such as the following:

—A person is standing on the corner making a speech regarding the overthrow of the government. He is drawing a crowd, and a certain amount of animosity is being shown toward the speaker, indicating future trouble. How would you handle this situation?

—You are working radar and you clock the mayor going 39 mph in a 30 mph zone. How would you handle this situation?

—You are walking a beat and a juvenile thrusts a stick between your legs causing you to fall to the pavement and tear your pants. What would you do?

The interview usually lasts about thirty minutes. The same questions are asked each candidate to allow comparison of answers. After the interview, the qualifications of each candidate are evaluated.

> The oral interview usually evaluates appearance, ability to present ideas, social adaptability, alertness, judgment, emotional stability, interest in the job, and communication ability.

Each candidate is given an overall rating which is combined with the scores of the other examinations to yield a composite (total) score. The following Oral Examination Rating Form is typical of how an oral interview is evaluated:

Figure 16-2.

```
                              MUNICIPAL - COUNTY

 CS-131                   ORAL EXAMINATION RATING FORM


 Name of Jurisdiction _____

 Name of Candidate _____ Date _____

 For Position of _____   USE ONLY ONE RATING FORM

 Place of Examination _____   FOR EACH CANDIDATE


  I      II     III      IV

 ( )    ( )    ( )      ( ) 100   Exceptional qualifications.  Recommend with enthusiasm.

 ( )    ( )    ( )      ( ) 95

 ( )    ( )    ( )      ( ) 90    High qualifications.  Recommend without reservation.

 ( )    ( )    ( )      ( ) 85

 ( )    ( )    ( )      ( ) 80    Good qualifications.  Recommended with confidence.

 ( )    ( )    ( )      ( ) 75

 ( )    ( )    ( )      ( ) 70    Acceptable qualifications.  Would probably succeed in
                                     position.
 _____

 ( )    ( )    ( )      ( ) 50    Doubtful qualifications.  Should not be considered at
                                     this time.


 Examiners:    I  _____   Send the oral examination rating forms to the State of
                                    Anywhere Civil Service Department, 215 State Adminis-
               II _____    tration Bldg.  By combining the oral examination score
                                    with the written score, a final score will be determined,
              III _____    and a suggested eligible list will be established.

               IV _____

 INSTRUCTIONS:

 Examiner I will place his check mark in one of the boxes in Column I and then sign his name
 after Examiner I.  Examiner II will place his check mark in one of the boxes in Column II
 and then sign his name after Examiner II.  Examiner III and Examiner IV, if there is a
 fourth, will do the same.  The Examiners may give different scores.  They need not concur on
 their ratings.  Our department will average their scores.
```

Candidates should prepare themselves both physically and mentally for the oral interview. They should be well groomed and present a professional appearance. They should have considered in advance responses to questions which are likely to be asked. It is critical to be well prepared since the oral interview generally disqualifies more candidates than it qualifies.

☑ CHECK POINT

1. What is generally included in the preliminary screening?
2. What impact did the Griggs v. Duke Power Company decision have on the use of tests for employment purposes?
3. What are most physical agility tests like and what do they test for?
4. What type of information is sought during the oral interview?

✱ Answers

1. The preliminary screening usually includes a written examination and a psychological examination.
2. Griggs v. Duke Power Company established that all tests used for employment purposes must measure a tested person's capability to perform a specific job. Additionally, all requirements and standards established must be business or job related.
3. Physical agility tests most commonly resemble a military obstacle course that must be completed in a designated time. They evaluate coordination, speed of movement, and strength.
4. The oral interview seeks information about the candidate's personality and suitability for police work including appearance, ability to present ideas, social adaptability, alertness, judgment, emotional stability, interest in the job, and communication ability.

The Medical Examination

Medical requirements vary from jurisdiction to jurisdiction, but the purpose is the same. With the modern emphasis on health care, more and more importance is being placed on the medical examination. Citizens, concerned about the possibility of early retirements due to poor health, are demanding physically fit candidates.

The medical standards usually include a variety of factors with some being more important than others.

> Vision, hearing, and the cardiovascular-respiratory system are of prime importance in the medical examination.

Good eyesight is of great importance. Candidates who wear glasses that correct their vision to meet the agency's requirements can qualify. Likewise, candidates who wear hearing aids that correct their hearing to meet the agency's requirements can qualify.

Because of the stress of the job and the hypertension that frequently accompanies it, the cardiovascular system is thoroughly checked. The respiratory and cardiovascular system play a critical role in fitness. To a great degree, endurance, the ability to continue exertion over a prolonged time, is directly related to the capacity of the cardiovascular-respiratory system to deliver oxygen to the muscles.

A physician who feels a candidate has a functional or organic disorder may recommend disqualification of that candidate.

The Background Investigation

The applicant's background is one of the most critical factors considered in recruitment. In most police agencies an applicant must submit a personal history. The background investigation serves two purposes: (1) it examines the past work and/or educational record of the candidate and (2) it determines if anything in the candidate's background might make him unsuitable for police work. The extensiveness of the background investigation is limited only by the number of candidates being investigated and time available.

> The background investigation includes:
>
> —Verification of all information on the application and history sheet.
> —Check on driving record.
> —Fingerprinting and a check on any criminal record.
> —Check on military records.
> —Interviews with personal references, acquaintances, past employers, neighbors, and teachers.
> —Check on financial status.
> —Check on past performance at school and previous jobs.

Normally all information given by the applicant on the history sheet must be verified. Birth and age records are verified through vital statistics, driving record through the drivers' license bureau. Adverse driving records containing drunken driving, driving after suspension or revocation of license, or a consistent pattern of moving violations may cause disqualification.

Candidates are fingerprinted, and the prints are sent to the Federal Bureau of Investigation in Washington to determine if the candidate has a criminal record. The candidate's criminal record is also checked on the local and state level, usually through fingerprints, name, and date of birth. Juvenile records are normally discounted unless a person has committed a heinous crime.

Ironically, because of the transient nature of our population, persons wanted on warrants in one part of the country have applied for a police officer's position in another part of the country. The criminal record check has sometimes resulted in the apprehension of such individuals.

Military records are usually checked to verify service and eligibility under the veteran's preference acts of some states. The check also determines if the candidate was involved in any court martials or disciplinary actions.

All personal and professional references, individuals with personal knowledge of the candidate, listed on the history sheet are interviewed. Interviewing of references is sometimes criticized because candidates obviously will list only those who see them favorably. However, these references may lead to others who know the candidates and have a different view of them. When candidates list out-of-town references, letters or questionnaires are usually mailed.

Neighbors of the candidate, past or present, are an excellent source of information about a candidate's character and reputation. No department wants police officers who have had prior association with the criminal element, who have been addicted to narcotics or drugs, or who abuse alcohol. Their reputation in the community should be high.

Previous employers are contacted to determine the applicant's work record. Inability to hold continuous employment may indicate trouble getting along with supervisors. A high absentee rate may indicate lack of interest, initiative, or health problems.

The financial status of the candidate is also determined, usually through a credit records check. Individuals whose expenditures exceed their total income may be candidates for bankruptcy or bribery. Good credit indicates the person can live within his means and possesses self control. The candidate may be required to submit a financial statement.

Educational records from high school, college, and any other schools attended are usually checked through personal contact. The education record may indicate interests, achievements, accomplishments, and social life style while attending school. The scholastic record reflects not only intelligence but study habits. Any degrees, certificates of achievement, or awards are usually noted.

The use of the polygraph examination as a follow-up to the background investigation is a widely increasing means of verifying the background of a candidate. Although some states have banned its use for pre-employment purposes, where it is used to screen police candidates, it is necessary to determine why it is being given. Some departments use the polygraph extensively, especially if they have many transient applicants from other parts of the country. Some agencies use it to determine if the candidate has ever engaged in criminal activity and never apprehended. Some want to know about the candidate's sexual behavior; is he a sex deviant? Others use it to verify the written information the candidate has given them on the application and history sheet.

It is imperative that the polygraph examiner be ethical and professionally competent. Any questions asked the applicant beyond those pertaining directly to the suitability of the candidate for police service could be construed as discriminatory and negate any information obtained through the use of the polygraph.

The Final Result

After all required tests are completed, they are analyzed and a composite score is given for each candidate. A list is made of eligible candidates, and they are called as openings occur in the police department. Some larger police departments keep their eligibility lists from one to two years, depending on civil service requirements or other requirements mandated by states or municipalities.

☑ CHECK POINT

1. **What factors are of prime importance in the medical examination?**

2. What occurs during the background investigation?
3. The final result of the selection procedure is based on the results of what six procedures? (What six steps occur in the selection process?)

✱ Answers

1. Vision, hearing, and cardiovascular-respiratory system are of prime importance in the medical examination.
2. The background investigation includes (1) verification of all information on the application and history sheet, (2) check on driving record, (3) fingerprinting and a check on any criminal record, (4) check on military record, (5) interviews with personal references, acquaintances, past employers, neighbors, and teachers, (6) check on financial status, and (7) check on past performance at school and previous jobs.
3. The candidate must successfully complete (1) a formal application, (2) preliminary screening including a written examination and a psychological examination, (3) a physical agility test, (4) an oral interview, (5) a medical examination, and (6) a thorough background investigation.

PROBATION AND TRAINING

When candidates are sworn in as police officers to uphold the laws of the state and the country and they swear to the code of ethics, they are on the way to their life ambition.

Some states have mandated that recruits must be given from 240 to 400 hours of police training within one year of employment. Coincidentally, this is also usually the length of time the officers are placed on probation.

> The probationary period is a trial period, usually one year, during which the officer is observed while obtaining training and applying this training on the streets.

Police officers may obtain their training in a state police academy, a city academy, or a specialized "rookie" school. The basic training of police officers varies with each jurisdiction and its needs, but most officers will be trained in constitutional law, laws of arrest, search and seizure, and in the various requests for service such as accident investigation, crisis intervention, and giving first aid.

While in training they may be required to come back to the department and spend a specified number of hours on street patrol. Some jurisdictions break up their training periods every two weeks, allowing an officer to apply on the street what was learned in basic recruit school.

While on the street the recruits ride with a "trainer," usually a sergeant, who monitors their movements and helps them apply principles learned in rookie school. While in school, the officers are evaluated and tested by their instructors who periodically send progress reports to the chief of police. After completing training, they continue to ride with one or more training officers who continue to evaluate their street performance.

Following successful completion of the probationary period, they are full-fledged police officers. After probation some states license the person to be a police officer. Legislatures in Texas, Michigan, California, Oregon, Minnesota, and other states have adopted standards for police officers which must be met to satisfy the state's training requirements for licensing.

States have also mandated a certain amount of in-service training to keep the license current. Many of these in-service training requirements revolve around the behavioral sciences so police officers have a better understanding of the entire criminal justice system. Guest speakers from the corrections system, the court system, and on many occasions from minority groups appear to give their philosophy and objectives to police officers.

PHYSICAL FITNESS TRAINING PROGRAMS

Because recruits and experienced officers often face situations involving physical restraint and self-defense, police departments have set up both mandatory and voluntary physical fitness programs for officers. Job-related stress has sometimes affected officers to the extent that many retire early because of physical disability.

Controversy over physical fitness programs exists; some police administrators feel the police are being singled out from other employees. Nevertheless, it is obvious that law enforcement officers should maintain a high level of physical fitness. It is not only desirable from the standpoint of being able to enjoy life to the fullest, for police officers it is a necessity because they are frequently faced with situations that place great demands on their physical capacity. Physical fitness may make the difference between success and failure on the job—sometimes even the difference between life and death.

As noted in *Physical Fitness for Law Enforcement Officers* (1972, p. 1): "The officer who lacks the muscular strength and endurance so necessary to successfully cope with these situations is not prepared to adequately discharge his duties."

In spite of this, many law enforcement officers have no opportunity to participate in an organized, supervised physical fitness training program; physical fitness is left entirely up to the individual officer. Consequently, it is important for each individual in law enforcement to understand what physical fitness is and how it can be achieved.

In general terms, *physical fitness* is a state of well-being which permits one to enjoy life to the fullest; it is the general capacity to adapt and respond favorably to physical effort. Many people evaluate fitness on the basis of appearance alone. Although personal appearance does have some bearing, what is going on inside is more important. The traditional image of fitness—the Charles Atlas physique—has given way to an image which stresses endurance and stamina as the true indicators of fitness.

Although many factors contribute to a well-conditioned body, the prime factor is the condition of the circulatory (cardiovascular) system upon which endurance or stamina is dependent. Other factors important in physical fitness are balance, flexibility, agility, strength and power.

The prime factor in physical fitness is endurance (dependent upon the circulatory system). Other important factors are balance, flexibility, agility, strength and power.

Endurance or stamina is the capacity for continued exertion over prolonged periods as well as the ability to withstand pain, distress, and fatigue for extended periods. Physical endurance is required in long distance running, swimming, cycling, and wrestling.

Balance is neuromuscular control—the muscles and nerves working together to perform various movements. Poor balance results in poor body control and may cause the individual to be "accident prone."

Flexibility is mobility of the joints, the ability to "bend without breaking." A flexible person has a wide range of movement; a stiff person has a very restricted range of movement. Loss of flexibility is frequently one of the first signs of physical deterioration.

Agility is the ability to react quickly and easily. Agility is needed to run an obstacle course, to jump or vault fences or barriers, to climb a ladder quickly, or to lie down and spring back up. Agility enables an officer to successfully cope with emergencies and minimizes the chance of personal injury.

Strength and power imply toughness, durability, and vigor, as well as the ability to exert force with the hands, arms, legs, or trunk. *Strength* is needed to perform routine or daily tasks. For example, hand and arm strength is needed to lift or pull heavy objects. Leg strength is needed to walk, run, and jump. Trunk strength is needed to support all movements of the arms and legs. *Power* is the explosive force which moves the body suddenly or which propels some object independent of the body. It requires power to run the sprints, to hurdle, or to high-jump.

SELF-EVALUATION

A self-evaluation may reveal some startling things about yourself. Just because you feel good or have no recognized diseases does not necessarily mean you are physically fit. The FBI's publication *Physical Fitness for Law Enforcement Officers* (1972, pp.19-24) recommends the following:*

Feel your arms, shoulders, stomach, buttocks, and legs. Are your muscles well-toned or are you soft and flabby?

"Give yourself the pinch test. Take hold of the skin just above your belt. Are your fingers separated by more than one-half inch?"[1]

Give yourself the weight test. What is your weight today compared with your weight when you were 21?"[2]

Ask yourself these questions:

Are you overweight, soft, flabby, tired, and under par most of the time?

Do you look, feel, and act ten years older than you actually are?

Does the slightest bit of physical exertion cause your heart to pound, make you gasp for breath, and leave you in a weakened and wornout condition?

Do you lack endurance, that inner reserve power which allows you to safely overcome situations requiring a maximum physical effort?

*Reprinted with the permission of the Federal Bureau of Investigation.

The self-examination as set forth above will no doubt give you a good indication of your physical condition and appearance; however, further steps should be taken to ascertain *dynamic fitness*. Dynamic fitness is evaluated by your response to physical activity.[3]

"The principle underlying physiological tests of dynamic fitness is based upon the general agreement that the capacity to perform continuous work in a temperate environment is related to the capacity of the cardiovascular-respiratory system to deliver oxygen to the muscles (the maximum oxygen intake)."[4]

The physical fitness tests that are set out as follows will enable you to evaluate all aspects of your cardiovascular and musculoskeletal fitness:

CARDIOVASCULAR TESTS

Cureton's Breath-Holding Test

One simple and acceptable way of testing your respiratory capacity, which is related to circulatory fitness, is to step onto and off a chair, bench, or stool (approximately 17 inches high) for a period of one minute and then see how long you can hold your breath. You should be able to hold it for at least 30 seconds. If you can't, it's an indication that your cardiovascular function has deteriorated below a desirable level.[5]

Kasch Pulse Recovery Test (3 min.)

This test can be performed by either sex and almost any age group. Only the infirm or the extremely unfit would find it too strenuous. You should not smoke for one hour or eat for two hours prior to taking the test. Also, you should rest for five minutes before taking the test.

EQUIPMENT:
12" bench or stool
Clock or watch with a sweep second hand

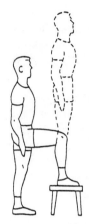

PROCEDURE:
a) Start stepping onto and off the bench when sweep second hand is at 11.
b) Step 24 per minute, total 72
c) Duration is three minutes
d) Stop stepping when sweep second hand is again at 11, after three revolutions, and sit down.
e) Start counting the pulse rate when sweep second hand reaches 12 on the clock, using either the artery located inside the wrist or the carotid artery in the throat. Count every 10 seconds and record for one minute.
f) Total the six pulse counts for one minute and compare with the following scale:

CLASSIFICATION	0-1 MINUTE PULSE RATE AFTER EXERCISE[6]
Excellent	71-78
Very Good	79-83
Average	84-99
Below Average	100-107
Poor	108-118

Cooper's 12-Minute Walk/Run Test

NOTE: Persons over 30 years of age should not take this test until they have had a complete medical examination and have completed approximately six weeks in a "starter physical fitness program."

Find a place where you can run/walk a measured distance of up to two miles. A quarter-mile track at a local school would be ideal; however, a nearby park, field, or quiet stretch of road can be used. The test is quite simple—see how much of the two miles you can comfortably cover in 12 minutes. Try to run the entire time at a pace you can maintain without excessive strain. If your breath becomes short, walk until it returns to normal, then run again. Keep going for a full 12 minutes, then check your performance on the following scale:

FITNESS CATEGORY[7]	AGE			
	UNDER 30	**30 TO 39**	**40 TO 49**	**50**
1. Very Poor	<1.0	<.95	< .85	< .80
2. Poor	1.0-1.24	.95-1.14	.85-1.04	.80-.99
3. Fair	1.25-1.49	1.15-1.39	1.05-1.29	1.0 -1.24
4. Good	1.50-1.74	1.40-1.64	1.30-1.54	1.25-1.49
5. Excellent	1.75+	1.65+	1.55+	1.50+

< Means less than   (distance in miles covered in 12 minutes)

BALANCE TEST

Stand on your toes, heels together, eyes closed, and your arms stretched forward at shoulder level. Maintain this position for 20 seconds without shifting your feet or opening your eyes. (FIGURE 1) [8]

FLEXIBILITY TESTS

Trunk Flexion

Keep your legs together, your knees locked, bend at the waist and touch the floor with your fingertips. (FIGURE 2)[9]

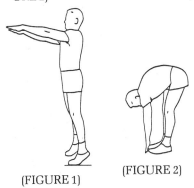

(FIGURE 1)   (FIGURE 2)

Trunk Extension

Lie flat on your stomach, face down, fingers laced behind your neck and your feet anchored to the floor. Now raise your chin until it is 18 inches off the floor. (FIGURE 3)[10]

(FIGURE 3)

(NOTE: Average for men students at the University of Illinois is 12.5 inches.)[11]

AGILITY TEST

Squat Thrusts

Standing, drop down to squatting position, palms flat against floor, arms straight. (FIGURE 4) Next, with weight supported on the hands, kick backward so that your legs are extended fully. (FIGURE 5) Immediately kick forward to the squatting position (FIGURE 6) and stand up. You should be able to perform four in eight seconds.

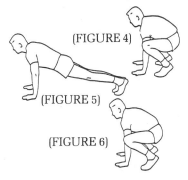

(FIGURE 4)

(FIGURE 5)

(FIGURE 6)

STRENGTH TESTS
Pull-ups

Hang from a bar, hands slightly wider than shoulders, palms turned away, arms fully extended. (FIGURE 7) Pull up until your chin is over the bar. (FIGURE 8) Lower yourself until your arms are fully extended and repeat. You should be able to perform four pull-ups.

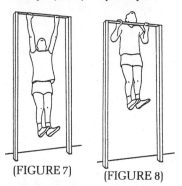

(FIGURE 7)   (FIGURE 8)

Push-ups

From the front leaning rest position, hands slightly wider than the shoulders with fingers pointed straight ahead (FIGURE 9), lower your body until your chest barely touches the floor. (FIGURE 10) Push up to the front leaning rest position, keeping your body straight. You should be able to perform 15 push-ups.[12]

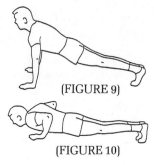

(FIGURE 9)

(FIGURE 10)

Sit-ups

Lie on your back with your hands behind your neck, with your legs straight and free. Flex the trunk and sit up, (FIGURE 11) and then re-

turn to the starting position. You should be able to perform 25 sit-ups.[13]

(FIGURE 11)

POWER TESTS
Standing Broad Jump

From a standing position, jump as far forward as you can, landing on both feet. (FIGURE 12) Do not take a running start. The length of your jump should equal your height.[14]

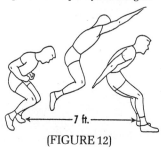

—— 7 ft. ——

(FIGURE 12)

Vertical Jump

Stand facing a wall, feet and chin touching wall, arms extended over the head. Mark the height of the hands on the wall. (A piece of chalk will do.) Now jump up and touch the wall as high as you can with one hand. (Use chalk). (FIGURE 13) Note the difference between the two marks on the wall. You should be able to perform a vertical jump of 18 inches or more.[15]

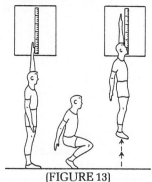

(FIGURE 13)

MISCONCEPTIONS AND FALLACIES CONCERNING FITNESS

TOO FAR GONE—Many people feel that they are either too old or have deteriorated physically to such a degree that it is impossible to get back into good physical condition. Actually this is not true. Regardless of age or how far one has slipped, a person who is organically sound can become fit through a good physical training program.

HARD WORK WILL KILL YOU—A rather common misconception simply stated is "The harder you work—the quicker you die." Not only is this false, it is just the opposite of the truth. We must exercise on a regular basis or we deteriorate. People "rust out" from inactivity more than they "wear out" from hard physical work.[16]

ANY KIND OF EXERCISE IS OKAY—Another fallacy is that any kind of exercise is okay, regardless of intensity, duration, or frequency. It is rather obvious that different exercises and activities have various degrees of value.[17] Short-duration exercises such as stretching or isometrics offer very limited benefits. Likewise, an hour of handball or three fast sets of tennis every three or four weeks by a sedentary person not only offers limited benefits, but it could be downright dangerous. The programs most beneficial are those which are performed on a regular basis and are directed toward all aspects of total fitness (endurance, strength, flexibility, et cetera).

THE EASY WAY TO FITNESS—Attaining and maintaining a relatively high level of fitness requires hard work. This is contrary to a great deal of the information and advertisements pertaining to fitness machines. This includes such things as motor-driven stationary bicycles, electric shock devices, and various forms of vibrators, et cetera. They imply that fitness can be achieved without work. This is not true. Fitness is attained after many months of regular endurance-type exercise and it is maintained only by regular participation in an exercise program.[18]

MASSAGE AND "SWEAT THERAPY"—Steam baths, sauna baths, mineral baths and various forms of massage have been advocated as increasing fitness. Although they have some tranquilizing and relaxing effects, they have no true fitness value.[19]

REFERENCES

[1]Allman, Fred L., Jr., M.D., Executive Fitness Desk Diary, (MB Productions Company, Dallas, Texas, 1969), p. 15.

[2]*Ibid.*

[3]Cureton, Thomas K., Jr., Physical Fitness and Dynamic Health, (The Dial Press, New York, New York, 1965), p. 22.

[4]Allman, *op. cit.*, p. 15.

[5]Cureton, *op cit.*, p. 49.

[6]Boyer, John L., and Kasch, Fred W., Adult Fitness, Principles and Practices, (All American Productions and Publications, Greeley, Colorado, 1968), p. 1.

[7]Cooper, Kenneth H., The New Aerobics, (Bantam Book by M. Evans and Company, New York, New York, 1970), pp. 29-30.

[8]Cureton, *op. cit.*, p. 44.

[9]*Ibid.*, p. 45.

[10]*Ibid.*

[11]Cureton, Thomas Kirk, Physical Fitness Workbook, (Stipes Publishing Company, Champaign, Illinois, 1944), p. 133.

[12]*Ibid.*, p. 138.

[13]*Ibid.*

[14]Cureton, Physical Fitness and Dynamic Health, *op. cit.*, p. 47.

[15]Cureton, Physical Fitness Workbook, p. 137.

[16]Cureton, Physical Fitness and Dynamic Health, *op. cit.*, p. 57.

[17]Boyer and Kasch, *op. cit.*, p. 3.

[18]*Ibid.*, p. 4.

[19]*Ibid.*, p. 3.

A Caution

Before engaging in a physical training program, everyone, including police officers, should have a thorough medical examination to determine if they are physically sound or they should limit their physical activity.

The Santa Monica Physical Fitness Incentive Program

Although many police departments encourage marksmanship proficiency, police officers are often offered no incentive to keep physically fit—an attribute required daily if they are to perform their duties at peak efficiency and protect themselves as well as the public. Some departments have taken steps to correct this situation.

The Santa Monica, California, Police Department instituted a physical fitness incentive program in 1976 which might serve as a model for other agencies wanting to provide such programs (Tielsch, 1976, pp.9-11).

In this voluntary program, participating officers train on their own time. The incentive structure is similar to the marksmanship incentive program in which participants earn a monthly bonus of $2, $4, $8, or $16, depending on their skill. Tests are administered quarterly; recorded scores determine the incentive pay for the following three months.

The test itself has a maximum score of 500 points and includes five events: sit-ups, squat thrusts, pull-ups, push-ups, and a one-mile run. Female officers are allowed to do push-ups and pull-ups in the style normally recommended for women. To encourage participation of all sworn personnel, points are added to each event according to the participant's age. For example, if the participant is 35-40 years old, 15 points per event are added to the score; if the participant is 41-45, 20 points per event are added; if 46-50, 25 points per event are added, and so on.

In addition to the incentive pay, to further encourage participation, a perpetual trophy has been established to honor the officer with the highest score each year. Although relatively new to the department, the physical fitness incentive program has encouraged officers to begin and expand individual physical training programs. It is hoped the program results in long-term benefits to each participant and to the police department as a whole by promoting better health and job satisfaction.

SALARY AND BENEFITS

Salaries among police departments in the country have little uniformity. A variety of factors influence a police officer's salary. Of utmost consideration are the community's ability to pay, the cost-of-living in the area, and the prevailing wages of similar police departments in the surrounding area.

Normally position-classification plans are implemented into a personnel ordinance or department rule book. Steps on the salary scale are established in each position-classification. New recruits start at the bottom of the salary scale and receive increment raises after six months and each succeeding year until they reach their maximum salary, usually after three to five years. They obtain more salary only if granted a cost-of-living raise. However, a promotion to the next rank would bring them into a different salary bracket. Sergeants, lieutenants, captains, and chiefs all have minimum and maximum starting levels, with the top salary usually reached after three years in the ranks.

To compensate individuals who do not attain a rank during their police careers, many police departments have adopted longevity plans whereby non-ranking officers receive a certain percentage more of their salary after the tenth year, the fifteenth year, and so on. This seniority system has been attacked, however, on the grounds that it discourages initiative and further education.

When salary schedules are formulated, fringe benefits such as hospitalization and dental plans, insurance, vacation, sick leave, and holidays are all considered. Police officers' indirect benefits from their employers are estimated to be approximately 33%, comparable to what business and industry currently allow their employees.

In addition to fringe benefits, most police departments give police officers a yearly clothing allowance to maintain their uniform wardrobe.

Policies vary regarding overtime pay for officers on the job, going to court while on duty, being required to attend training while off duty, and being called back to duty in an emergency. Some departments pay; others give compensatory time off.

Police departments may belong to unions which bargain for them. Usually all conditions of employment are clearly spelled out in their contracts.

Off-Duty Work Limitations

Moonlighting, working at a part-time job while fulfilling the obligations of a full-time position, has been a source of controversy in the police field for many years. Some administrators allow their officers latitude in the work performed and the number of hours worked. Other administrators are becoming more conservative as a result of poor work performance by some moonlighting officers and lawsuits against the officer and the city or municipality due to some incident while the officer was working off-duty.

> Most police departments restrict the type of work which can be done and the number of hours an officer can work while off-duty.

Some cities allow their police officers to work in only police-related areas; others allow them to work in only nonpolice-related areas. While there are advantages and disadvantages in allowing police officers to work off duty, most cities and municipalities have some limits on the officer's off-duty time. The following chart indicates the salary range of police officers in various cities throughout the United States and their policies on limitations on off-duty employment.

Figure 16-3.   Survey of 20 Cities.

CITY	Salary Range — Patrolmen	Limitations
Atlanta	$10,049–12,844	No jobs inside bars Vice, permits and narcotics bureau men cannot work in bars or night clubs. 20 hours a week.
Boston	$11,201–17,724	Can't work where sale or distribution of liquor is main business No guards or security work 20 hours a week.
Chicago	$13,000–21,000	No work in bars No security jobs in uniform
Denver	$12,432–16,200	Must wear uniform in bar and club security 32 hours a week
Detroit	$14,166–18,822	No police-related work
Fort Wayne	$12,340 (base)	Cannot be a bartender
Houston	$12,480–14,904	Two officers must work where alcoholic beverages are sold; 20 hours a week
Indianapolis	$9,836–11,773	No menial jobs while in uniform 20 hours a week
Jackson, Miss.	$7,094–10,064	Cannot work for less than $5.50 an hour
Memphis	$8,544–13,104	Employer or officer must carry at least $500,000 insurance for injury, false arrest or civil rights violations
Milwaukee	$14,720–17,111	No work in bars; 16 hours biweekly
Newark	$13,738–14,963	No work in bars 20 hours a week
New York	$13,000–17,000	20 hours a week No job where police action is required No guard or bartender
Philadelphia	$13,844–14,443	No wearing of uniform in performance of job No guard or security No establishment where alcohol is sold
Phoenix	$12,000–15,888	No job where sale of liquor is the principal business No work at "X" rated movies
Raleigh, N. C.	$10,500–14,500	No work where alcohol is sold No taxi driving No carrying groceries in parking lot
St. Louis	$10,624–13,598	No work where liquor is sold No taxi driving or bill collecting
San Francisco	$16,452–19,056	No uniform or badge on job No bartender or tow truck operator 20 hours a week
Seattle	$13,152–16,308	No selling or dispensing of alcohol No gambling establishment No operating tow truck
Washington, D.C.	$13,799–19,000 (appr.)	No guns or badges on job No security jobs, taxi drivers bill collectors No jobs where alcohol is sold or dispensed No work in pawnshop 24 hours a week

SURVEY OF 20 CITIES THAT ALLOW OFF-DUTY EMPLOYMENT*

*Source: Telephone interviews in 20 cities; a survey by the International Brotherhood of Police Officers; a 1976 survey by the International Conference of Police Associations.

☑ CHECK POINT

1. What is the usual length of the probationary period in law enforcement and what purpose does it serve?
2. What factors are important in physical fitness and which one factor is of most importance?
3. What restrictions are sometimes placed on police officers' off-duty employment?

* Answers

1. The probationary period in law enforcement is usually one year. The purpose of probation is to provide training and to observe the candidate both during training and while applying this training on the streets.
2. Factors of prime importance in physical fitness include endurance, balance, flexibility, agility, strength, and power. Endurance is the most important factor.
3. Police officers may be restricted in both the type of work and the number of hours they can work while off duty.

FEDERAL GUIDELINES AND REGULATIONS

In 1964 Congress enacted the *Omnibus Civil Rights Law.* Title VII of this law concerns employment opportunities and prohibits discrimination because of sex, race, color, religion, or national origin. The law also established the Equal Employment Opportunity Commission (EEOC) to administer the law and gave this commission authority to establish guidelines.

> The 1964 Omnibus Civil Rights Law prohibits discrimination in employment opportunities in *private* business.

This law affected only private business, not state and local governments; therefore, it had little impact on police agency practices.

However, in 1972 Congress passed the *Equal Employment Opportunity Act,* which modified Title VII to include state and local units of government. This law was passed because six years after the EEOC published guidelines for employment and promotion testing, few state or local central personnel selection agencies had taken positive steps to meet the guidelines. Although not legally required to do so, they should have been forward-looking enough to realize that if such guidelines were not voluntarily followed, steps would be taken to assure compliance.

> The 1972 Equal Employment Opportunity Act prohibits discrimination due to sex, race, color, religion, or national origin in employment of any kind, public or private, local, state, or federal.

MINORITY GROUP MEMBERS IN LAW ENFORCEMENT

According to the Task Force on the Police of the President's Commission on Law Enforcement and the Administration of Justice (1967), police administrators in most large cities are genuinely interested in attracting more officers from minority groups—Puerto Ricans, Mexican-Americans, Orientals, and blacks. However, in many communities, both north and south, discrimination in the selection and promotion of minority officers has occurred in the past and may still exist.

To gain the community's general confidence and acceptance, police department personnel should be representative of the community as a whole.

Additionally, an integrated department helps reduce stereotyping and prejudice. Further, minority officers provide a department with an understanding of minority groups, their languages, and their subcultures, all with practical benefits to successful law enforcement. For example, a police officer with a knowledge of Spanish can help to prevent conflicts between the police and Spanish-speaking residents of the community.

> A racially balanced and integrated police department both fosters community relations and increases police effectiveness.

A task force of the President's Commission on Law Enforcement and the Administration of Justice (*The Police*, 1967, p. 167), noted that black officers in black neighborhoods have special competence, as demonstrated in a study in Philadelphia in which three-fourths of the patrol officers thought that black police officers were more effective in black neighborhoods than white police officers: "Personal knowledge of minority groups and slum neighborhoods can lead to information not otherwise available, to earlier anticipation of trouble, and to increased solution of crime."

Reasons for the increased effectiveness of the black officers included: (1) they get along better with, and receive more respect from the black residents, (2) they receive less trouble from the black residents, (3) they can get more information, and (4) they understand black citizens better.

A need for minority police officers has been stated repeatedly. Accomplishing this, however, frequently poses difficult problems for police departments.

☑ CHECK POINT

1. What legislation prohibits discrimination against members of minority groups and women in employment practices?
2. What benefits are derived from having a police department whose racial makeup reflects that of the community?

✳ Answers

1. The 1964 Omnibus Civil Rights Law and the 1972 Equal Employment Opportunity Act prohibit discrimination against members of minority groups and women in employment practices.
2. A racially balanced and integrated police department fosters community relations and increases police effectiveness.

Recruitment and Selection of Minority Member Police Officers

Precinct police officers from minority groups are one of the best sources of advertising for minority recruits. However, police officers cannot honestly "sell" police work if discrimination exists in their departments. Police departments sincerely wishing to attract minority recruits must abolish internal segregation and discrimination. They must give minority officers full opportunity for promotion and assignment to prestigious units. Minority officers must not be segregated in patrols or in a particular part of the city, but must be welcomed warmly.

Minority community leaders and civic organizations may disseminate recruitment materials and provide opportunities for recruiters to address groups of potential applicants. Community leaders convinced of the sincerity of the police in recruiting minorities may refer applicants to them.

Certain selection standards may unintentionally bar large numbers of minority applicants who could actually perform police work very competently. For example, minimum height restrictions frequently disqualify many Puerto Ricans, Mexican-Americans, and Orientals from police work.

The Task Force of the Police cites national statistics which indicate the underrepresentation of minorities in law enforcement is partly due to the greater percentage of minority applicants who fail to meet police selection standards. This is hardly surprising as minorities are frequently disadvantaged both culturally and educationally.

To hire minority police officers, agencies might apply *compensating factors* to increase the number of eligible minority members. Compensating factors allow an applicant who fails to meet one qualification but excels in another to be employed; the area of qualification outweighs the deficiency. For example deficiencies in height, weight, or vision may be compensated for by an unusual language skill, leadership experience, or a high level of education. However, certain minimum qualifications such as moral character, mental ability, and psychological health must be met directly rather than by compensation.

An interesting finding of the Rand Study (*The Police*, p.331) was that salary and job security were *not* primary interests of minority applicants; minority applicants were motivated first by an opportunity to maintain law and order, second by the feeling that comes from helping people, and third by fringe benefits and job security. This study also found that most attrition after initial testing was caused by lack of motivation to follow through on the lengthy processing. At the time of the study, the New York Police Department took up to seventeen months to process an applicant. The Rand Study recommended accelerating the selection process and instituting personal contacts between police department personnel officers and minority applicants to sustain the applicant's interest during the selection process.

As noted by the Task Force Report (1967, p.169): "Any program to increase the proportion of minority group police officers must begin by persuading qualified candidates to apply. However, the hostility of blacks to police forces is so strong that black officers are frequently disliked by their fellow blacks." The minority officer faces a unique problem in that often members of his own group consider him a traitor, an Uncle Tom or a Tio Taco. Some of the young, lawless males resent police in general and hate anyone of their own group who goes into law enforcement.

Promotion

Increasing the number of ranking minority officers is as important as, and closely related to, recruiting new minority officers; successful recruitment and promotional opportunities are closely interdependent.

The limited number of minority officers promoted in comparison to the number recruited and selected is partly due to the recency of recruitment of many minority officers. It usually takes several years to work up through the ranks to supervisory and command positions. Additionally, the more limited educational background of some minority group officers may cause them to do poorly on promotion examinations. Still, to be responsive to the needs of minority neighborhoods, a police department needs several qualified higher-ranking minority-group officers. Minority groups should not feel they are policed by an entirely white police force; they should see that minority officers participate in policymaking and other important decisions.

Discrimination

The number of minority applicants will not increase if discrimination in the assignment and promotion of minority officers exists. The total police image will influence minority interest in police careers. The Task Force Report (*The Police* 1967) identified several policies which limit minority officers' authority to make arrests and restrict them to working only in minority neighborhoods and then with other minority officers.

> Discrimination has been found in the recruitment, selection, and promotional practices of police departments as well as in policies which limit minority officer's authority to make arrests and restrict them to working in certain areas on certain types of assignments and only with other members of their minority group.

Minority officers should be selected on the same standards as other officers and should compete on an equal basis for every assignment. They should be assigned to minority neighborhoods, but not exclusively; they should work with other minority officers, but not exclusively; and they should be allowed to advance within the field to positions in supervision, management, or administration. However, a National Advisory Commission on Civil Disorders survey conducted in 1967 revealed marked racial disproportions in supervisory personnel: one of every 26 black officers was a sergeant compared to one in 12 whites; one of every 114 black officers was a lieutenant compared to 1 in 26 for whites; one in every 235 black officers was a captain compared to 1 in 53 for whites.

Preferential Hiring and Promotions and Court Actions

Police agencies must recruit minorities and assure that the selection process is free of unwarranted cultural bias. The federal courts have forbidden cultural bias in the selection process. Some have gone further than that and have demanded *preferential* minority employment to rectify the effects of past discrimination.

Preferential hiring and promotion seeks to approximate the minority composition of the community within the employee ranks.

Carter v. Gallagher 452 F. 2d 315 (1971) dealt with discrimination in the hiring procedures of the Minneapolis Fire Department. The court found that certain selection requirements were not job related and were, in fact, discriminatory. The court ordered the city to correct the situation by hiring one minority group member for every three whites employed until twenty minority members were hired.

A similar decision requiring preferential hiring was made in Philadelphia. In Allen v. Mobile 331 F. Supp. 1134 (1971), Mobile, Alabama, was charged with discrimination in the assignment and promotion of black officers. The court ordered Mobile to consult with black leaders to develop a recruitment program and to directly advertise that Mobile was an equal opportunity employer.

The Detroit experience with recruitment, hiring, and promotion of minority group members has received national attention. In 1971 the Detroit Police Department found it had 13% minority personnel compared with 44% minority in the community. If the department continued its annual hiring ratio of 20% minorities, it would never approach an ethnic makeup reflecting the community. Over half the police officers hired would have to be from minority groups to achieve an ethnic balance by 1980. Therefore, recruitment efforts to attract minority applicants were emphasized in preference to general recruitment techniques.

In July, 1974, the Detroit Board of Police Commissioners adopted an affirmative action policy designed to promote equal numbers of blacks and whites, even if it required passing over highly qualified white candidates. At the time Detroit was 50% black, but the police force had only 15% black personnel. High ranking black officers were almost nonexistent: only 2% black lieutenants and 15% black sergeants. Detroit maintained separate lists of black and white candidates for promotion, placed in order of test scores and other criteria. When openings occurred, equal numbers of blacks and whites were drawn from the two lists. Consequently, blacks with lower total scores were promoted over whites with higher scores. This did not, however, mean the blacks promoted were not qualified to fill the position.

Reverse Discrimination

In March, 1978, as a result of a lawsuit filed by two hundred white officers on the Detroit Police Department, Senior Federal Judge Fred W. Kaess issued a permanent injunction barring the City of Detroit from promoting less-qualified black officers to the rank of sergeant ahead of whites. The injunction barred using racial quotas in promoting police officers to the rank of sergeant only; it did not bar all affirmative-action promotions. However, the blow to Detroit's affirmative action program may have repercussions throughout the country.

> Reverse discrimination exists when a more qualified person (usually a white male) is denied a position or promotion because it is "reserved" to fill a quota established by affirmative action plans.

The Detroit case is vital to virtually every large city in America. It will be appealed to the 6th Circuit Court of Appeals in Cincinnati, but the appeal could take three years. It might eventually go before the U.S. Supreme Court and could raise fundamental issues of civil rights.

The Fourteenth Amendment guarantees *every* American citizen equal protection under the law, and a long series of civil rights laws assert that a person must not be discriminated against because of color. Judge Kaess (court referee) noted: "While the purpose of the quota system is generally compassionate, its effect is intolerable because it denigrates individuals by reducing them to a single immutable birth characteristic—skin pigmentation." Kaess also rejected the commonly used term "reverse discrimination" as a misnomer: "Racial discrimination is as indefensible when practiced against whites as it is when practiced against blacks and does not become 'reverse' merely because it is practiced against whites."

A Promising Future for Minority Police Officers

Police administrators should aggressively seek out, employ, and promote qualified members of minority groups (or the courts may well dictate that they do so). Several recruitment techniques and programs are effective in attracting minorities. When it is necessary to overcome a distrust of the police, minority recruiters may establish rapport with minority groups. Minority recruiters have been successful across the country, especially in Phoenix, Washington, Kansas City, New York, and Detroit.

Although employment of persons from all ethnic groups within the community should be a recruitment goal, primary consideration should be given to employing the best-qualified candidates available, regardless of ethnic background. The ethnic make-up of the community should be a guide for recruitment policies, not a basis for quota hiring.

One way to assure well-qualified candidates from minority groups is to promote educational programs for minority group members. For example, in 1977 a little-publicized program to increase minority participation at master's and doctoral-degree level in criminal justice education was begun in eight traditionally black colleges. Participating colleges included Mississippi Valley State University; Itta Bena, Mississippi; Grambling State University, Louisiana; Talladega College, Alabama; Texas Southern University, Texas; Fayetteville State University and Shaw University, North Carolina; Bishop College of Dallas; and Shaw College at Detroit.

The program, known as Positive Features, Inc. (PFI), is conducted under an LEAA grant and seeks to improve the image of the criminal justice system in the black community by using black criminal justice students, graduates, and interns to conduct community relations meetings, workshops, and other related projects. Personnel involved feel confident that once LEAA funding is discontinued the participating schools will continue the program with their own funds.

Such innovations and others in the developmental stages should help to assure that minority-group members have the opportunity for a successful future in law enforcement.

☑ CHECK POINT

1. What discriminatory practices have existed against minority member police officers?
2. What is preferential hiring?
3. What is reverse discrimination?

∗ Answers

1. Discrimination has occurred in the recruitment, selection, and promotional practices of police departments as well as in policies which limit minority officers' authority to make arrests and restrict them to working in certain areas on certain types of assignments and only with other members of their minority group.
2. Preferential hiring is intentional hiring of members of a certain group (racial or sex) to make the composition of the department approximate that of the community.
3. Reverse discrimination occurs when affirmative action programs limit the employment opportunities for nonminority members, especially white males.

WOMEN IN LAW ENFORCEMENT

"Police Woman," portrayed by Angie Dickinson on television, is seen by millions of viewers each week. Sergeant Pepper Anderson sees more action in sixty minutes than many police officers experience in a career. Weekly she shows that a woman can be an effective police officer. Her role is far different from that performed by the first policewoman.

Initially women were restricted to processing female prisoners and to positions as police matrons. Many misconceptions about the female's ability to perform certain "masculine" tasks have been dispelled as a result of changing social attitudes, yet room for improvement remains.

Just before the turn of the century, a movement to employ women as regular police officers gained support and culminated in 1910 in the hiring of the first regular policewomen by the Los Angeles Police Department. By the end of World War I, over 220 cities employed policewomen. A major reason for this relatively rapid acceptance of female peace officers was a change in the public's view of the police function.

> The acceptance of women paralleled the newly accepted emphasis on citizen protection and crime prevention rather than exclusive concentration on the enforcement of laws and detection of crimes.

Despite early rapid progress in breaking into the police field, women have met with several barriers in becoming equal to their male counterpart. Many agencies have excluded women altogether by quota systems, discriminatory hiring, and promotional policies. Some women officers are not eligible to take the exam for promotion available to men. Only within the last five years have many agencies allowed women to take supervisory exams. Some agencies require women to have more education than male applicants. For example, before 1969 Washington D.C.'s Metropolitan Police Department required women applicants to possess a college degree; men needed only a high-school diploma.

Practitioners at every level within the police service have resisted the expansion of the woman's role in law enforcement. Some believe police work requires more strength and physical agility than most women possess; few women have the strength to perform many of the difficult tasks required of patrol officers. Some argue that if they allow shorter, lighter women to become patrol officers, they must also allow shorter, lighter men. They contend that physical standards should not be altered to bring women into the service. However, if standards are not altered, only 3.5% of the women in the country would be eligible for work in the police field because 96% of American women are shorter than 5'8" and 98% weigh less than 140 pounds (National Advisory Commission on Criminal Justice Standards and Goals, p. 345).

> Those opposed to women in police work feel women (1) are not strong enough to perform many of the required tasks, (2) are given an unfair advantage over men if height and weight standards are lowered for them, and (3) are not able to supervise male officers.

Another concern of police administrators is women's ability to supervise male officers. Some administrators believe all female supervisors should be assigned to the Juvenile Aid Division and supervise only policewomen. Some supervisors feel women supervisors are too lenient with their men, do not have the respect of the patrolmen, and fail to get voluntary compliance from subordinates. Other police officials claim deployment of women limits their command flexibility and that social, domestic, and disciplinary problems occur when "coeducational cop cars" are used.

In addition, many agencies neglect training of female personnel. Some conduct separate training classes for women, geared toward investigative rather than line functions of police work. Women are also excused from the qualifying examination in physical fitness and passed automatically. However, such exemptions perpetuate the image of "weakness" of women officers and promote an overprotective attitude in male officers. More important, the exemptions are a form of discrimination against male officers.

Further, in many agencies substantial numbers of policewomen are assigned to clerical duties, and many are not paid on the same basis as the men who perform similar functions. For example, five Detroit policewomen filed a complaint with the Michigan Civil Rights Commission alleging that their salaries were not equal to their male counterparts.

Often promotions are based on experience, knowledge, and ability as determined by an examination. Women, because of discrimination, have been unable or unwilling to compete successfully in this process. Their duties do not lead to attainment of comprehensive knowledge or experience in police work, especially in basic line functions. Since they cannot qualify for positions requiring such background, some agencies systematically exclude them from the promotional process.

Across the country, many police departments have tried to keep physical agility tests, height standards, and other requirements to restrict the number of women on police forces. However, the Equal Employment Act of 1972 forbids such practices demanding that *all* jobs must be open to both men and women unless it can be proved that sex "is a bonafide occupational qualification necessary to the normal operation of that particular business or enterprise."

Cleveland has had over a dozen suits on behalf of women, from the refusal of mandatory maternity leave to the right to wear pants on the job. The Justice Department and the LEAA have interceded on behalf of women in several cities, most recently Philadelphia and Chicago. LEAA has threatened to discontinue funding to law enforcement agencies which discriminate against women. In December, 1977, LEAA halted federal grant funds to the South Carolina Highway Patrol because of restrictive hiring practices.

Suits have charged that women have been discriminated against regarding promotions, job assignments, seniority practices, maternity policies, and physical requirements. Yet no one has proved that a taller, heavier person can perform the functions required of a police officer better than a smaller, lighter person. However, because most police work does require physical strength and agility, agencies must not establish criteria which will result in the hiring of police officers unable to perform police duties. Agency standards should *not* be changed to employ women at the cost of reduced physical effectiveness of individual police officers (although discriminatory height and weight restrictions may be changed).

Police agencies cannot maintain different hiring qualifications for men and women. They must establish criteria to facilitate the employment of both without restricting their capability to carry out their functions. The federal government has taken steps in this direction. In 1971 the Secret Service administered the oath of office to five women, the first in the history of the agency. In 1972 the nation's first female FBI agents were sworn in. Dallas, Miami, and New York City Police Departments have opened their promotional examinations to women. And Washington, D.C. Metropolitan Police Department has gone a step further in an innovative promotional policy that maintains only one promotional list including both male and female officers. When a vacancy occurs, the next eligible person is elevated, regardless of sex.

Effectiveness of Women on Patrol

In 1971 Miami promoted the first woman to sergeant to command a patrol sector of six to ten men from a mixture of ethnic backgrounds. The woman sergeant not only did a highly competent job, she helped change the departmental uniform regulations so female officers could wear slacks on duty.

According to Miami Chief of Police Bernard L. Garmire (1974, pp.11-13), female officers proved to be effective in all phases of police work in Miami. Women officers were well accepted by male officers and by the public. In fact, the classification of policewoman was eliminated with all personnel classified as police officers. As noted by Garmire: "Crime makes no distinction between sexes, and neither should law enforcement in its efforts to combat it (p.13)."

> Studies have shown that women perform as well as men in police patrol work.

The LEAA financed a seven-month study in New York City ("Women on Patrol," 1978, p.43) which found that women generally perform as well as men in police patrol work, although some small differences exist. The study, based on direct observation of 3,625 patrol and 2,400 police-civilian encounters, examined an equal number of men and women. It analyzed the actions required of the officers, their style of patrol, their methods of gaining control, their initiative, physical strength, and the reactions of the public.

The study found that the performance of policewomen is more like that of policemen than it is different, although the women made a better impression on the public. Citizens said women officers were more competent, pleasant, and respectful than the men. The women's performance created a better civilian regard for the New York Police Department.

The study also found that women were less likely to join male partners in taking control of a situation or jointly making decisions. However, in the few incidents judged to be dangerous, men and women were equally likely to attempt to gain control. Women were neither more nor less likely than men to use force, display a weapon, or rely on a direct order. In addition, the behavior of women who patrolled with women was more active, assertive, and self-sufficient.

Other findings of the study were that women were slightly less physically agile in such activities as climbing ladders or steep stairs. Women took more sick leave than men—consistent with earlier research showing that, in general, women are absent from work more frequently than men, perhaps because they are more likely to stay home when family members are ill.

The report attributed the small but consistent differences to socially-conditioned attitudes such as protectiveness, disdain, or skepticism by men and passivity by women. The study concluded that: "The results offer little support either to those who hold that women are unsuited to patrol or to those who argue that women do the job better than men. By and large, patrol performance of the women was more like that of the men than it was different."

According to James M. H. Gregg, acting LEAA administrator: "This report is another important step toward creating equal opportunities for women in law enforcement ... Today's police patrolwomen are pioneering in what has always been a man's world, and there are obstacles to overcome. This report makes it clear that they are being overcome."

A later survey of women on patrol (Bouza, 1975, pp.2-7) revealed that women were confident of their ability to perform all aspects of the patrol function, they could drive automobiles as well as males, they would rather work on the street than in the station house, they acknowledged their physical limitations but were confident of their ability to cope—either through persuasion or through the display of superior force, and the initial male resistance was subsiding and acceptance was growing; they felt accepted and respected by the public as well.

The current situation does seem to be improving for women. "Women on Patrol" (1977, pp.45-53) describes the gains made. From 1971 to 1975 the number of women police officers has doubled from 3,157 to 6,139, yet this number represents less than 2% of all police officers. Almost every city has some women on patrol. In 1978 Atlanta had 71 of 126 women police officers on the streets; Dallas had more than 50, San Francisco 46, Miami 35. Many cities are still experimenting with women on patrol. For example Houston had only five women out of 2,700 officers riding in patrol cars in 1978. St. Louis had fewer than twenty women on patrol and New York had only 112.

Washington, D.C., is the first city to assign large numbers of women to patrol. Currently more than 200 of their 299 policewomen are on patrol—walking beats and riding in patrol cars. They constitute almost 10% of the total police force (Kiernan and Cusick, 1977, pp.45-53). Women are assigned to each of the twenty-three divisions and bureaus, from traffic to homicide. Most are young, still in their twenties. Two-thirds are black. Only six have achieved the rank of sergeant, only one that of lieutenant. These female uniformed police officers have drawn great interest and undergone more professional scrutiny over the last five years than any other category of police officers in the country. The question inevitably asked is, "Can women perform patrol work as well as men?" And, almost without exception, the answer, from the women, their male partners, and the professionals who have studied them is: "YES."

Although the use of policewomen has been a success in many departments, problems do occur. The questions most frequently asked about putting women on patrol include:

—Can women handle situations involving force and violence?

—What changes in training and equipment must be made?

—Do women resent the loss of the "specialist" role they have usually had in police work?

—Should women compete with men for promotions?

—Does the law require police departments to hire women and put them on patrol?

As these questions are satisfactorily answered, less resistance to putting women on patrol should be encountered. It must be remembered, however, that women differ from one another as much as men do. Among the differences in the women on the Washington Police Force were the following:

—They range in height from 5 feet to more than 6 feet and in age from 20 to 44.

—All finished high school, but many had additional schooling; some had completed college.

—They joined for a variety of reasons: money, adventure, or to help people.

—Their views of their male colleagues ranged from complaints of continual teasing and harassment to glowing praise that the male officers "were like brothers."

The men on the force also differed in their opinions of the policewomen. Some women were described as "nice guys, people who want to help people." However, one woman was so aggressive she was nicknamed "Mad Dog."

In 1972 the Police Foundation funded a comparison study of male and female recruits in Washington. Completed in 1974, the study concluded that from a performance viewpoint it was appropriate to hire women for patrol on the same basis as men. Among its specific findings were the following (Kiernan and Cusik, 1977):

—Both men and women officers obtained similar results in handling angry or violent citizens. No incidents cast serious doubt on a female officer's ability to patrol satisfactorily.

—Women made fewer arrests and gave fewer traffic citations. However, they also had fewer opportunities to do so, as they were not given patrol assignments as often as men. Arrests made by women and men were equally likely to result in convictions.

—Men were more likely to engage in serious misconduct than women, for example, to be arrested for drunk and disorderly conduct while off duty. Women, on the other hand, were more likely to be late for work.

—A majority of D.C. residents approved of the use of women in patrol work, although they were "moderately skeptical" of women's abilities to handle violent suspects.

—There were no differences between men and women in the number of sick-days used, number of injuries sustained, or number of days absent from work because of injuries.

—Male and female partners shared driving equally, took charge with about the same frequency, and were about equal in giving each other instructions.

—Resignation rates were also similar: 14% for women and 12% for men.

Perhaps the most graphic illustration of the equal role played by men and women on police patrol is that of Gail A. Cobb who joined the D.C. Police Department in 1973 and had been assigned to patrol duty for only five months when she responded to her last police call.

Around noon one Friday in September, Officer Cobb was patrolling downtown Washington when she was called to help search for two suspected bank robbers who had exchanged shots with police and then fled. Officer Cobb saw a man dash down a ramp into an underground parking garage and followed him. Then, moments after entering the garage, she was shot in the chest. Only twenty-four years old, Officer Gail Cobb became the first United

States policewoman to be killed in the line of duty. As noted by Police Chaplain Reverend R. Joseph Dooley, her death "established the fact that the criminal makes no distinction between the sexes. It is the badge and the blue of the uniform that makes the difference."

☑ CHECK POINT

1. What movement paralleled the acceptance of women into police work?
2. What are some objections commonly raised against women in police work?
3. What do studies show when men and women on patrol are compared?

* Answers

1. The acceptance of women into police work paralleled the newly accepted emphasis on citizen protection and crime prevention rather than exclusive concentration on the enforcement of laws and detection of crimes.
2. Those opposed to women in police work feel women (1) are not strong enough to perform many of the required tasks, (2) are given an unfair advantage over men if height and weight standards are lowered for them, and (3) are not able to supervise male officers.
3. Studies have shown that women perform as well as men in police patrol work.

THE WIDE ARRAY OF EMPLOYMENT OPPORTUNITIES IN LAW ENFORCEMENT

Although this chapter has focused on the local police department, numerous other employment opportunities exist for individuals interested in a career in law enforcement. A review of Chapter 5 will provide several opportunities on the state and federal level.

More information about specific requirements for positions at the federal level can be obtained through the nearest Federal Job Information Center which is usually listed in the white pages of local telephone directories under "U.S. Government." If there is no listing, call the toll-free Information number (800-555-1212) and ask for the nearest Federal Job Information Center.

Information about opportunities in law enforcement at the state level can be obtained by contacting the state department of personnel or any local state employment office.

SUMMARY

The future success (or failure) of our law enforcement system depends in large part on the effectiveness of our police officers. Therefore, valid recruitment, screening, testing, and selection procedures must be used to assure that only well-qualified candidates are hired. Characteristics identified in "good" police officers include: reliability, leadership, judgment, persuasiveness, communication skills, accuracy, initiative, integrity, honesty, ego control, intelligence, and sensitivity. Individuals possessing such skills are sought through a careful selection procedure.

Police officer selection usually includes (1) a formal application, (2) a preliminary screening including a written examination and a psychological examination, (3) a physical agility test, (4) an oral interview, (5) a medical examination, and (6) a thorough background investigation. Most agencies require that a police officer candidate be a citizen of the United States, have or be eligible for a driver's license in the state, and not have been convicted of a felony. Additional requirements may specify height, weight, age, educational level, and residency in the community served.

Tests used in the selection process must be valid, as established in Griggs v. Duke Power Company that all tests used for employment purposes must measure a tested person's capability to perform a specific job and all requirements and standards established be business or job related.

Once candidates have passed all tests in the selection process, they usually enter a one year probationary period, during which they are observed while obtaining training and while applying this training on the streets. This probationary period allows for evaluation of the selected candidates. After the probation, the officers should continue to receive periodic in-service training to maintain already acquired skills and to achieve proficiency in new ones.

Physical fitness is of critical importance to police officers. The prime factor in physical fitness is endurance. Other important factors are balance, flexibility, agility, strength, and power.

In addition to local and state requirements for recruitment and selection of police officers, certain federal guidelines and regulations must be met. Most important are the 1964 Omnibus Civil Rights Law which prohibits discrimination in employment opportunities in private business and the Equal Employment Opportunity Act of 1972 which prohibits discrimination due to sex, race, color, religion, or national origin in employment of any kind, public or private, local, state, or federal. All individuals meeting the specific requirements of the department should be given the opportunity to apply for and successfully compete with other candidates.

Members of minority groups are highly beneficial in a police department. A racially balanced and integrated police department fosters community relations and increases police effectiveness. However, discrimination has been found in the recruitment, selection, and promotional practices of some police departments as well as in some policies which limit minority officers' authority to make arrests and restrict them to working in certain areas on certain types of assignments and only with other members of their minority group. Progress is being made in eliminating such discrimination. In some instances preferential hiring and promotion have been implemented to attract minority group members to police departments. However, preferential hiring and affirmative action programs have resulted in claims of reverse discrimination from white male police officers who feel their civil rights are being violated when quotas for minority group members are established.

Just as members of minority groups have a promising future in law enforcement, so do women. The acceptance of women into law enforcement paralleled the newly accepted emphasis on citizen protection and crime prevention rather than exclusive concentration on the enforcement of laws and detection of crimes. Women have not always been welcomed onto the force, however. Those opposed to women in police work feel they are not strong enough to perform many of the required tasks, are given an unfair advantage over men because of lower height and weight standards, and they are not able to supervise male officers. In spite of such contentions, surveys have shown that women perform as well as men on police patrol.

All police officers, be they white, black, brown, male or female, are subjected to the hazards of police work, and all are expected to fulfill the responsibilities of the job. Each must be given an equal chance to become a police officer, to be adequately trained, and to be promoted. Each offers the profession an added dimension and one more means of fulfilling its mission.

APPLICATION

A. Charlie Triserite wants to be a police officer. He passes all the Mytown Police Department preliminary examinations and has an appointment at 10:00 A.M. for an oral interview. He arrives at 10:15 A.M. wearing blue jeans and a T-shirt with a Budweiser emblem on it. He answers all questions fluently, but egotistically, and he occasionally uses profanity.

Do you think the interviewers would rate him highly as a candidate for police officer?

B. Barbara Szutz has passed all the preliminary tests for the position of police officer. She is disqualified because she cannot pass the physical agility tests.

Is her disqualification reasonable?

C. Officer Cody works for a police department which forbids off-duty employment in bars. He takes a job as a bouncer at a private party where gambling will take place and liquor will be served.

Is he right in accepting such employment?

*Answers

A. No, because characteristics of a good police officer include: reliability (being on time), judgment (his attire was inappropriate), communication skills (he has these, but profanity is inappropriate), and ego control.

B. Yes, because a physical agility test evaluates a candidate's coordination, speed of movement, and strength—all necessary in the performance of police officers' duties.

C. Technically it is all right because it is not a bar, but the job violates the spirit of the regulation. He should have checked with his superior officer about such employment before accepting the position.

DISCUSSION QUESTIONS

1. Why are veterans given preference in some departments? Won't this make the police more militaristic?
2. What is the most common restriction for off-duty work for a police officer?
3. Where are the U.S. Civil Service Commission offices in our area?
4. Is a newspaper advertisement placed by a police department requesting that only women apply for a job opening fair?

5. What is the most common reason for rejection during the selection process?
6. What employment opportunities in law enforcement are available locally? In our county? Our state?
7. What is the percentage of minorities and women on our police force? Is this "balanced"? How did this situation come to be?

REFERENCES

Bopp, W. J. *Police personnel administration.* Boston: Holbrook Press, 1974.

Bouza, A. V. Women in policing, *FBI law enforcement bulletin*, 44:9, September 1975, pp.2-7.

Garmire, B. L. Female officers in the department, *FBI law enforcement bulletin*, June 1974, pp. 11-13.

Indiana University develops police selection procedure, *Target*, LEAA, 6:8 September 1977, p.1.

Kiernan, M. and Cusick, J. Women on patrol: The nation's capital gives them high marks, *Police magazine*, 1977, pp.45-53.

National Advisory Commission on Criminal Justice Standards and Goals, *Police.* Washington, D.C., 1973.

Physical fitness for law enforcement officers. Washington, D.C.: Federal Bureau of Investigation, U.S. Department of Justice, March 1972.

The Police, President's Commission on Law Enforcement and Administration of Justice, Task Force Report, 1967.

Sturner, L. J. Personnel selection and promotion processes: Some considerations, *FBI law enforcement bulletin*, 46:6, June 1977, pp.6-12.

Swaton, J. and Morgan, L. *Administration of justice.* New York: D. Van Nostrand Company, 1975.

Tielsch, G. P. Physical fitness incentive program, *FBI law enforcement bulletin*, 45:8, August 1976, pp.9-11.

Women on patrol, *Minnesota police journal*, 50:1, February 1978, p.43.

Epilogue
Why become a police officer today?

With violence a constant threat in communities and to individuals in the form of hijackings, murders, assaults, rapes, and kidnappings, the future police officer must be a true professional dedicated to the American creed of justice and liberty.

It is evident that the general public has become somewhat suspicious of the rhetoric of politicians, and many citizens want simple solutions to the crime problem where none exist. Police agencies themselves have become more militant and political; some ambitious administrators have even used a police agency to launch themselves into high political office. Many police have problems with poor image, low status, and limited training, while at the same time they are asked to perform the most skilled, important, and dangerous police work.

What leads us to believe that the next ten years will be much better? Not much, on the surface. Only 1.5% of the convicted criminals are ever imprisoned. The odds are 99 to 1 that you could commit a crime and never go to jail for it. Besides, if we were to imprison every convicted criminal, we would have to build thousands more jails, and the public simply won't stand the cost.

The question today is whether our citizens can resurrect the determined pioneering spirit to succeed in controlling crime exhibited by our "heroes" in history. Seldom have city dwellers been as apprehensive about their safety as they are today, even though statistics show there is more fear of crime than actual crime itself.

Our forefathers fought to gain liberty for us; today we struggle to maintain and perpetuate that liberty. The police must enforce the law, but citizens must help. They must express their outrage at crime by reporting it. They must cooperate fully in its investigation and prosecution. They must give full support to law enforcement and criminal justice programs. As citizens see for themselves the correction of inequities in their communities, crime will start to be contained.

We need to rekindle the spirit of self-esteem in America, and police officers can provide the leadership. It will take intelligence, courage, and determination.

Assaults on the Constitution and the Bill of Rights

The assaults on the Constitution and the Bill of Rights continue incessantly, but the law is a living reality which encourages the opening of new avenues of human conduct. As Oliver Wendell Holmes puts it: "The life of the law has not been logic; it has been experience." People who view the Constitution as an outdated document fail to see that it is the best structure so far in history for a growing society with changing institutions.

The Second Amendment to the Constitution is one continuing source of controversy. Those who oppose gun control state that outlawing handguns would arm criminals and disarm law-abiding citizens. They say the criminals will get guns anyway. The question revolves around whether the government should regulate handguns—the Number One weapon of killers. Some 18,000 murders occur every year in the United States, often committed by "law-abiding" people shooting other "law-abiding" people. In addition, an average of more than ninety police officers are slain by handguns every year.

Some polls consistently show that the majority of United States citizens support sensible handgun legislation. However, when Massachusetts held a referendum proposing to ban handguns, it was defeated by a 70% majority. Possibly they realized what New York's tough gun law has shown: if only one state outlaws guns, a person can easily get one in another state. Nevertheless, it seems clear that the federal government should establish some uniform regulation of handguns before they cause more tragedy and terror.

Controversy also exists over the Exclusionary Rule and the Miranda decision. You recall that the Exclusionary Rule disallows the introduction of illegally seized evidence from a trial, and the Miranda decision forbids confessions as evidence if the suspects have not been informed of their constitional rights. The Exclusionary Rule has been regularly challenged in our courts. Opponents of the rule say that it penalizes society and rewards the defendant for any "mistakes" made by the police. When the Miranda decision was handed down in 1966, many people felt the criminals were decidedly given the upper hand; consequently the U.S. Supreme Court came under blistering attack from some police, prosecutors, and citizens. Since 1966, twenty-two states have sought to overturn the Miranda decision through the U.S. Supreme Court, but to no avail. Today's police officers are functioning and performing their jobs better than before Miranda; they are not hindered by it. Police officers, above all others, ought to obey the laws. Further, withdrawal of the rights provided by the Fourth and Fifth Amendments could lead to a police state.

Another controversial amendment is the Eighth Amendment, which forbids "cruel and unusual punishment." The question of capital punishment has been in the courts for the past quarter-century. In 1976 the U.S. Supreme Court ruled that states which used certain guidelines could pass laws allowing them to execute convicted murderers, but the court reserved any decision on whether the death penalty is constitutional for any other crime. Still unresolved are such questions as how far prosecutors can go in making emotional charges in their closing arguments to a jury in a capital punishment case and whether rape can be punished by death.

Effects of Television and Movies

The effects of television on both the police image and the fight against crime cannot be accurately measured. Certainly, it must be having its impact. In one evening a person can learn how to steal a car, rape a woman, rob a bank, mug a senior citizen, and commit murder in a variety of bizarre ways. This continuous diet of murder and violence is an insult to our citizens' integrity and a threat to our youth. Youngsters spend more time watching TV than they do in school classrooms. Each successful crime serves as an advertisement to entice and encourage some youths to commit crimes.

In addition, hardly an hour passes without an illegal search, a coerced confession, police brutality, and general violence dealt out by the police officers. Many modern day police "heroes" are shown blatantly using illegal and unconstitutional behavior, which in effect instills in the public the opinion that police misconduct is acceptable and, in fact, sometimes the only way to apprehend criminals. The same criticisms may be applied to our movies.

Law-Abiding Citizens Select the Laws They Obey

Many "good" citizens disobey the law every day and justify it as "not hurting anyone else." For example, countless citizens break speed laws, drive after drinking, and pilfer from their employers. Even more serious, many citizens, although abhorring organized crime in general, foster, promote, and support it daily by gambling and using its many other "services." Perhaps the deeply entrenched force of organized crime has gone beyond the comprehension of the general public. Many notorious criminals of the present era wear the mantle of respectability because they have bought into legitimate business with their illegal money or have simply strong-armed their way in. These criminals have gained social prominence and often community acceptance. Police officers and citizens alike must not lose sight of their responsibility to control organized crime through cooperation on the federal, state, and local levels.

The Future

There are presently discussions and plans for restructuring the federal government's financial aid to other governmental levels. Possibly the Law Enforcement Assistance Administration will be abolished and a new National Institute of Justice created. Perhaps all its functions will be reorganized in the Department of Justice. Whatever organization evolves, there is always need for more coordination, cooperation, and efficient work between police and the various levels of government.

So, why does anyone want to be a police officer today? Because, despite all that is terribly wrong with our country, the majority of citizens do not commit crimes, and they need protection. Law violators are a minority. Most people in our country are honest and good, and from among them are many men and women who, although realizing that no one ever said being a police officer is easy, nonetheless want the challenge of *service* to their community, which is implicit in being a law enforcement officer.

Glossary

Administrative service—those services such as recruitment, training, planning and research, records and communications, crime laboratories and facilities including the police headquarters and jail.

Affidavit—a statement reduced to writing, sworn to before an officer or notary having authority to administer an oath.

Affirmation—usually related to an oath.

American Creed—the national conscience.

Amphetamine—a stimulant taken orally as a tablet or capsule or intravenously to reduce appetite and/or to relieve mental depression.

Appeal—the removal of a decision from a lower to a higher court.

Arraignment—a court procedure whereby the accused is read the charges against him and is then asked how he pleads.

Arrest—to deprive a person of his liberty by legal authority. Usually applied to the seizure of a person to answer for a suspected or alleged crime.

Assault—an unlawful attack by one person upon another for the purpose of inflicting bodily harm.

Barbiturate—a depressant usually taken orally as a small tablet or capsule to induce sleep and/or to relieve tension.

Bill of Rights—the first ten amendments to the Constitution.

Bow Street Runners—the first detective unit; established in London by Henry Fielding in 1750.

Burglary—an unlawful entry into a building to commit a theft or felony.

Chief of Police—the chief law enforcement officer at the local level.

Civil law—all restrictions placed upon individuals which are noncriminal in nature. Seeks restitution rather than punishment.

Civil liberties—an individual's immunity from governmental oppression.

Civil rights—claims which the citizen has to the affirmative assistance of government.

Commission—the highest ruling body of the Mafia.

Complainant—a person who makes a charge against another person.

Complaint—a legal document drawn up by a prosecutor which specifies the alleged crime and the supporting facts providing probable cause.

Consent—to agree; to give permission; voluntary oral or written permission to search a person's premises or property.

Constitution—the basic instrument of government and the supreme law of the United States; the written instrument defining the power, limitations, and functions of the United States government and that of each state.

Contraband—any article forbidden by law to be imported or exported; any article of which possession is prohibited by law and constitutes a crime.

Coroner's jury—an inquest, usually before a jury of six members, to establish cause of death occurring under unusual circumstances.

Conviction—the legal proceeding of record which ascertains the guilt of the accused and upon which the sentence or judgment is based.

Crime—an action which is harmful to another person and/or to society and which is made punishable by law.

Criminal intent—a resolve, design, or mutual determination to commit a crime, with full knowledge of the consequences and exercise of free will.

Criminal law—the body of law which defines crimes and fixes punishments for them.

Data Privacy Act—the regulation of confidential and private information gathered by governmental agencies on individuals in the records, files, and processes of a state and its political subdivisions.

Defendant—the person accused in a criminal proceeding.

Defense attorney—the representative of the accused in court.

Delinquent gang—usually consists of youths who have joined together to obtain material profit illegally.

Deliriant—a volatile chemical which can be sniffed or inhaled to produce a "high" similar to that produced by alcohol.

Discovery Process—a system that requires all pertinent facts be available to the prosecutor and the defense attorney prior to the time of trial.

Diversion—bypassing the criminal justice system by assigning an individual to a social agency or other institution rather than bringing to trial.

Emergency situation—circumstances where a police officer must act without a magistrate's approval (without a warrant).

Equity—requires that the "spirit of the law" take precedence over the "letter of the law."

Evidence—all the means by which any alledged matter or act is either established or disproved.

Evidence technician—a police officer who has received extensive classroom and laboratory training in crime scene investigation.

Exclusionary Rule—a United States Supreme Court ruling that any evidence seized in violation of the Fourth Amendment will not be admissible in a federal or state trial.

Felony—a major crime, for example murder, rape, arson; the penalty is usually death or imprisonment in a state prison or penitentiary.

Field services—the operations or line divisions of a law enforcement agency such as patrol, traffic control, investigation, and community services.

Forcible entry—an announced or unannounced entry into a dwelling or a building by force for the purpose of executing a search or arrest warrant to avoid the needless destruction of property, to prevent violent and deadly force against the officer, and to prevent the escape of a suspect.

Frisk—a patting down or minimal search of a person to determine the presence of a dangerous weapon.

Goal—a broad, general, or desired result for a law enforcement agency.

Grand jury—a group of citizens, usually twenty-three, convened to hear testimony in secret and to issue formal criminal accusations (indictments) based upon probable cause if justified.

Hallucinogen—a drug whose physical characteristics allow it to be disguised as a tablet, capsule, liquid, or powder. Hallucinogens produce distortion, intensify sensory perception, and lessen the ability to discriminate between fact and fantasy.

Hard-core drug user—a person who is psychologically and/or physically dependent on drugs.

Homicide—the killing of a human being by another human being.

Immediate control—within a person's reach.

Indictment—a written accusation based on probable cause, returned by a grand jury charging an individual with a specific crime.

Informant—a person who furnishes information concerning accusations against another person or persons.

Information—similar to an indictment. The prosecuting attorney makes out the information and files it in court. Probable cause is usually then determined at a public preliminary hearing.

Informational probable cause—statements which are made to officers that can be relied upon and are generally sufficient in themselves to justify an arrest.

Instrumentalities of a crime—the means by which a crime is committed or the suspects and/or victims transported, for example, gun, knife, burglary tools, car, truck.

Intent—same as criminal intent for the purpose of criminal law.

Interrogation—the questioning of a suspect.

Interview—the questioning of a witness.

Jacksonian Philosophy—a spoils system which encouraged politicians to reward their friends by giving them key positions in police departments.

Justification—a sufficiently lawful reason why a person did or did not do the thing charged.

Juvenile delinquent—an individual not of legal age (usually under age 18, but in a few states under age 21), who fails to obey a law or an ordinance.

Larceny/theft—the unlawful taking and removing of the property of another with the intent of permanently depriving the owner of the property.

Law—a body of rules for human conduct which are enforced by imposing penalties for their violation.

Legal—authorized by law.

Legal arrest—lawfully taking a person into custody (with or without a warrant) for the purpose of holding that person to answer for a public offense. All legal standards must be satisfied, particularly probable cause.

Legis Henrici—made law enforcement a public matter and separated offenses into felonies and misdemeanors.

Limitation—a legal restriction of time or authority relating to an offense.

Loan sharking—lending money at higher than legally prescribed rates.

Mafia—an Italian word referring to the lawless, violent bands of criminals who engaged in kidnapping and extortion in Sicily in the nineteenth and twentieth century; used today to refer to organized crime.

Magna Carta—a decisive document in the development of constitutional government in England that checked royal power and placed the king under the law (1215).

Misdemeanor—a minor offense, for example breaking a municipal ordinance, speeding; the penalty is usually a fine or a short imprisonment in a local jail or workhouse.

Mobility—movable; not firm, stationary, or fixed, for example an automobile that is capable of being moved quickly with relative ease.

Narcotic—a drug that produces sleep and lethargy or relieves pain; usually an opiate.

NCIC—National Crime Information Center—the computerized files of the Federal Bureau of Investigation containing records of stolen property and wanted persons.

Nighttime warrant—a search or arrest warrant issued by a magistrate that authorizes a police officer to execute the warrant during the night.

No knock warrant—authorization by a magistrate upon the issue of a search warrant to enter a premise by force without notification to avoid the chance that evidence may be destroyed if the officer's presence were announced.

Nonconformist drug user—a person, usually of middle or upper middle income, who uses drugs to rebel against society.

Oath—a legal attestation or promise to perform an act or make a statement in good faith and under a responsibility to God.

Objective—a specific, measureable means of achieving a goal.

Offense—an act prohibited by law, either by commission or omission.

Offense report—a preliminary report filled out by the responding officer for all crimes, attempts, investigations, and incidents to be made a matter of record.

Omerta—a rigid ethical code which bound Mafia members together and required any member who suffered an injustice to take personal vengeance without contacting the law.

Ordinary care—such degree of care, skills, and diligence as a person of ordinary prudence would employ under similar circumstances.

Organized crime—conspiratorial crime involving a hierarchy of persons who coordinate, plan, and execute illegal acts using enforcement and corruptive tactics.

Parish Constable System—an early system of law enforcement used primarily in rural areas of the United States.

Pennsylvania Constabulary—organized in 1905 and considered the first modern state police agency.

Plain View Doctrine—evidence which is not concealed and which is inadvertently seen by an officer engaged in a lawful activity may be seized. What is observed in plain view is not construed within the meaning of the Fourth Amendment as a search.

Plea—the accused's answer to formal charges in court.

Plea bargaining—a compromise between the defense and prosecuting attorney which pre-arranges the plea and the sentence, conserving manpower and court expense.

Police authority—the right to direct and command.

Police power—the force which officers are authorized to use to obtain compliance.

Preliminary hearing—a court process to establish probable cause to continue the prosecution of the defendant.

Probable cause—reasonable grounds for presuming guilt; facts which lead a person of ordinary care and prudence to believe and conscientiously entertain an honest and strong suspicion that a person is guilty of a crime.

Prosecutor—an elected or appointed official who serves as the public's lawyer.

Rpr'd—released on personal recognizance—individuals are discharged or released from the jurisdiction of the court and are responsible for their own behavior and for appearing at their trial.

Rape—carnal knowledge of a woman through the use of force or the threat of force.

Reasonable—sensible; just; well-balanced; good sound judgment; that which would be attributed to a prudent person.

Reasonable doubt—when a juror is not morally certain of the truth of the charges.

Reasonable force—force not greater than that needed to achieve the desired end.

Reasonable search—a search conducted in a manner consistent with the Fourth Amendment.

Reasonable seizure—the seizure of evidence or persons according to constitutional standards set forth in the Fourth Amendment.

Reception center—a juvenile correctional institution where adjudicated delinquents are placed preparatory to beginning their rehabilitative program.

Relevant—having a direct relationship to the issue in question.

Restraint—to restrain; to prohibit; to bar further movement; to limit freedom.

Robbery—the stealing of anything of value from the care, custody, or control of a person in his presence by force or by the threat of force.

Roll-call—the briefing of officers prior to their tour of duty to update them on criminal activity and calls for service.

Search—examination of a person or property for the purpose of discovering evidence to prove guilt in relation to a crime.

Search warrant—a judicial order directing a peace officer to search for specific property, seize it, and return it to the court. It may be a written order or an order given over the telephone.

Seizure—a forcible detention or taking of a person or property in an arrest.

Sheriff—the principal law enforcement officer of a county.

Sir Robert Peel—often referred to as the "Father of Police Administration": his efforts organized the Metropolitan Police of London (1829).

Situational drug user—a person who takes drugs for a specific purpose and usually only periodically.

Social gang—youths who band together for friendship and a feeling of belonging.

Spree drug user—an individual who takes drugs for "kicks."

Statutory law—law passed by a legislature.

"Stop and frisk"—a protective search for weapons which could be used to assault police officers and others, for example, knives, guns, and clubs.

Submission—placing of one's person or property under the control of another; yielding to authority.

Supreme Court—the highest court in the United States and the only court established by the Constitution.

Task—a specific activity which contributes to reaching an objective.

Texas Rangers—established in 1835 as the first agency similar to our present-day state police.

Tithing system—established the principle of collective responsibility for maintaining law and order.

Tort—a civil wrong for which the court seeks a remedy in the form of damages to be paid.

U.S. Attorney General—the head of the Department of Justice and the chief law officer of the federal government.

Violent gang—usually sociopathic youths who join together and engage in violence for "kicks" and prestige.

Warrant—a written order issued by an officer of the court, usually a judge, directing a person in authority to arrest the person named, charged with the named offense, and to bring that person before the issuing person or court of jurisdiction.

Watch and Ward—a system of law enforcement which was used primarily in the urban areas in the eighteenth century.

White-collar crime—occupational or business-related crime.

Witness—a complainant, an accuser, a victim, an observer of an incident, a source of information, or a scientific examiner of physical evidence.

Index

A

accidents, 271, **272-88**
  causes, 279-80, 281
  reports, 280-4
  statistics, 271, 272, 276, 278-81
administrative duties, 251, 253, 254
administrative police boards, 18
administrative services, 179, 180, **188-99**, 192-8
  communications, 188-91
  coordination, 198-9
  records, 188, 189, 192-8
advancement, 470-1, 475-6
adversary system, 400-1
affidavit, 375-6, 377
Affirmative Action plan, 477
aggravated assault, 68, **69**
air patrol, 255, 256, 257
Alcohol, Tobacco, Firearms Tax, Bureau of (BATF), 154, 156
Alien and Sedition Act, 58
Allen v. Mobile, 477
alphabet, phonetic, 272
Amendments (*see also* Bill of Rights), 32, 33, **45-56,** 60, 61, 62, 204, 324, 334, 335, 347-8, 359, 368-9, 372, 373, 379, 384-5, 404, 412-13, 419, 432, 455, 478, 490
  First, **45-7,** 60, 61
  Second, 45, **47,** 60, 62, 490
  Third, **47,** 54, 60
  Fourth, 45, **47-9,** 60, 62, 347-8, 359, 368-9, 372, 373, 379, 384-5, 404, 490
  Fifth, 45, 47, **49-51,** 54, 60, 62, 324, 334, 404, 413, 432, 490
  Sixth, 45, **51-3,** 62, 324, 334, 335, 404, 413, 419
  Seventh, **53**
  Eighth, 45, **53-4,** 404, 490
  Ninth, **54**

Tenth, 32, **54,** 204
Fourteenth, 33, 45, 51, 54, **55-6,** 412-13, 455, 478
Twenty-sixth, **56**
Twenty-seventh (proposed), **56**
American Creed, 42
American Revolution, 42-3
amphetamines, 83, 85-7
ancient law, 5-6
Anglo-Saxon Period, 6-7, 13
application for police officer, 450-1
Argersinger v. Hamlin, 405
armed forces, 157
arraignment, 414-15, 429-30
arrest, 7, 13, 47-8, 192-4, 252, 254, 275, 343, **345-64,** 370-3, 378, 414-15, 418-19
  citizens, 7, 13, 349-50
  defined, 347
  lawful, 47-8, 343, 345-64, 370-3, 378
  record, 192, 193, 194
  report, 254
  warrantless, 348, 349
assault, 68, **69,** 254
  aggravated, 68, 69
  simple, 69
assembly, freedom of, 45, 46-7
assizes, 8
attorney, 147, 165, 402-3, 405-6, 407-8, 423-5, 426-8, 430-40
  (*see also* counsel)
  defense, 405-6, 433-40
  general, 147, 165
  prosecuting, 402-3
  state, 165
authority, police, 31-3, 35
automobile, 255, 257, 278-85, 293-4, 308, 385-9
  accidents, 278-85
  instrumentality of crime, 308, 389
  mobility, 385, 386, 387, 388-9

R

W

Table of Cases